Dewy & Carolyn,
Grateful thanks for your friendship, fellowship & hospitality over many years! Trust you will enjoy these stories from Asia.
Love & prayers,
Aletta Oct. 24/10

Sun Like Thunder

— *Following Jesus on Asia's Spice Road*

High Adventure Across Earth's Most Strategic Continent

by

W. Harold Fuller

**"A gem of a book—
a travelogue, but far more: a spiritual journey."**

– Patrick Johnstone, Founding Editor, *Operation World.*

Centre for Contemporary Christianity

Bangalore

2010

email: harold.fuller@hotmail.com

First edition: 2010

Asian edition: **CfCC**

Published by: **Dr. Siga Arles**
Centre for Contemporary Christianity
P.O. Box 4601
Bangalore 560 046, India
E-mail: <cfcc94@gmail.com> <arles@sify.com>

ISBN: 978-93-80548-00-5

Paper Back Rs. 600/- US $40

Printed at : **National Printing Press**, Bangalore.

D. Wetherby

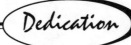

Dedication

For Olive Fuller of Dohnavur

Olive Y. Fuller ("Pramila Sitti"), 1919-2008

(See Chapter 8)

"May we serve our Lord as she did – caring for the needy, a shining witness to all."

– *Nesaruthina Carunia*, Amy Carmichael's Successor

About the Author

Following Jesus on Asia's Spice Road Today.

W. Harold Fuller, Lit. D.

AWARD-WINNING editor and author W. Harold Fuller's *SUN LIKE THUNDER–Following Jesus on Asia's Spice Road Today,* is the result of 15 years' research and writing. Third in his "Sun Triad",[1] and his 12th book, it comes out just as the world is increasingly aware of Asia's role as a major player in world affairs.

Fuller's books reflect 50 years of editing and writing, as well as leading seminars on six continents. Besides involvement in mission leadership (Serving in Mission), Fuller was a founding member of the Association of Evangelicals of Africa, vice-chair of World Evangelical Alliance, executive member of Evangelical Fellowship of Canada (EFC) and of World by Radio (itself a member of National Radio Broadcasters, USA), and member of the Secretaries of Christian Communities (Geneva). Fuller has been correspondent for *Christian Herald, Christianity Today,* and other publications.

---

1. The "Sun Travelogs": *Run While the Sun Is Hot,* 1967 (Africa), *Tie Down the Sun,* 1990 (S. America); *Sun Like Thunder* (Asia).

In Africa, Fuller was editor-in-chief of *African Challenge* (largest magazine in West Africa, plus continent-wide sales), *SIMNow* (international magazine), and several vernacular publications. Moody Press selected his first travelog, *Run While the Sun Is Hot* (about Africa), for their Book of the Month Club (1968). In 1991, EFC awarded first prize to his second travelogue, *Tie Down the Sun* (about South America). EFC's magazine, *Faith Today*, awarded Fuller its 1996 Leslie K. Tarr Award "in recognition of outstanding contribution to the field of Christian writing."

Dr. John R. W. Stott, former Chaplain to Queen Elizabeth II, wrote concerning Fuller's 150 years of evangelical history, *People of the Mandate* (1996): "It is more than a chronicle... informative and inspiring." Missions and college professors in several countries have used Fuller's book, *Mission-Church Dynamics*, as a text. Biola, one of USA's oldest Christian universities, in 1989 awarded him a D. Lit. for the book's "contribution to missiology."

Endorsements

- With sharp eye, warm heart, vivid writing, and two handheld bags, Harold Fuller makes a long pilgrimage across the most populous continent. Result: a sort of narrative missiology – hard, sometimes controversial issues of gospel and culture set out in real life, served in sausage lengths for easy consumption. Missiology is about coping with real situations, interacting with real people; framing issues within the narrative will engage many whom a more systematized or abstract treatment would leave cold.

Andrew F. Walls
Hon. Professor, University of Edinburgh
Professor, Mission History, Liverpool Hope University

****

- This compelling account of the impact of the gospel across the centuries over the vast continent of Asia is a remarkable achievement by a gifted observer, that will help a wide audience appreciate all that has been accomplished, as well as "the unfinished task" in Asia.

Gerald H. Anderson, Ph.D.
Sr. Contrib. Ed., International Bulletin of Missionary Research
Dir. Emer., Overseas Missionary Study Centre
Hon. Trustee, Theological Education, S.E. Asia Foundation

****

- Fascinating! Lively interviews with us Asians, as well as research into our religious heritage and contemporary Christian witness, provide a challengingly relevant missiological thrust.

J. T. K. Daniel, M.Sc., B.D., Ph.D.
Former Principal.
Serampore College (founded by Wm. Carey), W. Bengal

****

- ... Helps us navigate Asia's complex religious, political, and cultural histories, understanding the world's largest continent from the missions perspective, which other books do not normally provide. . . . Will help mission mobilizers and goers grasp essentials and articulate challenge of missions in Asia—the continent that will affect the global agenda for the next 100 years.

Andrew Ng, MD, FRCS
SIM Australasia, Far East D.I.D.

****

- Impressive–understanding of Japan and introduction of our nation to readers. Interesting, challenging, and analytical. I felt as if I were with the author as he meets many of my colleagues in the Lord's work.

Joshua K. Ogawa, Ph.D.
President, Evangelical Free Church, Japan
Evangelical Fellowship of Asia Board; OMF Council
Chair, SIM Japan Council

****

- Harold Fuller uniquely, compellingly demonstrates how the gospel impacts this complex, exciting part of the world. As the dominant continent of this century (according to analysts), could it lead in spreading the gospel in this new era of global mission?

Malcolm McGregor
International Director, SIM.

****

- Intriguing: development, style, and content flow well. Challenges mission stereotypes predominant in the West—especially those falling into the Mitchner mentality.

Richard Konieczny
Director, OMF, Canada (formerly Indonesia)

****

- Some of the greatest areas of church growth *and* of unreached people—that's Asia! If we are to do God's will, we need a greater understanding of this part of the world. *Sun Like Thunder* can help us do just that.

George Verwer
Founder, Operation Mobilization (former Asia missionary)

****

- From beginning to end, *Sun Like Thunder* holds my attention! Enormous work covering History, Culture, Religion, and Economics gives insight into what might have been Asia's conditions had Christ's Spirit not travelled the Old Spice Road. Useful in our Bible study groups and messages to inspire missionary service.

J. E. Dodla
Scientist (M.Tech., M.I.E.E, C.E. India)

****

- A *must-read*, because Asia already affects our daily lives more than we realize. Harold's skillful pen has done an incredible job portraying the nations—well researched and packed with fascinating 'people encounters' along Asia's Spice Road. This book will grip your heart and change your life forever.

Aletta G. Bell, MD/Administrator
AIDS consultant, Asia

****

- Like the entire book, the China section is well-researched, conscientiously attempting to solve what the author terms 'the Chinese Puzzle'—efforts are as painstaking as the end-product is stimulating.

Lena Lau
Hong Kong University (former Lecturer in Linguistics)
SIM Representative in Hong Kong; current SIM Canada Council

****

- Compelling, captivating, and astonishing—"must read" for anyone interested in missions in Asia! My greatest thrill has been to visit the house from which Father, 85 years before, had been expelled, forbidden to visit the Hmars [*Ch. 6*]. Now Hmar enthusiasm for God and incredible singing brought tears to my eyes.

Paul Watkin Roberts, MD, O.M.
Hon. Consul for Ecuador

****

- Having spent my early life in India, I was delighted to be involved in SIM and ICF's merger [*Ch. 7*]. I've found Fuller's book most interesting and informative, some reports quite moving. Excellent detail and knowledge of Asia's background and religions—valuable scholarly material not easily found elsewhere.

Clifford H.C. Edwards, CM, OM, QC,
Former Dean, Faculty of Law, U. of Manitoba

****

- *"Hearing something a hundred times is not as good as seeing it once"* (Chinese proverb). But this account is so realistic, it makes me feel as if I were with the author. Interesting and enjoyable, its insightful observations on different religious beliefs were highly beneficial to me. I strongly recommend it to others.

Stanley Ling, Ph.D, FRCS
Regional Director, SIM East Asia

****

- Astounding—hard to put down! Autobiographical approach accurately analyzes "distinctives" in Asia's societies—*balancing theological insights* without narrow or denominational focus. Footnotes and appendices are extremely important for the "serious student"—a current cross-cultural missions manual.

Rev. Harvey Sider, Bishop (ret.)
Brethren in Christ, N-E India

****

- Informative, challenging, encouraging—a very readable analysis of the complexities, dynamism, and potential of Kingdom impact. Christians around the world need to understand the dynamic of Asia and its strategic role in the Church's global mission.

Geoff Tunnicliffe, D. Min.
International Director/CEO, World Evangelical Alliance

****

- In *Sun Like Thunder,* Harold Fuller once again brings us a readable account of what God is doing in another part of the world—Asia with all of its exciting variety. Praise God he led SIM to merge with International Christian Fellowship—a great door of opportunity and challenge.

Ian M. Hay
SIM International Director
(at time of the merger with ICF, Ch. 7)

****

- Delightful fresh style! Personal yet international in ethos and expression of cultural, historical, economic and political developments. The book covers an account of the church in mission in all the Asian countries, while yet carrying a story-telling style that captivates, and interpretations that appeal! A worthwhile reading with challenging data for missional commitment and action in Asia.

Siga Arles, PhD
Editor, Journal of Asian Evangelical Theology
Director, Centre for Contemporary Christianity

****

Sun Like Thunder

—Following Jesus on Asia's Spice Road©

"On the road to Mandalay ... the dawn comes up like thunder, outer China 'crost the Bay!" —Kipling

"The Lord thunders over the mighty waters... From the rising of the sun to the place where it sets, God shines forth." –The Psalmist

---

Contents

With Grateful Acknowledgments to

1. Busy people, Asian and non-Asian, who gave time to pencil through early drafts, checking facts and concepts.

2. Veteran "Asia hands" from many agencies, who graciously put up with my enquiring research. Aging pioneers who shared their memories, before the Lord welcomed them with his accolade, "Well done, good and faithful servants!"

3.. Today's disciples (call them believers, missionaries, evangelists, pastors, teachers, or whatever) in countries of the Old Spice Road, serving all over the Asian continent and its islands, who allowed me into their lives and showed me what God is doing in their communities. "It is – God is at work," they insisted. "Please don't mention us so much."

"OK," I apologized. "I know you don't want attention, but readers need to pray for the people God is using—that includes you! They need to meet you and let you share your burden for the people God is reaching through you."

4. Mark and Elaine Maxwell, who generously gave me the key to their lake house. Between the swimming and skiing seasons, when their stretch on Lake Huron was deserted, I spent weeks writing without interruption—except for the stimulation of the lake's ever-changing face, Canada geese honking their way North or South (depending on the season), a fox or two, rabbits, and occasional deer.

5. Family: Lorna, patient with "separations" during research travel and stints of writing and editing. I didn't enjoy the separation, but was thankful Lorna looked after the home-end, including correspondence, church, and family matters. Our son, daughter, and our grandchildren, as well as our siblings and their families, encouraged and prayed for the project.

6. All our faithful friends who covered fifteen years of research and writing with prayer. I knew someone was praying as the Lord solved one or another problem in the project.

7. Leaders in Anthropology, Linguistics, Missiology, Theology, and other studies, who have been my friends and mentors through the years, adding to my understanding.

8. Not to overlook computer guru friends, Glen Coleman and Bryan Nixon, who coolly solved our "digital" problems when we were about to panic over some glitch.

Lorna (my patient wife and editorial advisor) and I thank the Lord for each one.

WHF, 2010[1]

1. (See "About the Author" at end of the travelog.) As Deputy General Director of Serving in Mission (SIM) and Vice-Chairman of World Evangelical Alliance (WEA), W. Harold Fuller travelled widely in Asia. A sister served in India (Dohnavur), brother Dave with OMF (Philippines), and nephew Jonathan on OMF's International Leadership Team (Singapore).

Foreword

HERE IS A GEM OF A BOOK. It is a travelogue, but it is far more than that! It is also a spiritual journey that shows both the growth of God's Kingdom in Asia, and the challenges of a task unfinished in that great and diverse continent. There is a spiritual insight and challenge that constantly peeps through the fascinating insights and interactions with Christian workers and ordinary people across a broad sweep of Asia.

Harold comes from a background of journalism, years as a frontline cross-cultural missionary, and as a Christian statesman. He applies all of this heritage as he travels through, what to him at the time was, a new continent. He sees the kaleidoscope of Asia's peoples and countries with the freshness and excitement of new discoveries.

This book is right up to date, and even such events as the recent natural disasters and their impact are covered.

May this book inspire interest, and, more, involvement by Christians in Asia in prayer and in taking the precious Gospel to the remaining unevangelized peoples of Asia.

Patrick Johnstone
WEC International
Founding Author/Editor, *Operation World.*[1]

1. Throughout this book, most country statistics are from Operation World , Carlisle: Paternoster UK, and Waynesboro: Paternoster USA. Used by permission. ISBN 1-85078-357-8. Cover photo: John Rose, SIM. All other photos: W. Harold Fuller.

At the Khyber Pass, the author and his armed guard look out over Afghanistan. Moments later the guard hustled Fuller into the covered back of their rented Land Rover, as a rebel lorry lumbered up the switchback trail of the Pass.

Pakistan stretches from the Himalayas southward to the Arabian Sea

The fabled Taj Mahal reminds visitors of the Medieval Mogul Empire

Outside Lahore's main mosque, the faithful worship before slaughtering their bleating goats and sheep for a Muslim festival

India holds great contrasts in everyday life: a lurid wall poster for a "Bollywood" cinema film forms an incongruous background for a sacred cow munching on the garbage of a Delhi street

A bedecked elephant slowed down traffic for miles before arriving at a festive celebration

In Bangalore, southern India, missionaries of SIM's related CIGM churches gather to be refreshed by Bible studies and fellowship

Outside Chennai (former Madras), a shrir memorializes the spot on which first-centu disciple/missionary Thomas reputedly wa martyred. Pilgrims hope for miraculous cu and other blessings

Dohnavur care-givers, themselves raised from abandonment as babies, cuddle recently-rescued new-borns

Dr. Nesaruthina Carunia, first Indian director of Dohnavur Fellowship, cares for shrubs planted around a birdbath–the only "memorial" that DF's founder, Amy Carmichael, would permit to be erected in her honor. "Nesa," raised in Dohnavur, was discipled by the author's sister, Olive.

"God just patted Old Tiger on the back!" Amy Carmichael comforted the children,
after hunters had to shoot this man-eating tiger that had staked out the Dohnavur compound for a kill.

Some of India's myriad deities adorn a towering stupa

Sitting in William Carey's chair at the pioneer's desk, the author muses on Carey's legacy, such as banning widow-burning, opposing social apartheid, and urging self-government-plus translating the Scriptures into 44 languages/dialects as well as establishing Serampore Theological College

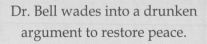

Dr. Bell wades into a drunken argument to restore peace.

Youth learn bicycle repair—a ready skill to earn a living in Bangladesh

In Japan, Fuller enjoys meeting Dr. Shin Funaki. Their fathers respectively had chaired the Japan and Canada councils of Japan's Evangelistic Band.

Kathy Bell leads Marwari women in worship.

The famed "Star Ferry" ploughs across the strait between Hong Kong island and the Kowloon mainland

The ubiquitous portrait of Chairma Mao looks on from the wall of the Forbidden City as the author view Tiananmen Square

James Hudson Taylor III chats with SIM missionaries Yu-Guang and Lily Hsieh. To the right are Leone Taylor and the author.

choolgirls visiting the Great Wall greet the author before reciprocating by taking his photo

Dr. Young Jun Son, Director of Korea's Missionary Training Institute, welcomes the author to teach church-mission relations and management/leadership development

Fresh from a Geisha festival, two women greet the visiting cameraman.

Laiu Fachhai shows other missionaries the area of north-east India from which he comes. He has since served in Sudan with SIM, becoming SIM area director at one time.

On the most southerly tip of the Indian sub-continent, Tamil friends point out that the Indian and Pacific Oceans stretch all the way to Antarctica and the South Pole. (In the background is Gandhi's mausoleum)

Olive Y. Fuller
Pramila Sitti
1919-2008

Publisher's Note

Dr. Harold Fuller has been a prominent leader who held high positions within the mission circles. When I met him at the Wheaton '83 conference, he gifted me a copy of his book *CHURCH MISSION DYNAMICS* in which from his years of experience in Africa he was dealing with an important area of concern in Christian missions. The fact that his sister Olive was a missionary in India (Dohnavur Fellowship) made our link that much more closer. Years later while at the twelfth conference of the International Association for Mission Studies at Balaton, Hungary, it was Dr Gerald Anderson who spoke of his friend Dr Harold Fuller who was looking for a publisher for his travelogue on Asia. Will I be willing to publish? I counted it a privilege to include this work in my series from the Centre for Contemporary Christianity. Soon we were in correspondence and here is the product - *Sun Like Thunder...*!

I am grateful that Dr Fuller has such a warm style of writing his observations, investigations, interactions and offer them in a lively way with his own interpretations, gentle critique, further input and added analysis, missionary challenge and a clear passion for people to find the Lord Jesus Christ who walks the silk road rather ably. I read through the pages with great interest and rapt attention. I enjoyed his graphic descriptions, scholarly interpretations, extra inputs and missional anguish.

Centre for Contemporary Christianity attempts to provide relevant literature to enhance the church in her witness. Global and local writings, both academic and experiential are published in different series. I am glad to include *Sun Like Thunder* in our Missiological Classics Series.

I commend this book to all who belong to the Lord Jesus Christ and are burdened to share Him with people, particularly in the large continent of Asia. I acknowledge my gratitude to Dr. Fuller for allowing CFCC to be the publisher of his work and for the financial grant towards the project. It is my prayer that this book will prove a blessing and a challenge for God's people in Asia and God's kingdom in the world in the years to come.

Siga Arles, PhD.
Editor

January 2010

SUN LIKE THUNDER – ***PREFACE***

Why the Sun Comes Up Like Thunder

"We learn history ... to know who we are."
– Leszek Kolakowski, Polish philosopher (1928-2009).

TRAVEL WITH ME across the world's largest, most restless continent to find out why the "Sun comes up like thunder" over Asia. I confess it was an arduous trip, but I invite the reader, without the sweat, to accompany me on this fascinating trek across our globe's most populous land mass. Mingle with its diverse people and cultures; sense their joys and struggles. See how today's world still connects with the bloodstream of the ancient Spice Road (sometimes called the Silk Road)—the arteries through which world commerce pulsates more than ever. Asia affects our daily life more than most realize; let its saga of life grip you as it gripped me.

Right up front, I admit to using "poetic licence" with fellow Canadian[1] Rudyard Kipling's classic poem, "Mandalay." His "dawn comes up like thunder" implies sunrise. So this is third in "The Sun" travelog triad.[2]

Sunshine or not, isn't it rather ambitious to try describing Asia's complexities in one brief volume?[3] Furthermore, *can we justifiably consider Asia as a unit,* rather than many unique ethnic groups crammed into the world's largest landmass? I hope this book examines these issues. However, the reader may have more basic questions:

---

1. *Canadian Quotations and Phrases* (Robert Hamilton, Toronto: McClelland and Stewart, 1966) includes English-born Kipling's poetry.
2. The two other travelogs: *Run While the Sun Is Hot* (Africa) and *Tie Down the Sun* (South America).
3. However, I refer only briefly to the Middle East and Central Asia. Those require a book of their own.

1. ***What has Asia's Spice Road got to do with readers today?*** Jesus sent forth his disciples to announce the "Gospel of Peace" in a fractious world—and that gospel travelled along the Spice Road. Now, Asia's dynamic influence on our world is greater than ever. Viewing the gospel at work all along "the Old Spice Road" (birthplace of the world's oldest faiths and ideologies) is a challenging experience. *Sun Like Thunder* refers not only to the gospel's history in Asia. Readers also meet followers of Jesus *today* in the continent that contains three out of every five people on earth.

Besides, our world is now feeling the impact of a resurgent Asia. "Historians and futurologists state that, with the rise of India and China's huge billion populations, the agenda of the world for the next 100 years will revolve around what happens in Asia," states Andrew Ng, international mission leader from Singapore.[4] If tall buildings illustrate that, the tallest is no longer in the West but on the Arabian Gulf, in Dubai.

India has called itself "India Shining" and, more recently, "Incredible !ndia." China and its neighbors compete with the West in manufacture, finance, and consequent political power. In Medieval times, the Spice Road was the main East-West conduit for interchanging ideas and trade—an early example of "globalization."[5] Even though today, travel and communication have changed exponentially (from donkeys and camels to jets and Internet), Asia's Spice Road still provides a vital link in *global* intercourse. But it is time to understand how this affects our world, apart from manufacturing the West's "widgets" in Asia. Christians need to awake to *the spiritual implications*: the Spice Road, metaphorically, revitalizes mission and ministry around the globe. (A special challenge is witness to Muslims, 70% living in Asia—the majority not even in the Middle East).

Perhaps our questions should be, "Why *not* Asia? Why haven't we paid more attention to earth's greatest population mass—three out of five of its population, stretching over a third of the globe? To rising nations *already* dominating the future of our world? To religions that today challenge the globe's liberties."

---

4. Letter from Andrew Ng, M.D., SIM International Deputy Director, Pacific/East Asia, 2007-10-01.
5. Nayan Chanda, *Bound Together: How Traders, Preachers, Adventurers, and Warriors Shaped Globalisation*. New Haven: Yale University Press, 2007.

✓2. ***Doesn't each country warrant a book of its own?*** Definitely—and I'm glad books on individual countries come out all the time.[6] But I suggest there's place for a single volume putting the jigsaw together. Surprise—the pieces *do* fit in an overall picture!

3. ***Hasn't this been done by others?*** Indeed, scholarly tomes such as Samuel Hugh Moffett's encyclopaedic two-volume *History of Christianity in Asia* (see Bibliography) do a more thorough job than I would ever aspire to. However, *Sun Like Thunder* is of a different genre. While I've tried to ensure its facts are academically accurate, this book is a narrative to help the reader enter the lives and worlds of Asians—to *experience* Asia.

5. ***Why follow Jesus on the Spice Road?***[7] Even before the time of Jesus upon earth, the Spice Road (call it the Silk Road, if you wish) was the world's main two-way conduit for trade, ideas, migration, cultures, and religions. It was no easy bridle path; courageous travellers faced armed robbers as well as icy mountainous trails (to the north), scorching sand storms (across deserts), and "perils of the deep" (to the south).

From the Mediterranean to the Pacific, this route over land and sea increased in activity with the Roman Empire's interest in the fabled fabric of the East: silk. Julius Caesar became the gossip of Rome when he appeared in the Coliseum robed in a toga of Chinese silk. Silk and spice trade followed. [8] Ubiquitous Jewish and Arab merchants plied the connecting strands of the Spice Road, dotting Asia with synagogues and mosques.

But my greatest interest was seeing the Holy Spirit at work all along that trans-continental artery. Not only did I follow the footsteps of Jesus' disciples; I also learned what it means to "follow Jesus" in Asia today. Scattered from comfortable Jerusalem, disciples fulfilled Jesus' promise: "You shall be my witnesses to the ends of the earth."[9]

---

6. See Bibliography.
7. "Road" (from Old English *rad*—ride, journey) included sea as well as land routes.
8. Europe's increasing gourmet appetite included perishable foods, which (in the absence of refrigeration) required spices to preserve them or disguise spoilage. Medieval magical "cures" also depended on spices.
9. Acts 1.8. While Jesus' instruction applied to the entire world, for his disciples, "the ends of the earth" extended from "The Pillars of Hercules" off Spain to the Isles of Nippon (Japan)—*i.e.* "the Spice Road."

In our current world of mega-churches, renowned TV personalities, and massive budgets, it is also instructive to realize that global church *growth* (vs. re-cycling) is taking place *today* along routes such as "The Spice Road," in places that never hit our headlines, led by very ordinary disciples whose names we wouldn't recognize. Budgets? In a subsistence society many groups don't have a "budget". Those believers are simply following the lowly Jesus along their village footpaths. All they have is the gospel—their "mustard seed." In our self-sufficient pews, we have lessons to learn.

In 1900, 80% of Christians lived in Europe and North America. Today, over half of the globe's Christians live in Africa, Asia, and Latin America. This book explores why the Christian faith—despite the expansion of Buddhism, Hinduism, and Islam—is once again exploding in Asia, where the early disciples first set out on the Old Spice Road.

Is There a Thesis in All This?

This is neither a beginner's reader nor a worker's manual—although I hope it aids all who minister in this amazing continent. Others have already produced "readers and manuals" (Bibliography). It's neither a catalogue of statistics nor a study in comparative religion, although it is loaded with both interesting and sometimes surprising facts.[10]

My **objective** in writing this book is to help the reader *experience* Asia—its rich history, its multiple peoples, its complex religions. I want readers to sense, with me, the burden of earth's greatest population mass, by visiting men, women, and children in their homes and markets. I intend to present more than simply facts and figures.

In researching how the gospel spread across Asia in response to Jesus' commission to his disciples, I came face to face with "another gospel"[11]

10. Readers may wonder why information on any one topic is scattered throughout the volume (e.g., details about various religions). I could have collated these on one page—but that would have created a catalogue, not a narrative. In life, we learn as we plod through our pilgrimage. I hope this narrative introduces readers to facts as part of life's adventures. (For those who want to assemble the bits, I list them in the index under topics.) For specific country profiles, see Patrick Johnstone's *Operation World*.

11. Galatians 1.6-9.

(in fact, many others) that forced me to think through the uniqueness of Christ and his claim to be "the Way, the Truth, and the Life." The multiplicity of religions also led me to examine the common desires and fears of mankind that underlie religions.

This overview of Asia therefore proposes a **thesis:** *All religions are responses to common human needs. Christ Jesus represents more than a religion or system. As God,*[12] *he is the only Way, the only Truth, and the only Life who can meet the world's spiritual needs.*

That's the distinctive of Christ's gospel (as opposed to Christendom): it is not a religion in the sense of rites hopefully meriting eternal life. It is a *life*—Christ living within the believer. This thesis will surface from time to time in the account, but I seek to support it in Appendices F ("Religions of the World") and G ("Christianity").

Before you read further, I confess that words intrigue me! How could language fail to, after I've tramped the globe and edited for half a century? This accounts for the innumerable footnote definitions of foreign or abstruse (I'll hold the footnote on that one) words. If you don't need them or don't care, just ignore them; I won't even know!

As an editor, I hope I've followed *a cardinal rule*: Even if a reader enjoys being stretched, the context's meaning should be clear, so he/she doesn't *have* to dive for a dictionary (except out of curiosity). After all, travelog reading should be armchair stuff—enjoyably inspiring, I trust. However, there's also in-depth content to study.

I hope *another editorial rule* shows through: In the first sentence capture a reader's interest and hold on to it. Therefore, if after tramping through one country, you feel you know Asia, think again—the next stop may surprise you! At least, that's what happened to me along the Old Spice Road. So enjoy the entire trip.

The story line is always important. Even a history book has a story line—that is, the history of a nation, a movement, a person, or whatever. *Dilemma*: how to create a story line in a book stretching over millennia

---

12. Jesus Christ, God incarnate, is a great stumbling block to many, who may infer a plurality of gods or idolatry. For explanation, see Appendix G: Christianity and Christendom.

of time and more than two-dozen countries, without reading like some academic "History of Asia"? *Solution*: a personal travelog across that space in time and geography. I trust that my own reactions along the way will help explain why the "Sun Comes Up Like Thunder," and put missiology in context.

Asia is huge. Fifty years ago, John Gunther, chronicler of the modern world, employed a team of 40 researchers. I haven't had that luxury. Instead, my research for this book included months of travel in Asia as well as much reading, over some dozen years. I've been able to use only 20% of my files and interviews. In the interest of space, I've had to skim off only the *top* of the cream. However, my footnotes also include documentation and additional detail. At times, a topic deserves more than a footnote. Since immediate comment would interrupt the flow of the narrative, I've lifted the additional information out of the mainstream and set it down in the marshland of Appendices. Marshes do serve a creative purpose, but they require more time (less adrenaline) to explore than "shooting the rapids" of travel. You can search the marshes *later* if you want. (The Bibliography lists a resource omnibus.)

Researching Asia has shown me how little I know. History can upset parochial assumptions and conceits. My travels helped my understanding of Asia's ancient peoples and cultures and the world's major religions. I hope that more than arousing interest, this journal helps the reader feel the pulse of Asia's remarkable peoples, and sense God's concern that "not any should perish" (2 Peter 3.9).

Working on *Sun Like Thunder* has also caused me to reflect on my own relationship with God. Spiritual lessons along the way have been an unlooked-for fallout of my research— "Meditations along the Old Spice Road," you could call them. You'll have to look for them, because you could bypass them on the roadside. I pass them on with the prayer that the Holy Spirit may meet someone's need on life's journey.

WHF, Toronto, 2010

Experiencing Asia

***Why Asia is what it is, how it affects our lives, and why the gospel's opportunity becomes the church's responsibility.*[1]**

"A JOURNEY OF A THOUSAND MILES begins with a single step," said Lao-tsu, 6c. founder of Chinese Taoism. And so it was for me, except that my first step was to board a flight for Asia, and the journey would be ten thousand miles.

Experiencing Asia has enriched my own life and has fascinated me with many surprises. I wish I had had this exposure at the beginning of my missionary life in other parts of the world. I hope it will be an immersion experience to help you feel the pulse, the heartbeat, of the peoples of Asia.

Of one thing I'm certain: an Asian may have written this book differently. Another thing: an Asian may *read* this book differently than a non-Asian. But my purpose is not to tell Asians about what they already know much better than I. My purpose is to transport readers to the Asia I saw, meet Asians I met, and put the whole experience in context of the continent's history and hopes.

I've gained my own impressions from a host of Asians I met, and from shelves of books by Asians and others who know Asia. I hope my verbal sketches will be informative to non-Asians. Maybe they'll also be a curiosity for Oriental readers to see how Occidental eyes and ears have interpreted the Orient. I think they'll agree with the Scot bard, that there's some value to "see ourselves as others see us."

---

1. 1 Thessalonians 2.4; 1, Corinthians 9.16.

Each country has its own worldview—that is, the way it looks upon the rest of the globe and intrusions into their world. Tramping around Asia helped me gain an Asia-centric view. At the same time, I became convinced we all take ourselves far too seriously. Religion and tradition, containing foibles and superstition, become our *identity*, triggering emotional defence if questioned or even seemingly slighted. This emotional attachment prevents people looking at themselves, culture, religion, and history objectively. Regrettably, it can lead to discrimination, anger, warfare—and even pogrom. So may the reader forgive me for occasionally taking a humorous swipe at some precious icon of society, even if it's a religious taboo![2] I do so not out of disrespect but because if I couldn't laugh, I would have to cry.

Each country also has its particular "hurts." In the case of Asia, I think the deep-seated hurt is that lesser powers and cultures subjugated the superior empires and more sophisticated cultures of the past. For instance, as a monarch, Emperor Babur of India was wealthier and more civilized (in terms of administration and culture) than his contemporary European rulers, Henry VIII and Charles V. Long before Columbus set out to find a westward sea route to the Far East, China possessed faster and larger ships.

Nevertheless, the hurts of nations affect worldviews—and that includes attitudes to the gospel and its messengers. The impact of the gospel—obdurately ignored by world media—will probably be one of the greatest surprises readers discover as they meet Jesus on the Old Spice Road.

"Differences Only Skin Deep?" Changing appearance across Asia, from Turkic heavy visages to Oriental fine facial features, would seem to indicate radical changes, yet genome research assures us that out of millions of genes, only 10 control superficial appearances. Far more radical are differences in culture, both between and within nations. Those differences touch the heart.

In spite of such differences, as I traveled across the continent, I was struck to observe how the gospel of Jesus Christ is relevant to each and bridges them all. Scripture does say, "[We are all] one in Christ Jesus."

2. God himself laughs (in pity, not amusement) at the absurdity of mankind's rebellion against him: Ps. 2.

East-West Two-Way Traffic

One major lesson of history is that the human story, in spite of nationalistic protest, is a never-changing sea. Cultures are dynamic, not static. Peoples, languages, cultures, and religions we see in Asia today have moved outward from their Middle East origins, washing across the continent in wave after wave, like a vast ocean. Although *Sun Like Thunder* follows migratory routes from Mesopotamia eastward, there has been westward migration as well. For instance, the "Roma" ("gypsies") of Eastern Europe originally migrated from Rajasthan in India, bringing their Sanskrit (an earlier linguistic export from central Europe) with them. Of course, our world today has multiple migrations—mostly for economic and refugee reasons.

However, as Medieval exploration in Asia opened up an entirely new world of opportunity for Europeans, the East shared the wisdom of the Orient with the Occident. Two-way traffic also broadened Asia's horizons. Yet the 20th century's Cold War and the 21st century's globalization awaken lingering resentment that inferior cultures have overtaken ancient cultures. It was ever thus. Greek philosophy overtook Egypt's engineering greatness. Wild Huns and Goths from Asia sacked Rome's imperial civilization. Persia's skilled arts buckled under unlearned Mongolian hordes. Arab nomads overran Mongol suzerainties.

After the Medieval period, Europe's Renaissance Man, with his ambition to rule, lust for gold, and appetite for spices, moved eastward even as he also moved westward. This travelog will show how it easily could have been the other way around (the East over-running Europe), dramatically rewriting world history. That would come in time—indeed it is already with us in some ways. In spite of what appears to be Western-driven globalization, Asian concepts and expertise are influencing the very powers that once upset their own balanced worlds.

I soon discovered that while I was following the footsteps of Jesus' disciples across Asia, I was really tracing my journey through minefields of revolution. Throughout history, the tectonic plates of Asia's peoples have rumbled, clashing periodically in revolution. In fact, the world's major religions, all of which have arisen out of Asia, in a sense have been revolutions in culture, religion, and politics. Each has sought to produce "The New Man"—from Aryan mythology to Buddhist philosophy, from

Confucius to the Aga Khan. Both Pol Pot and Mao Zedong rationalized their massacres as necessary to "create the New Man." Regeneration provided by Jesus Christ is itself revolutionary: "Old things are passed away; behold all things are new."[3]

Commercial intercourse destabilized peoples en route, so that the Spice Road became a pipeline for revolution, in effect. Travellers from both East and West unwittingly carried in their satchels new seeds, but they also returned home with new ideas, stimulating new religions, cultures, and even political change. The rise and fall of earlier empires shed light on today's remarkable renaissance of Asia and its effect upon the rest of our globe.

Did I come across any surprises, apart from the exotic? Yes. Two underlying facts came through: (1) Mingling and admixing ("globalization"?) of language, culture, religion, trade, and race have occurred more than we've assumed—long before the rise of the West. Solomon knew that when he stated, "There is nothing new under the sun." He'd already seen it all, as emissaries visited his courts.[4] (2) Wherever I went, Jesus, through his disciples, had already been there! I was "Following Jesus on Asia's Spice Road" today.

You'll smell and taste and see exotic cultures. But I hope that *Sun Like Thunder* proves to be more than an exotic experience, more than a surprising history, and more than a series of challenging stories. I'd like these journeys and interviews to combine all three, because experiencing Asia requires all three. (I was encouraged a wee smidgen—as the Scots would say—that Captain Cook's travelogs stimulated cobbler William Carey's interest in other lands.[5])

Everything Can't Be Told[6]

Everything in this book is true, as far as I have been able to verify—thanks to many checkers of the manuscript. However, I can't tell everything I've seen and heard. To do so would create difficulty and even danger for several of my sources.

3. 2 Corinthians 5.17.
4. Some scholars think Solomon may have written Psalm 2, with its phrase, "Sun Like Thunder."
5. See Chapter 10.
6. I don't fully identify all people and places, for security reasons. I've changed some names, but they still represent real people and situations. Legal cases specifically cited have been confirmed in the local press or by human rights agencies. Some occurred before present governments came to power.

For one thing, if I gave all the details about some countries, authorities might blame local Christians and expatriates for reporting these things. Life could become more difficult for them—including ostracism or imprisonment—and kidnapping or expulsion for selfless visitors who go to help. As I've scanned back over the stories of the people I met, recollecting their circumstances, tears have come to this veteran editor's eyes.

The truth is that great intolerance and denial of human rights exist in our world. In some communities, many are not free to express their true thoughts and must conform to the ideology, worldview, and religion of the ruling party—or face the consequences.[7] Women in particular, denied common liberties and expression, suffer verbal and physical abuse in silence. There's fear, anxiety, depression—very little happiness, joy, or hope.

Life *is* a desperate struggle. According to one religion, acceptance by God will depend on righteous deeds outweighing the pile of defilements stacked up. In some faiths, *suffering* paves the way to a higher status in the cycle of births—but there's always the fear of some slip-up that could result in a worse existence. Another belief sees "re-cycling" until ultimate "Enlightenment"—an amorphous suspension of all desire, eventual nihilism.

No wonder Christians long to share the good news[8] that Jesus can assure us of new spiritual life for our earthly sojourn, and eternity in God's presence!

Yet by the closing page, you may be wondering, "If God yearns for his creation to be saved, and if the gospel has reached the ends of the earth, *why hasn't "the good news" been more widely accepted?*" I hope *Sun Like Thunder* will help provide the answer. In some countries, the gospel's spread will surprise you. Other lands have seen slow growth.

Let's start at Afghanistan's Khyber Pass. See you along the way in deserts, jungles, valleys, and on mountain ranges, until the Pacific laps our feet on Japan's Pacific coast.

W. Harold Fuller, Toronto, Canada, 2010

7. Where I've departed from the "received wisdom" on any topic, I know readers are able to make up their own minds. In the interests of honesty, I try not to parrot "politically correct" but misleading lines. Whether readers agree or disagree, I trust such comments at least stimulate discussion and more: prayer! But I would not be honest to ignore religious practices that deny human rights—however cultural the practices.

8. "Gospel" simply means "good news."

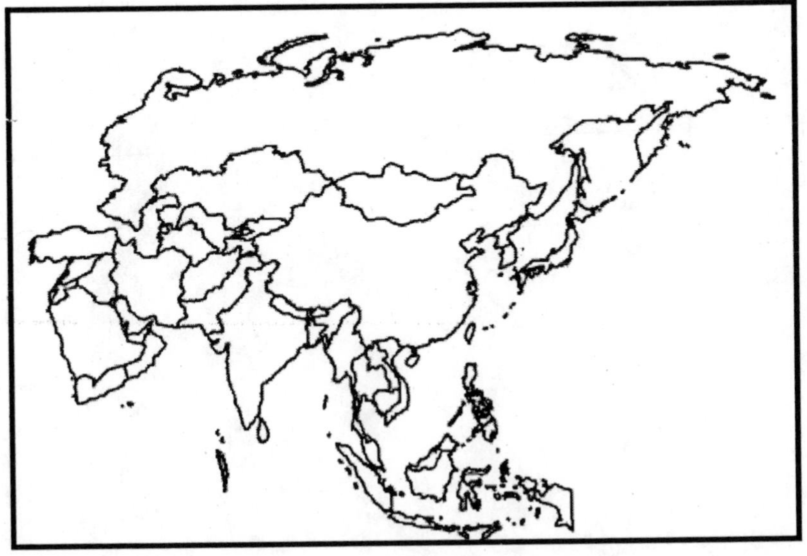

While *Sun Like Thunder* refers to the entire continent, it does not seek to cover the Middle East or Central Asia—separate topics.
It examines Asia's *major populations*, lying *east of the Afghan-Pakistan border.*

Maps courtesy of *EnchantedLearning.com*, 1996-2007; fobissea.org; Hist-geo.co.uk; and worldatlas.com

Cover : Montage of typical Asians - Courtesy John Rose.
All Others : W. Harold Fuller

Section – I
SOUTH ASIA

Pakistan stretches from the Himalayas southward to the Arabian Sea.

A – PAKISTAN

Where the Middle East and Orient Meet

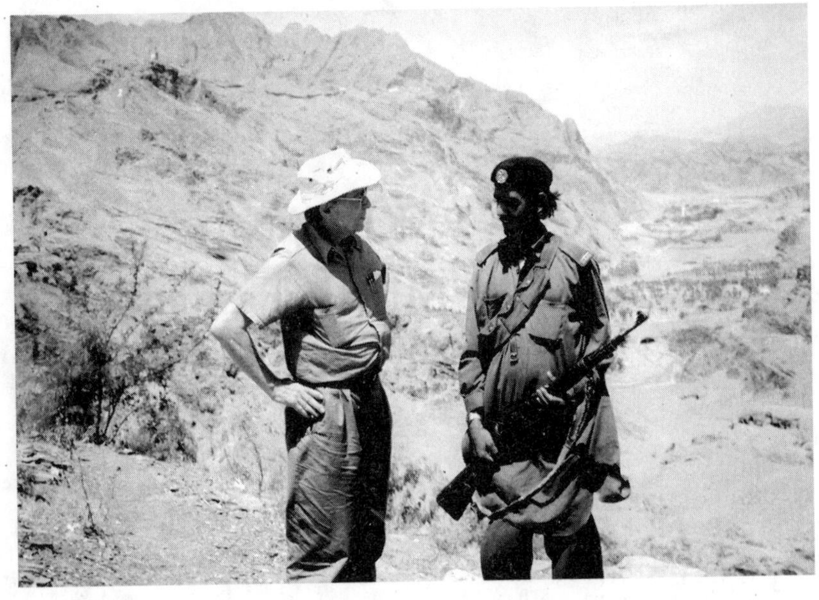

At the Khyber Pass, the author and his armed guard look out over Afghanistan. Moments later the guard hustled Fuller into the covered back of their rented Land Rover, as a rebel lorry lumbered up the switchback trail of the Pass.

The Khyber Gateway

"Why do the nations rage and the peoples plot in vain?. . .
Ask of me, and I will make the nations your inheritance, the ends of the earth your possession" (Psalm 2.1,8).

Pakistan: Pop. 199,744,986

I EDGED CLOSER TO OUR ARMED GUARD at the Khyber Pass. In the torrid air sucking up between the eroded sides of the Pass, I could almost hear the struggle of mankind's eastward march. Through the Khyber's rugged ramparts, cultures, commerce, religions, and armies have flowed and ebbed, like ocean waves washing across Asia.

Earlier, the sun had risen like thunder—or like a red-hot canon ball shot up from some boiling cauldron. Now it blazed down on the haze overlying the plain below us. At our feet were Afghanistan, Iran,[1] and Iraq. To the southwest, Arab neighbors surrounded Israel; to the northwest Turkey connected Asia with Europe. Below us lay ancient Anatolia and Mesopotamia—"the Middle East" that makes headlines today.

After the Greek general, Alexander the Great, conquered many of those lands, he and his soldiers urged their mules up these rocky defiles, fighting their way eastward through the Pass. Their goal was to plunder China's riches, for at the time Europeans thought India was only a narrow peninsula standing in the way.

1. In the heart of a region with quarter of the world's known oil, the nation was known as Persia, home of ancient Zoroastrians and other polytheistic religions, until Islam changed the name to "Iran" ("Aryan"?).

The Khyber was a gateway to Asia beyond the Middle East. It certainly was *my* gateway to the rest of Asia. In the weeks to come, I'd re-trace the trail of explorers and conquerors across earth's most populous continent.[2] All along the turbulent eastward flow of history, I'd find the "footprints" of Jesus. Even more—I'd meet courageous disciples treading in those footprints *today.*

But at this stage, I couldn't imagine the mind-boggling safari ahead of me.

Tourist Attractions Millennia Ago

Here I was, actually standing at one of the world's most historic gateways, The Khyber Pass—astride the trail from the Middle East into fabled Hindustan! If there'd been a tourist agency millennia ago, its brochures could have advertised an alternative to venturing through this gateway. Travelers could trek around the south end of Baluchistan's rugged range and desert, and sail across the Arabian Sea to the southern tip of India. Of course, they risked either being wrecked by a typhoon or boarded by real live pirates, the kind we see only in movie these tame days. These were hardly selling points for tourism or trade. However, the risks didn't deter the Apostle Thomas, Francis Xavier, and other pioneer Christian missionaries who braved the rigorous sea journey to India.

SpiceRoadTours.com (if there'd been an agency with that web site) could also have advertised a northern safari across Central Asia's plains around the top end of the Himalayas to the Middle Kingdom.[3] That route could have been promoted as "Extreme Safaris," featuring death by freezing or at the hands of robber barons—depending on the season. Marco Polo took that "tour."

Later in my travels I'd find out how early missionaries had penetrated from the shores of the Mediterranean to "the uttermost part of the earth."[4] For them, that was Nippon (Japan), and the "endless" Pacific.

---

2. Obsessed with a sense of destiny by the gods (*so* intimidating to enemies!), Alexander penetrated to Lahore on the east of today's Pakistan, before a shaman advised him to go no further. His weary army readily agreed. Sailing south down the Indus River to Karachi, he built an altar to the gods and headed back to Persia to solve urgent problems. There Alexander, only 32, died in Babylon (323 B.C.) of lingering fever—West Nile virus, new studies suggest. His final words: "Let the gods be my judges, for in every sign they gave me, they told me no lie."
3. Chinese emperors considered theirs the perfect "Middle Kingdom" (chapters 17, 18).
4. Acts 1.8 AV.

But the Khyber Pass held another amazing story—one illustrating the Apostle Paul's declaration to idolaters that even *before* Jesus walked upon earth, even *before* he commissioned his disciples, God had "not left himself without testimony."[5] It was likely through the Khyber Pass that the forefathers of India's Santel people pushed their way from Mesopotamia up on to the plains of the Indian subcontinent. In spite of idolatry around them, they maintained their trust in the one "Genuine God." *Thakur Jiu* they called him. Millennia later, in 1867, Norwegian missionary Lars Skrefsrud and a Danish colleague stumbled across the Santel in East India, and were amazed at the Santel's ready acceptance of the gospel, which confirmed the ancestors' faith in the "Genuine God."[6]

Looking westward, I thought of the courageous Christian communities in Iraq, Iran, and Afghanistan. Some had survived Islam's incursions centuries ago; others had found new life in Christ more recently. Right now, further north in one of Central Asia's republics, disciples were preparing at Operation Mobilisation's (OM's) Spice Road Seminary. I'd read of OM's remarkable pioneering work along "The Old Spice Road"[7]—one of several groups ministering where Islamic intolerance builds upon millennia of rugged militancy.

Understandably, we don't hear much about those valiant disciples or those they bring to know the Lord. Following Jesus on the Old Spice Road is dangerous for many. Wrote one seeker, "I want to follow Jesus, but they will kill me if they find out."

My guide to the Khyber, Peter —, had earlier been a missionary with O.M. in Iran. He helped me understand the background of what we were now viewing through the haze. We were on a southern branch of the Old Spice Road, running through the gateway to South Asia. Until European

---

5. Acts 14.17.
6. Don Richardson examines the evidence in *Eternity in Their Hearts* (Bibliography).
7. OM's Asia work may surprise readers, because its ship ministry is better known. Driving OM outreach, on water or on land, is the vision of its founder, George Verwer, to make the gospel's most powerful tool, God's Word, widely available. [Deborah Meroff, *Riding the Storm,* and Ian Randall's *Spiritual Revolution* (Bibliog.)]. A radio ministry in the Middle East, Pamir Productions, beams the gospel in several languages. Typical listener response: "We are 15 people who listen to your programs." "About three months ago, I found a Bible. I can see many changes in my life." (Kitchener: Afghan Christian Media, March 2007.)

fast-sailing "clippers" made sea routes feasible, the Khyber controlled east-west trade along this route.

Standing there, I imagined the straggly parade of merchants and adventurers—Jews, Arabs, Persians, along with Caucasians—yes, even the Huns! Between the rocky crags, up and over the crest of the Pass, they urged their mules, donkeys, or camels laden with commerce, carrying woolen textiles and trinkets eastward and returning with silk, dyes, spices, and sometimes gold. But it was the gospel Nestorian ("Syrian") Christians carried.

The Apostle Paul had met Jesus back on the Damascus Road near the Great Sea, but I knew that people were finding Jesus all along the Old Spice Road. I hoped to meet them in coming months. At this moment, Peter and I were gazing down on arid Afghanistan, where conversion to Christianity and even possessing a Bible were crimes.

Orphans Terrorize the World

Peter reminded me that in those hills far below, Afghan families were still being blown to bits by volatile detritus left from years of war. Traditionally a lovable people, although with rugged mien from marginal living, they practised their proverb, "*Let it be an onion, but let it be served with love.*" However, as farmers and herders unwittingly triggered landmines buried during the Russian-fedayeen[8] and more recent conflicts, they sadly remembered another proverb, "*If your hand is broken, you can still work; but if your heart is broken, you can do nothing at all.*"[9]

For a while, a new group, the Taliban,[10] had clamped the lid on that country. Angry Afghan youth, orphaned during the war with Russia, found common cause under the Taliban label. Most had never known a mother's touch. Instead, extremist Wahhabi-style Qur'anic schools fired them with intolerance and hatred, turning them into wild-eyed defenders of a legalistic medieval "morality." Life became drab gray, as

8. *Fedayeen*: resistance fighters. It may take 400 years to rid the country of buried mines.
9. Afghanistan has one of the highest child mortality rates (257 deaths per 1,000 live births)—UN, 2004.
10. *Taliban*: from Arabic name of cousin and son-in-law of Muhammad, Ali ibn Abi Talib.

puritanical authorities not only outlawed music (except Qur'anic chanting) but also banned youth from two favorite activities: playing soccer and flying kites.[11]

Women, the Taliban believed, had no part in their macho world—it was not God's will that a female should show her face in public, learn in school, or participate in male society. Even after the Taliban were turfed out, the Supreme Court's chief justice barred women from joining his court because they menstruate (!)—making them unfit to handle the *Qur'an* (the Court's basic working document) for several days a month.[12] Most recently, male zealots had sprayed acid in the faces of Afghan women college students

Even after Afghanistan's new democracy expelled the Taliban from power, insurgents kept the long-suffering population in a state of emergency. As in other parts of the Middle East, radical insurgent clerics demanded rigid Islamic totalitarianism, promising suicide bombers instant "Paradise" if they blew themselves up in crowded markets while shouting, "*God is great!*" Extremists found the impenetrable landscape an ideal base for international terrorism: assembling, indoctrinating, and training *jihadists*,[13] as well as plotting and disseminating global propaganda. Whereas Taliban rule had banned opium growing, after they had been ousted from power, they (and many Afghans) turned the area into the world's primary source of the opiate.

I bowed in silent prayer for the beautiful but abused Afghan people. Jesus speaks to them through courageous messengers—whose names we may never know. One Afghan team[14] is broadcasting six days a week, including a program on "Principles for Character Achievement," based on the Book of Proverbs. "These texts have changed my life!" said a listener. For Muslims, a favorite Christian program is "Prayer: Devotion with

11. Taliban banned football because Islam's enemies reportedly once beheaded a Muslim leader, kicking his head around a field. They also consider flying kites as an "un-Islamic" activity. (In 2005, a Russian born in Afghanistan wrote a best-selling novel, *The Kite Flyer*, which Hollywood turned into a film.)

12. More about the status of women under Appendix I: Women.

13. *Jihad* >Arabic: "struggle"—either in personal devotion or as holy warfare on behalf of Islam. Western apologists cite the first meaning, but *jihandists use the* latter interpretation.

14. For their security, we avoid further identification. —WHF

God." *(Islam's concept of prayer is vastly different from Christian prayer. See Appendix H.)*

I thought of the Afghan Christian who started a school in the rubble of Kabul. One day he gave a gospel pamphlet to a student who seemed curious. The next day the student brought a message from her father, asking to meet with the teacher. "I want to join the Jesus party," he said when they met. "I gave up the other way two years ago and have stayed awake at night wondering how I can reach God. What can I do?" He continued Bible studies with the Afghan teacher.

"Don't Mess with Us!"

The distant whine of a rusty Russian-built bus toiling up the switchbacks of the Khyber Pass caught my ear. The Khyber River had chewed through the earth's wrinkles, falling to the plains below. To me, the crumpled ridges seemed to mark The Great Divide between the Middle East, predominantly Islamic, and the hodgepodge of Hindu-animistic masses of Southern Asia. Given today's power struggles, that gave Pakistan great strategic importance in world affairs.

While the Khyber Pass itself is blocked by militants at times, flanking us right and left were some of the world's most dangerous badlands, the North-West Frontier Province (NWFP). Al-Qaeda terrorists holed up in a labyrinth of tunnels and caves. As Taliban regrouped, Pakistan's army waged a running battle with the restive tribes. The government eventually signed a peace agreement (which held for a while) with the insurgents—including imposing *shar'ia* law.

In Afgahnistan, one good thing the Taliban had done when in power, was banning the sale of opium, but now Taliban insurgents financed terrorism by *selling* illegal drugs—90% of heroin found in Britain comes from Afghanistan. "We must destroy poppy before poppy destroys us!" pled Afghan's President Hamid Karzai, a member of the Pushtun tribe that spans Afghanistan and Pakistan's frontier.

As the overloaded bus lurched toward us, two turbaned, heavy-browed guards straddling the front fenders shot off a volley from their Russian Kalishnakovs.

"*We're coming through!*" the gunfire warned our own armed guard, Adid. "Don't mess with us!" We didn't intend to. Adid spat through tobacco-stained teeth and motioned with his rifle for us to duck inside the army vehicle we'd rented in the border city of Peshawar. We'd be safer out of sight under the tarpaulin canopy as we headed back down the Pakistani side of the Khyber Pass. Bouncing along under cover, we still had a fair view past our guard squatted on the tailgate. His dark eyes observing every detail, Adid cocked his rifle at the ready. Even if the lives of a couple of two foreigners and two Pakistanis weren't worth much to a gangster, a LandRover in working order was worth seizing.

Peter, my guide, knew the customs and spoke Urdu, the official language. Obviously his mind was still off on the lands we'd left behind in the haze below.

"It's sad we no longer have missionaries in Iran," Peter reminisced. He'd once lived in that nation below us in the haze, south and west of Afghanistan. He served there with International Christian Fellowship (ICF). "Did you meet ICF's International Director before you left Canada? Keith Jones and his wife Ruth were among the last foreign missionaries in Iran."

Back in Canada, Keith and Ruth had indeed told me how they had had to flee with only 24-hours' notice. They got out with little more than their Persian Bibles.[15]

Heroin's Hero

Our guard motioned us to peep through an opening in the canopy. "We're passing the fortress of the Ruler of the Khyber Pass!" Peter explained.

"*Ruler?*" I queried.

"Yes—he was a lorry driver who made it big in the drug trade and became the world's Heroin Drug King. Ayub's his name. He's a Pakistani who can't go to any other country because he's a marked man. Interpol knows all about him!"

15. However, the Holy Spirit has never left. It wouldn't be wise to identify the continuing witness in the face of severe restrictions and persecution. Iranian Christians demonstrate that Jesus still walks Iran's paths.

"So he holed up here, smack in the middle of the Khyber?" I asked. "Must be a great place to collect bribes of passage!"

"That's right—no way around," Peter continued. "Ayub has two wives, five children, a palatial home inside the fortress walls, and a private militia of ten thousand."

"Can't the government dislodge him?" I asked as we bounced over rocks and holes.

"One of Pakistan's presidents tried a few years ago," Peter grimaced as we hit a bump. "Sent an army of ten thousand to arrest him. But Ayub's militia held out, and he's still the undisputed ruler of the Khyber Pass." He might have added that no one has tamed any of the proud fiefdoms in the swath of tangled ridges straddling the border of Afghanistan and Pakistan—really the western foothills of the great Himalayas. It's a riven, tortured region, difficult for outsiders to penetrate. Pakistani maps label it simply, "*Tribal Area.*"

Other powers that have tried to subdue the Frontier know it as one of the most rugged and lawless areas of the world. Pathans (the largest tribe in the area) call it, "Land of the Unruled." Their Pathan Code is simple: Revenge, Hospitality, and Sanctuary. This is also the land of the Pirs[16]—whose *spiritual* pedigree, their followers believe, traces back to the Prophet Muhammad; therefore they are highly respected and even considered holy. They ban their women from ever leaving their compounds, but other women (with a male relative) come to consult with them and purchase their holy amulets.

We passed peasants trudging alongside the trail, scarves wound around their heads, and hand-woven shawls draped over their discolored cotton robes. "Do these people keep goats or sheep?" I asked Adid, through Peter.

"Neither—the only trade here is smuggling," Adid replied, tugging the short black beard outlining his square chin. Obviously I'd brought up a topic he really didn't want to pursue with me. No doubt anyone (including smugglers) could employ Adid.

16. *Pir*: Persian "elder." Muhammad's direct descendents are called *Sayids*.

The Coming World Revolution

From the Khyber we drove back to the walled city of Peshawar, ancient border city. Peter paid for our driver, vehicle, and guard (until then, maybe our *lives* had been surety for a safe return!). At Adid's base, his chief was talking over his cell phone. In the guards' hut, a TV screen showed rioting youth throwing stones at helmeted police—somewhere. I couldn't read the Arabic captions.

Noticing my interest in the TV pictures, Adid gritted his teeth as he poked my arm with his rifle and pointed to the sky. An invisible aircraft was leaving a vapor trail. A commercial flight crossing Pakistan on its way from Beijing to Tehran? Or the Pakistani air force? Western Alliance spy plain? We couldn't hear it, but the vapor trail, coupled with the guards' TV set and cell phone, reminded me of the remarkable world we live in.

The Khyber may have echoed to sounds of past revolution pressing through its gate, but the airwaves around me crackled with potential for world revolution. Khyber Gate and Cyber-gate had met. How to put the vapor trail in the sky together with the belching lorry lumbering up the Khyber's switchbacks? I'd have to trek across Asia to understand the events that were affecting the entire world. It promised to be a challenging adventure. Asia was where human history's threads began, and Asia was now raveling before me as the place where it may all end. Through millennia, the clashes of tongue against tongue, tribe against tribe, bespeak mankind's innate sinfulness. Yet language has also been God's gift to develop, express, and preserve cultures worldwide as humanity expanded eastward to the Pacific, westward to the Atlantic, and north and south to the icepacks.[17]

The guard's TV monitor reminded me how Cyberspace, in a sense, reduces the world's babble of speech to one binary language. That's great—but every apple has a worm, it seems. Westward, far below on the misty plains we'd left behind, were the ruins of the Tower of Babel,[18]

---

17. Something God commissioned Adam and Eve to do in their pristine state (Genesis 1.28). Since Babel, fallen mankind has spread over all the earth, but often with greedy abuse rather than environmental care.
18. Heb. *Babhel* > Akkadian, "Gate of God." Are Asia's *stupa* (Skt: "mounds") reminiscent of Babel—man's attempt to reach to the heavens?

where the whole world once spoke a single language. For society's preservation, did God scatter that cozy cabal intent on ruling in God's place?

Now through the Internet, al-Qaeda sought to fulfill the Islamic dream of a global *umma* Caliphate. I was in one of the world's terrorist hotspots: Peshawar. This is where al-Qaeda started. In the surrounding untamed "Federally Administered Tribal Areas," many of its leaders and their henchmen were using the latest Internet technology to connect a loose amalgam of *jihadists*. Al-Qaeda provided global cohesiveness for terrorists through spreading an all-inclusive ideology of "Islam under attack." The self-image of victimhood unites disgruntled Muslims against "the Great Satan" (western democracies led by America), and provides know-how for terrorist attacks. Interestingly, although most terrorists come from neglected segments of society, al-Qaeda's "victim" philosophy also roped in affluent intellectuals as well.

Prayer Power-Walks

Although Peshawar has been a base for insurgency leaders, including the Taliban, the city has also been a center for aid organizations and missions seeking to help stricken areas. Peter and I arrived back inside the city in time for a prayer meeting of these agencies, held in a rented house. One missionary, Brian —, excitedly reported that Afghan authorities allowed his team to hold a "Service of Repentance" overlooking the nation's capital, Kabul. The back of his yellow polo shirt announced, "***Jesus is the Answer***."

"First we publicly apologized for the Crusades!" Brian reported rather triumphally, it seemed. "Then we told the crowd that gathered, about the love of God in Christ Jesus. Praise the Lord for this great opportunity!" Another missionary told about praying over the city "to bind the powers of evil."

This was all interesting to me, because I'd heard various opinions about "Prayer Power Walks" around "Target Cities." Some Christians feel it's the only way to open communities to the gospel—"binding demonic principalities and powers holding large groups of people under their control," according to one advocate.

Veteran missionaries question the wisdom of such headline forays, which they claim divert energy, time, and funds. Often devout people from overseas descend on a city—and on the missionaries who graciously board them. But it was not for me to judge. After all, for whatever reason, God told Joshua's army to march around Jericho! And didn't the walls fall? However, ancient Romans also marched around *their* fields, calling on the name of pagan gods to protect their crops. Anyway, who am I to argue against the concept of Satan having a geographic location, when John the Divine identified Pergamum as the city "where Satan has his throne"?[19]

I realized there's a fine line between *superstition* about the presence of evil and *recognition* of God's sovereign power over evil.[20] After travel in many lands, it seemed to me that Christians could fall into the trap of "evangelical animism"— belief that evil spirits consistently reside in specific items and areas. The Apostle John reminds us, "the *whole world* is under the influence of the evil one," yet God's Spirit is pre-eminent over Satan. Disciples of Jesus are right to "pray in the Spirit," claiming his victory and following his lead in spiritual warfare. I recalled Charles Spurgeon's prayer: *"Oh that Thy people might know they are contending with a vanquished enemy; that they go forth to fight against one who, with all his subtlety and strength, has already been overthrown by Him who is our Covenant Head, our Leader, our all."*[21]

Whatever one's views about public "prayer walks," I was glad to find that Pakistani Christians, pastors, and missionaries aren't about to discount the power of prayer and the reality of spiritual powers. I was in the Indus Valley, the land of "Praying Hyde," who'd agonized in prayer for conversions—and saw them take place.[22] So let me not seem to knock prayer, if it is with the right motive. I knew I would need "the full armor of the Spirit" as I continued along Asia's Old Spice Road.

---

19. Revelation 2.13. Theologians differ over the meaning. Pergamum was the *official* capital of the ancient Greek (and later Roman) Asia Province, a city of learning and libraries, site of temples to the four major pagan deities plus one for Emperor worship. It may have been the site of the first Christian martyr in the province, Antipas. Certainly it was a seat of pagan worship violently opposed to Christians and their faith.
20. Spiritual Warfare is too big a subject and too complicated to pass over lightly. For further reading, see Appendix F: Religion/Christianity/Spiritual Warfare. Also see Lowe, Mau, and Page in Bibliography.
21. Quoted by J. Oswald Sanders in *Prayer Power Unlimited*, p. 119 (see Bibliography).
22. More about Hyde in Chapter 3.

Stepping outside into the gathering dusk, I looked up at a crescent moon magnified by the still air, rising behind the prayer towers of mosques. God had created that moon, I mused, even if many religions had claimed it as their sacred icon. The vaulted sky seemed to loom over me like the dome of a mosque, yet sprinkled all across that dome were galaxies of stars, like pinpricks of hope. "Thank you, Lord!" I whispered. "You placed the moon and the stars there, evidences of your power—yes, and also of your love."

Suddenly the evening call to prayer shattered my reverie. Crackling through loudspeakers mounted on the local mosque's minaret, it announced time for one of Islam's mandatory five-time daily ritual prayers: *"Allah is the greatest. . . . There is no God but Allah. . . . Mohammad is the messenger of Allah."* Prayer is commendable, but this strident call was so demanding, so peremptory, so ubiquitous, that it sent a shudder through me. I knew that Muslim prayer was very different from my Christian understanding of communicating with the Lord God. But Pakistan's history stretched back before the advent of either Islam or Christianity.

Ancient Valley—New Nation

"Hindoostan," the whole sub-continent used to be called, from Old Persian, ***hind'u*** ("river"). Ancients called the great river Sindhu, because it flowed from *Sinh-kabab*—"the mouth of a lion". The surrounding peoples were therefore *Sind*. Like Ephraimites who couldn't say "Shibboleth" properly,[23] early Persian conquerors (whose empire stretched from the Mediterranean to India) had difficulty pronouncing "S." So the Sindhu population became "Hindu," the area "Hindustan," and the river "Indus."

Fed by glacial streams high in Tibet and the disputed Kashmir ranges (a frozen northern area "hotly" claimed by both Pakistan and India), the Indus snakes along the length of the country, from northern cataracts to southern arid plains. For 2740 km (1,700 m.) it flows before emptying into the Arabian Sea, where its brown silt stretches ten miles out to sea.

---

23. Judges 12.6. Invading Ephraimites revealed themselves when asked to say, "Shibboleth" (Heb. *stream*).

From the time of Abraham, the valley had boasted large cities. They evidenced city planning, with brick houses (some two-level) equipped with bathrooms. Garbage emptied down chutes into a covered sewage system. Farmers cultivated grain crops and cotton.[24]

This became the heartland of Hindu religion. It is an admixture of early idolatry from Mesopotamia (worship of cattle and fire, from ancient Sumeria and Babylon), astrology from Egypt, and later Aryan mythology from eastern Europe and western Asia, reflecting successive empires.[25] The province along the banks of the lower Indus is still called Sind, where the indigenes speak Sindhi. But among settlers of this fertile basin there have been enclaves of Babylonians, Egyptians, Greeks, Huns, Jews, and Tartars.

Syrian Arab armies invaded the Indus Valley early in the 8th c., defeating the Buddhist King Dahir. Under Islam, polytheists had the choice of either converting or fighting, but "People of the Book" (Jews and Christians) and Zoroastrians could pay a special tax and maintain their own faith under Muslim rule. In like measure, enclaves of Muslims lived among Hindu majorities in the Indian sub-continent under various emperors, including Afghans and Moguls (of Islamic Turkic-Mongol ancestry) up to the 18th c. They enriched local cultures with Arab, Persian, and Turkic art and language.

Muslims and Hindus "Play Cricket"

In the 16th c., Britain opened formal trade with India, and for the next 150 years competed with Portugal, France, and Holland. By the 18th c., internal strife had weakened Mogul rule, and in 1765 Robert Clive became the first British Governor of Bengal (on India's East). Ultimately, Britain ruled the entire sub-continent, by then known as India.

---

24. F. R. Onyedinefu, "The Indus Valley Civilization." Unpublished lecture notes, 1999.
25. Aryans began migrating from Europe/W. Asia ca. 5,000 B.C., invading Persia (now "Iran," derivative of Aryan) and the Indus Valley, c. 2,000 B.C. Archaeology links their Sanskrit with traces of Latin and Greek, and their rites (veneration of fire, sun, sky, mother-goddess) with Nordic Europe and Mesopotamia. Oral tradition formed the *Vedanta,* with Sumerian and Jewish concepts absorbed *en route* to the "Indian" sub-continent. (Cf. "Euro-Asians," J.R. Hinnels, *Dictionary of Religions*, 163, and other sources—see Bibliog.)

British rule at least brought together a semblance of national unity. Until then, the population had been splintered among 563 fractious kingdoms under successive foreign emperors. Now "the British Crown Jewel" of India (including the Empire's sport of cricket!) opened up a "new world" for Muslim and Hindu alike. All along the Indus Valley, British engineers planted trees and created an irrigation system with the world's largest network of canals (50,000 k./30,000 m.) based on a single riverain basin.[26]

However, the goal of Independence became a common motive among the sub-continent's politicians. Mohammad Ali Jinnah, respected Muslim statesman, and Mahatma Gandhi, a Vaishya (Hindu upper class), had already parted company on ideology and methods of achieving that Independence.[27] Gandhi pursued non-cooperation with the British (although non-violently). He wanted a united independent state. Jinnah, although a moderate but just as intransigent as Gandhi, at first opposed Partition, backing the constitutional path to a united democracy.

But Muslims would have been a minority within such a confederation, and Jinnah knew they already considered themselves a distinct community. The sheer number of India's Hindus made Partition essential for *Shari'a* to rule a Muslim community. In the Punjab (on India's West), poet-statesman Mohammad Iqbal (who once attended a Christian mission school), called for a consolidated Muslim state.

When tensions became violent, in 1947 the departing British sought to forestall civil war by hiving off the sub-continent's Indus Valley western area and its far-eastern riverain area from the rest of India. The result was two independent "Dominions" within the British Commonwealth.

---

26. While today's wisdom decries empire, it has been the story of mankind—for either abuse or benefit. Although every nation takes pride in its unique existence, even European countries are the result of the cross-pollination of culture, language, and breeding from other races—including Asian. Americans who condemn colonization forget the benefits it brought to North America (apart from the disgraceful abuse of First Nations peoples—who themselves had been earlier colonizers from Asia). It was the sense of justice and democracy in some early *British* settlers that led them to declare Independence from their inept king.

27. Both leaders earned their law degrees in Britain. Jinnah, a Muslim, became an exponent for controlled democracy. Gandhi, although a secular lawyer, used Hinduism as a powerful tool for Indian unity. Gandhi turned down the Prime Minister role in India, because it would have conflicted with his ascetic life style.

Islam-dominated Pakistan and supposedly "secular" India. Jinnah became Governor-General of independent Pakistan. A year later, M.A. Jinnah died of Tuberculosis. Pakistanis remember him as "Father of the Nation."

Most disturbing to Jinnah and Gandhi was the turbulence of Independence, when Muslims and Hindus clashed violently.[28] Partition had sought to solve their incompatibility by political and geographic surgery, but it unleashed seething anger, hurt pride, and frustrated ambition. As Muslim refugees sought sanctuary west in the Indus Valley, Hindu refugees fled eastward. In some places, only a foot-wide white line marked the new political border, but animosities were beyond measure. Partition exposed as myth 19th c. Europe's romanticism of "the Sacred East's" syncretism, tolerance, and non-violence. Liberal theologians had cited it as a model for churches to follow.

An estimated additional 30m Muslims moved from India into West and East Pakistan, some 15m people *exchanging* places—many on foot. Another million died in the melee, it is estimated. Women suffered most of all. An estimated 75,000 women were abducted or raped, some by brigands, others by angry males seeking vengeance on the families that ousted them, and many by zealots opposed to mixed (Hindu-Muslim) marriages—not uncommon in the sub-continent.

Pakistan suffered a further blow when its eastern wing—Islamic but considered "unorthodox" by some—declared its own Independence. After a war of secession in 1971, it became "Bangladesh." Pakistan and India clashed over the unresolved status of Kashmir,[29] sandwiched between them in the far north. Pakistanis felt as if under siege. Their former Hindu neighbors unhelpfully forecast the nation's collapse. Paranoia about external influences may have been heightened by the fact that all Pakistan's rivers rise from sources outside the country. It's still easy for some Pakistanis to blame both drought and flood on neighboring countries. And in spite of the intransigence of Jinnah and Gandhi, many still blame Britain for Partition.[30]

---

28. Within a year, both men died: Jinnah of illness; Gandhi murdered by a Hindu who objected to his conciliatory attitude to Muslims, including seeking peaceful relations with Pakistan.
29. When leaving the sub-continent, Britain handed Kashmir's unresolved dispute to local chiefs to decide. If they'd waited for resolution, they might still be there.
30. Yasmin Khan, *The Great Partition: The Making of India and Pakistan*. Yale University Press, 2007.

Immediate Identity—World Community

Learning of this background, I admired the young nation for pulling itself together. Across the border in the Indian sub-continent, Muslims had been used to a sense of power under Muslim (Mogul) rulers for over six centuries. Under British rule, Muslims lost that political dominance and withdrew into isolation. Those who moved into Pakistan represented many different Islamic communities. These in turn had to settle among multiple sects and minority cultures and faiths long established in the Indus Valley.

While Partition shattered dreams of restoring the Mogul emperors' power on the Indian sub-continent, Pakistan didn't collapse. Independence sparked new hope. The new nation (new, and yet with a multiplicity of ancient peoples, languages, and cultures) needed immediate identity and cohesion. Islam was the natural bond to unify the country. Muslims anticipated overcoming isolation by making the new nation part of a worldwide religious community. Suddenly despair turned to future hope, part of a global vision; for Islam foresees the entire world eventually being ruled by *Shari'a*—that is, the "Law of God," as revealed to the Prophet Muhammad and the *Ulama*.[31] (Reality required constitutional provision for the nation's non-Muslim elements, already ensconced.)

The nation's new flag, with its white crescent and star on a dark-green background, "emphasizes Pakistan's profound commitment to Islam and the Islamic world."[32] While in India Hindu zealots sought to dominate India,[33] Pakistani zealots sought to impose a strict form of Islam that would demonstrate what a truly Islamic country could become. Of course, in their thinking, "The Land of the Holy" (meaning of "Pakistan") would have to purge (or consign to museums) relics of

---

31. *Ulama*: Arabic "learned men"—custodians, interpreters of sacred knowledge of traditions and theology. Islam imposes on fractured nations orderly systems of living, cohesive veneer, and common identity. Pakistan's Constitution technically guarantees human rights. (More in Appendix H: Islam.)
32. M. Ajmal, *Pakistan*—Centenary Tribute for the Founder's Birth. London: Stacey, 1977, p. 69. Star and crescent appear on several Islamic national flags. Since the 18th c., Islam has universally used the crescent as its symbol, equivalent to Christianity's cross, although originally it was a Zoroastrian (Persian) symbol.
33. Actually, nearly as many Muslims still live in India as in all of Pakistan.

earlier idolatrous civilizations and practices. "Pakistan is a model of an Islamic welfare state," announced one of its Prime Ministers, Nawaz Sharif, in 1998.

Though the constitution guarantees other religions the right to exist in the nation (on the flag a vertical white bar represents some 2m Christians and other minorities), government did institute *Shari'a* (Qur'anic) Law, replacing the British legal system. Pakistan became an Islamic Republic in 1956. Successive governments have increased the rule of *Shari'a,* enforcing prayer five times daily for Muslims (see Appendix H.). In keeping with Orthodox Islam, the law perpetuates gender discrimination. For instance, if a woman is raped, she herself may be blamed and receive the death penalty—because while men need only one male defense witness, orthodox law requires women to find *four male* defence witnesses (unlikely!). Sex outside of marriage incurs death by stoning.

> Pakistan's newspaper, *The Daily Star,* Nov. 14, 2008, headlined: "1,019 Women Killed for Honour over Three Years." The article recounted: "National Assembly was told on Thursday Nov. 13, 2008, that more than 7,000 cases of rape and murders of women were registered 2005 to 2007, in addition to 1,019 cases of honour killings."

Jesus Finds Needy Woman on the Spice Road

In the strictures of a Muslim society, I wondered how Jesus could find receptive hearts. Although often unrecognized, his Spirit was indeed still passing along the Spice Road. He who was despised and rejected, was softly calling to downcast people: *"Come unto me, all you who are weary and heavy-laden, and I will give you rest."*

That's what Jesus did for Madame Bilquis Sheikh in her home on the Peshawar road, near the nation's capital, Islamabad. Daughter of a prominent Muslim family, she'd been devastated when her husband rejected her for another woman.

"I divorce you!" her husband had pronounced three times. That's all *Shari'a* law required. No messy divorce courts.[34]

34. The cell phone makes this even simpler, for a Muslim husband can now send, from anywhere in the world, the required triple pronouncement in a text-message—and the divorce is complete!

Feeling forsaken, Mdme. Bilquis looked to her holy book, the *Qur'an*, for comfort but found none. However, the *Qur'an* did mention "People of the Book"—Jews and Christians. Perhaps their holy book could provide some solace. She secretly sought for a Bible. When she found a copy of the forbidden book, she opened it at random. The first verse her eyes lighted on shocked her—and started a spiritual pilgrimage to find the Way, the Truth, and the Life:

"I will call them my people, who are not my people, and I will call her 'my loved one' who is not my loved one. And it will happen, in the very place where it was said to them, 'You are not my people,' they will be called ' sons of the living God'" (Romans 9.25-26).

Could this be true? Madam Sheikh, rejected by her husband, longed to give herself wholly to God. But she couldn't understand this prophecy. Remote and austere, Allah could never be a loving Father! To Muslims, it was blasphemous to even think of him as Father. Although the Qur'an teaches that an angelic visitation caused Mary to conceive, to Muslims the Trinity portrays idolatry and immorality—God having sexual union with the Virgin Mary, begetting a son!

The more she read, however, this educated woman understood that God is indeed one. She knew Islam also states that, even though it accepts the existence of the Holy Spirit. But from her Bible reading, Bilquis learned that God (because he *is* God) can be known as Father, Son, and Holy Spirit—yet he is truly one. And the Bible did not state that Mary was; she was only the human channel for a miraculous birth, conceived through the Spirit of God. Jesus was therefore the one true God in human form. Moreover, the Eternal Son of God gave himself for our sins—something that Islam does not accept. Although Bilquis had wondered if Jesus' disciples were idolaters, as Muslims charge and some "Church" rites seem to imply, she noted that the Bible clearly forbade idolatry. It was all confusing—even overwhelming!

However, the Holy Spirit started convicting Bilquis of her need for God who "so loved the world that he gave his only begotten son." She struggled and hesitated, but finally in desperation she dared to pray to the one true God as *Father*—Eternal Father, the personal God who *loved her*. Suddenly, instead of guilt, Bilquis felt free. She hadn't read *Pilgrim's*

Progress, but she had the same sensation that John Bunyan wrote about: a tremendous burden rolled off her back. She trusted in Christ as Saviour, and her life changed forever. Tragic events that had threatened to destroy Madame Sheikh's life, forced her to seek the Saviour and find eternal life.

So powerful is Madame Sheikh's published testimony that the government of the day banned her book, even though it's been published in some 30 countries.[35] The risen Saviour met Bilquis Sheikh on the Old Spice Road, and, like the Apostle Paul, she became an ambassador for Christ to her own nation and others.

As I travelled along the Old Spice Road, Madame Bilquis would be only one of several examples of "the Hound of Heaven" at work. English poet Francis Thompson first used that phrase in his 1893 volume of poetry, to refer to the Holy Spirit's relentless tracking of spiritually needy men and women. God, I mused, is more concerned about finding his spiritually lost Creation than humanity is about finding him![36]

Military/Civilian Seesaw

Further along the Peshawar highway, I visited Islamabad, the young nation's capital: gleaming white mosques, orderly boulevards lined with architecture reflecting Arab influence. Saudi Arabia had invested heavily in Islamabad, its strict Wahhabi sect greatly influencing the nation's practice of Islam. The city's Lal Masjid ("Red Mosque") has waved the flag for militant orthodoxy.[37]

Pakistan has seesawed between civilian and military leadership. Whether ruling or not, the military holds tremendous power economically. It has helped stabilize the nation, beset by internal factions and external pressures. According to Pakistani author Ayesha Siddiqa,[38] the military also looks after its own (!), operating five "welfare foundations" that include an airline, road-building, and light and heavy industries—$10 billion worth.

35. Bilquis Sheikh, *I Dared to Call Him Father*. Old Tappan: Chosen Books, 1978.
36. For further discussion of this topic, see Appendix G.
37. In 2007, the government had to take forceful action to oust militant *jihadists* who had seized the mosque.
38. Ayesha Siddiqa, *Military Inc.: Inside Pakistan's Military Economy*. Pluto Press, 2007.

A few of Islamabad's traffic circles sport a missile—symbol of Pakistan's military power. Those missile symbols hold more significance than the casual visitor might suspect, for one of the residents of a wealthy suburb is Abdul Qadeer Khan, "father of Pakistan's bomb." It was difficult to realize; although he's a metallurgist-business man and not a terrorist, until recently he was under house prisoner, confined by the government and denied any contact with foreigners—even use of the telephone!

Khan stole nuclear technology from a Dutch laboratory where he worked in the 1970s. Returning to Pakistan with his secrets, he set up a major enrichment lab in the Punjab and made a fortune selling parts and technology, inspiring dreams of an "Islamic bomb." Libya blew the whistle on Khan's global nuclear sales after Interpol intercepted a shipment of nuclear bomb parts in the Mediterranean. Khan's network included not only Libya but also China, Dubai, Iran, and North Korea—who else, no one really knows, except entrepreneur Abdul Khan. If a nuclear holocaust ever incinerates our world, Khan may be the most culpable single initiator.[39]

Regardless of Khan's mischief, this spanking new city illustrated for me the founding of an ambitious nation.[40] Islamabad is the Islamic centerpiece in a mosaic of ethnic groups, languages, and religious sects that inhabit the Indus Basin and borders. By constructing Islamabad ("City of Islam"), in 1967 the nation sidestepped rival claims of Lahore (capital of the Punjab[41]) and Karachi (major port city) to be the rightful capital.

Friendship in a Tea Pot

This was a good time to visit Murree, further north, perched in the foothills of the Himalayas. It was during the school break, when expatriates escape the most intense lowland heat by spending a few weeks at Murree. Several missionaries I knew would be there. Drinking in the crisp air, I

---

39. *Shopping for Bombs: Nuclear Proliferation, Global Insecurity, and the Rise and Fall of the A. Q. Khan Network*, by Gordon Corera. (Oxford: Oxford University Press, 2006); also *The Nuclear Jihadist,* by Douglas Frantz and Catherine Collins. New York: Twelve, 2008).

40. Formed 1947, Pakistan (Farsi/Persian: *Land of the Holy/Pure*) was declared an Islamic Republic in 1956.

41. Lahore—capital of India's prosperous geo-ethnic Punjab region before Partition split the area. Lahore became capital of Pakistan's Punjab State. India built Chandigarh as the capital of its share of the Punjab.

enjoyed the breath-taking mountain view. To the northeast sits majestic K2, second in altitude only to Everest. In between is Kashmir, where the Indo-China fault-line periodically triggers earthquakes.[42]

Many of the missionaries had children attending Murree's inter-mission school. Parents and children gathered from all over Pakistan, from the port of Karachi northwards. Although from different countries and agencies, they had one calling—Christ's Commission. The ways they fulfilled that calling nationwide were varied, including teaching children at the inter-mission school, preparing Bible programs for Marwari radio broadcasts, translating, distributing literature from a "bookvan," and publishing Bible study notes. A couple of missions worked on Theological Education by Extension courses—invaluable leadership-training tools.

I expected to hear about such projects, but what surprised me was *the ministry of serving tea!* It's a natural in a country that bans alcohol, but whose culture places the highest value on social friendship. The West has its ways to show friendship, but the pace of life rules out the most obvious way—spending time in hospitality. In Pakistan, that doesn't necessarily mean a table laden with food, but just a cup of tea (*chai*), and time to chat.

> An Arab proverb explains: *"A friend is one to whom one may pour out all the contents of one's heart, chaff and grain together, knowing that the gentlest of hands will take and sift it, keep what is worth keeping, and with the breath of kindness blow the rest away."*

"My record for serving *chai* is 50 cups in one day!" Anne Noble told me. She and her husband, Charles, were enjoying a needed "breather" from the desert heat of Sind Province. But serving tea had its local twist. Islamic culture prevented a woman from personally serving non-family males. So Anne kept out of sight as she boiled tea, sugar, cardamom seeds, and milk—then placed the brew in the hallway, where Charles could pick it up and serve it to the men who came to see him throughout the day.

Anne always wore women's Pakistani garments, never going outside without a head covering and floor-length shawl—in order not to offend. Wherever Anne went she had to be accompanied by her husband. Anne

---

42. In 2005, a devastating quake engulfed entire villages, killing 73,000, displacing 3m. More than 100 aid agencies rushed in to help, donors pledging $6 billion more than requested. Amazingly, Murree School was practically undamaged.

could never visit in a home if Charles and the husband of that home had not first met together. In the eighteen years she lived in Sind, she was never in the market place where fruit and vegetables were bought. Charles had to do the shopping.

Apart from the inconveniences of such restrictions, there were trying times of harassment—such as when the neighboring mosque pointed its loudspeakers directly at the Nobles' apartment. For 36 hours, the local maulvis screamed instructions, reprimands, and challenges to their parishioners. Living in the centre of the market area, they took the full impact of the verbal assault. The volume was so great that a pot of boiling water fell off the Nobles' kerosene stove and an iron fell off the ironing board. The spiritual darkness made it impossible to concentrate in prayer.

"Life was frustrating at times," confessed Anne, in spite of being a vivacious sort; "but we did it for Christ's sake. It was encouraging to know that family and friends were praying for us—even if they didn't know what we were going through." The Nobles couldn't even guess the lasting value of those cups of tea, with discussions about God's love in providing our redemption.[43]

Murree was placid when I visited, but it later exploded in terror as revolutionaries seeking foreign targets invaded the school compound. The amazing thing was the peace God gave staff and children (some Pakistani as well as expatriate), who barricaded themselves in rooms and closets or huddled under tables and desks. They quoted Scripture, quietly sang choruses, and prayed (one child prayed for the attackers' salvation) until police arrived. Three suspects committed suicide as police approached.

The school's thanksgiving for deliverance was mixed with sorrow over the death of six Pakistani staff, who had been personal friends. A couple of other staff suffered non-mortal wounds.[44] Around the same time, terrorists attacked other humanitarian projects in the area, including a Christian hospital.

---

43. However, some Islamists may regard a Christian missionary's proffered cup of tea as an act of proselytizing, according to Ray Tallman of Arab World Ministries.

44. See Sue Morton, *Angels in the Rafters.* Chiang Mai: Murree Christian School, 2002. Because of further threats, the school moved to Thailand temporarily but reopened in Pakistan in 2005.

Adding Insult to Injury

"BISHOP KILLS HIMSELF ON COURT BUILDING STEPS!" screamed the newspaper headline. Whatever caused that, I wondered! The good bishop was not a suicide bomber. Friends told me that Bishop John Masih set himself alight in front of the court to protest the victimization of Christians under the Blasphemy Law.[45] The Law makes it a capital crime to "insult" Islam or the Prophet Muhammad. "Insult" has wide interpretation. A radical Muslim could accuse someone of insulting the Prophet by using his name without adding the obligatory benediction, such as, "Peace be upon him." (Orthodox Muslims use a phrase that implies the highest veneration of the Prophet.)

The government of the day introduced the Law to win support of Islamic extremists, but it has since been a threat to both non-Muslims and Muslims. On the slightest pretext, anyone anywhere can interpret it to accuse a person of blasphemy. The accuser needs no witness, and the offense entitles a zealot to defend the faith by killing the accused—or at least having him or her arrested. If a judge requires a witness, only one Muslim witness is needed to prosecute a case, while a court requires *two* non-Muslims (or *four* women) for the defense. It's a great way to settle scores, let alone intimidate non-Muslims!

Bishop John came to the end of his tether when a court sentenced to death one of his parishioners, 26-year-old Ayub Masih.[46] Ayub and a Muslim had been arguing over a piece of land, when Ayub allegedly said he enjoyed Salman Rushdie's writings. The Muslim claimed that Ayub spoke favorably of Rushdie's novel, *The Satanic Verses*, that obviously parallels the Prophet Muhammad's life.[47] Enraged, the Muslim charged Ayub with blasphemy. I learned that Pakistani and

45. Compass Direct News, Istanbul, May 7, 1998. The actual law is *Pakistan Penal Code #1860.*

46. Masih is a common surname given Christians—from *al-Masih,* Arabic for "the Messiah."

47. Rushdie, a secular Muslim Britain knighted for his literature, has been under a death *fatwa* for insulting Islam with his book. Yet in early editions of the *Qur'an,* Muslim scholars called a section "The Satanic Verses"—they were so contrary to Muhammad's teaching, that Satan must somehow have inserted them.

International appeals later lowered the death sentence to imprisonment, but by then the good bishop was dead.

Thousands await trial under The Blasphemy Law. The death sentence is often commuted by the High Court. When Islamic sects upset orthodox Muslims, rivals sometimes charge fellow Muslims. Mohammad Yusuf Ali of Lahore was one of those. He had declared himself a prophet, thus "insulting" the one and only Prophet in Islam.[48]

The case of non-Muslims Rasheed (33) and Saleem (20) demonstrates the trivial basis for many charges. An ice cream vendor refused to serve them ice cream, because that would contaminate the bowls for Muslim customers. No doubt the brothers were annoyed, but the vendor had the last word by accusing the two of blasphemy.[49] The courts lowered the mandatory death sentence to 35 years in prison for these two young fathers.

The law at times causes summary execution, as in the case of a favourite teacher in a government school in one town I visited. The fact he was a Christian didn't bother the Muslim students. They all spoke highly of him. But other teachers resented his popularity, and one day someone put up a wall poster alleging that the Christian teacher had insulted Islam. The zealous son of the village butcher grabbed one of his father's butcher knives and stabbed the teacher to death, becoming judge and executor. There was no enquiry or arrest—instead village mullahs came to the butcher's house and placed garlands around the neck of the son to congratulate him for defending the faith.[50]

Pakistan does have a Minister of Religious Affairs, who is responsible for protecting religious freedom. However, a 2002 letterhead from his office pointedly quoted a Qur'anic verse: "Islam is the only religion acceptable to God."

---

48. Rather than "Prophet," a Sunni leader may be a Sheikh; a Shi'a may be an Imam or Ayatollah.
49. *Family News*, October 1999. Colorado Springs: Focus on the Family.
50. Compass Direct News Release, Istanbul, May 19, 2000.

Jihadis "Revolutionize" Islam

In spite of the region's stresses, Pakistan has been one of the most open Muslim countries, seeking to curtail terrorist elements. But I knew that Islamic teachers in the Qur'anic schools (*madrassas)*[51] of many countries drill into children's minds the classic definition of global *jihad* as a Muslim's duty to kill unbelievers. In fact, *jihadis,* led by Al Qaeda, have been changing the face of Islam worldwide. (For details on the two meanings of *jihad* and this "revolution," see Appendix H: Islam.)

Apart from fomenting international murder, arguably a religious school should be free to teach its faith. However, most Qur'anic schools in the Middle East do not also teach the academic subjects today's youth will need to find employment. That's potential unrest!

My mind struggled to reconcile radical Islamists with my tolerant Muslim neighbors back home, and those I met in my travels. Reformers have genuinely sought to bring Islam into the global mainstream. At the same time, well-advantaged *western* converts have joined in terrorist mayhem. It just didn't make sense.

While those who wage war against Islamic states are, understandably, considered as enemies, so are *peacemakers* in the eyes of radicals—for they try to prevent "*jihad*"! To *jihadists*, the Western concept of "peacemaker" is contrary to Islamic "struggle." Radical Muslims accuse peacemakers and aid workers of being "spies," imposing Western values (which they equate with "Christian") upon the followers of Allah.

In fact, Islam considers all non-Muslims ("infidels") to be legitimate targets of the struggle to bring everyone into the Islamic *Ummah*. They are enemies of God. As such, they can legitimately be lied to and, when possible, forced to convert or be killed. While moderate Muslim states do practise social democracy within certain religious strictures, representative democracy that truly participates

---

51. Although accurate figures are not available, there are likely tens of thousands of these in Pakistan.

in government is not in the thinking of core Islam—or any other type of theocracy, for that matter. Radical *jihad* and peaceful nation-wide ballots are simply incompatible. That's what Afghanistan's Taliban believe.

I still didn't understand the nation or its dominant religion—but Pakistan was teaching me much that would inform my travels across Asia. My mind was in a whirl. With such a myriad of Islamic views, small wonder that Christendom (which also is split into many streams) has various opinions of Muslim-Christian relations. I thought of the devout missionaries in Peshawar, apologizing for the Medieval Crusades. They saw the Crusades as a blot on Church history, making Christian witness ineffective if not impossible.

Next morning, I almost heard thunder in the sunrise as I boarded a train heading south to the vast Baluchi Desert. I wondered what Pakistanis themselves think of the Crusades.

Children cluster around missionary Kathy Bell to hear a Bible story

Pakistan
What "*Izzat*"?

"Our struggle is not against flesh and blood, but ... against the powers of this dark world and against the spiritual forces of evil in the heavenly realms" (Ephesians 6.12).

WHAT ARE YOU DOING in Pakistan?" my two traveling companions asked. We were in the closed compartment of a vintage steam train chugging across southern Pakistan's Baluchi Desert.

I presumed the two men were Muslims. Why did they want to know what I was doing? Many Taliban zealots took refuge in Baluchistan. How sympathetic to them were my fellow passengers?

A bigger question was buzzing through my head: what was this country called Pakistan? I'd heard how it had come about—how the area had been part of successive empires: Persian, Mogul, and British. How, under the British, it had been part of India and gained Independence in 1947. How civil strife between the Hindu majority and the large Muslim populations had resulted in Partition.

I could understand why predominantly Muslim Pakistan had adopted an Islamic constitution, and why sore feelings still festered between the new nation and the rest of the sub-continent it had found impossible to live with.

At the time, Pakistan was one of the more tolerant Islamic states. How did its Christian communities exist? Could they reach out to their Muslim neighbors? Were there still Hindus in Pakistan?

The questions stopped buzzing in my head as the train neared a watering station—the last before a vast featureless sandy plain stretching to the nation's borders with Afghanistan and Iran, according to my map. Earlier, I'd closed my window to keep out soot from the train's belching smokestack, but through the smudgy glass, I saw vultures wheeling above the station coming into view. A lone date-palm leaned over the station, as if begging for a drink.

Earlier, I'd peeked into the low-fare carriage, where goats and fowl nestled between men, women, and children, who sprawled on benches and on top of piles of baggage. (The latter position not only provided a resting place but also safeguarded one's possessions.) The atmosphere appeared to be as thick per square meter as the occupants. I saw why friends had advised me to go "Second Class," in which European-style compartments divided the passenger cars into compartments for four. That's where I shared a section with a uniformed army captain and a railroad accountant. Both sported a mustache, as did many Pakistani males. Introducing myself as "Fuller" from Canada, I learned the army man was Captain Said, and the accountant was Assad.

Prayers on the Train Platform

When the train stopped to drop off supplies and refill its water reservoir at this outpost, I slid open my window, trying to suck in fresh air. It almost needed cutting. My two travel companions disembarked, joining other males to pray on the station platform, in partial fulfillment of one of Islam's meritorious requisites: *Sallah*[1] five times a day, facing towards Mecca. They followed the same choreographed ritual I'd seen in other countries:

(1) wash hands and face from a kettle in order to be pure enough to recite sacred words;

(2) recite an introductory prayer;

---

1. Arab: *salat,* "prayer"; Urdu: *wamaz.*

(3) kneel, bending forward until foreheads touched the ground;

(4) sit back on folded legs to finger prayer beads while reciting Allah's 99 names;

(5) stand up to recite more prayer;

(6) conclude with Islam's basic maxim: "*God is great, and Muhammad is his prophet.*"

After the prayer ritual, worshipers dropped coins into the bowls of expectant beggars—a meritorious deed. During the prayers, the men's wives and other females stayed curtained off in the women's carriage.[2] I too stayed on board, to keep an eye on our bags, lest any *dacoit*[3] reach in through the cabin doorway or open window. I wasn't averse to giving alms to needy people, but that shifty-eyed beggar at my window seemed to have more on his mind than a few coins.

When my cabin mates returned, the dusty spots on their foreheads and knees piously testified to their complete submission to Allah.[4] They thoughtfully brought me an English-language newspaper and a bottle of Mecca Cola. Typical Arab hospitality, I thought. My mind went back to a visit a fellow missionary, Howard, and I once made to Arabia. In a bazaar, we dropped by a shop whose owner Howard had known in Somalia.

"No problem," Rashid had replied when we asked if we could borrow a few coins until we changed our foreign currency. He pulled a wad of local money out of his nightshirt-like garment. "Here—take this. Return what you don't use. And just a minute; I'll get my driver to take you where you want." Rashid never counted the money—not when he gave it to us or when we returned it. And he refused to take our money in exchange—not even for the use of his Mercedes Benz.

---

2. Our word for Islam's secluded women's area, "purdah," comes from Hindi/Urdu *parda*: screen or veil.

3. From Urdu *daakuu*: bandit.

4. The Arabic word, *islam,* means "submission." Although this is a desirable attitude toward God, orthodox Islam reduces it to fatalism controlling all of life. This may lead to accidents resulting from belief that "if Allah wills" an accident, nothing can prevent it.

Such thoughtfulness is typical of many Arabs, I learned. A Sanskrit proverb states:

He who allows his day to pass by without practicing generosity . . .
is like a blacksmith's bellows—he breathes but does not live.

Although the "Coke" was warm, it was wet—welcome in the 50 C. (122F) temperature. Our coach windows were now wide open, but when the train lurched into motion, I quickly closed mine to keep out soot from the coal-burning engine. Besides, the desert air blasting in through the open window felt like a blowtorch on my bare arms. On the horizon a thermal sucked up sand into a twister. Nomads call it a *djinni*.[5]

I consoled myself with the thought that Alexander's army didn't even have a train to cross this desert. We passed the kind of "train" he would have used—a camel train laden with baskets and bales, proudly lurching across shimmering sands. The way they seemed to roll and pitch, no wonder they were called "*ships* of the desert." I'd been told that only the camel knows the sacred one hundredth name for Allah. No wonder they all had a haughty, proud expression!

"Christians?—No Trouble!"

Now we settled down for the long stretch. That's when Captain Said and Assad asked: "What are you doing in Pakistan?" Until then we'd exchanged only pleasantries. But I sensed that curiosity rather than suspicion prompted the question.

"Visiting friends," I explained truthfully. "In Canada we have many Pakistanis, so I'd like to know more about their country." One doesn't have to tell everything, only the truth. We became quite chatty, comparing our respective countries—such as the difference between ice hockey and cricket. We even touched on religions.

"I've met Muslims, Hindus, and Christians in Pakistan," I probed, opening up the conversation further. "Is there any tension between them?"

"We don't have any trouble with Christians," Captain Said assured me.[6] "True Muslims should respect your Bible as a holy book and Jesus

---

5. Arabic: *demon* in Muslim teaching; but in folklore, a magic spirit or genie.
6. This interview was before the Islamic reactions of the 21st c.

as an historical figure." While they spoke, they fingered their prayer beads—a kind of security while discussing another religion, I imagined. A couple of times during our onward journey, the businessman spread a white cloth over his passenger bench, perching on it to recite his prayers while kneeling and squatting. "Islam affects whatever we do and all of life," they explained.

"Christians also believe our faith should affect the way we live," I ventured, wondering how far I could go. My mind searched for points of common understanding. I knew that Islam acknowledges the Spirit of God, even if not in a biblical way. "If our faith is real, the Holy Spirit gives us power to live as God wants us to. Unfortunately some Christians don't let him. They worship God on Sunday but they live for themselves the rest of the week." I waited for a reaction.

"Muslims and Christians are more alike than Muslims and Hindus," the two rejoined. "Hindus worship idols, but Christians don't—except maybe the Virgin Mary." Ah, Asia's concept of Christianity! I explained why I don't worship Mary, although I respect her. However, I admitted there are different views among Christians, even as Muslims have different views of Islam. At last I saw my chance to ask about the Crusades.

"What are *crusades*?" asked Assad. He'd never heard of them. (I wasn't about to tell him that Muslim destruction of the Church of the Holy Sepulcher in Jerusalem had inflamed Christendom, leading to the politicized Crusades, in much the same way as more recent Hindu destruction of Islam's Babri Mosque at Ayodhya, India, had inflamed Muslim passions.) Instead, Assad asked me why he'd never seen a Christian beggar but lots of Muslim beggars. The difference, I knew, was that in Islam, giving to a beggar is meritorious, and begging is an acceptable means of living. Christian agencies seek to provide skills that empower a crippled or impoverished person to regain the self-respect God intends for his creation. But I didn't want to get into that side issue.

Captain Said, obviously more widely read, knew of the Crusades as one of many foreign incursions, including Aryan, Persian, Turkic, Arab, and more recently, Communist. I'd heard that Urdu (Pakistan's official language that the two men spoke) had its origins in a conglomerate of

Arabic, Persian, and Sanskrit[7] dialects developed by a "crusading" Mogul emperor to enable him to communicate with all groups.[8] Surprisingly, it was a *British missionary linguist,* Henry Martyn, whose translation of the Bible codified poetic Urdu into a language of wider communication. It replaced *Farsi* (Persian) as the sub-continent's lower-court language, becoming Pakistan's national language. (Similarly, Medieval Bible translations had melded Britain's fractured dialects into English.).

"Does the memory of the Christian Crusades make Muslims resent Christianity?" I pressed the Captain.

"Before the Iraqi war, the average Pakistani hadn't heard of the Crusades," he replied, twisting the ends of his handlebar mustache. (That style of facial vegetation marked him as a genuine army officer of Imperial School pedigree.) "Besides, Islam has also had its crusades.[9] Muslims are generally peaceful, but there are always radicals who stir up trouble. They try to blame the Crusades and the Americans."

Wow—these were not the kind of Muslims I expected to find! I didn't know how widespread were the views of my two travel companions, but our conversation told me something about moderate Pakistanis—kind, understanding, compassionate. When a train porter came around with piping hot tea (one of the good customs the British Raj left behind) they even purchased a pot for me—and wouldn't take a rupee for it!

"They're Used to Me"

At the Quetta station, Kathy Bell's friendly face welcomed me. An Anglican serving with SIM, Kathy could have been a Pakistani, but for

---

7. Sanskrit ("perfected/noble"): Indo-Aryan (incl. Persian, Turkic) mix, shaped Bengali, Hindi, Punjabi.
8. Though now using Persian script, Urdu began as a verbal trade language—as did "Pidgin" in China, and conglomerate Swahili in Africa. "Urdu" >Turkic-Mongol *ordu*, "camp" (English added "h" to give us "horde"). After Partition, Pakistan promoted Urdu (used in the North of India before Partition) as the national language among Pakistan's 69 languages/dialects. For years, readers preferred Urdu newspapers hand-scripted, not printed from type. Estimates of Pakistan's literacy vary from 25-38%.
9. The Captain obviously knew history. Before the major Crusades to recapture Jerusalem, the Muslim commander, Saladin, had led Islamic "crusades" into Asia, Africa, and Europe, slaughtering thousands.

her blond hair discreetly tucked under a cotton scarf. White shawl over maroon *shalwar qamiz*[10] marked her as a respectable woman. (But in this heat, I wondered how she could stand those stifling layers!)

Quetta,[11] guarding a branch of the Old Spice Road, sat strategically between two mountain passes south of the Khyber Pass. When the British built a rail line across the Indian sub-continent, Quetta became the western end on the border with Afghanistan. Rebuilt since an earthquake leveled the city in 1935, Quetta has long been a haven for terrorists as well as a refuge for Afghans fleeing war and poverty beyond the hills. Many become miners; others city labourers or smugglers. Iran lies just across the border.

Kathy had rented a small car to transport us and my two small bags[12] back to her house. "Sorry I don't have my own car to fetch you," she apologized, adjusting her headscarf to cover her hair better. "I usually get around town in a rickshaw or on a motorized scooter."

"Must be an unusual sight in Quetta—a woman on a scooter!" I commented as we passed many men along the street, but no women. I knew that in some Muslim states a woman was forbidden to drive a car or to leave her house unless heavily veiled and accompanied by a close relative. "Do men object?"

"Women often travel in rickshaws—some with a curtain enclosing the passenger. Anyway, they're used to me on my scooter!" Kathy laughed. Just then we did pass a woman—at least a figure completely covered in a black *burqa*,[13] with only a narrow mesh-covered slot for her to peer through. The macabre figure stood alone, except for a lad near it/her—an eerie sight, like something out of Star Wars!

"OK to take photos of men," Kathy reminded me when she saw me reach for the camera around my neck; "but don't photograph women!"

---

10. A long, formless dress worn over loose "trousers."
11. *Quetta*: "Fort" in local Pashtu, spoken by Pashtuns/Pathans (Parthans). Eastern Pakistanis say the speech of these fierce Western Pakistanis "sounds like boiling water."
12. To save weight (also "airport *wait*") on this safari across Asia, I carried only two hand-held bags plus a shoulder camera bag. (No checked baggage; globally, 30m checked bags go astray each year!)
13. Arabic-Persian: "shroud."

When we turned into the compound of Kathy's rented bungalow, children playing around the entrance waved and cheered. Almond trees were ablaze with pink blossoms. At the time, Kathy was sharing her simple quarters with a visiting pastor and his wife. Rustic chairs and table sat on a bare concrete floor. In the washroom, water from a makeshift shower drained through a hole in the wall onto a flowerbed. Later, when I took my obligatory shower (a daily ritual in that climate), I first had to remove a wooden bung from the drain hole and replace it after—to keep out rats.

But this was home to Kathy. I soon saw why. Chattering children peered through her windows to see the "foreigner" (namely, me). Neighbors obviously accepted Kathy as part of the community, constantly dropping in to visit. She always had a drink ready,[14] taking time to sit and listen to them. Baluchis are rough and ready but lovable people, even if they have a reputation for lawlessness, including smuggling. Tradition has it that they immigrated from Syria or Babylon.

"This is a person-to-person society," explained Kathy, pouring tea to wash down flat bread hot from the local baker's oven. She sees herself as quiet, not gregarious. That's perfect for women in this culture. "People don't really believe anything unless it's told them and demonstrated personally. They don't seem to acquire concepts by reading.[15]

"I think Pakistan will skip the age of literacy and literature, moving right from illiteracy to audiovisuals and the Internet. Villagers will rent a video player for 24 hours, along with enough tapes to watch all day and night to get their money's worth. Businessmen more likely call international partners on cellular phones than write them.[16]

"Ministry among men is easier because there's a male network to spread word about meetings. But I can't expect a Pakistani woman to go from house to house informing women about a meeting. It just isn't done!"

---

14. In many non-western cultures, one always gives a visitor a glass of water or other drink—without asking.
15. In Islamic schools, children learn to read by rote—mechanical, unthinking memorization.
16. In many developing countries, businessmen save handsomely on long-distance calls through "connections" with friends in International Telephone Exchanges.

That Haunting Figure in Black

Instead, Kathy spends a lot of time visiting in the women's quarters, where they're free to express their joys and sorrows. They listen hungrily as Kathy tells them about the eternal Saviour who loves them. They often invite their neighbors to listen, over a glass of Pakistani tea. For Muslims, friendship has the highest priority.

"But that figure on the street corner, shrouded in black, cut off from the world around her—can you meet her in her home?" I interrupted Kathy.

"Yes, that's the kind of person I'm talking about," Kathy explained. "Under the *burqa* is a normal person. She likely doesn't think of the *burqa* as a restriction but as proper attire, protecting her reputation.[17] Once inside her house, she and her friends are fairly normal women. They enjoy putting on lipstick and eye shadow. But though they become so friendly, initially I can't go and knock on their doors. They have to invite me—and I still don't publicize my visits."

I couldn't get that shrouded figure out of my mind. The child beside her—a male relative, perhaps her son—made it legitimate for her to be out on the street. This dear mother could not step out of her home whenever she wanted. She had to wait until some male, if only a child, was ready to accompany her. She was completely hidden *for her protection*? From whom? What kind of society or ideology or religion would do that to God's wonderful gift of womanhood? Although the woman obviously accepted this banishment from sight, how did she really feel about being a nonentity in public? She could never fully take her rightful place as part of wholistic male-female humanity. The community itself ended up the loser—an incomplete, male-dominated society.

I—a man who loved my mother, respected my sisters, and honored my wife and daughter—felt my blood boil. All the more, I appreciated Kathy and other women who graciously seek to befriend women under male-imposed restrictions.[18]

---

17. And defence against the lust of men, who (women may consider) are "created weak," SIM Islamic scholar John Miller explained to the author. A woman missionary explained that a robe is a woman's constant friend: a wrap-around, rain shelter, prayer shawl, protection—and finally, death shroud. For more re. the *burqa* and inequality, see Appendix I, Women and Culture.

18. See Fran Love, Jeleta Eckheart, editors, *Longing to Call Them Sisters* (Bibliography).

Kathy knew where and when it's acceptable for her to walk and visit—usually with another woman missionary. She was not in the more conservative areas, where most females cannot read or write. Virtual prisoners in their own homes, they are confined to housework only. Even if a school opened nearby, most orthodox husbands would prevent their wives and daughters from attending, in case they became literate. Of course, husbands would not state that as the reason—rather to *protect* their womenfolk from corrupting influences![19] In some Islamic countries, even where women are permitted to shop in public, signs often bar access to videos and music recordings that theological police consider corrupting for females. Males, shop on!

I had a lot to learn about ancient male attitudes that continue to surface in cultures. In some, sight of a female's hair or shape is a clear invitation to immorality—"obviously" the woman's fault for allowing it to be seen. While male chauvinism shocked me, some cultures understandably view western society, with its in-your-face feminine freedoms, as licentious. I had to admit that sinful immorality is endemic, whether western or eastern, modern or ancient. Societies simply regulate it differently.

However, in order to protect their own testimony, Christian missionaries and pastors observe the etiquette imposed in their communities. Actually, under Pakistan's 1973 Constitution, technically women are protected from discrimination that is on the basis of their sex *alone*. That can be widely interpreted, including unfounded allegations that a woman *appeared* seductive. Sometimes missionaries feel like screaming when they see how men treat women. Instead of helping a rape victim, police may charge the victim herself with a sex crime.[20] One socially active Pakistani woman told me that 80 percent of women in jail are accused of having sex outside of marriage. As a result of such injustice, most women do not report sexual violations.

---

19. In ancient cultures, males are totally responsible for women. Therefore any suspicion (even if later proved groundless) of female sexual promiscuity reflects on the male—or "dishonors" him. This legitimizes "honor killing" in religions such as Islam—although scholars state the Qur'an doesn't teach it. A rape victim or a girl whose vaginal diaphragm (hymen) hasn't fully closed (a natural occurrence) can imply her "protector" was negligent or unable to protect. The "dishonored" male protector may legally kill her!
20. Such as allowing too much of her hair to show beneath her headscarf!

Accepting Inconvenience

But Kathy's main work among Hindu Marwaris[21] was a lot different. She would purposely attract a crowd by taking with her a group of singers, because Marwaris like the excitement of something going on. "It's OK for us to work among Marwaris," Kathy said. "Muslims think it's good for us to turn them from idol worship. It's also OK to worship with Marwari Christians—they're free to be seen in public. But the bulk of our church members are Punjabi."

Kathy had a vision of setting up a Christian workers' training school and a Bible school—at least a short-term one. "I'm one person and there's only a certain amount of time in the day!" she explained.

"My present quarters are ideal—folk can come to visit," she told me. "When I lived in another town, another missionary and I rented rooms over a row of shops. I wondered how I'd ever sleep—there were so many noises. The Muslim call to prayer before dawn. Roosters crowing—they loved to do so under roof eaves, enhancing their raucous calls. Loud record playing at parties well past midnight. During the Muslim fast (which is really only during daylight), neighbours enjoyed meals during the night, repeating the call to prayer. To make matters worse, across the street was a tinker's shop. The constant 'tap-a-tap' nearly drove me crazy, so I jokingly told friends to pray he'd move. Returning from a holiday, I was surprised to find his business had grown so much he had to move!"

Kathy accepted these inconveniences and other frustrations for the sake of the women she sought to help. But again my thoughts went back to that shrouded specter in black.

"Why do orthodox Muslim women have to be *incognito* when outside the house, under a shapeless *burqa*?" I wondered aloud. "Why are they confined largely to their houses?"

"For them, it's an indication of being a Muslim—of submission to God," she explained. "The Qur'an teaches that a woman must cover up.

---

21. SIM works among Marwari Bhils, who were cut off from their homeland in Central West India by Partition. (In India, Marwaris and Bhils belong to different castes, but not in Pakistan.) Although outwardly Hindu, they are really spirit worshippers from the bottom of the caste scale, living in fear of spirits.

But there's another good reason women feel they must not let men see them—except of course their husbands or close relatives. In Islam, people follow external controls more than internal moral convictions. So a morally upright woman may be vulnerable if she doesn't conform to custom. She feels safer under cover."

Such fears are real, illustrated by the gang rape of a female teacher right in nearby Sui, on Baluchi's western border. A Baluchi, Shazia Khalid alleged four non-Baluchis attacked her—one a security officer. When authorities whisked the *teacher* away to Karachi "for investigation," Baluchi tribesmen raised a public outcry. They protested not because of abuse of a woman, but because they saw her rape as *disrespect for their tribe.*[22]

Missionaries understand the strictures placed upon women. Typical was Maureen Hider, who responded to a challenge from ICF pioneer Raymond Castro. He realized the strategic role of single women missionaries.[23] Maureen was an outgoing London Cockney, but in order to enter women's sequestered world, she traded the rollicking sound of Bow Bells[24] for a mosque's sonorous call five times a day. However, in visiting village women, Maureen usually took another woman along, to safeguard against being considered promiscuous.

"Women trust no man," Maureen explained. "Not even a husband, a Muslim priest, or the government. We try to show women that Jesus is completely trustworthy. Better than any earthly priest or *imam,* he can link them with our Heavenly Father."

In my travels, I discovered that while *purdah* and the *burqa* provide controls for both men and women, they do not indicate a moral society—the rules of morality are simply different.[25] Earlier, when I visited Egypt,

22. *Economist,* 01/22/05 p. 41. The case was dropped "for lack of evidence" (BBC March 3/05), but the government re-opened it.
23. Castro pioneered with the Poona & India Village Mission, which merged with ICF and became SIM.
24. Definition of a London Cockney: "Born within sound of Bow Bells" (Church of St. Mary le Bow).
25. In the book, *Princess,* by Jean P. Sasson (London: Bantam Books, 1993), a Saudi princess reveals the infidelity of men (even though they rigidly control their spouses—up to four wives at a time).

Christians there told me that men from strict Islamic states were the greatest frequenters of Cairo's licentious nightclubs—belly dancers and all. At the same time, I realized that the West and Christendom have no moral high ground to stand on. And while Muslims may also use religious regulations to maintain male dominance, most religions do that in some way.

"Then there's also *izzat,*" Kathy continued.

WHAT'S "*IZZAT*"?

"*Izzat*? Whatever *is that*?" I queried, trying to make a pun.

"*Izzat* is respect, honour—'face,' you might say. But it's more than that. If a wife or sister gets into trouble, it's a great loss of face for her menfolk. They can be jealous, but they also could be seen as very caring. From the woman's viewpoint, she wouldn't want to be exposed to immorality or other problems. So her seclusion helps protect the family's *izzat*—and she dare not jeopardize that!

"*Izzat* penetrates the whole culture," Kathy continued, seeing my still puzzled look. "If two men notice they've dropped something, they'll first consider which man has more status—then the one with less honor will bend down to pick it up. If you understand *izzat,* you understand Pakistan."

On the streets I'd noticed men's one-fits-all sack-like robes—reminding Muslims that before Allah, they're all on the same level. "Doesn't *izzat* contradict that?" I asked. "On the train, my fellow passengers told me that Islam controls every aspect of their lives."

"That's the anomaly," Kathy agreed. "Publicly, everyone pretends to be on the same level, but privately, everyone wants to be one-up. That influences government and social groups—even churches. People gain position according to their *izzat*. So a church can end up with unspiritual members in authority, surrounded by their own power structures.

"The concept of *Loyalty* also affects the churches adversely," she added.

"Adversely?" I asked. "Aren't we supposed to be loyal to those the Lord places over us?"

"True," Kathy agreed. "But this concept of loyalty (maybe you'd call it twisted loyalty) means you cover up for someone else in the event of wrong doing. It's quite OK to tell a few lies in order to protect your colleague, supervisor, or even pastor. In this culture, loyalty is more important than truth, honesty, and integrity."

As the Army Captain on the train had said, Islam influences all of life. Since it greatly influences the culture of Pakistan, I suddenly understood why it's OK for a Muslim to tell a lie—especially to an infidel; that is, a non-Muslim. Of course our Western societies are riddled with lies and liars (witness top-level corporate scandals), but lying is not acceptable. So in many parts of the world, courts prosecute liars. However, our Western public doesn't understand that in Islam, lying can be a virtue—for the sake of loyalty, or to deceive an infidel. So the West's media unsuspectingly report Islamic government statements as "gospel truth."[26]

I was learning about both mosque and church in Pakistan, and questions buzzed in my head. "Christians, Muslims, Hindus, and animists talk about God," I pointed out. "Yet we don't believe in the same 'God.' How do you distinguish?"

"Aha," replied Kathy. "When leaving friends, we used to say "Kda hafiz"—or 'God be your safe keeper." When the government of Pakistan changed the farewell to "Allah hafiz," it sounded odd to Christians. But though everyone may now use it as a generic expression, Christians simply teach our belief in God as revealed in Jesus Christ."

I also wondered about witness to Muslims. "If Marwaris are coming to Christ, are they reaching out to Muslims?" I asked.

"There are obstacles," Kathy replied. "Marwaris are at the lower end of the economy. It's difficult for them to witness acceptably to Muslims, who consider themselves higher in social status." Kathy was being kind, I later discovered when I talked with Pakistani Christians and learned of the enormous problems they face in witness to Muslims.

---

26. Regrettably, our own governments at times are guilty of misleading—but we don't excuse them for that.

"Perhaps Marwari Hindus have been more responsive because they haven't faced the same social restrictions as Muslims. But therein lies a problem. Marwaris are so desperately poor that Christian workers are tempted to use the church or mission to improve their living conditions. Converts may want to become evangelists so the churches will provide them a living, not because they really feel a calling from God."

Kathy went on to explain that just when a church is growing to a level where it could support outreach, Christian sects may move in and siphon off some of the congregation. Western sects are well financed, offering social amenities and salaries. While evangelical missionaries also help needy people and assist with projects, they rightly feel that pastors should not become dependent upon foreign funds but upon their members' support—that encourages responsibility. However, some of the most promising believers, hoping to improve themselves and their communities, leave their churches and join better-financed groups. Charismatic preachers quickly gain a following because of Marwari love for excitement and noise.

"There is little unity among Pakistani Christians, who tend to factionalise anyway," Kathy continued, slipping her flip-flop sandals on in preparation for taking me to the railroad station for my onward journey. "For instance, Punjabi Christians look down on Marwari believers because of the clothes they wear. Yet Punjabis don't realize the Northern garb they've adopted is Islamic culture, while Marwaris have simply retained their traditional attire, which is Hindu.

"It's awfully disheartening when Christians don't accept each other in spiritual oneness. Add the hot climate sapping one's energy, poor health, and a religion so depressing to women and minorities—and you'll understand why many missionaries and pastors become discouraged."

Ah, I thought—that's why I'd heard Peter Hambrey, a Baptist missionary from our home church, ask for prayer "to serve joyfully" when he and his wife served in Pakistan.

"We don't live under romantic delusions regarding the commitment required," Peter told us. "We realize that, to fulfil our commitment, we need a firm sense of God's purposes and a spiritual and emotional freshness."

A Pakistani pastor told him and his wife, Cheryl, that even though we come to God empty, we never leave empty. That inspired Cheryl to write a praise song:

Here in Your Presence there is one thing I know:
Though empty I come, I'll not empty go.
Your Grace and Your Mercy and Love overflow—
Not empty, but FULL I will go!

"Kathy, isn't there *anything* to encourage you?" I wondered aloud as we arrived at the station. Kathy never left for the station until she could hear the unpredictable train shunting its creaking carriages into line.

"Oh, there's lots," smiled Kathy, as the steam locomotive complained about having to work under pressure. "For instance—the pastor who's staying with us. He and his wife are true disciples of Jesus. They uphold truth; they walk in humility. Like the Apostle Paul, they've laid their *izzat* at the foot of the Cross. Their loyalty is to Christ. Humanly speaking, they're what keep us plodding on. You'll meet more of their kind during your travels."

Patience may be one of the most-needed graces in Pakistan. The seed of the Word may take years to germinate—but that's true in many other countries. Operation Mobilization (OM) was encouraged when a Pakistani contacted them ten years after someone handed him a gospel leaflet. Using it as a bookmark, he'd forgotten it. Now he asked for the correspondence course it advertised. When he completed the course, OM put him in touch with a Pakistani pastor, and today the man is following Jesus.

Pakistan was looking a lot more complex than my irenic conversation with the two educated Muslims on the train implied. The complexity included not only Muslims but also Christians. The concepts that quiet, resilient Kathy had described would explain puzzling things I'd see on the rest of my journey through Pakistan and then eastward.[27]

---

27. Kathy Bell's novel based on fact, "Evangelizing the Moon," reveals her thorough understanding of Pakistani culture. Unfortunately it has never been published (available only from SIM Archives).

The train driver importantly announced his departure as only a steam whistle could—not an electronic wheeze, but a blood-curdling blast, like a dragon disturbed from its sleep. Enough to send scavenger fowl and felon flying! The train jolted into motion, and I was on my way to meet stalwart disciples of Jesus in other parts of Pakistan to the East.

I still didn't know what held the Pakistani puzzle together. Would traversing the Indus Valley leave me with more questions than answers? If it were anything like what I'd seen, it would hold several surprises.

Outside Lahore's main mosque, the faithful worship before slaughtering their bleating goats and sheep for a Muslim festival.

Walking the Valley with Jesus

"Even though I walk through the valley ..., I will fear no evil, for you are with me" (Psalm 23.4).

TELL YOUR SON TO STOP, or I'll send him back to you . . . cut up into small pieces!" a voice rasped when Pastor Daniel answered his telephone.

"What*ever* was your son doing?" I asked, shocked at what the mild-mannered Pakistani pastor had so casually told me.

"Witnessing to other students at his university," Daniel told me. "He's careful never to insult other religions—he doesn't even mention them. But he does tell his friends about Jesus, his Saviour. Some people think that insults Islam."

I looked at this gentle father and tried to place myself in his sandals. I imagined living in a country with a Blasphemy Law that makes "insulting" Islam or the Prophet Muhammad a capital crime.[1] I knew that

---

[1] Pakistan Penal Code—Criminal Law Ordinance XXI, 1991, Section 295-C. It has been opposed by some Muslims as well as minorities and human rights advocates. But Pakistan's Islamic scholar Abul Mawdudi states that death for apostasy is an unchangeable tenet of Islam. (Abul Ala Mawdudi, *The Punishment of the Apostate According to Islamic Law*. See Bibliog.) In Afghanistan, Islamic law conflicts with the nation's Constitutional support of the UN's Religious Freedom clause. (More under Appendix H.)

a *convert* from Islam to another faith (making him an apostate) risked death. But the new Blasphemy Law made even *being* a Christian dangerous. I'd heard how the charge of "insult" was sometimes based on envy or petty grievance—as had happened with a Muslim and Christian boy quarreling over pet pigeons. I wondered how a Christian could live under such a threat.

In fact, after religious-parliamentary tensions in neighboring Afghanistan, some observers pointed out that all five branches of Sunni and Shi'a jurisprudence (which interpret Islamic, or Shari'a, law) deny religious and civic freedom to the extent that full democracies allow it. A nation may have a democratic election *process* and yet forbid freedom of speech and of conscience. Many insiders consider that The Middle East demonstrates basic incompatibility between Islam and democracy: an Islamic state (under totalitarian Shari'a Law) can never be truly democratic, they state. The West's insistence on freedom for all explains the charge that "The West" is seeking to undermine if not destroy Islam!

To me, neighboring Afghanistan illustrated that. In spite of the nation's constitutional guarantee of religious freedom, an Islamic court found that a Muslim had broken the Shari'a Law by converting to Christianity. Abdul Rahman had changed faiths while working -in another country (Pakistan), but when he returned to Afghanistan *16 years later*, police nabbed him for having a Bible <u>in his house</u>(!).

On worldwide TV, a news clip showed the convert declaring in court that he now believed in Jesus and would never recant. Outside, a reporter asked a crowd if the convert should live. "*No*!" one of them shouted. "Fuel should be poured over him and set alight!" The crowd vehemently agreed.[2]

It was a critical test for the nation struggling to be a democracy. Only unprecedented international pressure (by nations which daily sacrifice their soldier's lives to protect Afghans) led to the man's release, in the name of liberty. The government lamely stated that Abdul lacked the mental ability to stand trial. In other words, he must be crazy! But he was still smart enough to accept asylum in another country—where he remains under protection while Muslim clerics, goaded by protesting devotees, still vow to kill him.

---

2 ABC News, March 24 and 27, 2006.

To be fair, Pakistan's government unsuccessfully tried to introduce procedures making it harder to misapply such a law. I respected the government for that. But Pakistan's many volatile factions vying for power make governing difficult. Not everyone was like the two moderates I'd met on the train. Extremists knew how to foment religious zeal for political ends. My question wasn't *why* such a law existed, but rather *how* Christians lived with it.

Gossiping the Gospel

The more I learned, the more I gave thanks for disciples like the Christian father who had told me about the telephone threat to his son's life. That haunted me.

"What about your son—what happened to him?" I remember asking.

"It wasn't the first threat we'd had," the pastor had explained. "We knew it was time to get him out of the country. Friends helped him head north into Russia, where he finished his degree."

"So did he end up as a Pakistani missionary to Russia?" I quipped, intending irony.

"That is so!" the father affirmed. "After Communism collapsed, university students there were eager to hear about our son's faith."

Echoes of the early church, I thought—persecuted disciples scattered afar, spreading the gospel! In early centuries, some reached the Indus Valley and even China. Even if earlier Jewish merchants hadn't been Christians, they at least told idolatrous people about the one true God. Christian travelers further declared that God revealed himself in Jesus.

But what about following Jesus in Pakistan *today*? When a Christian family invited me to dinner, I found out.

"Thank you for coming to visit us!" said Pastor Masih (yes, another with that common Christian surname). His wife, Miriam, had just placed a bowl of steaming *palau* rice on the family table.

Seated around were several of their sons and daughters. The chatter and giggles made me feel at home, as a dish of curried chicken and lentils followed the rice. I'd heard that the eldest, Yusef, had once vowed never to be a pastor. However, after studying outside the country, he now was a full-time evangelist. His English was excellent.

"What had earlier turned you against being a pastor?" I asked, breaking off a piece of *chapatti* (unleavened flat bread).

"There is so much quarrelling among church members!" he told me. "It's so sad, when we need to show we're one in Christ. But clan, dialect, status—even personal greed—these cause divisions. And outsiders are always ready to take us to court. My father wasted much of his time in a court case—a Muslim claimed he owned the property the church was built on, even though the government had signed the lease on it. The case dragged on for 11 years before the government threw out the case because the property had been a place of worship for a long time."

"OK—but what eventually changed your mind about Christian *ministry*?" I pressed, as I sipped sweet tea mixed with water-buffalo milk.

"Well, I read that the Apostle Paul faced a quarreling church in Corinth, and he also had many attacks from outside the church. But he never gave up. Why should I?"

"Your father tells me that apart from your evangelistic work among the Marwaris, you have a special concern for Muslims," I said, remembering that Pakistan's Ministry of Religious Affairs, responsible for ensuring religious liberty, on its letterhead quotes the Qur'an: *Islam is the only religion acceptable to God.* "How do you communicate?"

Yusef explained he simply tells people what peace and spiritual assurance he's found in Christ. That brings up many questions, because Muslims don't have peace and assurance.

"Our national Constitution ensures freedom of religion, and there's no law against my answering questions," he told me, swallowing another spoonful of rice. "I never mention other religions. You'd be surprised at the number of people who personally trust in Christ, even though they daren't make that public." Yusuf does make sure there's always someone else with him, and if a person becomes agitated, he ends the conversation.

I couldn't help admiring this quiet, intelligent young man who has such a burden for his own people. His father told me Yusef's life is more effective than an evangelistic sermon. Most Muslims stereotype Christians as licentious drunkards, from seeing nominal "Christians" reeling home. So they're impressed to see a young man living righteously.

"Why Are You Happy?"

In this kind of environment, truly Christian families can be a powerful testimony. For instance, the Muslim principal of a girl's school remarked that her missionary neighbors didn't spend a lot of money on themselves. Instead, they were constantly helping the poor. (To complicate life, however, some other Muslims despise missionaries for *associating* with poor Marwaris—just as the Pharisees despised Jesus for associating with the oppressed.) Muslim neighbors watch in curiosity when Marwaris turn from Hindu gods. They're amazed to see the difference in their lives. As a result, one Muslim came to ask for a Bible.

"Why do you want a Bible?" enquired the pastor, guardedly. It turned out that a poor Marwari widow lived on the other side of his compound wall. Not only was she caring for her children, but they all seemed happy. The man could hear them singing hymns. When he asked the widow why she was happy, she replied, "Because Jesus lives in me!" That made him so curious he came for a Bible to read for himself.

But male chauvinism can show up among Marwari Christians, as well. At the conclusion of a conference, when a missionary expressed appreciation for the meals the women had cooked and served, his translator skipped that sentence—it would have been culturally inappropriate to praise them. In some ethnic groups, men don't pass information on to their wives because the women aren't considered important. If a husband has something to say to his wife, he may inform her through a child—not directly. At the same time, women in such cultures often don't pay attention to a speaker, because they're not expected to think for themselves. At any time they can expect a beating.

However, some attitudes are changing. In major cities, such as Islamabad, Lahore, and Karachi, I found educated women serving in hotels, airline agencies, and larger shops. Acceptance of women apparently didn't extend to governments at the time of my visit, though. I read a comment in a Pakistani English-language magazine: "Women are totally invisible at every level of decision making." And in rural areas, I noticed the absence of women not only on the streets but also in shops and offices.

I found it depressing—public life lacked the grace that women contribute to society. I remembered how my two Muslim train companions had pointed out Pakistan's higher public sexual morality in comparison to the flagrant immorality of Indian society—implying that segregation accounts for this. Yet I heard that segregation has led to homosexuality among men and among women (difficult to prove or disprove). Confined together all day, women, especially, form intimate friendships—not a bad thing, yet it can allow a dominant woman to possess a reliant woman in a lesbian relationship. And AIDS is more prevalent than admitted—unfortunately increasing its spread.

Lusting at the sight of a female is really a *male* problem, I decided. Christian men know how they must constantly "walk in the spirit and not the lust of the flesh," as the Apostle Paul pointed out. Pure thoughts arise only from the Holy Spirit living in the believer. However, in a legislated religion that does not know inner spiritual regeneration, the solution is to cover up the object of lust. Yet, though sex may not be publicly displayed, men are still males. In the market, women missionaries are often aware that lustful eyes are following their every move.

"We get used to that," one missionary told me, "but we must admit it's a little disconcerting when we feel someone pinch us as we shop!" Deservedly, the men might say, because even though the women are properly robed and are with a female friend, a male relative does not accompany them!

"But remember, there are many real gentlemen—Muslim and Christian," Kathy Bell had reminded me. "Knowing the restrictions women face, they faithfully provide their daily necessities (such as milk, or fresh bread from the baker), and they go to all kinds of trouble to escort their womenfolk even on long journeys to visit relatives. If a husband didn't do so, a woman would be more upset by restrictions."

When I was with Pastor Masih, I questioned him about a ghetto mentality among Christians. "Their conferences are great to encourage each other, but do they result in outreach?" I asked. "Do they show concern for unreached people? I can understand fear of persecution, but is there any way to help them evangelize—as your son does so appropriately?" [3]

"The big need is for teaching," replied the pastor. "That's the greatest help your missionaries can give us."

I heard of different ways groups are helping. As to evangelism, the nation's animistic peoples provide unusual opportunities. For instance, Richard Twiss, President of Wisconi International of the Rose Lakota/Sioux Tribe (USA) reports, "Our Christian teams of traditional drummers and singers effectively communicate the gospel."[4] They've found ready response in Pakistan's rural villages. However, such seed-planting requires the watering of the Word.

Taking Revenge on the Rhino

Heading south to the coast, I found the most cosmopolitan city in Pakistan—Karachi, a busy seaport. There's even a Jewish synagogue. Contrasts abound—such as my taxi speeding past a camel-drawn freight wagon. Outside modern shops, male pedestrians mix with female—the latter often without any headscarves. However, on a large billboard, someone had tried to spray-paint over the picture of a young woman drinking Coca Cola. She was decently attired, but in a pant suit, appealing to educated youth.

In Karachi I learned how powerful is the concept of revenge. After a frightened rhinoceros, protecting her newborn cub, killed a careless zookeeper, the man's male relatives duly marched on the zoo and killed the rare offspring. Tit for tat! Revenge is not just about anger, I learned, but is an honor, a duty, to defend one's *izzat*. No wonder the prayer of Jesus from the Cross is so incomprehensible: "Father, forgive them ... "!

It was in Karachi, back in 1976, that delegates from 44 Muslim countries met for the first Islamic World Congress. They adopted a resolution calling on their governments to close Christian mission stations

---

3 Recently Yusef found it advisable to move to another country, where he still witnesses effectively.

4 *Books & Culture*, Jan-Feb. 2007, p. 33.

and activities in the Islamic world, and to insure the peaceful withdrawal of Christian missionaries."[5] However, today's Karachi showed me that Islam is not the monolithic religion many think of when they use the word "Muslim"—just as there are many different churches and sects in Christendom and divisions among Buddhists, Hindus, and Jews. One ex-Muslim quotes Muhammad as predicting there would be 72 different Islamic sects, and that they would destroy one another.[6] In fact, Muslims blame divisions for their weaknesses and for invasions by infidels. Through the centuries, Islamic variations have ranged from murderous 12th c. Assassins[7] to liberal Alavi Muslims in today's Turkey. Worldwide there are several schools (versions) of Sunni[8] Islam. The wife of a Turkish politician switched from Shafi'i Islam (a strict sect) to the more liberal Hanafi sect, so she could at least shake hands with foreign dignitaries! It was Wahhabi Islam, offshoot of the strict Hanbali school, that bred Afghan's Taliban.

So when I arrived in Karachi, I discovered that Sunni Muslims had bombed a Shi'a Muslim mosque, killing a number of worshipers. To understand this Islamic "civil war," I had to remember that Wahhabi-style Sunnis consider Shi'a shrines idolatrous—and Shi'as a greater enemy than Americans.[9] Since "struggle" (*jihad*) is part of Islamic doctrine, Sunnis feel meritorious feuding with Shi'as. They in turn believe they are the rightful heirs of Muhammad, tracing their legitimacy to the grandson of Muhammad, assassinated in the 7th c. Unemployed youth provide a ready source of suicide bombers—a promised shortcut to paradise.

In turn, Shi'as thrive on a sense of marginalisation and martyrdom as their own *jihad* in life, even observing an annual "Day of Martyrdom"—

---

5 Sherwood Wirt, *Evangelism: Next Ten Years* (G. Osei-Mensah quote, p. 59.) Wheaton: Word, 1978.

6 Abul Kasem, ex-Muslim author: nirribilli@gmail.com.

7 Arabic: *hashshashin*, lit. "hashish [narcotic] users"—from which we derive English "assassins." Like today's Islamic terrorists, they believed they earned immediate entrance to Paradise through suicide.

8 Sunni: Arabic, from *Sunnat*, Muhammad's "path," or practice—Islam's largest conservative grouping.

9 Antagonism dates back to conflict over Muhammad's successor. Resentment increased when Shi'as stole (and held for 22 years) Islam's most sacred relic, a large black stone enshrined in Mecca's Ka'aba. Though once a pagan fetish, Muslim pilgrims deem it sacred, circling it annually. Sunnis say overthrow of North Africa's Shi'a dynasties was a greater triumph than defeating Crusaders.

Ashura. They believe that "the Hidden Mahdi"[10] will eventually reappear and establish justice upon the earth. "Charismatic" Shi'as and Sunnis are the Sufi, a mystical folk Islam that builds shrines honoring spirits of the dead. Orthodox Muslims cannot condone such heresy. Another subsect of Shi'a is the Isma'ili, named after a bypassed ancestor. Their leader, the moderate Aga Khan, is honored for his benevolent projects, including schools and hospitals, in many developing countries.

Another sect is the Ahmadiyya movement, founded in India by a noble Mogul named Hazrat ("Honorable" or "Saint") Mirza Ghulam Ahmed, who announced his divine mission in 1889. Ahmadis believe Jesus revived from crucifixion and *walked* to Kashmir, where he is supposedly buried under the name of a prophet, Yuz Asaf (could that sound like a variation of Yesu?). Although not accepted by orthodox Muslims—therefore listed in Pakistan as a "non-Muslim minority"—Ahmadis are the world's most aggressive Islamic missionaries, with a following of some 15m. Their current leader (or *Khalifa*) lives in London, UK. They've built Canada's largest Muslim mosque.

Mohajirs, mostly Sunni from India immigrating after Partition, add to ethnic tensions; Karachi and Lahore share the largest number. Worldwide, there are other sects, some practicing syncretistic folk Islam incorporating local culture, such as placing rice on ancestral graves on feast days. Added to these divisions, individual imams (teachers) in mosques compete for followers within "dynasties."

Whew—Islam sounded to me as fractured as Christendom![11] With all these different Muslim forms and their distinctive ideologies, when people state anything about the nature of Islam, I first ask them, "Which Islam do you mean?" And I get the feeling that when Western

---

[10] "Divinely Guided One," the 12th Mahdi, who disappeared. Some sects identify him with Jesus' return.

[11] "Christendom": catch-all term I use for institutional, cultural, and political "Churchianity" distinct from the Church Universal—Christ's Body—in which believers enjoy unity in the Spirit. Sectarianism within Islam has significance because one reason Muhammad claimed God "gave" the Qur'an was the schism and sectarian division of Jews and Gentiles, and (Muhammad assumed) consequent corruption of the Bible.

–WHF. (From N.J. Dawood, *The Qur'an,* transl. with notes. Harmondsworth: Penguin, 1956, p. 10.)

governments think moderate Islamic leaders still keep too tight a grip on their people, they don't understand the leaders' problems. The West equates Islam's divisions with Christendom's denominations. But Calvinists don't usually blow up Pentecostal churches because of their charismatic teaching(!). Unless an Islamic dynasty eschews totalitarian ideology, any seeming "democracy" will exist only until the most powerful sect stacks the polls.

Drums and Prayer Mats

For a visitor like me, a Sunday service had unusual features.[12] I left my shoes on the steps of the one-room cottage-style church, along with everyone else's. I joined men squatting on colorful floor mats on one side; on the other squatted women (even expatriates dutifully covered their heads with shawls). I wondered at the sound of hammering just before the musical prelude—but it was only the drummer pounding wooden pegs deeper into the thongs that stretched the leather membrane over his drumheads. He and a couple of assistants provided a soft rhythm, tapping twin *tabla* drums, shaking castanets and a tambourine,[13] while we quietly sang hymns to a five-note scale. It was more meaningful than many a noisy service back in my own land. Afterwards, no one spoke until outside the simple room of worship. Reverance!

But, as SIMer Phil Parshall[14] points out, most Pakistani churches have not succeeded in winning converts in Muslim communities. There are understandable reasons, I found: (a) official strictures, (b) threat of persecution, (c) vested interest in property and structure, and (d) the stereotype Muslims have of Christians as licentious drunkards and inferior people. Result: most churches are paralyzed with a self-centered, ghetto mentality. Frustrated, many evangelical Christians by-pass churches, choosing to evangelize through other agencies. This is unfortunate for the life of churches, although currently it may seem a more effective avenue for the gospel.

---

12 Although Friday is Pakistan's official day off, at the time, Christians were allowed to take Sunday off.

13 From Persian *tambir*.

14 The Parshalls ministered among Muslims in East Pakistan before it became Bangladesh.

When Cheryl X—, asked a Christian friend what bothered Pakistani Christians the most about missionaries, she got an unexpected response: "Why do you missionaries give so much attention to Muslims?" Many Christians, already feeling marginalized, see missionaries as an asset to their status. But Cheryl's friend, who also seeks to witness, felt missionaries should give priority to meeting the great spiritual needs within the church.

This sincere Pakistani woman also had a burden for a forgotten group of Christians—an enclave tracing their Christianity back to Nestorian missionaries from Syria. Their ancestors were following Christ before the Prophet Muhammad was born, but through lack of Bible teaching, they had been over-run by Islam, absorbing some Islamic views while still calling themselves Christian.

Pastor Joshua[15] was one of these who found Christ as personal Saviour. To work among the Nestorians, he found it necessary to start his own church (which draws some 200 for worship) because other churches wouldn't welcome Nestorians—some have absorbed Islamic culture and aroused suspicion. Missionaries Bill and Arlene X— work with Pastor Joshua, who heads up a Bible correspondence course with several thousand members.

Heartbreak or Embarrassment?

I met Hugh and Jean Gordon, who had felt the effects of another aspect of *izzat*. The government had turned down their visa renewal, not because they'd broken any law or because Muslims didn't want them in the country. The believers of B— Synod loved them, appreciating their tireless ministry teaching Bible courses and distributing gospel literature. However, the Synod of D— was envious of the expatriate missionaries helping B—. That gave B— unfair status, so D— complained that the missionaries were working against the churches. A relative in Immigration made sure the complaint reached the "right" authority, which happily cancelled the return visas of several missionaries who had been helping B—. Hugh and Jean went home saddened, although they continued to pray and work on behalf of their beloved Pakistani friends.

---

[15] Name of the pastor and others in this chapter withheld for security reasons.

I recalled how the Apostle Paul had also met opposition from envious Christian leaders: "The important thing is that in every way—whether from false motives or true—Christ is preached."[16] The Gordons found that same grace.

"Our Lord is still meeting people on the Old Spice Road and saving them!" Hugh and Jean rejoiced after re-visiting Pakistan on visitor visas.

The same church attitudes prevent the rise of younger leaders. As a result, some Christian youth in main-line denominations turn to more flexible evangelical churches. In one city, several Brethren Assemblies baptized 65 the Sunday I was there. All came from mainline churches but had found the Saviour through evangelical youth ministries.

Missionary Mark O— told me his was the fifth generation of Britons to serve in the subcontinent. His great-great-grandfather had served with the East India Company (which at the time had responsibility for development in the area)—so he felt right at home with the language and the people. During his ancestors' era, the British had planted trees along the hillsides (until then denuded for firewood) and built an extensive canal system that turned the arid Punjab into fertile farmland. It is still in use.[17] During the Cold War, the Russians vilified colonizers and missionaries, but the Punjabis knew the benefits their colonizers had brought. In fact, Punjabi troops fought valiantly for the British Empire in several wars.

Then I met Ivan, a newcomer from Britain, who was embarrassed to witness to Pakistanis. I could understand hesitancy for a newcomer, and we should approach people of all cultures and religions in humility and acceptance. But *embarrassment*? Why?

"Because my people colonized these people!" he replied apologetically. I might have commended Ivan for lacking racial pride, but this was the opposite extreme. It was the same sincere but misguided apologetic philosophy I'd found in Peshawar.

---

16 Philippians 1.18

17 Punjabi Muslims planted cotton and wove it into a see-through fine cloth Europeans called 'muslin' (Arabic for Mosul, in Iraq). Portuguese traders brought blue *indigo* (Gk. *indikon*—"Indian substance") dye.

"What clever ways Satan finds to tie the hands of Christ's disciples—while many talk about binding *Satan's* hands!" I thought to myself. However, I did ask Ivan how he'd relate to an Italian, since the Romans had once colonized his own people! I suggested he talk with Mark about the *benefits* Mark's ancestors had brought to the subcontinent.[18] I also recounted my earlier conversation with the two Muslims on the train.

Quite apart from the problems inside or outside the churches, I discovered that missionary service in Pakistan is rarely a simple matter. One team thought they were making great progress preparing Marwari radio messages, only to discover they were using the wrong dialect of Marwari (one of Pakistan's 69 languages) for their listeners. They also discovered that a woman's voice for female parts in a Bible story was unacceptable! And their use of the term "blood of Christ" evoked blushes and giggles, because they were using the word for *menstruation*.

"Don't Change Our Urdu KJV!"

The Urdu Bible had urgently needed revision, I learned, having been translated some 160 years ago, long before Pakistan was founded as an Islamic state. Even when it was revised in 1935, translators intentionally chose non-Islamic words that the masses readily understood, but Muslims today find certain ethnic terms repulsive. It is not a theological issue, but a problem of translation.

However, as in the West, many Christians mistake an accurate cultural translation for the inerrant original Word of God. Therefore most Pakistani pastors look upon the early missionary translation as their "King James Version," and won't countenance any vocabulary change. Some also are concerned that a new translation would seem to confirm Islam's allegation that "the Bible has been changed."[19] Result: the Urdu Bible has had few

---

[18] For some people, a "politically incorrect" view.

[19] Muslims believe the Qur'an is the only infallible "Word of God," pre-existing Creation and later released in Arabic by the angel Gabriel through Muhammad, correcting other partial revelations (such as the Bible). Since they believe it was verbally dictated to Muhammad, no word may be altered. Only the original Arabic is genuine, written on slips of parchment, leaves, stones, or other materials collected by his followers under Omar, the 2nd Caliph. The Qur'an recognizes that God revealed his will through prophets and apostles to Jews and Christians, but Muslims think those corrupted scripture, dividing into schismatic sects. Thus, they reason, the world needs the new revelation of the Qur'an. For centuries no Qur'anic translation was approved. Now translations exist in major languages. (Dawood, *The Qur'an, op. cit.* p.10.)

Muslim readers, to the frustration of Christian leaders. However, the United Bible Society has now released a contemporary translation that half-a-billion Urdu readers worldwide can readily understand.

Endemic cheating is another frustration for teachers. Again I found that ubiquitous *izzat* is involved. "A low grade would mean losing 'face,'" Michael X— of InterServe explained. "They'll even share their answers with a failing-grade student because of class or clan ties."

"So cheating's really an honorable thing to do?" I asked, surprised.

"Precisely, even for some Christian students!" said Michael. "Status and loyalty take priority over honesty. Until now I've tended to be lenient because it's the culture, but now I notice that a Christian Pakistani teacher takes it seriously. 'The Bible calls lying a sin, and cheating is lying,' he states plainly."

I noticed police questioning a group of Marwari boys. "Why are the police interested in boys so young?" I asked missionary Graham X—, pointing with my chin (finger pointing would amount to cursing).

"They're not as young as they look!" he explained. "Marwari children are usually small for their age. That's why many are sold as camel jockeys. It's an international trade that has brought new wealth to the Marwaris! Smugglers ship them across the Arabian Sea to be camel jockeys. In our youth center and classes we try to reach these boys with the gospel before they disappear."

Besides such underground traffic, women are sometimes sold in rural markets, according to a Pakistani group, the Ansar Burney Welfare Trust. Police were investigating. The government is struggling as the population swells and poverty spreads. (Islam rejects any kind of birth control, and men may have four wives at a time) Infant mortality is officially 10%. Fifty percent of the population is under 15 years of age, only one in five children attend school, and one in four families have no safe water supply.

Group Bible discussion with both men and women present is next to impossible, because Marwari women must sit lower than men and turn their backs to the men. This leaves them out of things, adding to prevalent female illiteracy. And marriage is a constant problem for Christian families. Their daughters cannot marry anyone from the same clan, yet the only eligible Christian young men may be within their clan. At the same time, clans despise each other for various reasons.

Unfortunately some "Christian" parents resort to arranging marriage for their daughters with Hindu or even Muslim men. A Muslim father may promise to safeguard the bride's Christian faith, but after marriage the wife is either ostracized or the promise doesn't materialize. (It's OK to lie to an infidel.)[20] "It's a great problem for the future of the church," Pastor Masih had told me.

Sometimes well-meaning groups from overseas add to the burdens of sincere pastors.

One independent Baptist church in Texas felt it was doing the right thing to support a Pakistani evangelist, who sent glowing reports back to the U.S. Each year the Texas church sent mission committee members to see for themselves. The evangelist obliged by assembling villagers (who each received a bag of rice for turning up), and baptizing several. Mark X— told me he personally knew believers (some from other churches) who had been baptized two or three times over the years. Great rejoicing back in Texas; regret in Pakistan among pastors for whom life was always difficult. They knew honest evangelists who could do well with some financial help.

Pakistan's Psyche

Muslims take pride in their medieval science and art—including philosophy and poetry—absorbed from cultures conquered by Islam. However, while celebrating the birth of a new nation, Pakistan suffered from "post-*partum*" depression—a sense of rejection and trauma from the violence of Partition. Heightening (or should I say, *deepening*) Muslim depression is the dashed dream of an Islamic Indian sub-continent—dating back to A.D. 712, when Governor Hajjai of Iraq ordered the invasion of India. Under Muhammad Qasim, raiders "demolished temples, **shattered sculptures, plundered palaces, killed vast numbers of men, . . . and carried off their women and children to slavery."**[21] So while

---

[20] Westerners do not understand this basic Islamic ethic, neither Muslim "ethic" of suicide bombing.

[21] Serge Trifkovic, *The Sword of the Prophet: Islam History, Theology, Impact on The World.*

Pakistan boasts world-status scientists, it seems the nation hasn't developed pride in its own products. I found shops well stocked with imported goods, not locally made items.

Dr. Mohammad Ajmal, Pakistani educator and former Education Ministry Secretary helped me understand Pakistan's national psyche:

> Inward self-abasement and insecurity produced rumor, intrigue, blackmail, prejudice, and ferocious defense of clichés. . . . Moral inquisition can lead to a society's self-destruction, as people abandon self-development for the comforting authority of religion, government, and social planning. . . . But tension continues—tension between Islamic law [Shari'a] and knowledge [education's *gnosis*]. . . . Self-debasement also conflicts with material desires: importing cars and air conditioners, instead of manufacturing them.[22]

Meanwhile, Pakistan's population (now over 160m.) *doubles* every 30 years. As Professor Ajmal also foresaw, Pakistan's religion and tradition promote population explosion. (Of 160m. population, 85m. are younger than 19.) Consumer expectations coupled with unemployment of restless youth can lead to radicalism—a government concern. (Pakistan is at the bottom of a list of 26 "emerging nation" economies.[23]) Health and employment problems plague the nation.

Added to this background are multiple regulations governing licenses, investments, and employment and manufacturing—creating a restrictive atmosphere common to most orthodox Muslim countries. They account for 20% of world population but only 4% of world trade—and that includes oil! Pakistan's government is understandably concerned about unemployment as the population burgeons—particularly among male youth. Forecasts put the annual growth rate entering the labour pool at 30% (excluding the untapped potential of females in *purdah*) by 2015. Neighboring Afghanistan's labor growth rate is forecast at 43%.[24] That spells u-n-r-e-s-t in both lands.

What's the problem? Doesn't the West have lots of work for lower-cost Asian labor? It does, but many new Asian industries are utilizing the

---

22 *Pakistan, op. cit.* (WHF précis of pp. 228-230).

23 According to Gross Domestic Product per person: World Bank report, *Economist* April 29, 2006.

24 *Economist*, Jan. 14, 2006, p. 47.

automated machinery the West itself used to lower costs—and in Muslim nations, youth don't have the training needed. They want a piece of the nation's new-found wealth, but fiery imams direct their emotions against "Western Imperialism" instead of into developing employment. Dr. Ajmal's analysis of Pakistan's psyche is proving all too accurate. Feelings of rejection, impoverishment, and anger will fuel unrest in any nation.

"Illiterate masses become ready recruits for all sorts of unhealthy activities," stated Javed Ashraf Oazi, a more recent education minister. Officially, 53% of Pakistanis are literate, although observers put the figure lower, near 30%, for "literacy" may mean little more than ability to write one's name. Among women, the rate is as low as 3% in some areas. Yet only 52% of elementary-school-age children attend classes, and 3,500 "schools" have no building, 29,000 no electricity, 22,000 no toilet.[25] While the government is tackling these problems, the task is enormous.

Sacrifice of Bulls and Goats

Lahore was my last stop before flying across the border to India. This walled city of 13 gates was as far east as the Greek General Alexander had reached before he sailed down the Indus and back home. At the time, it was an animistic metropolis on river-fed agricultural plains ("Punjab" is Sanskrit for *five rivers*). King Osiris of Egypt (*circa* 3 BC), purported to be the first conqueror of the Punjab, introduced *cultivated* agriculture. His successor, Sosotries (2 B.C.) introduced the study of stars, which Egypt had learned from Mesopotamian astrology—important ever since to Buddhism, Hinduism, and Islam (whose rituals are governed by moon sightings). History has such unexpected links!

I arrived in Lahore, capital of the Punjab, during Id al-Addha, commemorating Abraham's proffering of his son (Ishmael, not Isaac, according to Islam). In compounds, tethered goats, sheep, and bulls expressed their frustrations. The next day would bring an end—literally—to their complaining. Prayers at the mosque started the day.

Lahore being a cosmopolitan city (on the border with Hindu India, and with large Muslim, Christian, and Jewish communities), no one objected to my wandering through the vast and impressive Bad Shahi

25 Figures are from *The Economist*, April 7, 2007.

mosque. Built by a Mogul[26] emperor (17th c.), the mosques boasts the largest courtyard of any mosque worldwide, its gilded archways framing a view of the mosque's red sandstone façade inlaid with marble designs. As I stepped among the male worshipers, they were proud to be photographed prostrating before Allah. (Their women were "off limits," segregated in a screened-off sector.)

Apart from the chief Imam's occasional sonorous chants over loudspeakers, and a murmured response like distant thunder, there was complete silence, broken only by the rustle of thousands of bodies kneeling, bending to touch foreheads[27] to the ground or rising to lift palms up to Allah. It was fairly eerie. Prayers over, worshipers silently disgorged from mosques all over the city and began slaughtering their goats, sheep, or bulls (depending on the wealth of the family). Feasting filled the rest of the day and night, with wealthy families sending choice cuts of meat to less fortunate neighbors. I could sense Islam's strong camaraderie—*Jama'at al-Ummah*[28] they call it.

The ancient city with its sprawling suburbs now has nearly 7 million inhabitants. Its brand of Islam is chiefly mystical Sufi[29] that arrived from Persia (now Iran) in A.D. 905. Unlike the more orthodox Sunnis, Sufis are tolerant of the arts, including decorations, literature, music, and dancing (fabled "whirling dervishes" are an offshoot of their orders). A syncretistic sect, their beliefs and practices reflect influences from Gnosticism, Persian culture, and Hindu tradition.[30]

---

26 *Mogul*: (Persian "Mongol")—Mongol, Turkic, or Persian Muslim conquerors of India, and their heirs.

27 Traditional dress allows Muslims to touch foreheads to the earth without removing their brimless fezzes.

28 Lit. "Assembly of the (Muslim) community"—a local and global presence.

29 Sufis also predominate in E. Pakistan (now Bangladesh)—hence that nation's earlier tensions with W. Pakistan's Sunnis. Lahore became the seat of a reformist Hinduism influenced by Islam. In the 16th c., Guru Nanak initiated the Sikh (*learner/disciple*) movement. Nanak rejected idolatry, espoused monotheism, but opposed Mogul rulers, who persecuted Sikhs. One order never cuts the hair and binds a metal dagger (symbol of divine power) under their turbans. Sikhs provide free food and shelter to any visitor.

30 Reflecting common roots, Hindus believe in *Nirvana* (subliminal "ceasing to be"—off the re-incarnation wheel); radical Sufis, in *fana'* ("extinction" in sense of "mystical union"). Hindus teach re-incarnation; Sufi belief may include transmigration (also accepted among exotic sects of Islam). Many variations exist.

Sufi Imam Moin-ud-din Chishti (12-13 c.) loved poetry and music, and preached "love of God for man." His teaching influenced Islam in the Indian subcontinent. Imam Mian

Mir (also 12-13 c.), whose tomb is in Lahore, inspired the vision of uniting "the two oceans of Islam and Hinduism."

However, orthodox Islam objects to Sufi use of music. Muhammad stated, "Music is deception." His meaning is not clear, but no doubt the music he heard on caravan routes would be pagan Arab and Persian, since Jewish merchants would *chant*, not sing. (Jewish Apostle Paul encouraged believers in Ephesus to sing "*spiritual* songs" instead of the idolatrous, licentious songs surrounding them, resulting in a Christian hymnology.)

Muhammad's comments caused orthodox Muslims to ban all musical forms. Islam is rich in science, literature, and *arabesque* design, but art restrictions (no depiction of human or animal form, no music) have severely stifled the creative potential of some ethnic groups who have come under Islam's restrictions.

"Give Me Souls or I Die!"

Lahore's eclectic background led some Christian leaders to view the subcontinent as a prime example of Universalist Brotherhood. Moreover, Christian unity (ultimately interpreted by many as union, or one world church) became the priority goal of liberal theologians, since Muhammad had cited earlier schism as one of the main reasons for the new revelation that would later form the Qur'an.[31] (Therefore, evangelicals were considered divisive, because they introduced division into otherwise peacefully slumbering Christendom and even sought to convert Hindus and Muslims![32]) I'd learn more about that view as I traveled on to India and Sri Lanka. Right now, I found Lahore to be Pakistan's largest center for evangelicals, able to function because the Constitution recognizes Christians as part of the nation.

---

31 Dawood, *The Qur'an, op. cit.* p.10.

32 Politicians and other faiths picked up on this, making "Conversion" a hotly debated issue in the Indian sub-continent. See Sunder Raj, *The Confusion Called Conversion* (Bibliography).

Less than 100 miles north at Sialkot, around the turn of the 20th c., "Praying Hyde" had fasted and prayed for the sub-continent. A Presbyterian minister's son from Illinois, John Hyde sailed for India in the 1880s. Burdened by India's spiritual needs and slow response, Hyde gave himself to prayer and fasting. "O God, give me souls or I die!" he prayed.[33] In 1908 he asked God for (and saw) one convert per day. By 1910 that grew to four per day. Christians felt the Punjabi revival of that decade answered Hyde's prayers, inspiring many others around the world. Memory of Hyde still inspires the Sialkot Christian Conference—an annual "Keswick" begun in 1904 to refresh Christian workers.

Although Nestorian Christians had brought the gospel to the Punjab as early as the 8th century and Jesuits arrived in 1594, Roman Catholic work was not established until after Britain gained control of the area in 1842. American Presbyterian missionaries arrived in 1849, soon joined by Anglicans, Methodists, and Lutherans. Before Partition in 1947, it was through Lahore that several interdenominational missions entered the area. At that time, Christian agencies sought to avoid duplication of earlier mission work. Since those missions were not working in the southern provinces, in 1947 churches readily welcomed CIGM/ICF[34] missionaries for the South. Officially registered in 1954, their work grew into the Pakistan Christian Fellowship.

Baptist missionary Eric Wright joined CIGM and moved to Lahore when he and colleagues saw the potential of literature and leadership training through production of extension courses—including Theological Education by Extension. A Pakistani Christian now heads up the program, which has more than 1500 students nationwide. The Brethren have their publishing house in Lahore. Several agencies help prepare literature. Nation-wide, the *Jesus Film* has drawn crowds, and Christian radio has many listeners.

Three groups bear the title of "Evangelical": (1) Evangelical Fellowship of Pakistan, (2) Pakistan Evangelical Fellowship Relief and Development, and (3) Pakistan Evangelical Alliance Churches in Evangelism (PEACE). PEACE is a member of the Asia Missions Association and Evangelical

---

33 Was this a paraphrase of the prayer of John Knox, "Give me Scotland or I die!"? Praising God for many *spiritual* children, Hyde, exhausted, died of cancer in 1912.

Fellowship of Asia. However, Patrick Sookhdeo, a knowledgeable Guyanese with experience on international bodies worldwide, regrets tensions he's noticed between some Christian Pakistanis—especially among locals who feel threatened by strong para-church groups—who therefore keep to themselves.

Through the years, Christians have influenced development in the area, beyond reckoning. For instance, President Musharraf is among the Pakistani government leaders and academics who have attended Forman College, named after Charles William Foreman (1821-94), an American Presbyterian missionary—one of the early Princeton student mission volunteers.

Lahore: Surprises Galore

Lahore was full of surprises for me. To begin with, I stayed in the home of a Muslim Pakistani married to a Christian Briton: Iqbal, a businessman, worshiped in the mosque, while Eunice worshiped at the church. He treated her with respect and affection. She respected him and his nation while helping the many lonely, marginalized women around her. Their home was always open to both Muslim and Christian guests. Iqbal reminded me of Captain Said, whom I'd met on the train (Chapter 2)—mature, moderate, and educated. Theirs was the tolerant side of Islam. However, I also was conscious that most Orthodox Muslims I met would not accept their brand of Islam as legitimate.

Isa, an African university student I met in Lahore, turned out to be a different kind of surprise. His father was a Muslim and his mother a Christian. In order to receive a scholarship,[35] he turned against his mother (whom he actually loved) and declared himself a Muslim. In Lahore someone gave him a Bible. Then he met Mark X— and Tim X—, who befriended him in this strange land. Soon Isa was asking them about their Christian faith, and he eventually trusted in Christ as his own Saviour. He promptly lost his scholarship but changed his course and took a part-

---

34 Ceylon and India General Mission merged with Puna and India Village Mission, in turn becoming International Christian Fellowship before it merged with SIM in 1989. Ch. 7 examines these as an interdenominational case study.

35 In Isa's country, a common sentiment is that "if the Devil offers you a scholarship, take it!"

time job to pay his fees. Back in Africa, his mother had wept when he disowned her; now she wept with joy over the news that her prodigal son, traveling all the way from Africa, met Jesus on Asia's Spice Road!

Not all the surprises are in Lahore. A Christian couple on an overloaded bus in Sindh province were enjoying typical Hindu folk-music blaring over the vehicle's loudspeakers, when they suddenly realized the words were right out of the Bible. The gospel tape was the project of Baptist missionaries who had studied Sindh music. It was so well done that a secular company distributed it through their regular music outlets. Within months of release, the pop music tape sold over one thousand copies. Jesus riding Pakistani buses!

But Jesus' disciples had been to the Indus Valley long before missionaries from the West arrived. Operation Mobilization is producing tapes of Punjabi hymns—rediscovered from some 400 *early* Christian hymns based on the Psalms. Today's churches had known only 50-60 of these. Now Punjabis can sing these authentic indigenous hymns.

Surprises—both happy and sad. So much to encourage; so much to discourage! At times human nature and culture hinder the gospel. From Kabul to Lahore, I could have thrown up my hands and asked, "What difference has the gospel made?" The Army captain had told me that Islam affects all of life. I'd told him that Christianity does too. But how much was the gospel transforming the lives of the average Pakistani Christian?

Then I thought of my own nation, inheritor of a rich biblical background. It has thousands of churches and millions of churchgoers, sated by Christian magazines, TV programs, and seminaries. Yet it's riddled with status-seeking (*izzat*?) and corruption. Pakistan has a different heritage, one that lacks a strong biblical heritage. But as I met disciples fully committed to honoring only Christ, I saw that Jesus really does make a difference.

But a press release made my heart heavy for my brothers and sisters in this nation. The government condemns violence, but it can happen. One news release reported:

"In Pakistan, some 2,000 Muslims armed with iron rods, axes and tins of kerosene ransacked and looted four churches, a convent, a mission-run school and several Christian homes in Sangla Hill on November 12, after the burning of the Qur'an led local mosques to appeal for Muslims to "teach the Christians a lesson."

"The previous day, Catholic Christian Yousaf Masih was gambling with his Muslim friend Saleem Sunihara near the Sangla Hill sports stadium. To avoid paying a large gambling debt, the Muslim set fire to old pages of the Qur'an kept in a nearby storage room and blamed the fire on Masih. Eyewitnesses told a joint fact-finding team from Jubilee Campaign and the Lahore-based Center for Legal Aid Assistance and Settlement (CLAAS) that they saw Sunihara throw a burning match into the room.

"Several busloads of Muslim men arrived in Sangla Hill to join the mob the morning of November 12, and hundreds of Christian families, mostly poor farmers and laborers, fled the area during and after the attack. Police not only failed to protect the Christian places of worship but also joined the crowd in vandalizing Catholic and Presbyterian churches. Sangla Hill police also arrested and tortured four of Masih's six brothers, prompting the alleged blasphemer to give himself up in exchange for their release. Masih was held at the Sheikhupura jail.

"The homes of Masih and his brothers were burned to the ground, with no one able to confirm the whereabouts of his wife and three children. Addressing a crowd of 3,000 men at the Jamia Masjid Rizvia mosque in Sangla Hill on December 2, Muslim clerics flanked by government officials demanded the public execution of Masih."[36]

"If God Wills, We'll Land . . ."

With mixed feelings, I left for the airport. It was time for me to leave Pakistan. Bold Qur'anic inscriptions decorated Lahore Airport's departure lounge walls. Two airport staff and a flight-crew member touched their foreheads to prayer mats. A Pakistani businesswoman in a fashionable pantsuit made a last-minute call on her cell phone. Then we boarded for

[36] Compass Direct, January 2006

the brief flight across the border and into Delhi, India. As we took off, an Arabic traveller's prayer used by the Prophet Muhammad wailed over the speakers. Islam affects all of life, the soldier on the train had said. I looked down at the sun-burnt countryside that seemed to be gasping for Monsoon rains to begin. "Lord, send spiritual showers too," I prayed. "May your living water flow through all of life!"

"If Allah wills, we'll land shortly," an attendant announced as we approached Delhi.[37]

---

[37] Although Christians might commend recognition of God's sovereignty (cf. James 4.15), Muslims could understand the announcement as (1) "talismanic," for safety, (2) religio-political, recognizing Islam, and (3) fatalism (maintenance and flight crews could not prevent a landing disaster, if "God wills it.")

India holds great contrasts in everyday life: a lurid wall poster for a "Bollywood" cinema film forms an incongruous background for a sacred cow munching on the garbage of a Delhi street.

B – INDIA AND SRI LANKA

Krishna and Buddha Meet Jesus

Disciples on the Old Spice Road

"You shall be my witness in Jerusalem, and in all Judea and Samaria, and to the ends of the earth" (Acts 1. 8).

India: Pop. 1,152,163,518

INDIA BURST UPON ME like the trumpeting of an elephant when I landed in New Delhi, the nation's capital. As dramatically as a stage backdrop changes a theater's ambiance, I was suddenly in a different world. No wonder Muslims and Hindus find it difficult to live together! A ceramic mural in the arrival lounge displayed a voluptuous goddess seducing a muscular god, both naked except for chastity belts—no doubt acceptable costumes for Hindu deities.[1] After learning about Islam's 8thc. invasion of India and 20thc. "rejection" (chapter 3), I could understand this flagrant Hindu defiance to Muslims boarding the return flight. A number were heavily bearded, shaggy-browed Afghans who had come to India to find work but instead found they weren't welcome.[2]

1. Islam bans even bare limbs, and depiction of gods, spirits, or humans is idolatrous. For a concise study of Hinduism, see Zaehner, *Hinduism* (Bibliography). Casual sex—including homosexual coupling—has been "normal," whether in markets or temples. India's flagrant sexuality follows the culture of Babylon and societies across Asia. In view of such neighbors, God gave the Jews laws requiring moral relationships based on fidelity among the betrothed; Islam later sought to do so through its own regulations.
2. Actually, more Muslims still live in India than in Pakistan. One can only imagine the distress Puritanical Muslims feel in the midst of the flagrant sexuality of Hindu society. India has the world's second largest Muslim population (after Indonesia).

Was I on a different planet from the one I'd just left? The busy, noisy streets of Delhi hit me with some of the reasons for tension between the two states. Nowhere did I hear the muezzin's call to prayer, so ubiquitous in Islamabad. Instead of prayers from crescent-crowned mosques rising to "the One God and his Prophet," Hindu dance music wafted from towering temples, ornately decorated with carvings of several of India's some 30m. gods and goddesses.[3]

Eve-Teasers and Holy Cows

After Pakistan's absence of women in public, I found Delhi's streets full of them, milling alongside men. Yes, women out in public! Many with bare navels between halter blouse and wrap-around skirts.[4] On a billboard, a sultry siren advertised Coca Cola, alongside another billboard promoting the latest made-in-India romance movie. Any Pakistani must experience shock, but some males in both nations have the same penchant for pinching females and making sexist remarks. Only it was more common in Delhi, especially for women waiting at bus stops or walking home from work. Each evening, undercover (no pun intended) policewomen arrested half a dozen "Eve-teasers," as police called them.

Unlike slaughter-bound bulls and goats in Pakistan, sacred cows placidly ruminated in the streets as if covered by life insurance. I could imagine the tensions when Muslims neighbors slaughter animals in their compounds on a holy day, to the horror of Hindu neighbors—who wouldn't think of hindering a wandering cow from eating a flower garden! In the middle of a road, without grass or water, a bovine may look pitifully hungry and thirsty but remain unmoved—secure in the knowledge it is sacred?

To me, a holy cow suggested several things. Although its safeguarded life would earn praise from a vegetarian or animal rights enthusiast, an environmentalist should be concerned that the bovine *annually* consumes

3. Figure varies from 30m-330m—anyone's guess. You may choose, placate, be blessed by a god fitting your particular need—whether love, hate, wealth, theft, birth, murder. Hindus may add other gods, even "Jesus," to their pantheon, implying that Hindus are tolerant, whereas "Jesus-the-only-way" Christians must be intolerant! But "Hindu" is a catchall term, covering a variety of cults, some intolerant of others.

4. Nothing new for the West, where bare midriffs became "mod" fashion.

its weight in food (food that India can ill afford to spare) and the cow belches methane gas, a pollutant. And surprisingly, the status of cows can result in cruelty to aging cattle![5]

But to a Hindu or Buddhist, isn't "Mother India" (as a cow is called) worthy of veneration? The bovine must be the re-incarnation of some righteous person—upgraded from miserable *human* existence. How could anyone disturb it, let alone slaughter it? Cows block traffic because no one dare push them out of the way. Was the sacred cow a parable about India? I'd find out as I crisscrossed the world's largest democracy and soon-to-be most populous nation.[6]

Fit for the *Raja*!

My driver through Delhi's streets was from the Evangelical Fellowship of India (EFI), which had invited me as guest Bible speaker at their nation-wide annual convention. Earlier, when I arrived at the airport, the driver was thoughtfully holding aloft a sign: *"Welcome Dr. Fuller!"* He said he'd take me to my lodgings.

After driving through exhaust fumes from vintage taxis, passenger buses, and motorized rickshaws, I was somewhat surprised when we pulled up at the peaceful entrance to the International Ashok—a five-star hotel, set in a manicured landscape of lawn and gardens. The resplendent porter—turban, handlebar mustache, red jacket with brass buttons, waist cummerbund, and white *jodhpurs*—opened the car door for me to alight like royalty. Picking up my two bags, he ushered me into the hotel. A house porter, similarly costumed, took over my bags, showed me to my luxurious air-conditioned room, and turned down the top bedding (a ploy to give me time to tip a few rupees into his out-stretched hand). Classy! Fit for the *raja*[7] himself.

---

5. In "The Cruelty of Vegetarianism," Indian professor Vishal Mangalwadi cites the plight of a destitute Hindu, whose cow can no longer give milk or produce calves—yet he cannot sell or slaughter it. Unable to provide fodder, he resentfully mistreats the beast or turfs it out on to the road.
6. China has held that top position, but its severe birth controls are allowing India to compete numerically.
7. Sanskrit: ruler, king.

I read the note my airport driver had handed me before he left. It was a welcome from the conference chairman. Thoroughly weary from traipsing sultry Pakistan, I gratefully noted that the driver would not pick me up before 11 A.M. next day. I sank into the massive king-size bed and was soon sound asleep between the spotless sheets.

Next morning, after a first-class breakfast, I donned a hotel bathrobe and went down to swim in the kidney-shaped pool. (At home I keep fit with regular swimming, but this was my first exercise, other than perspiring, on this trip.) Then while waiting in the palm-lined lobby for the driver, I thanked the Lord for this unexpected respite, and looked through my Bible notes for the conference. When the driver took me to its venue, a Christian college, I found the auditorium buzzing with some 500 Christian workers from all over India, representing a kaleidoscope of churches and missions.

"Welcome!" greeted the General Secretary, as he introduced me to the other main speaker, Richard Howell, president of EFI. Howell and I would share the devotional and Bible teaching messages for the next three days.

But the Secretary seemed to have something else on his mind. "There's been a little mix-up about your lodging," he finally said, clearing his throat apologetically. "It's true you are supposed to stay at the Ashok, but our office forgot there are two Ashok Hotels.[8] Do you mind if the driver takes you back to move your things before check-out time?"

Of course I didn't mind, and we returned to the International Ashok for my baggage. Later, when the driver dropped me at the *local* Ashok Hotel, it definitely wasn't the International one! As I lugged my two hand-held bags up a dark stairway to my room, I realized the difference. I was sorry EFI had incurred a night's expense at the other hotel—but it did show me a different side of India, and I had a swim! Now I was thankful for this one-star lodging, more in keeping with missionary life. However, that night I used my own towel, checked between the graying sheets, and covered the pillow with my shirt before laying my head on it. Something ran upside-down along a ceiling beam.

8. Emperor Asoka (3c. B.C.) unified India, making Buddhism the state religion. Today, commerce frequently trades on his name ("Ashok").

Curry[9] and Conversation

Back at the convention, meals were simple but tasty: rice, plantain, and either curried fish or cubes of meat—seasoned with very rich fellowship. Most of the nation's evangelical church, mission, school, and agency leaders were there. These were educated, intelligent men and women, "representing the salt and light" of their nation. EFI brought together denominational, non-denominational, and Non-Governmental Agencies (NGOs—charities, including missions, in other words).

It was an eye-opener to meet people such as video producers Paul and Sheila Samuel (a common surname in parts of India). Sheila got her start with Trans-World Radio, producing dramatized Bible stories. As Christmas approached one year, she courageously asked India's television service Director-General (for results, go to the top!) for a trial. He invited her to the studios, where she narrated the Christmas story with appropriate stills and music. After viewing the taped recording, the Director-General liked it so much he put it on national TV just as it was.

Sheila had one request—that John 3.16 (text in full script) take the place of the usual credits. And so it did. That was the beginning of Samuel Video Productions, which has been making Christian TV videos for special occasions ever since. Samuel Productions now tapes documentaries, musicals, and dramas—all culturally relevant and with an evangelistic message.

"Sometimes we patiently have to convince the station to show a particular aspect of our Bible stories, because they're afraid it might upset Hindus or Muslims," Paul and Sheila said. I asked, "Like what?"

"Our drama on the Crucifixion was OK—Hindus are quite ready to worship anyone or anything," she explained. "But not the Resurrection. They wanted us to leave Jesus in the grave, because they believe he's buried in Kashmir! Contrary teaching could have political repercussions. We're still praying that one through."

---

9. "Curry": >Tamil *kari*—condiment of pungent ground spices. Before the advent of domestic refrigerators, Europeans discovered that it disguised tainted foods in stew—a staple spicy additive.

"Thankful I'm Single!"

Joyce Khanna was another very special Indian Christian leader, nearing retirement age. I was surprised when she thanked God she wasn't married (unusual view in India), because she could devote her full time to being principal of Faith Academy, a secondary school in the heart of Delhi. Obtaining the property was in itself a miracle for the Presbyterian couple who had founded the work, and Joyce saw her role as the Lord's calling.

"We now have 1500 students, and graduates have 100 percent success in the state exams," Joyce told me, tossing one end of her eyelet shawl over a shoulder. "But it's a constant work of faith, looking to God for any extra finances needed beyond the fees, and insisting on our Christian standards and employing only Christian teachers—even though many students are not Christian."

External pressures are always a challenge to her faith. When she found an idol on the school property line, she protested but the local authority assured her it was only a small idol—it would be no problem to her. However, the inevitable happened. Hindus built a shelter over it, topped by a larger figure, creating a shrine 15 feet high. It is impossible to move anything that is being worshiped, so Joyce could only build a wall inside the property line, to fence off the shrine. She was also being watchful about a tree growing at the school's entrance. A guru claimed to have been "enlightened" under it—so people began to hang idols on the limbs. Joyce quickly removes these, before Hindus can venerate them. That would make the tree a sacred shrine.

"How do men accept you, a woman, as a leader?" I asked, tongue in cheek.

"Usually I have no problem. Our people's attitude to women depends on the level of education. There's more equality in cities, where there are more educated people. But in society as a whole, both Hindus and Muslims give women an inferior position in life. In rural areas, from childhood, a female considers herself worthless, the chattel of men."

I'd heard that, for Hindus, a husband is *patidev*, a wife's god. In fact, males thank God they weren't born as a woman or a dog.[10] One major

10. Interesting that certain Jewish Pharisees also thank God for that!

political party had issued an official statement on the status of women—conclusion: women are inferior to men!

"How do you reconcile that with the fact several outstanding women have been political leaders, and that Hindus worship goddesses?"[11]

"Goddesses?" Joyce smiled grimly. "That's no problem for a male, because men create the goddesses and then manipulate them—even using temple priestesses for sex. As to women political leaders, I agree we've had several. Most have been Brahmins—high caste—widows or wives of family dynasties, like the Nehrus or Gandhis. However, with increasing freedom for the lower castes, we'll likely see more women leaders emerging."

Culture of Despair

"I don't see much joy in people's faces!" I commented. I'd read that suicide rates are rising—so that some states pay bereaved families compensation for a breadwinner's suicide.[12] "I thought I left endemic depression behind, on the other side of the border."

"Oh no!" Joyce replied. "The general attitude of Hindus is despair. There's no assurance of anything in this life or the next. They're always afraid of doing something that will cause them to be reincarnated in a worse state than they are in now."

"How do you approach them with the gospel?"

"We stress that *now*, in this life, through Christ's salvation, people can have assurance of eternal life. That's the Good News for Hindus, Muslims, and everyone!"

Ah, I thought—Jesus here and now on the Old Spice Road!

"I'm always hearing about court cases—on the slightest pretext. Why?" I pursued.

---

11. Hindus teach that a husband is *patidev*, a wife's god. Hindus represent female deities in different forms. "Durga" (literally, the inaccessible) is the classical mother goddess. Bengalis know her as Kali, "the black (fierce) one"; villagers as Candi, protector from animal spirits; Brahmans (highest caste) as spouse of Shiva, member of Hindu "trinity" along with Vishnu. In 1st c., Brahma was highest in that "trinity," but was supplanted by Shakti, principle female deity.

12. Although this seems to increase the suicide rate, reported the *Economist* of June 23, 2007.

"We've had our share at Faith Academy," replied Joyce. "Litigation has always majored in Hindu society—although modernization has brought about more legal activity. Basically everybody is there to get something from someone else. There is not a strong work ethic. Society is lazy, looking for a handout, and court action is one possible way to get this. Unfortunately, Christians are among some of the worst troublemakers. That's a poor testimony, and it wastes our time, energy, and finances."

"You're educating children," I commented, changing the topic. "I read in India's *Liberal Times* about a dozen boys aged between 3 and 6 years smuggled from Bangladesh and sold to an agency in Delhi that shipped them to the Near East for camel racing. There was also an article about bonded children—as many as 200,000 in 'The Carpet Belt'—working up to 14 hours a day hand-knotting carpets. What can you do about that?"

"Our Constitution prohibits child labor, but the law is hard to apply," Joyce explained. "Conditions are appalling; those children should be in school. But it's not so simple. Many illiterate families depend on child income, even though it's meagre. Unfortunately, if the children weren't employed, they'd be into hooliganism or crime. The problem is larger than child labor. It involves parental attitudes to family and work, caste, females, education, and debt (parents use children to pay that off). It's regrettable, but if you solve only part of the problem, you make other problems. Through the gospel and training in Christian character we hope to bring about over-all change in communities. That's going to take time because our population is so large. And even though governments propose reforms, bribes make proposed changes ineffective!"

What heavy burdens this small woman carried, I thought! And what an uphill battle she and others faced in overcoming harmful practices!

I shuddered as I thought of ritual murders that priests of Kali still commit, although people suppose that the grizzly sacrifices ceased long ago. A Hindu cult believes that sacrificing a male child to the goddess Kali ensures protection and success. Holding great power over superstitious and poverty-stricken villagers, temple agents entice boys—or parents offer them—to the temples, where priests confine, mutilate, and kill the human sacrifices by degrees.[13] Torturous death supposedly placates the blood-hungry goddess most effectively.

In pre-Independence India, when Christians condemned such atrocities, many readers refused to believe the reports, and more than one writer toned down descriptions, for the sake of "polite" readership. Even today, to be politically correct, one doesn't talk about such atrocities; but thank God, not everyone thinks that way! In my travels, I'd be meeting courageous people combating hidden as well as public evil.

A Goldmine of Research

Meanwhile, in Delhi I was meeting quite a cross-section of the Christian community. Take, for instance, Christopher Raj, at the time the Executive Secretary of the Theological Research and Communication Institute (TRACI), grandson of a clergyman. With a doctorate in political science and studies in technology relevant to Asia, Dr. Raj had been a Fulbright scholar and Brooks Institute research fellow before lecturing in several countries. When I met him, he was giving full time to TRACI, analysing trends and views relevant to Christianity in Asia. TRACI has a number of projects going, including a film about AIDS. Although any group could use the film, viewers know that the medics shown are Christian: they examine and *touch* AIDS patients—something few Indian non-Christians would do, for their other patients would shun them if they did.

Dr. Raj proved to be a goldmine of information about life in today's India:

Christianity: Mainline denominations came together after Independence in 1947, to form the Church of South India and the Church of North India. The North tends to be more liberal in theology than the South, but there are evangelical elements within it. Along with such CSI elements, evangelical groups in the South send a wide range of missionaries to the North.

13. BBC World Report, April 11, 2006, broadcast a documentary on this continuing atrocity. Indian police stated they knew of 200 cases.

Indian Christians seek to be self-sufficient, but some agencies from overseas come in and offer finance to pay salaries and build churches.[14] "We don't endorse that, because it would only strengthen Hindu and Muslim allegations that Christianity is 'an imperialist plot and foreign religion that endangers social tranquility,'" Dr. Raj explained. In his book, *The Confusion Called Conversion*,[15] Ebenezer Sunder Raj demolishes that argument, documenting how Christianity has brought peace to warring communities. Rather, he points out, other religions have violently opposed the upward mobility of "Untouchable" (Dalits), while aggressively seeking expansion and political power.

Christian missions refused to endorse the caste system, but unintentionally they strengthened it by the good work they did in planting Christianity among the lower castes![16] Now churches full of Dalit[17] (low-caste, untouchable) members find it difficult to relate to higher castes—which look down on them.

In some states, church growth is chiefly among "Christianized" elements—out of their own church background, not from new outreach. To enhance their claims for attention (particularly overseas), a church or sect may inflate figures. I heard of one state claiming to have 500 churches, but actually it has very few. The other side of the coin is the good that many churches spread in their communities, prompting considerable growth. When radicals attack Islam, Muslims often seek refuge in churches.

Family Life: TRACI produces materials on Christian marriage. Dowry is a social issue, not a religious issue. It has been a custom for centuries. Abraham's wife, Sarah, brought gifts to her new in-laws. The problem is how to remove its economic evils, since it has become a matter of trade.

---

14. There are responsible non-denominational agencies careful to work with churches and not compete for leaders. However, potential leaders may join these agencies because of lack of opportunity in some older, established churches. They indirectly assist their denominations with new approaches and vitality.

15. Sunder Raj, *The Confusion Called Conversion*. New Delhi: TRACI, 1995.

16. In 1607 Jesuit De Nobili opened the Madurai Mission. Culturally aware, he trained priests to work among specific castes as the only acceptable way. Unfortunately it perpetuated caste among Christians. Some Christian leaders went to the other extreme, viewing church development among outcastes (now "Designated Castes") as hindering church growth among educated Indians (see Ch. 9 re. Telugu).

17. Dalit >Sanskrit: "broken down, crushed."

In the South, churches receive a tithe of the dowry. That's commendable in one way, yet it perpetuates the problem for Christians. In arranged marriages, dowry promotes greed, so families of grooms continue to demand money and gifts from the bride's parents. Sometimes the groom may beat or even burn his new bride because her parents haven't met the demands! Female infanticide adds to the carnage.

Christopher Raj and his wife, Punita, discovered how upset many women are about dowry—women feel that the groom and his family really want the money and goods, rather than loving the woman. Christopher and Punita have decided they will not give dowry for their daughter, setting an example to break the system. They will provide for their daughter in other ways as needed. Educated girls, already employed, can be independent of dowry.

Family planning is also a religious problem. Muslims oppose it because the Qur'an does not teach it. Hindus oppose it, to maintain their majority. They know that Muslims will have four wives and plenty of children, increasing their numbers. India's population is about to bypass China's—yet in an area one-third the size of China!

For newly Christian families, complications continue. Parents may be angry that their Hindu traditional religious ceremonies (on which they depend for successive births to the next level)—won't be carried out by Christian families. Grandmothers, an integral part of any family, may secretly teach Christian grandchildren Hindu views, convinced this is for the children's benefit. In fact, they have been known to strangle a female baby in their preference for male progeny.

***Hindutva* (Hinduism):** In this concept of national religion and culture, India is a Hindu nation; non-Hindus are aliens. The nationalist Bharatiya Janata Party would like a law prohibiting conversion—a political concept.[18] Even as Partition increased Pakistan's histrionic reaction to other religions, it increased Hindu reaction to anything that threatened

18. Several states passed such a law, but Tamil Nadu recently repealed it; Christians hope other states will follow. A former prime minister proposed a national debate on Conversion (Bibliography: Raj, *Conversion: A National Debate*). Pressure has made some pastors nervous. One told enquiring Hindus, "If you want to become Christians, find an evangelist. Converting someone isn't my job. I'm a pastor." (Unbelievable!)

their faith and political power. In the Hindu mind there still lurks deep resentment over Islam's Mogul domination of Delhi (1526-1858), driving fear of a perceived Muslim threat.

Although Hindus have not always had centralized leadership, they have learned from Muslims, whose emphasis on Allah supersedes Islam's sectarianism in times of unrest. Some westerners think Hindus really are monotheistic, and that their multiple gods are only varied depictions of a supreme deity. However, these gods are often in tension and conflict. So Hindutva's strategy is to emphasise one deity, Rama, as supreme. This, some Hindus believe, would cut across the caste system and unify the Hindu religion. But to cover the bases, parents dedicate children to specific gods whom they tenaciously worship, regardless of which god may be supreme.

"*Hindutva* portends a total crippling of our national energies by its unforgiving, malicious, and hate-obsessed spirit and outlook," writes Raj's colleague, Valson Thampu, TRACI's editor. That's not the idealized view most Westerners have of Hinduism![19]

Protesting Discrimination

These tried and tested leaders blessed me as I learned their stories. Richard Howell's expositions enriched us all. One hundred percent a son of India,[20] Howell represented a younger generation of devout, educated Christian leaders, free from caste and clan, making an impact on their own nation and other nations. EFI gives voice to over 20m evangelicals. When a political leader in another area vowed to make his state "Christian-free," Howell protested to the Prime Minister himself. When a Hindu organization sent a "state-wide protest against Christian schools" for not displaying pictures of Hindu gods, there were Christian voices that spoke up in defence.

What courageous people, I thought—living for Jesus on the Old Spice Road! The leaders I met at the EFI conference represented many

19. Re. Hinduism, see Appendix F. Valson Thampu has also written a helpful book: *AIDS—Heresy and Prophecy*. New Delhi: TRACI, 1993.

20. Not only in India but other areas, for generations grateful families have customarily adopted the surnames of benefactors from different nationalities.

sons and daughters of India who stand for the gospel and religious liberty, in the midst of an often hostile culture.

For instance, in the northern state of Gujarat, a state-run grammar test for grade 12 students contained questions that likened Christianity to Nazism. A prominent Mumbai lawyer, Atul Setalvad, stated, "The last ten years have seen a consistent, organized campaign of hate against Christians and Muslims in Gujarat."[21] This certainly was not the attitude of Pandit Jawaharlal Nehru, India's first Prime Minister:

> **"If any man raises his hand against another in the name of religion, I shall fight him till the last breath of my life—whether I am in Government or outside."**[22]

However, India has the same problem curbing extremists that many other countries have. Sectarian tensions brought the destruction of the Ayodhya Mosque, built on one of Hindu's holiest sites. A Muslim mob retaliated by burning a busload of Hindu devotees, leading to a cycle of extremist retaliation. In January 1999, anger got out of hand, and rioters turned against Christians, bursting on to both national and international headlines.

Burned Alive for Jesus' Sake!

A mob, incited by a Hindutva militant, attacked the vehicle in which Australian Graham Staines and his two sons were sleeping after a Bible study among the grateful villagers of Manoharpur, in Orissa. The village was more remote than "the end of the road"—reached only by a trail, without electricity, piped water, sanitation, or effective education. The people of Manoharpur were typical of 40,000 Santhalis (served by one dysfunctional school). Although others despised them as "only tribals," Graham learned their language and spoke it like a native. He even composed peaceful hymns for the Christians to sing in place of their traditional songs to dreaded spirits. Graham and Gladys had brought to these marginalized people health, agriculture, education, and most of all, spiritual hope.

---

21. REC News Exchange June 2002, quoting ENI/Compass Direct.
22. Quoted by Valson Thampu, Director of TRACI, Delhi, in a letter to India's Prime Minister, Nov. 25, 1998. Popularly called "Panditji," Nehru was a Kashmiri Pandit (high caste Hindu/ Brahmin).

For some thirty years, Graham and his wife, Gladys, cared for "untouchables"— leprosy patients and the poor. Local villagers loved them. The night of the murders, villagers rushed to rescue Staines and his sons but were prevented by the machete-wielding intruders. They broke the car windows, shot the occupants with arrows, and poured gasoline over the vehicle before setting it ablaze. The thugs hung around for nearly two hours, to prevent anyone trying to rescue any trace of the Staines.

The Staines were the kind of martyrs the author of Hebrews had in mind when he penned his tribute: *"The world was not worthy of them."* For most of us, discipleship doesn't include martyrdom, yet Jesus told his followers, "...any of you who does not give up everything he has cannot be my disciple." A parallel passage includes one's life.[23]

At a community memorial service, saffron-robed Hindus and Buddhists, white-robed Muslims, Catholic priests, Protestant pastors, and laypeople wept together. Radicals sought to blame the Staines for "forcible conversions," ironically alleging that their help to "untouchables" was destructive to their traditional way of life.[24] However, a Commission headed by Supreme Court Justice D. P. Wadhwa absolved the Staines and indicted radicals for the grisly murder. The Commission described the murders as an attempt by religious extremists to subvert "the secular foundations" of the nation by inciting violence against people of other faiths.

"Lies, deception, and misconception have no place in religious faith," stated the Commission's frank report (which included the testimony of witnesses). "It is necessary to see the truth of the Christian faith as a way of life and the teaching of the gospel and the teachings of Christ as an integral part of their tenets. This is a fundamental right of the Christian minority community . . . zealously protected by the constitution . . . . [the murder of the] Staines was

---

23. Scriptures cited in this paragraph: Hebrews 11.38; Luke 14.33; Matthew 10.37.

24. "Untouchables" believe they must endure rejection and poverty in order to (hopefully) be reincarnated to a better existence. Therefore, helping them would interfere with their destiny.

plainly to prevent missionary activities amongst the tribals so that they would not embrace the Christian faith."[25]

Forgiveness Beyond Human Comprehension

India's President said the murders belong to "the world's inventory of black deeds." A government minister resigned, stating, "My head has bowed in shame. I am shaken and I want to atone." National TV and newspapers reported the crime, but what drew even greater attention was the amazing attitude of Gladys Staines (who had not accompanied the family on that fatal trip). Instead of hatred and revenge, she showed love and forgiveness. "*I forgive those who killed my husband and darling boys. I pray they will come to know God's love.*"

"The Bible reveals a God of love who sent his Son, the Lord Jesus Christ to die for the sins of the world," she told the Press. "When the Lord Jesus was brutally treated and nailed to the Cross, he prayed: 'Father forgive, for they know not what they do.' Jesus is the role model for all Christians, and it is His example that gives me strength."

It was beyond comprehension—the "peace of God that *passes all understanding*."

"This is true spirituality," commented Samuel Kamaleson, at the time president of Friends Missionary Prayer Band,[26] later a vice president of World Vision. "And there are a whole lot of . . . Indians, who . . . have been killed and buried quietly, . . . for the sake of the gospel."[27]

"Mrs. Staines has gone far ahead of us along the path of spirituality," stated Swami[28] Agnivesh, weeping. "She was not the 'official spokesperson

25. Eight months later, the same radical group burned to death a Muslim trader in Orissa—far to the east. (There are actually more Muslims in India than any other country except Indonesia.) Inter-faith violence caused a nation-wide debate on Conversion. (See Bibliography: Raj, *Conversion.*) Major reaction threatened in 2001 when nearly one million Dalits—of the caste formerly called "Untouchable"—decided to break from Hindu discrimination and become either Christian or Buddhist. Hindered by a campaign of misinformation and obstruction, only 100,000 turned up in Delhi for the mass ceremony, in which many publicly opted for Buddhism—more acceptable for the pro-Hindutva party then in power.

26. By 2005, FMPB had formed over 1,000 congregations, with one new group every two days.

27. Shubin, R.G., *Mission Frontiers,* September 2000, p. 31. Pasadena: USCWM.

28. A Hindu ascetic or religious teacher, from Sanskrit: *svamin*—"lord, owner."

of the Church,' but only a simple housewife. But we have not seen a better witness to Jesus than Gladys, who has committed herself to serve leprosy-affected people of Baripada. I draw inspiration from her." Maulana Rafique Quasmi, the General Secretary of a Muslim organization, stated, "The more we see of Gladys, the greater our admiration for her grows."

The Swamiji, one of the founding members of "Religions for Social Justice," later arranged for Gladys to meet the Press, where she again stated her love for the people of India and her forgiveness to the murderers of her family. The national press and TV stations reported the meeting, to the astonishment of all who heard. The Swami described Gladys as the source of a possible spiritual renewal in society.

Gladys stayed on in India to look after her larger "family"—the leprosy patients. Ten days prior to the loss of her husband and sons, she and Graham had discussed the news of violence against Christians in another state. "Shouldn't Christians learn to forgive, even as Jesus did?" Gladys had exclaimed. She could still picture Graham agreeing with her. "God was preparing me!" she said.

I know that, in myself, I don't have the grace that Gladys shows, but I also know that God could give me that grace in the moment of need. As someone has said, "You won't have emergency grace until the emergency."

Attacks still continue in Orissa, as militant Hindus strive for political power to ensure a privileged status for "a culture that is racist, fatalistic, and immoral . . . in which struggle Christians often suffer as the pawns," according to the World Evangelical Alliance.[29] In 2008, thousands of Christians were killed, their houses and churches burned by Hindu extremists, after a militant Hindu leader was killed. Rioters blamed Christians, even though a Marxist group had claimed responsibility. Evangelical Fellowship of India reported eye-witness accounts of pastors being beaten and threatened with death. "Even if you kill me, I'll not turn my back on Jesus!" one pastor told his attackers. He escaped into the forest when the mob turned on his parishioners.

29. *Faith Today,* Evang. Fellowship Canada, Nov. Dec. '08; *EFC Release Feb. 26/09.

Another was indeed hacked to death when he refused to undergo Hindu "reconversion" rites. Prime Minister Manmohan Singh described the situation as a "national shame."*

Dalit Problem "Untouchable"?

Many Dalits become Christian—being more open to the gospel (and change) than the self-sufficient "higher castes." While the government, modernizing in so many ways, does try to overcome discrimination against "untouchable" Dalits, the problem seems like trying to move a sacred cow lying on a busy roadway. Stated a 2006 news release:

> In a year of weekly incidents of violence against Christians and the introduction of a bill that could make Rajasthan the sixth state restricting religious conversions in India, the Supreme Court on November 28 deferred for the third time ruling on whether Dalit Christians (low-caste untouchables) can be denied job and education rights. Dalits belonging to Hindu, Buddhist, and Sikh faiths qualify for a government plan that reserves 26 percent of jobs and educational places for them. Under current laws, Dalits who convert to Christianity or Islam lose this "reserve" privilege.
>
> Christian leaders said India's 16m Dalit Christians are extremely frustrated and demoralized by the government's position. In October, government attorneys had delayed a ruling by telling justices that a commission had been set up to study a broad range of issues surrounding government reservations for Dalits. That commission, which Christian leaders dismissed as a way of stalling the issue, is due to finish its work next year. Additionally, throughout 2005, police routinely refused to register complaints from Christians who were assaulted by Hindu extremists.[30]

Joseph D'souza, International President of the Dalit Freedom Network and President of the All India Christian Council, works tirelessly to overcome the Dalit problem. A prolific writer, and author of the book, *Dalit Freedom Now and Forever*, Dr. D'souza addresses organizations and the public in many countries. An activist for human rights, including Christian liberty, D'souza has addressed UN and government Commissions and spoken on news networks in UK and America.

30. Compass Direct, January 2006. Other sources list the Dalits as 22% of the population.

"Joseph D'souza is one of our most capable leaders," George Verwer told me. "He's OM's Associate International Director, as well as Executive Director of OM India." D'souza also works with agencies such as People's Church, Toronto,[31] to place in Indian villages large TV screens, tuned to show educational and Christian programs and films.

Others are taking an active interest in Dalit needs. One is Ivan Kostka, Global Discipleship Pastor at Bramalea Baptist, Toronto, who plans to publish a biblical magazine for Dalit readership in India.

Meanwhile, Communists see the marginalized as a growth opportunity. India's Prime Minister stated that a Maoist group, the Naxalites, posed "the single biggest internal-security challenge ever faced by our country."[32] Originating in the 1960s in Naxalbari's district of West Bengal, they have grown into a nation-wide force by promising land and freedom to marginalized peoples. They intimidate through gruesome killings and rumors. For instance, when they killed a Hindu leader in north-east Orissa state, they blamed Christians—provoking violence that took a number of lives.

Obviously, I had a lot to learn about cultures and religions in this vast country. For one thing, although caste identity may be losing its importance among India's growing middle class, even among them, maintaining caste still provides Dalits' only real social network as they move to urban centers. But I couldn't have anticipated discussing how many times a Dalit—or anyone else—would have to be re-incarnated to move up the ladder of existence.

---

31. Toronto is North and South America's most cosmopolitan city.

32. *Economist,* Aug. 19, 2006.

A bedecked elephant slowed down traffic for miles before arriving at a festive celebration.

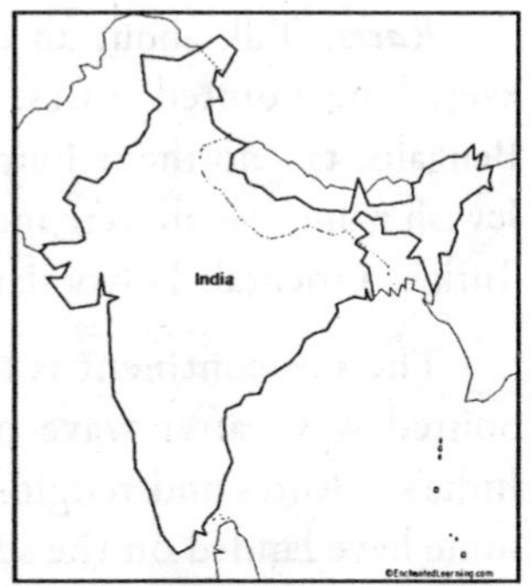

New Birth or 26,000 "Births"?[1]

"I am the light of the world. Whoever follows me will never walk in darkness, but will have the light of life" (John 8.12).

I HAD A COUPLE OF DAYS, following the EFI Conference, before my flight to the Himalayan foothills. That gave me time to experience in detail what had earlier burst upon me after landing at Delhi airport. Walking around the crowded streets of the old city, I felt perfectly safe. People chatted in front of teashops and in the bustling markets. What I saw in Delhi was fairly typical of other major cities in India:

People![2] All kinds of them: men, women, young, old, tired, depressed, aggressive, anxious, lethargic; in robes, saris, shirts, slacks, dhotis, and pantsuits; colorful, drab, attractive, dirty, smart, and ragged. Hindu shawls, Sikh turbans, Muslim veils, coiffed bobs. Some hawking their wares, others sleeping on top of them—in one of the lowest-cost cities in the world. Annually, ½ m. newcomers swell the 12m. population further.

1. Hinduism's *Janma* ("next birth") is not *re-incarnation*, as some dub it. Only gods can be re-incarnated (*i.e.* the same god in different form). The Hindu "life cycle" ("birth after birth") is re-emergence after death into another *level* of existence—higher or lower, depending on one's *karma* from the previous cycle.

2. India has nearly 5,000 people groups, totalling about as many *people* as China's but in 1/3 the area.

Now I understood the last words of a CIGM missionary, repatriated home with terminal cancer: "So many people! So many people!" she murmured in her last breath. The unreached of India were on her mind. She'd loved them; she'd given her life to tell them about Jesus. And India is bypassing China as the world's most populous nation.

Races: Talk about an ethnic melting pot! Small eyes, large almond eyes, long pointed noses, bulbous noses, swarthy southerners, short Bengalis, tall northern Euro-Indians (some with Portuguese, English, or Jewish names[3])—all were Indian, but with admixtures of African,[4] Arabian, Turkic, Oriental, Polynesian, Caucasian—you name it.

The sub-continent is true to its shape—a funnel into which have poured wave after wave of different ethnic groups, each adding to India's cultures and religions. Most have come in through the top, but some have landed on the southern tip or along the coasts—a potpourri of humanity. In a pedestrian underpass, a ceramic mosaic displayed symbols of the three major religions: Hinduism (Aryan swastika[5]), Islam (crescent), and Christianity (cross). "***We are all one***," the mosaic declared.

Sounds: I used to think rural India, particularly, would be quiet. Actually villages can be quite noisy because of Hindu and Muslim loudspeakers, church bells ringing, cassette tapes and radios blaring, donkeys braying, dogs barking, roosters crowing, mechanics tinkering, vehicles honking, or trains blowing their whistles—as well as people shouting at each other. The majority of adults smoke, I noted.[6]

That's Old Delhi: Narrow streets, old buildings, vendors under lean-to shelters. Colorful *saris*, sparkling ornaments, fragrant perfumes, savory aromas—but also grime, filth, perspiration, open gutters, vultures wheeling

---

3. One could guess a person's area of origin (such as Hindi north, Tamil south-east, Portuguese Goa, British /Jewish Bombay, "Christian" Kerala, etc.) by either the first or family name.

4. For centuries, Africans had crossed the Arabian Sea, seeking work. In India, Britons sometimes released slaves rescued from ships they'd intercepted on the Arabian Sea. Many of these stayed and intermarried.

5. Sanskrit: *svastika*, "well being"—ancient symbol found in many cultures. (The German "w" in Swastika is pronounced "v," as in the original Sanskrit.) Nazis borrowed the sign from an earlier Austrian anti-Semitic party, as the symbol of their Aryan purity.

6. India is among the world's 25 top-smoking nations, an enormous market the tobacco industry targets as western sales dwindle. The government is seeking to curb harmful effects.

overhead. Pitiable beggars. Lurid posters promoting heavy romance movies. A determined sun struggling to penetrate smog, glinting off gold-tipped temple roofs.

I discovered that cows weren't the only sacred animals in Delhi. At the time, some 6,000 monkeys roamed the city—the incarnation of the Hindu monkey god, Hanuman. (Delhi's High Court has since ordered the city council to consider their expulsion.)

I was glad the municipality thoughtfully provides public toilets—sometimes in an elevated row of stalls. I easily located a vacant stall to use, for while the partial (for ventilation) "bar-room" doors block head and torso from view when people sit, they don't hide users' feet—or their shoulders and back of their heads if, as men are wont to do, they stand up to the task.[7]

Then there's New Delhi, laid out by the British Raj with wide roads and high curbs radiating out from Connaut Circle. High-rise offices, five-star hotels, one-star hotels, starless hotels. Fashionable shop windows displaying the latest from Gucci and Chanel. Billboards promoting "Bollywood"[8] romantic movies. Green foliage! A parakeet surveys me from a tree. India's new breed of economic maharajah reflects the nation's increasing prosperity. One economist forecasts that average incomes will triple by 2025, the middle class growing more than tenfold.[9]

Yet the contrasts of expensive and low-cost conditions result in the lowest quality of life on an index of 30 cities worldwide—less than ½ New York's, and 1/3 Tokyo's. Authorities were sprucing up the city's image for the Commonwealth Games in 2010. No one has objected to banning the 60,000-odd beggars who harass pedestrians and motorists, but there have been protests by Animal Rights groups against rounding up the monkeys, and by Hindus for corralling stray cows off the streets. Delhi will never savor the same if some 300,000 cooking stalls are banned!

---

7. Some Asian cultures reject as "dirty" the use of toilet paper, hankies or tissues. Instead, people "clean up" with the left hand—using the right hand to give/accept something or to eat with. For cleanliness, many prefer to *pour* water over the hands, rather than use a basin with standing water (considered unsanitary).

8. Nickname for the film industry city: Bombay (Mumbai).

9. *Economist*, June 2, 2007.

Driver's Sport: Playing "Chicken"

Traffic! Buses, buses, buses; cars, cars, cars—nearly all alike, made in India; tricycle taxis (rickshaws)—some pedal operated, some propelled by scooter motors. Weaving in and out, disregarding lanes. At an intersection, a hapless traffic police stood on a pedestal placarded with posters. Yellow cabs jockeyed for position—where there was no space, they forced an opening by blowing their horns. Honk! Honk! Truck air horns blasted, exhausts spewed black smoke screens. Yet surprisingly, I saw few accidents. These had to be the best drivers in the world!

Driving was a different story when I journeyed outside the city. Occasional bullock carts slowed us down, but my biggest surprise came after our vehicle had crawled for miles in a long line of traffic. I discovered the reason when we came to a Hindu festival, where a festooned elephant (which had been up at the front of our traffic), turned off. Perched on top was a Hindu priest. We had all been travelling at elephant speed—in low gear. Our driver was not in the least upset by the slow-down, however. He told us the appearance of an elephant is a very good omen.[10] Maybe so, except for making time on a highway. But every good omen must help, in view of the small shrines and offerings I noted at crossroads—where demons are believed to dwell. So now we know—*spirits* account for all the road accidents!

Anyway, India is full of surprises, full of the new bumping into (or along with) the old. Talk about contrasts—in the 2004 federal elections, electoral officials rode into remote villages on their "good luck" elephants to supervise the electronic terminals that *all* voters used!

Outside the cities on the "open" road, a favorite passing trick is to play "chicken" head-on with an approaching vehicle. The first driver to blink suddenly pulls back into his lane or veers to the opposite shoulder, scattering pedestrians. Passengers hang on to the side, back, and roof of already crammed buses—at times ending up a mass of broken bones.

I was especially alarmed passing through villages where shops had been built right to the paved edge of the tarmac, leaving no shoulder.

10. "Ganesha" is the elephant god, widely worshipped.

Although fields may stretch behind the buildings, owners prefer to build right up to the road's edge, leaving as much precious land as possible behind their shops to grow food. I instinctively tried to shrink as our vehicle passed a slow-moving, exhaust-belching truck on a two-lane road, while oncoming traffic filled the other lane. Meanwhile, another car was passing on the *other* side of the truck. Incredibly, cyclists and rickshaws were passing on *both* sides!

Mumbai: Persian Bazaar & Indian "Bollywood"

To the west of Delhi lies historic Bombay—now Mumbai. It had been one of Britain's coastal trade ports before the sub continent became part of the empire. Overlooking the Arabian Sea, it has its own eclectic character—traces of Arab kasbah, Persian bazaar, Hindu bungalow, and British colonial canteen. Beneath ornately carved railings and shutters on projecting balconies, squatters slept in lean-to shelters and sold everything from (a) betel nuts to (b) bully beef.[11] I caught whiffs of ginger-laced coffee, ginseng tea, and curried rice. If I'd been a "druggie," I could have bought the narcotic of choice.

Bordering Mumbai airport, Dharavi's slums shelter some 100,000 dwellers doing their best to keep body and soul together. Some earn enough to put their children through college. In fact, they're part of India's "alternative economy," an unofficial industry topping $500m annually that manufactures items for city shops. More than 8m people live in the city's shantytowns. (Nationwide, cities need some 25 m more houses, one consultancy estimates. Developers plan to provide small affordable units.)

As I threaded my way through puddles in Dharavi's narrow lanes, a cacophony of sound, smell, and sight assaulted my senses: tinker and blacksmith anvils, bread ovens, smelting ovens, and garbage-burning kilns. Tanneries raised a stink as only drying leather skins can. Potters turned clay jugs next door to smiths shaping reclaimed metal scraps into utensils. Workers sweating in unventilated sheds produced the colourful plastic bags or smart leather purses visitors buy in the airport departure lounge.

11. (a) Nut & leaf with astringent orangey juice, chewed by laborers; (b) corned beef in tins (French *boilli*).

Mumbai may be India's commercial capital, but the exotic city earned its "Bollywood" title (when it was still called Bombay) by making India the world's largest producer of full-length movies—over 900 annually, many of them "soft porn." (Colonial law barred homosexuality but in 2009 the High Court declared the law unconstitutional. Hinduism considers sex an essential exercise to attain *Moksha.*)[12] An estimated 90% of the population view these in local cinemas or on touring screens. Christians face this challenge through indigenous agencies such as Galilean International, which writes and produces theater-quality films, training churches to use them in evangelistic outreach.

Not all the films are sleazy romance, however. India's noted director, Deepa Mehta, has produced a controversial film, *Water,* portraying the tragic plight of widows—even though today they aren't burned on their husband's funeral pyre. In the film, a fictionalized Ghandi helps a six-year-old child-bride and a middle-aged woman, both consigned to social banishment, find child-mother affection and flee their ashram.

Just released, *Water* is so controversial that Mehta had to film it all over again in Sri Lanka, under a false working title. She'd actually produced the film earlier in the pilgrim city of Varanasi, but Hindu fundamentalists destroyed the original negative and all copies. They also burned down the production set. However, Asia's Pusan Film Festival applauded an advance showing of the re-produced film, and a British film critic called it "the finest Indian film for a generation."[13]

"The Half Has Not Been Told"

For exposure to India's cultural glory, friends insisted I see the historic Red Fort and the Taj Mahal—as do 3m. tourists annually. Emperor Akbar (16c.) built the fort just outside Delhi. To unify the kingdom, he married a Hindu, a Muslim, and a Christian. The Emperor's bedroom impressed me: he enhanced romantic evenings by "air-conditioning" it! That is, cooling water ran in a trough surrounding the room, behind sandstone latticework. The fort's domes are Islamic, the pillars Hindu, and the frescoes Mogul.

---

12. *Moksha*: "Paradise". If this or other comments don't fit readers' impression of Hinduism, Hindus have no official canon. They have as many religious variations as they have gods.

13. *Economist*, October 22, 2005.

Ironically, white marble Stars of David sparkle in the main archway. At least I thought of them as the Star of David, but centuries ago, the six-pointed star became a Hindu symbol (eclectic bunch, these Hindus!). Although the judgment hall is 120 X 75 ft., acoustics are so clear that everyone could hear the Emperor snap his fingers. To defend the fort, soldiers in a gallery above the entrance could give invaders a warm welcome by pouring boiling water and oil down on them. Even if intruders survived scalding, after that deluge their camels and elephants couldn't ascend the slippery ramp leading to the courtyard.

Bahadur Shah Zafar II, "The Last Mughal,"[14] holed up in the Red Fort during "The Sepoy Mutiny." Scars on the Fort's walls testified to Britain's punishment of Delhi as it put down the nation-wide rebellion of its Hindu soldiers ("sepoys") by devastating the Fort and Delhi city in 1857.

The restored Red Fort was only a foretaste of the famed historicity awaiting me some 300 km. (200 m.) south at the Taj Mahal. I'd booked a convenient return flight to Agra, giving time for my onward flight later in the day. (Nothing could go wrong! Before leaving Canada, I'd purchased an Air India pass, which allows travel anywhere, ensures bookings, and costs half normal fare.) All went well until I arrived at Delhi's airport.

"Flights are already full!" the surly airline agent in Delhi announced without looking up from a romance pulp. Fortunately back in Canada, my Indian neighbor who'd been an Air India pilot told me to expect this, and how to cope: Either (1) press a few US dollars into the agent's hand (as many booked on the "full flight" would have already done), or (2) wave my international pass with a public flourish. I opted for the latter approach, and *presto!*—I was on the early flight to Agra.

A millennium ago, Christian Armenian traders had established a community in Agra, as they did in several Indian towns. The Armenian Church in Agra flourished for centuries, although it was finally swept aside by Mogul invasions. I hurried to view the Mogul Emperor Shah Jahan's historic memorial to his wife, the Taj Mahal.

---

14. See William Dalrymple's book by this title. Bloomsbury/Knopf, 2006. Mughal (or Moghul/Mogul): Muslim rulers were descendents of Mongol, Turkish, and Persian invaders of India, for 350 years.

Even though I'd seen tourist postcards of the Taj, the sight before me took my breath away. Shimmering in a long pool was the almost ethereal reflection of the 17th c. domed mausoleum. The Emperor built it as the last resting place of his wife, who'd died in childbirth. To honor his wife's beauty, he imported white marble. Twenty thousand men and 1,000 elephants took 17 years to complete the Taj.

The Queen of Sheba's comment to King Solomon, "The half has not been told!" came to mind, as I walked the white marble corridors.[15] My fingers traced the intricate mosaic inlay of semi-precious stones, whose colourful designs glowed in reflections from sunbeams spotlighting marble floors.[16] "A teardrop on the cheek of time!" the Bengali poet Tagore described it. As I thought of the emotions this earthly building raised, I could only imagine viewing the "mansions" Jesus said he's preparing for us—more splendid than any earthly marble.

Later, in a stone-masons' workshop, I watched artisans creating inlaid patterns for tourists. Using the same methods as their ancestors, they squatted beside large grinding wheels operated with one leg lying across a treadle. I was impressed how they could shape, with such rudimentary tools, minute pieces of colourful stone to fit into white marble tabletops or cup coasters—precisely inlaid, just like stonework in the Taj! Well-heeled tourists bought inlaid coffee tables (for several thousand US dollars each), but I contented myself with $30 coasters to take home as mementos of skilled artistry, patient workmanship, and Indian antiquity.

Back to the airport I headed to catch my return flight to Delhi. "No flight coming—cancelled!" the airport attendant announced without looking up from his newspaper. Neither bribery nor pass would have made any difference. I was only one of several tourists stranded in Agra. And I was supposed to catch the last connecting flight out of Delhi that evening, for the Himalayan town of Mussoorie! Vishal Mangalwadi and his wife Ruth were expecting me to stay with them, and Vishal had invited me to speak at their weekly prayer meeting.

---

15. After the Emperor built the Taj Mahal and Peacock Throne, "the world ran short of gold," it was said.

16. On the 350th anniversary (2004) of completion, curators refused to open it to the overflow crowds after dark, because one must see the Taj in sunlight, in order to appreciate the white marble's ethereal glow.

"There's a train coming through at six," the attendant at last announced, nonchalantly. "We've booked you all on it." Six? *The flight to Mussoorie leaves Delhi at six.* I'd obviously scheduled things too close. There was nothing to do but board the train and then arrange alternative transport from Delhi to Mussoorie—bus or even bush taxi![17]

My Cup of Poison

Back in Delhi I hailed a cycle taxi and hurried to the bus terminus. Nothing available. Anyway, road transport wouldn't reach Mussoorie, up winding mountain roads, until the next day—if then. Exhausted by pre-monsoon heat and humidity, I needed to get some sleep and re-think my plans. I booked in for the night at a nearby three-star hotel (a lower rating than three stars usually wasn't advisable). The first thing I spotted in my room was a thermos flask of water. India's tourist board advises visitors not to drink tap water; so decent hotels usually provide filtered water in flasks for foreigners. Weary and perishing from thirst, without a second thought I unscrewed the top and gulped a long draught. By the time my parched palette had tasted the water, it was too late. I'd just swallowed stagnant water! Likely a maid had filled the flask from a tap, and the contaminated water had stagnated while the room was vacant for several days. I nearly retched at the thought of the polliwogs I'd just swallowed. I fell asleep with a prayer for my health.

In the night, I awoke in a sweat. I'd come down with the traveler's nightmare—"Delhi Belly."[18] What else, I didn't know. Yet I had to find less expensive lodgings over the weekend until my next scheduled journey, skipping the Mangalwadis in the highlands. I tried to telephone them to explain my non-arrival. When it proved impossible to get through, I sent a telegram—which they never received. I'd been looking forward to the Mussoorie visit, not only to be with the Mangalwadis, but also to get relief from the increasing humidity and soaring temperatures of the lower plains.

---

17. India's railroad system, installed by the British during colonial years, is the nation's largest mover of people and goods—and has more employees than any other commercial organisation worldwide.

18. Euphemism for "the runs," or diarrhoea.

In the local phone book I found the YMCA number. Their hostel should be clean if not fancy. Yes, the "Y" has a swimming pool, the voice on the phone confirmed. Maybe a good swim would refresh me. At the "Y," I was ready to jump into the blue water. But a sign on the door leading to the pool bluntly stated: CLOSED.

"The pool's *closed*?" I asked incredulously. This was the last straw!

"Yes," replied the receptionist, annoyed I should ask. (*Couldn't I read?*) "This morning a dog fell in and drowned." I knew healthy dogs don't fall in and drown; rabid dogs do, crazed by thirst.

Dripping with feverish perspiration, I checked into my room and swallowed a couple of anti-malaria pills. (Malaria parasites hibernating from my years in Africa tended to surface whenever other infections weakened my defenses.) Sitting on the edge of the army-type cot, I understood the feelings of pioneer Brethren missionary John Ollie: "I had a little argument with God!" That was when his hut on the edge of the Sahara burned down. In the ashes was his life's work—his hand-written translation of Scripture in a Saharan language he'd laboriously reduced to writing. *He had no copy!*

My aborted visit to Mussoorie wasn't *that* devastating, I tried to tell myself, but maybe the contaminated drink made me feel depressed. I did wonder why the Lord let me miss the Mangalwadis' invitation to visit them high in the Himalayan foothills (providing relief from the heat) for an important segment of my research. I had to admit that God wasn't obligated to relieve my own stupidity.[19] "Stop feeling sorry for yourself, Fuller!" I said—and dragged myself down to the cafeteria.

There I found two other guests: an Indian who didn't understand my English, and a young woman (tourist, I presumed). Hearing me greet the cafeteria staff in English, the woman greeted me in a German accent. Foreign travelers, I've found, have an immediate sense of camaraderie.

---

19. Was God teaching me to be more vigilant? From then on I carried bottled water. I didn't know I had come down with two infections: bacterial and amoebic—diagnosed when I arrived home months later. Meanwhile answered prayer came in the form of strength to continue the rigorous travel, in spite of occasional fever, diarrhoea, and loss of energy. Back home, it took me a year to recover.

The Yoga Disciple

"I am Mona. Do you mind if I sit at your table?" she asked after filling her tray. "It is good to practice my English—yah?" Mona said she had arrived with a tour group several weeks before and had stayed on in India after the others returned to Germany. But pickpockets stole her money and passport while she was in town shopping. She was stranded in Delhi getting a new visa from the German embassy, which had lent her cash to stay at the "Y" until she could transfer money from home. A sturdy Teutonic, she was no hippy but well spoken, educated, and decent. I guessed she'd be 25 or 30—but guessing a woman's age is reckless!

"Did your tour group see all the famous sites?" I asked to make conversation.

"Yah," she replied, sitting across the table from me. "We saw the Taj Mahal and the Red Fort. But our reason for being here was to attend a Yoga seminar. Our yogi invited us to stay and become his disciples. I'm the only one who could stay—others had family or business to attend to. I came back into town to do the shopping for my yogi's *ashram*.[20] But pickpockets got everything. It's bad *karma*[21]—I just know!" Mona seemed near tears. "That cockroach in my bathtub—I shouldn't have killed it! But shopping for my yogi will earn me *good* karma."

"I'm so sorry you were robbed!" I commiserated. I remembered how devastated I'd felt when pickpockets in South America filched my wallet—money, credit card, I.D., and all. Better change the subject. "How are you becoming a disciple?"

I was curious—yogi, disciple, shopping? I wanted to learn more about Hindu belief, but I hadn't anticipated it would be through a stranded German studying Yoga at an *ashram* in India! I didn't know how orthodox Mona's views would be; I'd heard there are different "schools" of Yoga across Asia. But she at least could tell me what she knew about Hindu yogis. They seem such gentle people. Several times a day devotees repeat the hypnotic word "Om," considered a sacred sound from its Sanskrit character.[22]

---

20. Sanskrit. *Yogi*: Hindu teacher of *yoga*—suppression of body, mind, and will, leading to ultimate "liberation" from existence. *Ashram*: "religious exercise" in a secluded retreat center.
21. Sanskrit: "fate," affecting one's form of re-incarnation. "Good" *karma* can balance out "bad" *karma*.
22. See Appendix F, Asian's Religions: Hinduism, Buddhism.

"My Master—that's my yogi—is teaching me. He's probably near the state of 'Sublime Yoga' himself. When he meditates, his teeth chatter, his tongue—how do you say? ..."

"Fibrillates?" I suggested. Mona nodded and continued.

"And he speaks in tongues. In fact, his tongue has pierced the roof of his mouth and entered his brain cavity. ... X-rays confirm that!" she quickly added, noting my querulous look. "He says he'll experience sublimation when his tongue reaches his gland–what's it called?"

"Pituitary?"

"Yah!" Mona agreed enthusiastically. I knew Mona was referring to the longed-for state of all Hindus and Buddhists—to be freed from the wheel of "birth after birth." They'd be absorbed, not into the presence of God (Buddhists don't accept the existence of a personal deity) but into "nothingness": non-existence, luminosity, sublimation, the sublime Yoga. The greatest goal is release from the trammels of existence, to suppress all bodily impulses so that "the inner self" can achieve union (meaning of Sanskrit *yoga*) with the Ultimate Reality.

"Uh huh," I grunted, toying with my cold and greasy curried omelette. Acculturation doesn't go down easily in the morning, especially when one feels ill anyway. "How are *you* progressing?"

"I've been interested in Yoga since I was 16," Mona confided eagerly, happy to share her faith. "I'm trying to be purified in all my thoughts and desires so I can become a true yogi. Repeating our sacred mantra is soothing.[23] Hinduism and Buddhism don't try to convert people. You have to be *born* a Hindu. I'm trying to earn enough good *karma* to come back as a Hindu in the next incarnation."

"Do you find discipleship difficult?" It wasn't yet time to debate anything. I just listened, but I knew Yoga demands intense concentration, deep meditation, and prescribed posture.

Mona hesitated and looked out a window. "What I find difficult is... how do you say, *squatting?* ... for so long! But Master says not to give up.

23. Mona was referring to the sound, *OM* (with the "m" held in a prolonged hum), repeated endlessly in hypnotic meditation. It is said to derive from *AUM,* the first letters of the three main Hindu deities.

He says he needs me to help him set up a university. Foreign students don't understand Urdu, so I can help explain with my English and German. Many Germans come to India to study Yoga."

"Rational" Germans Believe *Myths*?

I'd always thought of Germans as highly rational, but I later learned that they've long been fascinated with Hinduism and Buddhism. How had this arisen in the land of Martin Luther's earlier Reformation, I wondered? Germany experienced a spiritual vacuum when many leaders in the state church (ironically still called "Evangelical Lutheran")[24] replaced Bible faith with naturalistic philosophy ("Higher Criticism"). Eastern mysticism, with its Aryan roots, seemed to fill that vacuum.

There was a fascinating sequence to this shift, from pre-Darwinian evolutionists, through a series of liberal theologians, to atheistic secularists. Perhaps the ironic aspect is the church background several of these humanists had.[25]

Hermann Hesse (1877-1962), son of a Lutheran pastor, was one who helped link Eastern thought with Karl Jung's psychoanalysis. His novel, *Siddhartha* (the Buddha's name) later made into a sensuous film in India, widely influenced German and Indian intellectuals and students with its romanticized, idealistic portrayal of Buddhism. It even included instruction in achieving "Enlightenment." Hesse received the Nobel Prize for Literature in 1946.[26]

In the West, Yoga and Hare Krishna were among popular Oriental mysticisms during the "Hippie Era" of the 20th c.[27] Many Westerners

---

24. "Evangelical Lutheran" does not imply evangelical theology. The term distinguished the Protestant state church from Roman Catholicism, which early Lutherans saw as ritualism, not "The Evangel" (Gospel). That was before humanism and liberal theology permeated the state Church.

25. These included Thomas Paine, Immanuel Kant, Charles Darwin, T.H. Huxley, Hermann Hesse, Sam Harris. For the sequence and analysis, see Appendix F: Religion, Secularism/ Humanism.

26. Recent European authors have continued to popularize Buddhism, including Oscar Wilde in *The Picture of Dorian Grey* and W. Somerset Maughan in *The Razor's Edge*.

27. Hare Krishna combines one of the names of Shiva (*Hara:* fertility god) with Krishna (i.e. Vishnu or Brahman, supreme deity). Swami Prabhupada founded the movement in USA in 1965.

revere Oriental religions for their "spirituality" (that is, versus secularity). In USA alone, 15m practice Yoga. One yogi, Bikram, aims to franchise his style of Yoga to 900 "studios" worldwide. His fleet of expensive cars and his Beverly Hills, Hollywood, villa attest to his popularity. Self denial? "Ya gotta live!"

I was interested that a current global best seller by German "spiritual teacher" Eckhart Tolle (*A New Earth—Awakening to Your Life's Purpose*) repeats the 18th c. sequence, but twists Bible quotations (including Jesus' own words) to support what amounts to Buddhism. *The End of Faith: Religion, Terror, and the Future of Reason,* by another contemporary philosopher, Sam Harris, also dismisses Christianity and all religion except for Buddhist "spirituality" (which he wouldn't consider "religion"). So atheists, agnostics, and liberal theologians repeat the same arguments. Over and over again. Century after century.

And so European departure from biblical belief infected the Indian subcontinent. Although evangelical Christianity grew in the years following William Carey's work, the rot of liberal theology also set in. By the early 1900s, the Welsh missionary Watkin Roberts published in India a booklet, *The Ravages of Higher Criticism in the Indian Mission Field.*"[28] Widely circulated throughout India, it attracted a lot of adverse criticism from liberal church groups.

Eastern Mysticism or Aryan Mythology?

And now I was talking with a product of this East-West synthesis, Mona. Back in Germany, she would have known only sterile Christendom, not the life-giving gospel of Jesus Christ. In spite of the "oriental" mystique that captivated her, she would have been surprised to discover it was Caucasian Aryans who invaded the sub-continent, subjugated the earlier population, and imposed their venerated *Veda* on the indigenous Dravidians.[29]

---

28. Ruth Roberts, personal memoir, 1993. See Ch. 6 re. Ruth's father, Watkin.
29. Sanskrit—*Veda*: sacred knowledge; *Dravida*: dark-skinned people in S. India, likely Arab-Africans mixing with others en route (F.A. Onyedinefu, "The Dawn of Civilization," unpublished lecture, 1999).

Although there are several theories about where Aryans came from, they seem to have emerged from Central Asia north of the Caucasus, in Eastern Europe or central Asia. Being nomadic, they drove their herds southward seeking pasture, leaving traces of their language and culture as they passed through Mesopotamia and the Indus valley, until they settled in the Indian sub-continent, becoming known as Euro-Asians.

Today's New World views, although actually recycled ancient mysticism, are called Post-Modern because the Modern Era's "scientific logic" didn't solve the world's problems—it ended up increasing them (e.g. Industrialism vs. Nature, the argument goes). The younger generation seeks a mystical ("spiritual") element. Buddhism, it seems, provides the ideal compromise—human enlightenment by self-effort, without a supernatural being or need for salvation from sin. It provides self-improvement "spirituality." New Age tune; Old Age lyrics.[30] "I'm interested in Buddhism," a secular Iranian student told me. "I'd believe in Jesus if only you didn't claim he was divine." Sure, just another mystic guru!

"East is East and West is West, and ne'er the twain shall meet," wrote Rudyard Kipling.[31] Actually, they did meet, millennia before Christopher Columbus. He was searching for India when he stumbled on "The New World"—since called "the world's melting pot." The Indian subcontinent already was that. Secularism of the west is still meeting mysticism of the east.

I felt like saying to Mona from Aryan Eastern Europe, "What goes 'round, comes 'round!"[32] But she was about to add something....

"I'm doing OK. Only ... ," the Yoga disciple hesitated and sighed, "... only I thought I'd have more time for meditation. But I have to do cooking for the Master and students."

---

30. See Bibliography: Mangalwadi, *When the New Age Gets Old*. Also Appendix F: Religion.

31. Rudyard Kipling, "The Ballad of East and West."

32. Though each religion claims originality, commonalities arise from human philosophy. Greek Gnostics and the Jewish Kabbalah share basic concepts with Aryanism, Buddhism, Islam, Christendom (not evangelical Christianity), atheism: self-effort or knowledge as salvation, dualism (evil material world vs. good spiritual world), astrology, meditation freeing inner sublime force or "light."

I knew that meditation has a beneficial calming effect, but Buddhist meditation doesn't hold the same meaning as it does for Christians. It's not spiritual communion based on God's revealed Word, but the inward-gazing path to sublimation. That's extremely important in a self-help religion.

Self-help religion assumes many different forms. India's Mahatma Gandhi, for instance, thought of Jesus as a good man, but believed that many paths could lead to sublimation. Like Mona, I respected Gandhi as a great man, but I didn't have the heart to tell the German "disciple" that the Mahatma practically disowned his eldest son, Halilal, who wanted to marry an accomplished German member of their *ashram*. To avoid a family feud, Halilal became a Muslim named Abdulla (and taking the German as his *frau*.)[33]

Yoga—the Only Way of Salvation?

It was time for Mona to go to the Embassy, so we decided to meet again over dinner. Meanwhile, I got some needed sleep. Over the weekend, Mona and I continued our conversation whenever we were both in for meals. She was convinced that Yoga gave the true explanation of the universe and liberation from evil.

"Other religions are selfish. Their idea of heaven is to get things. The objective of Yoga is to meditate until you are rid of selfishness and evil. That is liberation, and Yoga is the only system in the world that can liberate us."[34]

"If a yogi desires to sublimate himself so he won't be reincarnated, isn't that selfish?" I suggested gently.

Mona thought about that. "I suppose it could be, but that shouldn't be the main motive for meditation. Bad *karma* from the past life influences us now. If we were evil in the past life, we'll be evil now."

---

33. Wolpert, '01, Bibliography.

34. Mona neglected to mention Hindu and Buddhist constant fear (while eating, walking, sitting—anything that might break "code"). *Sila* and *Eightfold Path* sound like Christian morality, but these are to earn good *karma* to attain "Emptiness" (annihilation), not to express the Holy Spirit's fruit. People who have never trusted Christ, but seek to earn salvation through "the Golden Rule," may find self-help religion attractive.

"Is there any hope for change?" I pressed.

"Oh yah— by trying to change, adding up good *karma*. That will help us be reincarnated in a better form. You can't do it by faith. It has to be deeds."

"How many incarnations will it take to achieve sublimation?"

"Humans are midway between lower incarnations and higher incarnations," explained Mona, finishing some curried fish. "Life is meaningless—the only goal is to achieve liberation of the spirit. To do that, the number of incarnations would . . . how do you say? . . . "blow your mind"—maybe 26,000. It's a lengthy evolution, going on for eons!"[35]

Life is meaningless? OK, I thought: the wisest man in the world, Solomon, agreed. In fact, he even called life a meaningless cycle, from a human standpoint. However, his solution was not in successive births but finding meaning through obedience to God.[36]

I reminded Mona that the Apostle Paul had discovered there was no good thing in him—life *is* meaningless apart from Christ, who gave his life for our sins. But Mona didn't believe in sin or the Devil. She explained that there is only "downward gravity." We have to resist it by struggling upwards through many incarnations. There's no such thing as sin, only ignorance of the "Ultimate Reality" within us.

"I agree that something drags us down," I responded. "The Bible calls it sin. Although we should do good deeds, I haven't found we can drag ourselves upwards out of sin. We're trapped. That's why I'm thankful God so loved us that he sent his Son to redeem us. The Bible says Jesus came when we were without strength, when we were dead in sin."

"Jesus was a good person," Mona conceded. "He must have come to India at some stage and learned from Hindu gurus and yogis, because some of his sayings are the same as Hindu writings—which are older than the Bible.[37] I had a Bible in Germany and read about Jesus. I think he

35. In fact, estimates range up to 600,000—although the number is anyone's guess.

36. Scriptures: Ecclesiastes ch. 1; ch. 12.13.

37. Hindu teaching includes the *Vedanta*—an eclectic collection describing mythological activities of deities, brought to India by Aryans (circa 2c. BC) and added to through the centuries. Hindus and Muslims picked up Old Testament teaching from traveling Jews, and Jesus' sayings from Nestorian Christians. Christian evangelists now use these as points of contact with non-believers.

probably achieved liberation for himself. When he said we should follow him, he meant we should follow his example of meditation and good deeds and suffering. That's what St. Francis of Assisi did. But to say that Jesus is the only way of salvation is arrogant. My yogi accepts *all* religions—he's studied the Bible too. After all, if you believe God created the world, he must have created all the religions.

"...But if there *is* a God, why does he allow so much suffering?" she quickly added.

"The Devil has seen to that," I replied, aware Buddhism doesn't believe Satan exists, but Hinduism—out of which Buddhism arose—teaches there are devils, or evil spirits. "He wants to destroy God's creation." (Tongue in cheek, I thought, "If only God had created us as robots, unable to choose evil!" But Adam and Eve used the priceless gift of free will to yield to Satan rather than obey God. Today all mankind has that option of choice.)

As to Mona's question, I knew that many (including Charles Darwin) have tripped over the problem of suffering. Injustices I saw in Asia brought inward tears, and I could imagine the heartbreak God feels, watching his creation suffer. Regrettably, many religions believe that salvation (or sublimation) comes *through* suffering—and perpetuate it. We may never understand the struggle between good and evil, nor why God allows it. Yet Abraham affirmed, "Shall not the judge of all the earth do right?" I remembered also the Apostle Paul's reassurance: "Where sin abounded, grace abounded *much more*."[38]

Finding Meaning in Life

After reminding Mona that, according to her, there's no meaning in life and no assurance of coming back in a better form, I told about the meaning and assurance I had found in Christ: "It's true there are many religions, but only Christ died for our redemption, and only he assures us of eternal life. To Christians, that is true 'spiritual liberation.'"

I knew that Hindus and Buddhists find it impossible to comprehend "the peace of God that passes all understanding."[39] As one Hindu journalist

38. Gen. 18.25; Rom. 5. 20 (italics mine—WHF).

39. Philippians 4.6.

told me, "Without worry we cannot live. It's our main motivator. If we overcome one worry, we'll create another."

"We don't say, 'Jesus is the way of salvation,' in pride or arrogance, but because he himself claimed it, and we want to share that good news with others," I reminded Mona.

"I can't believe that!" Mona exclaimed, stacking her dishes to take to the kitchen. "The only way to liberation is through Yoga meditation.[40] My yogi says that Mother Teresa's help for thousands of suffering children was nothing compared to what Yoga can accomplish in releasing even one soul from the cycle of births."

Interesting! This intelligent young woman said Jesus' claim to be the only way of salvation was arrogant, but now she's declaring that Yoga was the only way![41] She favored Yoga because it didn't proselytize—but helping someone find sublimation through Yoga was of greater value than Mother Teresa's Christian compassion.

"Have you met Jesus Christ in person?" Mona asked, perhaps to put me on the spot, or maybe out of curiosity. Not physically, I told her, but through his Holy Spirit and his Word, the Bible. I understood Mona's inability to relate faith to Jesus, because Hinduism has no Founding Father. The system is built on practicing *Dharma*, the code of life. "Hindus are guided by their own 'inner law,' not an external, revealed truth."[42]

No more time to talk. Mona had received a temporary visa and was about to travel to her *ashram*. She went to pack her knapsack; I returned to my room. Half an hour later there was a knock on my door.

"May I use your washroom?" Mona asked. "I turned in my room key before I realized the public ladies' room downstairs is closed."

---

40. Hindu/Buddhist "liberation" ultimately leads to annihilation, *yoga* "suppressing all activity of body, mind, and will, that the self may attain liberation from them." Miriam-Webster's dictionary (11th Edition).

41. "Hinduism incorporates all forms of belief and worship without necessitating the selection or elimination of any" (Indian Supreme Court). Sunder Raj, *The Confusion Called Conversion, op. cit.* p. 144.

42. Defined by David Weston, board member, CNEC/Partners, Canada, who has traveled extensively in Asia. *Dharma*: Sanskrit derivation of "firm," implying *duty* to observe cosmic principles of existence.

"Sure," I replied, not wanting to seem suspicious. But questions did race through my mind. Was this a test or a trap? If a test, did Mona want to prove her Buddhist "purity of thought and desire?"—or my Christian morals? Each bedroom had a small en-suite washroom. I stood in the hallway *outside* my room. "You needn't have stayed out of your room!" Mona remarked when she came out.

I asked this German college graduate if she thought it was accidental she had been robbed and I had missed my flight. "Is it possible God brought you to India to find Jesus as your personal Saviour?"

"Oh, I found Jesus before I left Germany!" Mona quickly assured me. Jesus was still just an historic figure to her. No use arguing. Only the Holy Spirit could enlighten her spiritual understanding. I had to trust him to water the gospel seed.

Since my "poison cup" experience three days earlier, I knew how important water is to the traveler. I'd stocked up with bottles and asked Mona if she had a supply with her, but she was too short of cash. I gave her one of mine.[43] She also accepted a pocket New Testament. After she left, I flopped down for a feverish nap, praying Mona would yet meet Jesus as *Saviour*, even on the Old Spice Road.

When I went down to the cafeteria for dinner, I noticed a sign on the door of the ladies' washroom: *Closed—Out of Order.*

Amazing how God turned my disappointment over a missed flight into a weekend of learning about Yoga and witnessing to a yogi's disciple![44] The Mangalwadis would forgive me for not showing up; I had to get back on my travel schedule. Feeling better, I headed south instead of north, further into the vortex of this funnel called India.

---

43. Later I thought of how Jesus encouraged his disciples to give "a cup of cold water" in his name.

44. Buddhist-Hindu literature includes ancient wisdom. Some church leaders, noting universal values in other religions, have hoped for ecumenical unity with them. By the end of my Asian travels, I was able to list those values and also reasons Christianity and other faiths can never be reconciled (see Appendix D).

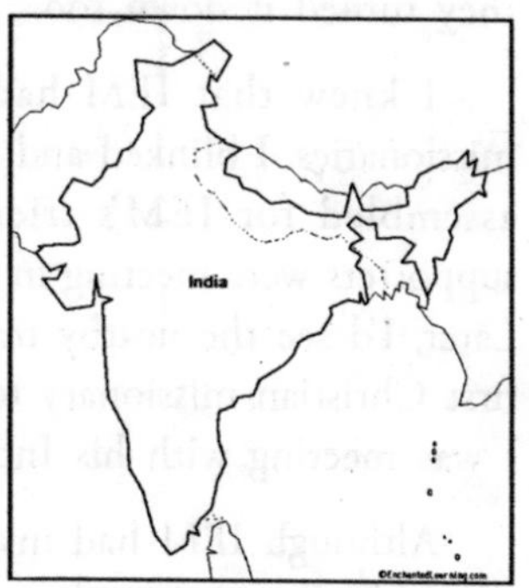

Meeting Apostle Thomas` Successors

[Thomas said]: "My Lord and my God!" (Jn. 20.24).

YOU REALLY TURNED DOWN A GIFT of one million dollars from Coca Cola?" I asked, a trifle incredulously.

"Yes, we did," replied Theodore Williams, General Secretary of the Indian Evangelical Mission (IEM) at the time.[1] "They offered it to Friends Missionary Prayer Band (FMPB). I was president. It was our policy not to accept funds from foreign organizations."

"Why did Coca Cola offer you that kind of money? I hadn't thought of them as fund-raisers for missions!" I quipped, stepping under a shady fig tree. It was the humid rainy season, the monsoon vacation break, when conferences could find an empty school campus for accommodation.

"At that time, India's foreign exchange laws made it difficult for companies to export earnings," explained Williams. He paused to return

1. Like most missions in India, IEM is a member of the India Missions Association, a strategic network linked internationally with World Evangelical Alliance, of which I was vice-chair at the time.

the traditional greeting[2] of a sari-clad missionary walking by. "While the spiritual message of the gospel may not have been important to Coke officials, they saw its side effects—uplifting neglected villagers with hope, self-respect, hygiene, literacy, agriculture, and education. They figured FMPB was a worthy investment. They also offered the money to EFI, but they turned it down too."[3]

I knew that IEM had the policy of no foreign support for its missionaries. I blinked and looked around at the 450 Indian missionaries assembled for IEM's triennial missions conference. They and 400 supporters were meeting in Chennai (Madras), on India's southeast coast. Later, I'd see the nearby traditional site where the Apostle Thomas, the first Christian missionary to India, was martyred. He didn't die in vain; I was meeting with his Indian successors!

Although IEM had invited me to bring the Bible messages, I felt I should be listening to *them*. I'd never been in a gathering of such devoted missionaries. Several in faded and ragged shirts and saris looked as if they could do with some of Coca Cola's million. They'd come together from the icy Himalayas, the arid northwest, the southern rain forest, the rugged coastal hills, and the isolated islands of the Indian Ocean. Each morning began with simultaneous praise to God for his mercies, in languages and dialects from all over the nation. I almost thought I was reading the book of John's Revelation!

Facing Demons and Mobs

During report time, these missionaries told of casting out demons, of being chased from town by stone-throwing mobs, of struggling in prayer for a couple who wanted to follow Jesus but couldn't bring themselves to throw their idols on to a bonfire, of Satanic oppression and human depression in lonely situations. They also told of failures, of new believers who buckled under the pressures of relatives or communities and turned back from following Jesus.

---

2. *Namaste*: palms together (like Christianity's "Praying Hands"), raised to the face—originally a Hindu way of saying, "I worship the god in you." To most, it's now a cultural greeting without religious meaning.
3. For a time, India banned the sale of Coca Cola, but it is now available almost everywhere. During a recent drought, protesters closed down a bottling plant, blaming it for the water shortage.

But they also reported surprising opportunities. One Indian missionary couple lived in the pilgrim city of Varanasi, on the Ganges—sacred to Hindus. Although a red dot[4] on the forehead is in honor of the god Shiva, it also signifies marriage; therefore the missionary wife used it to show she was not a prostitute. (She carried her Bible prominently, to show she wasn't a Hindu!)

"Thousands of pilgrims come from all parts of India and from around the world to wash in the Ganges River,"[5] reported the couple. "Pilgrims are surprised we have a Bible study in our home, and sometimes they drop in. One Buddhist yoga group asked many questions about the Bible. They explained they were seeking peace and fulfilment. We told them how we found both in our Saviour, Jesus Christ."

While the Holy Spirit often used a believer's witness, in the case of one young Hindu, Chandra, God spoke directly through his Word. Chandra longed to know God, but nothing satisfied his spiritual hunger—not meditation, rituals, sacrifices, or religious festivities. Finally Chandra made pilgrimage to the sacred Ganga (Ganges), "the flowing hair of the Hindu god Vishnu." Sitting on the riverbank, he prayed, "Mother Ganga, show me that Vishnu is my spiritual father and has accepted me as his son!"

After three disappointing days, Chandra wandered back to his village. He noticed a Bible a friend (the human factor God used) had given him. He again prayed, "O God, if you are real, show me you're my father and have accepted me as your son!" Randomly opening the Bible, he was startled to read Psalm 2.7: "Thou art my Son; today I have begotten thee." Regardless of that psalm's real intent, it was enough for Chandra. In that moment, he trusted in the living God and embraced Christ as his personal Lord and Saviour. He paid a high price for his newfound Saviour, rejected by family and friends. He married a former Hindu, and today both are evangelists.[6]

---

4. *Bindi*—"Devi's Footprint," after patron goddess of women—may have originated with custom of a warrior placing a drop of his blood on his wife's forehead, to establish his claim during wartime absence. Educated girls now consider it ornamental, using different colors, sometimes ringed with tiny beads.
5. The annual pilgrimage is the world's largest religious event, an estimated 80 m. bathing "to wash away their sins" and break the cycle of "birth after birth."
6. SIM evangelist Benji Devadason, friend of Chandra (substitute name), told me his story. –WHF

Two single women gave thanks for God's protection when a mob burned down their house and threatened them with rape and death. Another single woman described the crosses embroidered into the hems of Tibetan women—their only remaining cultural evidence of Christianity since missionaries were driven out of the area during World War I. Now this slight woman was teaching them about Jesus, who died on the cross and rose again.

One missionary couple worked in Chennai among the city's 40,000 rag-picker caste. Society considered them "untouchables" but this couple devoted their lives to tell them of Jesus.

"We Feel Re-Commissioned!"

At the close of the session, the leader warned, "There's always the danger Satan may attack those who've given reports and the converts they've named." He asked the 800 of us to break into groups to pray for them. Prayer, rather than triumphalism!

Between sessions, as daily temperatures climbed, these missionaries sat under trees or on the shady side of buildings, sharing stories of God's faithfulness. Parents played "pat-a-cake, pat-a-cake"[7] with their children, their faces dripping with perspiration. Families slept together on mats in humid college classrooms—vacant for school break during the hottest season. This year the monsoon rains were late, making water scarce.[8] Mothers scrubbed their children's clothes in buckets of water they'd scrounged during the night, when faucets did more than drip. Fathers played with their children. I could see the missionaries' joy at simply being together, studying the Word and eating together *with fellow believers!*

"My wife and I had decided we wouldn't go back," a missionary from the isolated Andaman Islands, off Malaysia's coast, told me. "We were discouraged . . . burned out. But God has refreshed us through his Word and fellowship here. We feel recommissioned!"

---

7. A British hand-clapping children's game that doesn't require running around in a hot climate!
8. Somewhat repulsive for people culturally used to showering three times daily because of the humidity. "You must consider me dirty," I joked. "As a boy, in winter I hated taking even my *weekly* bath!"

During the conference a light-skinned man introduced himself to me. "I'm Laiu. Your mission has just accepted me for Africa!" he exclaimed, his eyes bright with enthusiasm.

I was taken aback. Did he mean IEM? No, he'd been an IEM missionary for several years, and now had applied to SIM through IEM to serve in other parts of the world.

But Asia needed missionaries, I thought, and here was an Indian telling me he had joined SIM to serve in Africa! Rev. Laiu Fachhai, who had almost oriental features, told me he was a Mara from Mizoram (also known as "Mizoland")—a state in India's eastern panhandle, separated from the main part of India by Bangladesh, and bordering Myanmar. Laiu's grandparents first heard the gospel from British Puritan Congregational missionaries, whose pioneers arrived in 1905. Earlier in the 1800s, Presbyterians had pioneered among these headhunting tribes. Methodists and Baptists followed. Now the population is estimated at over 90% Christian.[9] To raise funds to send their own missionaries to other parts of India and neighboring lands, villagers daily put aside a handful of dried rice.

As a young teacher, Laiu took for granted he was a Christian because he was born into a Christian family. Fellow teachers led him to personal faith, and his church sent him to Bible school. He then manned an isolated pastoral outpost in neighboring Myanmar.

"I was very lonely!" he told us. "But I learned to meditate and commune with God." (How many missionaries have learned to do that, under similar circumstances, I thought!)

As Laiu also learned more about the wider world, he felt a definite call to overseas missionary service. His home church already supported 14 missionaries but added Laiu to their list of people supported through handfuls of rice! They put him in touch with IEM—which in turn referred him to its overseas partner, SIM. After he started receiving their magazine, *SIM NOW*, he felt a burden for Africa, applied, and was accepted.

9. Some 1.5 million claim descent from Israel's lost tribe of Manasseh. Exiled in Persia, they travelled further along the Old Spice Road, ending up in north-east India. Traditions, appearance, and DNA reflect Jewish ancestry. Israel's Law of Return has welcomed back many (*Toronto Star*, June 07).

To me from the jaded West, where some churches are questioning the need for missionaries, Laiu was a shot in the arm. Since I met him, he's taught Bible in Africa, and now also has administrative responsibilities.[10]

Obviously, the missionary calling knows no political borders. Another missionary channelled by IEM to Africa is an Egyptian medical doctor who came to India to study at the Missionary Training Institute (MTI). He went on to work with SIM's Nigeria associate, Evangelical Missionary Society, among the animist/Muslim Magazawa. Overseas Missionary Fellowship sent a Japanese couple to study at MTI. Men and women come to MTI because of its thoroughness in preparing candidates. "We've learned a lot from other missions, such as Latin America Mission, OMF, and SIM," they told me.

The Lost Book—and Lost Jewish Tribe?

I was learning how much we current missionaries owe to the pioneer work of earlier disciples on the Old Spice Road. Laiu Fachhai had told me about the entry of the gospel to his people on the border with Myanmar. They were one of several tribes of Northeast India reached through courageous pioneer missionaries. Their stories have been well told, including the prophecy of strangers bringing "a great light from the west."[11]

Dr. Paul Roberts, a physician friend of ours in Toronto, is the son of one of those pioneering couples, Watkin and Gladys Roberts. Paul confirmed how his father came upon the prophecy among the Hmar. The story traces back a century ago, when Watkin had become fired up through the Welsh Revival. That spiritual renewal (1904-06) changed entire communities: it cut the Welsh crime rate in half, magistrates had no murder charges to try, and many drinking saloons closed for lack of patrons. The revival also awakened Christians to the needs of others—even in other lands. Watkin could no longer keep this good news to himself.

10. Laiu married Debbie of Singapore. He became SIM Director for Sudan, later for N.E. India.

11. See Don Richardson, *Eternity in Their Hearts,* p. 88-100 (Bibliog.) re the persistence of similar prophecies among peoples of India, south China, and S.E. Asia.

After reading a Welsh General's account of the ferocious Hmar in NE India, he felt a call to take them the gospel of peace. The Hmar had fought their way from Mongolia across China, settling among the hills that, like a mammoth welding seam, join together the Indian sub-continent and Indo-China (as S.E. Asia was then called).

Roberts, a chemist, arrived with a Presbyterian medical doctor friend in 1908, trekking inland to set up a clinic in Manipur State, on India's border with Myanmar. After officials barred his entry to the warring Hmar, Roberts, occupied himself translating the Gospel of John into Lushai, understood by neighboring tribes.[12] He gave copies to clinic patients.

When a roughly attired group turned up from over the distant range, no one at the clinic could speak their language, Hmar. But the wild-looking men did accept Lushai gospels. At the time, Roberts and his friends didn't know of the Hmar prophecy about "the Lost Book"—reportedly a golden book that a white man would restore to them.[13] So villagers were amazed when one of the Hmar who could speak Lushai later returned with a strange booklet ("Wordless Book") a white man had given him. It wasn't made of gold, but it had a golden page. Could it be "The Lost Book"?

The chief sent him back with a request: "Please come and teach us about this book and your God." That's all Roberts needed, but the British administrator still refused to let him go—too dangerous. This could be a trick, to take the white man hostage . . . or worse.

"They are notorious head hunters. I'd never go there, unless with one hundred soldiers!" the official told the young Welshman. Roberts, only 21, went anyway, taking a Hmar as his guide and several Lushai translators. Over hills and through jungle they trekked 14 days. However, Roberts got

12. On India's side of the Indo-Myanmar border, Lushai people are known as Mizo.

13. [Had this prophecy filtered down from N.E. India's **Bnei Menashe** (*children of Menasseh*), who vigorously claim to be descendants of "the lost tribe of Menasseh"—one of Israel's 12 tribes that Assyria banished to distant lands? In Manipur and Mizoram they came to Israel's attention when they applied for Israeli citizenship under that nation's "Law of Return." Israel's Chief Rabbi met with them and confirmed they were descendants of Menasseh, observing all Jewish laws, such as circumcision, Sabbath keeping, and kosher diet. In 2006 a rabbinical court began formal conversion to Judaism of those who wished to return.]

nowhere when he told the Hmar chief and his elders the strange news of a Saviour who gave himself to redeem them. Blank looks all around.

"Sahib, what you are saying sounds like our peace covenant," a Lushai translator told Roberts as they enjoyed the chief's roast boar and fried plantain. "If we want to make peace with another tribe, and they agree, we draw a boundary line between us, sacrifice a goat, and spill its blood along the boundary. Then the opposing chiefs place their hands on the sacrifice while they repeat three times, 'Peace has come!'

"The two sides embrace, roast the animal, and have a feast! Sahib, my people cannot understand what you say about God, but maybe our Peace Covenant would help explain."

When Roberts used the Hmars' own peace covenant to illustrate his message, the chief and his elders grunted with understanding. They'd heard about tribes on the other side of the range, who could raise their families and grow their food without warring. The Hmars were tired of being terrorized by evil spirits. Could this "Jesus sacrifice" also make peace with the spirits?

Roberts moved in to teach the gospel. As he sat with them one evening, the campfire glinted off the gilt-edged King James Bible he'd brought along to supplement the translated Gospel of John. "It's the Golden Book!" gasped villagers. From then on, Roberts and his colleagues could teach in any Hmar village. The people drank in the news that the Apostle Paul had written to the Ephesians: Christ "himself is our peace, who has made the two one and has destroyed the barrier, the dividing wall of hostility." Roberts explained this meant even more than making peace with their enemies—it was a covenant with God himself, through Christ Jesus.[14]

While on furlough in England, Watkin became engaged to Gladys Dobson,[15] whom he met at the Keswick Bible Conference. They married in India in 1915. Watkin re-named his Thado-Kuki (initial tribal areas) Pioneer Mission as the Indo-Burma Pioneer Mission[16] to evangelize other

14. Ephesians 2.14-22.
15. Capable artist and hymn-writer—her most famous: Stanzas 2-5 of "Wounded for Me.")
16. Now with indigenous leadership under the name, Partnership Mission. A strong-minded entrepreneur, Roberts also founded the Thadu-Kuki Mission, and a printing press.

areas, including Burma/Myanmar. Until then, Hmars subsisted by "slash-and-burn" methods—clearing virgin land, then constantly moving on to new clearings, instead of replenishing the soil for annual planting. Many feared that planting trees and deep ploughing might disturb and anger "earth spirits." To avoid periodic famine, Watkin planted fruit trees, distributed more productive seeds, and fertilized the farmland.

The people found they could settle and live off the earth. Spiritual "seed" also took root, and soon bamboo churches, schools, and clinics began to appear on hilltops and in valleys. The whole area became peaceful and self-supporting, led entirely by indigenous people. Watkins introduced the printing press and even sewing machines. Because of his youthful vigour, even later in life, people called this peripatetic missionary, "Mr. Youngman." One observer, Howard Dinwiddie, stated, "The hand of the Lord is here in a steady work of salvation as perhaps nowhere else in Asia."

But progress wasn't without opposition. Fearing losing their traditional control, spiritist priests beat villagers who listened to the gospel, and at one stage the British administrator expelled the missionary for creating a disturbance![17]

From Head-hunters to Ambassadors

Rochunga ("Ro") Pudaite was the son of one of the first five Hmar who came to Christ. Ro's father dedicated his son to God, to translate the Scriptures into Hmar. Ro married Mawii, daughter of one of the other first five Christians, studied at Bible school and launched into translation work. Roberts and a young Bob Pierce, who later founded World Vision, raised funds so Ro could go to Scotland and USA to develop skills in linguistics and translation. (Ro's grandson, Jonathan Pudaite, recently completed a thesis towards his Master of Theology in the History of Christianity: "The Legacy of Watkins R. Roberts.")

---

17. Watkin's son, Paul, provided the sequel. *The Ride of Our Lives!*, unpublished memoir, tells how the Hmar people invited Paul and Barbara in 1994 to see the result of pioneering by Watkins and others: about 85% of Hmars are now Christian, with their own churches, schools, and a small hospital. No longer head-hunters, many farm and follow other peaceful pursuits. (Paul, with his wife Barbara, became a medical missionary with Radio HCJB in Ecuador. The government appointed him as its Consul in Canada.)

"After my people received the Bible in their own language, they became one of the most advanced ethnic groups in all of India," wrote Dr. Pudaite in *The Book that Set My People Free* (see Bibliography). It turned out that the Hmar live on some of the best land to grow coffee and fruit. Hmar Christians support their churches, missionaries, and themselves. Hmar are educators, medical doctors, politicians, and ambassadors for India in several countries. Rochunga went on to found Bibles for the World, based in Colorado Springs, USA.

And now I was speaking to Laiu, who came from that general area and was going to Africa with SIM! He spoke Lushai, into which Watkin Roberts had translated the Gospel of John. It is the language of the Mizo, Laiu Fachhai's extended people group. Nearly 100% of them are now Christian.[18]

I was amazed to learn this, for back home I'd heard Dr. Paul Roberts mention only that his father had been "a missionary in India." I had no idea of the remarkable details. Later, however, I was surprised to find no trace of Watkin Roberts (who died in 1969) in biographical dictionaries of missionaries. Here was a young man who had only one passion—not the motivation often blamed on missionaries by anthropology's elite: high adventure, colonial expansion, and racism. Finding spiritual life himself, he was ready to do anything to pass on the Good News.

Of course, some might think he'd pretty well wasted his life by leaving the heather downs of Wales and going to the wild head-hunters of Manipur State. After all, they had their own religion, didn't they? They were happy "savages," weren't they? Why corrupt their culture with "European" ideas, as some charge?[19] Those critics forget that the gospel came from *Asia* to Europe while Europeans were still barbarians worshiping trees!

---

18. Readers may have heard the Mizo Choir, sponsored by Partners International (CNEC) to tour the West. People of the area are often termed "Zo" ("hill") as belonging to S.E. Asia's "hill people."
19. Among denouncers of the gospel (which he dubbed "European") was German Anthropologist Hugo Adolf Bernatzik, who did "research" in the area in the 1930s (*The Spirits of Yellow Leaves*. London: Robert Hale Ltd., 1958-English Ed.) Don Richardson (*Eternity in Their Hearts, op. cit.*) points out that although Bernatzik may have known anthropology, he failed abysmally in research. [Like Meade (Ch. 15), he refused to recognize the gospel's amazing power to release culture from superstitious fear. —WHF.]

Wasted life? Roberts, a gifted linguist, had *only* learned several local languages, translating the Scriptures, and teaching people to read their own languages! *All* he and his colleagues had accomplished was to free villagers from the tyranny of spirit worship, tribal warfare, and alcoholism. They'd *only* emancipated an ethnic group from age-old traditions and superstitions, making them self-supporting. Freed from fear of spirits, the Hmar *only* become one of India's most advanced peoples, no longer threatened by periodic famine!

As to the practice of missions, he championed women's ministry as well as indigenous leadership—neither a priority with several fellow missionaries. Ambitious home council members resented his entrepreneurship, finally expelling him from the mission he had founded! Watkin simply packed up his bags and started another mission.

"I read about the Judsons, Boardmans, Youngs, and other pioneers, but I don't see your Dad's name in any list of missionaries!" I told Paul Roberts. As usual, Dr. Paul was in a hurry, shipping containers of supplies to poverty-stricken areas in Ecuador—something his father had done in Asia by organizing the Evangelical Medical Missionaries' Aid Society.[20]

"That's just as Dad would have wanted it!" he said. "If he were still alive, he'd tell you that Jesus was glorified by many Hmar having their names written in Heaven's books. It's all that mattered."

Paul was right, I knew. We've all read about remarkable pioneers, but alongside the likes of William Carey and James Hudson Taylor are a host of "unsung heroes"—many shunning the limelight; occasionally other names purposely omitted from any roll of honour, because of colleagues' feelings. It's no secret that some rugged individualists have been impossible to work with (I think of Mary Slessor of Calabar)—but God has used that very characteristic to open up difficult corners of the earth, where others feared to venture. Some have upset the status quo with their vision, but that has sometimes led to innovation—which secular agents were bringing in anyway. In spite of a few horror stories, the Holy Spirit has brought good out of the motley crew called "missionaries." All have

20. Dr. and Mrs. Roberts founded Radio HCJB's hospital in Ecuador. That nation made Paul honorary citizen and its Consul in Canada. He once served as deacon at our church, chairing its building committee.

been clay vessels, but in his day, missionary Paul concluded, "Christ has been preached."

Now a new generation—Laiu and the other IEM missionaries around me at the conference—were part of God's ongoing global strategy.

Unreached Hill People's Call to Missions

"How did your mission start?" I asked IEM's founder, Theodore Williams, at the conference. Theodore was born in 1935, in the Tirunelveli District of a largely "Christianised" southern state, Tamil Nadu. His own Christian roots went back five generations, from the pioneer work of Anglican missionaries;[21] when he was nine, he and his parents moved to Chennai, where they attended Emmanuel Methodist Church.

"I thought I was a Christian because for five generations my family had been Christians," Theodore told me, giving an Indian head waggle. "At the time, the pastor of Emmanuel, from England, didn't preach the gospel, and the church was losing members. An American pastor replaced him, but he taught only social good works—no salvation.

"However, in the 1940s God used India's Bible-teacher Bakht Singh[22] to bring spiritual revival to Chennai. Our pastor knew he himself had no gospel message but had enough sense to invite evangelical speakers, because people came to hear them. One night at an evening service in his own church, the pastor himself went forward to accept Christ."

Theo realized his own need to repent and personally trust in Christ. He was 19, in the midst of taking a Master's degree in Statistics. His ambition had been to earn lots of money.

Now he thought more about equipping himself in God's Word. He assumed every Tamil in his home state had heard the gospel, ever since two German missionaries, Bartholomew Ziegenbalg and H. Plutschau had arrived in 1706.[23] But while in Bible school, Theo was astounded to learn that only 90 miles away, hill tribes had never even heard of Jesus.

21. Apart from its Anglo-Catholic "High Church," Britain's Anglican Church has several missions, including the Church Army, Church Missionary Society, Society for the Propagation of the Gospel, and South American Missionary Society. Most are still evangelical, although liberalism has entered some.
22. Bible Expositor Bakht Singh had great influence on the churches in India as well as overseas.

"I visited their villages—and that was my life-calling to missions!" Theo recalled. Later, teaching at South India Bible Institute, he married Esther, a missionary from Kentucky.

Like Theo's family, Christians in many mainline churches had become nominal in their faith, losing their vision to reach unevangelized neighbors. That caused young Christians such as Theo to seek outlet through non-church agencies. He, his fellow college student Sam Kamalesan,[24] and other young Christians worked with the Union of Evangelical Students of India and Scripture Union.

"Until then, in my generation, most churches had been content just to hold their own services," Theo told me. "They'd lost their missionary vision. Several of us from the Tamil area got together to pray for unsaved peoples."

A number of young people found Jesus as Saviour at Vacation Bible Schools led by P. Samuel. They formed the VBS Friends Fellowship—which grew into a vision to reach out to the entire nation. After prayer and fasting, in 1958 they formed the Friends Missionary Prayer Band (FMPB), with Theo Williams as President. But at the time, FMPB didn't yet send out missionaries.[25]

Influenced by the example of William Carey and Adoniram Judson, Naga Baptist Ben Wati challenged the Evangelical Fellowship of India (EFI) to develop a missionary vision, and in 1954 it did support an Indian in Kenya. Wati went on to become a worldwide Bible speaker and president of World Evangelical Alliance. By then, Theo Williams had become a member of EFI's executive and urged it to found a mission arm. In 1965 it formed the Indian Evangelical Mission (IEM), appointing Williams as

---

23. Tamil Nadu was a Dutch colony at the time. They had studied in Halle, Germany, and at the University of Holland, and were ordained in Denmark. It was an international network: Germans allowed into India by the Dutch, and financed by the King of Denmark! They produced the first translation of the New Testament in any Indian language, and started orphanages and India's first girls' school.

24. Dr. Kamalesan became internationally known as evangelist-at-large for World Vision.

25. I'd heard of the FMPB through my sister Olive, serving with Dohnavur Fellowship (also in Tamil Nadu). FMPB later sent out missionaries (total over 600). Upon Olive's retirement, FMPB made her the sole exception to their policy of not accepting funds from overseas—since she'd been a founding member.

its first General Secretary. Eight months later IEM sent out its first missionary, supported entirely from India. Currently IEM accepts 40 new missionaries a year, supported through their own churches or adopted by other churches. Throughout India, several hundred volunteer representatives keep churches informed of the mission's needs.

Vision, Faith, Sacrifice

"We founded IEM on three pillars: *Vision, Faith, and Sacrifice*," Williams explained. "From the first, we decided the president would take no salary from IEM and would accept no foreign support for missionaries. My home church in Chennai and EFI provided my salary. Although Kerala received the gospel before other parts of India, most of our missionaries were Tamils—maybe because Ziegenbalg had translated the New Testament into Tamil more than 200 years earlier. It became the first Bible in an Indian language. But now churches all over India send and support missionaries through IEM."

No funds from overseas! That seemed unusual, from what I'd seen in contemporary India. However, I also had followed the history of India since its Independence.

"How widely is this indigenous finance principle followed in India?" I asked.

"It's not a new policy for India," Theo explained. "In 1903 and again in 1905 Bishop Vedanayagam Samuel Azariah and others started two indigenous missions,[26] both supported entirely by nationals. In the 1920s, the Anglican missionary, Roland Allen (1868-1947) revived the teachings of pioneers Rufus Anderson and Henry Venn, recommending indigenous funding for churches. At the time, British and American mainline missions were paying the salaries of Indian pastors.

"In IEM, we wanted to develop the grace of giving among our churches. We find that Christians generously support fully indigenous

26. Indian Missionary Society (1903) and National Missionary Society (1905). Azariah C.1874-1945) became the first Indian bishop of the Anglican Church in India, Sri Lanka, and Myanmar, and blessed missions world-wide with his book, *Christian Giving*, published in 55 languages (see Bibliography). (In Africa, I'd studied it as a member of a group led by a Nigerian Anglican—WHF.)

missions, but even overseas missions with indigenous arms have difficulty raising local support. If people know that foreign support is available, they'll depend on it rather than give themselves.

"Another thing—we don't want to be looked upon as foreign agents of a foreign religion. We once turned down 40,000 rupees from an overseas mission. But increasingly Indian Christians who've moved overseas want to send financial help, and so do some missionaries. We came to realize there could be a place for overseas help for projects—not personal support—such as housing, travel, and development."

I asked Theo what he thought about fund-raising agencies in the West. I knew he'd seen foreign and indigenous mission work in Africa, Latin America, and Asia.

"Several fund-raising agencies are extremely helpful in supporting projects we could never afford," replied Theo, who personally knew several agencies and their leaders. "But it's best for them to partner with indigenous missions which can be accountable and can provide supervision. Otherwise, the danger is that overseas funding can encourage abuse. Evangelists can say to their own churches, 'I'm supported from overseas, so I'm not accountable to you!' Also, even with the best of intentions, fund-raising agencies could end up controlling evangelists they support, as 'their' workers.

"Send Money, not Missionaries!"

An Indian friend had told me he knew evangelists who were supported *simultaneously* by groups in Australia and USA—the supporting groups never knew the men were fully supported twice! Another evangelist annually made two trips to USA to "thank" his supporters. My friend had seen funds raised for evangelists misused for building grandiose churches and offices in his home state.

"Your friend is quite right," Theo confirmed. "It's unfortunate that financial help can be abused, whether in India or in your own country. Some of the agencies you mention have learned Western tactics of fund-raising, and their appeal to support 'nationals' is strong. At this end, there are some pastors who misrepresent their work in order to receive funds. We know one man who has been baptised 25 times over successive years, for that purpose! But of course there are also worthy projects that

Christians overseas can help fund. We're grateful for that kind of help, and we know we have to be accountable. That's the key—*accountability*!

"I've also heard fund-raisers say, '$1 a day can support an evangelist.' That's not true. No evangelist in this country can do his work and live on $30 a month. Such tactics make people feel guilty. They imply, 'Send your money, not your missionaries.'"

I asked Theo if there was still any place for foreign missionaries.

"Expatriates need to consider their costs carefully," he replied, "to make sure they're worth what they accomplish—such as mentoring nationals and meeting needs we can't because they are so overwhelming. Foreign missionaries still need to live simply—maybe at the level of a university professor in India. But I have no right to say to churches in other parts of Asia or Africa or the West, 'Don't send your people.' The Apostle Paul would never have gone to Asia Minor if he'd listened to that. Every church should help spread the gospel as God directs."

Theo Williams had arranged for me to preach at the church where he'd been converted. Founded in 1878, Emmanuel Methodist Church still had its original pipe organ, powered by bellows the church custodian pumped with a long lever.[27] Yet it was expanding its building by a third. I wondered how it retained its spiritual life. I had little doubt when I read the church bulletin, headed: "Following Jesus: reach out, press on. Phil. 3:12-14." I asked the young pastor what would happen if the Methodist bishop would assign them a liberal minister. "He never would," Pastor Peter M—replied. "He knows we wouldn't pay his salary! Our elders examine even invited speakers very closely."

"Take all the time you need," he leaned over and whispered during the pre-sermon hymn. "Preach the gospel of Jesus Christ." I thanked God that even among some long-established denominations that have become spiritually cold, there are still clergy who preach the saving gospel of Jesus—right along the Old Spice Road. Thinking of Methodism, I remembered the strategic ministry of J. Waskom Pickett, Moderator of the Methodist Church during the turmoil of India's Independence, protecting Christians and other minorities.[28]

---

27. Since replaced with an electric system.

28. McPhee, Arthur G, *The Road to Delhi,* Bishop Pickett Remembered 1890-1981. Bangalor: SAIACS Press, 2005.

Typical of the dedicated ministry of evangelical agencies in Chennai, is (Madras) Christian College (MCC). Founded in 1837 as a result of the vision of the Scottish missionary, Alexander Duff (1806-1878), the first overseas missionary of the Church of Scotland, the college met the thirst of young Hindu men for literature and learning, set in a Christian context.[29] In 1988 MCC inaugurated the Institute of Advanced Christian Studies (IACS) to fulfil the mandate of offering theological studies as an integral part of the College's holistic mission. For a while IACS became dormant, but in 2007, it was re-constituted to include "Christian responses to contextual challenges" as a special focus for theological learning and research.

India's First Missionary

One more thing I wanted to do before leaving Chennai: visit the traditional last resting place of India's first missionary—the Apostle Thomas. The site is on the highest point around Chennai, 300 feet above sea level.

"Why are the steps wet?" I asked my guide, Rao, as we climbed to the site. A millennium and a half after his death in A.D. 72, Portuguese Catholic missionaries built this shrine on the spot where "Saint Thomas" purportedly was speared to death while praying.

"Don't step in it!" Rao exclaimed, pulling me back from a wet-looking step leading up to an "altar" and crucifix. "That's wax—not water!" The tropical sun had melted votive candles pilgrims had placed at the base of a crucifix as they prayed to Saint Thomas. The hill was called "Calvary of St. Thomas." To Muslims, this was revolting idolatry. To Hindus, it was perfectly appropriate—simply a Christian addition to some 30m Hindu idols and gods!

Thomas himself would have been appalled at such syncretism. When Jesus told his disciples he would be leaving them, and that they knew the

---

29. Duff's work led to modern medical and other university studies, transforming missionary methods. Declining Calcutta University's (chapter 10) Vice-Chancellorship, he became Moderator of the Free Church General Assembly and leader in its Foreign Mission Committee. (Stephen Neill, Gerald Anderson, John Goodwin, *Concise Dictionary of the Christian World Mission.* London: USCCL, 1970, p. 171.)

way, it was Thomas who remonstrated, "We don't know where you are going, so how can we know the way?" Certainly Thomas could not have known the way he himself would take in *following Jesus on the Old Spice Road*. But if tradition has it right, I was standing on the spot where Thomas declared to the people of India the reply Jesus gave to his question, "*I* am the way, the truth, and the life."

India's cinema viewers can hear "Doubting Thomas" once again exclaim, "My Lord and my God!" The indigenous Christian film service, Galilean, has produced a movie on his life.

But to trace the journey of pioneer missionary Thomas, I had to travel farther south, to the tip of India.[30] On my way, I'd find myself in the midst of today's followers of Jesus, at a church conference in Bengaluru (Bangalore), due west of Chennai.

30. See Chapter 8.

Outside Chennai (former Madras), a shrine memorializes the spot on which first-century disciple/missionary Thomas reputedly was martyred. Pilgrims leave offerings, hoping for miraculous cures and other blessings.

Chips and Garlands

"We wrestle not against flesh and blood but against principalities, against powers, against the rulers of the darkness of this world, against spiritual wickedness in high places" (Ephesians 6.12).

"We national Christians must accept our part in fulfilling Christ's Commission, but overseas missions still have a part to play," the founder of one of India's largest indigenous mission agencies, Theodore Williams, had told me in Chennai. "We can benefit from their spiritual experience, Bible teaching, research and organizational skills, and professional assistance—such as medicine and agriculture."

In India that kind of commitment among early denominational missions—Anglicans, Baptists, Brethren, Lutherans, Methodists, Presbyterians, plus—impressed me. Their stories fill volumes. There were other missionaries with those same church backgrounds, who played their part through non-denominational missions, because of particular objectives. A couple of missions with unusual titles aroused my curiosity: Ceylon and India General Mission (CIGM), and Puna and India Village Mission (PIVM). What had motivated them? What did they accomplish? They eventually merged as the International Christian Fellowship (ICF), which joined SIM in 1989. What was involved in all this? I decided to check out the original missions as a case study of church-planting in the sub-continent.[1]

1. **Benjamin Davidson**, Scottish pearl agent in Ceylon (Sri Lanka), founded CIGM in 1893 after a Tamil challenged him to become a missionary. To better reach Southern India's masses, he moved from Sri Lanka to Bangalore, juncture of several large language groups: Tamil, Telegu, Kanarese.

When I met CIGM's Gene and Ruth Tozer in Bangalore (as the city was then known), some 200 miles west of Chennai, I knew I wouldn't be disappointed: case study it was! I'd see the beautiful and the ugly sides of "the care of the churches"—something that burdened even the Apostle Paul. I stayed with the Tozers in the old mission bungalow—its airy windows, roof overhang, and long veranda harking back to the colonial era before air conditioning.

On my way from the airport, I had discovered that the city is by no means "colonial" today. Bangalore? Of course, back in Canada I'd heard of Bangalore[2]. One day when my computer and I weren't on the same wavelength (computers do have a mind of their own!), I telephoned the Technical Support Line. The technician's Indian accent didn't surprise me, for I live in North America's most cosmopolitan city. However, knowing trends in "outsourcing," I asked the lady where she was located. "Bangalore," she responded.

Still no surprise. Founded as Bangalore in 1537 in the ancient Vijayanagar (Dravidian) Empire, the city became capital of modern India's Karnataka state. Often dubbed "The Garden City" (in spite of its original name's reference to "cooked beans") Bangalore/ Bengaluru has the ideal climate in India because of its geography and elevation. It attracts tourism, business, and industry alike, an example of what politicians called "India Shining."

Major cities in India have been booming economically ever since the nation emerged from protectionism. After Independence, business regulations, meant to encourage Indian initiative, unfortunately resulted in a "Hindu rate of growth"—a term formerly used to describe business bogged down in socialist bureaucracy ruled by "the Licence Raj" and "Inspector Raj."[3] Although 10m. "Raj" bureaucrats slow nation-wide

---

Meanwhile, a visiting Indo-Aryan soldier had challenged **Charles Reeve** of Tasmania, Australia, to evangelize the pilgrim, military, and intellectual center of Pune (near Mumbai) as well as nearby villages (hence PIVM's unwieldy name). Reeve arrived in 1893. Reeve couldn't have anticipated the amazing results.

2. Later (2006), the city became **Bengaluru** ("City of cooked beans," after the legend of a 14th c. woman who provided a bean feast for her monarch). European pioneers mispronounced the name as "Bangalore."

3. Indian Institute of Planning & Management cited a 2004 report that a manager spent 16% of his day dealing with officials, including 40-60 inspectors a month.

growth, government has loosened fiscal policies to encourage not only foreign investment in India but also remittances from nationals living outside the country (no taxes on their remittances). India became the world's largest recipient of such, but also one of the highest on a scale of corruption. The nation heads the global list of domestic companies in "emerging markets."

India's Potential and Poverty[4]

Bengaluru (as we'll name it from here on) is a window on India's ambitions to make up for decades of stifled potential. The outside world is catching on to India's advantage of a huge reserve of intelligent, educated, English-speaking men and women. Some 300,000 agents staff India's call centers. Based on Bengaluru alone are 140,000 Internet (IT) professionals—20,000 more than in California's Silicon Valley.[5] While the city provides employment opportunity, I was sobered to read that it also has India's highest rate of suicides—mostly skilled workers.[6]

Although many Indians once considered computers as "man-eating machines" and the English language as "brain fag," now 50 colleges state-wide turn out 40,000 IT pros annually. Chipmaker Intel employs 1,500 in research (R&D) "as complex as any other project on the planet," says its president. India's Wipro is "probably the world's biggest R&D-services firm."[7] Westerners aren't particularly happy to see these jobs disappear overseas, but they still represent only a small fraction of the West's economy—which must adapt to global economy fluctuations.

Staff for satellite-linked call-centers take courses to smooth out local accents—just as heavily accented Cockneys and Texans go through a similar process for positions in Westminster or Washington, D.C.

---

4. See Appendix I, Asia and World Economy.
5. Impressive as such figures are, they need to be viewed in the context of India's domestic potential. Its population has one of Asia's lowest *percentages* of IT users *per capita*—under 2%. Japan, and S. Korea are higher, with Singapore at 36% (*Economist*, September 2000). In '04, India ranked only 51st for "openness to information technology"—based on technology and social factors (IDC, *Economist* Nov. 20/04).
6. In a different category, nationwide in 2006 more than 17,000 farmers killed themselves—mostly because of unpayable debts incurred during failed monsoon rains (*Economist,* March 8, 08). By 2009, India accounted for 60% of heart-disease deaths. (Source for this sentence and the next: *Economist* March 21/09).

Bengaluru is only one of several Indian cities that have moved into the Third Millennium's world of technology. Surgeons at the Indian Heart Centre saved the life of a boy *in Pakistan* by remotely guiding the repositioning of his heart (a procedure not then possible among India's neighbors). Over the Internet, one-on-one Indian tutors (who charge only $100 per month) help students in the West and other parts of the world upgrade skills in mathematics, English, or other subjects. Infosys has introduced a new bio-metric I.D. card it hopes to provide for India's 1.2 billion population, which will quickly identify holders to validate everything from welfare to passports and land registration. To overcome corrupt interests blocking the system, the government gave the card's developer, Nandan Nilekani, ministerial status to run the system.

Such IT developments can distort our understanding of India's industrial economy. Its core relies on myriad entrepreneurs in cottage industries. But government leaders are concerned about the rural poverty of some 700m (over 70% of the population) who barely subsist in 600,000 villages. An estimated 40m unemployed look for work, and impoverished masses such as 300m Dalits[8] are 90% illiterate.[9] With loosening restrictions, enterprising Indians are providing some hope. For instance, a businessman is giving rural areas access to markets for industry and agriculture, using solar-power and satellite links. And this is only the beginning. The next generation of technology promises to use "low-frequency open spectrum" to connect villages anywhere without cable or satellite (See Chapter 10 re Kolkata, and Appendix J re. other industrial factors.)

In other continents, including Europe and North America, men and women from India are making their way to the top in industry and professions. For instance, the chief technology officer of America's giant IT, Motorola, is Padmasree Warrior. An engineering graduate from India, she receives credit for helping turn around Motorola's fortunes with her "seamless mobility" concept. Then there's entrepreneur Vinod Khosla,

---

7. *Economist* Business Report '04—though in 2009 the World Bank banned it for two years because of a scam.

8. *Dalit:* >Sanskrit for "broken people." The lowest caste, formerly known as "Untouchables."

9. Karnataka State's concern for those "left behind" through lack of English prompted its ruling in 2006 that all schools (including private ones that had been teaching solely in English) must teach in *Kannada*—the local language. However, all schools will also teach English as a foreign language from age five.

graduate of the Indian Institute of Technology. Having made billions with Silicon Valley technology and investments, Khosla tries to wean industry from its thirst for oil, developing substitutes.

Indian firms continue to lead globally. Tata, a small iron foundry in early 1900 British-ruled India, has bought the Anglo-Dutch steel-maker, Corus, making Tata Steel the world's fifth-largest producer of steel (it had already purchased Singapore's NatSteel and Thailand's Millennium Steel). The largest is another Indian-owned company, Mittal. Smaller steel companies are setting up integrated iron-and-steel plants in India, which has ample coal, iron ore, and low-cost labor. Meanwhile, Tata Tea has reversed commerce along the Old Spice Road by purchasing, among other foreign companies, Britain's Tetley Tea—once a proud jewel in the crown of the British Raj! Tata has also expanded into other industries, including truck manufacture and Internet services. (For a while, global economic downturn removed some of the "shine" of India and other Asian lands.)

Bengaluru, I discovered, is also the base for a number of Christian organizations, including mission, theological, and publishing. The Centre for Contemporary Christianity (CfCC) is an example of the outreach these agencies have. Begun by Professor Siga Arles, Ph.D., as a spiritual renewal and study center for Christian workers, CfCC developed academic and publishing departments. Finding that most texts were beyond the resources of Asian students, CfCC economically produces publications by Asian and international theologians and missiologists. They include works by Bosch, Bush, Jongeneel, Kraemer, and Walls.

Between Bats and Bytes

All this was the context in which I now found myself sipping tea on the veranda of the Tozer's mission bungalow. As evening approached, bats swooped from under the eaves to scoop up insects. Was I in some kind of time warp? All I needed was a pith helmet! Computer chips and websites hadn't even been invented when CIGM's pioneers arrived. Back then, the Internet wasn't the communication channel of choice. The first open-heart surgery had just been performed (in 1967 in South Africa) when CIGM merged with PIVM to form ICF (1968). However, those missions had to retain their original names within India, because of legal complications.

What had happened between the eras of colonial bungalows and Internet bytes, I wondered. The pioneers had planted the gospel; the Holy Spirit had watered it through the ministry of others. Had it resulted in national churches led by Indians? Was Christianity a foreign import or an indigenous plant with deep roots? In Bengaluru, I asked the Tozers about Theodore Williams' statement concerning missions. Was the church able to take responsibility? If so, was there still any part for missions to play?

"To answer your question about nationals taking responsibility," replied the Tozers; "we'll take you to the annual conference of the CIGM Telegu-speaking[10] churches tomorrow. That's where you'll be speaking. You can see for yourself!"

And so I did. We arrived on Sunday morning at a secondary school (vacated for monsoon break) operated by a Brethren mission. Some 700 pastors, evangelists, and adherents had already gathered to sing hymns accompanied by a traditional zither and hand-tapped drums. A young man in slacks and flowery shirt led the singing, a sari-wrapped woman read the Scriptures, and a suited pastor made announcements at great length. I noticed that Gene was huddled in a corner with several older pastors, deep in discussion.

Divine Healing and Frangipani *Lei*

"Any problem?" I asked Ruth.

"They're discussing the other speaker," Ruth whispered. Another man was to bring the devotional messages, while I was supposed to bring Bible studies. I assumed there was a mix-up as to which of us should speak at the next session.

"No problem!" I exclaimed, loud enough for the huddled group to hear. Telegu Christians ran the entire conference, so it was only

10. After arrival in Bangalore, CIGM absorbed the smaller Anglican (CMS) Telegu Mission. Brahmins considered the Telegu and other ethnic groups of the South as lower caste—some as outcastes (now termed "scheduled castes"). Anglicans, Baptists, Methodists, and Lutherans were among several missions evangelising these, resulting in mass movements to Christianity. Ironically, some religious leaders worried that inclusion of lower castes in the churches would lower the social and educational levels of the church in India. Missions *raised* the levels of these. (Anderson, Goodwin, Neil: 1970, p. 272. See Bibliog.)

appropriate that they have a Telegu speaker instead of a foreigner. "I'll just sit and enjoy the meeting instead of speaking."

"That's not the problem," Gene said, overhearing me. "The pastors want you to teach the Word! That's why they're here." He explained that the conference leaders had invited the other speaker before realizing he was an exorcist. Spirit-worshiping villagers looked upon him as some kind of guru, but CIGM churches weren't into that kind of thing, neither were the owners of the high school.

"As disciples of Christ, we need the empowering of the Holy Spirit," they acknowledged. "And to combat evil forces, we depend on the Holy Spirit. He sometimes answers prayer in spectacular ways—including divine healing. But that is up to him, not up to our manipulation of God's power. We're afraid of mass campaigns that seem to promote Christian 'gurus,' not the Lord."

The evening before, the other speaker had spoken on Jesus' ministry—emphasizing exorcism. The man had also urged other manifestations. Conference leaders explained the tension to the speaker, and he graciously agreed not to conduct his planned exorcist session following Sunday morning's service. People could come to him outside the auditorium after his message, if they wanted to.

"You see why we need you!" the conference chairman told me. "We know our members need to be aware of spiritual warfare, but most don't have the maturity to see the difference between warfare in the Spirit and pagan superstition. Many have just come out of Hinduism. We'd like you to tell us what the Bible teaches."

"*Help, Lord!* Why did you get me into a fix like this?" I protested inwardly. The Bible study I'd prepared wasn't on this topic. And to complicate matters, the charismatic brother would be sitting in the audience! I lofted a quick prayer for guidance.

The exorcist spoke first. A capable communicator, he clearly stated his ministry. How should I follow that? I had to keep positive. I certainly did not want to attack the man. He was a brother in Christ. As I walked up to the platform, the Lord turned my thoughts to 1 Thessalonians 5—Paul's guidelines for a New Testament church. It was a radical change from what I'd planned, and I had no notes with me.

"Keep the barrel full, so you can dip in anytime, anywhere," I remembered my preacher father saying.[11] During the preliminaries, I flipped to the passage, which provided a wide range of teaching. I was to speak twice, and by my second session, the exorcist had excused himself to go to another appointment. By the end of the morning, sticky and fairly drained, I doubted whether I'd been of any help.

"Thank you! Thank you for that Scriptural balance!" several pastors said afterwards. "You made the Word clear to us. We'll preach from that passage in our churches next Sunday."

After the Sunday service, the chairman (himself a converted high-caste Hindu) placed a necklace of frangipani blossoms around the neck of the local Commissioner, a Hindu, who'd been sitting on the platform as the guest of honor representing the community. The chairman also bedecked me with a fragrant *leu*. I wondered why the Commissioner quickly removed his floral necklace. Was he embarrassed by the Christian attention? I didn't realize he was only showing his humility—I later discovered it was the cultural way of saying, "I don't deserve this honor!" Instead, I left mine on, to show appreciation for the gesture. Talk about a *faux pas*!

The Church at Three Levels

The afternoon heat closed in like a wet blanket when we went outside for lunch, but the organizers had set up lean-to shelters all around the school walls, shaded by colorful local cloth draped across bamboo poles. We sat down on benches at "tables" of planks laid across trestles. Young men came around with buckets of steaming food—*basmati*[12] rice with bits of vegetable, and curds, followed by tapioca dessert—which they ladled on to our banana leaf "place mats." To catch the drips between the planks, we covered our laps with hand towels Ruth had thoughtfully brought in her bag. But a banquet in the five-star Ashok International couldn't have produced more happy chatter than this simple communal feast.

---

11. "Sermon Barrel," referring to the widow's flour barrel that miraculously stayed full (1 Kings 17.16).

12. *Basmati*—a fragrant rice of southern India.

This conference was very different from the other two at which I'd spoken. The one in Delhi had impressed me with the capable leadership God has raised at the national level. At the second, in Chennai, the vision and dedication of national missionaries heartened me. In Bengaluru, I was at the grass roots—Christians witnessing to their own community in their own generation. Like the early churches of Asia Minor, they did so out of poverty, often under persecution, and riven at times with misunderstanding.

As I viewed those stages across India, I wished the dedicated missionary pioneers—who had poured their lives into planting the Church of Jesus Christ—could see the results. The stories of their heroic sacrifice had challenged many of us. For instance, our family had come to know Peter and Kathleen Paget, who served with CIGM, financially helped by our own Melrose church. We didn't know how God would test their commitment—not in India but while returning there from furlough. Their story told me of God's protection—yes, but it also reminded me that we all are frail creatures.[13]

That Promise—Cruel Joke?

It was near the start of World War II. The Japanese were sinking ships. As the time for the Pagets' return to India drew near, they knew the travel dangers and health problems lying ahead. They worried about taking their three-year-old daughter. Then at our farewell service for the Pagets, Kathleen felt she had received the promise she needed:

> **"Be not afraid of sudden fear, neither of the desolation of the wicked, when it cometh. For the Lord shall be thy confidence, and shall keep thy foot from being taken."**[14]

However, their faith was to be sorely tested, as the Japanese army kept them hostage under harsh circumstances. Kathleen was tempted to doubt the promise: they *were* afraid, "their foot " *had* been taken! It was three years before US paratroopers could free the emaciated prisoners of war.

---

13. Kathleen Paget, *Out of the Hand of the Terrible.* 1949 (SIM Resource Center, Charlotte, NC).
14. Proverbs 3.23-26, KJV.

It was then that Peter and Kathleen realized the verse *was* true: it hadn't promised they wouldn't suffer, they'd experienced amazing peace in the dreadful ordeal, and they had emerged alive! Instead of returning home, the Pagets sailed on to India, and eventually Peter became director of the CIGM in USA.

The Pagets' struggles with tests of faith reminded me that "we have this treasure in jars of clay."[15] I'd seen a village potter carefully fashion a vessel, yet it could easily crack and crumble. The fragile pot became strong and more beautiful only after the potter placed it in a fiery pit.

The ordeal also helped them prepare others for full commitment to God's will. One was Dr. Aletta Bell, who enrolled for medical service with CIGM in India. Later I'd meet her in north-east India (Chapter 11).

A much different example of "fiery trial" took place during a more recent war—the invasion of Kuwait by Iraq's dictator, Saddam Hussein. This story involved the Barnett family, who served with CIGM/SIM in another part of Asia.

Delivered from Lion's Den in Baghdad

I remembered watching a TV news clip of a 15-year-old Scottish schoolboy with the Iraqi dictator. I didn't know the story behind this scene, until I met an SIM missionary couple in Asia. It turned out that the schoolboy was their son, Allen, returning to a missionary boarding school in India after vacationing with his parents in Britain. The family had been on home leave.

"Allen had to return before we did, to start his last year at the mission school," Bill and Anne Barnett told me. "It was the first time he'd traveled by himself. But just before his flight took off from London, he phoned from the departure lounge to say that others from the school were on board the flight to Chennai in southern India. One was the daughter of Billy Graham's Indian associate evangelist, Abdul Haqq. The woman was taking her three children back to school. That was re-assuring."

15. 2 Corinthians 4:7.

But next day came the alarming news: the airline told the Barnetts the flight had been detained *in Kuwait* during a re-fuelling stop, and passengers had been bussed to Baghdad! Was Allen all right? Did he have any of his baggage—especially his carry-on bag, which had a change of clothes and his Bible. The airline didn't know.

Meanwhile, in Iraq, Hussein pumped his seizure for maximum propaganda, parading the Europeans and Americans before him. That's when the Barnetts glimpsed their son on the TV news. He was wearing a pair of shorts—that meant he had his handbag, including his Bible! The Barnetts prayed; the mission prayed; many other friends prayed. During the suspenseful concern for their son, Bill and Anne were amazed that they could even sleep!

Two days passed, and no further word. The British Foreign Office told the Barnetts that the prisoners were lodged in a deserted hotel in Baghdad. Did the Barnetts want to send a brief message? Bill gave the official this: "Many people are praying for you. Remember our family verse."

The official was curious when he learned the "verse" was not a poem but from the Bible. "Do you mind telling me what the verse says?" he asked. "We also need help over here!" Bill repeated the promise the oft-separated family had made theirs:

> **"God has said, Never will I leave you. Never will I forsake you. So we can say with confidence, the Lord is my helper, I will not be afraid. What can man do to me?"**

The third day brought discouraging news—the passengers had been moved, and the Foreign Office didn't know where they were. Iraq and the Western allies exchanged threats. Then on the fifth day, the telephone rang. It was Allen, yes—their 15-year-old!

"I'm coming home!" he told his astonished parents. "No, I don't know what airline. I think we're in Jordan. I don't know when we'll travel. I'm O.K. Don't worry!"

The Barnetts worked the phones of every airline flying out of Amman, Jordan. It was only after they held their son tight at London's Heathrow airport, that they got the details. When Hussein was checking on his captives, enquiring about their nationality, a woman passenger pointed out Allen: "This boy is traveling alone."

"What do you want to do?" The President of Iraq asked Allen.

"Go home, Sir!" Allen replied without hesitation. Hussein barked orders in Arabic, shook Allen by the hand, and suddenly the boy found himself on a bus headed for Amman, Jordan. He told his parents that the evening before, he'd asked God to get him home for the weekend. On Saturday he burst through the arrivals door into the family's arms!

"The ordeal wasn't easy at the time," recalled Anne. "But as we look back, we count the Lord's small mercies that strengthened the faith of each of us: friends unexpectedly on the same flight, another hostage passenger's unsolicited plea for release of the boy traveling alone, the peace each one experienced—and our son's faith."

But most precious was Allen's Bible reading from his Scripture Union notes. "It was weird," he later told his family. "There I was in what used to be called Babylon, and the daily readings were from Daniel! The night I prayed to be home for the weekend, the reading was about Daniel in the lion's den!"

"We knew only God could have timed that reading, because the syllabus would have been set a couple of years earlier!" Bill added.

Pursuing the Original Goals?

This was the kind of "stuff" that impressed SIM's International Director, Ian Hay, when CIGM and PIVM, under the initials of ICF, approached him and the rest of us on SIM`s Council in the late 1980s. SIM wasn't interested in enlarging, but Hay could not ignore ICF's commitment under exhausting circumstances.[16] In God's providence, the Chairman of SIM's Board of Governors—Clifford Edwards, a law professor

16. This wasn't SIM's first contact with CIGM. Rowland Bingham, founder of the original Sudan Interior Mission (1893) knew CIGM from the formation of its Canada Council, established by Davidson in 1914 with encouragement of Bingham's close friend, A. B. Simpson, founder of the C&MA. Bingham's own fledgling mission in Africa faced great needs, but Bingham sent gifts to CIGM missionaries one Christmas, aware of their sacrificial living. (Reported to author by retired CIGM missionaries in UK.)

with international experience—had been born in India, son of a British railway official. Cliff and Ian Hay became burdened for ICF. They understood the context of its struggling work and realized God might want SIM to encourage it—Barnabas-like. Certainly ICF needed a wider home base, and SIM`s offices in Australia and New Zealand were natural "neighbours"[17] for assistance and missionary outreach.

Now I wanted to ask whether the churches still pursued the original vision of ICF pioneers. Certainly at the conference, church and mission were getting along well together, and the number of churches was growing.[18] But how about evangelising unreached communities in India's exploding population? The Tozers introduced me to men and women who soon removed all doubt about the continuing vision.

Several had been Hindus, a few Muslims, and many nominal Christians who had found the Saviour. One farmer from the north of CIGM's Telegu area told me his church had no pastor, but he and other farmers constantly witness in outlying areas. All around, tiny groups of new believers meet for worship. Gene said he'd been invited to the opening of three churches, all in separate villages, within a two-day period. At one there was no pool of water for a baptismal service. So each new believer climbed into a barrel of water and, at the appropriate time, the pastor pushed him or her down under water!

At a professional level, one academic and his wife told of amazing opportunities to witness as the government assigned him to different parts of the country. When local officials complained he was trying to convert people, he explained he was only holding "discourses on Christianity." The nation's constitution guaranteed freedom of religion even if it discouraged conversion, he pointed out. What could officials say, when they valued his specialization so highly!

A pastor, X—, told me how he despaired in his youth after his mother died and his illiterate father couldn't support the family. Their Hindu gods hadn't helped them. Unemployed, one day X— thought of

17. Luke 10.29; Mark 12.31.

18. Telegu churches: About 100, with some 11,000 adherents, in two states. Within India, all are registered under the CIGM name for legal reasons.

jumping off the bridge he was crossing. Incredibly, as he paused before leaping to the crocodiles below, a Bible verse popped into his mind: *"Believe on the Lord Jesus Christ."* He'd heard Christian friends quote it as they played together. He changed his mind and returned home, where a friend invited him to the Layman's Evangelical Fellowship (one of many independent churches). The message was so made for him, he thought someone must have told the evangelist about his life. That led to his salvation.

After studying at the Oriental Missionary Society under my colleague, Wesley Duewel of World Evangelical Alliance, X— pastored with CIGM. Church members took him to court when X— supported the mission's view that the property belonged to the church and not to individuals. The members' angry attitude so discouraged X— that he left the pastorate for some time. After CIGM (ICF) and SIM merged, he returned to the pastorate.

A New Day—New Problems

Now as I sat beside the conference chairman, Pastor **Yesurathinam**, his story impressed me. It encapsulated the role of earlier missionaries as well as the ongoing vision of church and mission today.

He'd lived like any unsaved teen, until he heard a message by CIGM's memorable preacher, Silas Fox. Now decades later, he still remembered the topic ("Mary weeping over her sins, her tears falling on Jesus' feet"), and the exact time of his repentance for his own sins: 11.30 p.m. That not an unusual hour for Silas Fox, who was known to preach on until 4 a.m. to attentive groups.[19]

CIGM missionaries helped the young man study the Bible. Hearing about unevangelized areas of the North, he moved there and studied Urdu and Hindi. His first convert was a Muslim leper, who'd been cast out of his village. But when Pastor Yesurathinam witnessed to Hindus, some threatened him, shouting, "Hinduism is India's religion!"

---

19. Silas Fox was a peripatetic evangelist of international repute. Once on furlough in my home city, he boldly paraded downtown with a sandwich board emblazoned with Scripture calling on sinners to repent!

The young pastor had to return to the Telegu area to put his children into a Telegu-language school. In his village, a prominent Hindu trusted in Christ. Pastor Yesurathinam taught him from the Bible, finally pointing out that if the man had really become a follower of Christ, he shouldn't keep idols in his house.

"The man eventually destroyed them all," the pastor told me. "That really upset his wife; she feared that the gods would take revenge. That's at the heart of Hinduism—fear of idols. Hindus have to appease them."

"What did the villagers do?" I asked.

"Nothing!" replied Pastor Yesurathinam. "They couldn't say anything, because he was an important man in town."

A Brahmin who trusted in Christ eventually asked the pastor to cut off his pigtail (a sacred Brahmin sign). Low-caste sweepers also came to Christ through his ministry. With his use of northern and southern languages, this humble pastor had an unusual ministry among both high and low caste, right up to the time of his death (since my visit).

"We're in a new day," Gene Tozer later explained. "We know missionaries who worked for thirty years without response. Dissatisfaction with politics and the economy has changed that. Last week a thousand people gathered when they heard that an evangelist was coming to a town further north. But there's a backlash. In a nearby town, Hindu militants have twice burned down a church. It's a mixed picture."

"In Canada I heard a TV evangelist report that 5,000 new churches had been established in Maharashtra state," I said. "Could that be true?"

"That's another problem," Gene answered. "Visiting evangelists make amazing claims to gain support. I can tell you, those 5,000 new churches in Maharashtra don't exist! But where there's real turning to the Lord, we're concerned that churches won't be ready to disciple converts. That's why Pastor Yesurathinam is so keen on Bible teaching."

Litigation: National Pastime?

Prasad has suffered persecution, chased out of a few villages. But the problem that weighs most heavily is the waste of time and stress in court cases, similar to what the Tamil pastor had told me about. I asked Prasad why there was so much litigation going on in India, including in the churches.

"Yes, a lot of my time right now is tied up in a church court case," he admitted, waggling his head ruefully. "Our people are poor, especially in rural areas. It's true some pastors have no salaries. But the problem is that lawyers tell them they could win property or money by taking a church to court. They also use the courts to settle grievances, even over small or imagined things."

Gene Tozer added some background: "All missions and churches face these cases.[20] They are usually over the land the British government gave missions because of their humanitarian work—land for hospitals, schools, and churches. Many of these sites are now prime property, and people want to get their hands on it. Pastors and employees refuse to move out, once they've been allowed to stay for a while. Instead, they go to court. Villagers sometimes bring cases simply to harass Christians. Of course, bribery makes all this lucrative for lawyers and court clerks. Christian lawyers who won't give bribes face great frustration.

"We wish we'd been able to turn over mission properties to the national church years ago, with safeguards preventing individuals claiming property for their own benefit. In India, that's now a lengthy and difficult process because of claims.

"Ironically, CIGM's ownership once saved property for the church. An angry pastor, upset with his superintendent (also an Indian), appealed to the state high court to disband the CIGM and disburse its assets. The court refused, because the properties were registered in the name of the Mission!"

When elders (who often try to exert authority over pastors) took their pastor to court, the Hindu judge complained, "These men have no respect for the house of God or for the men of God!"

---

20. Litigation has a lengthy history. In the early 1800s, "Syrian" churches were suing over church property.

Earlier, when I had visited Pune, a board member of Union Biblical Seminary in Yeotmal[21] told me about a theology student who took the school to court. "I'm a Hindu," the judge told the appellant; "but I know that your Bible says a believer should not take another believer to court. Case dismissed!"

Litigation seemed to be the national sport. It provides steady employment for lawyers. Hindu lawyers delight in stretching church cases out: postponing hearings, "losing" papers, changing the case or court site on some technicality, and finding obscure counter charges. Some courts have 100,000 cases pending, I learned. A godly professor in another part of India told me his family had given up their rice paddies rather than renounce their faith when threatened. "I find it ironic to see Christians going to court over property," he said.

I remembered how the Apostle Paul wrote of his "concern for all the churches"—apart from a litany of hardships he had suffered. He also endured Demetrius, "who loves to have the pre-eminence"!

Churches' Greatest Need

"Tell me, what's the church's greatest need now?" I asked Pastor Prasad.

"CIGM has been outstanding in preaching the gospel and motivating young men to study to preach and evangelize," he told me as he finished off his tapioca and wiped his fingers.

"Now there's the problem of power. Members want to control the preachers, and pastors want to hang on to assets and authority. They all need teaching from the Word of God, and spiritual revival. The mission can help us train more pastors, and also can teach the churches how they should support their pastors."

The Director of a Christian Medical College cited the lack of a servant attitude in Hindu society as a whole. Servants there are aplenty,

21. UBS is one of a few evangelical seminaries among some 40 degree-granting theological schools. There are 300 Bible schools. Pune (the "e" is pronounced as "eh") was the "Poona" of PIVM, which merged with CIGM to become ICF. ICF helped provide teachers for the Seminary and nearby Yeotmal, a missionary and Bible-training center.

but that's because it's their caste or employment. "The idea of success is to have power at the top—the Brahmin maharaja syndrome," he said. "Unfortunately, this has infected the churches. They should follow David's servant-shepherd model."

"One of the churches' greatest problems is from within," a Bible teacher told me, although external persecution has been mounting. "Nominal Christians allow compromise and syncretism, and churches give negative witness before Muslims and Hindus." I realized afresh how Christians in every generation—whether in Asia or overseas—must renew their spiritual roots in repentance, faith, and the Word of God.

CIGM and PIVM pioneers for the most part had ministered to the poverty-stricken masses, considered by the highest caste (Brahmins) to be "untouchable." Lower castes looked upon Brahmins ("the twice-born") as gods. To many a Christian evangelist, proud Brahmins (Euro-Asians, or "Aryans") may have seemed "unreachable"—but the Holy Spirit was also working among them. It was a Christian Euro-Asian who challenged Charles Reeve, founder of PIVM, to come to evangelize in Pune, at the time India's intellectual capital and a Brahmin stronghold. Reeve could never have imagined his part in the spiritual pilgrimage of Brahmin Sanskrit scholar Sastri and his daughter, Ramabai.

Jesus on the High as well as Low Road

For Ramabai Sastri, related to the ruling family (*Peswa*—"Prime Minister") of Pune, that amazing pilgrimage began in a forest. It could seem dramatic to call Ramabai's pilgrimage "a jungle-to-fame" story. But her father, Anant Sastri, had attained to the third-highest stage or *ashrama* of Brahmin: forest dweller or *vanaprastha*—for the purpose of meditation and isolation. (The fourth stage, *sannyasin*, is total renunciation of the world and all human ties.)

Then a major famine struck. Ramabai watched her parents and siblings starve to death. But her father, a most unusual man, had already given her something very precious—knowledge of sacred Sanskrit, the language women were not supposed to learn. Both her parents had modelled learning and initiative. Both also shared their disillusion with Hinduism.

Although the family continued rites with the hope of eventual emancipation from birth after birth into different levels of existence, they viewed the religion as fraud.

Sole survivor of her family, Ramabai supported herself by giving discourses in Sanskrit—to everyone's amazement. By the time she was 20, the *Shastris* (religious teachers) of Calcutta honoured her with the title *Pandita.*[22] Her own disillusion turned to anger as she witnessed society's treatment of women and the poor. At the same time, the love and compassion of Christians brought her to an intellectual acceptance of Christianity—but at the time she knew Jesus only as a historical figure.

She finally found Jesus Christ as Saviour, the Son of God, through reading the Gospel according to Luke (which a missionary had translated into Sanskrit). Christian friends further explained the way of salvation. She eagerly learned more from Bible teachers, Indian and expatriate. One was none other than the missionary who came all the way from Australia to Pune, Charles Reeve![23] Pandita Ramabai founded a school for widows and girls at risk, a ministry similar to Dohnavur Fellowship, founded by her contemporary, Amy Carmichael. Six months after she started a prayer meeting to pray for "the true conversion" and spiritual empowering of Christians, a remarkable revival broke out, spreading to other parts of India. The *Pandita* also founded the famed Ramabai Mukti Mission.

During her lifetime, Hindu zealots cast insults at Ramabai, blaming her for the destruction of women.[24] But in 1989, India issued a postage stamp in honor of the *Pandita.* Professor A. B. Shah of Maharashtra State explains why:

> "Pandita Ramabai Saraswati[25] (1858-1922) was the greatest woman produced by Modern India and one of the greatest Indians in all

22. *Pandita*: Sanskrit, feminine of "learned one" (*pandit*)—from which English derives "pundit."

23. MacNicol, *What Liberates a Woman*, p. 142 (Bibliog.). Friends from Ramabai's overseas visits also deepened her life and supported her ministries. Appendix A gives a précis of her full story.

24. To them, she was "damning" women to bad *karma* by freeing them from male domination and abuse!

25. Hindus called her "Saraswati" (goddess of language, literature, and learning), though she rejected that.

> history. ... a pioneer in the fields of women's education and social reform. ... She was the first to introduce the kindergarten system of education and also the first to give a vocational bias to school education in India. Most important of all, she was the first to rebel against the inhuman slavery to which widows were subjected in Hindu society and to lay the foundations of a movement for women's liberation in India."

It was the gospel that enabled seeds of greatness sown by her parents to blossom. This accomplished woman passed that gospel on to women who found asylum with her.

Today, a select group of missionaries and Christians in the professions all over India encourage Indian pastors and missionaries in their own witness. You won't read their names, and they won't appear in mission videos. But while keeping in the background, people like Bill and Betty X[26]— see God at work through daily contacts.

"Christian friends asked us to visit one young man at the end of a major festival," they recently related. "Government doctors had given him up as terminal with a brain infection. Sleepless, he hadn't spoken for two months; neighbors shunned the family. We read the Scriptures, prayed, and talked about the eternal life that Jesus gives. We later heard he slept for three days and then talked! His change was so dramatic that the family's been attending Bible studies. When everyone else had shunned them, they were impressed that Christians showed them love."

Such are small spiritual victories in the face of overwhelming need. I heard of many such instances all across the nation. Most church growth is taking place in village house groups. Some of them reminded me of the early disciples—"the church that meets in the house of Onesiphorus," as the Apostle Paul wrote to one group. Medical doctor Victor Choudhrie and his wife Bindu have seen several thousand such "churches" spring up in their region of India.

"We do not *go to church*, as we *are* the *Ekklesiya*, wherever we happen to meet, in a house or anywhere else. The house *Ekklesiya* is not a series

26. Name withheld at their request.

of meetings on a particular day, at a certain time, led by a particular leader. It is a household of God consisting of twenty-four-hours-a-day and seven-days-a-week relationships."[27]

Such "house churches" don't hit the headlines. They reminded me of Anglican missionary Roland Allen (1868-1947). When his home board asked for spectacular stories, he replied: "I do not trust spectacular things. Give me the seed growing secretly every time."

Rescued from the Serpent's Coils

In every land there are instances of spiritual victory and of spiritual defeat. Nevertheless, I was shocked to hear that one of the outstanding Christian leaders I had met had fallen into sexual temptation. (I need not reveal actual names, for the lessons learned are the important point of the story, which illustrates the spiritual battle all of us face. I'll simply call the leader and his wife Rimi and Sippra.)

The crisis could have ended Rimi's public ministry and his marriage, but instead it resulted in a powerful testimony to the grace of God. Both his wife and his church showed the same grace. In the global context of famous public figures, major moral lapses among Christians, and society's sexual promiscuity, the pilgrimage of this couple has been of great significance to me—outstanding example of biblical restoration.

"The Lord has manifested his great mercy and grace to me and set me on the path of restoration," Rimi later wrote me.[28] "Sippra has been a great source of blessing though I had betrayed and hurt her."

The path to restoration was not an easy one to follow. Although Rimi was in demand as a public speaker and had played a prominent role in several organizations, he resigned from all leadership posts and ministry. In contrition, he submitted to biblical discipline under his church, later describing the painful process:

---

27. *Books & Culture,* Jan.–Feb. 2007, p. 32.

28. Personal letter to author Oct. 19, 1994. Though Rimi and Sippra gave permission to mention this episode, it was my decision not to use their names; that would serve no good purpose. –WHF.

> "Can a person who has walked with the Lord and served him for many years fall so badly? ... Can such a person be forgiven and restored to fellowship with his Lord?" he wrote, recalling his sense of failure, self-recrimination, and depression. "This is the story of my life in recent times."

Rimi told how, under the pressures of successful ministry, he became numb to reality. Unknowingly, he neglected his two most important priorities: relationship with Christ and with his wife. He illustrated temptation with the story of a snake charmer who thought he could control the deadly python he had made his pet when it was tiny. But it grew strong and one day crushed him to death.

With contrite honesty, Rimi compared his story to King David's, recorded in Psalm 51: temptation, sin, defeat, repentance, forgiveness, and restoration.

"It is not easy forgiveness," Rimi reminded us. "There were consequences of David's sin in his kingdom and his family. . . Failure is not a waste when it is confessed and repented of." David's repentance had to be genuine, his desire had to be restoration of fellowship with the Lord—not of ministry or public respect. Rimi wrote in his diary: "Lord, my prayer is not that I may accomplish something for you, but that I may please you."

As Sippra and fellow Christians remained faithful to the healing process, God eventually granted Rimi a new, fruitful ministry in teaching and counselling. After an appropriate period of discipline, his church asked him to conduct a series of Bible studies based on Psalm 51. He did so "with fear and trembling, trusting the Lord." At these gatherings, Christians pledged to pray for Rimi as he took up ministry. The couple have demonstrated that "*failure is not final with God*."

My friend's pilgrimage holds lessons for us all: (1) perils of over-busyness in a successful ministry, (2) subtlety of sin, (3) pain of moral and spiritual collapse, (4) catharsis of true repentance, (5) mercy of forgiveness, (6) healing grace of restoration.

With much to think about, I headed off to the tip of India's "southern cone."

Surging Tides Clash

"A furious squall came up, and the waves broke over the boat. ... [Jesus] got up, rebuked the wind and said to the waves, "Quiet! Be still!" (Mark 4.39).

IT'S A RATHER EERIE MOMENT—standing on the most southerly tip of India. Water and sky stretch before me until they meet at the horizon. Of course, they never do meet—they reach far beyond. There's no land—from my feet southward, first crossing the Indian Ocean, hurdling the equator, then on, on, and on for thousands of miles, right to the frozen wastes of Antarctica.

Deep under the blue-green swells are the tectonic plates, demonstrating the Creator's engineering genius. Or should we call them "titanic" plates, imperceptibly yet relentlessly, pushing the subcontinent northward, colliding with the rest of Asia, thrusting up the Himalayas' crumpled ranges like a monstrous welding seam.[1] Their writhing arrests our attention when "faults" trigger massive undersea quakes, sending *tsunami* tidal waves racing to devastate distant shores.[2]

I'm standing on historic Cape Comorin—now called Kanyakumari. The Arabian Sea is to my right; the Bay of Bengal to the left. Here the

1. In case welding seam "seems" an inept analogy in view of the lofty Himalayas, geologists tell us that if the earth were shrunken to the size of a billiard ball, the globe would be smoother than the ball!
2. See Chapter 15, "Where Was God when the Tsunami Struck?"

"tides" of water and culture and faith have clashed for millennia. Behind me is a different "sea"—people pushed down into the cone of India by wave upon wave of northern invaders. Aborigines and Dravidians[3] were the earliest inhabitants. Wind and tide brought many to these shores. Coastal ranges (the Western *Ghats* and Eastern *Ghats*) angle off northwards like an embossed V, angling hundreds of miles northwards to the West and East of my vantage point.

Between those coastal "walls" lies the Deccan Trap—perhaps earth's oldest plateau.[4] The amazing Indian sub-continent contains every type of climate and terrain—from glaciers to fertile valleys, from treeless deserts to rain forests. Fauna include multiple species, from mountain goats and elephants, soaring eagles and jungle parrots, to rock-dwelling snakes and marshland crocodiles.[5]

Between the two southerly states of Karnataka and Tamil Nadu, the jungle provided the ideal redoubt for India's most notorious bandit, "Veerappan." It took a 750-strong special police unit 14 years and massive funds to put an end (in 2004) to his flamboyant reign of terror, which included ivory poaching, smuggling, extortion, kidnapping, and 124 *known* murders. In a way, the generous bribes he gave did help the local economy—he became the villagers' hero and some officials' main source of personal wealth. They might have written as his eulogy: "He will be missed!"

Fathering Nation of Triumph and Tragedy

But on India's most southerly tip, a mausoleum commemorates India's quiet hero, the revered *Mahatma*[6] nationalist (1869-1948). A tourist attraction, the structure houses the urn for Mohandas Gandhi's ashes. On each anniversary of his birthday, October 2, the sun's rays beam directly through a window on to that urn.

---

3. Anthropologists trace aborigines to Australia. The polytheism of Dravidians (ancient dark-skinned people) modified and added to the later-arriving Aryan pantheism (Zaehner, 134, etc.—Bibliography).

4. International geologists are currently puzzling over the possibility that primordial volcanic explosions from this plateau triggered several catastrophic phenomena all over the globe.

5. There are nine crocodilian subspecies in India.

6. *Mahatma*: Sanskrit, "great-souled," a term of highest respect.

The Mahatma earned the title, "Father of the Nation." Even though he was from the northern Vaishya (Hindu upper class) elite, he lives on in the nation's hearts at every level. A brilliant thinker who studied Law in Britain and practised in South Africa during *apartheid's* early years, he also picked up Christian values of work and democracy.[7] He believed his people not only should be free from colonial rule, but should also free *themselves* from their dependency syndrome. A master strategist, he cloaked such alien (at that time) principles in Hindu culture.

Returning to India, Gandhi faced Britain's imperial power with passive resistance. He gave up business suits, recasting himself as an ascetic guru—recognized worldwide by his slight, stooped figure wearing a loincloth *dhoti*, peering over owlish spectacles. His was a most unlikely figure to lead a movement, compared with the impressive parade of India's rulers through the centuries—from ancient Persians to turbaned Moguls and ostrich-plumed British Raja.

Like the tides off the Cape, many thoughts surged through my mind as I stood overlooking the Mahatma's memorial. On top of the mausoleum, I noted the symbol of Gandhi's other great crusade for India's independence—the *dharma* wheel.[8] Conscious of the nation's burgeoning population and their feeling that the rest of the world owed them everything, Gandhi motivated peasants to grow their own food, spin their own yarn, and take pride in manual labor. He spun his own cotton on a wheel and wove his *dhotis* on a handloom. Self-reliance brought a much-needed social revolution.

After the twin triumph and tragedy of Independence and Partition in 1947, another Brahmin, Jawaharlal Nehru, became Prime Minister

---

7. Some South African churches opposed *apartheid*. Supporters, often unknowingly, had a racist Aryan view but later repudiated their unbiblical position. Gandhi may not have recognized the connection between *apartheid* in South Africa and *caste* in India, but both came from the same pagan Aryan (Euro-Asian source)! The West rightly condemned decades of apartheid in Africa, but governments disgracefully closed their eyes to millennia of a more iniquitous form of *apartheid*—India's caste system. Though Scripture forbids discrimination, people generally accepted it until evangelical Christian conscience roused public opinion. Carey condemned caste's denial of human rights (Ch. 9, note 22).

8. Ancient Sumerian symbol, the *dharma* is an allegory of the cycle of "birth after birth." It appears on India's national flag in the middle of three panels of saffron, white, and green. Gandhi cleverly tied it in with his self-help spinning wheel. Most Westerners think it is just that, but Hindus embrace it as *dharma*.

and turned self-reliance into isolationism. Cottage industries were indeed right for India, and stiff bans against imports were necessary for a period, to break consumer dependence on foreign imports. But a stifling brand of socialism unfortunately perpetuated state dependence that left India economically trailing other emerging nations.[9] Although antiquated technology appeals to romantics, it has its own injurious "fallout." Environmentalists are chagrined that indoor pollution from "dirty fuels" (charcoal, crop residues, and cow dung) may cause up to 2m. deaths annually![10]

However, the present government has awakened to two pressures as inexorable as the tectonic plates under the Indian Ocean: (1) Before 2020, India will be the most populous nation on earth (with only one-third the land of China), and (2) every year the working-age population will increase by more than the combined workforce of Europe and USA![11] Officials realize that investment from successful Indians overseas, other foreign investing, and two-way globalization could overcome the potential unrest of the rapidly growing 300-million educated middle class.

"Beyond the squalor of India's city slums, its broken down infrastructure, infuriating corruption and mind-boggling bureaucracy, lies a consumer market of epic proportions," reports *The Financial Post*[12] of Canada, a nation with many educated Indian expatriates who remit large sums to their homeland. "A fundamental shift in the economy and the way it is governed, coupled with globalization, will see India become the world's third-largest economy by about 2040, behind China and the United States."

But the sub-continent's major tensions will continue as long as its newfound wealth doesn't trickle down to the impoverished masses. In 2005, India's Prime Minister Manmohan Singh gave his view of the

9. Although China's Maoism also throttled development, after China opened to free enterprise it outstripped India three to one in some sectors. Now India is opening and catching up.
10. *Economist,* February 10, 2001.
11. India and China are becoming the world's leading emitters of carbon dioxide (*Ibid.*), yet as "emerging nations" neither is bound by the Kyoto treaty—which explains why USA (condemned by others but actually instituting national pollution regulations for its own survival) did not sign "Kyoto."
12. *Financial Post,* April 16, 2004.

problem: "There is an India that wants to move ahead even faster. There is an India that is unable to catch up."[13] The tension is increasingly evident in the spread of "Naxalite" influence. Named after their birthplace in West Bengal in 1967, these Maoists oppose conventional government, thriving on the dissatisfaction of poverty-stricken communities. They now form a revolutionary band that stretches from the southern tip of the sub-continent northwards through India's heartland and northeastern states, linking up with Maoists in Nepal.

India's enormous population makes it difficult to put any figure into perspective. Depending on what they want to prove, reporters (and politicians) paint a picture of millions enjoying great wealth or of millions suffering abject poverty. Or they state there are millions of Christians, or more Muslims than in Pakistan's Islamic state. But such isolated "facts" do not portray the overall picture. "Land of contrasts" is a common title travellers could give to most countries, although some display starker disparities than others. India, land of advanced technologies, and reputed to be the first nation to employ hypnosis as a surgical anaesthetic (in 1845),[14] also has educated people who recommend drinking a glass of one's own urine daily for health's sake. Many mothers still use dry cow dung to scour children at "bath time." Progress and archaic tradition can be cousins.

A Greater Driving Force

India's breakthrough into the modern world is undeniable. What really brought it about? Historians regard non-violent resistance to British rule as the turning factor in India's Independence as well as new era, but there was a stronger driving force. Contrary to accepted wisdom, Indian philosopher/historian Vishal Mangalwadi has documented the role played by evangelicals in Britain's parliament. They held Britain to an earlier pledge to grant India Independence.[15] While Gandhi deserves

13. *Economist,* November 26, 2005, p. 52.
14. *Time,* March 27, 2006.
15. See Ch. 9 for details. An intellectual who has lectured worldwide, Mangalwadi has exposed Hindu gurus as fakes and also been jailed for protesting poverty. [Vishal Mangalwadi, ***India: the grand experiment.*** Mussoorie: Good Books, 1997.] See Bibliography for his other books.

credit for motivating the masses in India, evangelicals in far-off Britain were the ones laying the groundwork for the establishment of the world's largest democracy—one that still functions.[16]

Mangalwadi goes further, presenting historical records to show that Christian parliamentarians and social reformers introduced to India the rule of law, which had not been "part of the Indian psyche," according to noted Indian jurist Nani Palkhivala.

Instead, for millenia astrology has ruled the lives of the people of the sub-continent. Tantric astrology includes numerology and Sanskrit characters. From birth to marriage to death, from travel to farming, people still seek the guidance of astrologers, fearing to act without auspicious signs. In the West, astrology may often be entertaining, but Tantric astrology has occult connections, according to Dr. A. P. Stone, a life member of the Indian Association for History and Philosophy of Science.[17] Whatever else, astrology's effect is loss of initiative and misadventure.

"The traditional Hindu world view stifles initiative, perpetuates poverty, and promotes endemic corruption," states Mangalwadi. As to the future, he warns that the *Hindutva* movement, a totalitarian political force cloaked in traditional culture, is antagonistic to Christianity but favorable toward fascism. Its youthful followers study Nazi writings—Adolph Hitler has been the second most popular non-fiction author in India.[18] Only a nation-wide spiritual revival will save India from sinking into totalitarianism, Vishal Mangalwadi warns.

Syncretism's Conundrum

One who illustrated the Indian sub-continent's syncretism—and the clashing of tides swirling around it—was none other than the "Father of

16. Britain's problem was knowing to which of the 563 petty kingdoms it should turn over power. Gandhi understood nationalist sentiment and positioned his political party for rule. (Facts in this and the next paragraph are from Mangalwadi, *Ibid.*)

17. A. P. Stone, *Light on Astrology*. Bombay: Gospel Literature Service, revised 1994.

18. Appealing to many educated Indians, Hitler's ideal of ethnic superiority was based on the Aryan cycle's evolution into perfect manhood. Four bent arms make a swastika seem to rotate, like wheel spokes. The main Hindu deities have at least four arms. (*Swastika*: Sanskrit "well being,"—ancient Aryan-Hindu sign.)

the Nation." The Gandhi era may seem remote today, but it still holds important lessons for understanding India's eclectic worldview. Unquestionably a great man, Mahatma Gandhi was also somewhat of a conundrum. Which of the following was he?

a. Practical secularist, who recognized Hinduism's stifling effect and sought change?

b. Brahmin reformist, who cloaked needed change with religious mysticism?

c. Astute politician, who organized the grassroots masses to oppose colonial rule?

d. Nominal disciple of Jesus, invoking the Saviour's lifestyle but not his salvation?

Answer: all of the above. For instance, the Mahatma had a certain admiration for Hitler,[19] the epitome of ruthless power. Yet Gandhi completely opposed war. His concept of pacifism led him to regard Roosevelt and Churchill—who ended World War II's slaughter and genocide—as "no less war criminals than Hitler and Mussolini"!

Pleasant to Christian ears, the Mahatma's early dictum was, "God is Truth." But Gandhi ended up with a neat Hindu inversion: "Truth is God."[20] He appreciated the medical services of Christian missionaries, but rejected conversion to Christ. Although he openly broke Hindu caste taboos, he vehemently opposed any mass movement of "untouchables" to the freedom of Christianity. That fuelled fears an independent India might restrict the religious liberty of Indian Christians and missions.

The Mahatma so modeled his lifestyle on Jesus, that some Christian leaders considered him to be Hindu in culture while Christian in faith. To theological liberals, he was Exhibit No. 1 that there are many "ways

---

19. Wolpert, 2001 (Biblio.). July 23/39, Gandhi addressed Hitler as "Dear Friend," pleading to avoid war.

20. Gnostic concept in Buddhist mantra: "He who sees the truth sees the Buddha, and he who sees the Buddha sees the truth." Jesus stated: "I *am* the truth, the way, the life"—goals sought by all religions.

to God"—contrary to evangelicals, who stressed the uniqueness of Christ and necessity of spiritual regeneration. Yet the Mahatma's lifestyle did deserve the respect of Christians.

"I bow to Mahatma Gandhi and I kneel at the feet of Christ," stated the well-known American missionary, E. Stanley Jones. "A little man . . . has taught me more of the spirit of Christ than perhaps any other man in East or West."[21] Certainly Gandhi portrayed Christian virtues, including kindness even to traditional enemies. In fact, a Hindu fundamentalist murdered him because he protected Muslims at risk in Hindu-Muslim riots.[22] In Hyderabad, a largely Islamic city, mourners commemorating Gandhi's death carried his photograph surmounted by a cross.

Hindu or Christian? Though Gandhi admired Jesus as servant leader and said the Sermon on the Mount went "straight to his heart," he never claimed that Christ was his Saviour. He did challenge Christians to live the gospel instead of just talking about it—a much needed emphasis. While Gandhi's interest in Jesus the Man interested Hindus in Jesus, they looked upon his suffering as a means of earning good *karma*. Wasn't *Janma* (Hindu "birth after birth") the same as being "born again"? Some Hindus saw Gandhi as the East's incarnation of Christ. For Buddhists, Jesus' suffering fulfilled one of their dogmas: "Existence is suffering." They accepted Jesus as an Enlightened One to emulate. Nominal Christians considered Gandhi as universalism's "Saviour-of-the-world" example.

Evangelicals wondered how many accepted Jesus Christ as their *personal* Saviour (liberals dislike that term—"selfish" they think!): the bearer of *their* sins, *their* Redeemer, the resurrected Lord of *their* lives. Semantics? Or the difference between mental assent and heart faith, social emulation and regeneration?

As I learned more about Mahatma Gandhi, however, I had to acknowledge that God's workings are beyond our planning or

21. E. Stanley Jones, *Gandhi: Portrayal of a Friend*. Nashville, Abingdon Press, 1993, p. 8. Jones (1884-1973); Methodist Episcopal missionary in N. India; member, International Missionary Council, which the World Council of Churches absorbed as a department. His books contained cross-cultural insights but also increasingly Universalist views influencing the WCC.

22. Marie Louise Gude, *Louise Massignon: The Crucible of Compassion*. Notre Dame: University of Notre Dame Press, 1996, pp 193-194.

understanding. For instance, over in the Middle East, Mazhar Mallouhi, a Syrian Muslim who read Gandhi's writings, was impressed with the Mahatma's respect for Jesus. Mazhar decided to find out more about this Jesus, whom Muslims regard as a prophet, but one superseded by Muhammad. The Bible gave him further information, but the call of Jesus also reached into his heart: "Come to me, all you who are weary and heavy laden, and I will give you rest."[23] Although Mazhar had no contact with Christians or a church, he cried out to Christ for the "rest" the Lord had promised. While retaining his Arab culture, Mazhar has continued his spiritual pilgrimage, until he is now involved in publishing the gospel for other Muslims—all in an Arab, non-Western format.

Perhaps the Mahatma was in the same position, spiritually, as the teacher of the Jewish Law, who came to discuss with Jesus. Mark 12.34 records that Jesus told him, "You are not far from the kingdom of God." So near, and yet not in.

"I want all the cultures of all lands to be blown about my house as freely as possible," Gandhi explained as his philosophy. "But I refuse to be blown off my feet by any."

While I could not agree that Asia's religions are all simply different ways to salvation, I recognized that throughout our world, God has placed pointers to truth. The Apostle Paul implied as much, while condemning those who distort the witness of nature (Romans 1:18-21). I also realized that God can use a person who is "not far" to interest another to search further for the Truth, and that only the Holy Spirit knows the heart of man.

Yet I could not accept a syncretistic worldview that values "truths" while rejecting the one who is Truth—as noted Bengali poet Rabindranath Tagore penned for Yuletide:

> *Great-souled Christ, on this blessed day of your birth, we who are not Christians bow before you. We love you and worship you, we non-Christians, for with Asia you are bound with the ties of blood.*[24]

---

23. Matthew 11.28.
24. Quoted by E. Stanley Jones, in *Christ of the Indian Road.* London: Hodder & Stoughton, 1925, p. 51. Note that Tagore gave Christ the same title ("Great-souled" or "Mahatma") that Gandhi bore.

The Malabar Coast—Cultural Crossroads

Millennia before Gandhi, "the cultures of all lands" blew over India's most southerly coast, westward of the Cape. Before the Christian and Muslim eras, its cities traded even with Egypt during King Solomon's reign over sections of the Middle East. Later, Jews found refuge during Babylon's conquest of Judea. Tradition avers that the Apostle Thomas came as an evangelist in AD 52, followed in AD 68 by ten thousand Jews after the fall of Jerusalem's Second Temple. Syrian Christians arrived in the 4thc.[25]

Knowing that kind of background, I was surprised to find a far different ideology predominant in today's state of Kerala.

"How did Kerala—India's most literate, most populous, most prosperous, and most Christian state—also become the first *Communist* state?"[26] I asked Bishop Key Michael John, Church of South India, Kerala.

"Hold on!" protested Bishop John, throwing up his hands. "You've really asked three questions—or a question with three main answers.

"*First*—the Kerala coast had contact with the rest of the world right back to Solomon's time. Ancient Chinese coins buried in the sand indicate a sea route even to China. It was called the Malabar Coast, and was open to new ideas and change.

"Logically, the Apostle Thomas chose this spot, already with its Jewish community. We can't document his arrival in A.D. 52., but we can show you evidence of the seven churches tradition says he founded. When migrant Christians arrived from Mesopotamia, those churches became Syrian Orthodox.[27] But they had no open Bible.

"In 1288, Italy's Marco Polo visited South India, and in 1498 Portugal's Vasco da Gama landed on the Malabar Coast with missionaries. A century later, the King of Portugal sent Francis Xavier as papal legate to this coast.

25. R. Leela Devi, *History of Kerala*, p.286 etc. Kottayam: Vidyarthi Mithram, 1986.
26. Part of Kerala's prosperity came from production of "calico" cloth, named after the city of Calicut.
27. Called "Syrian" to this day because they and their successors use "Syriac," a literary-liturgical language/script—based on an Aramaic dialect used in several Middle East churches.

These all founded Catholic churches, yet for 19 centuries the churches weren't propagating churches. Only after evangelical missionaries arrived did some churches reach out to the unevangelized.

"*Second*—CMS missionaries translated the Bible into Kerala's main language (Malayalam), taught literacy, and in 1817 established our first printing press. *Pallikkudam*, the indigenous word for 'school,' literally means, 'the building next to the church.' Some districts became 100% literate.

"Now, *third*—why did Kerala become Communist? Delhi's government at the time was socialist, and Kerala's seacoast was open to ideas from the rest of the world. The Mahatma said, 'Christian missionaries from overseas taught the nation to read and Communists gave materials to read.' Communists had money to fill the vacuum with colorful literature. When the state was unable to overcome poverty, people thought Communism could."[28]

I thought that over, for I'd heard that Kerala had become one of the most prosperous states in India. For instance, fishing income[29] has greatly improved—surprisingly, the result of using mobile phones! Formerly, catches used to rot in outrigger holds because a fisherman's village would have a glut of catch, while a fishing village up the coast had none. Now fishermen phone each other to find out where the big shoals are, and phone village markets before deciding where to land with their catches.

"One more point," I pressed the patient bishop; "these days, in spite of Kerala's new prosperity, its suicide rate is India's highest. Why?"

"That follows from the spiritual vacuum when people become educated, with high expectations," explained the bishop. "When you call the state 'the most Christian,' remember most are nominal Christians—they don't know God's peace and power. Instead of worshiping him, they worship material things. Those never satisfy the soul."

28. In some respects, Hinduism and Buddhism lend themselves to Communism. Besides, while secular education often freed students from Hindu superstitions (even if they continued rites to protect their caste status), Britain *excluded* Christianity from government education. Many expatriate teachers were atheists, rejecting the Christianity of their homeland. Encouraged by the Enlightenment's rationalism, these tolerated any "superstition except Christianity" (Eds., *One Hundred Years*. London: CMS, 1808).

Hammer and Sickle

A friend I met, K. Mathew Abraham, had been a teenager at the time of Independence. He verified Bishop John's assessment and added some historical background.

"Kerala is a combination of the former kingdoms of Travancore, Cochin, and Malabar," he explained. "When India became a Republic in 1950, a governor replaced the Maharajah as ruler, and in 1957 a free election ushered in the world's first *elected* Communist government.[30]

"**Dr. Rajendra Prasad**, India's President, congratulated Kerala: 'I am happy that this great experiment ... being made in your state, is going to serve as a great lesson ... to the country as a whole, as an example of co-existence ... for the good of all.'

"I saw the red flag of hammer and sickle all over Kerala," Matthew recollected. "I remember shouts of *"Inquilab Zindabad"* ("Long Live Revolution"), as people anticipated a new era of plenty for all. But violent class warfare broke out, as Communist ideology pitted poor villagers against rich landowners. Life for 'the masses' didn't change, as special interest groups opposed land and education reforms. Many unemployed people left for major cities further north."

Matthew also recalled the religious fervor of his early childhood, as Christians, Jews, and Muslims had mixed freely. Hymn singing greeted both sunrise and sunset. Christian worshippers filled the churches. But the new Communist ideology opposed religious groups, often with bloody clashes. Caught up in materialism, many "Christians" became only nominal church members.

"What the prophet Isaiah proclaimed long ago has become true in the case of Kerala," Matthew continued. "'... *These people draw near with their mouths and honor me with their lips, but have removed their hearts far from me.*' Spiritually, Kerala lags behind some other states, although economically it has seen boom times."

---

29. If you buy sardines, they may well have been caught in the teeming waters off Kerala's coast.
30. Speech at **a public meeting in Trivandrum August 14, 1957. —K.M. Abraham note to the author.**

The Malabar Coast (the area's general name) potentially had been one of the brightest hopes for the gospel. Instead, it represented a tragedy in the missionary history of the church. What was the basic cause in Kerala as well as in North Africa and Mongolia? In each case the problem has been similar—no open Bible; therefore no deep roots and no outreach in witness. Believers started well but failed to follow up on Christ's Commission "to go into all the world and preach the gospel." These became ghetto churches, soon swallowed up by other forces.

Those Who Followed in Their Train

In spite of lost centuries, I thanked God for those who have followed in the train of Thomas, India's missionary Apostle. Although after the Resurrection he had demanded proof (and therefore has been dubbed "Doubting Thomas"), he obviously became so convinced that he braved the hazards of this missionary journey in obedience to the final commission of his Lord. What difficulties and dangers he faced back in the first century! He courageously left his homeland and culture, sailed on a frail *dhow* across pirate-infested waters, landed on a hostile coast, and preached the revolutionary gospel in a resistant Jewish colony and fractious Hindu villages!

"Have any of the churches stemming from the work of Thomas experienced spiritual revival?" I asked, returning to Bishop John.

"Some survived as a mixture of Christian backgrounds," Bishop John replied. "By the 1800s, the Syrian Orthodox Church invited CMS missionaries to teach in its Seminary. But the CMS couldn't agree with doctrines such as prayers for the dead, Eucharist (communion) for salvation of the dead, and worship of the Virgin Mary. Before leaving, they mentored a monk named Abraham Malpan. They taught him the Word, and the Lord used Abraham to revive the seminary and the churches. You might say that the Mar Thoma (St. Thomas) churches really took off from that point. Now they're doing missionary work all over India!"

Bishop John sees great opportunities for the gospel. "We have an open Bible now. I spend most of my time preaching the gospel. Traditional Christianity is formal and lifeless—evangelicals are the only hope for reviving it. Our land needs the Word of God!"

Not only the bishop deplored India's moral degeneracy. *The Times of India* quoted a former Chief Justice of the Supreme Court: "The judiciary in India has deteriorated in its standard because judges are appointed [such] as are willing to be influenced by lavish parties and whisky bottles." Another former Chief Justice in Patna stated: "Corruption is now a way of life, and there is corruption in the judiciary also."[31]

Nevertheless, the early missionaries and those who followed them[32] did make a great impact on the South of India. Men such as D. T. Niles,[33] T. Alker, H. Somerwell, and F. R. Hemingway (of the Indian Civil Service) had a wide influence in India as well as overseas. More recent leaders such as Anglican Bishop Stephen Neill have continued to uphold the evangelical message.

Vedanayagam Samuel Azariah (1874-1945)[34] was born in Tirunelveli District in the southern state of Tamil Nadu. He resuscitated his home village and started a grassroots movement to Christianity among the lower castes. Although most villagers wear sandals (if any foot-ware), one caste group, the Nadars[35] were *prohibited* from wearing shoes, or using umbrellas, or milking cows. Through the gospel, Azariah freed these "untouchables" and thousands of others. Although he was the first Indian Anglican bishop, he used common means of transport, including bullock carts and bicycles, to crisscross the sub-continent with the gospel—years before his contemporary, Mahatma Gandhi, opposed the caste system and made his celebrated "Train Tour of India." Secular historians, however, have generally ignored Azariah's influence on India—no doubt because Gandhi was a key political figure.[36]

---

31. Valson Thampu, "Christian Response to Corruption." New Delhi: TRACI, April 1995.
32. RC, Lutheran, CMS, Methodist, Baptist, Salvation Army, Pentecostal, and other denominations.
33. Son of a Congregational/Methodist clergyman in Sri Lanka, Niles was an evangelical ecumenist who insisted there was a "true and essential discontinuity" between Christianity and other faiths.
34. Also mentioned in chapter 6.
35. Nadars, classed among "agricultural workers," were the palmyra tree climbers, collecting sugar-rich sap.
36. Susan Billington Harper, 2000 (see Bibliography).

"Let the Little Children Come to Me"

Bishop Azariah was among church leaders whose work prepared the way for a remarkable woman missionary, Amy Carmichael, when she came to live in Tirunelveli District. An Irish Presbyterian, she had stayed in the home of the founder of the Keswick Convention, and in 1892 became its first missionary. She went to Japan, but after illness, moved to Sri Lanka and then India, where CMS leader Thomas Walker[37] of Tirunelveli greatly influenced her. The need of India's little ones stole her heart, and in 1901 she opened her home to children at risk.[38] "*Amma*" (Mother), everyone called her.

I had more than a passing interest in visiting Dohnavur Fellowship (DF), the work Amy founded. For one thing, a spiritual revival had spread from Dohnavur to other conferences in other parts of the nation—one of the influences that led to the formation of the Evangelical Fellowship of India.[39] But I had a more personal interest: my sister Olive served there for some 36 years.

"Pramila Sitti's *thambi*!" welcomed a dignified woman in rose-colored sari when I arrived there. (I knew that *Pramila* was the name Amma gave my sister, and *thambi* meant *younger brother*.) "I'm Nesaruthina Carunia. Just call me Nesa." Nesa was then president of Dohnavur.[40] She told me that Olive had helped mentor her, the first Dohnavur girl to earn a university degree, and first Indian president of Dohnavur. (Her sister has succeeded her.)

Crowding around Nesa's skirts were olive-skinned children—laughing, clapping, and hopping from one foot to the other in wide-eyed excitement.

37. Walker (1859-1912), chairman of Anglican Tirunelveli District, sought to purge clergy of indiscipline and immorality. He resigned chairmanship to concentrate on evangelism and revival, bringing the Keswick Conference tradition to South India. He was a fervent supporter of Amy Carmichael and Dohnavur. Bishop Steven Neil was another, more recent evangelical leader, who had great respect for Dohnavur.

38. Dohnavur became a center like Ramabai Mukti Mission, founded by Pandita Ramabai (Ch. 7).

39. William Nagenda and Joe Church, from East Africa's Revival (which continued for over 30 years) along with Indian evangelists, visited Dohnavur in the '50s. *People of the Mandate, op. cit.*, p. 158.

40. I use the name to refer to Amy Carmichael's work, and not the adjacent village of Dohnavur.

They offered me bunches of fragrant blossoms and carried my bags to the terracotta brick guest-room, which they'd already festooned with purple *bougainvillea* blossoms. Almond-eyed *accals* ("older sisters") in saris of red, blue, or green shepherded the children. Each had a twist of blossoms in her pulled-back black hair. I noticed these *accals* playing with groups of neatly clothed children—mothering those assigned to their clusters of compound huts.

Between cups of tea and many greetings from staff, Nesa showed me around Dohnavur Fellowship village. Amma's bedroom was much as she had spent the last 20 years of her life—except that senior staff had replaced the wooden bed frame with a circle of chairs for their daily team prayer time. That was fitting: before Amma died, each morning they'd met around her bed to share with her and the Lord the concerns of the larger "family." Only four little square marks, left by layers of wax wiped around the bed legs, reminded us of the 20 years of pain that had crippled Amma. That began in 1931, the night she fell into a pit left uncovered by workmen. Indomitably, she refused to be invalided back to Ireland for surgery. Like her predecessor in India, William Carey, she never returned to her homeland.

Instead, for the latter two decades of her life, the Irish missionary guided the work from her bed—penning some 600 poems, more than 40 books, and personal letters that touched people all over the world.[41] I saw the bedside stool on which my sister had taken her turn communing with Amma, personally learning from this senior disciple of Jesus, while discussing and praying together. A screened veranda surrounded the room on three sides, enabling Amma to look out on a garden of blossoms, songbirds, and butterflies. Sometimes, when a door was left open, a songbird would fly into her room and sit on the end of her bed—even on her shoulder. Birds and flowers figured in many of her poems, for she felt it important to teach children—rescued from hideous abuse—to enjoy God's creation as signs of his love rather than objects of Hindu worship.

On Amy's bedroom wall, I read her favorite motto: *"By one who loveth, is another kindled."* It summarized her life.

41. After another fall in 1948 she became completely bedridden until she died in 1951. She did not have access to today's medications—nor air conditioning to relieve the oppressive humidity.

In stark contrast to birds and butterflies, on another wall was the head of a man-eating tiger! "How did that get on Amy's wall?" I asked, it seemed so incongruous to Amy's gentle, nature-loving poetry. Besides, the children's Hindu background gave great status to a tiger.

"Oh, the beautiful tiger reminds us not only of the Creator but also of his protection," Nesa replied, going on to explain that the golden-furred, black-ringed tiger had killed several villagers before hunters shot it.

"Your God has protected you and your children!" the awed hunters exclaimed as they presented the head to Amy. "We traced his paw prints to the children's open veranda, where they were sleeping on hot nights. We don't know why the tiger didn't snatch any of them!" Amy felt sad the hunters had to kill the magnificent creature, until she discovered it was aged and had lost its incisor teeth—causing the tiger to seek easier prey than wild game. (Game animals there were. I later learned that wild elephants, driven by encroaching settlers and drought, had rampaged through the DF forest, causing staff to flee for their lives.)

"God just patted Old Tiger on the back!" Amma told the children, typically seeking to console them. So the Dohnavur Family viewed the vicious tiger's head mounted on the wall not as a symbol of cruelty, whether of animal to man or man to animal, but rather God's love for his majestic creation and for his trusting children.

Amma had taken in her first child while she lived in Pannaivilai (Tirunelveli District). She moved to a bungalow set in an empty field on the outskirts of Dohnavur village—a field that became a village of its own—with school, hospital, chapel, workshops, and farm. Another community has grown up outside the DF "Village" gates—mostly Palmyra Climbers[42] who had found refuge and God's saving grace. But also outside DF's garden wall is a contrasting counterpart of the Christian Palmyra Climbers: a Hindu temple looms above the garden wall, periodically blaring religious chants and a priest's expositions of Veda classics. Although

42. "Low-caste" palmyra tree climbers, employed to tap and collect the sugar-sweet sap.

these kept me awake at night, they remind the children of what they'd escaped.[43]

No Monument for Amma!

After reading Amma's books, men and women with professional skills wrote to ask if they could help at Dohnavur Fellowship. When Nancy Robbins, a British medical doctor, enquired, she received this up-front information: "We have no salaried workers, Indian or European. . . . We live as a family, each contributing to the good of all."

"I still have Amma's first letter to me when I queried about helping at Dohnavur," recalled Dr. Nancy Robbins. "Her concern was that I should be absolutely certain of God's call—and so should everyone at Dohnavur's end. She could not offer me a big spectacular work, but 'a field in which to die.'"[44]

Volunteers did come—teachers, engineers, doctors, nurses, accountants, and agriculturalists. An Indian environmentalist, great-grandson of one of Amma's first converts,[45] re-organised the farm, using only natural fertilizer, with rotational planting and recycling. Another staffer used the "System of Rice Intensification" (SRI) method developed in Madagascar. A model in environmental care, the farm keeps the Dohnavur Family supplied with eggs, milk, poultry, rice, vegetables, and fruit. Some of the volunteers who came to help never returned to their home countries. I saw their graves in the nearby cemetery.

"Where's Amma's grave?" I asked. "Is it true she asked you not to put up any memorial?"

---

43. Traditionally, Hindus considered "marriage to the gods" (becoming *Devadasi*) the highest honour for daughters, and meritorious. The girls often became temple prostitutes, for (as in ancient religions) many males considered orgasm the consummation of idol worship. To escape that fate for daughters (among other reasons), sometimes mothers sought refuge for their babies. Some older girls fled temples. Though after Independence, Indian's government made *Devadasi* customs illegal, it is difficult to stop (Rashme Sehgal, "Law Unable to Curb Devadasi System in Karnataka." Bangalore: *The Times of India*, 21/12/1999).

44. Jesus' words in John 12.24. Author Elisabeth Elliott used the phrase in the title of her biography, *A Chance to Die* (see Bibliography). Above quote is from Nancy Robbins to WHF, written Jan. 28, 2005.

45. See Carmichael, *Mimosa* (Bibliography).

"That's true!" Nesa replied, waggling her head from side to side. I'd seen my sister do that—the Indian sign of assent. "But since Amma loved birds, before she died she agreed we could place a memorial birdbath in the garden in place of a tombstone. She said that would refresh the birds."

Although Amy was always self-effacing, she had a pragmatic reason for refusing a memorial monument. As she aged, she knew that the children really looked to her as "Mother" with love and respect—perhaps with some awe, which could turn her memory into almost worship, in the context of India's gurus. She had seen Hindu tombs become objects of worship, shrines. She would leave no memorial that would take the glory away from her Lord.

Dohnavur's on-going "memorials" are Indian men and women living for their Lord all over the sub-continent. One couple working with the Bible Society of India had qualms about their son going as a missionary to Himalayan tribes.

"I wouldn't have a godly mother if missionaries hadn't left their country and culture to come to Dohnavur," the young university graduate said. "Mother, you cannot go out as a missionary, but I can go instead of you." His sister, a nurse, regularly sends financial support to the place that raised her mother.

Several "Old Boys" and "Old Girls" (to use a British school term for a former student or member) play the role of grandparents at Dohnavur. One was Vineetha.

"Whom are you looking forward to meet in Heaven?" I asked the frail woman.

"I'll see my grandchildren!" she replied, wrinkles in her face transforming her smile into a wreath. "They're already there, so they will take me to see Jesus! I'm so happy about that!"

I couldn't doubt her happiness. But then Vineetha told me why she was so sure. She'd just had a vision of four men standing beside her bed, each dressed in a different color, holding a book of the same color as his robe. White was the Book of Life. Red, Forgiveness. Green, Remembrance. Black, Judgement.

"Is my name written in your book?" she asked the man in white, who held the Book of Life.

"Yes," he assured her—and with that they all vanished.

"Father, I adore you!" she remembered praising God. Then she had a second vision. She was climbing a ladder, but it had no rungs. When she looked below, she noticed the bottom was cut off. Looking up, she saw that the top was cut off. She wondered how she could be suspended like that in space. But then a voice re-assured her: "You are not going down anymore; you are going to go up." She awoke with assurance of being prepared for heaven.

But little ones were still arriving in Dohnavur.[46] One four-year-old, rescued from a tribal area after a mob had beaten her Indian missionary parents, still had night-mares. Parents working in untamed tribal areas sometimes beg Dohnavur to care for their children, for no child is safe from idolaters who kidnap young boys or girls to sacrifice to their gods.

I saw abandoned baby girls who had been brought in baskets to the caring staff. Seven arrived in one day, but two died. So that new mothers won't kill unwanted girls, government hospitals "thoughtfully" provide baskets on the porch outside delivery rooms—for anyone (or no one) to take. No questions asked. (For poor families, girls are a liability to raise, parents paying for the eventual obligatory wedding and exorbitant dowry. Readily available ultrasound tests lead to increased abortion of female fetuses.)

Staff learn to handle the usual pains of growing up: children aching for attention, rebellious boys, angry teens, romance-hungry girls attracted by preying philanderers. Tense moments send staff and children to prayer

---

46. 2008: Documentation of certain facts are on file but not made public, for security reasons. As part of a nation-wide effort to prevent baby smuggling, a regulation later prohibited Dohnavur receiving any child under two. But after an appeal by Dohnavur, the state government allowed babies already there to stay. The government appreciates Dohnavur's work; Tamil Nadu State follows its pattern of village centers to help women and children. All over India, mothers, fathers, and professionals I met serving their communities with integrity told me they owed their lives and training to Dohnavur.

when men come to claim children, trumping up law court and even government departmental challenges. After several infants were spared being uprooted from their new loving "family," one little girl, only 3½ herself, exclaimed, "We sent a letter to Jesus. He has big hands, and he kept the babies safe!" The children become very attached to each new child, and the staff to all.

Packing my travel bag, I pondered my own sister's leaving a promising career in Canada to live with abused children in a Tamil village. She'd never been physically robust, but she didn't need "fulfillment"—she'd already received a silver cup and a plaque for excellence in her dental nursing. She'd won collegial recognition for her slogan: "Do It Now!" She had many good friends, including Elisabeth Elliot, Amy Carmichael's later biographer. But her highest commitment was to her Savior and Lord, and that meant going anywhere and doing anything she genuinely felt he wanted. It had meant lonely nights, struggles with abused and abusive children, and debilitating illness. (Olive was invalided to Canada twice for treatment of intestinal parasites that resisted treatment.)

Why had she done it, I asked myself. As an attractive single woman, she'd sacrificed much more than I ever had as a missionary. Olive took young women who had grown up in DF, and lived with them in the nearby village where Amy Carmichael had earlier kept her first child. Protected since infancy, these women needed to re-integrate with their own culture and society. So Olive lived as one of them, all her belongings in one small box—sleeping on a mat, shopping in the open market, preparing food, and discussing problems during daily Bible study, until the women were oriented to village life.

"We hated it when your sister woke us early for prayers," Nesa told me, "but she prepared us to face life as adults. We're grateful." Olive suffered small indignities in order to relate to the marginalized women with whom she lived. (For instance, along with her female companions, she would step out of a narrow path into viper-infested grass to allow a man to pass.) After all, Jesus had sat where the people sat, and Olive walked where he walked.

"Let the little children come to me, for of such is the Kingdom," the Lord had told his disciples. For Olive, that meant giving herself in India.

Jesus is still welcoming little children on the Old Spice Road. Right in Dohnavur Village, among the Tamils.

That reminded me: it was evangelist "Tamil David" who challenged CIGM's founder to help evangelize his country. But India was not the evangelist's home country[47]—his people had crossed the narrow Palk Strait to the Buddhist Island state of Sri Lanka.[48] Although I was aware of tensions between Tamils and Singhalese, I had no idea how quickly I'd find myself at a flashpoint of that conflict over there. Wasn't I headed for the peaceful "Pearl of the Indian Ocean"?

---

47. A Salvation Army missionary led Tamil David into deeper life. In 1892 David teamed up with a missionary in Kerala to spark a revival, which spread to other states. (Duewel, *Revival Fire*, 1993, 231).
48. Buddhism crossed from India to Sri Lanka in '03 BC, according to tradition. Instead of passing through the mainland, monks from Northeast India (where the Gautama claimed to have found "Enlightenment") likely arrived along with merchants in coastal dhows.

Dr. Nesaruthina Carunia, first Indian director of Dohnavur Fellowship, cares for shrubs planted around a birdbath–the only "memorial" that DF's founder, Amy Carmichael, would permit to be erected in her honor. "Nesa," raised in Dohnavur, was discipled by the author's sister, Olive.

Serendipity Shattered

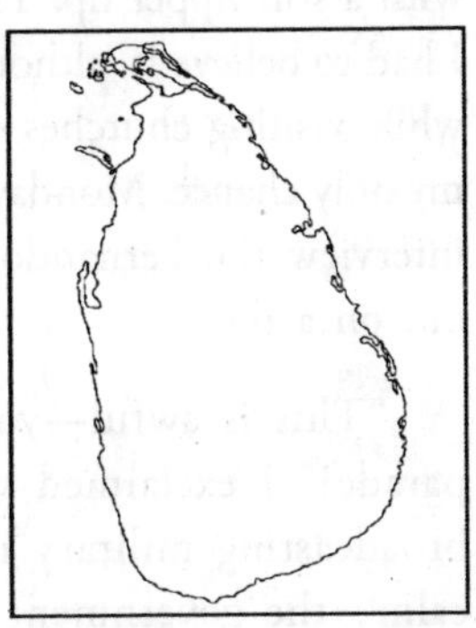

"What though the spicy breezes blow soft o'er Ceylon's isle, though every prospect pleases, and only man is vile?" ("From Greenland's Icy Mountains," Reg. Heber, 1783-1826.)

Sri Lanka: Pop. 20,869,505

"THE PRESIDENT HAS JUST BEEN SHOT!" exclaimed Ajith Fernando. I blinked, trying to take in what I was hearing. I was staying with Dr. Ajith Fernando and his wife, Nelun, in Colombo, capital of Sri Lanka. I'd arrived in the nation's capital on May Day, 1993. Exhausted from my travels, I fell asleep instead of viewing the traditional May Day Parade, which was to pass nearby. I knew I needed to be rested for next day's church services. Now, stumbling out of the guest room, I expected the cup of tea Nelun had promised. But Ajith wasn't announcing teatime.

"*The President was leading the May Day parade, when an assassin walked up and shot him!*" Ajith exclaimed. "Only a couple of blocks away from us! The whole city is under military curfew. Everyone is ordered to stay off the streets."

If I hadn't fallen asleep, I would have been out with my photojournalism juices flowing, getting as close as possible to the President for an action photo. How could this happen in this "Resplendent Land,"[1] known for its gentle people? How could such violence take place among a highly literate population, one with income per head twice that of India's.

1. Meaning of "Sri Lanka," 270 miles (434 km.) long by 140 miles (225 km.) wide, off India's South tip.

"Colombo is closed down for mourning and security!" Ajith made it clear. "We won't be able to have the Sunday services we'd lined up for you to speak at tomorrow."

"Well, the Lord knows what we should do this weekend!" I replied with a stiff upper lip. That was the pious thing to say, I figured. Anyway, I had to believe it, although I'd looked forward to worshiping in Sri Lanka while visiting churches on Sunday. With my tight schedule, it was to be my only chance. Monday I had to fly north. But right now, I could at least interview the Fernandos while sipping the orange pekoe tea Nelun set out on a tray.

"This is awful—your President shot while leading the May Day parade!" I exclaimed when Ajith turned off the radio. It had been broadcasting military marches between calls for everyone to remain calm—the government was in charge. "How can this happen on the island that Arabs called 'Serendib'?"[2] I asked.

"You know our history!"[3] answered Ajith. "Actually, generations of Buddhist Sinhalese and Hindu/Christian Tamils lived peacefully together for years—proud of our island. Since Independence, however, many Sinhalese see Tamils as intruders, and feel that British colonisers favored them; some Tamils feel neglected by the economy. A militant group, the Tamil Tigers, sought a homeland, or at least self-government, for the northeast of the Island. It was a situation somewhat like Cyprus. But let's not get into politics!"

"Agreed," I responded, coming back to my purpose for being there. "So tell me about what CIGM did here. I'm curious why they left. I've read how Tamil David from Sri Lanka challenged the Scot, Benjamin Davidson, who had been in business in Ceylon, to return as a missionary to help evangelize the island."

---

2. From this name, British writer Horace Walpole coined the word "serendipity" in his 1754 fairy tale, "The Three Princes of Serendip." In it, happy discoveries came about by chance.
3. Singhalese (probably Aryans from the Indus River area) arrived by sea (600 to 300 BC?) and imposed their caste culture upon the aborigines. Tamils (Dravidians) emigrated from India in early A.D. centuries. The President's death was just one of a series of continuing political assassinations.

I'd read of the great missionary heritage pioneers such as John and Harriet Scudder had left in the Ceylon of the 1800s. Dr. John, an ardent evangelist and medical missionary,[4] founded a hospital in Jaffna, day and boarding schools, and a medical school. The major denominations had set the pace for missions. But I was curious about the rise of non-denominational agencies. In 1883, Davidson landed in Colombo with eleven volunteers."[5]

Within a year those 12 opened two bases in Sri Lanka and three in India. Tamil David led them across the narrow Palk Strait to India. I wondered where they had worked in Sri Lanka, and why they soon left the island. Had Ceylon's currency exchange regulations made it difficult to maintain a central office there, for sending funds on to the work in India? Were there other reasons? We may never know. Without thinking, a CIGM couple had later found boxes of old papers up in the rafters of the mission bungalow and thrown them out. Those happened to be CIGM's pioneer journals and archives—lost to posterity!

"As far as I can assume," Ajith said as Nelun poured him another cup of tea; "CIGM noted that Methodists on the island were strongly evangelical at the time, so Davidson turned over the work to them.[6] CIGM's ministries in Hindu India were growing more rapidly than in Buddhist Sri Lanka. India would soon require all their resources of people and finance."[7]

---

4. American Board of Commissioners for Foreign Missions. Scudder's children became missionaries; but granddaughter Ida rejected mission life—till three girls died at her doorstep in childbirth. Becoming an outstanding surgeon, she founded "wayside clinics" for poor areas and the Medical and College Hospital, Vellore, Asia's largest medical center. Her nursing school became India's first graduate nursing school.

5. The granddaughter of one was from our home church. CIGMers Doris and Bruce Sinclair became members of SIM when the two missions merged. They'd worked near the village where Doris' parents were buried.

6. One CIGM missionary, Bruce Kerr, became an independent missionary so he could stay in Sri Lanka.

7. "CIGM founder Davidson's heart was always in South India," pioneer Raymond Castro, author of *Advancing Together* (see Biblio.), later wrote me (Aug. 14, 2000). "Ceylon was a sort of stepping stone." He moved to Bangalore, being central to Deccani-Urdu, Kannada, Marathi, Tamil, Telegu and others.

"That reminds me," I said, scooping up a handful of freshly roasted cashews. "When I visited Chennai, I asked Theodore Williams if India still needed expatriate missionaries. What's your opinion about Sri Lanka? After all, missions have been around for a long time, and you have strong evangelical groups."

"We're thankful for all that," replied Ajith. "And of course our needs are different from a century ago, in Tamil David's day. Each generation has to assess its spiritual needs. Do you know where expat missionaries would fit in now? Asia has lots of zealous young believers, but the pressure on experienced leaders is enormous. We're called to lead churches, speak at conferences, train future pastors, train evangelists. You know, I'm even thankful when I have to fly overseas to speak, because I find time to meditate, reflect, read, and rest while traveling!

"The kind of missionary we need is a mature servant leader who can mentor men and women for ministry—to teach our future leaders the Word, applied in daily life."

Rediscovering Culture

I asked this quiet but vibrant leader how he himself had found the Lord. His devout Methodist mother had been saved out of Buddhism. Ajith followed all the rituals of Christianity—prayer, Bible reading, worship—but had no assurance, only great spiritual wrestling. One night at 2 a.m., aged 14, he woke his mother to complain he couldn't pray.

"That's because of your sins!" she told him. "Repent and give your life to Christ."

"And you did!" I chimed in. "But how did you know that Jesus had saved you?"

"Until then, I had a terrible temper. That gradually went, and I found great peace. Right away, I wanted to become a preacher, and I wanted to write! Our minister was a godly Irishman who helped me grow spiritually. The story of the missionary to China, Hudson Taylor, and others inspired me."

Graduating from a University near Colombo with a Biology degree, Ajith went on to study at Asbury Theological Seminary, USA. He took further studies at Fuller Seminary, earning an M.Th. When he returned to Sri Lanka in 1976, he became national Director of Youth for Christ. In that role, he's made a great impact at home and also overseas. I'd heard him preach, and I had several of his books.

"The Portuguese, Dutch, and then the English Europeanized Sri Lanka as a colony," Ajith went on to explain. "Christians worshiped just like Western church members. We were comfortably Europeanized! Many became Christian for status and economic gain, but they lost sight of the uniqueness of Jesus. After Independence, most mainline churches rushed to disassociate themselves from the colonialists by becoming pluralistic and liberal in theology. To seem tolerant, they threw out Christ's uniqueness; however, they lost the heart of the gospel. Overseas, liberal theologians held up Sri Lankans as models of tolerant ecumenism. We got along fine with everybody—but we weren't reaching the hearts of Sri Lankans!"

"Why don't you have the same mentality?" I asked. "After all, you were raised in an ex-colony and you studied in the West."

"You know how most anthropologists accuse missionaries of destroying culture?" Ajith continued. "In my case, it was a *missionary* who helped me *reclaim* my culture! Professor J.T. Seamands of Asbury had been a missionary and convinced me how important culture should be to me as a Christian and in reaching others. Until then, Christians rarely witnessed to the unsaved. We got along fine with everybody, but precious people were going into eternity without even hearing about Christ's salvation! The churches were dwindling too."

"So how did you break through that indifference?" I asked.

"Believe it or not, music was the initial way," Ajith explained. "Although Buddhists don't use it much, Sri Lankans really love their own music. So for a couple of years I cut myself off from foreign music. I studied only local music. We held music concerts. Some 6,000 people flocked to our first concert in a park—not massed choirs, but small groups singing the gospel to indigenous tunes.

"Since many of our churches had become liberal in theology, the Lord used para-church organizations to revive us. In the '70s, Back to the

Bible Broadcast, Youth for Christ, Campus Crusade, and others helped revive churches. Because they're interdenominational, they've helped all churches, teaching methods and practising evangelism."

After attending a student mission conference in Holland (similar to InterVarsity's Urbana in North America), Fernando and his colleagues started *Navodaya*, meaning "dawn of a new era," among the churches. They were surprised when 900 attended the first conference, 1500 the next—and the numbers kept growing. Many who've attended the Navodaya conferences are now out evangelizing. "Music and the challenge of Christ's commission play a big part in this movement," Ajith added.

"You're working among youth a lot," I noted. "Are they any different nowadays from when you were a youth?"

"*Are they!*" Ajith exclaimed. "Your country has taken decades for social values to change, but here it's been almost overnight! Media from the West have promoted sexual licence, so now pornography, rape, and teenage pregnancy are common. Migrant workers leave their families without moral controls."

Compassion for Buddhists

The phone rang and Ajith had to handle several urgent calls, so I helped myself to more Sri Lankan tea. Ah, this was the real thing: "Ceylon Pekoe."[8] A few hours earlier, I'd flown in over rolling green hills of tea plantations—planted in rows like a woman's plaited hair. Outwardly, Sri Lanka lived up to its title of "The Pearl of the Indian Ocean." But this Buddhist state was a puzzle to me. On a hilltop overlooking Colombo was a mammoth stone statue of the Buddha, squatting in traditional meditative pose, the picture of calm.

Yet tensions were especially high on this "Pearl," I knew. The month of May was an auspicious month for Buddhists. Siddhartha, the Gautama Buddha, became "enlightened" during May's full moon, a holy day (*Wesak*),

8. Pekoe: Chinese *pek-ho*, new growth of tea. "Orange" Pekoe: small and tender orange-blush top leaves. The traditional tea plant (*Camellia sinensis*) is native to Asia, and has assumed various names from the areas in which it is grown, and from the process used to prepare its leaves (*e.g.* "black" or "green" tea). Sri Lanka is ideal for growing tea, which does best in warm humidity, on hillsides providing drainage.

and died on an anniversary of that day. Sri Lankans mark *Wesak* with three days of abstinence (no meat, drink, or alcohol; no lying, robbing, or other misbehavior) and celebration—banners, lanterns, and balloons. Shops and even tourist hotels close.

"How do you reach out to Buddhists?" I asked when Ajith returned from his phone calls.

"We have many good friends who are Buddhists," Ajith replied. "It's important to respect their values and to show them compassion,[9] even as we hold to the supremacy of Christ."

"Is the colonial background a barrier?"

"*Big* problem!" Ajith replied. "You can understand, because some early colonists forced people to become 'Christians' or lose their land. Of course, we don't believe in the use of force or enticement—faith in Christ must be a free choice of the heart. But each week some newspaper will publish an inflammatory article charging that churches are paid agents. That's ridiculous, because the government supports Buddhist institutions, not churches, which are much poorer.

"Then our critics allege we're 'buying' poor people to convert—but both poor and rich are coming to Christ. And the funny thing is that relatives of new Christians complain about just the opposite—family members who become Christians aren't given anything. Relatives see the Christians 'slaving away witnessing to others without any monetary reward!' They can't understand a person's turning to Christ only out of inner conviction. Actually, this view is the thinking of many people—low self-esteem, and material benefit. Sri Lankans have a welfare mentality—receive, receive, receive. Even when beggars come to us, they say, 'You are doing yourself a favor by helping me!' Merit, in other words."

"Are Buddhists fatalistic?" I wondered.

"Well, to some extent, because whatever happens is the result of previous *karma.* Although Buddhist fatalism is not in the absolute sense of Islam's—that whatever Allah has decided will happen and cannot be

9. Fernando calls for such attitudes in *The Christian's Attitude Toward World Religions* (see Biblio.).

changed. Buddhists hope to change their fate in the next life through doing good deeds in this life. Their goal is to attain "Enlightenment," as they believe Siddhartha Gautama did.[10]

"So how do you witness to them *effectively*?" I pressed.

"We show friendship and love within our communities," Ajith explained. "We must never be blatant or arrogant. But we still must declare the uniqueness of Christ, even if that doesn't make us popular. I wrote my Master's thesis on 'Universalism.'[11] I wanted to show why the gospel itself is unique. Honest Buddhists or Hindus admit they can't buy or earn salvation, because of human weakness.

"Buddhism believes in a kind of evolution and doesn't accept the thought of a transcendental God, so the gospel causes people to think new thoughts about God and Creation. Grace is also a new concept. Answers to prayer are convincing—a number of people come to Christ after seeing answers to prayer."

While Buddhists appear to be placid souls, I learned that many live in fear of doing anything not approved by their ancestral spirits.[12] That includes the way they walk, talk, eat, and other activities. Too bad that Christians are not nearly as concerned about living in a way pleasing to their Lord, I mused, even though there is no saving merit in doing so.

Curfew Lifted!

Just then the phone rang. After hanging up, Ajith was smiling. "The curfew will be lifted at dawn, so churches can hold their services," he announced happily. "Praise the Lord!"

The next morning as the Fernandos took me to several churches, the streets were largely deserted, except for knots of gun-toting soldiers at

---

10. I hoped later to visit the village in India where Siddhartha Gautama is reputed to have found Enlightenment, making him The Buddha. See Ch. 10; also Appendix F: Religion, Buddhism, for detail.

11. Gordon-Conwell Theological Seminary, Boston, presented Fernando an honorary doctorate for his extensive work on the topic, including "The Uniqueness of Christ in a Pluralistic World."

12. Since the 80s, suicide rates have increased by eating yellow oleander seeds.

main intersections. Neat little shops with signs in Sinhalese calligraphy lined downtown streets. On a garden wall, I noted graffiti, including a Buddhist/Aryan swastika. The Marxist Worker's Union had scrawled a hammer and sickle. We passed a church Ajith said had Marxist leanings. I asked how that could be.

"When that church lost the uniqueness of Christ, Marxism posed as the solution to human problems," he explained. "Evangelicals need to show that the unique Christ embraces poor and unjustly treated alike."

I noted the respect churches gave Ajith. They looked to him for leadership as Honorary President of Sri Lanka's Evangelical Alliance (EASL). Earlier, EASL had been a meeting place chiefly for educated English-speaking churches. Now members include many who are uneducated and don't speak English. EASL has a role in strengthening these new rural Christians. Ajith insists that all its conferences must be held in both Sinhalese and Tamil.

Three churches had invited me to preach that morning. Starting out at 8 a.m., we went from one to the other. I learned from each, thanking God for their loving-yet-sure stand for the unique Christ in a pluralistic nation. Each was full—and different: Methodist, Community Fellowship, and Bakht Singh Assembly.[13] I also met the General Secretary of EASL. He told me that although there are some 36,000 villages in Sri Lanka, fewer than one thousand have any Christian presence. But EASL is encouraging outreach, equipping pastors with study materials, and providing help for thousands of displaced refugees, whatever their religion. This lack of discrimination has impressed people.

I asked the EASL leader about backlash from Buddhists, who seem so gentle.

---

13. Born a Sikh, Bakht Singh (1903-2000) hated Christianity, turned atheist before finding the Saviour. A dynamic Bible teacher supported solely "by faith," he led worship in New Testament simplicity, planting Assemblies across India. His godly life, faith, vision, and indigenous principles influenced evangelicals in India and the West. Billy Graham asked Bakht Singh to open his Madras (Chennai) crusade with prayer. Benji Devadason, leader of SIM's Tamil ministries in Canada, once pastored a Bakht Sing assembly.

"They *are* gentle," he replied, kicking off his sandals as we sat under a shade tree. "But as Buddhists started coming to Christ in greater numbers, radicals attacked us. They've put pressure on the government to write an anti-conversion law.[14] In one village where a number of people turned to Christ, a mob attacked a gospel center and injured the staff. But they weren't typical. Other villagers came to defend the Christians, because we were part of the community. Several Buddhists came to sleep in our center overnight, to protect it against further violence. As Christians stand for truth, they can expect persecution and suffering—Jesus foretold that! It's good for praying friends to understand what is happening."

I wanted to ask a Buddhist about his views of life and death. A business man, Sri —, "enlightened" me.

"Do Buddhists pray to Buddha?" I asked.

"No—not as a god," Sri replied. "We only pay Buddha respect as the 'Enlightened One.'

In our ancient *Pali* language I thank him for showing the right way of living—right thinking, right speech, and right action. That leads to Enlightenment, so the mind is most important. There is no god, no mediator. Buddha told people he couldn't even save his own mother—we all are responsible for our own actions."

Sri said he does pray for his wife and children. "Who helps them?" I asked.

"I don't know who helps them," Sri admitted, for a moment looking a little helpless. "There are things we do not know. I don't know what I was in my previous existence, nor what I shall be in the next. When I'm dead, I'm dead. There's no possibility of forgiveness, for there is no God to forgive us. We pay for our own sins. The best we can do is to repent of our misdeeds, and to balance them with good deeds."

"*I don't know!*" rang in my ears as I headed back to the Fernandos' home.

14. The government was considering an Anti-Conversion Bill, but left it in abeyance following the 2004 *tsunami,* which brought massive assistance and compassion from the West.

Unique Christ or Universal Brotherhood?

"You mentioned that the ecumenical movement had once looked to Sri Lanka as a model for religious tolerance," I reminded Ajith. "Although recent events have shattered that concept, I remember when the Indian sub-continent was "Exhibit A" to show how different religions could dialogue together. In fact, there are church leaders, even a few famous evangelists, who think Buddhism, Hinduism, Islam, and Christianity are only different approaches to God and thus can live together in peace. How can those leaders think that way?"

"People are having second thoughts!" Ajith responded. "Of course, it's true that God 'has not left himself without testimony' throughout history. The Apostle Paul reminded idol worshipers in Lystra of that. On Mars Hill, in Athens, he recognized man's search for truth, even quoting pagan philosophers as an introduction to preaching the gospel of Jesus Christ. When I'm preaching to a non-Christian group, I often do the same, quoting one of their traditional proverbs.

"As I wrote in my book, *The Uniqueness of Christ*,[15] churches that deny Christ as the only way of salvation, can easily relate to non-Christian beliefs. When Christianity and colonialism were being lumped together, church leaders wanted to be pluralistic, accepting every faith as valid. Other faiths do have worthy values, but they don't have a Saviour who gave himself to redeem us from sin."

"What do you want Christians overseas to do for Sri Lanka?" I asked Ajith and Nelun Monday morning as I threw my things into the two small bags that held everything I was travelling with. It was time to go.

"Ask them to pray for us," they replied without hesitation. "Don't just pray for evangelism—pray for depth of teaching in our churches, and for our leadership training program. Our up-coming leaders are going to face tougher times in the future. Ask people to pray for strength and grace for pastors and their family members—many of them widows and orphans. They sometimes feel very much alone in all the ethnic and religious violence."

15. See Ajith Fernando, in Bibliography.

As we headed to the airport, we passed police barricades still blocking off the area where the terrorist had killed the President only 36 hours earlier.

Believers Are Not a Forgotten Island

I commended the World Evangelical Alliance (WEA) for demonstrating the concern of Christians worldwide, by presenting the annual Religious Liberty Award to the courageous widow of a pastor murdered in the Buddhist south of the island.[16] After her husband's death, she continued his ministry. In the north, Hindu radicals had slit the throats of a pastor and one of his church members. Sri Lankan evangelicals were proving the words of John's Revelation: "They overcame him by the blood of the Lamb and by the word of their testimony; they did not love their lives so much as to shrink from death" (Rev. 12:11).

Sitting in the airport departure lounge, I thanked the Lord for Ajith and Nelun Fernando, who so clearly stand for Christ as the One who is uniquely "the way, the truth, and the life."[17] I also had time to think more about Ajith's comments on religious unity.

As my Sri Lankan host had said, Christendom and other religions get along just fine, as long as Christians don't witness about Jesus the Redeemer. When they do, the liberal ecumenical chimera vaporizes, because other faiths reveal their rejection of the unique Christ. Jesus had forecast that.[18] "Christendom's" denial of the gospel's core truths failed to gain any greater acceptance for the gospel. Yet remarkably, the Grand Illusion persists! I recalled how one church denomination in India opened its synod with prayers in the name of the Hindu god Shiva, the Gautama Buddha, Islam's Allah, as well as Jesus Christ. No doubt the synod felt a cozy sense of ecumenical brotherhood and tolerance.

I noted how Sri Lankan evangelicals promote respect and friendship between people of all faiths, yet without compromising faith in the

16. Sponsored in 1988 by Friends of the Martyrs, which assists persecuted Christians in difficult areas.
17. John 14.6. For discussion on good in every religion vs. the uniqueness of Christ, see Appendix F.
18. John 15.18,19. In spite of that, Jesus also told his disciples to be "wise as serpents and harmless as doves" (Matt. 10.16). For more on witness to followers of other faiths, see Appendix D.

unique Son of God as Saviour. I also realized how well-meaning people can confuse values for beliefs: common values are indeed shared among several religions, but Christian belief trusts in Christ's sacrifice that provides eternal life. In substituting "common values" for "biblical truths," people can develop a romantic view of religion. Not wanting to be doctrinaire or divisive, they may overlook systems that deny the gospel. What, for instance, does a religion really mean by using familiar terms such as God, salvation, faith, or grace? Semantics can so mislead!

Sri Lanka helped me realize that the true nature of a religion or system of morality shows up when its adherents reveal their hatred of the gospel. Mobs incited by religious leaders continue to kill pastors, destroy property, and intimidate worshipers. Politicians get involved by passing sectarian bills that restrict freedom of speech and of association.

"Flight 104 to Calcutta is ready for boarding!" The loudspeaker announcement shattered my reverie.

It seemed a long weekend—so much had happened. But as my flight lifted off, I was sorry to say "Goodbye" to this idyllic island off the southern tip of India. It had inspired the hymnist Reginald Heber to write of it, "... where every prospect pleases, and only man is vile." Sri Lanka (smaller than Eire or New Zealand's North Island) truly is the "Pearl of the Indian Ocean." However, I'd seen something of the violent tides swirling around it: Buddhist transcendentalism, Hindu idolatry, socialist ideology, capitalist trade, Christian liberal theology, ethnic violence—and in addition, satellites were beaming down the decadent values of the West.

Yet Jesus stands ready to say to people tossed by society's swirling tides: "Peace, be still!"

* * * *

Caught Up in the Holy Spirit's Network

ON INDIA'S SOUTHWEST COAST, I'd learned about the nation's first missionary, the Apostle Thomas of the first century A.D. Now I headed to Calcutta, on the northeast border of India, to learn about the work of another pioneer, decades later. William Carey is sometimes called "the Father of Modern Missions." The label sets an arbitrary time line, but the title likely arose from Carey's "Manifesto for Modern Protestant Missions" drafted in 1792. He wrote this before he became a foreign missionary—solely on the basis of understanding Christ's Commission and his disciples' responsibilities. Without doubt, the work William Carey and his colleagues accomplished was prodigious.

I needed to understand Carey's missionary calling in the context of the Holy Spirit's long-range strategy. Few people realize that Carey first set sail for India with an experienced lay missionary, Dr. John Thomas. In fact, even before Carey and Andrew Fuller initiated the Baptist Missionary Society, Dr. Thomas, a former naval surgeon, was ministering in India. He got there as a ship's doctor with the East India Company but stayed in Bengal to treat the sick, learn the language, and translate the first two Gospels into Bengali—while telling as many as possible about Jesus the Redeemer.

Returning to England, Dr. Thomas started a fund for a mission to Bengal, East India. Hearing of him, William Carey told Andrew Fuller, Secretary of their fledgling Baptist Missionary Society—and the Mission accepted John Thomas as their *first* missionary. Thomas again set out for India, but this time with a "suitable companion"—William Carey, the second candidate![19] The invaluable experience of the one complemented the zeal of the other, and both fulfilled the missionary vision God had given them.

I learned that there's much more to the Holy Spirit's networking in the subcontinent. How many know about the missionary vision of the King of Denmark and Norway (yes, they were both under one ruler at the time) before Thomas and Carey were born?

A century before Carey's arrival, Frederick IV, a devout Protestant, appealed for missionaries to evangelize his colonies in India. In 1706, German missionary Bartholomew Ziegenbalg responded, arriving in the Danish colony, Tranquebar (on the east coast, south of Madras/Chennai).

19. Mary Drewery, *William Carey* (see Bibliography). These fascinating details in no way diminish Carey's contribution to missiology. (Anyway, he would never have accepted prominence.) Rather, history should encourage us to recognize God's sovereign hand in the global spread of the gospel. Our part is to obey.

He translated the Bible into Tamil and established a missionary seminary. In other parts of the world, Count Nicholas Zinzendorf and his Moravian Brethren were "modern missionaries" who preceded Carey's era.[20] When did "the Modern Era of Missions" really begin, anyone?

A millennium earlier, first-century Nestorian missionaries were taking the gospel throughout much of Asia. I was following the trail of another traveller, Cosmos, who found Christians in Sri Lanka in A.D. 525. He tracked down others on the Old Spice Road along the Ganges Valley, and in North Vietnam and Thailand.[21] Did they have flaws? Yes. Do we as missionaries today have flaws? In spite of these, the Holy Spirit still allows us to participate in his global network. My research was underlining that we "know-it-all" 21st century missionaries should walk humbly.

Dates and eras aside, I realized that God has commissioned his missionaries throughout history, and has not been limited by race, nationality, or church denomination. Christian work in the subcontinent—from the Apostle Thomas through to today's resourceful missionaries—has made a significant impact on the work of the church worldwide.

As I flew northward, high above this fascinating sub-continent, in my shirt pocket was a special reason for visiting Calcutta and William Carey's nearby base at Serampore. In my heritage was another, personal reason.

---

20. Zinzendorf's motto: "I have but one passion: it is He, He only." Both Zinzendorf and Ziegenbalg were influenced for missions while at the pietistic University of Halle in Germany, to which Frederick had appealed for missionaries. King Frederick later founded a college to prepare missionaries.

21. Alex G. Smith, *Siamese Gold*. Bangkok: Kanok Bannasan (OMF), 1982, p. 23.

Sitting in William Carey's chair at the pioneer's desk, the author muses on Carey's legacy, such as banning widow-burning, opposing social apartheid, and urging self-government —plus translating the Scriptures into 44 languages/dialects as well as establishing Serampore Theological College.

Carey's Stamp on India[1]

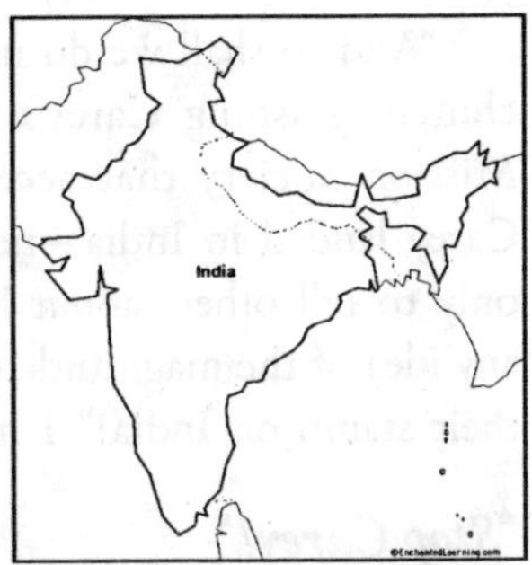

"Is not this the kind of fasting I have chosen: to loose the chains of injustice and untie the cords of the yoke, to set the oppressed free...?" (Isaiah 58.6—favorite Scripture of Christians in India.)

FLYING INTO CALCUTTA airport, I felt in my shirt pocket to make sure something I'd retrieved from my carry-on baggage was there—a precious postal stamp. I'd searched for the stamps in a number of post offices: in Delhi, Mumbai, Chennai, and Bengaluru. That issue was sold out, everyone told me. But at last I found it: a six-rupee stamp commemorating the 200th anniversary of the arrival of a missionary in India! Rather surprising, to find a missionary on any government's postage, I thought. But the face on this bit of philately was William Carey's.

India's President launched the issue in 1993. These days—in the political ferment and religious tension of the Indian sub-continent, it seemed incredible: Carey (1761-1834), a balding English leather worker, an evangelist—honoured with a national stamp? Gandhi and Nehru had each appeared on stamps—understandably. But an English *missionary*?

That little gummed rectangle held additional meaning for me. A distant namesake, Andrew Fuller,[2] attended the Baptist church where

1. *Candle in the Dark,* produced by Ken Curtis of *Christian History films,* portrays Carey's life, now available in English and six major Indian languages.
2. "Fuller"—common family name among Huguenots, hounded out of Normandy, France, because of their Protestant faith and commercial success. A century after Andrew Fuller's missionary plea, my father, William Fuller (member of the same church that Carey had earlier attended) applied for China. Turned down medically, he ministered among settlers in Canada but prayed his children might be missionaries.

Carey had pled on behalf of the unevangelized.[3] A clergy told him, in essence, to shut up. "Sit down, young man!" he shouted. "When God pleases to convert the heathen, he will do it without your aid or mine." Such was the hyper Calvinism of the era, which both Carey and Fuller opposed.

"And so shall we do nothing?" Andrew asked on the way out of the church, grasping Carey's arm. In 1792 they helped form the Baptist Mission Society that accepted William Carey for India. A year later, Carey landed in India—never to return to his homeland. Carey wanted only to tell others about his Saviour. But neither he nor his board had any idea of the magnitude of the revolution they were starting. "They left their stamp on India!" I mused, fingering my six-rupee collector's item.

"Stop Carey!"

The sprawling metropolis (now renamed Kolkata) I flew into wasn't the squalid city Carey arrived in. No president would have been there to honor him with a postage stamp! In fact, the orders were out: "Stop Carey!" Earlier, the East India Company (Britain's trade agent and *de facto* administrator) wouldn't even let the little Cobbler board a ship for India.[4] The company threatened to revoke the sailing license of any ship that gave him passage. Contrary to the popular allegation that missionaries were agents of the colonizers, British agents didn't want meddlesome missionaries talking nonsense about liberty and justice—or Jesus! They might upset merchants and oppressive religions.[5]

That didn't stop Carey. He boarded a Danish cargo ship for the arduous, six-month voyage (stopping at many ports-of-call) around West,

---

3. Awakening vision for world evangelization took years. Influenced by American Jonathan Edwards' mid-century treatises on Free Will and Missions Carey and Fuller opposed Predestination. In 1784, Fuller published an essay: "The Gospel Worthy of All Acceptation," and in 1791 preached, "The Pernicious Influence of Delay in Religious Concerns." In 1792, Carey published his "radical" treatise: "An Enquiry into the Obligations of Christians to Use Means for the Conversion of the Heathens." He followed this up with his ringing message: "Expect Great Things; Attempt Great Things," based on Isaiah 54:2.
4. The same company had opposed the earlier work of Ziegenbalg among Tamils (Ch. 9).
5. F.A. Cox, *Baptist Missions.* London: T. Ward & Co., 1842, records Fuller's backing of Carey amid vested UK opposition. (A resultant meeting in London, termed "the cradle of the missionary society," led to 1795 founding of London Missionary Society. –*Ibid,* p. 103.)

South, and East Africa, across the Arabian Sea, past Sri Lanka, and up into the Bay of Bengal, to Calcutta (as it was then known)—at that time capital of British India. Unwelcome in British territory, Carey camped in India's Bengali villages until he made the Danish enclave of Serampore his headquarters in 1800. Jesus was a carpenter's son. The missionary he sent to Rome was a tentmaker. The one he chose to do his work in Bengal was a shoe-repairer.

Now I found Kolkata bulging with 18m people—2m living on the streets. I flagged the Bengali driver of one of the city's ubiquitous, made-in-India yellow taxis to drive me to Serampore, about an hour away. As the cabby negotiated streams of vehicles, cyclists, and people streaming between the close-up rows of tiny shops, tropical air sagged from the sullen sky like damp burlap. I wanted to punch a hole in the atmosphere so I could breathe. This was the squalid city (ironically known as "The City of Joy") to which Mother Teresa and her companions sought to bring some final joy for terminally ill humanity, through their Missionaries of Charity order.[6] Unfortunately, in spite of the Albanian Roman Catholic nun's commendable dedication, her recently published diaries reveal her own lack of joy because of anxiety, even doubting God's existence.

The monsoon rains had started. Kolkata is the world's largest city most vulnerable to tidal flooding. But poking through the tropical smog was a backdrop of glitzy high-rises—the new "shiny India." Earlier, Kolkata had deteriorated after losing its status as India's national capital, but now it competed with other major cities for a share of the world's expanding technology market. From one of those corporate towers, industrialist Yogesh Deveshwar says he's transforming "the rural life of India" through the E-*Chaupal*.[7] "Distance has been killed!" exclaimed one farmer, who uses the Internet to check out the futures market, whether in Chennai or Chicago, for the soybeans he grows. Now he's no longer at the mercy of high-take village brokers. Kentan Sempat, president of Intel India, believes the nation is "on the cusp" of a rural transformation.

---

6. Before Teresa arrived, an Assembly of God couple, Mark and Hulda Buntain, had arrived from USA to found the Calcutta Mission of Mercy. An SIM Africa pioneer, John Hall, had challenged them to give their lives in missionary service. Globalization? God has his own international networks!

7. *Chaupal*: "public space", where villagers of all ranks and ages can sit together and discuss anything.

Right now I was looking forward to exploring the source of a major spiritual transformation that began two centuries ago in Serampore. My sister Olive (retired from Dohnavur) had introduced me by letter to Dr. J. Thomas K. Daniel and his wife Beulah. Earlier, Olive had known Thomas in the South, where he'd found Christ through a Scripture Union camp. For a short period, he became General Secretary of Friends Missionary Prayer Band. He, Olive, and others prayed together for revival in the North, never dreaming that one day Thomas would become President of Serampore College, India's most historic academic institution, founded in 1818 by William Carey.

Emergency Heart Surgery

"*Welcome to Serampore!*" Dr. Daniel's voice rang out as I arrived at the College. "Just call us Thomas and Beulah." No stuffed shirts, these! Beulah soon put before us tea and fresh-baked *chapattis*, served on their cool verandah overlooking the Hugli, a channel in the Ganges's vast delta. From that same verandah some two centuries earlier, Carey had watched in horror as mothers pushed their infants down the opposite river bank to their death, sacrificing them to fulfill vows or assuage sins. Responding to Carey's protests, in 1804 the British administration made this religious practice illegal.

"That point is called the Gandhi Ghat,"[8] Thomas explained, motioning across the river. "It had always been considered a sacred spot, so Mahatma Gandhi's ashes were scattered on the river from across there."

"But," I interrupted, "my guide at Cape Comorin said *the Mausoleum* there contains the urn for Gandhi's ashes."

"That's right—and the *urn* is still there," explained my host, "but the government later transferred the *ashes* here, to the waters of the sacred Ganges Delta."

This delightful couple told me how God had led them to Serampore. Confirmation came through Thomas' amazing recovery from a serious

8. *Ghat*: (Hindi/Urdu) broad steps on a river's bank—used in religious rituals.

heart attack. That happened in USA, where the Billy Graham Center Director, James Kraakevik[9] had invited him for the bicentennial of William Carey's arrival in India.

Without warning, two blocked arteries threatened Thomas' life. His vision for Serampore College back in India seemed about to evaporate. But the Graham Center arranged emergency bypass surgery.

"Usually people in your condition aren't brought in alive!" the doctor told Thomas as he came out of the anesthetic. He would ever be grateful he'd been staying in the home of Lynn and Jim Kraakevik at the time of the attack, and that he could recuperate in the country home of their friends, David and Phyllis Howard of (at the time) World Evangelical Alliance. To Thomas, the remarkable timing, arrangements, and care all confirmed that God would enable him for the task ahead.

Sleeping in Carey's Bedroom

"This is where you'll sleep," announced the Daniels, showing me around the rambling colonial-style building. The bed in the high-ceilinged room had a mosquito net suspended from its four posts. "Carey, Marshman, and Ward slept in this room until their wives arrived.[10] People sometimes forget that Carey's work was teamwork. Joshua Marshman and William Ward arrived in 1799 and became a vital part of 'The Serampore Trio.'"

Later Dr. Daniel took me to the little cemetery in town, where simple plaques marked the trio's three flat graves. We had to step carefully, because monsoon rains had flooded the cemetery. "Baptists are always under water!" my host joked apologetically. The university had wanted to move the graves into a mausoleum overlooking the Hugli, but Thomas foresaw it could become a religious pilgrimage shrine.

---

9. Dr. Kraakevik had earlier served with SIM and was an SIM board member.

10. Carey's first wife, Dorothy, has been portrayed as uncooperative and mentally unbalanced. She later joined William, but few understood her stressful plight. An illiterate who had never ventured from her village, she set out on an eight-month voyage, alone with a baby and two children, to an unknown culture and hostile environment, feeling isolated—while William's colossal tasks consumed his time and attention. Missions have become more understanding. (Carey survived two wives; his third survived him by a year.)

The university library holds Carey's memorabilia. On one wall hangs the original charter, signed by the King of Denmark, granting the College authority to award degrees.[11] I was amazed that even today as many as 40 leading theological colleges in India are affiliated to Serampore College (University) through the Senate of Serampore College, established by *The Serampore College Act IV of 1918*, a fitting honour for the College which had already served the people for 100 years. The annual convocation for all theological colleges affiliated to Serampore, with more than 2,000 students, is held in one of the theological institutions, and at Serampore itself almost every third year.

"There were only 30 students in the Department of Theology of Serampore College when I arrived," Thomas told me. "Now 80 are currently enrolled. It's impressive to watch them receiving theological degrees after successfully completing studies in one of the affiliated colleges. There is hardly any other institution in India giving theological training along with secular disciplines—as the founders established from the beginning. It's a rare privilege and responsibility for the Administrative Council of Serampore College.

"Of course, since the government took over the university, it's included many shades of theology," continued Thomas, at the time Principal (President) of the college and secretary of the entire university. "But we're glad there's still a strong evangelical student movement in a number of institutions within the Serampore family." At Dr. Daniel's request, I found it a stimulating privilege to give three lectures on "Mission" to the theology undergraduates.

Revolutionizing Breakthrough

As I stood at William Carey's pulpit and sat in his chair at his oak desk, I recollected his challenging motto: "***Attempt great things; expect great things.***" Although it was seven years after arriving in India that Carey saw his first convert to Christ, he lived to see some "great things." However, he could not have anticipated how those words have challenged

11. Carey couldn't work or receive a salary within British territory at the time. Britain later embraced him. Secular universities were established in Calcutta, Bombay, and Madras in 1857, 39 years after the establishment of Serampore College in 1818 by the Serampore Trio.

succeeding generations of missionaries. For instance, a century later, Rowland Bingham, founder of SIM,[12] stated, "If there was one who influenced my thinking more than others—one who should influence the thinking of the SIM—it would be William Carey. I would like his watchwords to ring in our ears: *Attempt great things **for** God; expect great things **from** God.*"[13]

Financially, Carey and his colleagues also exemplified a walk of faith. They and their wives "drew up the celebrated Serampore Covenant, in which they pledged never to call anything they possessed their own. Even later, when [they] earned large sums of money [teaching], they insisted in putting the whole into their common fund for furtherance of the whole work. . . Carey remarked that 'if we continue to live this life of denying our own rights for the work of the whole, the day will come when thousands in India will rise up to pronounce us blessed.'" When the Indian government offered to pay Carey a large sum for a few hours' translation per week, he said to his wife, "We lived on [5% of that] last year, let us so continue to live."

Here in Serampore, I paused to thank God for the monumental achievements of Carey, Ward, Marshman, and their colleagues. The needs they faced were both rudimentary and enormous: (1) They had to translate God's Word into the languages of the people. (2) They had to print those translations. (3) In most languages, they had to provide literacy primers and teach people to read their own languages, which were only oral, not written.

Although self-educated, Carey had a natural linguistic gift. Even in his teens he could read the Bible in six languages—including Hebrew, Greek, and Latin. But he knew that Jesus spoke in the language of the

---

12. SIM began in 1893 as Sudan Interior Mission. The name, Serving in Mission (approved June 2001) incorporates the former Africa Evangelical Fellowship, Andes Evangelical Mission, International Christian Fellowship, Sudan Interior Mission. Members from 37 countries, serve in some 50 lands. Globally, over 15,000 SIM-related congregations (though not bearing SIM's name) care for some 9m members/adherents.
13. J.H. Hunter, *A Flame of Fire*. Toronto: SIM, 1961, p. 31, 297(this and next paragraph quote). Years of quoting added "for God ... from God" to Carey's original motto, but in keeping with his intent.

common people (Aramaic). So in India, he reduced *vernaculars* to writing and, along with Marshman, translated scripture into 44 languages and dialects.[14] He and his colleagues translated classical literature and compiled dictionaries and grammars.

Today this may seem only a colossal task, but it was more—*it was revolutionary*. In most of the world, education was the monopoly of the elite, priesthood, ruling class, and academics. In India at the time, there was no such thing as a *Hindu* religion, and it was a *crime* for lower castes and women to study. According to Brahminical law, an "untouchable" who recited a verse in Sanskrit should have his tongue cut out; if he dared even to *hear* the god's sacred language, molten lead should be poured into his ears.[15]

And here were Carey, Marshman, and Ward publishing the Christian's Holy Bible in the sacred Sanskrit as well as in vernaculars! In their fledgling college, they insisted on teaching in the local language, Bengali, as well as in English. Whereas orthodox Muslims believed they must recite the *Qur'an* only in Arabic, and at the time Roman Catholics read the Bible in Latin, a*nyone* could read the sacred Word of God in his/her *own language*. What a revolutionary breakthrough—an irreversible precedent!

Globally, the West's Enlightenment and the French Revolution, although unleashing forces of darkness as well as of light, provided a climate for change. To evangelicals, this meant the spread of God's Word and proclamation of the gospel to people of all cultures. This was the key to bringing people to trust in Christ as well as discipling them. But it didn't simply serve a "religious" purpose. Even as 16th–17th c. translations of the English Bible had stabilized the eclectic English language (which freely borrowed from other languages—exotic spellings and all), Bible translations did the same for languages in India. Contrary to the Enlightenment's denunciation of missionaries for destroying

14. On Carey's arrival, only 67 languages had Scripture portions. Carey's translations made the Bible or portions available to over 300m people. Two other missionaries, Henry Martin and a colleague, Gilbert, established modern Hindi as India's national language (Mangalwadi, *India*, p. 339). India has some 1,652 languages, 4,635 ethnic groups. Translations now include 53 Bibles, 42 New Testaments, 40 portions.
15. *Sanskrit*: combination of two Indo-Aryan words—literally "he makes together," hence "perfected."

cultures of primitive innocence, Bible translation actually helped preserve cultures.[16]

Multi-tasking Missionaries

Carey, along with colleagues Marshman and Ward, had more on the go than linguistics, translation, and printing. His mind worked faster than a *punkah*[17] on a hot day. He produced studies in agriculture, astronomy, economics, education, geology, health care, horticulture, and other subjects—all related to India's needs. As Christians became outcastes (for "breaking caste" when they accepted believer's baptism) the Serampore team encouraged them (as well as all villagers) to become self-reliant. If they had no local school for their children, they should start one! No wonder that even 200 years later, the nation honored him as agriculturalist, educator, linguist, and social reformer! Bengalis honored him for preserving their culture.[18]

For missions, Carey advocated two important principles: (1) equality of missionaries and nationals; (2) self-sustaining missions. In fact, before founding the work at Serampore, he had supervised an indigo[19] factory and purchased an indigo plantation to support his mission station. Using these principles, Carey established mission work in other parts of India and in Burma and the East Indies. One of Carey's sons, Felix, became a missionary to Burma, where he translated some Scripture—work that Adoniram and Ann Judson later carried on. But when the King of Burma, who approved the work of Felix, appointed him as his ambassador in Calcutta, Carey complained, "Felix is shriveled from a missionary into an ambassador!"

---

16. Yale Linguistic-Anthropologist Lamin Sanneh cites the protection Bible translation has provided culture in languages under assault from trade, migration, and foreign ideas (see Bibliography). Critics of widespread Protestant Bible translation should ask why other faiths did not similarly help preserve language and culture by translating their own scriptures into the vernacular.
17. Ceiling-mounted hinged canvas, pulled up and down as a fan by a *coolie* (Hindi: "laborer").
18. Nobel prize poet and international lecturer, Tagore (1861-1941) "father of modern Bengali literature," reflected richness of Bengali culture as well as Christian influence. Although son of a Calcutta Hindu noble, he developed high regard for the Christian faith. See Rabindranath Tagore (John Thorpe, trns.), *Let My Head Bow Down.* Charlotte: SIM, c. 1960.
19. Plant producing blue dye used for textiles. Mission pioneer C. T. Studd's father owned an indigo farm.

I've heard that quoted in Missions classes. Regrettably, some have used it to make negative comparisons between witness through secular or missionary service. Carey's criterion was that obedience to God must be the criterion, whatever one's calling. He knew his son's motives better than we. In fact, Felix fell to the temptations of status, luxury, and liquor. A year later, he even had to abandon his ambassadorial post.[20]

Although the "missionary vs. ambassador" quote was typical of William's single-eyed commitment to missions, he well knew how government service could play a strategic part in the work of the gospel. In fact, William Carey's appointment as Professor of Bengali at the government's Fort William College brought tremendous support and recognition for the work of the Serampore Mission. I also was aware how God had used evangelicals in Britain's civil service and parliament to bring to India the human rights that Carey and his colleagues had campaigned for.

The "Calcutta Three" were constantly burdened by the spiritual plight of the people around them, and sickened by atrocities carried out in the name of religion. Before they decried the evils they saw, they studied Brahminical law and Hindu Vedas to show that those sacred writings didn't teach such crimes. Twenty years earlier, renowned Scottish economist-philosopher Adam Smith, who pioneered global economic analysis,[21] had *reported* these evils (and their effect on South Asia's economy), but Carey and his colleagues *did* something about them.

Shocking Britain into Action

When Carey sent his documented report back to the British Parliament, both government and public were shocked that Victorian Britain could allow such evils to continue in any of its territories: widows writhing to death on their husband's funeral pyres;[22] innocent infants,

20. May Drewery, *William Carey*. Grand Rapids: Zondervan, 1979, p. 167.
21. Adam Smith, An *Inquiry into the Nature and Causes of the Wealth of Nations*, 1776.
22. *Sati*: "holy service" to a widow's god-husband in the next life and supposed shortcut to cycle of births. A widow's life was so unbearable that society accepted *sati* even as Western culture has accepted abortion.

sacrificed to the gods, drowning in the Ganges; shrieking devotees bursting asunder under the rolling juggernaut that bore an image of Krishna.[23] It was a hideous nightmare in the name of religion, but the missionaries carefully documented it all. For skeptics today, those unaltered records are still available. And what they described was only the top layer of deep wounds in Indian society—including caste, denial of human rights, male domination, female infanticide, injustice, and poverty.

The sub-continent has so earned our respect for its progress that it's difficult to imagine how chaotic it had been in earlier centuries.[24] Over 3,000 years of tyrannical oppression from wave upon wave of invading emperors had left it fractured into some 562 autonomous kingdoms (similar to England's petty kingdoms of the 5th c.) containing over four thousand distinct ethnic groups and 1,652 languages. Elite Brahmins[25] controlled illiterate peasants by creating fear of religious taboos. Caste prevented people realizing their potential and kept the economy abysmal.

Although some Muslim-Turkic "Mogul" emperors, such as Akbar (1556-1605) had tried to introduce a form of government, others (including Akbar's son Jahangir) lived in opulence and licentiousness, neglecting the populace. Most of the rulers humiliated their own nobles into servility and exploited the people (one petty ruler demanding 2/3 of a farmer's crops in taxes). Communities could not prevent starvation from famines because no one dared interfere with the gods (who supposedly controlled monsoons) by irrigating or by stockpiling grain. (Godly Joseph defied Egypt's astrologers by doing that in Egypt). Millions of Indians died from successive famines, depopulating many villages and farms.

Britain at first administered India through trading companies, as Holland and Portugal had done in their territories. The amalgamated East India Company (EIC) not only proved powerless to make changes,

---

23. English "Juggernaut": from Hindi "Jagganath," a title of Krishna (<Sanskrit *Jagganatha*—"World Lord").

24. I realize Britain had also come through chaotic centuries. There again, the Gospel brought change.

25. From early Aryan mythology, *Brahmanas* ("sacred") include the Vedic scriptures; the *Brahmans* ("sacred," of the gods, or "twice born") were the highest caste; a *Brahmin* both supervised and embodied the sacred. Their earlier domination has currently caused resentful reaction from lower classes.

but also for the sake of commerce played along with corrupt practices. Dutch as well as English companies opposed missionaries, who often exposed their corruption and excesses. An evangelical member of the British Supreme Council in India, Thomas Babington Macaulay, dubbed the EIC "a gang of public robbers," providing "the rule of an evil genii." (Mangalwadi adds that although "historians rarely discuss the economic conditions in the non-British territories in India . . . . they relish discrediting the Raj."[26])

In the charter Act of 1813, the British Parliament revoked the company's blanket ban on missionary activity. Finally the British Crown took over direct governance of India in 1858, based on a "constitutional charter" drafted five years earlier. Queen Victoria declared her reliance on "the truth of Christianity" but disclaimed any plan to impose her convictions on her new colony. All citizens would "enjoy the equal and impartial protection of the law." However, inexperienced administrators made great blunders, and some continued to oppose education. Hinduism's worldview did not allow reform; commercial interests didn't want it. Several national and expatriate leaders opposed a free press.[27] So it took mostly Christian reformers in India as well as in Britain to bring about the changes missionaries were calling for. Lord Macauley, Charles Grant, and William Wilberforce (all followers of Christ) put pressure on their government to honour its word; they also urged education at all levels.

On the Road to Freedom

"No people ought to be free till they are fit to use their freedom," administrators argued. But Macauley countered, "If men are to wait for liberty till they become good and wise [while] in slavery, they may indeed wait forever!" Like William Carey, Macaulay opposed caste. Yet, in the name of "tolerance" in a Hindu country, mainline missions that were losing their biblical bearings increasingly avoided presenting Jesus as the

26. Vishal Mangalwadi, *India—the grand experiment*, pp. 210, 221. Farnham: Pippa Rann, 1997.

27. Opposing a free press, Governor Thomas Munro of Madras (*op. cit.* p. 188) wrote in 1821: "I have no faith in the . . . rapid improvement of the Hindoos, or of any other people. [Their] character is probably much the same as when Vasco da Gama first visited India, and it is not likely that it will be much better a century hence." By 1858, missions had started several publications, annoying government (*op. cit.*, p. 191).

only way of salvation. They presumed education alone would bring freedom from caste discrimination. Commendably, they began many of India's outstanding academic institutions, but without a clear-cut Christian message—Bishop John of Kerala (Ch. 8) had cited this as the cause of his state's mix of nominal Christianity and Communism. Indian historian/philosopher Vishal Mangalwadi roundly condemned such diluting of the gospel message.

In India, there was little use in replacing the fatalism, lethargy, and intolerance of caste (which at least had a sense of community) with the greed of individualistic capitalism based on education and industry without morality and justice. Macaulay knew that caste was ingrained in the Hindu belief system. Only a spiritual change could break its tyranny. (In case anyone thinks this is ancient history irrelevant to India now, the British-based news magazine, *The Economist*, of October 30, 2004, reported a highly significant Indian celebration of Macauley's birth—precisely because he opposed Hinduism and caste! There is more than meets the eye in that report. The gospel seed is still bearing fruit, even if often unrecognized.)[28]

By 1917 Parliament promised to set India on the road to self-rule, although at the time there was no united body strong enough to form a government. By 1931, Viceroy Lord Irwin, a committed Christian, was able to sign a pact with Gandhi for "Dominion Status" (similar to Canada's and Australia's), but British Parliamentarians dragged their feet. Evangelical leaders continued to press for Independence, and India accepted human rights, the rule of law, and a free press. It became an independent Dominion in 1947 and a Republic within the Commonwealth in 1950.[29] Earlier, Keshab Chandra Sen, one of India's great reformers, had written:

28. Although nationalists normally vilify their erstwhile British rulers, yet in Delhi, India's capital, on October 25, 2004, Dalit writer C. Prasad publicly celebrated the anniversary of Lord Macaulay's birth. Prasad commended Macaulay's "anti-Hindu, anti-caste views." To break their degrading status, Dalits have been turning to Buddhism and Christianity and are now a political force.

29. Britain learned much in India. Later in Africa its colonial administrators intentionally worked toward self-rule, responding to "the winds of change" (Prime Minister Harold Macmillan, 1956). Few people realize Africa's most populous nation, Nigeria, actually asked Britain to postpone Independence until 1960.

"We breathe, think, move in a Christian atmosphere under the influence of Christian education; the whole mature society is awakened, enlightened, reformed. . . . None but Jesus ever deserved this bright, precious diadem—India—and Christ shall have it."

Mangalwadi quotes Keshab Sen and also documents the work of other reformers in his definitive book published for the Fiftieth Anniversary of India's Independence, *India—the grand experiment*, cited above.[30] Mangalwadi recognizes "the grand experiment" that has made India the world's largest democracy. He loves his nation and reminds us of the phenomenal feat of governing a billion people. India encompasses over four thousand "people groups" under an elected parliamentary system that guarantees basic freedoms.

Fear of Fascism Arising

But Mangalwadi also voices concern that India's democracy could quickly deteriorate into fascism if the nation ignores its founding principles.[31] Certainly, India's first Prime Minister, Pandit Jawaharlal Nehru, a high-cast Kashmiri Brahmin, rejected violence. "If any man raises his hand against another in the name of religion, I shall fight him till the last breath of my life—whether I am in government or outside," he declared.[32]

However, in the name of nationalism, militant Hindus declare that India's Constitution is anti-Hindu and call for changing it. Back in the 1940s, their likes charged that Mahatma Gandhi himself was anti-Hindu, because he opposed untouchability and other human rights abuses. He declared they were not *dharma* (religious duty). Learned guru Dr. Kurtaakoti alleged that Gandhi's non-violent resistance "uproots the very principle of Hinduism and Aryan philosophy" (*Ibid.,* 278). A radical Hindu assassinated Gandhi.

---

30. Prof. Prabhu Guptara describes this book as "possibly the most important for the future of India, and certainly the most important for understanding the central difficulties and opportunities facing India today."

31. Mangalwadi shows how fascism takes root in universities through intellectualism, citing a study by Gene Edward Veith, Jr., *Fascism: Modern & Postmodern.* Mussoorie: Nivedit Good Books, 2000.

32. Quoted by Valson Thampu, TRACI, in letter to incumbent PM, Nov. 25, 1998.

The Mahatma likely gained these principles from Christian (including Quaker) contacts in Europe. ("I like your Christ, but not your Christians," he once said.) In order to make his views acceptable in India, he linked them to the non-violent and ascetic

Jains[33] of his native state, Gujarat. He adroitly cloaked his views in Hindu symbols, so that his movement seemed to arise from Hindu spirituality. He was a master strategist!

If abolition of the caste system and provision of democratic rights for everyone is anti-Hindu, the values that created the world's largest democratic state must have come from elsewhere. Through government records and statements by Indian and expatriate officials, Mangalwadi traces those values directly to evangelical Christianity.

Proponents of *Hindutva* threaten those very values with other imported ideas from Europe—in this case, fascist Europe (again, full circle!). Mangalwadi cites the strong ties India's early leaders had with German and Italian fascists (*Ibid.,* 282-284). Cleverly, they disguised fascism under the cloak of "Hindu nationalism" and religion, harking back to a supposed "Golden Age." However, Mangalwadi believes that the Hindu caste system and astrology contribute to India's poverty: "The culture of astrology enslaves us because it says our times rule us."

Respected journalist Khushwant Singh recollects that although at Independence, Indians believed that "our Gandhian principles of simple living and high thinking would set an example for the rest of the world, . . . [now] we have become a corrupt, violent people who are unable to work together as a team" (*India*, op cit., 280.)

It would be ironic—frightening—if the world's most populous democracy reverted to its earlier Aryan culture. As we've already noted, far away, on the other side of the Hindu Kush, the Nazis used Aryan

33. Jains: Hindu sect (3c B.C.). Like many Buddhists, they loathe the body. Asceticism can lead to self-torture and extreme austerity. Priests (*fakirs*) of one branch wear no clothes. To assure fertility, women may publicly kiss a *fakir's* genitals. Jains worship Shiva, whose figure often combines a stylized male genital (S'skrt: *lingam*) with a female genital (S'skrt: *ulva).* Sumerian/ Babylonian worship also featured the phallus. Gandhi discretely chose to wear the loincloth allowed by moderate Jains. But his asceticism included sleeping naked with a niece, to demonstrate his sexual abstinence (Wolpert, 2001—see Bibliog.).

mythology to develop a Master Race concept. Encouraged by evolutionary theory and elitist free thinkers, Hitler embraced eugenics to eliminate mentally and physically weak elements of society, as well as the Jews, whom he considered inferior to Aryans.[34]

In India, ancient Aryan views "legitimized" Hindu caste (marginalizing "the weak" to the benefit of a master race), female infanticide (eliminating a future dowry liability)—even *sati* (ridding society of unwanted widows)—basic to *Hindutva's* worldview.[35] All were "ethical" in Aryan-Hindu philosophy, for the greater goal of reincarnating a master caste or race. While enjoying sexual pleasure with "lower-caste" maidens, Aryan descendants rejected "bastard" offspring, to preserve their own "racial purity" (*discrimination*!). The more I learned of the caste system, the more complex I realized it to be.

" It's very difficult for non-Indians to understand Hinduism," Indian scientist J.Edwin Dodla, who has studied Hinduism in depth, explained to me. "It divided all human society into five hierarchies in descending social order. The first four are recognised as higher human beings and the last one as lower human beings. These are based on their community occupations:

[1] Priestly and educated, [2] Business people, [3] Warriors, [4] Farmers and artisans, [5] Shoe-making and mending, excrement (night-soil) and other dirty jobs. This has become an oppressed class, treated as *untouchables* by higher classes. Recently they were re-named *Dalits,* since they do not have any main caste name (only sub-castes). There are 200m. *Dalits*—18% of India's population.[36]

---

34. Historians disagree on Aryan origins and date of their invasion of N. India (3-2c. BC?). Lighter-skinned, they pushed the darker, earlier peoples southwards, leading to Hinduism's 6,400 castes (vicious form of *apartheid* originally based on color, but now most with some admixture) of continuing social importance.

35. Though eugenics—putting weaker people to death—rightly shocks us, some Western elitists embraced it in early 20thc. Swiss psychologist Carl Jung's writings taught that Aryan and Jewish psyches differed drastically), and encouraged Hitler. They now inform New Age thinking. (Goggin & Goggin, *Death of a "Jewish Science": Psychoanalysis in the Third Reich.* Purdue Univ. Press, 2001.) Humanistic philosophy (Nietzsche, Heidegger, *et al*) led to European Nihilism, in India to Buddhist Emptiness—same result.

36. For further details, see J.E. Dodla's explanation in Appendix F: Asia's Religions - Hinduism.

The Gospel's Far-Reaching Effects

William Carey and his colleagues could not excuse such discrimination as simply "Indian culture." They saw that millions of men, women, and children—with all the potential abilities of God's creation—were trapped in abysmal ignominy and segregated in hideous discrimination. Hinduism branded them and their children with an inescapable stigma—unless, *perchance* after countless re-births, they attained to higher birth. It was so much part of Hindu worldview that only the regenerating gospel of Christ—the spiritual second birth"[37]—could bring about the changes that one day would break tradition's vicious grip.

Few historians realize "the stamp" that Carey and his colleagues put upon India. No one would have guessed how far their carefully documented reports would go. They stirred the British to establish human rights in India, and then held them to their promise to grant Independence. As Mangalwadi states, the nation's Independence and democracy could never have succeeded without the basis of law, order, and ethics for which evangelical parliamentarians pressed. In a reversal of Britain's earlier opposition to missionaries, Sir Bartle Frere, a British administrator, later reported back to his government:

> **"Whatever you've heard to the contrary, the teaching of Christianity among 150 millions of civilized and industrious Hindus and Mohammadans in India is effecting changes—moral, social, and political—which for extent and rapidity of effect are far more extraordinary than anything you or your fathers have witnessed in modern Europe."**
>
> **"Bishop Cotton of Calcutta . . . who had gone to India, with, to say the least, no prejudice in favour of missions, wrote home ... : 'I intreat you never to believe any insinuations against missionary work in India.'"[38]**

Other British administrators joined in opposing traditional religious malpractices. In the 19th century, British General Sir Charles Napier

37. As Jesus explained to the Jewish intellectual, Nicodemus (John 3.3-6).

38. *One Hundred Years*—short history of the Church Missionary Society. London: CMS, 1898, p. 105

came across a Hindu group about to burn to death a Hindu widow, according to the Hindu custom of sati (burning alive).

"You say it is your custom to burn widows," the General told the group. "Very well. We also have a custom: when men burn a woman alive, we tie a rope around their necks and we hang them. Build your funeral pyre; beside it, my carpenters will build a gallows. You may follow your custom. And then we will follow ours."

Freed from destructive traditions, democratic India has produced from all strata of society outstanding philosophers and creative thinkers, influencing their own and other cultures. They are the strongest argument for the intellectual and ethical creativity that God brings to mankind by his Holy Spirit, as Jesus Christ walks a nation's paths. Names of Christian leaders since Carey's day, serving in Asia and overseas, would fill a book. In this brief overview, Pandita Ramabai (Ch. 7) and Sadhu (*Holy Man*) Sundar Singh (Bibliography) will have to represent past decades. In both cases, God's Word reached into the heart of Hinduism, bringing a seeking woman and a searching man into the light of the gospel to make a great impact on the world.

Creative Christian Witness

Among more recent leaders are Venkateswara Thyaharaj, who demonstrates a personal obedience to Christ's call to discipleship and witness.[39] Born a Brahmin, Thyaharaj found Christ as Saviour and wrote his story in terms understood by Hindus. There is Anand Chaudhari, a Brahmin priest who became a Christian evangelist and leader of innumerable ministries. These were two among a host of many active witnesses all over the nation, engaged in all kinds of effective ministries.

In India, I met leaders of indigenous missions,[40] such as Ken Gnanakan, founder of the Agriculture, Crafts, Trades, and Studies (ACTS) Bible Institute. I also met Indian leaders of *international* teams, such as Joseph D'Souza of Operation Mobilization, which links 1,200 full-time Indian workers. SIM's Pastor's Book Project provides Christian workers with

39. Venkateswara Thyaharaj, *A new motive for Living.* Bromley: Pilot Books, 1997.

40. There are some 440 Indian agencies, with 44,000 workers.

study books they could not otherwise afford. India helped expand the missionary vision of Ethiopian churches when a visiting team of ten pastors and evangelists found instant rapport and mutual encouragement with Indian counterparts.

"It was a life-changing experience for the Ethiopians!" remembers team leader Howard Brant. "They'd endured suffering in their witness for Christ in Ethiopia, especially under a Marxist regime. But now they faced a totally different world of Hindu culture. My heart was touched as each told the Lord, with tears, he'd be willing to die for the soul of even one Hindu person. Such dedication won more than a thousand to the knowledge of the Saviour. And Indian pastors were blessed to think that their Ethiopian counterparts cared that much for India. It demonstrated the global Body of Christ working together." That was the first of several such encounters.

Other international agencies, including Bible societies and radio stations, along with missions encourage Indian Christians.[41] The "Jesus Film" *daily* communicates the Good News in 55 languages, 500 film teams showing it to a daily average of 100,000 people. Annually, 2-3m watch an Indian film on Jesus, "Karunamaidu," available in 21 languages. Knowing the proliferation of cults, the indigenous Gospel for India agency beams in-depth yet simply explained Living Truth Bible lessons.[42] Ebenezer Samuel, local Director of Gospel for India (founded by K.P. Yohannan, International Director), operates Bible schools and helps marginalized people start micro-enterprises. "We don't want to make 'rice Christians,'" says Ebenezer. "We help people help themselves."

The Apostle Paul stated that "where sin abounds grace abounds." In overcrowded India, one paraphrase might be, "Where population abounds, help abounds"—from Christian agencies. The list of ministries of grace, local and international, is encouraging to see. But as India's population

41. Scripture Gift Mission sends India some 5m Scripture portions (in 39 languages) annually. World by Radio's ministries broadcast to people who cannot otherwise hear the gospel by radio *in their own tongue*.

42. Ministry of Charles Price, The People's Church, Toronto, (the church founded by Oswald J. Smith, known for his missionary slogan: "Why should any hear the gospel twice when millions haven't heard it once?") which provides wide-screen TV monitors in village squares for showing the Bible lessons.

swells, they aren't surfeited with help. Among more than one billion people, vast needs will continue to exist.

A visitor faces two extremes in summing up India's spiritual state: [1] the nation's needs are so enormous and Christian presence such a minority, that goals of evangelism and discipling seem hopeless; [2] Christian witness is so strong that agency reports can seem triumphalistic. You've seen one or the other in some mission reports. The truth is bi-polar: India's population and needs *are* vast, and Christian ministry *is* outstanding—like a candle burning in a dark room—"a city set on a hill" that cannot be hid. At the same time, because of concern for the safety of believers, I've had to refrain from identifying many fruitful projects, for which only God must get the "credit line." And that's as it should be.[43]

I'd see more fulfillment of Carey's vision at Raxaul, a remote outpost on India's northern border with Nepal. Westerners may know its more famous neighboring town, Darjiling, from whence comes Darjeeling Tea—considered by aficionados as the world's finest.

Where the Buddha "Saw the Light"

Canadian medical doctor Aletta Bell had invited me to visit Duncan Memorial Hospital in Raxaul. En route to Raxaul, I passed through the important Hindu center of Patna, on the sacred Ganges, abode of the goddess Ganga. Hindus believe gods provided the river to wash away mankind's sins. However, the gods must have been angry when the Kosi, a tributary of the Ganges, burst an embankment, sending a devastating flood down an old channel that had been dry for a century. Thousands of settlers in the valley drowned, and more than 3m were displaced.[44]

---

43. Agencies, needing to be accountable to their supporters, truthfully report encouraging results. Naturally, they don't attempt to tell about the fruitful work of others. Therefore, supporters may infer that *their* agency's work is the *real* work being accomplished. For security reasons, we cannot identify some projects.
44. Although receding Himalayan glaciers threaten the Ganges, upon which 40 million people depend for drinking water, livelihood, and "sanitation," this channel change tragedy occurred in 2008.

Patna benefits from nearby *Bodh Gaya* (Buddha Gaya), where, tradition says, the wandering ascetic philosopher, Sakyamuni[45] (6th c.) sat under a *bodhi* tree and through meditation became enlightened. Suddenly aware of all things on earth and in the heavens, including his own birth and death, even good and evil, Buddhists believe, he became the human representation of "Enlightenment," the Buddha.[46]

Each May, thousands gather to celebrate his birth. On the anniversary, lamas and their disciples parade "relics" of Buddha around the city. Buddhist and Hindu beliefs merge as Brahmins recite sacred texts and pilgrims dab holy ashes on their foreheads in honor of their personal deities. (Conveniently, priests have stashes of the ashes for purchase.)

Some 120 miles (nearly 200 km.) farther west, on a commanding bend of the great river, is Varanasi ("Land of Sacred Light")— pilgrimage center of the Hindu world. Ancient *vedas* and other texts refer to the city, said to have been founded ten centuries before Christ's birth. On any given day, pilgrims gather to offer sacrifice to their gods and pray for divine favors. Since anyone dying in Varanasi reportedly goes straight to Paradise, many elderly stay to await death. (What great tourist promotion to fill the hotels—except that most pilgrims are penniless and sleep in the open!)

On an appointed day each year, rays of the rising sun part the morning mists to signal the auspicious moment when pilgrims rush down the *ghats* into the polluted water for ritual cleansing from "mundane sufferings" and "worldly sins."[47] Cadavers, strapped to funeral rafts, float down the sacred river for the gods to carry off as they wish. Some "holy men" threaten to boycott the event because the water registers 3,000 times

---

45. His clan's name was Gautama, or Gotama, and his personal name was Siddhartha (c. 563-483 B.C.).

46 "Buddha" (>Sanskrit *bodhi:* "enlightened") originally was a sublime state, not a person's title. Seeking to reform Hinduism, Siddhartha adapted its basic concepts for Buddhism: humans should revere "holy men" rather than worship idols. (Appendix C: Buddha's Elephant, and Appendix F: Religions.)

47. *Varanasi Guide and Map*: India Tourist Offices, c. 2000.

acceptable levels of pollution, from human waste and a paper mill's effluent. Naturally, medics also express health concerns.[48]

Adding to the surreal atmosphere, sacred cows and bulls roam along the riverbanks as cremation pyres crackle into flame. The acrid odor of burning bodies mixes with the heavy smell of drugs, perfume of incense, and aroma of curried rice loudly hawked by vendors. For a donation, *fakirs*[49] and priests strew the ashes on the water. The scene would be carnival if it weren't for the sadness of it all.

In the city, Banaras Hindu University (founded in 1915, based on the Central Hindu College founded in 1896), teaches "the inner lights" of wisdom and philosophy—carrying on the city's tradition as the ancient seat of Sanskrit and philosophical learning.

"Lord," I breathed; "thank you for the light of the gospel. Only your Spirit can enlighten any of us, at the foot of your cross! And thank you for those who live among these sincere pilgrims, to share your love with them." My mind went back to the eager young couple I'd met at the conference in Delhi. I knew it wouldn't be wise to name them or give details of their work—but they are among those who today are "salt and light" at Varanasi's center of Hindu/Buddhist superstition.

Today's humble servants of God follow in the train of pioneers such as Welsh missionary agriculturalist, Sam Higginbottom, who studied Philosophy at Princeton in the USA. A century ago, he observed Hindu worshipers bathing in the Ganges at Allahabad.[50] He realized that in spite of the devotees' ritual cleansing, no Hindu guru could lift them out of their dismal poverty or their sins. He was saddened as he discovered that higher-caste Hindus even hesitated to help lower castes, for fear of angering the gods and accruing bad *karma*. That would interfere with fate!

48. Current research on "mad-cow disease" (*bovine spongiform encephalopathy*) raises the possibility that in the 1960s and 70s, a human form of this virus (CJD) could have been transmitted through the infected bones of cadavers set afloat during Hindu funeral rites. Indian agents supply the bulk of bonemeal for cattle feed, and unscrupulous scavengers could sell them human bones recovered from infected corpses. Scientists continue to investigate this yet unproved possibility (*The Economist*, Sept. 3/05, p. 71).

49. Ascetic mendicant or fortune teller; <Arabic for "poor man." (*Not* to be confused with "faker"!)

50. Further west on the Ganges, Allahabad boasts the world's largest religious gathering, *Kumbh Mela* ("Hindu religious gathering"), held when the sun enters the Aquarius Constellation. Astrology, with Sumerian and Egyptian roots, governs Hinduism.

Presbyterians had sent Higginbottom to India to evangelize among "low-caste" Indians. He became convinced that they needed more than just Christian "wisdom and philosophy." Colonizers' earlier humanistic attempts to upgrade living standards had failed, for they did not change the Hindu world-view or caste system that discouraged improvement and hindered farming. As he surveyed the eroding but fertile floodplains of the Ganges, he regretted (in his words) "the appalling loss of human life and stupendous economic waste." Indians needed a spiritual change along with knowledge of improved farming methods, he realized.

Samuel returned to USA to study Agriculture and reflect on the ministry of Jesus. Once again back in India, he founded the Allahabad Agricultural Institute, which has helped break the stranglehold of hunger in India and other Asian lands. This evangelist-agriculturalist followed Carey's lead in applying the gospel to daily life. Alongside improved farming methods, his Institute taught the Bible without apology, for "better plowing or larger crops are not going to save India—important as they are—but faith that comes from knowledge of Jesus, the world's Savior."[51]

India's Contribution to World Christianity

As Vishal Mangalwadi documents, evangelicals have contributed much to India's spiritual and social revolution. I was impressed, moreover, by the evangelical contribution *India* has made to the rest of the world. India formed a committee of the Evangelical Alliance in 1849, shortly after the EA was formed in Britain.[52] In 1860, a letter from India requested that the EA's annual week of prayer be made worldwide. India's Imchaba Bendang ("Ben") Wati was a key leader in forming World Evangelical Fellowship (Alliance) and became one of its early presidents. Theodore Williams of Chennai was another. An Indian bishop, Alexander Mar Theophilos, led the opening "Procession of Nations" at the 1966 World Congress on Evangelism, sponsored in Berlin by the Billy Graham Evangelistic Association.

From India, God has raised up contemporary leaders of Christian thought and Bible teaching to revive the West—Samuel Kamaleson, Ravi Zacharias, and Vishal Mangalwadi among others. The influence of the

51. Samuel Higginbottom, *The Gospel and the Plow*. NY: Macmillan, 1921, p. 128 etc.

52. J. W. Ewing, *Goodly Fellowship*, p. 23 (see Bibliography).

gospel in India has not been a one-way street. It has been reciprocal throughout the world.

In fact, India has contributed much to the study of church and mission. The Indian sub-continent has experienced the whole gamut of Biblical (Jewish and Islamic) history, as well as Christian experience: apostolic, Nestorian/Syrian, Iberian Catholic, Protestant; mainline, evangelical, inter-denominational, charismatic; indigenous, acculturated, syncretistic, cultic. It has experienced outright opposition and persecution, as well as "re-conversion" by traditional religions, and opposition not only to indigenization, but also to spiritual revival and "people movements" to Christ.

Students of global mission will recognize names such as Roland Allen, Alexander Duff, John R. Mott, and Henry Venn. The list could continue. They all developed their theories and strategies from experience gained in India. Duff's work, for instance, paved the way for modern medical studies, and led to development of university education. From Kolkata I headed further north to learn more about practical Christian witness today.

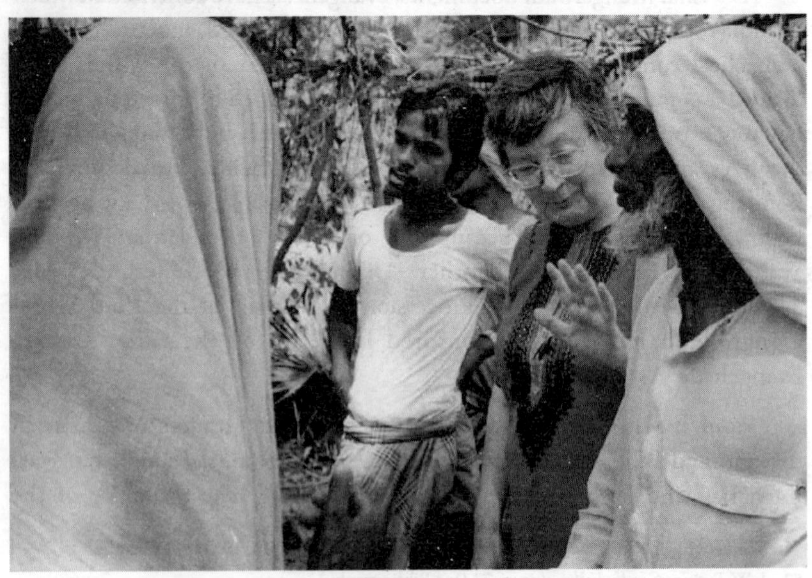

Dr. Bell wades into a drunken argument to restore peace.

Jesus' Disciple Wears a Stethoscope

"Whatever you did for one of the least of these brothers of mine, you did for me" (Matt. 25.40).

THE MONSOON RAINS were now pelting down upon us in earnest. When I reached the sprawling bungalow-style "Duncan" in Raxaul, I found Dr. Bell ready to drive her four-wheel-drive Jeep along muddy trails to Champak Community Health Centre.[1]

"Just call me 'Aletta'!" the hardy doctor said as I hopped in. While we bounced along, I popped into my mouth juicy lychees, thoughtfully brought along by the doctor to slake our thirst.[2] I also had plenty of questions. I knew that Champak would find cultural problems in undeveloped rural areas, where adults believe spirits cause fevers, idols need placating to prevent disease, and a drink of cow urine is a cure-all. I'd heard an alarming report about "Rat Children" in a neighboring area. A Hindu mother, to ensure that her other children would be normal, reportedly would dedicate a baby to serve the Idol of Rats in a shrine. Priests used devices to stunt head growth. Mentally retarded, the growing child became an alms-collector for the shrine.[3]

---

1. To villagers, "Duncan" was synonymous for "hospital." Dr. Cecil Duncan, born in India of Scottish missionary parents, opened the hospital in 1930, turning it over to Regions Beyond Missionary Union when he served in the Army in World War II. RBMU turned it over to India's Emmanuel Hospital Association. "Champak," name of a fragrant flower, also forms the acronym of three villages the Center served when it first began. Dr. Bell opened the Centre as a rural health outreach of Duncan Hospital. There are similar centers in other areas, such as Chetna and Prem Jyoti.
2. Although lychees come in grape-like clusters, each soft, white fruit surrounding a nut is "packaged" in its own shell—making it quite safe for travellers to eat the flesh without washing.
3. BBC World News T.V. (with photos) June 29, 1998. Many consider rats sacred, devoting temples to them, even though rats destroy 20% of India's food grain (*Revolution,* p. 140, K.P. Yohannan, see Bibliog.)

Arriving outside a village in which Champak had a project, we got out and walked its narrow lanes. I almost felt as if I were walking along with Jesus. Except that Jesus, when he walked in Judea and Samaria, didn't wear a stethoscope.[4] Here in an Indian village, laughing children crowded around their favorite visitor—and no "disciple forbade them"! Anxious mothers brought feverish infants. Squatting down to balance a child on one knee, Dr. Bell checked a baby's glands and listened to its breathing. Adults also got her attention. She stooped to enter a shack where a woman had dysentery. "How many times have you had a movement today?" Aletta asked, in Hindi.

"Fifty times!" the woman answered weakly but without hesitation. Aletta patiently asked her to count to fifty.

"One, two, three, one, two, three," the woman counted. Obviously, "fifty" was a nice-sounding figure she'd heard. But because dysentery is the most common ailment (and cause of death by dehydration), Aletta gave her an oral re-hydration packet.

At Champak Community Health Centre, we watched children making those rehydration packets. Sitting on mats, the children filled small plastic bags with a mixture of sugar and salt. One child carefully spooned out the right quantities, while other children filled bags and carefully sealed them with heat—from a candle.

Children Learning to Care

"We pay these children for their work, and use the packets in the villages and back at the hospital, which buys them," Aletta explained. "That's one of several ways we make Champak self-supporting. The children use their money for school books and pencils. And villagers use the small bags over and over."

This was certainly not the child slave labor we hear of and rightly oppose. It was an educational experience—the children learned that evil spirits don't cause dysentery, and that illness could be overcome with the

4. Not intending to be irreverent, I remembered that Jesus needed no stethoscope, for he "knew what was in every man" (John 2.25). And that included their physical needs and ailments, as shown in his miracles!

right treatment, not with sacrifices at the local shrine. Moreover, they learned to follow directions, measure accurately, and earn money for schooling while helping their communities. The World Health Organization talks about wholistic, sustainable development. This was it!

But that was not true of India's 70m children under the age of 18 who labor "without benefit of education" (10m bonded/enslaved, paying off family-inherited "debts"). This is in addition to 2m "children at risk" living on the streets, including 575,000 child prostitutes, plus 1.4m orphans and 13m considered homeless.[5] I asked Aletta what could be done about child labor.

"Child labour is illegal in India," she replied. "But it still exists because of poverty. No one is convicted of it, because the parents don't admit it, and employers never will. Besides, a bribe can quickly divert justice. We oppose exploiting children, of course, but we also realize it's more complicated than people overseas realize. If the children don't work, there will be less food for the family—and in most cases children would be sitting idle around the village. Working children are a family tradition. The only way we'll get rid of child labour is by improving opportunities for the poor and making school attendance compulsory."

Helping Villagers Help Themselves

I was amazed at all that this medical doctor was doing to accomplish both goals—plus others. Raised on a farm in Canada, she knew the value of self-reliance. Aletta was determined to alleviate grinding poverty, ignorance, and abuse in villages. Through the Centre, she sought to meet the most basic preventive health needs: sanitation and clean water.[6] She

---

5. Figures from TRACI (New Delhi), World Bank (Geneva, 2002), *Operation World* (Paternoster, 2001). In 2003, the UN reported 47% of under-five children are underweight.

6. International Water Management identifies these as most cost-effective ways of helping the poor—who suffer from (1) lack of delivery systems for drinking and plumbing water; (2) macro-irrigation priority, to benefit rich farmers, not poor villagers. In India, 160m lack access to clean water. Unsafe water lowers India's life expectancy (63 yrs.) and raises infant mortality (90 per 1,000 under five)—*World Bank* '04.

discovered that even though an area had a government school, sometimes it had no pupils because teachers, equipment, and books were missing.[7] Winning the confidence of authorities, she encouraged communities to build their own one-room schools: villages provided labor and half the cost; the Centre donated cement and basic equipment—and paid a responsible teacher for the first three years.

Champak improved farming yields, developed fish "farms" (villagers dug the pond; the Center stocked it), and introduced rabbit breeding. Aletta developed a tree nursery and encouraged men to plant bamboo for building projects. She urged villages to benefit from government house construction. For villagers, she opened up new worlds through adult literacy and small business seminars, so peasants could start cottage industries (one of Gandhi's goals), such as candle making, sewing, and other handcrafts.[8]

"We don't press projects on villages—they'd only collapse after a while," Aletta explained, as she felt for a child's pulse. "We wait until the people see the benefits a neighboring village receives. When they ask for the same, we're ready to help. Our formula for leadership? Teach as many people as possible, give responsibility, and require accountability."

That made sense in any management language! Aletta had the gift of organizing. She started by numbering the houses—an unknown practise at the time. Now it became possible to list every household, every child, access to water and sanitation, immunization, illness (especially TB and leprosy), habits hazardous to health (such as smoking and drinking), and an economic scale of 1 – 5. These statistics enabled the Clinic to identify health needs quickly, and to charge patients according to their ability. (The lower the income, the less the charge—right down to zero.) Staff asked patients to identify their problems and suggest remedies. And villagers knew that those who cared for them were followers of Jesus.

---

7. World Bank (2003) states that in India 25% of teachers are absent (38% in two states); therefore 25m children (6-14) are out of school, in spite of a promised but uncertain midday cooked meal.
8. Assistance for Champak projects comes from many sources, including TEAR Fund, Friends of East Champaran Dist., Bread for the World (Germany), SIM, and Teaching Aids Low Cost (TALC)-Britain.

The contrast between villages was dramatic. One village had refused medical treatment for their children and wouldn't provide a plot for a school. I noticed men lounging in the shade of a dilapidated hut, smoking while they gambled. A wrinkled grandmother, who looked to be 80 (but was likely under 50) held a coughing baby, obviously malnourished. Her 30-year-old daughter, wearing soiled clothing covered with flies, looked listless—likely from parasites and dysentery. Village women and children suffered contamination from crop residue and cow dung used as fuel in smoky huts.[9] Instead of attending school, girls carried water pots on their heads from a distant muddy hole. Refuse littered lanes; the smell of decay hung over the village. A wizened woman staggered along, a far-too-heavy water pot on her head. She didn't know any other life than hauling water for the males in the family. She believed she was worthless, and finding any paradise depended on serving the men-folk well. Men and dogs would get to drink first—the woman having her turn last, if any water were left.

In the next village, people looked healthier and were better clothed. They'd accepted the doctor's help. We could hear children reciting lessons in a classroom. We saw men tilling gardens, and women adding peelings to compost heaps. In one villager's hut, a sow was tethered to the center pole; six piglets slept on a raised platform. Beside the village market, I noticed a community water pump surrounded with guava trees. Aletta told me that when Champak started its project in that village, 70% of the children under five had been malnourished. Now, five years later, only 10% were malnourished.[10]

India was an example of the revolutionary effects of diet. I recalled that in the 1960s environmentalist Paul Ehrlich had forecast India's doom, predicted for much of the world by Thomas Malthus in the 18th c. — the world could not support its burgeoning population. But then my sister Olive, in India, told me of hybrid wheat they were using. It had shorter stalk, greater yield, and earlier harvest cycle. What we heard at

9. Females account for most of 2m Indian deaths caused annually by "dirty fuels" (*Economist,* Feb. '04).
10. The Food and Agriculture Organisation now doubts that the 1996 World Food Summit goal of cutting in half global malnourishment by 2015 is likely to be met. In South Asia, 40% of children will still go hungry by 2020. India tops its list of malnourished populations, followed by China and Pakistan.

the time was that M.S. Swaminathan of India's Agriculture Department had invited an American named Norman Borlaug to introduce this hybrid grain—and "The Green Revolution" brought India back from the brink of starvation.[11] What I wouldn't learn until I reached Japan, was the remarkable origin of that revolution (see Chapter 28).

Strategy to Uplift Women

Since then, India as a whole has not lacked basic food. But Indian women have had other problems to face, and those also affect entire communities. Dr. Bell was out to help them. First, she faced men who opposed educating women. They claimed that to enrol in the government's free small business course required a grade-ten level, which no village woman had ever reached. Aletta found it wasn't required, but she still had to fight for places in courses, because males claimed all places were taken.

Champak then organized a program to provide piglets for anyone who'd look after them. The Centre chose pigs because the only ones who would keep pigs were low-caste—the people the Centre wanted to help the most. Village men weren't interested, but women were—again, the most needy sector. So Aletta organized community committees that placed pigs and arranged breeding. When a sow gave birth, the owner had to give away two piglets to two neighbors—and so the benefits spread. Since the district veterinary, a Muslim, wouldn't come to inoculate pigs, Aletta found a Hindu vet who would—except he usually couldn't be bothered travelling to villages to treat pigs kept by *women*!

Aletta recalled how people had helped her earn her education in Canada. That was when rural society didn't expect farm girls to go into professions such as medicine. But perceptive teachers and principals noticed this girl who was at the head of her class, and urged her on. One even arranged bursaries to pay for university. With those memories, Aletta was a constant advocate for helping women.

"I've noticed the men around here give you respect," I commented after we'd dropped in at an administrator's office. "How come" I continued, tongue in cheek, "when you're not only 'a woman' but also single, at that!"

11. Nourishing diet lowers birthrate as the death rate reduces (*Economist*, Dec. 24/05), relieving poverty.

"Ah-ha!" Aletta chuckled. "Partly because of my professional training. Indians respect that. But another reason is my willingness to work in the villages, where professionals don't want to be. That administrator once told me, 'Most of our own people aren't willing to do this, but you—a foreign doctor—you come and *live* among the poor!' So he's very cooperative."

More than officials respected Aletta, the next village proved. A hubbub drew us to its little market, where drunken men from another village were trying to drag away a health worker. The man was brother of the chief, who wouldn't allow the intruders to sell or drink beer in the market. The drunken brewers wanted to beat up the young man in revenge. Disregarding the cursing and shouting, Dr. Bell waded into the melee, which suddenly became hushed.[12]

"Now, tell me what this nonsense is about!" she demanded in Hindi. After listening to the complaints, she told the intruders to leave—and all was over!

"Thank God I'm Not a Woman or Dog!"

"OK— you're certainly respected here!" I agreed. "But is it true that a traditional male thanks his god he wasn't born as a woman or dog?"

"Sadly that's true," Aletta confirmed. "The treatment of women is really dreadful. At a Hindu girl's wedding, the customary greeting of guests is, 'May you be the mother of a hundred *sons*.' That's also the name of a book exposing the treatment of Hindu women. The author cites bride killing, female infanticide, forced abortions, and widow burning—all outlawed but secretly perpetrated in some places. Bribery and status make prosecution difficult." However, in 2006, a court did sentence a doctor and his assistant to two years in prison for agreeing to perform an abortion after illegally revealing the sex of the foetus. Annually, India accounts for an estimated 10 million abortions.[13]

---

12. Shades of Mary Slessor, the Scottish pioneer in Nigeria. When I had visited that area, villagers told me how she would separate armed warriors, make peace, and proclaim the gospel to them!

13. Some 20,000 ultrasound clinics identify female foetuses, leading to female infanticide. With other conditions, this reportedly results in an estimated population imbalance of 40m females. UN estimates that 113m-200m are demographically "missing" worldwide. Globally, 1.5m-3m females die annually from male abuse and violence, killing more women than does disease (including cancer). "Women in an Insecure World" labels it "hidden gendercide." —*Economist,* Nov. 26, 2005, p. 58.

I knew that Hinduism not only condones but also glorifies some crimes in the name of religion. For instance, millions of Hindus deify widow burning by honoring the victim with the title of *Sati-Mata* ("Mother Goddess").

Aletta told me that if a husband or his family is not satisfied with dowry payments, or his wife's servitude, or lack of a male heir, he simply douses her with kerosene and sets her alight. One newspaper reported that police recorded 4,000 bride burnings *in one state* ("and if those are the recorded ones, the total is likely double," commented Aletta). Few come to trial because of corruption. In a nearby village, Aletta knew a beautiful bride whose bruised and strangled corpse was dumped in a pond. No inquest was held.

"Even for women who survive, life is miserable," Aletta continued. "Both Muslim and Hindu men restrict the movement of their wives, keeping them virtual prisoners and slaves. Their women have no say in life—in fact, most men do not want an educated wife, because the woman would speak up against injustice. While husbands may commit adultery at will, women are punished severely, if not killed.

"Although most women are malnourished (family males eat first), they are baby factories," Aletta added. She ought to know—having personally delivered some 20,000 babies and supervised a total of some 45,000 births. One mother was only 14. "If a woman doesn't produce a baby, or only a female, she's to blame. If she's sick, she's sent back to her parents, for them to look after. Since many husbands are far away working, a relative may not bother taking a woman to hospital—and she's not allowed to go by herself. If she needs blood, most male relatives are reluctant to give it."

Women as Leaders

"If that's how many men look upon women, how do you account for the great women who have risen to leadership in Asia?" I puzzled.

"Interesting paradox!" Aletta responded. "Women are becoming educated, especially in the higher caste. It hasn't filtered down to the illiterate masses yet, but literates are becoming more aware of human rights. There are a lot of women's movements. However, we're not involved in politics—only in doing what the government agrees needs to be done—helping the common people."[14]

"So how's the best way of doing that?" I asked, remembering that ailing mother who couldn't count past three.

"Of course, the gospel is the answer," Aletta said. "But as William Carey showed, communicating the gospel means a number of practical things. We must educate women, which we're doing through village health workers. They become human beings in their own eyes then. The husbands will respect them when they begin to earn money and become a useful member of the household. And for those who come to know Jesus Christ—that's when they find true liberation!"[15]

In my travels I'd heard allegations that missionaries "bribe" the poor by offering them material things—and then claim them as converts. That, I found, is a hollow charge made by people who aren't doing much, if anything, about uplifting the poor. Some seem jealous of obvious benefits from programs like the Centre's. In fact, higher castes oppose uplifting the poor in lower castes. If pressed, knowledgeable critics know that so-called conversion is meaningless if it's for material benefits. The Champak staff know that also and are careful not to attach any strings to their work. For those who ask for spiritual help, an evangelist is always available. Other staffers at the Centre include a teacher, agriculturalist, nurse, and crafts instructor.

When we returned to Raxaul, patients were lined up to see Dr. Bell. It would be a long day for her! Others on staff had their own line of patients waiting. Men, women, and children come to this 200-bed hospital from many parts of India and from across the border—Nepal. It's not that there aren't excellent hospitals elsewhere.

"India has one of the finest medical services," staffers told me. "That is—on paper. The problem is that many government doctors are also busy

14. In some lands, people vote for a woman who represents the dynasty of an assassinated leader. Males who despise women, may worship a goddess to ensure their wives' fertility, and as part of temple sex rites.

15. Caste still affects even Christians because of family pressures and social status. Some 6,400 castes segregate the population with social barriers, and 80% of the nation faces some form of discrimination.

in private practice and may not show up in hospitals. Medicines are often missing. People know they'll find devoted doctors, nurses, and other staff here, and also the medicines they need."

AIDS—the Threatened Explosion

On one of India's busiest truck routes, attractive young women lounge seductively in their doorways, waiting for the next truck to pull up. N— village is a convenient stopover point for weary truckers. At night, light streaming from bedside lamps temptingly silhouettes the figures lounging in doorways. A BBC report claimed that virtually every girl in N— becomes a prostitute.[16] Among nations globally, India has the second-highest number of people infected with HIV, forecast to overtake South Africa's infection statistics within ten years. The estimate ranges between 2.5 m. and 5 m. Some officials project 9m by 2010; other estimates are higher.

Predictably, in such towns AIDS is a major threat, and truckers carry HIV (the AIDS infection) back home and across the nation. Aletta knew of Sarabjeet, whose husband was one of them, but he didn't tell his wife. Their baby daughter was born infected and died before her third birthday. When Sarabjeet's husband also died of AIDS, her in-laws blamed her for both deaths. The distraught widow only wanted to kill herself when a worker with AIDS Care Training Services (ACTS) took her to Shalom, a Christian clinic. Today Sarabjeet has hope—and a job that provides her support.

"We help with projects such as ACTS in Delhi,"[17] Aletta explained. "Our mission also sponsors Hope for Aids projects here and worldwide. We empower churches by training volunteers in a Christian approach to sexual health education and to work with sufferers. That's really needed—

16. July 7, 2004. Although itinerant Muslims also visit prostitutes, Islam blames both Hindus and Christians for prostitution. Nominal "Christian" villages, where inner morality has not replaced traditional strictures, unfortunately are known for sexual promiscuity and drunkenness. Muslims don't understand Christianity is based on spiritual regeneration, not legislated behavior (as is Islam). Islam lumps all Christians together.
17. HOPE for AIDS partners with the Shalom Care and Training Centre in Delhi. SIM also helps homecare and prevention projects in partnership with CANA (Christian AIDS/HIV National Alliance).

a recent India-wide survey showed that 36% of respondents thought infected people deserved their fate and should kill themselves!

"I still see the face of Shanti, a beautiful child," Aletta says. "The Hindu temple had thrown her out when her mother, a 23-year-old temple prostitute, died. A pastor found Shanti sitting in the rain holding her baby brother, and brought her to our Home of Hope. Shanti found more than food and shelter—she found Jesus. Now her eyes sparkle."

But another prostitute, Meena, 19, told Aletta she'd been forced into the sex trade to pay off the debts of her mother—who also was a prostitute. Meena was emaciated and infected with HIV and TB.

Duncan and other hospitals tackle problems like these. Although presently AIDS affects only a small *percentage* of India's burgeoning population, the World Health Organization predicts it will explode unless the government takes urgent measures. (For several years, India denied any outbreak.) In spite of the blatant lewdness of temples, Indians don't like to discuss sexual disease. Now the federal and several state governments have programs of treatment and education, with industry and NGOs (including missions) assisting. BBC and Star TV join in campaigns. However, education departments tend to remove discussion of sexual activity, instead teaching "life skills: nutrition, decision-making, and communicating with parents."[18]

Adding to India's misery is the plight of 10m blind—more than one quarter of blind cases globally. in most of the world While the World Health Organization (WHO) has controlled polio in most of the world, pandemic blindness is still resistant in India. In rural areas, poverty and poor diet often increase its occurrence. Fatalism, class distinction, and belief in the cycle of births help spread infection and cause discrimination. Vermin (to a Hindu, re-born ancestors) harbor and spread disease.

A Disciple Takes Up Her Cross

"How did a doctor from rural Canada end up here, on Nepal's border?" I wondered. Aletta described for me her pilgrimage—a somewhat

18. *Economist,* Sept. 15, 2007.

roundabout trail. She had spent a short term with a hospital in the Trucial States, UAE,[19] before serving in India. Once here, she signed up with Emmanuel Hospitals Association, formed in 1970 by evangelical Christian Indians and expatriates. EHA now encompasses 20 hospitals, 26 projects, 4 schools of nursing, and 5 primary schools. Staff total 1500, including 128 doctors, 450 nurses, 200 project staff, and 160 administrators. EHA-member hospitals list a total of 1240 beds, and annually handle some 530,000 patients, 25,300 surgical operations, and 15,700 deliveries. They also provide 379 villages with community health teams. Some three million people live in the areas the teams serve.

EHA is the largest Christian indigenous medical mission in the world. Like Duncan and Champak, its members tackle underlying problems, resulting in elimination (rather than just alleviation) of poverty and poor health.[20] They also tackle ancillary problems, such as caring for children orphaned through AIDS. For instance, Duncan's hostel cares for some fifty orphans, providing medical and educational attention.

Another well-run hospital is Ramabai Mukti—offspring of the mission founded by Pandita Ramabai (see Chapter 7). Today it provides for both physically and mentally challenged patients, and has an active evangelistic outreach. The mission also teaches crafts to some 450 girls.

Dr. Bell, herself from a struggling rural Canadian family, became CIGM's first medical doctor. She founded and supervised CIGM's Prem Sewa hospital, upgraded from a clinic in Utraula, in the middle of India's northerly states. When EHA re-assigned her further eastwards to Duncan, she was not happy. Duncan had major tensions, in which she, as CEO, soon became entangled.

---

19. Sponsored and managed by The Evangelical Alliance Mission (TEAM).

20. Staff know that "poverty" is a relative term. Comparison with Western income is meaningless; a villager in India may be better off than a laborer in New York (where a haircut could cost a month's food in rural India). Poverty might be better defined as whether a person can afford to look after himself and family.

A departmental manager, raised by a missionary benefactor, and secretary of his church committee, tried to cover up a fatal car accident. EHA planned to transfer him. Refusing to move, he instead arranged for police to charge Aletta and her staff with making and selling drugs illegally! That started a dragged-out court case in Bihar State—which holds the record for the longest case in history (33 years).[21] For 17 years unable to go on furlough (or, if she left the country, unable to return) without court permission, Aletta experienced the inner Cross that Jesus told his disciples they must bear daily—dying to self and being alive to God.

"I was invited to Raxaul as Duncan Hospital's Medical Superintendent," Aletta explained. "Instead, because of the internal conflict, EHA designated me as Director of Community Health—a position that I didn't know a thing about. It was a blow! At Utraula, I'd been in charge, full of self-confidence. Now I was exhausted, out of control.

"I told the Lord I couldn't handle it. *He* told me his grace would be sufficient for me and the job. I had to die to my own ambitions and let God live through me in whatever circumstances he chose. That's how I found peace!"

(And look at what God has accomplished through her ever since, I thought. William Carey would thank God for her![22])

India is an amazing admixture of bio-diverse humanity. East of Raxaul, people take on Oriental characteristics. They live in the valleys or on the forested slopes of the Himalayan foothills, vying with tigers and some 2,000 elephants for living space. A few groups, like the Bodos, demand independent homelands—a constant threat to the unity of a nation with 6,635 people groups.

Raxaul, on the border with Nepal, was a favorite border crossing for smugglers. People in other parts referred to "those *rascals* up on the Nepal border." "Rascal" in a Bengali accent, morphed into *Raxaul.* However,

---

21. India had only 11 judges for every 1m people (*Economist*, June 7, 2008).
22. Dr. Bell has also made medical visits to Nepal and China.

many of the border crossers were genuine patients who came to Duncan for help. Some of them returned to their country healed in spirit as well as body. I decided to visit Nepal and see for myself. I was about to enter the only Hindu Kingdom in the world.[23]

In India, I'd seen both sides of the coin of reality—the down side and the up side. Every nation has both those sides. But uppermost in my memory of India are the intelligent, capable, courageous, and faithful men and women who daily honour their Lord and are a credit to their nation. I left the country feeling that the message of the gospel is in good hands—hands dedicated to the Lord and directed by his Spirit.

Now I looked forward to visiting Nepal, where the man who became Buddha was born. There and in Tibet, both on "the Roof of the World," I'd learn more about Buddhism. Later in my travels—even as far as Japan—I'd see Buddhism in different forms.

---

23. India, although predominantly Hindu, is officially a *secular* republic. Hinduism is Nepal's *state* religion. For an analysis of Buddhism, see Appendix F: Religion, Buddhism.

C – NEPAL, TIBET, AND BANGLADESH

Asia's Highlands and Lowlands

Jesus on the Roof of the World

"How beautiful on the mountains are the feet of those who bring good news, who proclaim peace, who bring good tidings, who proclaim salvation" (Isaiah 52.7).

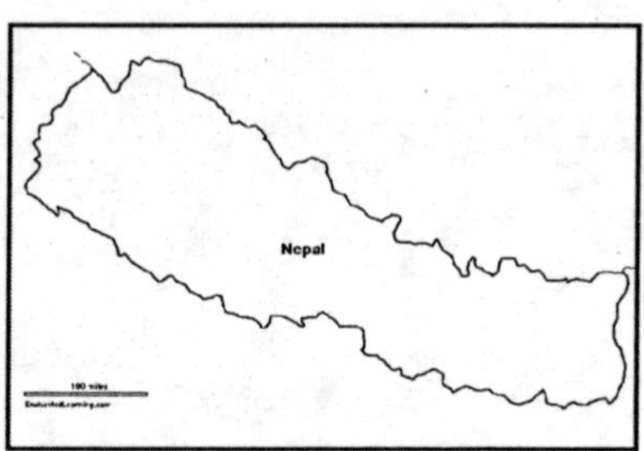

Nepal: Pop. 13,790
Tibet: Pop. 2,500,000

I COULD *BREATH* AGAIN! That's how I felt when I stepped out of the plane at Katmandu airport. A fresh Himalayan breeze rippled Nepal's unique flag—two-tiered triangular red pennants. A cotton shirt was plenty when I left India's plains, but now, at 1,400m. (4,600 ft.), I was glad to use one of the "layers" stowed in my carry-on bag.

To the north rose the higher ranges of the Himalayas. "The Roof of the World," the travel books call the lofty area of Nepal and neighboring Tibet. Nepal, only 400 miles long and some 100 wide, is the world's only Hindu Kingdom[1] and boasts eight of the world's ten highest mountains—topped by majestic Mount Everest.

Ah—clear, crisp air! The pastor who was to meet me wasn't at the airport, so I hopped on the courtesy bus a five-star hotel had waiting for other passengers. That at least took me to the hotel in town, where I telephoned the National Churches Fellowship of Nepal (NCFN). My letter giving travel details hadn't arrived, but the General Secretary would

1. Some readers may have thought of India as a Hindu nation also, but officially it is a secular republic. The Gautama Buddha was born into an aristocratic Nepalese family but developed his beliefs in India.

be on his way. I savored a cup of thick coffee in the luxurious International Hotel lobby before the Rev. Dr. Simon Pandey rolled up at the impressive main entrance—on a noisy motorcycle.

With no limousine door to open for me, the turbaned porter looked a little puzzled. His arms, complete with gold braid on the cuffs, hung helplessly by his side. Of course I tipped him anyway; but he must have felt somewhat dissonant as this "tourist" tied his own two bags on the motorcycle's rack. Without ceremony, I swung on to the rear saddle, hanging on to my host as we roared down the landscaped boulevard.

As Pastor Pandey negotiated the heavy traffic through town, black diesel exhaust filled my lungs. Where did that fresh, clean air go? Keeping close behind laboring trucks and buses, he quickly darted around them at the first gap in traffic. I gulped in two-lungs' worth of less toxic air each time we roared past, before we tailgated the next vintage vehicle. I was grateful the General Secretary had picked me up, but I was more thankful when we arrived intact at the modest office of the NCF, where the air *was* fresh after all!

I holed up in the guest room kept for visitors. It wasn't just the cooler air that gave me chills. The sudden change in altitude activated the infections I'd picked up in Delhi.[2] I fell into a fitful sleep on a cot. Unconnected bits of memory drifted through a haze. I was on a rickshaw chasing elephants—no, an elephant was chasing me. The rickshaw would not go fast enough. The elephant became an Indian lorry, then an airplane. It landed on Everest, sliding down its snowy slopes as I was about to fall off my narrow cot.

In a feverish sweat, I lay thinking about "lofty" dreams that bring mountain climbers to Nepal—such as scaling Everest, the world's highest peak. My goals were a trifle more down-to-earth: (1) learn more about the people of the Roof of the World; (2) discuss NCFN's ministry;[3] and (3) visit the United Mission to Nepal (UMN)—a consortium of 50 agencies from some 20 countries.

---

2. Higher altitude means lower atmospheric pressure and less oxygen.
3. On behalf of World Evangelical Alliance.

General Secretary Pandey had told me how early bearers of the Good News came from Darjiling in northeast India, where Presbyterians had pioneered.[4] In the 50s, a Nepali who went to India for work, found Christ as his Saviour and returned to evangelize his own people. By the 80s, several new churches formed the Nepal Christian Fellowship. However, since it was a denomination in itself, NCF and other groups had worked with WEA to form a wider coordinating body, the NCFN. Its members included a number of small groups that had been forming for some thirty years, through the quiet witness of Christian teachers in schools, through missionary medical work, and through Nepalis who had returned from India with the gospel.

Until 1990, Christian groups were not legal, officially. Hindu villagers ostracized Christians, and religious leaders sometimes confiscated their crops and livestock, even their land. Converts went across to India to be baptized. Theirs was an underground church. This was very true of the Nepali believers Aletta Bell had told me about at Duncan Hospital.

But in 1990, Christians were euphoric when the king publicly pronounced freedom of religion on the radio late one Sunday evening. The following Sunday was Easter, so some 300 Christians paraded through Katmandu with banners in Nepali and English, proclaiming the resurrection of Christ the Lord. I could only imagine what that meant to Nepali Christians, after decades of repression. Now Nepali men and women train at the Nepal Mission Training Center to take the gospel to other parts of Nepal and other lands.

(Christians have since lived through a Hindu backlash, political unrest, and a massacre within the royal household. More recently a Maoist insurgency joined "republicans" in a coalition government that abolished the monarchy.)

Together for a Common Purpose

Now awake, I splashed water in my face and headed out into the sunshine. I was eager to visit the UMN offices, for I had mail for David

4. Roman Catholics worked in 17th c., Indian evangelicals made later visits. Cindy L. Perry, *The History of the Church in Nepal*. Wheaton: The Graham Centre Nepal Church History Project (1989).

and Carol Stevens. Their offices were only a kilometer away, so I headed there on foot, for a little cultural exposure.

The streets of Katmandu, Nepal's capital, were filled with rural people seeking employment and refugees fleeing neighbouring totalitarian governments. Land-locked, the country also seemed locked in poverty, so tourists back-packing along the streets helped the economy.[5] However, Maoist violence greatly reduced the number of foreign mountain climbers.

The 1990 popular uprising had restored the oft-banished monarchy—only to have an unhinged member[6] of the royal family massacre the others (in 2001) beforeshooting himself. A new monarch, a former Hindu businessman, sought to hold the country together at the time and improve its economy—not an easy task, with an ongoing. Maoist insurgency (that claimed thousands of lives) and the population projected to reach 30m by 2010. Reacting to the insurgents, the king consulted his astrologers and imposed autocratic rule. Nation-wide rioting later toppled the government, nationalized royal property, and led to a democratic assembly that re-wrote the constitution, abolishing the monarchy. The former palace became a museum.

This land on the edge of the Himalayan Ridge continues to "live on the edge" politically. However, Hindus revere Nepal for being the world's only Hindu (at least in name) Kingdom. To be legitimate, the government must still receive the blessing of a living goddess, *The Kumari*, a female regarded as an incarnation of the Earth Mother.[7]

As I walked through the capital's crowded streets, pedal-powered rickshaws pulled up alongside me, their cyclist drivers hoping for a fare. Shops reflected Tibetan and Indian architecture. Awnings draped from peeling plaster walls provided shade for hawkers of everything from fresh produce to pirated tapes and counterfeit watches. On the whole, Nepalis seem more laid-back than their neighbors to the south—but I shouldn't generalize. After all, this is a land of many different peoples, although

5. Nepal holds top place for farming, in a list of 27 poor nations. Agriculture provides 39% of Nepal's economy (GDP). Some 10m Nepalis have left the country, to seek work in other lands.
6. Reportedly, he was high on drink and drugs.
7. We published her photograph (taken by our photographer): *Celebrate* (see under Fuller in Bibliog.).

most trace their ancestry to Indo-Aryan or Tibetan stock. Their most famous fighters are Gurkhas, outstanding soldiers of both the British and Indian Army for a couple of centuries.[8] This proud country has never been colonized.

At the offices of UMN, David and Carol helped me understand the country. They'd been seconded by InterServe, one of 50 Christian agencies that make up UMN, with staff from all over the world. Missions familiar to praying friends everywhere are among them.[9] Entering years before Nepal officially permitted Christian work, UMN registered as a development agency and won the respect of people and government with health, agriculture, reforestation, livestock, education, and energy projects. The latter included biogas for cooking, produced from manure and water in an underground tank—a boon in Nepal's hills, where most of the trees have been felled for firewood.

There seems no end to the area's medical needs. The altitude and dazzling snow of the Himalayas increase the incidence of eye cataracts. The majority of the world's 22 million blind people live in Nepal and Northern India.[10]

Specialists from different countries and various missions or churches work together to find "sustainable"[11] solutions to Nepal's needs. Miriam Krantz was one of these—a nutritionist working with rural mothers. Miriam remembers seeing Chini Maya carrying her malnourished son Samu—literally skin and bones. Miriam and other UMN staff patiently urged the listless child to swallow nourishing porridge Miriam had formulated from local grains and pulse (bean). After the first few gagging swallows, the child began to lap it up. In a few days Samu was reaching for his plate and refused to give it up until he'd licked it clean! In 17 days Chini returned home with Samu walking, normal weight for height.

---

8. Currently Britain's Army has 3,400 "Gurkhas" from several clans, though originally from a dominant clan. However, dubbed "lahure" after the Indian city of Lahore, where many soldiers once served, some 10% of Nepalis who work abroad are known by the name.
9. Including major denominations as well as inter-church agencies and missions.
10. Report of NBC News and World Health Organization, Sept. 28, 2003.
11. UN/WHO jargon for projects based on local materials, skills, and manpower.

"This is a wonder!" Chini tells her neighbors. "We have all these things in our village, but we didn't know how to use them!" Samu is now a "poster child" in the government's nutrition program, which promotes Miriam's formula as "Sarbottom Pitho."

Out of these projects, Nepali leadership has developed. While studying at UMN's Butwal Technical Institute, Nwang Singh Gurung started reading the Bible but covered his bases with instruction from Hindu priests and Buddhist monks. Comparing what he learned, he concluded that Jesus is the Way, the Truth, and the Life.

Nwang went on to work for UMN's hydroelectric projects and caught the vision of providing energy for Tibetan communities. He became a skillful leader in energy technology but he also co-founded a Christian vocational organization for marginalized peasants. His brilliant leadership has helped communities in Tibet and Nepal.

"Even before 1990," UMN staff reminisced, "the government welcomed all the help we could give the country. Of course, we had to be low-key as we showed God's love through serving the needs of one of Asia's poorest countries. We 'let our light shine' through our lives—and people noticed the contrast. Now we can openly worship and teach Bible."

"Congratulations for Your Stupid Allegations"

Observers outside Nepal also took note. In Pakistan I'd heard of a fundamentalist Muslim newspaper that sounded an alarm about Nepalis turning from Hindu idols to the living God. That was rather odd, because Muslims officially represent only 3.5% of Nepal's population. And shouldn't Muslims rejoice that Hindus were turning from idolatry?[12] Perhaps the editor wanted to provide readers with an illustration of Christian "subversion," to forestall Christian evangelism in Pakistan. The newspaper listed Christian agencies working in Katmandu, making allegations against them, such as being spies and working against the nation. Here was one classic:

12. Muhammad thought Nestorian monks in Sinai worshiped religious *icons* in their monastery. In Hindu lands, Muslims conclude Mary and Jesus are Christian equivalents of Hindu *avatara* (manifestations of Vishnu). Islam's rallying cry seemed apt: "There is one God, and Muhammad is his prophet."

> **Christian doctors give placebos to patients, who of course do not get well. Then they come and pray over them and give them real medicine, after which they improve!**

One or two offices whose telephone numbers were listed, did receive a couple of threatening calls, but they also had several interested inquiries about their work. It turned out to be good publicity! In Pakistan, another Muslim paper, in opposition to Islamic fundamentalists, thanked the fundamentalist paper for its "expose."

"Congratulations!" read the editorial in the other Muslim newspaper. "You have just kept several thousand Christians from converting to Islam, because your allegations have been so stupid."[13]

Muslim allegations of Christian medical atrocities were nothing new. Extremist Hindu groups have made similar allegations. In 1999, Nepali Christians had been concerned to see one of India's most violent Hindu sects establish a political party in Nepal, with the declared intention of opposing any conversions. Their leader claimed Christians had grown from six thousand to one million in just a few years—an obvious scare tactic, although the actual figure may be 1.5m. A government official accused Christians of a range of atrocities, such as sneaking into hospitals to give patients wrong medicines.

"This is an affront and very irresponsible," Nepali Christians declared. "It's clear the main parties feel they must make extremist noises against Christians in order to placate the militants." But the leaders of a citywide evangelistic event were dumbfounded when a politician, invited because of his promotion of religious *freedom*, publicly railed against Christians for supposed atrocities and fake healings.

Things got worse when police admitted killing two young men just graduated from a Nepali-run Bible college, for no apparent reason—they were not involved in any political activity. Two other Christians from the same village also died in police custody under suspicious circumstances.

---

13. Later, in the Iraq war, Muslim terrorists murdered 12 Nepalese kitchen staff employed by the army. The Muslims claimed to be "executing God's judgment" against "Buddhist invaders." That didn't make the front pages in Muslim newspapers, but next day, *Al Ahram,* Arab world's largest daily, headlined news that rioters attacked a mosque back in Katmandu (not bothering to explain what had provoked the riot).

In western Nepal, Maoists admitted bombing a Lutheran office involved in humanitarian assistance. (However, not only Christians suffer from Nepal's violence, and Maoists are not sole perpetrators. In one recent year, more people were listed, "Disappeared," than any other country claimed in that category.[14])

Hari Prasad was one of many Nepalis who cross the border into India looking for work. While living in one of Champak's community villages, he read the Gospel of John. When he came to John 3.16 ("God so loved the world that he gave his only begotten son..."), he trusted in Christ for salvation, meeting to worship with other new Christians. When radical Hindus heard that, they prevented Christians from using village wells and working their fields. Rather than stir up further trouble, the Christians met in one-room houses instead of in a church building. Their faith was more important than a building.

Moving to another village, Prasad asked the headman for permission to preach, but the chief was afraid to approve even his living there.

"I'm not a lion to eat you!" Prasad told him.

"I'm afraid because you'll make Christians," the chief replied.

"I'll tell people about God's love," explained Prasad. "How will that make Christians?"

"Ah, Muslims make followers by the sword, but Christians make followers by love!" replied the chief.

New Testament Miracles

The number of people turning to Christ has obviously drawn opposition. But news of amazing healings that accompanied early years in Nepal's church growth has been no secret. Most Nepali believers have come in ones and twos, but the story of the Tamang "people movement" (to use missiological jargon) remarkably combines courageous missionary obedience with dramatic conversion—much like New Testament experience.

14. BBC World News, June 24, 2005.

The saga began in 1952 with two intrepid women missionaries. Lily O'Hanlon was an English medical doctor; Hilda Steele was an Irish agriculturalist who lived in the northern Indian town of Nautanwa—not far from Raxaul. The spiritual and physical needs of India were enormous, but Nepalis who streamed across the border told the two women that their land had been closed to the gospel for a century, and no one could identify a Christian in all the country. The women knew that Nestorian missionaries had once reached the lofty ramparts of Nepal and Tibet—but that was a millennium ago. All traces of the gospel seemed to have died out as Hinduism and Buddhism swept across Asia.

The Holy Spirit laid these people on the hearts of the two women, and when the monarchy was restored in 1952, allowing foreigners to enter, these two and a few colleagues formed the Nepal Evangelistic Band (NEB). They trekked along trails that climbed and descended range after range, until they arrived in the Pokhara Valley, at the foot of the Annapura Massif (8,000 m. /26,000 ft. above sea level) on Tibet's border. There they opened the NEB hospital. As other medics joined the team, patients trekked in from all over Nepal and Tibet, and bordering parts of China and India.

One of the tribes-people treated was a Tamang, who populate many of the valleys. A strict Buddhist, nevertheless the man gladly accepted a Nepali New Testament as well as medication. When a nephew came to visit him in his Pokhara home, the uncle told him about the strange news he'd heard at the hospital—about the God who can even heal the sick. When the nephew, Lok Bahadur, returned to his own village, a four-day walk, he took with him the New Testament.

But during Lok's absence, his daughter had become ill. In vain, the Buddhist shaman[15] attempted to heal her. Lok told his wife and neighbors what he'd heard in Pokhara—but they weren't willing to risk angering the shaman. That night, however, Lok found the courage to pray to the God he really didn't know, yet somehow he believed God could heal, just as he'd haltingly read in the Gospels. Then he fell sound asleep. In the morning, he wasn't surprised that his daughter was completely well. The

15. *Shaman*: (Evenki, a Siberian language.) Priest/priestess who uses magic to divine events and heal.

rest of the family said it was just a delayed response to the shaman's rituals.

But someone else in the village fell ill a few days later; again the shaman's magic didn't work. The person's family were desperate, so they agreed to have Lok pray in Jesus' name. The sick person was well the next morning. These healings continued, despite village antagonism.

"Lok is in league with an evil spirit!" cried the shaman. Persecution increased as more villagers deserted their Hindu gods and worshiped the God Lok told them about, reading from the New Testament. Violence broke out, until the new believers realized they should move. They took advantage of a government re-settling plan and moved to the untamed land of Duradara. They were pioneers in every sense of the word, having to clear and terrace land to grow food. But they persevered, and other Tamang believed and joined them. They all tried to follow the communal life the Bible portion described. Some believers returned to their original villages as missionaries—hadn't Jesus said his disciples should be witnesses? Still, opposition to the new faith was brutal: believers beaten, crops destroyed, livestock stolen, houses set alight.

"The Mad Woman Is Healed!"

Then the most dramatic healing took place—in a woman whose husband had accused her of being a witch when their baby died. Under such stress, the mother became mentally deranged. Everyone in the valleys heard of Flechya, the uncontrollable mad one. Wherever she appeared, villagers cursed, threw stones, and drove her out.

In desperation, she found her way to the Christian village of Duradara. There the believers showed her love, prayed for her, and nursed her back to mental health. She decided to return to her own village and tell what Jesus had done for her. Flechya was like the man born blind—no one could deny that this "mad woman" was now entirely normal, and sick people she prayed for in Jesus' name also got well. It was sensational news, spreading throughout the valleys like brush fire. Entire communities believed; shaman priests burned their own fetishes.

That "people's movement" (rather—movement of God's Spirit) has tamed one of the most lawless parts of Western Nepal! What happened? Two women (with no sponsoring organization or "strategic planning") had a missionary vision. Others joined them in obedience to Jesus' command. The Holy Spirit used Christian compassion to open a door and his Word to transform lives. That's quite a saga![16]

By 1953, the Nepal Evangelistic Band (now International Nepal Fellowship) had received official permission to enter for humanitarian work, followed in 1954 by the United Mission to Nepal. Trevor and Patricia Strong, both medical doctors at Duncan Hospital in Raxaul, made trips into Nepal to treat the royal family. They also strengthened the few known believers.

Until 1960, there were only unofficial house churches, unrecognized by the government. Groups began to multiply in the 80s, and Gurkha soldiers who'd become Christians while overseas built Katmandu's first Christian church. Other redbrick churches appeared in the capital. However, anyone who changes his/her religion is liable to a year's imprisonment, and anyone responsible for a conversion faces a six-year sentence.[17] In spite of such laws (only occasionally applied), multiplication of Christians has been remarkable.

Besides, "Nepal and Tibet" had a sacred aura in their mountain steadfastness. "The Roof of the World" must be closer to the gods![18] Isolation (only mountainous trails, no roads at the time) kept its valleys almost inaccessible to the corrupting influences of the outer world. But mountain ranges and religious laws couldn't keep out the Holy Spirit—so Krishna, an Indian student, discovered. His story began back on the Indian lowlands.

---

16. Thomas and Cynthia Hale, former medical missionaries in Nepal, tell the full story in *A Light Shines in Central Asia* (see Bibliography).
17. At time of this author's visit.
18. Mountains inspire awe by their durability and grandeur. Through the ages, many religious people have substituted their awe, for worship of the transcendent, eternal, omnipotent Creator they did not know.

Suicidal Student Finds Eternal Life

"I only want to die!" Krishna cried out to his father, Ravi, one day. He was still quivering after narrowly escaping suicide by jumping off the tracks as a train thundered by. A bright student, in college he'd become disillusioned with life and decided to end it all by lying across the tracks. But as the train approached, he couldn't end it all.

In shock, Ravi looked at his trembling son. The farmer had named his first-born in honor of a powerful god, hoping the boy would receive good *karma* and do the family proud. In fact, Krishna faithfully studied the Hindu scriptures and worshiped "the five idols." But by his teens, he found life empty and meaningless.

"Son, you've been affected by foreign ideas at college!" Ravi told his much-loved son. "I know the best place for you! We'll pay for you to study in Nepal, where you won't be bothered by these wrong ideas." So Krishna found himself in Katmandu, studying in the capital of Hindu orthodoxy.

In Katmandu, no one from Krishna's family could check his lifestyle, so he tried to drown his unhappiness in drink and highlife. One day a Nepali handed him a gospel tract. Curious, Krishna read about the peace Jesus Christ could give. He'd never heard about Jesus. The message was so different from anything he'd learned, Krishna searched for the man, who turned out to be a Christian preacher.

"I invited the man to my room." Krishna later recalled. "He showed me a beautiful book called the New Testament. It was in Nepali. For three days and nights I was so disturbed by the message that Jesus was speaking to me, I couldn't eat or sleep.

"Finally I went to see the preacher again. He told me that Jesus loves me, and if I confessed my sins to him, Jesus would come into my life and give me his peace. I did that and suddenly felt I was the happiest, most peaceful, joyful, and confident person in this world. Tears rolled down my cheeks as I really trusted in Jesus."

Krishna felt God was telling him to go back and witness to his family. They cursed him and threw him out of the family. Wanting to know more of God's Word, he studied at a theological college in India. Four years later, he hesitantly visited his family. The shock came when his father said he'd also like to read the Bible.

"The family finally accepted me and even attended my marriage to a Christian girl!," reported Krishna, who attended Singapore's Asian Cross-Cultural Training Institute (ACTI), and with his wife is now witnessing among their own people.[19]

"Where can I flee from your presence?" the psalmist asked (Psalm 139.7). "If I go up to the heavens, you are there!" Krishna found Jesus on "The Roof of the World."

How Fatal Is Fatalism?

One Hindu belief that depressed Krishna was its inherent fatalism. I'd read an interesting book by Nepal's leading anthropologist, Professor Dor Bahadur Bista, *Fatalism And Development*.[20] I asked the Executive Director of UMN what he thought of the book, since the UMN is heavily involved in development.

"I know the author well," the Director said. "Dr. Bista has personal experience in trying to help develop communities—he started a brick and tile factory, for instance, as well as other local industries. He has international experience, having served as Nepal's Consul- General in Tibet and on international commissions.

"Since Dor Bista is a Hindu scholar, I was interested that he attributes the problems of Nepal to Buddhism and Hinduism. He points out that Nepalese have the qualities to sustain development, but an alien culture has stifled their initiative through fatalism. He doesn't come to any solution—only asks questions about the future. I asked Dor if he'd agree the solution really is in changing from fatalistic Hinduism to Christianity—with its sense of self-worth, personal responsibility, and work ethic. The professor only pointed out that Christian societies also

19. Krishna's précised story (with names changed) is from April 2004 *News Bulletin* of ACTI, Singapore.

20. See Bibliography. Fatalism is at the core of Hindu and Buddhist belief, although they believe human effort *can* influence passage into the next existence. Millennia ago, Aryans introduced this "alien culture."

have their problems. He describes himself as an agnostic, non-practicing Hindu."

"So some educated people see the problem but aren't about to change the culture?" I asked. "What can churches do about that kind of view?"

"The difference between churches in India and churches here is that Nepalese members are first-generation Christians," the Director of UMN went on to explain. "For instance, thousands of Tamang believe in Jesus as healer—and God honors their faith. But many don't yet know Jesus as Redeemer. They've thrown out their idols, and their lives have been changed, but they have little teaching from the Word of God and can easily be misled by cults. There's always the danger of syncretism. Most people don't even know the distinction between Buddhist and Hindu. Hindu temples have Buddhist figures and *vice versa*. How many know the difference between 'religion' and the Christian life? That's the greatest need here—teaching and discipling in the Word."

Underground Church Surfaces on "The Roof"

Rishi Acharya shares that vision, not only for Nepal but also for the whole area called "The Roof of the World." He told me his grandfather had been a Hindu priest, and his father was a strict Brahmin—the highest caste. As a child, he felt very proud of that and when he was eight, a Hindu priest officially inducted him as a Brahmin, marking his forehead with a sign. That meant he could not cut his hair short,[21] eat in a non-Brahmin's house, eat meat except goat on special feast days, or learn English (which might corrupt him with non-Hindu learning). He studied the Hindu scriptures, but when a cousin opened an elementary school, he studied English in secret.

He also met a Nepali Christian who shared with him the gospel story and gave him a Scripture portion from the Christian Literature Centre at Duncan Hospital. Rishi became a believer and read other books from the Centre. He kept his new faith secret at first, but when he returned to his people along the Rapti River, he couldn't help spreading the good news he'd found. Small groups of believers sprang up along the

21. He could fudge on that restriction, if he left one strand longer than the rest.

southern valley. At the time, they couldn't register as a church; so they formed and registered the Rapti Development Committee. Several believers have been imprisoned; but in a recent year, 15 villagers were baptized in the river.

"Now churches can register!" Rishi told me. "We've seen amazing growth in the Rapti Valley. There are now more than 25 churches.[22] But we need to teach God's Word!"

The International Bible Society, along with Living Bible Publishers, asked Rishi to work on a new translation of the New Testament. They produced 25,000 copies of the first portion (Mark), releasing it in the east of the country. Churches are introducing it to every household in the area. Another 10,000 copies went to Prison Fellowship of Nepal, and Rishi has visited every prison in Nepal with copies. When I interviewed him, he was picking up another order of Scripture portions.

Nationwide, several agencies have distributed 30m Bibles or scripture portions, although literacy is officially only 40%, and divided among 124 languages. An indigenous agency, Human Development and Community Services, also ministers through Bible correspondence courses, radio, and Christian films. A Nepali founded the Sower's Ministry, now working out of Hong Kong with 100 workers in eight lands. The Nepal Christian Fellowship includes 10 agencies, with 80 personnel from 12 countries.

"Waste of Time"?

In Katmandu, I met Paul and Clare Hudson. I should say, I caught up with them there, for I first met them years earlier in Ethiopia. Over there, Dr. Paul had been doing what he was now doing in Asia—bringing healing to patients' bodies and telling them about the Saviour who had brought healing to his own soul.

"Me—a missionary?" medical student Paul would have scoffed earlier, while studying medicine. Paul hadn't even believed there was a God. Anyway, who needed one? But while backpacking through Europe, he

22. For the most part, these are house churches: perhaps a dozen people squatting on the mud floor of a room, maybe 3m /10 ft. sq., to read, pray, and chant words of a psalm or hymn—without the gadgets of many churches in other lands.

bunked in at L'Abri, Francis and Edith Schaeffer's spiritual retreat center in Switzerland—low-cost lodging! After a few days, the sceptical backpacker asked the evangelical philosopher, "How do you know the Bible is *really* true?"

As a guest in the Schaeffer's home more than once, I'd seen how Dr. Schaeffer answered questions of atheist and agnostic backpackers who dropped in at the Alpine chalet. He'd verbally back them up against the wall of their own logic, until they had to admit they had no answers to life. In Paul Hudson's case, L'Abri started him on the road to faith in the Saviour. After completing medical college, the new-fledged doctor served stints in East Africa with Africa Inland Mission and SIM. That's when I met him in Ethiopia.

"Tell me," Paul had asked me back then, in SIM's mud-and wattle Addis Ababa guesthouse; "what's your opinion of development work as a means of reaching people with the gospel? Someone just told me, 'Development work is a waste of time, money, and effort. Just preach the gospel!'" To Paul, that sounded like the opposite pole of the social gospel (doing good without preaching). To be effective, how about combining good *and* preaching?

I'd long forgotten Paul's question and my reply, but when I later caught up with him in Asia, he told me I'd apparently given him a biblical "rationale." I'd conceded that although development work *could* be wasted effort, it was really *the handmaiden of preaching*. Jesus certainly did a lot of what we'd call "development work." And in some communities it was the only permitted way to show the Saviour's love. As a medical doctor, Paul went on to serve in Nepal, India, Thailand, and China. He eventually headed up SIM's HIV/AIDS program in Asia.

"It's exciting to see suffering people find relief, plus hope in Jesus Christ!" he enthused, still the tall and lanky backpacker when we met on the trails of the Old Spice Road. I kept thinking of his summary as I learned more about neighboring Tibet.

****

Tibet—Peak of the Roof

"How beautiful are the feet of those who bring good tidings." (Romans 10.15.)

TRAVELERS TO NEPAL aspire to keep climbing to the Peak of the Roof of the World—Tibet.[23] Mountaineers gaze up at Mount Everest and wonder if they can make it to 29,035 feet (8850 m.)—the globe's highest peak. Since New Zealander Edmund Hillary[24] and Sherpa Tenzing Norgay conquered the summit in 1953, some 2,000 other climbers have made the ascent, and more than 200 have died in the attempt. On the border of Tibet and Nepal, it dominates the Himalayan skyline. Although named after a Victorian map-maker, Everest's local title is "Mother goddess of the earth." Durable Sherpa[25] guides who lead adventurers up its slopes are testimony to the "high living" (altitude, that is, not attitude!) of Tibetans. They don't even need oxygen tanks!

Tibet's ancient history includes King Gesar of Ling, still its greatest cultural hero. Probably a pre-Buddhist ruler, he has become a messianic figure who, Tibetan Buddhists believe, will yet return to vanquish all forces inimical to religion—and also make Buddhism (despite its claims not to be a religion) universal. Wandering bards have carried his fame and philosophy as far away as Mongolia.

The lofty mountains of Tibet naturally inspire awe—and worship. Maybe it's their massive height that make humans feel puny—as if they are in the presence of powers beyond their control. Buddhists frequent "prayer mountains": the highest monastery in the world nestles on the

23. Remote and exclusive center of Tibetan Buddhism, the capital, Lhasa (pop. 110,000) was long closed to foreigners and was known as "The Forbidden City."

24. "Sir" since the British crown knighted him.

25. From Tibetan *Sharpo*: "Easterner"—member of Everest-area tribe, skilled mountaineers.

flanks of Everest. Destroyed during Chairman Mao's "revolution," it has now been rebuilt.

Apart from inspiring awe, the Tibetan Plateau and entire Himalayan range are the source of life for large areas of China to the north and the Indian subcontinent and south-east Asia. Their glaciers feed the major river systems that water the plains below, supporting well over a billion people. Some climatologists predict that global warming may threaten that serpentine ecology: rapidly melting glaciers and changing rain patterns. Chinese climatologists predict that by the middle of this century, the icy area feeding their rivers will have shrunk by more than a quarter since the middle of the last century. And India's plight may be greater, as the "Asian Brown Cloud" hangs over northern India-possibly formed by cooking fires and power stations.

Increasingly, scientists debate whether mankind is the cause, or whether this all is part of millennial climate cycle. Whatever the cause, plague and starvation may threaten massed populations dependant upon the great river systems, unable to sustain current agriculture. Adding to South Asia's unrest, down on the Bangladesh Delta millions of refugees (one estimate is 35m by mid-century) may be fleeing rising sea levels flooding inland. All these threats worry governments. While scientists debate causes or even the forecasts, superstitious folklore blames unseen powers in the sky.

Ancients were sure that spirits dwelt in mountain peaks, but Hebrew prophets warned the Jews against sacrificing on "the high places"—common site for pagan altars. I thought of the Samaritan woman, who reminded Jesus that while Jews claimed Jerusalem as the place to worship, her people worshiped on the mountain. Jesus replied, "The time is coming when you will worship the Father neither on this mount nor in Jerusalem. ... God is spirit, and his worshipers must worship in spirit and in truth."[26]

---

26. John 4.21. The ancients sacrificed and worshipped on mountaintops—hence Jehovah's ban of idolaters' "high places." While Psalm 121.1 may seem to look "unto the hills" for help, the psalmist is more likely asking a rhetorical question in the context of hilltop idolatry—"Shall I look unto the hills for help? [*No!*] My help comes from the Lord, the Maker of heaven and earth."

Bon and Buddha Buddies?

When Buddhism did spread to Tibet in the 7th and 8th c., it found the indigenous spirit-worshiping Bon religion with its Lha-Dre—two major classes of deities: *lha* (gods) and *dre* (demons).[27] Buddhism accommodated these as "deities of the world, distinct from the "symbolic deities" that embody Buddhism's qualities of enlightenment. (To a Buddhist, the former are in the same category as Hindu deities imported from India.) Prayer flags of various colours hang from lines or poles along Tibet's passes. Each time they flutter in the chill mountain breezes, they offer petitions that monks have prayed into them (for a certain fee). Tibet's population is 80% Buddhist.

Most of Tibet's quiet, shy people knew no other life than clambering up and down mountain trails with water pots and hand hoes, herding their grazing flocks. Their world exploded in misery after China annexed Tibet in 1951, renaming it Xizang Autonomous Region. Communists unleashed Mao-inspired violence against "class enemies"—ruthlessly throwing Tibetans into slave-labour camps, confiscating property, and scattering family members.

Tibetans' spiritual leader, the Dalai Lama,[28] fled into exile in 1959. Leader of the nation's Buddhists, recipient of the Nobel Peace Prize (1989), the Lama is internationally known as an affable spokesman for peace, his infectious giggle typical of Tibetan shy friendship. Although Buddhism does not recognize God, the Dalai's message to the world calls for "human" or "secular" values that make us "good, warm-hearted, and sensible."

The Dalai, whose actual name is Tenzin Gyatso, was born in 1935. Reputed reincarnated 14 times as the incarnation of "the Living Buddha," the authority he has among Tibetans causes concern among Chinese officials—who insist that only the government can appoint a Dalai Lama. Suggestions that the current Dalai could be reincarnated *outside* Tibet don't reduce government anxiety.

---

27. In early Bon religion, a *shaman* (magic-performing priest) showed ancient Zoroastrian elements, but current Bon practices include elements of Buddhism, which arrived later.
28. Idiomatically "Grand Monk": *Dalai*: (Mongolian "ocean"—i.e. "vast") and *Lama* (Tibetan, "monk").

Tibetan Buddhism follows the Mahayana school of early Buddhism. This gradually evolved into the Tantric-Vajrana form about the 9th c. The other branch follows the Hinayana school, found chiefly in countries to the southeast. Later I'd come across Chinese, Mongolian, Korean, and Japanese forms of Buddhism, all variations of the Mahayana school followed by Tibet.

"In Buddhism, there are three key elements earlier introduced to the area by Aryan invaders," states Thomas Hale, who with his wife Cynthia served in Nepal as medical missionaries.

(1) Universal, impersonal being called Atman or Brahman—source of all reality.

(2) All existence is simply part of the Atman. There is no essential difference between a person, a star, or an insect—or between good and evil, love and hate.

(3) What our senses tell us is an illusion, from which we can awaken only by 'Enlightenment.'[29]

Hale points out that from these basics developed "the greatest motivating force in Buddhism: re-incarnation and *karma*"—every action carries a consequence, good or bad, into the next life (in this respect, similar to Hinduism). Mahayana Buddhism provides one short-cut to the endless cycle of re-incarnations: a *bodhisattva* is an "enlightened" Buddhist, counterpart of Christendom's "saint," who "sacrificially" foregoes final sublimation *after death* in order to remain on earth (represented in a clay figure) helping to save others through 'enlightenment.' He is guaranteed liberation. (Could one say he's reached the point of "no return"?)

This accounts for thousands of Tibetan young men who spend most of their lives in monasteries, meditating as monks. At one time, 46,000 monks lived in 1,780 monasteries, but political events have reduced that number. The universal custom for monks is to gather their daily food by begging—or to put it nicely, by allowing lesser souls to gain merit through giving the monks food.

---

29. Definitions from Hale, *A Light Shines* (see Bibliography).

Since China's absorption of Tibet, the capital, Lhasa, has become dominated by Han Chinese, provoking Tibetan resentment. China's major project in the area has been to build the world's highest altitude rail, now linking Lhasa with Beijing. A remarkable feat of engineering, it traverses quake-prone and perma-frost terrain—now threatened by a cycle of freezing and thawing resulting from climate change. Crossing points provide for migrating Tibetan antelopes. Passenger railcars have to be sealed to ensure oxygen supply. Tourists, mostly Chinese, marvel at the Potala Palace—historic residence of Dalai Lamas. However, the rail line also brought many more Chinese to work and live in Tibet.

Leading up to the 2008 Olympics, many Tibetans joined in public protest over China's dominance.

One unexpected element of Chinese immigration has been the presence of Christians. Some have started house churches, but most worship in secret.

There are some half-million Tibetans living in Nepal, India, and other lands, to escape the grinding poverty of their rocky homeland. Tibet still has fertile valleys, but these are over-grazed and over-cultivated by farmers who subsist mainly on millet, goat's milk, curds, and cheese.

A number of Tibetan "expatriates" have come across the Bible, awakening interest back home in the Christian's Holy Book. In the 19th c., the Bible Society completed a translation in the Tibetan language, but publishing it proved to be almost as difficult as climbing Everest! It seemed as if Satan determined to keep the Word of God out of Tibet. Christians point out that satanic blood covenants, made by Bon animists before Buddhism arrived, have never been rescinded.

It took 90 years to translate and publish the Tibetan Bible, through many hardships. The first manuscript courier who attempted the 50-day mule journey into Kashmir was a Tibetan named Sandrup. He vanished in an avalanche. Months later, a Christian named Bahadur made the journey with a new set of proofs. But at the highest pass he faced the most frightening storm he'd ever witnessed.

Sleet turned into egg-sized hailstones pelting his terrified horse. Flash after flash of lightning glanced off the rock around them, with the heavy smell of scorched earth. Thunder roared as though the demons of hell had gathered to defy the terrified traveler. Bahadur lay in terror on the heaving belly of his horse. Never had he seen a storm like this. He felt the hair rise on the back of his head.

"Oh God," he cried, "deliver me from Satan and his host. Protect your Book!"

Stone deaf from the storm, he staggered to his feet and made it to the town, only to discover the manuscript soaked to a pulp from the rain. The trip was for nothing. When the Bible Society heard this they rallied churches across India and abroad to pray. Through great opposition but also wonderful miracles of God's favour, the third proofs of the manuscript made it through and after 90 years of effort, the Bible was published. The battle was won when Christians all over joined in prayer.[30]

Smoke on the Roof of the World

I'd seen the gospel at work in the Himalayan valleys and on mountain slopes. Now I had to press on to South-East Asia. My good pastor friend Pandey deposited me at Katmandu airport in ample time for my morning flight. Waiting for the plane to arrive gave me time to dictate notes on my pocket recorder. But by noon, the waiting passengers were pacing the lounge and plaguing the flight attendants with queries about our overdue flight.

"It's been delayed, but it will soon be here," they assured us. As the sun dropped below the distant range, we knew we weren't flying out that day. Instead, an airways bus took us to a quaint hotel that still had rooms available—for obvious rustic reasons. By then all of us on the flight list had developed camaraderie—such as cruise-line passengers find when shipwrecked on a coral reef with only one palm tree for shade. Asians, Europeans, North Americans—we idled away the time swapping stories of being marooned in exotic places. We even learned each other's names.

"My name's Cable—Michael Cable," a well-built man at our dinner table announced, extending his hand to the rest of us. Obviously an outgoing guy—sales?

"Yup, I'm the Reynolds Tobacco sales rep. for East Asia," Michael proudly informed us as he dug into a bowl of curried rice. He'd been in

30. Allan Maberly, *God Spoke Tibetan*. Rockwall: Evangel Bible Translators, 2001.

Tibet drumming up tobacco sales. Half in jest, I asked if he were related to Mildred Cable. Beyond probability, I realized, but it made conversation. Should anyone ask if "Mildred Cable" were a famous movie star, I could reply she was a missionary of the China Inland Mission. If that didn't quickly change the topic, I could go on to explain she was one of my boyhood heroines. I'd devoured the adventures she and her colleague Francesca French wrote about trekking across the forsaken Gobi Desert that straddles China's border with Mongolia.

"Yeh—I'm her grandnephew . . . I guess!" admitted Michael, looking as stunned as I.

"Mildred Cable—never heard of her," diners murmured sleepily. (Interpretation: "*Bor-r-ing*!") They already knew I was religious, because I'd paused to give silent thanks before eating. Most visitors to Asia thought missionaries were some kind of misguided nerds who wasted their lives messing up the culture of quite contented "natives." Michael looked as if he'd rather drop dead from tobacco carcinogens than explain who his great aunt was; so I recklessly volunteered a reply. After all, everyone in the dining room was a traveller, and this travel story would top the best of theirs!

"Mildred Cable and another missionary woman trekked across a desert north of here, right up near the Mongolian border. Not many explorers had crossed it, let alone two single women. Safer to go around, a further thousand miles."

"Wasn't that *raw-thah* risky?" an English traveler drawled in British understatement.

"Maybe they was lookin' for damned diamonds!" an American joked with an unmistakably Southern twang.

"They'd heard there were desert nomads camped in the oases, who lived in fear of the evil *djinni* the people thought inhabited the dunes," I explained. "The missionaries wanted to tell them not to fear *djinni*—there is a living God who loves them. In fact, he loves them so much he gave his only Son to be our Saviour." Table chitchat suddenly faded. *Djinni*? Missionary? Saviour? Glazed eyes turned on the tobacco salesman; he had *seemed* a regular enough kind of guy.

"I remember Aunt Mildred from my childhood," Michael confessed lamely. "She really believed in what she felt called to do!"

"Yes," I chimed in. "She saw the gospel free people from fear and harmful traditions."

Travelers at other tables were heading off for some sleep, and our table suddenly thought that was a great idea. We needed to be up at six for breakfast and the bus ride back to the airport. I took an aspirin and passed the night on a lumpy mattress—better than sitting up in the departure lounge anyway. I ruminated about the Divine Travel Agent that could book Michael on the same flight on the same day, out of a remote airport, with someone who knew about his missionary aunt!

By mid morning, a relief plane had flown in, and we soon lofted high above the clouds. Poking through their blanket was Everest's proud peak. Monarch of the Roof of the world, I thought—or was it a giant, contemptuously shrugging off human ants that had the gall to disturb its solitude, attempting to scale it?

Eastward along the Himalayan spine, tiny Buddhist Bhutan, "Land of the Thunder Dragon," covers only 47,000 sq. km, rising steeply from 200m above water in the south to 7,000m in the north, with only 16% of the land arable. A law protects the rest of the land from being denuded of trees—country-wide, trees must cover over 60%. The nation doesn't encourage a lot of tourism, for youthful King Jigme Singye Wangchuck struggles to retain traditional values while cautiously improving quality of life for his estimated 2.75m subjects (government figures are much lower). The city of Thimpu claims to be the world's only national capital without a traffic light. Until 1999, the nation had no TV or Internet access. The king has healthier things in mind for his subjects, seeking to involve youth in such activities as sports. He himself plays competitive basketball.

Michael Cable wouldn't have signed any cigarette contracts in Bhutan, for in 2004 that nation became the world's first country to *ban* tobacco. Instead, big-hearted Michael handed out sample packs of cigarettes on our flight, which served neither food nor drink.

After all, this fresh-faced businessman was only doing his job. He explained there was no "established scientific link" between smoking and cancer (seems I'd heard that before), and his company had no plan to hook younger smokers or women. As to marketing cigarettes in Asia, these people had been smoking for centuries, so he wasn't introducing them to anything new. He didn't bother to explain that traditional smokers had used pipes or water *hookah* chambers—less risky.

Nor did Michael mention the powerful lure of smoking a "superior" American brand (a youthful status symbol), and the convenience of carrying a packet anywhere—instead of being tied like an umbilical cord to a *hookah*. (I did wonder why critics say it's O.K. to change a culture's smoking habits but arrogant to change religious fear of *djinni.*)

Obviously, Asia has tremendous marketing potential, as sales in health-conscious nations dwindle. I read that in China, 300 million people now smoke—more than in all the developed world combined. The Chinese government makes $10 billion a year in tobacco tax. In fact, the BBC reported that 84% of tobacco is now sold in developing countries; annually, 5m. smokers die prematurely. By 2020, 7 out of every 10 of the world's population will die of smoking-related problems.[31]

What was that I said about enjoying clean, fresh air?

The Himalayas dwindled into one of many wrinkles in the globe's vast stretches northwards into China and southwards into India and Bangladesh. Looking out the aircraft window, I thought of the enormous task the gospel faces in Asia—how impenetrable its cultures and religions seem. Yet to the One who "sits enthroned above the circle of the earth," they are all part of the world he loves—*so loves* that he sent Jesus to give his life to redeem them. They aren't hidden to him.

Amazingly, ever since Jesus first sent his disciples "to the ends of the earth," messengers of the gospel had been penetrating those valleys and plains and ranges—however inscrutable they might seem—with the Good News. Mission outreach wasn't the brainchild of the latest upstart evangelist, but ever since Eden the strategy of the sovereign God. I prayed that many more gospel messengers would get involved in spreading the news of eternal life. Yes—in the lowest valleys and on the highest passes of the Old Spice Road.

---

31. Reports from *New Scientist* (quoted in *Servant*, PBI, Summer 1999) and BBC World News, Feb. 27/05.

Great River Banks' Deposit

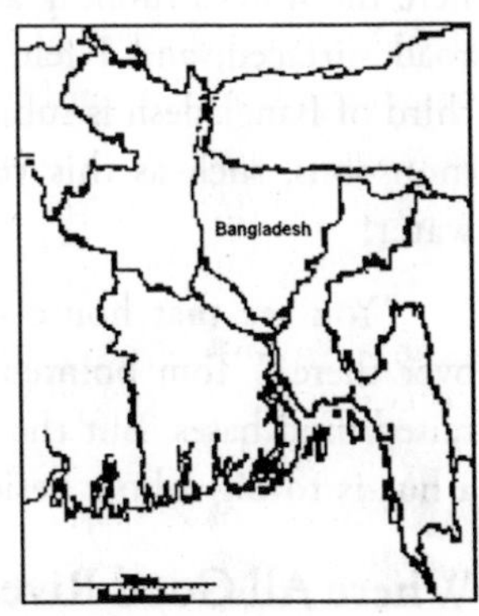

"All streams flow into the sea" (Ecclesiastes 1.7).

Bangladesh: Pop. 151,799,126

WATER, WATER, EVERYWHERE—and not a drop to drink." So penned the poet Coleridge.[1] That seemed true as I flew across Bangladesh, awash in post-Monsoon flooding. There were patches of dry land, but towards the coast it was difficult to know where land and sea met on the Delta into which the great rivers flow. From the air, I could see their turgid effluent stretching out into the Bay of Bengal some 400km. (250mi.). That's more than the length of the Bangladesh coastline!

Fortunately, Jessore airport (actually not far from Serampore, but on the other side of the India-Bangladesh border) was above water. I wanted to see one of SIM's rural development projects, so Tom Olson met me there and drove me to his farm project in Kushtia. At times it appeared our four-wheeled-drive LandRover was crossing a vast sea. Water stretched all around, right to the horizon on one side and to "islands" of villages on the other. Incongruously, isolated *single* huts also dotted the water's expanse.

1. S.T. Coleridge, *The Ancient Mariner*

"What are we driving on—or is this an amphibious vehicle?" I asked, trying not to sound alarmed. Only spotty ridges marked the road's edges along parts of our route.

"We're on a built-up road you'll see further along," laughed Tom. "Just here the water's running across the road too." Sure enough, up ahead the road surfaced, and I felt re-assured. During normal rainy seasons, one third of Bangladesh is submerged. People are used to that. But after heavy monsoons, such as this year's, *two-thirds* of Bangladesh could be under water!

"You see that house sitting by itself in the water? And those 'way over there?" Tom pointed out. "They're actually on stilts embedded in raised mud bases. But the land is so flat, the only way to raise a road or a hut is to dig a hole beside it—a 'borrow pit"—to get the extra earth."

Where All Good Rivers Meet

A quick glance at the map Tom handed me showed the reason for all this water. Bangladesh could be called "The Main Drain," although that would seem irreverent to Bangladeshis—a loveable people in a land with its own kind of lunarscape beauty. To them, the gods had blessed Bangladesh with "a land flowing with milk and honey."

"Flowing" is certainly descriptive, but "water" would be more accurate than "milk." The whole country provides drainage for the main rivers flowing from the Himalayan watershed. The Ganges, Brahmaputra, and Meghna Rivers all converge here in the armpit (so to speak) between the Indian subcontinent and Southeast Asia. Myriad smaller rivers join them. Together, a network of nearly 250 rivers has formed a delta as large as Illinois, USA—only here, the delta is called Bangladesh. Even the mighty, sacred Ganges loses its identity in a maze of rivulets, mangrove swamps, and inlet channels as it empties into the Bay of Bengal.

"In Bangladesh, monsoon rains are like pouring water on a tabletop," Tom explained. "The water has nowhere to go but across the land until it reaches the sea."

Drainage ditches don't help; dykes can't resist the unstoppable flow. Earth from "borrow pits" elevate some houses enough to "borrow time" for households to survive, with the aid of rafts and hollowed-out canoes, until rains stop and flat earth re-appears. Annually, hundreds die from a natural disaster people blame on the water gods. Actually, hillside peoples in the north increase the perennial problem by felling trees and overgrazing their pastureland. Global warming also is melting ice on mountain ranges north of Bangladesh.

"How do Bangladeshis cope with this, year after year?" I asked.

"Most accept it as you accept snow in Canada," Tom answered, to my surprise. "Annual flooding fits their fatalistic way of life. They don't know any other. But it's worth wading through, because each flooding deposits a new layer of rich silt. Some farmers get three harvests a year! Rice is the mainstay. They can always fish. So in most places they have food, even if it's lacking some nutrients. *'Rice and fish make a Bengali,'* people say."

"At least they have water to drink!" I commented, mentally contrasting Bangladesh with the desert I'd crossed in Pakistan.

"That's a problem, though," Tom cut in. "Rainwater is potable, but waste drainage from thousands of villages in India and the Himalayas brings pollution, including human waste, dead animals, and people drowned in floods. That means pandemic diarrhea!"

"Can't the Mission help people dig wells with built-up sides and covers?" I pressed, revealing typical Western confidence in technology to solve everything.

Tom explained that aid agencies and the World Health Organization had done that, only to discover a disastrous problem.[2] The Delta's alluvial soil contains high deposits of arsenic and mercury salts, which seep into wells. Suddenly villagers using their new wells were dying of poisoning.

Without doubt, Bangladesh has water problems—however, I'd found that most of Asia has, only of a different nature. There's no *over-all* shortage of water, but it's not evenly distributed. Governments provide it

2. Bangladesh has the world's greatest number of registered aid agencies (NGOs)—20,000.

free, as a basic human right. The problem comes with two abuses: wealthy landowners irrigate their fields non-stop, while village women fill their water pots from village standpipes—often leaving them running because it's free! Rainwater runs off into gutters instead of water barrels and reservoirs.

As a result, Asia suffers from enormous water wastage. Drought and famine could be avoided with basic resource management. True, water should be available to everyone, regardless of caste or status. It's the delivery system that needs to be paid for (at a high rate for landowners and a nominal rate for villagers, to prevent wastage). Taxes either aren't collected or are not applied fairly. But those are such political issues, governments haven't dared introduce water management or an equitable tax base. Some that tried have been shouted down with riots.[3]

Adding to the problem are disputes over irrigation canals and diverted rivers. Our world may yet see "water wars." And ironically, global warming could threaten the livelihood of millions of Bangladeshis. While scientists and politicians debate whether our globe is going through a 10,000-year (or more) climate cycle, or is facing the cataclysmic result of human pollution, in South Asia all worry about the human calamity resulting from diminishing water sources in mountain ranges and watersheds to the north.

Recycling All but the Quack

"Here's our farm project!" Tom announced as we pulled up to a neat bungalow in the village.[4] After sipping lemonade that Tom's wife, Ruth, had just squeezed, we toured a remarkable experimental project. On a small property, Tom and his national colleagues "farmed" fish in tanks, hatched and raised ducks and goats, grew vegetables, and recycled compost and manure to produce everything from fertilizer to animal feed to

3. Comfortable westerners demanding free water for the world may not realize how taxes finance their community water management infrastructure, water meters charging only for the amount they use.

4. "Bungalow"—from Hindi/Urdu *bangla*, originally a shack; later a house of *Bengal's* one-level style. Of course, it is the core of the nation's name.

methane gas for cooking fuel. When fish tanks become overloaded with nutrients, staff use water hyacinth plants to restore balance, then grind up the hyacinths for compost.

Demonstration gardens show how rice and other grain production increases with wise use of *natural* fertilizer along with hybrid seed. I was amazed that all this takes place on one acre of rented property *within* the town limits!

That's what I'd call "sustainable development." Any community can do it, given a little help to start up. The project regularly draws visitors from other villages, schools, government departments, industries, and aid organizations. It also gives Christians credibility as worthwhile citizens.

"I guess people see we aren't some useless sect!" Tom commented. "We're helping to provide the protein (vegetable and animal) that most communities are lacking—to go along with rice and fish! Villagers can come here and get a duck or rabbit or goat to raise for their very own. Anyone can do what we're doing."

The Olsons invited one of the farm supervisors, Habib,[5] to have dinner with us, so I'd have time to hear more about the effects of the gospel. "Everything on the table comes from our farm!" Ruth announced as she set before us piles of *chapatti*, bowls of rice and lentils, and a platter of fried fish.

"How did you come to work at the farm project?" I asked Habib.

"My father was a farmer," replied the stocky supervisor. "He raised enough food for the family and sold cash crops, so he could send me to a private school with a high standard. I became curious about the Bible.

"I was surprised to read that Jesus actually claimed to be the way of salvation! I read other passages that said I could be sure of salvation. I knew that Muhammad never made such claims. The Qur'an never freed me from a sense of sin and fear, but the Bible did. So I believed that Jesus really was the Way. But when I went to a Catholic priest for baptism, he refused, because he was afraid of being accused of proselytism, since I

---

5. This and other names changed for security.

didn't come from a Christian background. I finally found a Baptist pastor who questioned me about my faith and led me deeper into understanding the Bible. He finally baptized me."

Habib's parents were Ahmadiyyas, not strict orthodox Muslims. They didn't oppose his new faith, although his brothers and sisters became very angry.

Mango Theology

"You're surrounded by other faiths—how do you explain the gospel to them?" I asked.

"Most Muslims think Christians are idolaters, because they don't understand the Trinity," Habib replied. "So I start by agreeing with them that God is one. Then I hold up a mango and ask how many there are in my hand. After all, a mango has a skin, flesh, and a seed. Yet it's one. I know that's not a full illustration of the Trinity, but it helps them realize we believe in the Father, the Son, and the Holy Spirit as one God, not three."

Another staff member, Iqbal, used a different illustration to explain his faith to his family.

"I point out that the sun has heat and it has light—yet it's only one," he said. Before becoming a Christian, he heard his Qur'anic teacher warn, "Never touch the book of the Christians!" Yet in the Qur'an, Iqbal read references to Jesus. He became curious when he found a gospel portion that told the story of Jesus. What impressed him was the statement that Jesus was sinless. He knew that he himself was a sinner, and that even Muhammad acknowledged he was a sinner and so could not save others.

He heard a Campus Crusade radio broadcast and wrote to the address given, requesting a Bible correspondence course. They sent him the course that operates out of Pakistan. Still not knowing Jesus as Saviour, he met a Bengali working with ICF missionaries.[6] They gave him helpful literature. Although the Qur'an, like the Bible, teaches the need for faith and good

6. ICF and SIM merged in 1989 (see Ch. 7).

works, the Bible told him that *salvation* could be received only through repentance and faith—not *earned* through any number of good works. Iqbal finally trusted in Jesus to save him. When he joined a youth group started through OM, his former friends threw garbage and curses at him. He's still having interesting discussions with his family. One had been a Communist but turned back to Islam, at least nominally. Another doesn't believe any religion.

"The Bible has been corrupted!" his family tell him. "The Qur'an is the only true book from God, because it has been preserved in Arabic."

"Can you read Arabic?" Iqbal asks. They admit they can't.

"So how do you know what it says?" he questions. "Do you know what the Bible says about Jesus?" (They admit they don't.) "It says he is sinless. But the Qur'an says Muhammad admitted he was a sinner and couldn't save others." His brothers can't answer that logic, and so the discussion continues.

A side project of the Kushtia farm is the Savings Cooperative Program (SCP). Participants take a literacy course, learn management skills, and pool savings to purchase equipment for small businesses. One unemployed couple bought a sugar-cane crusher, and from the proceeds were able to install a simple "tube well." As their children saw what their parents could do, they too started saving, pooling enough to begin their own cottage industry—competing with the adults! The Savings Coop has helped downtrodden people gain self-respect and motivation. They've also learned about God's love for them.

In the world's most densely populated agricultural nation, SIM's Community Development Project helps farmers improve their crops while protecting their rented narrow plots of land from deterioration. Composting, crop rotation, improved seeding and spacing of plants are a beginning. Most participants soon move up from subsistence to surplus farming. They contribute to SCPs groups and in some cases form village health projects. As their livelihood improves, they also absorb spiritual lessons from Bible reading and the godly example of their Agricultural Field Worker, who is responsible for 120-150 partner farmers.

"Shooting" the Flood

The Olsons needed to drive to the capital, Dhaka to stock up on supplies, so I rode with them in their LandRover. Once again we seemed to be driving across an endless lake. We came to a cluster of shacks on stilts identifying the western bank of the Ganges—in flood but still a mighty river, not sluggish as it becomes among the coastal marshes. There was no bridge, but there was a floating platform manned by muscular men with long poles. The Olsons called it "a ferry." I tried to believe.

"This may be a little tricky," Tom warned, something I'd already thought of. "But we'll make it!" We inched our vehicle on to the "ferry" amidst unintelligible (to me) shouted instructions—warning us of impending death by drowning, I was sure. Our raft suddenly lurched into the swirling flood, shuddered, swung around 180 degrees—and we found ourselves free-floating downriver, swept along by the relentless current.

"Don't worry!" the Olsons assured me (was I looking nervous?), as the mad boiling cauldron swung us crazily. No need for a motor or rudder; ferrymen thrust long poles into submerged sandbars to keep the wayward raft headed at the right angle downstream. Suddenly, we shot into the main channel. Just as I thought we were about to update "St. Paul and the Shipwreck," a ferryman's pole snagged a sandbar, his pole acting as a fulcrum. The river's momentum abruptly swung us out of the deep central current and catapulted us toward the far bank. (White-water rafting, anybody?) Amazingly, it turned out to be the exact place the crew had planned to land, where the road continued. How they did it, I don't know. Uncanny. It took skill even though it appeared to be reckless chance![7]

And so we arrived on dry land—not (like the Apostle Paul) on pieces of the broken-up vessel, but in the Olson's trusty LandRover. Driving into Dhaka, we found it not yet flooded—although later I heard it did flood,

---

7. The flooding inland was nothing compared to coastal damage of typhoon-driven tidal waves that displace extensive sandbars fishing communities repeatedly build on. Millions live among the *Sundarbans* (islands of "the tide country"), subject to daily tidal flooding and crocodiles. One cyclone drowned some ½ million Bangladeshis.

with backed-up sewage flowing through the streets. Dhaka (with some 11m residents) is capital of a country the size of Maine, New Hampshire, and Vermont combined, but with a density of more than 1,500 people per square mile. Each year 3m more swell the nation's 150m.

In spite of the low-lying land, Mogul rulers built imposing buildings, and the British lined broad avenues with trees. Since secession from the Pakistan Federation (in 1971), the Bangladesh government has added its own landmark—a vast, ultra-modern railroad station. Yet the city streets had an eerie feel. I didn't understand why, until a pedal rickshaw nearly ran me down—I hadn't heard it coming. Across the border, in Calcutta, motorized rickshaws and scooters sounded like fleets of lawnmowers or leaf blowers. In Dhaka, most public transport was by pedal power. Streams of rickshaws silently paraded past me, while other pedal pushers loitered around shop fronts and street corners, hoping to snare a fare for a few "takka."

There were motorized rickshaws around, but a shortage of trained mechanics left many rickshaw owners resorting to pedal power when the small motors broke down. International Christian Fellowship (ICF)[8] had started a repair-training program, "STC." STC fills an important niche, equipping youth who otherwise would be hanging around tearooms hoping for a fare. The course is registered, and the government would like STC to take in more students, but space and facilities are limited. The yearlong course teaches the basics of small motors, auto-mechanics, and welding.

The school has three auto rickshaws for training purposes, but those three also bring in enough revenue to pay property rent, a Bengali instructor's salary, and food for the students. STC selects unemployed youths, who sleep in bunks on the property. More "sustainable development"—this is a self-contained, self-financed project, all in a rented shed. On the roof of the workshop, I noticed chicken coops. Students use the eggs for cooking. Each student has to take a turn at cooking meals for the others, and upon completing the course he receives enough cash to help start his own repair shop.

8. ICF, as mentioned earlier, a merger of CIGM and PIVM, opened work in Bangladesh in 1958.

Apart from that, STC holds seminars that bring up to 18 students for elementary or refresher courses. All have the opportunity to hear the gospel message.

Poverty and Cow Power

Pedal power told me something of the poverty of this nation, which has a 38% literacy rate, with 55% of the populace subsisting below the poverty line—one of the world's poorest countries. Under India's Mogul emperors, Dhaka was the wealthy capital of Bengal. However, Calcutta superseded it in the British era. In 1947, when the area became East Pakistan, it was richer than West Pakistan. But Partition (from India) cut off most of its trade with Calcutta—jute, cotton, textiles, and fish.

Politicians siphoned off any remaining wealth, and still blame each other for continuing corruption. Perhaps they established a pattern. During my visit, Dhaka's *Telegraph* cited "the unbridled corruption that pervades every sphere of national life." Transparency International has ranked Bangladesh as the most corrupt of 159 countries examined for "misuse of public office for private gain."[9]

One consequence of grinding poverty is endemic theft. Rickshaw pedal-pushers have to keep a sharp eye open for missing sewer covers—a favourite item to steal and melt down for pig-iron. That's a great hazard when streets are flooded with water! A pedestrian wading through the run-off could fall right into a sewer.

In market stalls, for a low price, I could buy watches, videotapes, and even computer programs, pirated from name brands. Bangladeshis are not alone in this kind of profitable trade. Throughout Asia, "authentic" replicas of equipment bear the faked stamp of countries that really do manufacture the originals!

Even without corruption, piracy, or theft, consecutive flooding and cyclones hinder economic recovery for this nation of some 153 million. Bangladesh currently keeps afloat with foreign aid and repatriated funds from citizens living elsewhere. But these resilient, resourceful people have learned to live with their circumstances. They have turned silt into social life.

9. *Economist*, Oct. 22, 2005.

In Dhaka I noticed construction going on (some on high-rise apartments), but I didn't see any construction cranes or booms. I didn't hear power machinery. Instead, laborers bash away at rocks with hammers, making crushed stone and gravel. Workmen hand-turn cement mixers. They pour concrete into casings until completing a floor; then a second floor starts on top of the first one. Floor by floor these buildings rise and miraculously stay up—miraculous from the fact that the foundations rest only on delta mud.

Bangladesh does not lack entrepreneurial skills. In 2006, economist Mohammad Yunus and his Grameen Bank received a Nobel peace prize—for developing what "had appeared to be an impossible idea": loans to people who have no collateral! Typical would be a woman who borrows the equivalent of $30 to purchase a sewing machine to start a small business making clothes, or purchases a cow and sells its milk. She pays back her loan and buys a second cow. The Bank has 1,300 branches serving some 3.5m. people in 46,000 villages. Repayment rate has been 98%. Dr. Yunus' model can now be found in 50 countries. He's also linked up with a French yogurt manufacturer, Groupe Danone, to provide free yogurt to Bangladeshi children as a protein supplement to their normal diet of thin rice gruel.

Iqbal Quadir, a Bangladeshi who moved to USA and became an investment banker, convinced the Grameen and a Norwegian mobile phone company to help him form Grameen-Phone (GP). Villagers, such as a small shopkeeper, use micro-credit to buy a mobile phone—which enables them to communicate with suppliers or increase sales to shoppers in a land where road transport is undependable. GP is now the nation's largest telecom operator, topping 6m. subscribers, and inspiring five other mobile operators. Quadir has now moved into local electricity supply. A villager borrows enough to buy a small generator that can provide lighting for 20 houses or shops. But how to power the generator in the first place? An American friend designed a generator that could use the methane gas produced by manure that cows "churn out."

"It's so much better to help people develop from the bottom up," comments Quadir. "Top-down assistance creates bottlenecks and can empower bureaucracy."

Villages end up with three enterprises from one simple idea. The electricity project "generates": (1) bio-gas from composted manure; (2) fertilizer from the disposable manure; (3) electricity from local generators. Each is owned by a different villager, who employs neighbors, so avoiding monopoly and sharing the prosperity. Meanwhile, shopkeepers keep their doors open longer, students study better, families enjoy safe lighting at home, and cows munch blissfully on.

Result? "$5 billion in micro-loans, 7 million borrowers, 265.000 village organizations, 52,000 schools, 8.5 million jobs, and new ventures in eight other Asian and African countries."[10]

Female Suffering: God's Will?

The nation has had women political and government leaders with ties to powerful families. Bangladesh has also produced brilliant women academics and professionals. Unveiled businesswomen work with male colleagues in city offices—although their pay is much lower than that of men.

Sadly, there's a large sex trade of shipping abducted females to other countries. The reaction is to strengthen religious taboos that prevent rural women appearing in open areas, such as rice paddies—that's the work of men and boys. Rural women stay home, tending family garden patches or fruit trees. To help develop community economies, Aid agencies make micro-loans to such women. A widow can obtain a loan to buy a fruit tree, cow, goat, poultry, or a sewing machine, and start a cottage industry. One agency reported 90% loan repayment within two years. But many men become furious at this economic independence. Radicals sometimes uproot fruit trees and let animals escape.

Traditions, especially male attitudes towards women, don't seem to change, in spite of outward signs of progress. A visitor whose car hit a child (who ran on to the road and died) was thankful that the police dropped their charge against him. But he was shocked when the judge gave the reason for dismissing the case: "It was only a girl!"

---

10. October '08 Conrad Hilton Foundation (LA: CA) annual humanitarian award to BRAC.

Respectability often hides abusiveness. One Christmas day in Dhaka, neighbor Hawa arrived at missionaries John and Jana Thorpe's back door. Wife of a prominent businessman, Hawa herself was successful, educated, and the mother of two lovely children. Yet the family's home life was a disaster.

"I've never spoken with you, but I saw that you have a happy family life," Hawa said through tears. "I just had to come to talk with you!"

"I can't have faith in any religion that teaches men to act like my husband does!" she cried. "He beats me, and when I was expecting our last child, he sent me to live with his parents, who abused me. They wouldn't even give me food, even though I was with child. They said women are meant to suffer—and they made sure of it."[11] Lowering her dark eyes, Hawa whispered that her husband showed no affection, not even when they were in bed together. She lived in fear of him.

"Tell me, please—what does your religion teach about men and women?" Weeping with the distraught woman, Jana gave her a copy of the Bengali New Testament. After the two prayed, Hawa slipped out the back door. "I haven't seen her since," Jana told me, "but I pray for her, wherever she is!"

Other women live in bondage to evil spirits, fearful that someone might put a curse on them—the Evil Eye, they call it. As protection, women buy expensive fetish necklaces and amulets with Qur'anic inscriptions. However, since creation of Bangladesh, orthodox Muslims (Sunnis in particular) have sought to purify Folk Islam and curb these errant concepts. To Islamic conservatists, this is of the Devil. That's why, on Dhaka's streets, I saw no monuments of people and animals, such as the heroes on horses I'd seen in Katmandu. And it was unusual to hear any music.

Flowing with Silt and Homily[12]

But there were other sides to life in Bangladesh. Even if the land didn't flow with "milk and honey," it could be said to flow with silt and

11. Hawa's religion teaches that women can enter heaven only by serving their husbands.

12. Greek *homilein*: conversation, discourse—now often a short inspirational sermon.

homily. The alluvial silt was inevitable—and also of great benefit to farmers. Did the resigned attitude of the people to the inevitable, produce poetic homily? I learned more about the nation's poetic soul from the Thorpes. John and Jana both studied Bengali art and music. I'd noticed that Bangladesh and Pakistan were markedly different in social atmosphere—with Bangladeshis more easy-going. This is a land of hospitable homily. Groups of men socialize in teashops, women chat with friends in their homes. Over our own cup of Chittagong tea,[13] the Thorpes explained the culture.

"Generally, Bangladeshis enjoy ethnic unity—the majority are Bengalis,"[14] John pointed out. "So they've never had to 'prove' their national identity. In fact, they may be reacting more against Hinduism from India and Islamic orthodoxy from Pakistan, than from a need for identity.

"We found something else interesting," Jan chimed in. "Bengalis love music and art. Of course, orthodox Islam prohibits those (except art in "arabesque" designs), because one tradition of Muhammad quotes him as saying, 'As water sprouts grain, so songs deliver deception.'[15] We'd almost agree these days, because of the morally corrupt music from the West now available anywhere in Asia, via an I-Pod or CD! Muslim orthodoxy has interpreted Muhammad's comment as a ban on music. But in Bangladesh, Islam comes out of a Sufi tradition overlaid on Hindu culture, with its love for mysticism, art, music, and poetry. As we studied Bengali culture, we discovered people actually *love* the arts."

Culture: Carey and Tagore

Of course, Rabindranath Tagore (1861-1941) was the embodiment of this love. This respected Bengali poet came from a wealthy family of the Brahma Samaj ("The God Society"), an Aryan-Hindu sect that developed out of the British-Indian Unitarian Association, founded in Bengal in

13. Exotic blend grown on the Chittagong Hills, on Bangladesh's panhandle bordering Myanmar (Burma).
14. 96.9% in fact. Altogether, there are 61 ethnic groups and 35 languages. The split from the Pakistan Federation came after Islamabad sought to impose Urdu as the official language for East as well as West, it is said. The newly named "Bangladesh" proudly made Bengali its official language.
15. Licentious songs along the caravan routes may have repelled Muhammad's morals.

1827. Unitarians made friends all around, because they didn't accept doctrines of sin, eternal punishment, the Trinity, deity of Jesus and the Atonement. That suited Brahmins, Muslims, and liberal Christians (who had never much cared for the Bible's absolutes). In fact they looked upon amorphous universalism as a bridge of understanding between all religions.

"Rabin" Tagore learned about Christian monotheism but not about the Redeemer—about God but not about the Way to God. However, he distilled beautiful thoughts from several sources. S.P. Carey, son of William Carey, states that Tagore (known as "the father of modern Bengali literature") built on the work of Carey, who studied and advanced Bengali prose.[16] Bengali is India's only language in which a Nobel Prize for literature has been won: in 1913 by Tagore's poetry, which includes the beautiful prayer:

O let my head bow down and meet
The dust at thy feet;
Let all my pride, all my pride
Drown in the tears I have cried.

All of the self-glory that I have gained
Has only myself disdained;
Encircled in my own self I wander—
Wander around in ceaseless shame.

Let me not ever, ever proclaim
My own self-made skill;
Rather let thy wish, only thy wish
My whole life fulfill.

O for thine ultimate peace I plead;
For my soul, thy glorious beauty I need;
Secretly plant it to dwell secure
Within my heart's deepest-most core.[17]

---

16. "SP" knew Tagore, and documents his father's influence on Tagore and Bengali (Biog: S.P. Carey). Pundits had considered Bengali "fit only for women and demons" (*sic!*). East India Co., unable to find one qualified teacher of Bengali, invited Carey to Calcutta to teach it. (Mangalwadi, *op cit.* p. 171.) William Carey's initial vision had been for Bengalis, who now number 240m. worldwide.)
17. *Let My Head Bow Down*, "thirty-nine Bengali songs by Rabindranath Tagore, translated as poetry by John Thorpe." Dhaka: ICF/SIM, c. 1980.

Tagore is the best known of Bengali bards. He embodied the temperament and history of the Bengalis of Bangladesh, conducive to philosophical thought and poetic expression. Christian missionaries found Bengalis open to discussion, or "homily," and learned much from chatting with them in tearooms.

Incarnating the Gospel

In the 70s, a group of missionaries seeking more effective approaches in Bangladesh, noted that most Christians were the result of outreach from Calcutta (before Partition split Bengal) and chiefly from Hindu background. Naturally, the Bengali Bible used Hindu terminology. This made the Bible's message plain to Hindus, but gave Muslims the impression that it was some kind of Hindu text—therefore idolatrous. Contextualization needed to be re-oriented! So the missionary group set about making the gospel intelligible to non-Hindus.

For instance, in 1981, David Coffey, son of a businessman in Bengal, and his wife completed a new Bengali translation, avoiding expressions from Hindu culture. They and other missionaries became more sensitive to Islamic culture. They quickly discovered how Muslims abhor pork. "Do you eat pork?" a Muslim neighbor would ask the first time they met, in order to "check them out." So missionary parents even adapted their nursery rhymes. Instead of saying, "This little piggy went to market" as they playfully pinched their babies' toes, they recited, "This little *doggy* went to market."

Before 1975, there was no known group of new believers from non-Hindu background who met together. Since then, they've been forming small churches that are culturally relevant to their communities. They have songbooks with indigenous melodies. This was a new era for the gospel in the region. At the same time, orthodox Muslims became concerned about the increase in Christian churches—although in reality all Christians (including Protestant, Roman Catholic, and others) have never amounted to more than three-quarters of one percent of the population!

Before 1988, the majority of Muslims looked upon Hindu gurus, Buddhist Yogis, and Christian clergy as simply religious leaders in their own infidel communities. To identify with the culture, some Christian missionaries grew beards and wore Bangladeshi attire. But orthodox leaders twisted this innocent acculturation into attempts at deception. Attitudes stiffened when the nation declared itself an Islamic state in 1988.[18]

There were many non-Christians who supported the good work of missionaries, however. A few years ago, when one missionary received a deportation order, a Muslim friend, Ayub, went to ask the responsible government department the reason.

"Because he's converting our people!" the official fumed.

"How?" Ayub asked. "Is he paying them money? Is he forcing them? No Bangladeshi will become a Christian unless through his own belief. You know that! Isn't this a free country? You can't deport the man because a few people become Christians!"

Ayub used the same arguments with other officials. To the missionary's surprise, the government rescinded the deportation order, and dismissed the official who had signed it!

"You've Got to Be Joking!"

Although I'd already seen a variety of cultures in Southern Asia, in Bangladesh I learned new things that helped me understand the area, its religions, and attitudes to the gospel. Take, for instance, Jesus' exhortation to "turn the other cheek."

"Your religion teaches that if a person strikes you on one cheek, you should turn the other cheek to him?" an incredulous Bengali asked Phil Parshall as he visited in a Muslim home. "What a ridiculous religion you have!" Others joined in laughter. In their obligatory prayers five times a day, Muslims call upon "Allah, the merciful," but most have no concept of forgiveness or divine love.[19] To them, Christian repentance, confession, forgiveness, and humility are signs of weakness.

---

18. Phil Parshall, SIM Islamics scholar, encourages understanding and friendship but rejects any compromise in approaching Muslims with the gospel. He helpfully describes distinctions between contextualization and syncretism. (Phil Parshall, *Evangelical Missions Quarterly*, October 1998, p. 404. Wheaton: EMIS.)

19. Although Sufi Muslims desire to love *God*.

For a Bengali Muslim, righteous living is a matter of legalism, observing certain rituals to receive God's mercy. True, they recognize the Spirit of God, but almost as some kind of Aladdin's *jinni*. They acknowledge the need for a blood sacrifice to atone for any laws they may have broken (don't call that sin, though!). However, they don't have the concept of righteousness being *imparted* to them, or of God's Spirit enabling repentant sinners to live righteously.

Then there's "thankfulness"—an alien concept for sure! There's no proper word for "Thank you" (although foreigners supply one), and there's little concept of thanks.

Instead, people have a patronage concept: others owe it to Bangladeshis to give them things and do things for them. They rely on others. Everybody else is the cause of the nation's problems. Even rich people call themselves poor, saying, "We are a poor nation."

For instance, a group of wealthy businessmen couldn't understand why they should assist a community project. "We receive from others, but we're not in a position to *give* to others," they explained without embarrassment. Church members often have no concept of helping someone else, each other, or even their own church. Therefore it's very difficult to make genuine friendship; although people are friendly, that's often with the hope of a handout. When that's not forthcoming, friendliness may fade.

Freedom Fighter Turns Church Leader?

As an executive of World Evangelical Alliance at the time, I was interested to meet Christian Bangladeshis who are practising the nation's constitutional religious liberty.

I found Rev. Amitar K— in his small study at the back of his church. The office, lined with books and files, also serves as headquarters for his denomination, of which he was General Secretary at the time.

"I hear that some officials once considered you an enemy of the state," I began after the usual exchange of greetings.

"That's right," laughed Amitar. "That was after I came to Christ and witnessed to anyone around me. You see, although our nation has a constitutional guarantee of religious freedom, the problem comes when activists of other religions want to stifle freedom and quash minorities."

"So how did you overcome that charge?" I asked.

"For one thing, I'd gone through college with men who became politicians and government leaders. In student years, they had the same leftist views as I had. So when the accusation of 'enemy of the state' came to the government's attention, the Prime Minister's office threw out the file!"

"Were you like the Apostle Paul, turning from political zeal to Christian faith?"

"As a youth, I was a zealous Communist," replied Amitar. "I became a freedom fighter. But what I saw happening across the border in China was failure. Mao couldn't make his ideals work except through force—and China was going downhill at the time.

"Would you like a lychee?" Amitar paused to offer me a bowl of fruit. My parched throat was grateful.

"So I began looking at other religions. I couldn't accept the caste system of Hinduism, and in the Qur'an Muhammad says he is not a saviour. I didn't know what to believe. But one of my college friends had a New Testament. I was amazed to read that Jesus plainly said he was the Saviour, and his words and miracles backed that up.

"After I broke an arm in a rickshaw accident, I began studying the Bible while recovering. Slowly I found what I hadn't found in Communism or religion—pardon for my sin and assurance of eternal life.

"Now I could start helping my country, not through ideology or armed struggle or even religion, but through the living Saviour, Jesus Christ!"

"What do your former college friends think of that?" I asked, sucking another juicy lychee.

"We have to be wise in this world," replied Amitar, like a man who had experienced trials. "For instance, it was very hard to get out of the

Communist party. If they'd known I believed in God and was a Christian, they could have finished me off. I had to be tactful, but I got out. Then I had to face my family. My parents disowned me and my wife left. Later she asked why I'd left her religion. I explained that the writings of other religions were full of superstitions, but I didn't see that in the Bible. It told the truth.

"Finally my wife came back to live with me, and she also has trusted in Christ as her Saviour. We both got jobs teaching, until I studied theology and came into the pastorate."

What Holds the Church Back?

I asked this fearless preacher why the gospel wasn't making better progress in Bangladesh. Churches didn't seem to be reaching out to unsaved neighbors.

"You know why?" he responded without hesitation. "Many churches have lost their convictions and no longer preach the true gospel. They evade the uniqueness of Christ. That's the Christian distinctive. He's the only Saviour."

"But I keep hearing of harassment," I interjected. "Are Christians afraid to witness?"

"Jesus said we'd face tribulation in this life," Amitar countered. "But we do need to be wise. For instance, we never use the words 'evangelical' or 'crusade,' because those are aggressive terms to Muslims. They know their own history of crusading and evangelising others by force. They measure us by their own yardstick. So they view Christian compassion as a form of coercion to win converts. They don't understand that spiritual regeneration through Christ can never be forced—it must be voluntary, from the heart.

"Both Hindus and Muslims keep a close eye on Christian activity. Local leaders twist things to upset the people—like claiming that a Christian leader visited a rural village in order to buy property. One missionary was even charged with kidnapping a man's son—but the man confessed that he'd made up the story in the hope of extracting money from the missionary! Some reports of Christian activities turn up in world publications of these other religions, which make it appear that Christians are about to take over the country! But we're only a very tiny minority."

"So what's going to convince Bangladeshis of the gospel's truth?" I asked, packing up my papers. The lychee bowl was nearly empty.

"The root of our nation's problems really is sin," the pastor summed up. "We aren't trying to undermine other religions or fight them. Our aim must be for God's Spirit to change the hearts of people spiritually. Then the gospel will become convincing."

Doctor Prescribes Amazing "Cure"

Cynics might say they'd expect Pastor Amitar to talk so courageously—as a clergyman, that's his job. But how about Christians in the work place, "in the real world?" I heard of a Christian medical doctor. When I went to his office (his "surgery," the Brits would call it), the brass plate on his door announced, Mr. Saidur Ghosh, M.D., F.R.C.S. That too was British terminology, adopted in the Indian sub-continent. Physicians use the title "Mr." followed by their professional degrees. I knew he was well qualified.

His patients also knew that Mr. Ghosh, Fellow of the Royal College of Surgeons, was a practising Christian. He lived like one! And because of his professional standing and moral living, no one challenged him about the Bible at the side of his desk, nor the Bible verse on a wall.

"Your patients know you are a follower of Christ," I began when Dr. Ghosh had a free period. "Your name is not typically 'Christian,' so some of your patients from other faiths must ask you about your faith. How do you answer?"

Dr. Ghosh slowly removed his stethoscope from around his neck and leaned forward on his desk. "It's very important to let our citizens know we can be followers of Christ without changing our family names," he told me. "Unfortunately people have this stereotype—that a Bangladeshi Christian follows a foreign religion, changes his name and his clothes, and disowns his culture. They think that makes him a Christian!"

"So when strangers assume, from your name, that you aren't a Christian, and yet they notice a Bible on your desk, what do you say?" I asked.

"Sometimes they ask me, 'Are you a Muslim?' So I ask them, 'What is a Muslim?'

"The questioner may reply, 'Someone who submits to Allah.' Then I quote from the Qur'an to show what 'submission' really means, and ask whether my visitor knows any true Muslims. Usually he admits he doesn't!"

Dr. Ghosh then asks which of the Prophets is able to save us. The man admits that all the prophets, even Muhammad, have sinned and that only Jesus is called the sinless one in the Qur'an. About then, the doctor asks whom we should follow.

He knows that the Qur'an speaks of faith as well as good works, but it provides no *assurance* of salvation or *knowledge* of the way. Through statements from the Qur'an, which Dr. Ghosh knows thoroughly from his own background, the visitor comes to realize there is no salvation apart from "the Sinless One," Jesus Christ.

Dying of Thirst

Christian ministries in Bangladesh respond to needs as they appear. Jeannie Lockerbie, a Baptist[20] who served as a missionary nurse, noticed the dearth of Christian literature and teaching aids in Bangladesh. Joining with Bengali John Sircar and others, she opened the Bible Literature Centre to develop a Literature Division of their work. They produced Bengali editions of Gospel Light's Sunday School curriculum, vernacular Scripture portions, teaching aids, and gospel tracts—most on their own presses. David C. Cook, Christian Literature Crusade, and other literature organizations gave a hand. India and even countries in Europe began ordering materials for Bengali readers. Jeannie and her team were meeting a deep spiritual thirst.[21]

People who serve Jesus in Bangladesh develop a deep love for a distraught nation. I began to feel that way as I packed my bags for the

20. Member of the Association of Baptists for World Evangelism, born in Canada, raised in USA.

21. See Bibliography: Jeannie Lockerbie, *Write the Vision.*

next lap of my trek. There were thirsty people all around—thirsty in spite of flooding rivers and overflowing wells. Spiritually, the parallel was that some religious "rivers" and "wells" they drank from delivered death.

I thought of Jesus' offer to the Samaritan woman drawing water: "Everyone who drinks this water will be thirsty again, but whoever drinks the water I give him will never thirst."

Here in Bangladesh, on the flooded trails of the Old Spice Road, I could almost hear Jesus calling as he did to the milling crowd two millennia ago: "If a man is thirsty, let him come to me and drink. Whoever believes in me, as the Scripture has said, streams of living water will flow from within him." What an offer—the safe, pure, and unlimited water of life—free! *"Whoever is thirsty, let him come; and whoever wishes, let him take the free gift of the water of life."*[22]

22. References for Scripture quoted in the last paragraphs: John 4.10-11; 7.37-38; Rev. 22.17.

In Japan, Fuller enjoys meeting Dr. Shin Funaki.
Their fathers respectively had chaired the Japan and Canada councils of Japan's Evangelistic Band.

Section – II

SOUTHEAST ASIA

Green Buddha, Son of White Elephant

"They are full of superstitions from the East; ... Their land is full of idols; they bow down to the work of their hands" (Isaiah 2.6,8).

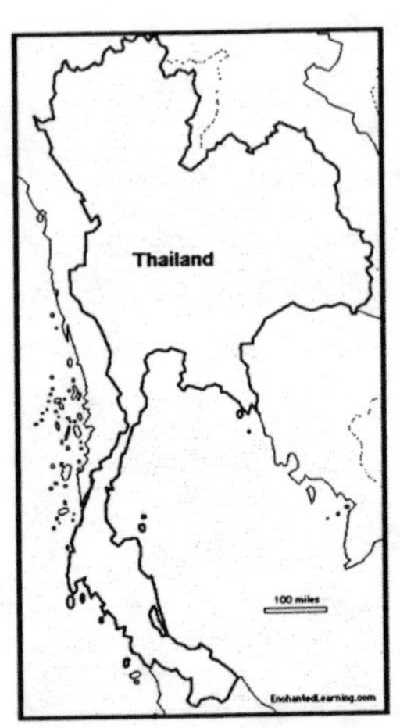

Thailand: Pop. 66,510,844

I FOLLOWED THE STREAM OF DEVOTEES to Thailand's most sacred shrine, Bangkok's Temple of the Jade Buddha. The soft shuffle of sandals provided a rhythmic accompaniment. Around the temple, gold-covered pinnacles of ancestral *stupas*[1] glistened in the tropical sun. Men and women threaded their way between ornately carved pillars and pagodas.[2] A market woman who, it seemed, could hardly afford to buy a handful of rice, pressed her gold-leaf offering on to the head of a sacred cow—that is, the life-size replica of one. Others added their own gold-leaf offerings. (Thailand's 27,000 Buddhist temples seem to do fairly well!)

Worshipers kicked off their sandals and entered the temple's archway, kneeling or reclining on the temple floor. While inching forward, they

---

1. *Stupa*: Sanskrit—a cairn or monument mound erected over the ashes of a noted personage; shrine. The Tower of Babel was a stupa, or *ziggurat* (>Akkadian: "to build on a raised area")—a pyramid-shaped series of levels, topped with a shrine.
2. Portuguese explorers in Buddhist Sri Lanka, across the Bay of Bengal, mispronounced *dagoba* (Sanskrit: temple tower with curving eaves), as "*pagoda*," which term survives to today.

respectfully pointed their feet *away* from the distant icon shrouded in burning incense. Sitting on the tiled floor, I too kept the soles of my feet behind me, so as not to show disrespect. As wreathes of incense cleared, my eyes adapted to the temple's shadows. Ah—there was the figure of Buddha, serenely cross-legged on top of a lofty *stupa.*

The rotund figure benignly gazing down on us was carved out of semi-precious green jade. His rippling belly hardly portrayed the image of an ascetic denying all sensual pleasure to earn eternal sublimation. Perhaps he symbolized the good life these devout people longed for on earth—a Santa Claus figure. Not to worry—I knew that Thai Buddhism had its own genre. Anyway, the disciples meditating on the tiled floor hoped to inch towards Nirvana.[3] *"He who sees the truth sees the Buddha, and he who sees the Buddha sees the truth,"* monks explain, "truth" being "the absolute aspect of the Buddhist nature."[4]

Even though, in theory, others could become a Buddha, so far there is only one—although there are "bodhisattvas." These "good bods" (if I may be so irreverent) postpone entering Nirvana in order to help non-achievers get off the re-incarnation cycle. How, no one explained, but they made me recall the Psalmist's description of idols: "They have mouths, but they cannot speak; they have eyes, but they cannot see; they have ears, but they cannot hear. . . . Those who make them will become like them, and so everyone who trusts in them."[5] Anyway, the "bods" don't charge for their sacrificial services—although the monks who present the devotees' supplications to them do need financial support—*thank you!*

Not just anyone can be a Buddha—a state more than a person. Monastic centers have compiled a list of 32 characteristics by which they

---

3. *Nirvana*—Sanskrit, pronounced *Nibbana* by Buddhists and Hindus—highest form of peace, happiness.
4. Sanskrit: *dharma* (truth). Suddenly I understood religions and Jesus' declaration, "I am the truth," in a new way. Eternal truth is more than my secularized concept of *truth-as-fact.* Because Jesus is the Truth, Satan seeks to mislead mankind with falsehood disguised as "truth" (see Appendix F: Religion).
5. Psalm 115.5-8. Of course, orthodox Buddhists would strongly object that *bodhs* are idols—even as members of some churches in Christendom, praying to "saints," would deny belief in ancestor worship.

can recognize a prospective Buddha (or "lama"). Besides character traits, there are physical "earmarks"—yes, including lengthened ears, a curl or mark on the forehead, and a topnotch of either hair or skin. When a chief monk or lama dies, it takes a while for the "college of monks" to identify all 32 auspicious signs before anointing the next spiritual leader.

Now as I stepped back outside the temple, I squinted in the dazzling sunshine glinting off the gilded pagodas of the Grand Palace. They reminded me of the battle between good and evil, at least as seen through Buddhist' eyes—a carry-over from Persia's ancient Zoroastrians. The picturesque upturned edges on layered roofs serve more than artistry. I learned that "they keep evil spirits from landing in the Palace courtyard." As the little devils slide down the roofs, the pagodas' curled-up edges send the aliens shooting back up into space (like a skateboard jump?).[6] But there is a scientific reason for the layers: in earthquake-prone Japan, pagoda towers flex as the earth shakes. Result: only two have collapsed during the past 1,400 years.

Sacred whitewashed bovines sported more gold offerings.

Knowing orthodox Buddhism's rejection of idolatry, I asked a tour guide about the worshippers in the temple. "The people are not *worshiping* the bulls and cows, or the Buddha," the guide corrected me. "They're only showing *respect* to the Buddha and their ancestors."[7] (Must protect Buddhism's non-idolatrous facade!) Any Thai monk worth his saffron[8] would explain that, like Folk-Islam, there is also Folk-Buddhism—a syncretism with pagan superstition. No problem, if that makes folk feel comfortable?

In fact, the monks at Thailand's Tiger Temple solemnly declare that the tigers they keep are reincarnated monks or family members. The

---

6. If any Westerner looks patronizingly upon such superstition, let him glance up at the grotesque gargoyles on the corners of European buildings. Their function in earlier centuries was scaring off evil forces from landing on buildings. (Of course, during rainfall, roof water spouted from their contorted mouths, dampening the spirits of hapless pedestrians below!) Superstition still affects buildings in the West—including our apartment building, which has no 13th floor or Unit 13 on any floor.

7. Certain churches also explain that's what icons, paintings of saints, or holy images are. But mankind's innate desire to worship usually turns meditation aids into objects of worship. This tendency accounts for reformers' iconoclasm (condemned by today's elite as "bigotry"—but sometimes a needed corrective).

World Wildlife Fund appreciates the monastery reserve in which the tigers live: they help preserve the globe's tiger population, endangered by souvenir-seeking tourists and traditional Asian medicine concocters, who pay big money for Tiger pelts and parts sold by poachers.[9]

After all, Thais cite cause to respect, if not worship, the spirit world. "Land of the Free,"[10] they call their country, crediting a guardian angel, Phra Sayam Devadhiraj, with protecting it. Thailand was never colonized by a Western power, even though invaders have ruled all its neighbors. The nation is now nearly 93% Buddhist, but many worship (excuse, me, I mean "respect") the nation's golden image of Guardian Angel Phra Sayam.

(Many missionaries think that since Orthodox Buddhists do not believe there is such a being as God, it does not affect the way Christian converts think of Jehovah God. However, Buddhism does affect the views of many Christians. See Appendix F.)

Historians agree that since the 13th century, a king ruled the Thais, although there have been political changes. The first time I visited Thailand, I noticed a photograph of the monarch in offices, shops, and restaurants. At the time, he helped preserve the stability of this heartland of South-East Asia. Its borders touch Myanmar (West), Laos and Cambodia (East), and Malaysia (South). During the British Empire era, Myanmar was "Burma."[11] France colonized the countries to the east, known as French Indochina. That included Vietnam, which curves around the others, like the thick fibrous husk encasing a coconut. Its southern end faces the tip of Thailand across the Gulf of Thailand.[12] The rivers of "Indochina" wash South-East Asia's effluence into the South China Sea.

---

8. Arabic *za'faran*, orange-yellow dye from the crocus. Considered the colour of some bird faeces and used by monks to dye their robes to signify their "worthlessness" and self-denial. Yet some monks reportedly shed their robes to frequent prostitute parlors, causing public resentment.

9. A tiger penis fetches $800, a pelt $6,000.

10. *Thai*—pronounced "Tie" (English is unique in soft pronunciation of the "th" diphthong) means "free."

11. One benefit was the Empire's global connection: Britain introduced rubber trees to Malaysia (from slips smuggled out of Brazil and nurtured in London's Kew Gardens), and palm-oil trees from Ghana.

12. Only part of Malaysia is on Thailand's isthmus, the rest sharing islands with Indonesia. (See next chapter.) Thailand's southern tip, bordering Malaysia, has a Muslim secessionist movement.

"Siam" was the explorers' best attempt to pronounce the land of the Thai, the dominant tribe. That label became world famous in 1829, with the birth of conjoined twins, Chang and Eng. "The Siamese Twins" toured on exhibit for 45 years. They died in 1874.

Oh, for Life of a White Elephant!

This ancient kingdom also was the source of the term, "White Elephant." According to mythology, all elephants originally were white. In fact, they also *flew*, companions of the fluffy clouds. (That reminded me of Nigerian Airways' logo: a flying elephant!) Millennia ago, one of them entered the womb of Queen Sirimahamaya. There are no medical records to indicate whether gestation was elephantine (nearly two years) or human (nine months), but in due time Queen Siri gave birth to Prince "Sid." You've got it—that was Siddhartha, the future Gautama Buddha, born in Nepal. He wandered off to India, where I'd seen the *bodh* tree under which he became enlightened.

I was glad for this "enlightenment" about the Buddha's genealogy.[13] Now I could understand why white elephants were considered sacred.[14] As good omens, they became pampered guests of the king, fed but never made to work. Tradition describes attendants shading the albinos with parasols, chefs feeding them trays of delicacies, and musicians calming them with exotic melodies. The latter might be a good idea, because some white elephants have been nasty characters. One went amok[15] and for years had to be penned in a very strong cage.

As if that wasn't bad enough, the white pachyderms have been the "cause" of war! In 1767, the king of neighboring Burma fought with the king of Siam over white elephants. When he heard that Siam's king had received a gift of seven elephants, he invaded the country in a

---

13. As I learned in India, "Buddha" is not a proper (or person's) name but a state: meaning "Enlightened." Buddhists believe Siddhartha Gautama (ch. 11) has been the only human manifestation of this state.

14. They aren't all that white, but have very little pigmentation in their eyes and between skin folds. Because they consume a lot of food but don't work, foreigners call any useless object, "a white elephant"—is that "BIGotry"? (For Buddha's elephant illustration of "The Eternal," see Appendix C.)

15. A Malay word for the murderous frenzy of demon-possessed dancers.

fit of jealousy.[16] His army destroyed the four-century-old royal capital, Ayutthaya, 50 miles north of today's Bangkok. The city lost irreplaceable treasures (including Siam's historical records and several magnificent gilded pagodas).

Since then, Thailand's palace has kept a white elephant as a tradition and zoological curiosity. But all elephants—of whatever color—are immortalized, somewhat as cows are in India. Few of the nation's 5,000 elephants now work, because the forests have been almost logged out. However, they are a tourist attraction. Every November (during a festival called Surin), there are elephant contests in Thailand. These include races and a tug-of-war: 100 men pulling against one elephant.

"Musician" must be the most unusual elephant "calling," so to speak. An American musicologist and a veteran elephant trainer formed the Thai Elephant Orchestra. Six pachyderms keep time as they flap ears, swish tails, beat drums and gongs, clash cymbals, strike dulcimer-like tubes (Thai *renats*), and even blow mouthorgans gripped in the end of their trunks. The finale is a chorus of natural elephant "trumpeting." A CD recording with 13 "tracks" is popular among New Age enthusiasts. The music is a little "heavy," but their concerts are a great tourist attraction!

It was elephant *art* that intrigued me at the Elephant Conservation Center, where two Russian artists gave art lessons *to elephants*. Tourists pay $2,000 and more for the novel paintings—as good as "abstract art" gets. The income, along with contributions at Big Band Concerts, helps maintain the Center. All this appreciative attention must give the redundant elephants self-esteem. Before the Center opened, unemployed *mahouts* (elephant keepers), unable to feed the pachyderms, let them beg in cities. They became a hazard, blocking traffic and causing accidents. Even if you are driving a tank, give an elephant the right of way! And they could become very deadly if they broke into village granaries. In India's northeast Assam, they did that and became intoxicated after gorging on fermented rice—trampling six people to death.

---

16. *National Geographic*, May 1991, p.29.

Bangkok—Bustling Mega-City

My first visit to Bangkok, Thailand's burgeoning capital (8-10m.) was at the invitation of the Christian and Missionary Alliance. Their "Field Chairmen" (Directors) gathered from countries in Asia, the Pacific, and Latin America. Most had pastored churches, but they kept me busy for a week, leading a seminar on management and leadership.

I had a great deal of respect for this "alliance" that had become a denomination. Albert B. Simpson, a Presbyterian, founded it with the vision of world missions. The pioneers of my own agency studied at his Missionary Training Institute. "The Alliance" has had one of the world's highest ratios of missionary-to-church-member support. Missionaries first have to serve in a pastoral role in their own country. Therefore, in first-term assignment to another land, many are older and more experienced, pastorally, than the *average* new missionary.

"We're glad for that pastoral experience," they told me, adding with a touch of frustration, "but we were unprepared for this role of mission administration!"

So we looked in God's Word for management and leadership principles. They were all there: "case studies" such as Jethro's advice to son-in-law Moses (delegate responsibility), and Paul's instructions to Timothy (prepare and appoint leadership). The Holy Spirit could use these principles as we trusted him to guide us. The Alliance impressed me by recognizing the need to further hone the gifts and skills God had given these seasoned missionaries.

After the course, I took time to browse around the bustling metropolis, dubbed variously "the city of angels" or "the city of sin" (depending on one's viewpoint!). Although its canals were polluted with industrial and human waste, on market days, they came alive with bobbing conical straw hats (actually sunshades over other headgear).[17] Market women and their produce filled dugouts and plank-sided skiffs, their design unchanged through the centuries. It was an easier way to travel than through the city's main streets, clogged with exhaust-spewing buses, trucks, and motorized rickshaws. But one had to be alert to "charity ambulances"[18]

17. *Bangkok* is the name of a fine straw used in making the hats.

18. Privately owned, but registered as charities.

racing along side streets. Eager to be first to reach the scene of an accident, their owners earn good money by delivering a victim, dead or alive, to the hospital with which the driver is registered.

Looking for a washroom, I called in at a hotel. In the lobby, a sign informed me, *"No Durian or Alcohol."* (Durian, I knew, was a tropical fruit one could either love or hate; gourmets braved its foul smell to enjoy its luscious flavor.) In the washroom, a sign instructed, *"Please use cared all items provide. Sing* [*i.e.* ring] *for what you want take."*

Back on the street, I chose to ride a *tuk-tuk*[19] because it could squeeze between traffic jams and take side streets. And it cost only a few *satang* (pennies) per ride. On every corner and down dark lanes, it seemed youth "hung out," waiting for their next sex "trick." I sadly remembered that Bangkok is known as the tourist sex capital.

Aircraft, watercraft, and buses arrive in Thailand in waves, filled with businessmen who have signed up for a romp with some of the country's prostitutes—they can choose from 100,000 males and 700,000 females. Most of the prostitutes are little more than children, under adulterers mistaken belief that adolescents are "safe"—they won't have AIDS yet. Destitute parents sometimes sell their children to agents, believing they'll find honorable employment. Other children are runaways from home, but if they attempt to run away from their pimps, they receive beatings and rapes until they submit.

It's a notorious and evil trade, involving an estimated 2m and accounting for some 14% of the nation's GDP revenue. The Thai government is trying to restore the nation's traditional moral concepts. In 2002, the Interior Minister instituted a "new social order," cracking down on under-age drinking, corruption, and the sex and drug trade.[20] "The family is the best instrument to prevent crime and instil ethics and moral values in children," said the Minister, a Buddhist who has a doctorate in criminology from Florida State University.

---

19. In Thailand, a motorized rickshaw's nickname because of its two-stroke motor's sound. *Rickshaw* is from Japanese *jinrikisha*: a two-wheeled, man-pulled cart.

20. Thais now use imported as well as traditional drugs. Neighboring Myanmar manufactures and exports *ya baa,* a popular new form of "speed" dubbed "the crazy pill," inducing disastrous addiction.

The Ministry has an uphill battle, facing corruption at every level of society, including monasteries.[21] Some Buddhists have refused to give rice to mendicant monks (a religious duty), because of numerous sex and drug scandals. (Monks take that stoically, because the Gautama Buddha taught, "Existence is suffering.") The media reported the arrest of a prominent abbot for impersonating an army officer. He was filmed with a prostitute, his saffron robe hidden under an army uniform.[22] Unfortunately, Thailand is not alone for scandals among its religious communities. It happens all over the globe.[23]

If they will, foreign governments can help reduce the tourist sex industry, as it's politely called. I gave thanks for the Christian men and women who intentionally live in "red-light" districts, to introduce unfortunate youthful victims to the Lord. I thought of the words Jesus spoke to an adulteress, "Go and sin no more!"

The promiscuity of today's youth is one of the unfortunate downsides of the nation's overseas contacts—including immoral entertainment accessible over the Internet and satellite TV. Otherwise, as one of the "Asian Tigers" in economic growth, Thailand has been an industrial powerhouse, with 94% literacy. Although the nation has a population of only 64m and only one in 12 owns a car, it became Asia's global production base for some vehicles. At one time it was the world's second largest producer of pickup trucks! Asian, European, and American automobile manufactures have had plants in Thailand.

Clothing manufacturers, competing with China's lower labor costs, seek an edge by designing and marketing their own fashions. In medical treatment, Thailand attracts more patients, including high-tech surgery cases, from outside the country (1m. in one recent year) than even India. The economy can stand all the help its industries provide, as it recovers from the property crash in the 90s. Bangkok's elevated Skytrain wends among impressive downtown towers, but many are still under-utilized.

---

21. Thailand expects every male to join a monastery for at least three months. There are 31,000 temples.
22. *Economist,* December 2, 2000.
23. Kevin Bales, *Disposable People: New Slavery in the Global Economy*. See Bibliog.

"Taken for a Ride"?

I was interested in seeing the city market, where industrious tailors and seamstresses create the latest fashions for Thailand's booming textile and garment trade. I bought a length of raw silk to take home for Lorna, who likes to sew. Thailand is famous for the silkworms that feed off cultivated mulberry leaves. After visiting the area, I headed back to the Alliance guesthouse in a *tuk tuk*. With the suddenness of a theatre curtain drop, darkness had descended, as it does in the tropics. Through the traffic's exhaust smoke I kept track of where we were by the outline of building roofs along the route (I learned that from my navy days: a sailor's tactic for finding the way back to dockside after exploring a foreign port.)

Suddenly I couldn't recognize buildings along the way. Well, no problem—probably the driver was smart to turn off the congested main road, I reasoned. It's still "rush hour" in downtown Bangkok. Or maybe he's taking a shortcut, I comforted myself. ... No lights along this back alley, though. Looks like a red-light slum ... flickering oil-lamps silhouetting curvaceous females in doorways. A bandit could easily jump me. A lone foreigner in an open rickshaw must be a sitting duck (so to speak).

My imagination went into high gear. Maybe rickshaw mahouts are in cahoots with thugs and share the booty. What was that high crime-rate figure? And the drug trade? I tried to fade into the canvass hood that stretched over the open passenger bench.

"Lord, keep me safe!" I breathed, patting my buttoned-up inside pocket, to make sure my wallet and passport were still there. In a strange city, it was always advisable to carry one's passport in case police check foreigners. Saves hassle, if one doesn't care to bribe. And not even mission guest houses advise leaving valuables in one's room. (Result: walking tourists make attractive mugging victims!)

I'm fairly used to exploring strange cities, but now my heartbeat quickened as the *tuk tuk* stopped in a lane. Now what! A dark figure hopped in beside the driver. Shades of another country on another continent, when my airport taxi stopped to pick up a passenger—who turned out to be a secret service agent. Instead of taking me to my destination at the mission home, the cabbie had taken me straight to Security Headquarters, where an army captain interrogated me, detaining me the rest of the day. I ended up in a holding cell until a friend recognized me.[24]

"Lord get me home safe!" I prayed, a little more intensely. Just as I felt my blood pressure mounting, our rickshaw jettisoned on to the main thoroughfare. Ah—I hadn't realized how bright streetlights could be! We'd bypassed the downtown gridlock, and now I recognized landmark buildings again. The unscheduled passenger turned out to be the driver's friend, acting as a bodyguard through the back lanes. All was well! "Thank you, Lord," I sighed as we reached the guesthouse. I also thanked the rickshaw driver with a little wad of extra *satang*.

Central Keyhole in S.E. Asia's Door

Later as I looked at a map of South-East Asia, the shape of Thailand and its position in the area made me think of a keyhole in a big doorway. That's how pioneer missionaries saw this ancient land of Siam, because of the other countries it touched and the many immigrants from those lands.

Today's global industry sees Thailand in the same way—central, friendly toward other nations, and with a capable potential workforce. Thailand is a member of the Association of South-East Asia Nations (ASEAN), an influential grouping of ten countries with a combined population of half a billion. Several mission agencies base administration there. OMF has long had offices, originally to minister to the Chinese *diaspora*. Now it helps other needy communities, strengthening their related churches, and reaching into remote parts. I've already mentioned the Alliance work. More recently, in the northern city of Chiang Mai, SIM opened its Central and South-East Asia (C-SEA) offices. Several faith-based agencies maintain facilities there, including a joint school for children of their personnel. Major denominations, including Anglicans, Presbyterians, and Southern Baptists provide missionaries throughout the nation.

---

24. I later learned that the city was under threat from "foreign mercenaries."

The Holy Spirit's Missionary Network

As to neighboring Myanmar (Burma), I remembered that back in Carey's era, God was preparing his instruments in a surprising way. In New England, USA, youthful Adoniram Judson seemed an unlikely candidate for missionary work.[25] Son of a Congregational minister, he nevertheless opposed the gospel—maybe it was too convicting! But the death of a close friend turned his thoughts to eternity, and he became a devout believer in Christ as Saviour. After he graduated from Andover Theological Seminary, the Congregationalists licensed him to preach, but a mission book on Asia led him instead to apply for service in India. The newly formed (Congregational) American Board of Commissioners for Foreign Missions accepted Judson and three friends as its first missionaries.

On their four-month-long voyage to India, Adoniram and his wife Ann, knowing of William Carey's work as a Baptist, studied Baptist doctrine in order to confute it (since they themselves hadn't been baptized). However, by the time they reached India, the Judsons realized that "believer's baptism" was a powerful witness to one's faith—and quite biblical. How could they baptize others if they themselves had not followed his example? So paradoxically, upon arrival in Calcutta, the two Congregationalists asked William Carey to baptize them. Ironically, this act brought about formation of the American Baptist Mission Society back home—and the Judsons became its first and most famed members, already in Asia!

But the British-American war of 1812-1814 forced the American couple to leave Calcutta, taking refuge on the French-governed island of Mauritius, southwest in the Indian Ocean. Eventually they re-traced their route back along the east coast of India, intending to start a mission across the Bay of Bengal on the island of Penang, off the southern tip of Siam. No foreign power ruled Siam (Thailand). At the time, it stretched that far south, and was seen as potential for evangelizing the Chinese who had migrated to Siam and Penang.

En route, their ship put in to the Indian port of Madras (Chennai). When British authorities threatened deportation to England, the Judsons took the only available alternative—a ship to Rangoon, Burma, which was not under the protection of any European power at the time. It was a risk, residing in a Burmese despot's territory, but the Judsons had already been through many risks. (Sounds like missionary Paul's "journeyings oft"!)[26] Though intending to pioneer in Siam, instead they arrived in Rangoon July 13, 1813. Authorities later jailed Adoniram on suspicion he was a spy.

In Burma the Judsons came across camps of Siamese prisoners (the two countries were traditional enemies, although both were officially Buddhist). Ann felt so concerned for these unfortunates, she learned their language and translated Matthew's Gospel and a catechism prepared by Adoniram in Burmese. Ann then held Siamese reading classes!

Ann Judson (also called Nancy) was the first known Protestant missionary to evangelize among Siamese.[27]

The Holy Spirit's Networking

That intrepid pioneer, William Carey, pops into the picture once again! In Burma, the Judsons lodged in the home of Carey's son Felix, who had gone there with others to start mission work. In 1819 William Carey's press in Serampore printed the first Christian literature in Siamese: Ann Judson's translation of Adoniram's Burmese catechism and gospel tracts.

Buddhism had long been ensconced in Burma, dating back centuries to an edict in the ancient capital of Pagan. Mogul (Islamic) invaders sacked the city in the 13th c., but today the Rohingya Muslim minority suffer as much persecution as Christians, causing thousands of minorities to flee across the border into the panhandle of eastern Bangladesh. Obviously the gospel is making an impact, for The Institution of Buddhist Clergy has called for a ban on FEBC gospel broadcasts—because "they are a threat to Buddhism." While the world applauds the

25. See Courtney Anderson, *To the Golden Shore: A Life of Adoniram Judson* (Bibliography).

26. 2 Corinthians 11.26, KJV.

27. Not the first Christian witness. however. There was a Nestorian bishopric in Siam in A.D. 800. Roman Catholic Dominicans arrived in neighboring Cambodia 1555. A converted Buddhist priest became the area's first martyr in 1568. Charles Robinson, *History of Christian Missions*, p. 165 (see Bibliography).

courageous opposition of Aung San Suu Kyi's pro-democracy party, the West ignores the harsh repression of Christians among the northern Karen tribe—forced into labor camps, tortured, raped, and killed at random.[28]

Again the Holy Spirit's networking impressed me: The journals of British missionary to the "American Indians" David Brainerd and his friend Jonathan Edwards (New England), had influenced William Carey (UK/India), who in turn helped Adoniram and Ann Judson (USA/Burma) with their productive ministries in East Asia, which resulted in formation of the American Baptist Mission (ABM). On opposite sides of the Atlantic, the ABM and Britain's Baptist Missionary Society (resulting from Carey's missionary call) have blessed peoples all around the world. Amazing! I acknowledged afresh that God is more concerned about the world than we are; he puts together his global network, giving us the privilege (and responsibility) of involvement.

> At the time, I was unable to enter Myanmar (Burma), strategically located between eastern India, China's south, and Thailand on its eastern border. Its southward neck stretched almost to Indonesia. Britain granted Independence in 1948, but for over four decades the nation has suffered under a repressive, secretive military regime. It has rejected most Western aid organizations that stand ready to help victims of natural disasters.
>
> (Most of the population is Buddhist, and monks have periodically led protests.[29] However, in spite of state persecution, Christians continue to worship, but in secret. Some Muslim minorities have fled the country.)
>
> Though rich in natural resources, Myanmar is listed as the world's riskiest investment, and second-largest (after Afghanistan) producer of heroin and opium.[30] For income, the Military sold large areas to concessionaires, who strip the land of timber, minerals, and animals.

---

28. REC News Exchange, Nov. 1999; *Family News*, Oct. 1999. Colorado Springs: Focus on the Family.
29. Mandalay, to which Rudyard Kipling refers in his classic poem, is a center of Buddhism in Myanmar.
30. "Emerging Market Indicators," *Economist*, September 30 and June 24, 2000.

The Military seek the advice of astrologers, who in 2005, determined the site of a new capital to mark the regime—following the custom of predecessors. Myanmar's superstitious junta moved their capital to the northern jungles, isolated and only half-built, but—conveniently for the regime—more easily defended, and closer to the border with Communist China. Government offices ordered staff to move—without their families. And no resignations allowed!]

Fishers "Net-working"

Jesus told his fishermen disciples they'd become "fishers of men." In Asia, I saw "net-working" in today's world. Thai evangelists go in teams to neighboring countries. Chinese missionaries work among spirit-worshiping northern villages, which have been losing their children to big city attractions. A few secular anthropologists are quick to blame missions for "destroying village culture," but that is not the result of missions. Instead, mission agencies often seem to be the only ones doing anything to overcome this social problem in remote communities. They preserve dialects, languages, and cultures, providing camps where tribal children learn traditional crafts, songs, and grammar.[31]

Koreans Lee Jung Son [actual name withheld at their request] and his wife Siu felt called to be missionaries in today's Thailand after his church sponsored a medical mission trip there. "I was touched by the kindness of the people," Jung Son reported. "Even though they were so poor, they smiled and provided us cool water. They listened closely to Scripture and asked us to pray." The couple trained at the Asia Christian Training Institute in Singapore before returning to Thailand.

Men and women from other parts of the world joined their Asian colleagues in this networking. Most were specialists who could fill niches on teams—folk like Paul and Clare Hudson, whom I'd last seen in Nepal. They'd moved to Thailand and were handling logistics for an SIM Pacific-Asia Regional Consultation (PARC III). Dr. Paul, wiry as ever, was taking a break from backpacking on medical forays to remote areas.[32]

31. Linguistic anthropologists Lamin Sanneh and Sherwood Lingenfelter document this (see Bibliography).

32. Dr. Paul Hudson has since become SIM's Area Director for C-Sea, based in Thailand.

"Only God Is Big Enough for AIDS"

The day after the conference, this medic planned to set off for China's northwest, to survey the AIDS outbreak there. "What should we know about this global threat?" I asked. "I know you're very concerned."

"I certainly am," Paul replied. "The problem of HIV/AIDS is growing at an alarming rate, especially in China and neighboring countries. Since 1998, the number of reported HIV infections in China has increased by thirty percent yearly. Susan Hunter, in her recent book, *AIDS in Asia*, says that 'although the world has already conditioned itself to AIDS deaths numbering in the tens of millions in Africa, predications of several hundred million AIDS deaths in Asia, accompanied by shifts in political boundaries and economic chaos ... are less easy to shrug off.'

"The Chinese government has spent millions to improve water, roads, schools and clinics in so-called 'AIDS villages' in central Henan.[33] Posters and school campaigns to fight AIDS are much more visible. In 2004, China's prime minister announced an official figure of one million HIV-infected people in China and asked for international help."[34]

Dr. Hudson pointed out that AIDS programs in most of Asia are based on technology, not on social behaviour. From his earlier experience in Africa, he observed the main reason for Uganda's dramatic reduction of infections—acclaimed worldwide—was based on moral teaching by the churches in Uganda. Paul and his colleagues help Asian churches to understand their strategic role in curbing the plague. They see the burgeoning church in China as key to forestall the pandemic forecast by government and medical officials.

"The core solutions to this crisis are not technical solutions, such as condoms, medicine, or even money. Rather, solutions involve relationships: ministry, passion, volunteerism and the hands and feet of Jesus. Let's keep the gospel central in all our efforts. There is something worse than dying with AIDS—and that is dying with AIDS *without Christ*. Transformation

---

33. Poverty triggered an AIDS pandemic, as illiterates sold their blood without using sterile needles.
34. Paul J. Hudson, *HOPE for China: The HIV/AIDS Context for Ministry*. Fullerton: *China 20/20*, 6/2005.

is through the cross. We have a wonderful opportunity to balance word and deed. The problems underneath HIV—corruption, sexual sin, oppression, injustice, and stigma—are 'ready made' for the gospel. Only God is big enough for HIV/AIDS. It is a disease of broken relationships, and our God—our mighty, powerful and gracious God—heals broken relationships."

C-SEA Welcomes PARC III

Networking[35] was the name of the game at SIM's administrative center for China and South East-Asia (C-SEA) in Chiang Mai, north of Bangkok. Back in 1974, Lorna and I had welcomed Elmer and Elvira Warkentin to Nigeria, rookies fresh from Canada's prairies. Now seasoned veterans serving on the other side of the world, during my visit they were welcoming PARC III to Chiang Mai, where they had moved. "PARC III" was the Pacific and Asia Regional Conference III, organized by SIM's Howard Brant and his wife, Jo-Ann. Of course I was also happy to see our daughter, Rebecca, and our grandchildren Stacey and Geoff helping in the parallel children's program.

The 173 delegates from 23 countries (most of whom paid their own way, some helping others with their costs), met for worship, Bible study, report sharing, and strategy discussion. SIM's International Director, Malcolm McGregor, in his engaging Scottish burr, gave us a brief daily challenge. Medical pioneer Robert Foster, retired General Director of Africa Evangelical Fellowship, shared his vision with us.[36] Both Asians and Caucasians led us into a fresh sense of the Holy Spirit's presence and guidance. Pastors and missionaries who sometimes feel isolated strengthened each other in team spirit, resulting in new networks of communication and assistance. I'd met several of them on earlier trips I'd made along the Old Spice Road.

"Do you remember me?" asked one beaming Chinese woman. "You accompanied Elizabeth and me into China!" I did indeed remember

35. In Thailand, OMF provides partner registration for C-SEA. New Enterprise International (with missionaries from India, East Asia and China) is one of several other agencies partnering with C-Sea.

36. Dr. Foster had led his mission, originally South Africa General Mission, through a number of changes, including adoption of the AEF name. (Later, AEF and SIM merged.)

Christine and that memorable trip before Hong Kong's re-unification with the rest of China.[37] Since then, Christine had served with SIM in Ethiopia and now in Thailand. A businessman I'd stayed with in Hong Kong, Albert Li, was also at PARC III—as an SIM Hong Kong Council member.

Missionary Hak Jin Chun reminded me he'd been in a class I'd taught in Korea 20 years earlier. I'd previously met others in places as far apart as Pakistan, the Philippines, New Zealand, West Africa, and points in between. What a privilege, I thought, to have part in what God is doing around the globe! We were blessed to see Asians from one or other Asian country now serving as missionaries in another country. We knew that meant a lot in cultural, emotional, and physical adjustment, along with spiritual warfare.

A lot of useful sharing went on, especially at meal times, over ample servings of spicy Thai chicken, Chinese egg-drop soup and "sticky rice," Indian curry, fresh pineapple, reliable western omelet—or whatever one chose from the sumptuous buffet.[38] For all of us, PARC III was a refreshing instructive experience, fulfilling the theme: "Sharing the gospel and our lives."[39]

Recovering the Lost Book

After the conference, Rebecca, Stacey, Geoff, and I enjoyed rides (and elephantine art!) at the elephant park and dropped in on Brian and Linda Crawford and their family, OMF missionaries who were from our home church. After the China Inland Mission withdrew from China the end of the 1940s, CIM had changed its name to the more inclusive Overseas Missionary Fellowship, with the vision of evangelizing other parts of Asia. Although Thailand's population is 80% Thai, the other 20% includes a mosaic of ethnic groups, each with a colorful culture. Some are from tribes that have spilled across neighboring countries of South-East Asia, many originating in China. OMF "China hands" could readily

37. See Chapter 17.

38. Food and accommodations made affordable by the low, off-season rates of the resort where we met.

39. From Paul's words in 1 Thessalonians 2.8.

communicate with the many Chinese-speaking citizens. The northern tribal groups obviously could do with medical and other help—including the message of liberation from fear of the spirit world.

I was curious whether the prediction about the Lost Book, told me by Paul Roberts (Ch. 6), had spread this far. I was able to check, when Brian and Linda took us back to the remote village where they'd first lived in Thailand. On the way, we drove under an umbrella of verdant forest, filled with calls of exotic birds.

In the village, the Crawfords asked an elderly Christian if she'd ever heard of "the Golden Book that was lost." Yes, the woman nodded, breaking into a grin. Her parents had told her the prophecy—how "a man from where the sun sets" would bring a Golden Book with a special message people should accept. (Burma, of course, was to the West).

Similar prophecies were more widespread than I'd realized. A Muslim traveler in Burma had left a copy of the Anglican *Book of Common Prayer and Psalms* in a Karen village, telling the people that one day a man would come to explain it. "You must listen to him," the Muslim had said, "because that book speaks truth!" They treated it as a sacred oracle until one day a Karen evangelist, Ko Thah-Byu, led Baptist missionaries George and Sarah Boardman to the village. When the chief and his priest unwrapped the sacred book, the Boardmans were able to point the people to the God about whom the book spoke.[40]

In turn, James O. Frazer, China Inland Mission (now OMF) pioneer sought the help of a Burmese Baptist Karen to evangelize the Lisu of Southern China. With the evangelist (whose Karen language was similar to Lisu), Frazer translated Scripture portions that spread the flame of the gospel like a grass fire across Lisu land. As had the Karen before them, the Lisu had long been waiting for the prophesied "teacher with a white face" who would restore their lost book of God—in their own language![41]

As Brian translated for me the village woman's response that day, shivers went down my spine. I thought of Isaiah's prophecy away over in

40. Richardson, *op cit.*, p. 91.

41. Isabel Kuhn, *Nests Above the Abyss* (Bibliog.), describes the "people movement" of tens of thousands.

another part of Asia—Israel: *"Prepare the way of the Lord, make straight in the wilderness a highway for our God."*[42] That had happened here in South-East Asia! In a great arc, from India's Assam, through the southern tribes of China, to South-East Asia's delta, the Holy Spirit had prepared the way for gospel messengers. In several related ethnic groups, hundreds of thousands had gladly received the news of Jesus Christ, the Savior—in spite of centuries of superstitious shaman, Buddhist, and Hindu worship surrounding them.

"You can have a mass movement without individual conversions," Eugene Morse, Disciples of Christ, warned when I enthused over the amazing response I'd seen in Thailand. Fourth generation of a line of missionaries, he spoke from experience. "It's as if you cleared the jungle to plant crops. Farmers know that if they don't cultivate several times a year, weeds will grow and choke the seed sown. They also have to winnow and prune. Even though the chaff looks like grain, it is empty husk. That's the story of world evangelism: *without biblical teaching, there is little spiritual growth.* Opposition and persecution aren't pleasant, but they, too, are part of the process of building the church."

Sacred Bread of the Yao/Yiu/Jew?

American missionaries Eric and Helen Cox and their OMF team knew the value of God's Word in grounding disciples. In the mid-20th c., they began translating the New Testament to enable Yao converts to grow spiritually. It was mostly hard work, not very exciting—but it had its own surprises.

"As we worked on Mark's Gospel," Eric recalled, "I described the Old Testament 'showbread' that David and his men ate.[43] I mentioned that even today, Jews set it out in a row of 12. My Yao informants broke into smiles."

"We have sacred bread too!" they exclaimed. "Only we set it out in two piles of six, instead of a row of 12."

---

42. Isaiah 40.3.

43. Sacred, unleavened bread, also spelled "shewbread." *Scripture*: Mark 2.26 KJV. Details are from "Yao Beginnings: A Jewish connection?" by Eric Cox, *East Asia Millions*, April/May, 1979. Robesonia: OMF. Ann Burgess later completed the entire Yao Bible, published 2007. (Re. Jews in ancient China, see Ch. 17.)

Eric thought little of this strange coincidence, even though it differed slightly from the Hebrew practice he knew about. But one day his mouth dropped open as he was checking a dictionary of Jewish customs. In David's day, Hebrews set the showbread in *two piles of six*! Where had the Yao learned this? The mystery grew as Eric learned that the Yao call their clans, "The Twelve Tribes," and they preface their aboriginal name, Mien, prefixed by Iu/Yiu. (Hence the Chinese called them Yao, sometimes pejoratively.) Eric realized that "yiu" was exactly the way a Yao would pronounce "Jew." In several ways, their worship rituals, although animistic, paralleled Old Testament practices!

The Coxes and colleagues lived in primitive bamboo huts, open to the elements and the villagers, but their faithfulness bore fruit, as first a headman and then other Yao rejected the spirits that had controlled their lives, and turned to the living God. Others completed translation of the Bible, and eventually, Christian groups sprang up all over South-East Asia and in China's south, among scattered Yao villages. Christians excitedly told their neighbors the news of Jehovah God, the God that Jewish merchants and travelers must have told them about, centuries before. Or were the Yao actually an inter-marriage of Jewish settlers and Chinese?

They came "from across the water," according to Yao legend. Characteristics indicate they either arrived via China or intermarried with Chinese. Their custom of clearing virgin land and never planting on the same soil for two consecutive years has driven them southward, seeking new areas to cultivate. Central to their culture is the accumulation of wealth. They'd had knowledge of a supreme being, but it took centuries, maybe millennia, before they met Jesus on the Old Spice Road.

The Yao/Myen[44] are only one of myriad ethnic groups that populate the riverain nations of South-East Asia. Apart from British-governed Burma and independent Thailand, the area became known as French Indo-China after WWI. When the French left, the ex-French colonies succumbed to local forms of Maoist-Leninism—introduced by the elite, who picked it up from Beijing, and by students studying in Paris. Communism still rules life in neighboring Laos and Vietnam.

44. Mien/Myen ("The People") is one of the Hmong-Mien (Miao-Yao) linguistic groups.

Sun Like Thunder – **15: South-East Asia's Upheavals**

Terrifying Nightmare

"They were put to death by the sword . . .
– the world was not worthy of them. . . .
These were all commended for their faith"
(Hebrews 11.37-39).

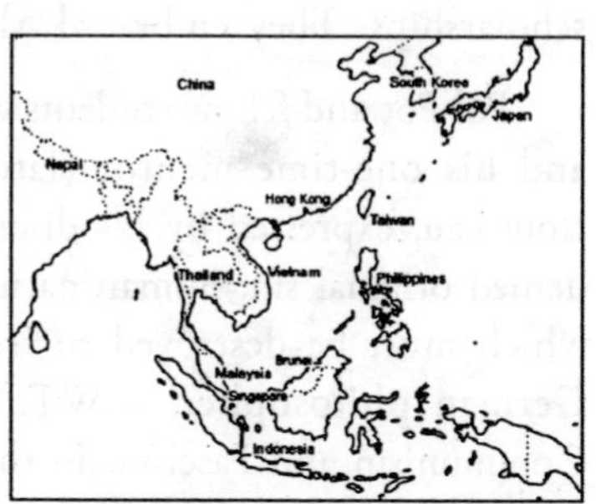

Cambodia: Pop. 13,250,035
Laos: Pop. 6,964,623
Vietnam: Pop. 90,764,274

CAMBODIA, Thailand's neighbor, is still reeling from effects of the Khmer Rouge ("Red Khmer") pogrom, in which Maoists from the dominant Khmer tribe systematically slaughtered a quarter of the nation's population, giving rise to the term, "the Killing Fields." Hundreds of thousands more fled Cambodia to escape state slavery that permanently disabled equivalent numbers of the nation's beautiful people.

I'm still puzzled—stunned—how a handful of Maoists engineered the social destruction of an entire nation. Tell me this was only a terrifying nightmare! *It was unimaginable.* I'd always thought of Cambodians, like their South-East Asian neighbors, as some of the most beautiful people in the world—milk-chocolate complexion, doll-like faces, graceful bodies. Adam and Eve must have looked like them, I mused. The world thought of Cambodians as peace-loving people. But for many, placid beauty was only skin-deep. Underneath Buddhism's inscrutable veneer were immorality, corruption, deceit, and abuse. Historically, Cambodia's Khmers have been a cruel, feuding tribe.

Amazingly, the ideology that drove this atrocity came right out of academic elitism in *France*. In colonial Indo-China, French educators had already passed on to their students the libertarian concepts of the French Revolution. France's colonial policy was to develop a limited but highly educated elite *evolue*, who became part of *francophonie*, with French citizens' rights.[1] In the '50s, Saloth Sar (the notorious "Pol Pot") and other Khmer intellectuals studied in France under government scholarships. They embraced Marxist-Leninism.[2]

Pol Pot and fellow students would have studied Jean-Jacques Rousseau and his one-time mentor (later rival), Voltaire.[3] The philosophy of Rousseau, expressed by his disciple, Jean-Paul Sartre. Rousseau (19th c.) denied original sin; human nature was innocent apart from societal evil, which must be destroyed to free mankind. Adding to this concept, a German philosopher, G.W.F. Hegel (1770-1831), influenced both Communism and Fascism. In the Hegelian process, a concept (thesis) is fulfilled by its antithesis (e.g., black is white; injustice is just), resulting in synthesis.

At last these young Cambodian intellectuals had a philosophical basis for righting all wrongs ever done to the Khmer: India's Brahmin invasion of the riverain peninsula, imposition of Buddhism over their ancient spirit-worship, incursions by Chinese, Thai, and Viet, colonization by the French and—worst of all—current evils of corrupt capitalism! Revolution, they learned, had transformed France, Russia, and Germany. (Although Hitler followed the fascist route, revolutionaries thought he was on the right path by eliminating millions of wealthy Jewish "oppressors" to create a super race. The Nazi Party, ironically, embraced socialism; so Vichy French sided with Hitler.)

---

1. In contrast, British colonial policy sought to raise the general educational level, rather than an educated elite. The British Empire also had its share of atheists, but Britain's 18th c. spiritual revivals awakened social conscience to change society through work ethic and humanitarian compassion, rather than destructive revolution. Evangelicals in Parliament urged moral justice. Later, InterVarsity Graduates' Fellowship placed many evangelical academics in overseas universities and the Foreign Service. Britain's colonies (a popular Cold War "whipping boy") reflected this difference from most other colonies. However, the popular destination of colonial scholarship students was the (then Marxist) London School of Economics.
2. *Communisme,* a French word, became synonymous with Marxist-Leninist ideology.
3. Though epitomizing conceit and hypocrisy, Rousseau became a cult figure to revolutionaries, along with Voltaire, as the greatest expression of reason and philosophy—*and worldwide is still required reading!* (Alan Jacobs, "The Only Honest Man." *Books and Culture*, Carol Stream, May-June 2000.)

Chairman Mao's takeover of China gave them a made-in-Asia model. A dedicated core could overthrow corrupt bourgeois oppressors.[4] The educated class could never be reformed—turf 'em out of their comfortable cities to serve the downtrodden masses! They deserved to become slave labor. Pol Pot's cadre would simply eliminate anyone who resisted their lofty goals.

"Organization on High"—out of Hell!

Revolution! Heady stuff, this. Pol Pot returned to Phnom Pen to form the Communist Party of Cambodia, with a core of 21 dedicated ideologues. They'd restore the nation to the glories of the Angkor Empire that had dominated northeast Cambodia and west Thailand for five centuries.[5] Of course, they'd replace its religion with a "patriotic faith," *Angka Loeu*, "The Organization on High." Once they'd overthrown the current regime, there would be no god but Angka, and Pol Pot would be his prophet. Western politicians considered the Khmers Rouges a curious but confused mix of animist, Brahmin, Buddhist, Islamic, and socialist dialectic—ending in Hegelianism.[6]

But the Khmers' deceptive plan worked! The Communist Party slowly wormed its way into power, as it captured the people's vision of ancient glories and cashed in on society's anger over corruption. Through clever pseudo-religion, deceitful promises, and intimidation, Pol Pot took over the capital April 17, 1975. Cambodia fell—into a man-made hellhole, a totalitarian "people's republic."

Communism had taught the young revolutionaries that humanity needed "A New Man" to change their world. The uneducated masses would help overthrow society's elite, but even the masses would then have to be destroyed if hard labor didn't change their worldview.

---

4. *Bourgeois*: French for "townsman," hence capitalist.
5. Heart of ancient Khmer Empire, Angkor contains the world's largest single group of religious buildings (402 acres). Some temples resemble Sumerian and Mayan sacred pyramids. City and empire fell in 15th c., and jungle covered the ruins until 1860. Khmers Rouges realized Angkor's symbolic importance, but because of their atheism, banned access to the religious site. Jungle again covered it. Now its treasures are acclaimed internationally. In 2007, Berlin mounted an exhibit: "Angkor: Sacred Heritage of Cambodia."
6. Hegelianism: see above re Hegel's philosophy. Hardly a new concept: Isaiah 5.20.

"Communism" they called it, but it really was Arian doctrine all over again—an elite breed of "New Man" who would loft the nation to its destiny (on the backs of the deluded masses). The Khmers Rouges ("Red Khmers"), they called themselves. They followed a devilishly simple plan:

(1) They tricked the respected wartime veterans and army into thinking exiled Prince Sihanouk would meet and reward them in a field—*instead, they met their death there.*

(2) They asked citizens for advice in solving Cambodia's economic and social problems. Once these had revealed their capitalist knowledge and culture, they were marched out to "the killing fields" and mercilessly shot.

(3) Khmer Rouge cadres told residents they must vacate all towns and cities for their own safety, to escape enemy fire. (There had been some aerial bombing.) Not to worry—they could return in three days. *Most never returned.*

(4) The Khmers Rouges put weapons in the hands of teenagers and children, who exulted in their newfound *power of the gun.*

(5) After they'd reduced the population to perhaps 1m (from some 7m), the new order would rebuild the nation: with the offspring of forced marriage (the "New Man").

Within days, Khmers Rouges were looting the empty towns and cities, while the erstwhile residents, whether judges or laborers, packed the roads on their way to "safety"—they thought. Instead, gunmen force-marched weary fathers, fainting mothers, and crying children to remote rice paddies, where they became slave labor to feed their well-fed predators. The dehumanized stream of humanity included educated university professors and magistrates—especially anyone wearing spectacles. Crippled patients and the elderly straggled on, collapsing until teen-age thugs kicked them back on to their feet.

It is obscene even to read about. "This book stunned me," veteran author Elisabeth Elliott said of Don McCormack's *Killing Fields, Living Fields* (see Bibliography). "It is Hebrews 11 in the 20th century," wrote reviewer Eric Alexander. Ray Lockhards, vicar of Christ Church, Jerusalem, likened the brutality to the Jewish holocaust.

OMF missionary McCormack, among the last expatriates to leave and first to return, vividly relates the eye-witness accounts of his Cambodian friends: gleeful children shooting their kin, spies mixing with weeping evacuees (who included hospital patients and the aged) and summarily executing anyone who complained. When a cadre member ran out of bullets, he used the butt of a hoe to kill a victim with a blow on the head. Young thugs ripped babies from the arms of wailing mothers, dashing infants' heads against a wall or tree. Although the elite may have started out with lofty ideals, their followers reverted to the cruel jungle practices and rites of the ancient Khmer Empire, sometimes ripping out a living prisoner's liver and eating it in front of his relatives.

The rest of the world knew all about Communist atrocities in Vietnam and China, it seemed, but overlooked the Khmers Rouges atrocities. Officials treated refugee reports as if they were fantasizing in order to obtain food. Pol Pot, responsible for the slaughter of 2m fellow countrymen in the '70s, lived in Cambodia until age took him in 1998.

> The prophecy of Isaiah, given in a different era to his own people, came true in Cambodia: *"I will make boys their officials; mere children will govern them . . . . The young will rise up against the old; the base against the honorable."*[7]

"Never again!" the world said, but it had said that after WW II liberating troops uncovered Hitler's death camps. "*Never again!*" the world more recently vowed after Bosnia's "ethnic cleansing," Darfur's slaughter, and Rwanda's genocide. The list will continue. The frightening fact is that such atrocities periodically overtake humanity—evil is inbred in the human heart. Jeremiah was right: *"The heart is deceitful above all things, and desperately wicked. Who can know it?"*[8] Evil needs only an opportunity to flourish. Scripture hints that evil would be even more rampant worldwide except for "him who restrains"—that is, the Holy Spirit.[9]

---

7. Isaiah 3.4,5.
8. Jeremiah 17.9 (KJV). The NIV reads: ". . . and beyond cure. Who can understand it?"
9. 2 Thess. 2.7, etc. This is one interpretation of a puzzling passage, but elsewhere Scripture speaks of the Holy Spirit restraining evil (*e.g.* Genesis 6.3).

"We Will Stand Firm for Jesus"

Understandably, suffering Christians pled with God to end the tribulation, but McCormack's book hints at the other side of the story—the faithfulness of believers facing torture, imprisonment, and death. He tells how his own heart was wrenched when missionaries were ordered out. He will never forget his pathetic farewell to a Cambodian Christian, who cut short his training in U.K. in order to return to strengthen the churches.

Missionaries knew if they stayed, it would only further endanger Christian brothers and sisters. By 1975, as the Khmer Rouges closed in, church adherents dropped from several thousand to only 300. Those who remained true showed tremendous courage. "We will stand firm for Jesus Christ, even to the shedding of our blood!" students at one Bible school declared. And thousands did lay down their lives rather than deny their Saviour. Their resolute commitment attracted other distraught Cambodians, and thousands turned to Christ and were even baptized. They crammed makeshift bamboo "churches," disregarding Communist persecution. As the regime murdered leaders and burned churches, believers met in "underground" groups.

I think we read about such faithfulness "even unto death," in the book of Revelation!

By the time disillusioned Khmers, led by Vietnamese forces, ousted Pol Pot in 1979, his evil regime had killed one quarter[10] of the population and expelled most of the rest to the countryside. They murdered virtually all church leaders and 90% of the Christians, destroying churches as well as Buddhist temples.[11]

Yet even in the midst of this dreadful pogrom, somehow God was at work.[12] The C&MA (which had ministered among the Khmers since the 1920s), OMF (which had entered Cambodia in 1974 in response to pleas from Chinese and Khmer Christians), Anglicans, Presbyterians, and other

---

10. ABC World News, Feb. 2, 1999. Some estimates reckon between two and three million.
11. I was interested to learn that Buddhist monks employed Vatican artisans to restore one of their most famous temples, burned by the Khmers Rouges (TVO documentary on Buddhism, Feb. 22, 2006).

church groups returned to find an amazing work of the Holy Spirit. In one Thai border refugee camp alone, several thousand believers were meeting for worship. McCormack reports that the gospel seed had sprouted, ripened to harvest, gone through winnowing, and now had sprung up again in the soil of great trial.

During those years, World Evangelical Alliance continued as an advocate for prayer for the suffering church. Previously many factions had split Christians, but in 1996 WEA rejoiced that Cambodian believers had formed the Evangelical Fellowship of Cambodia, now a full member of the Asia Evangelical Alliance. Mission agencies formerly in Cambodia returned to help rebuild the nation, physically and spiritually. World Relief set up camps to teach children hygiene (Cambodia has an extremely high child-mortality rate). Using puppets, drama, and song, the program teaches them how to have "healthy bodies and spotless hearts." In place of the violence they had witnessed, thousands of children hear of God's love and salvation. World Vision worked among Phnom Penh's estimated 15,000 children involved in prostitution.

"The Killing Fields will be renamed the Healing Fields, because of the Holy Spirit's work," stated Kim Chong Pae, Asia Director of Global Mission Society, visiting Cambodia with other agencies, including ACTI, Partners (CNEC), and World Team.

In 2004, Cambodian church leaders took part in a Forum for World Evangelization, held in neighboring Thailand. The Lausanne Committee for World Evangelism (an international and interdenominational group initiated by Evangelist Billy Graham in 1974) sponsored it. Cambodians prayed and dined and studied with Thais—no longer enemies or aliens, but members of Christ's worldwide Body. Nearly 2,000 participants from 120 nations discussed such issues as the impact of religious nationalism, ministries to children and non-traditional families, and post-modern "spirituality."

Cambodia is making a valiant attempt to recover its economy and standard of living. Manufacturing clothing is one logical way, given the number of unemployed and unskilled people, along with wages that can compete with China's. Clothing constitutes over three quarters of exports, supporting nearly one-fifth of the population.

A thriving sex trade plagues the nation. Many of the women are from Vietnam (despised after years of Viet colonization), and young girls are lured to cities with promises of gainful employment. The majority of "customers," most from other parts of Asia, regrettably believe that sex with a virgin will "rejuvenate and purify" the man.[13] To increase their sexual virility, Viet men favor a potion of snake blood.

Now Arab nations are taking an interest in Cambodia. They have oil money but need food. Rather than contracting to *buy* Cambodian rice, Kuwait and Qatar are among Islamic states preferring to *lease* (for 99-years) thousands of hectares (acres) of prime farm land, in exchange for building roads and dams (*Economist* April 25, 09). The mix of Islamist and Buddhist cultures in S.E. Asia is going to be interesting, to say the least.

Enemy Number One?

Elsewhere in S.E. Asia, there are Christian disciples who daily go through the fiery furnace of persecution. There is LAOS, forested but landlocked between the other nations of former Indo-China. There is also VIETNAM, world's second largest exporter of rice (and major producer of "pirated" computer programs), but economically strapped by Communist ideology. The loveable people of both nations deserve better, but live under repressive totalitarian socialism.

Vietnam has one of the world's highest abortion rates (two out of every three babies), while HIV/AIDS, drug addiction, and child prostitution are rampant. Wartime land mines and unexploded bombs still maim and kill farmers. Decades after the Vietnam War, mothers give birth to deformed babies, and their breast milk contains dioxin residue from the war's "Agent Orange" defoliants.[14] Now China, which colonized Vietnam for 1,000 years, would like to mine the country's vast bauxite reserves—which would leave valuable farmland scarred by strip-mining and contaminated by toxic red sludge.

12. This in no way implies God willed the pogrom—it was *evil* at work, evil that God sought to overcome.

13. *Economist,* Sept. 15, 2007

14. CBS "Sixty Minutes," December 12, 1999.

Two million Vietnamese have fled to live in other lands, where many are responding to the gospel. Unfortunately, the nation's name has been besmirched by criminal gangs that carry on their activities in the lands of refuge.

Since the civil war, America's name has also been associated with the violence of war that USA (as well as the Communist antagonists of North Vietnam) carried out. Many American veterans (known as GIs, for General Induction) and their families are still hurting from the slur of "the Ugly American" thrown at them. That label actually was the title of a wartime book detailing the ***humanitarian care*** that a beloved GI (whose face had been scarred by an explosion) gave to Vietnamese villagers as he sought to defend them from Northviets. "Ugly American" became an ironic epithet thrown around by western people who had not read the book but had heard its title!

The Religious Liberty Commission of Asia Evangelical Alliance (AEA) constantly receives reports of repression, discrimination, torture, and even killings in both Laos and Cambodia. The totalitarian Lao government labels Christianity as "a lying religion which violates Lao custom"—the number one enemy of the state. (Hello?) Amazingly, a person can be arrested even for listening to FEBC, Christian radio that beams into Asia. In Laos and Vietnam, believers tend to meet in "house churches"—unpublicized small groups.

Typical reports showing that Jesus still walks the Old Spice Road in S.E. Asia come from the animist Hmong people. They spread over several countries. Laos and Cambodia somewhat disdainfully call them "the hill people." Historically, they have resisted intruders and alien ideologies. Until recently, they have been open to the Good News that frees them from the terror of evil spirits.[15] Now governments try to suppress what amounts to a people's movement towards the Christian faith. Authorities

15. Alliance missionaries Linwood Barney and William Smalley were instrumental in developing the Roman-written form of the Hmong language in the 1950s [Gerald Anderson note to author, Jan. 5, 05]. Although other religions may form a veneer over traditional spirit worship in Southeast Asia, ancestor and spirit worship maintain a strong hold. The Malay word *amok* (absorbed into English as "amok" or "amuk") describes a violent frenzy induced during spirit ceremonies, thought to be demon possession.

are naturally suspicious of Christians, because Hmong mythology anticipates the arrival of a messianic figure as ruler. Church leaders assure officials that Christians have no political ambition—only to share the gospel with others.[16] Many meet in house churches. "We've heard the truth of the gospel," one persecuted believer told a visitor. "How can we *not* believe!"

However, tribal prejudice plagues Southeast Asia (as it does most of the world, we admit). For instance, when a Christian Thai and a Hmong member fell in love, their clans both refused permission to marry, even though respected church leaders pleaded for reconciliation, believing that in Christ, "we are all one." Clan tensions pale in contrast to national persecution Christians face, as revealed by a recent international press release:

> Vietnam Prime Minister Phan Van Khai's historic visit to the United States, an equally historic human rights agreement between the two countries, and supposedly less restrictive religion legislation introduced in November 2004 all made headlines but had no effect on continued high levels of persecution of Christians. The Mennonite church continued to face the kind of harassment documented by missionary X—[17], who submitted testimony to the U.S. Congress showing how local officials abused administrative powers to harass the denomination. The Rev. X—, a Mennonite pastor convicted of an offence he denied, was freed from prison on August 30 as part of Vietnam's National Day amnesty after enduring more than a year of harsh conditions and pressure to renounce his faith.
>
> Typical of persecution, authorities in Quang Ngai Province incited a mob to burn down the home of evangelist X— because he would not sign a paper denying his Christian faith. Authorities in the same province destroyed the homes of 10 ethnic Hre families because they would not renounce Christ. In 2005, the U.S. listed Vietnam as one of the world's worst violators of religious freedom.[18]

16. Letter to WEA from an observer, a personal friend and colleague, who does not wish to be named, for security reasons (April 26, 1994). –WHF
17. Names in Vietnam withheld for security reasons.
18. Compass Direct, Jan. 2006

Crumbling Temples and Empires

Wave after wave of proud empires have washed over Southeast Asia, including (alphabetically) Brahmin, British, Buddhist, Chinese, Communist, Dutch, French, Hindu, Japanese, Mogul, Mongol, Portuguese. Each has sprung up, blossomed, and withered. Once impressive but now deteriorating ruins are their monuments.

As I flew on my way to "discover" Asia's Pacific islands, I mentally mulled over the ruins of temples and empires all across Asia. We can all end up like those ruins, I mused. We can carve our material idols and worship them in our temples of conceit. We can set up petty kingdoms of success and extend our empires of fame. But they'll crumble into the dust, to be trampled on by the next generation. No wonder Solomon, who'd seen it all and had it all, concluded: *"All is vanity!"* Isaiah's statement is so true:

> *"All men are like grass, and all their glory is like the flowers of the field; the grass withers and the flowers fall, but the word of our God stands for ever."*[19]

19. Isaiah 40. 6-8

Along Asia's coasts, some people live on the water, travelling from island to island, always aware of the threat of a *tsunami.*

Sun Like Thunder – **16: Islands—Drops in a Bucket?**

Exploring Asia's Archipelagos[1]

"Surely the nations are like a drop in a bucket; they are regarded as dust on the scales. He weighs the islands as though they were fine dust" (Isaiah 40.15,16).

Singapore: Pop. 3,885,328

WARM ZEPHYRS[2] TEASE the turquoise sea into laughter, caressing palm "necklaces" adorning exotic isles. Giggling children—bodies glistening like milk chocolate—frolic on golden sands. And for the romantic, almond-eyed maidens sing "*Aloha!*" to the gyrating sway of their grass skirts as they place fragrant *frangipani leu* around visitors' necks.

That's the Pacific Island World—at least in tourist brochures. Explorers returning to the dank docks of Le Havre, Lisbon, Liverpool, or other ports, sketched these idyllic pictures with their embellished reports of a Pacific Paradise. Romanticism had a lengthy history with explorers, including Amerigo Vespucchi (1454-1512), narrator of Columbus' voyages to the "New World."[3]

---

1. An expanse of water with many scattered islands, first used to describe the Aegean Sea.
2. *Zephyr*: "Gentle breeze," from Latin/Greek: god of the west wind.
3. Amerigo's embellishments included not only lions and baboons (never found in the hemisphere prior to importation by zoos!) but also "implausibly superior savages" in a golden age of innocence—descriptions vital to financial backing by Columbus' royal sponsors, and even to hiring crews. (Felipe Fernandez-Armesto, *Amerigo: The Man Who Gave His Name to America*. New York: Random House, 2007.)

This exotic mirage lent credence to The Enlightenment—the 18th c. philosophic movement that rejected Europe's traditional social, religious, and political ideas, in favour of rationalism.[4] Philosophers Voltaire and Rousseau rejected the biblical concept of original sin (mankind's spiritual Fall); it was "society" that corrupted mankind—a seemingly valid truth, but a half-truth, for human beings shape society! Humanist philosophers latched on to Darwin's writings as "evidence."

French Post-Impressionist Eugene Henri (Paul) Gauguin (1848-1903), son of a Frenchman and a Peruvian Creole, settled in Tahiti and depicted island life as a languid paradise. He developed *Synthetisme*, and his carvings of their idols reflected the inspiration he found in primitive peoples. His views on art influenced Pablo Picasso. Gauguin's contemporary, Robert Louis Stevenson, transported readers there in his novel, *Robinson Crusoe.* Budding anthropologist Margaret Mead (1901-1978) immortalized the concept of "Noble Savage" with her misguided "research" among Samoan Islanders.[5] In the novel, *Hawaii,*[6] Mead's contemporary, James Michener, made consequent sport of quaint Victorian missionaries, "warping the innocents with the Ten Commandments."

[While Europe's churches generally rejected violent revolution (a tragic exception was several state churches' later acquiescence with Hitler's pogroms), theological liberals swallowed the concept of innate innocence, changing their view of the missionary mandate from

---

4. Europe needed reform, but education does not guarantee rationality. Breaking Rome's religious and political stranglehold and medieval superstitions, 16th c. Protestant Reformers, led by Martin Luther and like minds, prepared the way for further transformation, but secular philosophy demanded an alternative to Luther's spiritual basis. The Enlightenment rediscovered Aryan concepts of (a) faith in human prowess, (b) native innocence and goodness, (c) independence of science and reason, and (d) individual sovereignty.

5. "Noble Savage": Myth promoted earlier by 19th c. Jean-Jacques Rousseau, who denied original sin: people possessed innate innocence, virtue. Graduate Mead set out to support this. She may have understood anthropology but not culture—islanders told their naive guest whatever she wanted. *Coming of Age in Samoa* (New York: Columbia U., 1928) "established" that societies undisturbed by missionary morals were islands of Utopia. Mead became "one of the most famous women of her generation, particularly for her views on educational and social issues" (Crystal, *Ibid.*)—unquestioned until the 1990s, when a *secular* NZ anthropologist debunked her myth (Freeman, *Margaret Mead the Heretic: The making and unmasking of an anthropological myth.* —Bibliog.). But Mead's views still pervade academic texts.

6. James Michener, *Hawaii* (see Bibliography) The novel was later made into a popular movie.

conversion to welfare. Those who used "innocent nature" to underpin their antagonism to evangelical Christianity, still influence education and society today.]

Nevertheless as a boy, I devoured Pacific Island adventure stories, such as *The Swiss Family Robinson.* The heroic ventures of missionary John G. Paton[7] captured my boyish imagination. At the same time, I began to suspect that all was not Utopia in Paradise. When I later sailed the Pacific, I discovered how ironic is its very name! Its "pacific" face at times rages with savage fury.

Adventurers, whether in dhows or "tall ships," braved not only unpredictable seas but also fearful legends of disappearing expeditions, vanishing islands, and even lost empires. Over centuries, the biblical story of the Garden of Eden had surfaced in legends around the world—whether Atlantis in the Atlantic, the Tamil empire in the India Ocean, or Mu in the South Pacific. To each, campfire tales attributed imagined glories mixed with gleanings from traders and travellers, with glimpses of ancient kingdoms such as Egypt and Persia. This is not to deny that any race can highly develop its society. After all, critics at one time cited accounts of the Bible's references to the sophisticated Hittite Empire as evidence of the Bible's fictional nature—until archaeologists unearthed tablets listing their kings. Most races have had not only real but also imagined empires.

In a world dominated by stories of lost islands and desert spooks, sailors and camel owners feared being zapped by unseen powers—even though intrepid explorers wanted to press on in search of fabled riches.[8] Because of a bad omen, Greek General Alexander ventured no further east than Lahore. Portugal's Columbus faced mutiny by his crew, who feared falling off the world's edge. Just in time, they spied land. The porters of pioneer missionaries downed loads whenever they spotted a fetish on the trail.

Polynesia's Easter Island became Exhibit A of legendary lost empires. Theorists asserted that the volcanic outcropping, nearly 4,000 km. (2,350

7. Scottish Presbyterian Paton (1824-1907) faced great hardship in the New Hebrides. After his wife and infant son died, he moved to Australia, viewing it as the natural source of missionaries for the Pacific.

miles) from the nearest mainland, was the remnant of the lost Mu civilization. Its South Sea inhabitants sculpted more than 600 stony-faced heads, some 20m (65ft.) tall, stationing them along the shores like sentinels facing inland. That was nearly 1,000 years ago, but Europeans developed the legend of forgotten Mu after Dutch Admiral Jacob Roggeveen spotted Rapa Nui on Easter Sunday in 1722 and named it for Easter. A crewmember recorded seeing islanders burning sacrifices (presumably) in front of the monoliths. Perhaps they were imploring deities to save them from the strange "white birds" (tall ships) that hove over the horizon.

Nearly half a century elapsed before the next visit from Europeans, when Spaniards arrived in 1770. They found most of the mammoth heads toppled. Archaeologists have righted several—erect, they attract tourists (and research funding).

Archaeologists and historians have pieced together a saga of survival, environmental collapse, civil war,[9] and slave raiding (by Peruvian kidnappers). Hardly Shangri-la![10] After Europeans landed in the 18th c., disease, unintentionally imported from Europe, decimated the remaining population. However, New Zealand's head of the Institute of Polynesian Languages and Literature, Steven Roger Fischer, doesn't buy the "noble savage" concept, nor the European romance that the island had enjoyed "a thousand years of peace" before Western contact—although he is sympathetic to the islanders' plight.[11]

Other authors are now rejecting the concept of Utopia in primitive societies around the globe. "Wishful Rouseauian thinking has led academics to overlook evidence of constant violence," declares Steven LeBlanc of Harvard University.[12]

---

8. I've sailed "the Bermuda Triangle," in which many ships have mysteriously vanished—to this day feeding fearful superstitions. Fierce winds and clashing tides generate powerful squalls that can quickly sink unwary mariners and even suck down low-flying light aircraft. —WHF
9. "Short-eared" newcomers fighting "long-eared" aborigines, who sculpted extended earlobes on the heads? Contrary to utopian views, reefs were inhabited by warring cannibals and subject to destructive forces of nature. Steve Jones, *Coral: A Pessimist in Paradise.* Little Brown, 2007
10. From James Hilton's novel, *Lost Horizon* (1933)—a remote, idyllic land, "Utopia."
11. Fischer, *Island at End of the World: Turbulent History of Easter Island.* Auckland: Reaktion Books, '05.
12. *Economist*, Dec. 22, 07.

Stony Faces and Cargo Cults

Certainly the gigantic stone figures pre-date any European contact. But who sculpted them and why? Scientists have come up with no proven answers. Idols to worship? Departed ancestors? The "Rock-head Mystery" nonsense prize may go to egghead psychologists who suggest the monuments were a "make-work" project to overcome the boredom of isolation. (Really? A lot of work for nothing!)

The *tsunami* of 2004 that devastated the Indian Ocean rim suggested a possible reason. While nature struggles to survive on the earth's surface, titanic forces struggle under-ground. Shifting fault lines trigger undersea earthquakes, unseen but felt. If they are high enough on the Richter Scale, they trigger *tsunami,*[13] sending walls of water racing across the ocean, smashing on to distant shores with irresistible force. Most *tsunami* occur in the so-called "*Pacific*" Ocean, where sensitive monitors warn Pacific Rim countries.

I may be wrong, but why not venture another theory, since none so far has been "carved in stone"? Easter Island's grim-faced monuments could have been totems to ward off *tsunami*. With their backs to the sea, they would have been strong enough to withstand great force. Did the stern faces re-assure worshipers that powerful gods were watching over them?

Certainly island dwellers everywhere believed that spirits and gods caused volcanoes, earthquakes, tidal waves, and other disasters in nature. Islanders, in constant fear of unseen powers, surrounded themselves with taboos[14] and fetishes, on occasion sacrificing infants to appease the spirits. To overcome (and absorb?) the ancestral spirit power (*mana*) of slain enemies, they boiled and ate their bodies.[15]

Among Melanesian islanders today, Cargo Cults practice occult rituals, expecting their "ship to come in," literally—filled with material benefits.

13. Japanese: "harbor waves."

14. Polynesian *tabu*: forbidden to touch or use because of inherent dangerous supernatural power.

15. John Hinnells, Ed., *Dictionary of Religions*. New York: Facts on File Publications, 1984, p.200. Perhaps this gastronomy gave rise to the stereotype of the cannibal cooking pot!

The myth developed during WW II, after American soldiers set up bases on many islands to counterattack Japanese invaders. They generously provided food and medicine, the latter marked with the Red Cross symbol. Now red crosses dot some of the islands, and inhabitants wait for the return of a mythical John Frum in army uniform.[16] A local chief prophesied that Frum would turn up some February 15th with a cargo of gifts. Villagers have built an airstrip for him to land on, a thatched hut for his abode, and churches where they worship him. Cargo Cults are a serious problem, since they hardly motivate islanders to cultivate a living! And while their syncretism includes Christian symbols, it also calls for a return to pre-Christian traditions, including drunken orgies.

"Before the gospel came to us, our people lived in superstition; they didn't know what peace was," Fijian Aisake Kunanitu told me. A gentle but gigantic Polynesian, he was a fellow member of our World Evangelical Alliance International Council. "Jesus freed us from our superstitions. It's true that churches also contend with other churches at times, but that's not the Spirit of Christ at work. That's the spirit of this world—pride."

So what are the Pacific Islands really like? Balmy climate, beautiful scenery, with attractive people. But islanders are like humanity anywhere in the world, with their sorrows and joys, their struggles to live and fears of death. They may develop an island mentality, but so do people in isolated communities in the middle of Asia. Islanders vary as much as the islands in size and other features.

The Pacific Ocean covers more of earth than all the globe's land surfaces, over twice the size of the Atlantic. It stretches from the Artic to the Antarctic and has the earth's deepest trenches—one plunging almost 25% *deeper* than Mount Everest soars *above* sea level. The moon could rest in its basin. But in a sense, the Pacific is also like a vast fishing net, its islands snagging people of different race and creed as humanity's tide flows through the "mesh" of volcanic outcroppings and coral reefs: fishermen seeking larger catches, sailors blown hundreds of miles off course, farmers looking for greener pastures, refugees fleeing for their

16. *Toronto Star,* Jan. 4, 1997. "John Frum" could be short for "John from America," or a mispronunciation of "Brown"—from soldiers' stories of John Brown's crusade against slavery in the U.S.

lives, merchants selling their wares, explorers seeking new routes, conquerors enlarging empires. Some stayed, intermarried with earlier arrivals, and developed new cultures, dialects, and languages.

How did the Pacific Ocean get involved in this account of my travels through Asia? Actually, most of the islanders drifted from Asia, carrying their religions and legends with them. But, apart from recognizing Asia's influence on the entire Pacific, this chapter must focus specifically on *Asia's* Pacific Islands—those considered part of the Asian context. Geologically, Singapore, Indonesia, and the Philippines are high points on undersea extensions of Asia's continental shelves. (Eruptions further South result from pressures of the Indo-Australian shelf.) And so I headed off to Singapore, an Asian island-state that used to be part of an Asian Federation.

The Lion City State

"Where are the lions?" I asked my host in Singapore, Dr. Andrew Ng, as he drove me in from the island's airport—one of the most beautiful and efficient I've landed at. The city-state's name means "Lion City," I'd heard.

"In the zoo!" laughed Andrew. "But in 1819, when Sir Stamford Raffles of the British East India Company leased the island from the Sultan of Johore,[17] it was an overgrown wilderness—rumored to hide lions in its tall grass. So he got it for a song."

Sir Raffles[18] had an eye on Singapore's strategic location, with a deep-water harbor positioned in the main trade channel between the Indian and Pacific Oceans. Once Sir Raffles tamed the flora and fauna, the legend of the lion (traditional Chinese icon of prosperity) attracted Chinese traders from the mainland. Singapore became Britain's main naval servicing center in the Far East, and a key colony. After Independence, it was part of the British-sponsored Malay Federation, but in 1965 it became the Republic of Singapore—with a parliamentary form of secular government.

17. Johore is on the southern tip of the Malay Peninsula, separated from the island by a narrow waterway.
18. Raffles briefly administered Indonesia's islands for Holland during the Napoleonic Wars (1803-1815).

"There's the Raffles Hotel," my host pointed out as we passed a sprawling rose-tinted building. The hotel was developed from Sir Raffles' official residence. Now a turbaned porter, gold braid decorating his raja-style uniform, stood ready to open the doors of vehicles that pulled up to the lobby, had we taken time to stop. I gained the impression that Singaporeans were more than a little proud of Sir Raffles and the heritage he left them—including law and order, world-class industry concepts, global trade connections, and—you guessed it—cricket. They remembered their former colonizer for opportunity, not oppression, it seemed. And the Empire even honored the Old Boy with a burial plaque in Westminster Abbey.

Swamp or Oasis?

Early in Singapore's history, its ambitious business community had to be creative to survive—a swampy island surrounded by behemoth sectarian nations. No natural resources,[19] no space for heavy industry. Only people. Solution: develop specialists and technology; sell services.[20] Were the neighbors floating on oil reserves? Then Singapore would build refineries to process their oil. As tankers came to load and unload in Singapore's safe harbor, high-tech industries sprang up to meet consumer needs. Now swinging cranes outline its container terminal. Foreign shoppers "drop by" its malls to purchase jewelry, watches, calculators, cell phones, video players, and other light-industry products. The Internet has opened up the world.

Singapore now has desalinization plants and a plant that recycles waste water. Even Credit Suisse has opened a branch in Singapore. Investors across the region see it as an offshore financial services base, competing with Switzerland. (One private banker—*whisper it!*—has even moved from Dubai.) Financiers appreciate its strategic location and legal system. As a plus, the Wealth Management Institute runs courses for bankers and investors alike, with everything from studies in exotic funds to banking etiquette.[21]

---

19. Formerly solely dependent on fresh water piped across from Malaysia, Singapore now desalinates sea water by reverse osmosis, and also recycles waste water.

20. In this, Singapore was a century ahead of the West, which now promotes services in sectors where it cannot compete with Asia's lower-cost manufacturing.

21. *Economist,* Aug. 19, 2006.

The tiny state's entrepreneurs developed a free trade zone, Jurong, on reclaimed land crowding 1400 factories along with even shipbuilding. A bioscience park, the Biopolis, recently helped inspire Hungary's Semmelweis University to create its own "life sciences research consortium." Jurong also boasts recreational parks and a bird sanctuary—where the *visitors* are "caged" (in mesh-covered walkways), while exotic birds flit freely around them in lush, humid rainforest created under a great dome. Macaw parrots, resplendent in red, yellow, and green feathers, add piercing cries to the chorus of tropical birdcalls. I saw even the rare hornbill, its banana-like horn perched atop its head.

So the little swamp has become a thriving oasis, with the highest Gross Domestic Product (GDP) per head in all of Southeast Asia. In rating 159 countries, Transparency International placed Singapore ahead of Britain and USA.[22]

"What's the island's population now?" I asked Andrew, at the time SIM's Director for East Asia. Once Professor of Surgery at Singapore University, Dr. Ng resigned from a promising professional career to go to Africa as a medical missionary on the edge of the Sahara, along with his attractive and capable wife, Belinda. Andrew was well aware of the Far East's tension—Communists kidnapped his father when the family lived in Malaysia. SIM later appointed Dr. Ng to head up the Mission's East Asia Region.[23]

"Population? Four and a half million, they say," Andrew replied. "There are 59 other islets in the Republic, but most people live here on the largest island—90% in this city. See those high-rises? Four out of five residents, including our family, live in them."

"I guess the only way for so many people to live in such a small area is 'on top of one another'!" I smiled, noting apartments floor upon floor. In fact, shops also stack in high-rise layers. I'd heard that Singapore was the place to buy electronic and other items. When I shopped for a wristwatch, I went from one trader's cubicle to another—not along sprawling lanes, but on multi-levels in high-rise shopping "malls."

---

22. *Economist*, October 22, 2005.
23. When Dr. Ng became Deputy International Director for the South Pacific and East Asia in 2006, Dr. Stanley Ling, born in Hong Kong, became East Asia Director.

"Eating Out" in the Open Air

However, one market kept our feet on the ground—the bustling open-air food market. The Ngs took me out to lunch there, after we picked up Belinda at SIM's offices. Singaporeans "eat out" a high percentage of the time. It makes sense, considering customers' busy life styles, limited home kitchen space, and myriad restaurants and food stalls serving tasty food, strict hygiene inspection, and low prices.

Talk about "fast food"! My taste buds fairly exploded as we passed rows of steaming cauldrons, offering a gourmet's menu to choose from. A non-expert in Chinese cuisine, I followed Andrew and Belinda's example, starting with a bowl of bird's-nest soup, followed with fish sauce on noodles—and side orders of steamed prawns wrapped in rice flour. Andrew and I collected the meals while Belinda waited to lay claim of the first table to free up. That was only the first of a series of delicious meals at food stalls or in restaurants, as SIM Council members and friends entertained me. I soon became adroit with chop sticks—more suitable than forks for eating Chinese food.

An electronic "credit card" on Andrew's Nissan automatically paid a fee for entering the city's core—a system to control traffic congestion. (Without that, he'd receive a summons to pay a fine.) Most people commuted on the efficient bus and train services, but a car was rather essential to the busy Director's activities.

"If you're out walking, don't ever drop a Kleenex," Belinda warned me. (The Ngs' impeccable English impressed me. That, I discovered, is fairly typical of Singapore— English is the language of education.) "And don't jay-walk, spit, or drop your chewing gum! All carry automatic fines."

The "In" joke is that Singapore is a "fine" city. But fines keep Singapore orderly and attractive, in spite of high density. Another plus is that waiters and other service people do not expect tips. Anxious to preserve its reputation for integrity, city council long debated whether to allow a casino to open: how to attract tourists but control crime? Solution was to open "Integrated Family Resorts" entertainment for the whole family, as well as restricted casinos.

To explore Singapore while my hosts caught up with their mission work, I could have traveled by bus, subway, train, or taxi. I chose the latter, which I found readily available and low in cost.[24] The driver of one confirmed the city's strict environmental laws. He'd been fined S$200 for dropping a torn-up coupon. The driver wasn't angry, even though his plea of "First Offence" made no difference. The law was the law.

"In Singapore, we know where we stand," he told me as we flowed with orderly traffic along tree-lined avenues. "When we go to some other countries, we don't know—because of corruption and lack of laws being applied."

Back home, I marvel when I read criticism of Singapore's regulations, even though they've made the Republic the wealthiest, most efficient, least corrupt city in the Region. Economists recently ranked it fourth in the world for *lack* of corruption (USA ranked 16; Germany 20), greatest transparency of business (USA was next), highest "current account" surplus (e.g. lowest government debt), and lowest financial risk in Asia (lower than that of USA). In risk, the rest of Asia ranked between 20 and 45.[25]

Western media criticism of Singapore's "restrictive rules" saddens me, for it reflects the flabbiness of Western society. For instance, in the West a major howl went up when police arrested an expatriate youth for spray-painting graffiti on parked cars. (He'd grown up in Singapore and knew the penalty for vandalism was caning with a rattan cane.) "Police state!" Western critics protested.

But Singapore must be doing something right. Moral integrity plus disciplined living equals a city I'd be happy to live in at any time!

"*Clean and Green* is our city's motto!" architect Loh Hoe Peng later told me over a bowl of won ton soup. "When I draw up plans for projects, I make sure to include suitable species of trees to be planted, or the plans have no chance of approval."

---

24. All I had to do was raise my arm, and a taxi pulled up. My drivers were Buddhist, Muslim, Christian (from a 15,000-member church), and a Free Thinker ("I'm too busy for religion!"). Never have I had such variety of opportunity to witness—while being driven around! Singapore enjoys religious freedom!

25. References: Reader's Digest *Guide to Places of the World*; *The Economist* 2001, 2004.

A Christian Oasis

Sunday, from 8 A.M. to mid-afternoon, Hoe Peng whisked me on a preaching tour of several churches. Each church or assembly was packed with a mix of youthful and elderly, students and business people, women and men. They reflected Singapore's large Christian presence— about 15% of total population, one-third of university students.[26]

"What shall I preach about?" I asked, always glad to know what local Christian leaders see as a needed emphasis.

"Missions!" my hosts told me. "Our responsibility is to pass on the Good News to others." We made an appearance part way through a service, I spoke, and then we headed off to another meeting already under way. If we'd stayed long enough, we could have joined in a church luncheon at each stop!

Singapore's missionary activity goes back to the year Sir Raffles clinched his lease (1819). That same year, the London Missionary Society[27] established a base in Singapore. Now Singapore churches have one of the world's highest church/missionary ratios—almost one to each Protestant church. Loh Hoe Peng and his wife, Alice, are among them. After retirement from business, the Lohs went to Bolivia, serving with fellow Singaporean Henry Cheah in ministry designed to build up witnessing churches in cities. Evangelicals are re-vitalizing main-line denominations.

In Singapore, there are 20 or more seminaries, Bible schools, and missions training institutes. Pastors, evangelists, and lay workers came to one of those—the Haggai Retreat Center—from all over the world for leadership seminars. Several international missions have offices in Singapore. The city has 60 Christian bookshops. And in business and government services, Christian Chinese[28] serve, sometimes with a mix of Confucian and Calvinist work ethics.

26. Of the total population, Muslims also form about 15%, Buddhists nearly half.
27. Famed LMS pioneers include Chalmers (New Guinea), Moffat, Livingston (Africa), Morrison (China).
28. More than three quarters of the population is Chinese.

OMF spawned two of Singapore's training centers, both of them independent ministries. Discipleship Training Center concentrates on theological studies in a community atmosphere, whereas the Asian Cross-cultural Training Institute (ACTI) prospective candidates for cross-cultural missions. When I spoke at these centers, the caliber of men and women impressed me. At ACTI, most were Asian university graduates who had thought they could naturally minister within other "Third World" cultures. Rubbing shoulders in a small, communal relationship showed how insular any nationality could be, and opened them to learning from one another. However, at times the insular views made it difficult to enroll students.

"It's indeed a problem, but the reasons are several," explained Andrew Ng, listing examples: "(1) Many megachurches have limited mission programs. (2) Smaller churches face increasing costs. (3) 'Too many studies' for some. (4) Preference for on-the-job field training. (5) Prolonged time to prepare candidates. (6) Shorter mission terms."

A Wider Vision

The Ngs' hearts beat with the call of missions. As a professional medical veteran who has handled horrific trauma, Andrew learned not to reveal his emotions with tears. Except once, revealing what kind of heart he has.

"The only time I remember shedding tears was when Belinda and I returned to Africa to pack up our personal effects," Dr. Ng quietly admitted after I asked. "When I realized we wouldn't live there on the edge of the Sahara any more, I wept over the desperate needs of the people!"

The Ngs' consolation was that now they would be able to help prepare and send others.

"God has blessed SIM with a century of experience and administrative skills that we need to put at the service of Asian churches," he told me on a visit in the late 1980s, before SIM developed its current Asia-wide administration. "Now that an Asia-centered mission[29] has joined SIM

29. International Christian Fellowship (see chapters 1-13).

agencies, we have an increasing number of Asians who are asking where they can serve on their own continent. Some serve with OMF and other experienced Asia-based agencies. That's good. But if SIM doesn't provide opportunities in areas where we already have experience, many of these eager young people may join new inexperienced agencies that mean well but can't prepare and maintain them.

"A large number go directly from their churches, with no mission to help them. You know what happens. Fine young people crash and return home disillusioned."

"And that disillusions their sending churches," I added, thinking of the reasons Andrew had listed. "We've seen that on other continents. Zeal without understanding. The worst case I've run into is a young South American who went off to Africa with no preparation, independent of any mission that could guide him. When he became fatigued, depressed, and discouraged, the local Muslim imam showed him friendship. Within a year he stopped witnessing for Christ and became a Muslim, attacking the Christian faith.

"So I hear what you're saying," I continued. Switching to the role of a "devil's advocate," I asked: "You're accepting Asians for service in Africa and South America. You and your staff prepare them well. But as to service in Asia, why not refer all enquirers to other missions already here?"

"But we *are* here!" Andrew persisted. "And potential missionaries know that. Some feel called to serve in Asian countries where SIM, through its ICF heritage, has ministered for up to a century. For instance, SIM had already been in Hong Kong for 15 years before the colony reverted to China. When that happened, we were already in China!"

I knew Andrew was right, and his vision was refreshing. He and his wife have been able to put that vision to work in Australasia and the Far East, since SIM appointed him as Deputy International Director for those areas (in his place appointing Dr. Stanley Ling Regional Director for East Asia). But at the time, I wondered how OMF felt. I had a lot of respect for that sister mission. My father had applied to the former CIM,[30] and one of its General Directors, J. Oswald Sanders, had served on SIM's New Zealand's Council.[31] I also had relatives serving with OMF. But that wasn't why I hesitated—SIM should respond to the promptings of the Holy Spirit, regardless of what others did. For my own satisfaction, I wanted to be sure we were moving in complete harmony with others of similar calling and greater experience in the area.

"We have Council members who also serve on OMF's Council," Andrew told me. "Anyway, why don't you talk with OMF's General Director, Dr. Taylor? I hear he's in town just now." (That was in the '90s.)

JHT III Extends Warm Welcome

So Andrew Ng dropped me off at OMF's International offices—set among verdant palm trees. James Hudson Taylor III extended a warm handshake as we sat down beside a little table holding a pot of jasmine tea and rice cakes.

"Just call me Jim!" my host said, setting me at ease. He and his wife, Leone, had worked among university students in Taiwan before OMF appointed him as General Director at the time.[32] I explained SIM's thinking about recruiting Asians for service in Asia.

"I'm glad to hear that," Jim replied. "Your General Director, Ian Hay, also mentioned deployment in Asia the last time we were together at a conference. Asia is such a vast area, and it has so many needs—we can't handle the job alone. No one mission could. We welcome SIM's active recruitment and appointment throughout Asia."

---

30. When Mao Zedong forced the former China Inland Mission out, the mission restructured and became Overseas Missionary Fellowship (OMF). Rather than headquartering in the West, OMF located in Singapore—strategic for administering work in a number of Asian countries. OMF and SIM cooperate with personnel and ministries, meeting the calling and skills of candidates in different locations.
31. Precious to this author and his wife was the Sanders' prayer partnership for many years.
32. The JHT with whom I met was JHT III, even though fourth generation from the CIM founder, because the founder's son was named Howard, who wrote his father's biography (see Bibliog.). Upon retiring from leadership, JHT III and Leone served in Taiwan for several years. In 2007, a region in China made JHT III an honorary citizen. (He died in 2009). Current OMF International Director is Dr. Patrick Fung.

I knew that this veteran "China Hand" meant what he said. It was all encouraging: an initial sense of call from Asians (not Westerners), and the genuine hand of fellowship from veterans of the area. The Holy Spirit was confirming his leading.

One ACTI alumni couple, Dr. Sng Kong Chee and Chay Gek, became missionaries in Zambia, Africa, before taking a staff position at a Singapore hospital. As I learned their story, I knew they were still very much missionaries. Among the remarkable cases Dr. Sng described was one that illustrated the Holy Spirit's prompting. He felt the Lord leading him to accompany an elderly patient, suffering from heart and kidney complications, to his home village across the border in Malaysia. The man desired one last visit before he died. The doctor, patient, and the man's daughter set off in an ambulance. Dr. Sng's description of the trip:

> "Looking at the state of the patient and his anxious daughter, I leaned forward and prayed aloud that he would have peace and come to a deeper knowledge of God. His daughter responded excitedly, for she had flown from Canada to be with him in the Intensive Care Unit. The only believer in her family, she'd felt helpless to witness in the tense relationships but had prayed God would send a messenger.
>
> "While the ambulance was speeding through a thunderstorm, the daughter and I quietly prayed together, until I felt I should share with this man several Bible verses in Mandarin. Spontaneously he cried to God and prayed with me the sinner's prayer. Tears of joy ran from his daughter's eyes the rest of the journey. His family rejoiced to receive their father, who showed no signs of stress."[33]

If I began to think I was in a Christian world, I had only to look at a map to realize that Singapore is a tiny enclave surrounded by Islamic nations. That's why the government, while allowing religious liberty, frowns on indiscretions that neighboring lands might interpret as political provocations against them, their cultures, and their religions. Singapore has to "mind its manners" in order to survive. However, the island's Christians serve as missionaries and pastors in surrounding lands. The Ngs even sent me northwards across to the Malaysian peninsula (at the

33. *ACTI News Bulletin*, Singapore, Feb. 2006.

south end of Thailand) to preach in churches there. In one Chinese church I slept in an apartment at the back of the building and enjoyed the fellowship and hospitality of a vibrant group of young believers.

Malaysia's constitution grants freedom of religion to its people, although several Christian converts from Islam have not been allowed to change their identity card religious designation. The Malay-language Bible uses the word "Allah" for God along with the word "Tuham" for Lord. However, in 2009 a government official told the Catholic News Agency it must stop using the term "Allah" in its publications "because it would confuse people." "Only Muslims can use the word," he decreed, adding that church publications should be circulated to Christians only. Church officials protested.

I realized why Singapore seeks to remain neutral in religious controversies, surrounded as it is by strongly Islamic neighbors. Indonesia borders it on the south, across the Strait of Malacca—only 1½ miles (about 2 km.) wide at one point. It's one of the busiest shipping lanes in the world—up to ¼ of the world's sea trade and ½ of all sea-borne oil sailing through it, a strategic route (and also bottleneck!). As shipyards produce larger and larger tankers and container ships, "Malacca Max" is the designers' limit—the maximum size of a vessel that can pass through the Strait.

Sun Like Thunder – 17: Indonesia

The Pacific's Jade Necklace

"While people are saying, 'Peace and Safety,' destruction will come on them suddenly" (1 Thess. 5.3).

Indonesia: Pop. 239,026,778

LOOKING SOUTH across the Strait from Singapore, I could see the coast of Indonesia. On a map, the archipelago forms an ornate necklace of some 17,000 islands and islets, like a string of green-jade gems adorning the warm bosom of SE Asia, strung across three time zones and 5,200 km/3,200 miles—further than from Los Angeles to New York. Its steamy climate promotes growth of valuable hardwood forests. The country is one of the world's major exporters of rubber.[1] Its volcanic soil is ideal for rice growing, and it holds rich deposits of metal ores, oil, and natural gas. Yet some islands are practically wasteland.[2]

Lying along Asia's great sea-trade route, Indonesia felt the impact of successive waves of traders, migrants, and religions funneling into the archipelago. There's a saying that ACEH, at the most north-western tip, is an acronym for **A**rab (Islam), **C**hina (Buddhism), **E**uropa/Europe (Christian), and **H**ind (Hindu). Indeed, Indonesia's extremities illustrate its tensions, illustrated more recently when Islamic militants in the

1. Thanks to Britons' smuggling seedlings out of Brazil (which had a world monopoly), to London's Kew Gardens, and on to Southeast Asia—initially Malaysia. Fuller, *Tie Down the Sun*, p. 293 (see Bibliog.).
2. Rising sea level from global warming threatens to inundate some 2,000 of the islands.

western province of Aceh called for secession,[3] while far to the east, "Christians" (mostly Iberian Catholic) regained East Timor, the half island annexed by Indonesia after Portugal granted Independence.[4]

In between those extremes, restive communities tangle along ethnic and religious lines. The Muslim population (88-90%, making Indonesia the world's most Islamic nation) dominates politics, although the government maintains a creditable democracy. Indonesians have remained generally tolerant, but diplomats viewing the Islamic world's ferment worry that terrorists could easily hide in the archipelago's labyrinth.

Indonesia's Constitution espouses "Unity in Diversity" (*Pancha-sila*: Five Principles). These require citizens to adhere to one of five recognized religions: Islam, Protestant Christianity, Catholicism, Hinduism, and Buddhism. In each, however, people mix animistic fetish.

Although Aceh is the only province governed by Islamic *Shari'a*, following the Regional Autonomy Law of 2000, more than 50 regencies in 16 of Indonesia's 32 provinces passed some 600 *Shari'a*-influenced laws. The central government can block regional laws, but politicians often court support from Islamist groups, who declare that *Shari'a*-based law is divinely ordered—and to oppose such amounts to blasphemy. Implementing such laws could lead to Hindu, Buddhist, and Christian demands for their own local religious laws—thus threatening the unity of the country.

"We've Outgrown That!"

I think of Indonesia when I hear Westerners criticize Christian missionaries for their "arrogance" in attempting to share the gospel with people of other faiths. Secular pundits insinuate that evangelists must be racist—feeling that their faith is superior and taking advantage of poverty and disease to impose it.

---

3. The 2004 Tsunami put this agitation on hold.
4. For 420 years, Portugal extracted its colony's resources but neglected development. Indonesia's invasion (1975) brought more development but also slaughter of 200,000 Timorese. When Indonesia gave East Timor independence in 1998, departing soldiers left only mayhem in one of earth's poorest countries.

Racism, did I hear? I suspect there's a bit of racist superiority in the allegation itself. I think of the puzzled look on the face of my fellow passenger on the flight out of Singapore. He was returning from a business conference. "What did you say you did on your trip through Asia?" he asked.

"Asian churches invited me to speak at their Bible and missionary conferences," I replied. I figured I'd soon know what this European thought about spiritual matters.

"You mean there are *churches* in those countries—and they hold *conferences*?" he asked, obviously trying to grasp the incomprehensible. I went on to describe the Christians I'd met *and* their personal faith in Jesus Christ as Savior and Lord. (That was more detail than the dear man probably wanted—but he had asked and was buckled in next to me!).

"I guess we've outgrown religion in the West!" he commented after a long silence, as if to find some explanation for the anomaly without sounding negative. Since then, I've run into variations of his statement, giving me the impression that Christian faith is for the . . . how to put it tactfully? It is *not* for advanced societies. So I ask myself, who is racist?[5]

Although it doesn't matter, I asked myself who *first* imposed foreign religion and culture on Asians? Take Asia's islands, for instance. They've been inhabited longer than assumed. In fact, in 2004, Indonesian anthropologists excitedly claimed discovery of *Homo floresiensis*—a distinct human species differing from *Homo sapiens*, they claim. Seven fossils excavated on the island of Flores are said to date back 13,000 years.

Whatever their pedigree, the people now called Indonesians practiced indigenous spirit-worship long before the first century A.D. (or BCE[6]), when Hindu and Buddhist traders brought their own "foreign" religions

5. Racist elitism, even among clergy, is not imaginary. At the 1998 Anglican Lambeth Council, when African and Asian bishops defeated a motion to ordain homosexual clergy, some North American bishops dismissed the non-western delegates as uneducated (read "backward") and not progressive. However, an Oxford Ph.D.'s analysis revealed that the average academic level of non-western bishops was higher than that of their North American counterparts (*The Alberta Report*, Nov. 22, 1999).

6. BCE: Before Christian Era—a term preferred by some historians and scientists.

and cultures to the archipelago, resulting in Java's mystical *Kebatinan* religion. Later, in Islam's early centuries, Muslim traders and teachers introduced *their* faith, which became the islands' dominant religion after the old capital of East Java fell to Muslim conquest. But for the most part, Indonesia is now a mix of animist (spirit worship), Hindu, and Islamic belief. Muslims and Hindus make offerings to spirits supposedly indwelling rocks spewed out by the volcano Rinjani.[7]

Companies Oppose, Governor Welcomes Missions

Indonesia's Christian churches date back nearly as early as Muslim mosques. In the mid-1500s, the Jesuit pioneer, Francis Xavier, spent some three years in the Malacca area establishing Roman Catholic churches. The Maluku Protestant Church is Asia's oldest *Protestant* denomination, founded in 1605.[8] In the intervening years, churches of all the major denominations have opened. On the adjacent northeast tip of Sulawesi, the Minahasan have been Protestant for more than 300 years. Indonesian Protestants have suffered persecution from varied sources, including traditional animists, Catholics, Japanese invaders, and Islamic militants.

The early history of Christianity in Indonesia, however, marks one of the church's sadly missed opportunities. In the same way that the British East India Company suppressed Christian activity in order to safeguard trade, so did the Dutch East India Company. Tragically, the Company ignored its charter: *to spread the Word of God and enable the church to fulfill its calling.*[9] Commerce ruled, and for some 200 years the church ministered only to its own members (mostly expatriates), failing to spread the Good News to a vast population that could have embraced its uplifting message of salvation. As a result, Islam (not the gospel) converted the majority of the population.

Ironically, events in Europe on the other side of the world opened a window for the gospel. During the Napoleonic Wars of the early 19th c., France took over Holland and, accordingly, all Dutch colonies. The French flag flying over Indonesia sent the British into action, for France had

---

7. Rick Love, *Muslims, Magic, and the Kingdom of God*, traces magic's influence on Islam (Bibliog).
8. Although the Armenian Orthodox Church dates from 4th c., Armenia joined Council of Europe in 2001.

declared war on Britain. The Governor General of India, Lord Minto, had noticed a genius of strategy in nearby Singapore—none other than Stamford Raffles himself. In short order the French flag came down, replaced with the Union Jack (September 11, 1811). Only thirty years of age, Raffles temporarily became Lt. Governor of "Java and its Dependencies"—Indonesia, in other words.

Although born in the same village as his personal friend, William Wilberforce,[10] Raffles was no colonial ambassador for the church. In fact, earlier he had written, "[I] wish that Christians did as much justice to their Redeemer as Muslims do to their Prophet." He affirmed that he respected "the religions of every persuasion." But he also was appalled at the "corruptions, superstitions, and ridiculous observances" of the islands' religions. Simple Christian faith could help free the people, he felt. The Word of God could bring enlightenment.[11]

Although British administrators and traders continued to oppose missionary activity throughout the area, even as they had done upon William Carey's arrival in India, Raffles welcomed missionaries from Europe, including some who had served in China, and India.[12] By the time Britain returned the territory to Holland in 1816, the Dutch Reformed Church had awakened to its missionary responsibilities. The Dutch minister Dr. J. Werninck, as director of the London Missionary Society (LMS), commissioned one of the early Dutch missionaries to evangelize the indigenous people of Java.

Islands Teach Missiology 101

Indonesia has taught us lessons in "Missiology" (that's jargon for obedience to the Great Commission). As happened in Indonesia, other

---

9. David Bentley-Taylor, *Java Saga*. London: OMF Books, 1975. Richard Konieczny, OMF Canada Director who served in Indonesia, ranks Bentley-Taylor (d. 2005) with Dutch Reformed missiologist Johan Herman Bavink (1895-1964) in "grasp of, and missional directions for, life and ministry in Indonesia."
10. As cited in Chapter 10, British Member of Parliament, an evangelical emancipator on India's behalf.
11. Raffles later wrote his cousin in England, "Do you know of any layman who would go to Singapore and China as an agent to the Bible Society?"
12. Robert Morrison, pioneer of Protestant Missions to China, alerted LMS to Java's spiritual needs.

parts of Asia, and in North Africa, the church that doesn't reach out with a missionary vision soon stagnates and may fall prey to other forces.[13] There are other lessons for missions, which aren't above learning from mistakes. In spite of stereotypes used in films and novels, critics have no idea how much mission agencies critique themselves and the entire missionary movement.

I heard of the reaction missionaries met on one island, when they innocently held reading classes for children. After all, that's what a colleague and I once did in Northern Canada for First Nations (aboriginal) children—and the parents were grateful. Why not in the Pacific? But on one Indonesian island, animist parents, fearful of child slavery, thought missionaries planned to steal their children. They rioted, chasing the missionaries off the island. Missionaries analyzed the violent reactions, and when they went to another island, they intentionally ignored children. Instead, they sat with village elders and established friendship first—culturally essential.

"Why have you come from over the horizon to sit with us?" the elders eventually asked.

"We've come to tell you that God loves you, and that he can free you from fear of evil spirits," they replied. "Our book tells about this." The elders asked the missionaries to read to them from their book, which they did day after day for several weeks. One day the village headman stood up and declared that he and all the elders wanted to follow the Jesus Way. By now culturally sensitive, the missionaries did not press for separate confessions of faith until the entire group opted to follow "the Jesus Way"—a group confession *made only after each member personally committed to follow Jesus.*

"Would you also teach our children, so they won't be hurt by evil spirits?" they added. In some cultures, the elders would have told the missionaries, "This is good news, but we are too old to understand. Please teach our children instead." Missions 101![14]

---

13. By the 3rd c., North Africa had more than a thousand Christian bishoprics that ministered to European immigrants but had no vision to reach out to others around them. Islam later swept Christians aside. A church that doesn't reach out to others may have a beleaguered fortress mentality or lack a vital faith.
14. Personal interview with David Samuel-Morse, Gospel Missionary Union, 1970.

There are other lessons to learn from Indonesia—although, as Professor Hendrik Kraemer pointed out, "Christians should not think deductions could be drawn from Java which would enable them to achieve similar results elsewhere."[15] The nation's distinctive religious background and Javanese characteristics put it in a class of its own. However, Indonesia has experienced the world's largest "people movements" of the past century.

These include Bataks, East Javanese, Irians, Minahasans, and Simalunguns. Populations of entire villages—even islands—have come to Christ over the past forty years, so that nation-wide, 16% of the population calls itself some type of "Christian."

"Whole communities have experienced movements of God's Spirit that we can only long for," OMF Canada Director Richard J. Konieczny told me. "The people's strong sense of community has contributed to their group acceptance based on individual decisions." Theologian Konieczny and his wife Kathleen had earlier served in Indonesia.

What effect had all this Christian history had upon life in the nation, I wondered. Indonesia, of course, covers a wide area, but instances of spiritual and social advance testify to the power of the gospel to change the deepest traditions. For me, Indriani Bone's story was an example:

> "My mother gave birth to five girls before three sons and another girl. Because of the patriarchal and patrilineal structure of our family, to produce a male heir used to be the most important responsibility of women in marriage. Therefore, my brothers received the most attention; girls and boys are not treated equally.
>
> "When I became a Christian in my teens, I came to understand that Jesus loves boys *and* girls. As I was often sick, it was such a comfort for me to read the story of Jesus healing Jairus' little daughter (Mark

15. Bentley-Taylor, *op. cit.*, p. 138. Historian, theologian, and Islamist scholar, Kraemer (1888-1965) was an early leader in the World Council of Churches, but at variance with its more liberal members, who objected to his distinction between "biblical realism" and non-Christian religious experience. Indonesia's government banned his two-volume study of Islam (1928 and 1933), yet more than one Islamic scholar asked him to write the Foreword to their books because of his knowledge of Islamics. He helped revive the Netherlands Reformed Church missionary vision.

5.21-24a, 34-35). I saw that Jesus loves me as he loves my brothers, and he will always take care of me. God fashioned male and female, after his own likeness, so Jesus taught equality."[16]

Astounding Revival Phenomena

Years earlier, one of my mentors in the practice of missions was German professor George W. Peters, respected evangelical theologian, anthropologist, and psychologist (yes—he earned a doctorate in *each* of those disciplines). In the 1970s we asked him to lead sessions at conferences in Nigeria. We'd all been wondering about amazing reports of revival on the Indonesian island of Timor. Christian publications were filled with reports of mass conversions, accompanied by confession, repentance, and destruction of fetishes and idols. Church growth figures amazed observers.

Added to these reports were remarkable stories of divine healing, tongues of fire, visions, prophecies, resurrections, and walking on water. Even stones and trees proclaimed the gospel. With such persistent reports coming from the Pacific, many mission supporters wondered at the rather dull plodding in other areas of the world. Charismatics felt encouraged to expect spiritual phenomena in worship.[17] Christian leaders agreed that the global church could neither ignore such reports nor fail to check their authenticity.

"But to even enquire about a report, or to ask who saw a phenomenon—that was tantamount to questioning the Holy Spirit!" I remember Dr. Peters saying, when I asked about the Timor Revival. "However, I felt I was on biblical grounds, since the Word tells us to 'test the spirits.' God doesn't need his divine working embellished, and checking a report doesn't diminish his power but rather corroborates it in the eyes of skeptics."

---

16. Indriani Bone, in *2000 Years since Bethlehem* (condensed). Nashville: Upper Room Books, 1998.

17. New Testament theologian Thomas A. Smail helpfully examines biblical teaching on the gifts of the Spirit in *The Forgotten Father* (see Bibliog.). Smail led the Anglican Charismatic Movement in Britain for several years before his "reappraisal" of it. His conclusion is that obedience to the Father is central to our faith, and that undue emphasis on "Jesus Only" or "gifts of the Spirit" are distortions that can lead to error.

Peters documented remarkable church growth based on genuine conversions. However, he discovered significant factors in the reports, unrecognized by reporters:

> (1) In most cases, no one had personally witnessed the phenomena. (2) The average Timor worldview, occult background, and emotions accepted the phenomenal. (3) A cultural "participation mentality" meant that if a person *heard* a report or *if a thought went through his mind*, the event or phenomenon had indeed occurred.[18]

The latter point, incomprehensible to Western rationalism, was key to understanding the sensational reports. To an islander culturally immersed in the world of spirits, how could a thought enter his head, or a report come to his hearing, unless it actually happened? Not only was it unreasonable to question, but also for Christians, doubting was blasphemous!

Peters, a professor at Dallas Theological Seminary, unlocked a mystery that had long plagued missionaries from the West—the obvious lack of any separation between fact and fantasy, reality and non-reality. Inflated conversion figures and sensational miracle reports did not indicate dishonesty—they reflected sincere belief that whatever someone wished or thought was an actual fact.

In deciphering the Timor revival, however, Peters did not disparage genuine results. He described his own uplifting experience of meeting with believers, some straight out of stone-age conditions, including headhunters. He noted genuine repentance and faith as spirit-worshipers threw their paraphernalia into a fire. He quoted the wisdom of church leaders, who understood that non-Christian experience could also be accompanied by astonishing reports of phenomena. "We are on our guard against demonic influences," Pastor J. M. E. Daniel told him. "This is one of the dangers accompanying revivals."

The final question Peters asked was whether the Revival had produced lasting fruit, even though reports of phenomena have subsided. He answers positively:

18. George W. Peters, *Indonesia Revival—focus on Timor* (see Bibliography).

> (1) the vibrant life of the church; (2) strong biblical teaching; (3) love for the Lord and fellowship with other believers; (4) an effective core of Christian workers; (5) biblical openness to the Holy Spirit; (6) and continuing impact on life in Timor.

A Timorese leader once confirmed to SIM's Phil Parshall that among his people, the boundary between spiritual "reality" and physical "reality" is very small. Yet Parshall also cites positive results of the revival, adding a seventh point to Peters: *a strong missionary vision*. Many Timorese have gone as missionaries to other islands and even other nations— Suriname, China, and Greece, being three.

The Christians of Timor were at opposite poles from the dormant churchianity that had characterized Christianity during the first two centuries of Indonesian church history. Aspects were undoubtedly extreme, but God says he would rather have his church either hot or cold—not lukewarm. A cold church can be revived; a hot church can mature from initial startling combustion, into coals that continue glowing spiritually.

Vision Becomes Plan for Nation

Timor was only one island that experienced such spiritual movements. But as the number of believers increased, where were the trained leaders to help them grow to maturity? There was always the danger of syncretism or reversion into spirit-worship. Several Bible schools and seminaries were training men and women. Stephen Tong, a Presbyterian evangelist, became a strong leader. God was also raising up a man of vision from a most unlikely place—Nila, a speck of an island towards the eastern end of Indonesia. Born in Nila in 1941, Christoffel ("Chris") Z. Marantika became a Baptist pastor.

When Campus Crusade provided Chris a scholarship to study in the U.S., the young pastor earned Master's and Doctoral degrees. The burden to see Indonesians evangelizing Indonesia developed into a strategy that matched his nation's motto: "Many but One."

"I asked God to give us ways to reach the nation, and a vision was born," he later recalled. "I named it Indonesia One-One-One. I came to the conviction that in order to evangelize the whole nation, we needed to plant one church in every village, and do it in one generation. . . . Even though 150 million of my people are Muslims, I cannot dream less than finding ways to make sure that each one of them has heard clearly that Jesus Christ is Lord and Saviour."[19]

Chris looked for an agency that would provide a bridge between mission-minded Christians in other lands and his vision for his own land. It was one of his professors, my friend George Peters, who recommended him to Partners International (Christian Nationals Evangelism Commission). Although some missions question his strategy, they give thanks for a leader with more than a desire or vision—an actual plan to develop Indonesian evangelists and church leaders.

Needing a registered financial base, Marantika formed the Faith Foundation, to which churches in Asia, Australia, and the West give. The Evangelical Training School of Indonesia (ETSI) and Immanuel Christian University train leadership. Capable academics, businessmen, and theologians are on the boards and staff. These developed branch seminaries for different islands, and students started churches in their own communities.

Horrific Backlash

As expected, such Christian growth in Java and other islands provoked reaction from Islamic militants. Before European colonization, Indonesian rulers had converted to *Islam*, in order to benefit from its trade connections. After the colonial powers withdrew, Muslim purists expected to increase their monopoly, but by then democratic values influenced government and were enshrined in the concept of *Pancha-sila*. Understanding only legislative control and military power, Muslims couldn't comprehend internal, spiritual regeneration that belonged to "a kingdom not of this world." The number of Christians multiplied even though "Christian" colonizers no longer ruled.

Convinced that Islam is the only pure religion, Muslim militants have attacked churches, particularly in the Maluku group of islands.[20] Thousands of armed insurgents have over-run Christian communities, causing violent counter-attacks. Actually, the Muslim majority need not

19. Ray Wiseman, *I Cannot Dream Less*, p. 56 (see Bibliography).

feel threatened, for they constitute the largest Muslim population in any nation (80.3%). Most Indonesians have been moderate, and the nation does have a relative degree of religious freedom. However, I found the following report disturbing:

> Indonesian judges sentenced three mothers to three years in prison for allowing Muslim children to attend a Christian Sunday school program. Judges found Rebekka Zakaria, Eti Pangesti, and Ratna Bangun guilty of violating the Child Protection Act of 2002, which forbids "deception, lies or enticement" causing a child to convert to another religion.
>
> Sunday school teachers had instructed the children to get permission from their parents before attending the program, and those who did not were asked to go home. None of the children had converted to Christianity. Muslim parents had been photographed with their children during the Sunday school activities, but when Islamic leaders lodged a complaint, no witnesses testified or provided evidence of the charges that the women had lied, deceived, or forced the children into changing their religion. The three defendants were relieved they had not been given the maximum five-year prison sentence but were devastated to be separated from their children.
>
> Islamic extremists made murderous threats both inside and outside the courtroom. Truckloads of extremists arrived; one brought a coffin to bury the accused if they were found innocent. Islamic radicals threatened the defendants, witnesses, and judges with death if the women were acquitted.[21]

No doubt the worldwide resurgence of orthodox Islam has encouraged Islamists to purge the nation of Islamic syncretism and Christian influence. Radicals attempt to provoke Christians into religious warfare, as another report suggests:

> A bombing on May 28 in the Christian market of Tentena left 22 dead and at least 49 injured. Two witnesses in the ensuing trial were shot dead in Poso district, as was a policeman involved in the

20. Reminiscent of violent Muslim reaction to an attempted Communist coup in 1965 (killing 500,000).

21. Compass Direct, January 2006.

investigation. In Poso, three teenage girls walking to their Christian high school were beheaded. A fourth is still recovering from serious injuries. All three heads were found in plastic bags with a note stating in part, "We will murder 100 more Christian teenagers and their heads will be presented as presents."[22]

Open opposition is not the only problem Christians face. Sometimes opponents use subtle trickery to stir up trouble. Back in March 1998, a teenage girl, Khariyah Enniswah, begged a pastor, Rev. Yanwardi Koto, for asylum, claiming her family threatened to kill her. For her safety, the pastor sent her to a Christian school under the care of another pastor and his family, while members discussed how best to help the girl.

All seemed in order, until Khariyah's uncle turned up and charged the Christians with abduction, rape, and forced conversion to Christianity. A court duly sentenced the two pastors, the school principal, and their wives to ten years' imprisonment. Suspecting that the girl had been "planted" by the uncle to incriminate the Christians, the church appealed the sentence—but to no avail. Finally, the defendants referred their case to the President, who has the power to grant a pardon.[23] "Wise as serpents, harmless as doves," Jesus told his disciples to be.

Where Was God When Disaster Struck?

IT WAS TIME TO CONTINUE MY JOURNEY. Flying eastward along the string of islands, our aircraft passed over some of Indonesia's 100 active volcanoes—part of the Ring of Fire that encircles the Pacific with seismic activity. Galunggung's ash nearly brought down a giant airliner in the '80s. The eruption shot a stream of volcanic dust into the upper atmosphere, reducing sunlight and warmth around the globe. The airliner over-flying Indonesia sucked ash into its jet engines, sending it plunging thousands of feet before it recovered power.

Now as we flew eastward, humans, not nature, caused the thick haze below. Slash-and-burn farming and land clearing for development, domestic cooking fires, and traffic smog contribute to the air pollution. In 1997,

22. Compass Direct, January 2006

23. Compass Direct, April 25, 2001.

thick haze blanketed the entire archipelago, closing airports, schools, and businesses, causing thousands of infant deaths.

Illegal logging across these verdant islands is part of the environmental tragedy—unfortunately abetted by the global market for wood. Entire villages depend on logging for income, much of it legal and controlled. However, corrupt companies and courts conspire to fell timber beyond the quotas—an evil that robs communities of future livelihood, governments of licensing revenues, and legitimate companies (and their employees) of income. That also depresses global timber prices—which may reduce the price of the chair you sit on and the newspaper you read, but it also feeds the world's voracious appetite for wood beyond reasonableness.

That's not all. The island of Borneo has the richest diversity of trees in the world, as well as living creatures. The World Wide Fund for Nature reported 361 *new* creatures discovered in *one* recent decade. Their habitat is fast diminishing.

While nature struggles to survive on the earth's surface, titanic forces struggle underground. Subterranean fault lines along Indonesia's southern edge trigger undersea earthquakes, unseen but felt. If they are high enough on the Richter Scale, they trigger *tsunami*[24] that send walls of water across the ocean. Most *tsunami* occur in the Pacific, where sensitive monitors warn Pacific Rim countries. However, the devastating earthquake of December 26, 2004, sent 30-40-foot tidal waves smashing into shores around the Indian Ocean and even as far as East Africa's coast.

The true death toll will never be known, because many bodies were buried under tons of rubble. Estimates range between 200,000 and 300,000 deaths, half a million injured, and millions more homeless. Property damage reached $6 billion. Entire coastal towns and cities collapsed in debris. In Sri Lanka, 80% of the island's fishing vessels were damaged or destroyed, irrigation channels were destroyed, and fields and wells rendered useless by saltwater that penetrated three km. (nearly two miles) inland. The tidal wave destroyed much of the three most important revenue sources of tropical islands: tourism, fishing, and agriculture. The UN estimates it will take ten years for affected areas to recover.

24. Japanese: "harbor waves."

"Where was God?" the world asked. One secular TV interviewer, describing the disaster as of "biblical" proportions, asked a Muslim imam, a Hindu priest, and a Christian theologian to explain how God could allow so many people to die. Each faith has its way of coping with death, and the answers may not represent everyone. But did represent three different religious viewpoints others hold.[25]

1. Islam: "God punished them for bad things they've done," declared the imam. "But we should feel glad they are now released from all suffering. Since Allah willed this disaster, he has sent them straight to Heaven."

2. Hindu: "The people died because of bad *karma,*" explained the priest. "Now they have the chance to be re-born in a better form. That's good!"

3. Christian: "We don't know the spiritual condition of each person," replied Fuller Theological Seminary Dean, theologian Doug McConnell. "But we do know that God loves the whole world. He has provided Jesus Christ as Saviour from sin for all who believe in him. Christians show God's love to those who suffer or have been bereaved."

Denial of a Human Right

As the *tsunami* swept westward across the Indian Ocean, McConnell's comments took on practical meaning. Nowhere was this more evident than in the Maldives, southwest of India. When the *tsunami* completely inundated those coral islands (most only a meter/yard above sea level; the highest less than an average Fijian's height), Christian agencies rushed to save lives and provide shelter, water, and food.

[The Maldives (pop. some 300,000) are a vacation paradise. Tourists, lounging in some 80 hotels, account for almost four-fifths of the idyllic islands' economy.[26] Yet in 1998, the government terrorized *Christians*—arresting, imprisoning, and torturing 50. Authorities said they'd be freed if they recanted their faith—in writing and signed. International condemnation brought about eventual release,

25. ABC News, Jan. 4, 2005.

26. Only some 200 of the 1,190 islands are inhabited, but warming and rising seawater threaten islanders and tourists, who add their own pollution to atmosphere and ocean.

but Christians are forbidden to meet for worship—even in their own homes. Bibles are banned.

On July 3, 2000, the Maldives' President, Maumoon Abdul Gayoom, decreed that no religion should be allowed in his country other than Islam. Speaking at a special meeting held at Dharubaaruge on July 3rd to commemorate the day the Maldives became Muslim, the President claimed that his country had been able to sustain its sovereignty because of its adherence to the principles of Islam. ... Introduction of any other religion would harm that sovereignty.][27]

The ABC News cited above also reported there was one meteorologist in Southeast Asia whose equipment registered the undersea earthquake. He knew it was severe enough to trigger a *tsunami*. But he chose not to pass the warning on to his government or other countries. He knew that many of his superstitious countrymen likely would blame him for causing the inevitable destruction (how else would he have known it was coming?). Most coastal villagers and tourists could have fled to higher ground before the advancing wall of water swept them away. They had no warning.

They had no warning! **They-had-no-warn-ing!**

Like a power drill, the words bore into my brain, right down to my heart. In Asia there were men, women, and children who had no knowledge of spiritual dangers they were in, or how to escape. In the words of Romans 10. 14: *"How can they believe in the one of whom they have not heard? And how can they hear without someone preaching to them? And how can they preach unless they are sent?"*

****

27. WEA Religious Liberty Commission 7/12/2000. Christians (some 300) keep faith despite suppression. While the UN Declaration of Human Rights insists on freedom to choose religion, the Islamic Conference (co-coordinating global Muslim body) does not accept the UN Declaration but has drafted its own.

OUR FLIGHT CONTINUED NORTHEAST, across the island of Borneo, which Indonesia and Malaysia share, along with tiny oil-rich Brunei. Far to the East, Indonesia shared another major island, New Guinea. An island second only to Greenland in size, it's jungles continue to excite zoologists with new exotic finds—such as a rodent five times larger than common city rats, and a pygmy 'possum.[28] Its western half is Indonesia's Irian Jaya. The eastern half is Papua New Guinea (PNG). Many of the island's spirit worshipers have found new life in Christ. (Most PNG families belong to a Christian church.) Of the many tribes, probably the best known is Irian Jaya's Dani tribe, described by Don and Carol Richardson in *Peace Child*.[29]

I gained a great deal of respect for missionaries—local and expatriate—who have taken the gospel into the islands of the Pacific. I had got to know some who joined a course I led on management and leadership.[30] I admired their courage and commitment as they braved isolation (no roads in or out for them or supplies), physical hardships, disease, and discouragement. I could sense their weariness, struggling with exotic linguistic patterns, worldviews, and strange "values" (deception and murder are *values*?), patiently reducing the tongues to writing and then teaching stone-age people to read their own languages. But there was the upside, as spirit-worshipers suddenly realized that God was speaking to them through those black marks on white paper—and God really loved them. He freed them from terror!

These gospel messengers had become the victims of their own success, hounded by "the tyranny of the urgent."[31] So much to do, so few trained people to help, so little time!

"Why didn't we learn this forty years ago?" asked a veteran during the course, as we studied principles of management and leadership used by Moses, Paul, and the Lord Jesus himself. The principles were all there in Scripture: planning, time management, delegation, leadership

---

28. *Have a Good Day*, Carol Stream: Tyndale House Publishers, April 2008 issue.
29. Richardson, *Peace Child*—see Bibliography. This also was made into an award-winning film.
30. Sponsored by SIM, along with other agencies, in Sydney, Australia—a relatively short hop from PNG.
31. Title of a booklet published by InterVarsity Press, 1967.

development, and more. I agreed that we'd all been zealous in spreading the gospel—not bad—but hadn't been prepared for what Paul called, "the care of the churches."[32] Some missionaries end up "burnt out," unable to finish their tasks.

Flying over the Pacific, I thanked God for these dedicated disciples. Now I understood more of what it took to follow Jesus through the paths of the sea. These messengers carried with them something more precious than any cargo cult could imagine—the life-giving gospel. Not even angels had that privilege![33]

"The Spratlys! *To our left!*" my fellow passenger was shouting in my ear as he jabbed the air. So what? I peered down at specks sprinkled like pepper on the South China Sea. Are *those* what Brunei, China, Malaysia, the Philippines, Taiwan, and Vietnam all tussle over? Not that anyone would want to live there. But those desolate coral reefs are a symbolic outpost on which neighboring nations want to plant a flag and claim fishing and underwater oil rights—from here to that flag's country. The reefs sit astride rich natural resources.[34] Periodically, some nation's warship churns around the Spratlys, like a race contestant rounding a marker buoy. Front-page photo for *The National Bugle* back home!

Ahead, through the heat haze, lay the seven thousand (plus) islands of The Philippines. Our flight slid into Manila airport on the largest island, Luzon. When the airline doors opened, someone must have wrapped me in wet burlap—or so it seemed.

---

32. 2 Corinthians 11.28.

33. 1 Peter 1.12 may imply this.

34. The Spratly Islands are only one of several clusters off Asia's coast that are tension points between China, Japan, Korea, and (further north) Russia.

Sun Like Thunder – **18: The Philippines**

Land of the Jeepney

Philippines: Pop. 90,544,498

"God moves in a mysterious way, his wonders to perform; He plants his footsteps in the sea, and rides upon the storm." (—William Cowper)

"DAVE—*COME QUICKLY!*" Dave sensed urgency in Bev's cry. She'd been baking bread—a family treat in their diet of local rice and roots. But Bev had suddenly noticed a tiny flame around the pump of the kerosene "camp stove." Dave sprang up from the bamboo table where he was preparing his Bible class outline. He scooped up the two-burner stove and the pan that protected it from drafts whistling through the hut's woven split-bamboo walls.

With a blinding flash, a ball of flame enveloped Dave. Although kerosene oil is normally stable, an unnoticed leak had dripped fuel into the pan, its fumes exploding in Dave's arms. Hungry flames leaped into the low thatch. Dave pushed the children, who had been in an outer room, through the open doorway of their house-on-stilts, and Bev dropped from the window opening as grass and bamboo blazed like a bonfire. No time to rescue precious documents or anything else!

Dave plunged into the nearby mountain stream while Bev calmed their traumatized children. Mariano, the Alangan Bible teacher, and his students raced up the hill from their classroom to help their missionaries.

As everything the family possessed burned to an ash-heap, Dave's face, chest, and arms began to turn white from second-degree burns.

"*Laki* Dabid, I'll go with you out to the road to find a ride to the hospital in Calapan!" Pastor Mariano exclaimed.

That meant trekking eight miles over the hills to reach the road—then waiting for some vehicle to pass. Once on board, they'd still have a bumpy journey over the pot-holed road, some 12 miles (16 km) to Calapan, the nearest town with a hospital. Could Dave make it? No alternative! The two headed off. Halfway down the mountain trail, Dave sagged under the merciless sun. "I have to rest a minute!" he gasped, stopping in the shade of a straggly tree. "Mariano, please pray."

Would God Hear a Hill Tribesman?

Alangan looked to missionaries to pray for *them*, but now one of them was asking an Alangan to pray for the *missionary*! Simply in his own dialect, Mariano pled with God: "Great Father, please help us reach the hospital in time. Protect *Laki* Dabid from the sun!" Propped against the tree trunk, Dave was fading.

"*Laki*—we must keep walking!" Mariano urged.

Dave's skin was blistering, but Mariano was right. They had to keep moving or he'd go into shock. When they reached the flat plain and came to a stream, Dave lay in it for a few minutes. Then for hours the two slogged on until they reached the road. Somehow the sun hadn't felt as scorching, and when they looked back, they saw why. A cloudbank had risen, its leading edge casting a shadow all along their trail. Rain would have turned the clay into a slippery bog, but it was raining only behind them.

Waiting at the roadside, they heard a motor in the distance. While Dave sagged under a tree, Mariano flagged down a fuel tanker laboring towards them. The driver made room in the cab for Dave—he even let Mariano sit beside him.[1] As the lorry jolted through potholes, Dave's swelling blisters throbbed, but he couldn't feel his arms any more. Did he have any?

---

1. Hill people normally had to sit on top or, in passenger lorries, at the back. Missionaries often chose to sit in the back, to be with the people. That's how Bev and children later traveled to the hospital.

Another hour and they were at the hospital in the provincial capital. Dave lapsed into semi-consciousness as nurses began first aid until a doctor arrived. When they started peeling off skin and applying salve and bandages, Dave wanted to explain this wasn't the way to treat burns any more, but his swollen lips couldn't form words.

Bev and the children later slid down the now wet trail and arrived to spell off Mariano in the hospital, sitting with Dave. Anxiously they held water to his blistered lips, coaxing him to eat the food they brought (local hospitals don't cater). Painfully over weeks, Dave recovered enough to trek back again into the hills with Bev. The Christians had built a new hut for them, stocking it with whatever they could. That evening Mariano and others joined Dave and Bev in a praise meeting. Dave described the clouds that sheltered Mariano and him on the painful trek to the road.

"Truly, God answers the prayers of you missionaries!" the Alangan nodded solemnly.

Dave and Bev Fuller looked at each other. They'd come to love the shy Alangan, one of several linguistic groups that made up the Mangyan. The tribe had taken refuge in the hills when lowlanders confiscated their farmlands and cut down their forests. Even before Dave Fuller met Beverley Erickson, she and another OMF missionary, Morven Brown, had studied the language. They trekked for eight days across Mindoro's hills and valleys, contacting the reclusive Alangan and other hill tribes.[2] Morven had already analyzed the language, so they had an alphabet to help them construct sentences. The two women overcame suspicions as they used dialect greetings. On a hand-wound turntable, they played Bible portions produced by Gospel Recordings. One by one, hill people turned from placating the spirits that had terrorized them, as they trusted in Jesus. Little groups formed churches and met together in conferences.

Spiritually awakened to new life in Christ, new believers wanted more. They asked the missionaries to train pastors and Bible teachers for

2. Years before, U.S. soldiers based on the islands following Japan's invasion, had called the remote wilderness "the boondocks"—from Tagalog *bundok* (hill, mountain), giving rise to slang, "boonies."

them. And they erected a Bible "school" (at first a bamboo shelter like their own huts) in the village where Dave and Bev lived. The students drank in the Bible teaching.

But there was one problem that wouldn't go away—decades of oppression from lowland insurgents had left them with no self-esteem. Believers were free from the tyranny of spirit worship, but when would they be free from their paralyzing sense of inferiority? Could they lead their own people spiritually? Would they ever realize they were just as important to God as the educated people in the city—or as the white-skinned missionaries? When would they pray in their own dialects, instead of in the "superior language" of Tagalog—which, they felt, God would hear—not their "inferior" dialects.

As Dave and Bev's eyes met, their hearts ached. They remembered the difficult years of deciphering the language, patient translation, evangelism, and teaching, of watching the Holy Spirit bring to spiritual birth new babes in Christ among a downtrodden people. How would God overcome the sense of inferiority that bound these dear people?

Dave spoke softly but firmly: "Remember, I wasn't *able* to pray. It was Mariano who prayed—*in your own language!* God heard him pray. See, it says right here in James 5.16, 'The prayer of a righteous man is powerful and effective.' God answers the prayers of hill people!"

The islanders had learned not to reveal emotion on their faces. That often made them inscrutable. In Bible classes, were they comprehending or not? Who could tell? But now murmurs of approval went around the group, like palm fronds fluttering in a fresh breeze.

"*Truly!*" whispered Mariano, rubbing the back of a weathered hand across his moist eyes. That whisper went all over the hills, into hundreds of villages among some 50,000 hill people. For Dave and Bev, the house fire, painful burns, and family trauma came into new perspective. Today there are strong churches all over the island—and Mindoro Christians can hold up their heads even in the big city over on the main island.[3]

3. Dave Fuller is my brother, whom I didn't see for nearly 30 years. At the time, our OMF and SIM areas of service were on opposite sides of the globe. Yet, in one of life's interesting coincidences, Bev, whom my brother married, had been a Bible school classmate of Lorna, the girl I married. —WHF

The Tawbuid's Prophecy

The Alangan are only one of half a dozen dialect groups among the Mangyan people. A few believers from another group, the Tawbuid, also attended the Bible school. They and the Alangan had once been afraid of each other–as they were of any stranger. A mountain ridge stood between their villages. Now Alangan and Tawbuid squatted beside each other on the split-bamboo floor, learning more about the strange message of peace.

These Tawbuid were there because of a tribal prophecy. Three-and-a-half centuries earlier, one of their elders, Long Neck, foretold the arrival of white people. "When they come, they'll teach you a new message of peace," he told his people. "You must follow their teaching." Really? The Tawbuid wondered. Long ago, white people had arrived on the coast. A few in long black robes had even come as far as their ridge, but the Tawbuid hid in the jungle. Those strangers *seemed* peaceful, but with them were men carrying swords and also magic sticks they could just *point* at a baboon or man, and he would die!

Recently they heard of newcomers. Coastal traders said their skin was white, like the pithy inside of the tree bark the Tawbuid used for loincloths. Could these even be human? They must be evil spirits! Anyway, none of the coastal people could understand the strangers' tongue. That reminded the Tawbuid of the rest of Long Neck's prophecy:

"You'll know the ones to listen to, because they'll speak our language." Now *that* would be convincing proof! No stranger ever learned their language. Even the lowland people considered Tawbuid and other highland languages gibberish fit only for jungle monkeys.

What a shock a Tawbuid farmer got, when he ventured to the coast for supplies! He heard that there were *two white people in town who spoke Tawbuid*. Nervously, he sought them out, and sure enough, he could understand all they said. White people! Amazingly, they could also understand him.

The encounter also shocked the fair-skinned strangers—Russell and Barbara Reed, OMF colleagues of Dave and Bev. For eight years, they'd struggled to learn Tawbuid. It almost seemed wasted time. They'd come to give the Good News to the unreached people *inland*—but here they sat on the coast. No other foreigner or lowlander spoke Tawbuid.

But suddenly, here was a *Tawbuid* asking them to teach his people "the message they had"! Excitedly, they went to Tawbuid villages and did just that. For years they didn't know about the prophecy. Long Neck's descendents had kept it as *their* secret—even from the spirits, they hoped. But years later, the Reeds asked a believer to explain why so many of his people were destroying the fetishes of the spirits that had so terrified them. Until then, they had unsuccessfully trusted those fetishes to protect them from evil omens; now they trusted in Jesus for eternal life. The clan finally revealed the prophecy.

"My spine tingled!" Barbara later said. "We were part of God's plan for the spiritual release of the Tawbuid. Those years of preparation on the coast weren't wasted!"[4]

Learning to Hold Their Tongues!

"People at home lightly ask God to bless their missionary's language learning," years later I said to Dave and Bev when I visited them in the Philippines. Bev had studied four Filipino languages. "It's that simple, isn't it—just memorizing a new vocabulary?"

"I guess folk who haven't struggled with a language might think so," replied Bev, smiling at my tongue-in-cheek question, because she knew I'd also studied language (in Africa). "One of our most fluent missionaries thought he was getting along well. After giving a sermon, he asked a close Filipino friend how he rated.

"'You sounded arrogant!' the friend told him. Unlike most polite villagers, the man understood his missionary friend enough to be blunt with him."

The nonplussed missionary and Bev discussed the problem with informants. They weren't sure why, but they also thought the taped sermon somehow didn't sound "polite." Finally Bev clued in: it wasn't the vocabulary but the inflection and sequence of noun-verb-object. In some

4. Barbara Reed, *Beyond the Great Darkness*, p. 299 (see Bibliography).

languages, the speaker interjects pauses to show politeness. Instead of saying, "Listen—I am going to tell you a story!" a Filipino would gently suggest, "Maybe you this . . . ah . . . story might like . . . er . . . to hear told—yes?" (That's not a translation, but it gives the drift.)

With advice from an SIL (Wycliffe) linguist and Filipino informants, Bev's team found keys to comprehension: sentence and even paragraph construction, verbal patterns, and use of discourse. Many missionaries hadn't realized these subtle differences.

"We're sure we're using the right vocabulary and grammar. Why do villagers look as if we're talking Greek?" frustrated language class members complained to Bev. When Bev and consultants listened to students' taped messages, a linguist identified the problem.

"They're teaching like foreigners!" she said. "They should be using Filipino *discourse*." That sent Bev and team back to re-format their teaching materials, which missionaries are still using.

If friends at home only knew the frustrating complexity of language learning!

Mega-City World

After visiting Dave and Bev on Mindoro Island, I stayed in the nation's capital, Manila. I found a world full of different issues. I stayed at a splendid international hotel, where I took part in the General Assembly of the World Evangelical Alliance. People raise their eyebrows when they hear of evangelical gatherings in posh hotels—hardly representative of the simple living Christ's followers usually follow! But as a member of WEA's executive, I knew the logistics of bringing together several hundred delegates from around the world: need to meet near an international airport, in a hotel with catering, audio-visual and medical facilities, security, local volunteer support, and (most important) *off-season low rates*. Rather than lose experienced staff, the hotel provided their facilities at little more than cost. Besides, Manila rates lowest on an index of major cities' cost of living.

So meeting in Manila, a mega-city of some 12m at the time, made sense. Our triennial WEA conference went off without a hitch, capably hosted by the Philippine Council of Evangelical Churches. Local gifted pastors (including WEA's then International Director, Agustin "Jun"[5] Vencer, a Filipino) led Bible studies and prayer sessions that edified everyone.

Circus "Jeepneys" and Happy Bees

After the convention I risked my life on a "Jeepney." I could have increased the risk by sitting up front beside the driver, where highly respected passengers and foreigners expect to sit. I declined, squeezing on to an already full bench—for with each new passenger, custom requires everyone else to exhale and fold like an accordion.

The Jeep[6] wasn't a risk in itself. Like thousands of fare-earning vehicles that ply Manila's streets, this one had a wooden passenger platform built over the chassis. Our resultant "Jeepney" was well equipped, painted red, green, blue, and orange, 24 leaden galloping horses festooning the engine hood ("bonnet" to Brits)—no doubt to increase the "horsepower," or at least the passengers. An oversized, hand-operated, rubber-bulb horn completed the vehicle's high-tech paraphernalia. My jeepney of choice lacked nothing.

The risk was with Manila's traffic—a circus. Nowhere (not even in Rome) have I been in such heavy congestion and riotous driving. A herd of hooting vehicles (bulls with horns?) vied to lead the pack—although there was no front-runner as far as one could see. Four or five lanes squeezed together where there should have been two. I admired the skilled drivers, who obviously knew the width of their vehicles (even the thickness of paint on them). If there had been a breeze, it couldn't have squeezed between us and the Jeepneys on either side. Somehow, we scraped through—without a scrape!

Though much of the nation's population is poor, Manila's economy is as bustling as its traffic. Because the nation turns out so many engineers

5. "Jun": popular Filipino nickname, from American "Junior" for a son bearing his father's full name. Brits add Roman numerals instead—as in John Q. Smith II.

6. "Jeepney": a "jeep" used as a "jitney." When the US Army closed its WWII base, thousands of jeeps became available at low cost. The Jeep was already popular among enterprising Filipinos. For a series of children's missionary stories, see Eva Doerksen, ***Adventures of Mr. Jeeponary***. (See Bibliography.)

(100,000 p. a.), it does a lot of other's out-sourcing—even China's, although its labour costs are higher.

Felipe de Leon, professor at the University of the Philippines, cites surveys that rate Filipinos as the happiest citizens, whether in the Orient or the Occident.[7] They are neither individualistic, as in Western culture, nor "collectivist"—as in Confucian or other cultures that value hierarchy. The Tagalog term is *kapwa,* "shared being."

That's why entrepreneur Tony Tan's family chose the bee for their company logo, because it epitomized Filipino light-hearted happiness and collective activity. His Jollibee hamburgers outsell all the American competition. The Tans have even opened "Jollibee Foods" outlets in USA.

"The strongest social urge is to connect, to become one with people," says de Leon. Some 97% of Filipinos believe in God, the majority feeling "extremely close to him." Notably there is little drug abuse, suicide, or depression among Filipino maids (who are usually overworked and sometimes mistreated) employed in many countries with those problems. Their families dub these overseas workers their *bayani*, from the traditional way of moving a house: the community surrounds the hut and carries it to its new site—*bayanihan*: a shared effort.[8] The government estimates that 10% of the population works overseas, making them one of the biggest sources of foreign exchange.[9]

However, that carries a heavy social price: children growing up without their father. Ironically, it also means a shortage of nurses, who train in the Philippines but serve overseas, where their skills and gentle bedside manners are in demand. The poverty-stricken nation faces a dilemma: it needs the overseas revenue, but will use it to educate the next generation preparing to migrate—unless there's radical change in the economy.

A third of the Republic's 80m citizens live below the poverty line. One sad result of such poverty is Manila's high level of prostitution.

7. *The Economist,* Dec. 22, 2001, p. 43.
8. *Bayani* can also mean "hero."
9. In 2006, their remittances amounted to $15 billion.

Unscrupulous agents offer poverty-stricken parents cash for their daughters, promising lucrative employment. Girls, many barely into puberty, are forced into at least a dozen sexual "tricks" nightly. They end up beaten, half-starved, diseased—and unloved.[10]

Friendship and Street Evangelism

On a downtown street, I found Phil Parshall sitting beside a table displaying literature with a difference: Christian literature for Muslims. There were stories, tracts, and Scripture portions in English, Tagalog,[11] and Arabic. Filipino literacy is rated at 95%, so book tables are common, and often vendors spread out their magazines along sidewalks.

"I sit here four times a week," Phil explained. "Although the nation is the only predominantly Christian country in Asia,[12] about 5% of the people are Muslim. That's some four million! Right here you're in a Muslim district—15,000 around us." Earlier, Phil and his wife Julie had served with ICF (now SIM) in Bangladesh, gaining experience in cross-cultural witness among Muslims.[13]

"Do many stop by your table?" I asked. "And when they do, what's their attitude?"

"Occasionally people stop," Phil replied. "The main thing is to be available when the Lord prompts someone to browse. Muslims love to discuss life—anything. For some this is an opportunity to practice their English."

"What's the main requirement for sidewalk evangelism?" I wondered.

"Friendliness!" Phil answered without hesitation. "Muslims are very community conscious and appreciate friendship above all. Each time I'm here, someone invites me to his home or accepts an invitation to ours."

"How are Christians going to reach Muslims?" was my next question.

---

10. CBC World News documentary, April 6, 2007.
11. Tagalog, language of a tribe in the Philippines' largest island, Luzon, is the national trade language. All languages total 169, plus dialects.
12. 93% call themselves "Christian"—mostly Spanish-Portuguese (Iberian) Catholic. Easter tourists watch Filipinos being nailed to crosses (in 2006, one man for the 20th time). One way to earn merit—and cash!

"By their godly lives," Phil replied. "Although Christians are such a mixture, Muslims have formed a stereotype that defines us all. In an Islamic country, the state's Islamic laws govern every Muslim. So when they meet a Christian in a so-called Christian country, like the Philippines, they assume every Christian reflects Roman Catholic teaching and rules: the impression of idolatry and immorality because they make offerings to statues of the Virgin Mary as the Mother of God. Islam reacts to the perceived idolatry of churches that revere icons.

"In non-Christian countries, Christian minorities often give Muslims a false picture of our faith. For instance, in certain countries, the very poor and marginalized have responded to the gospel. So Muslims, who value success, aren't attracted to members of a 'poverty-stricken faith.' Then there are communities and nations that call themselves Christian but are known for prostitution and drunkenness.[14] It's going to take the witness of a godly life to even get a hearing for the gospel. It's an uphill struggle.

"Oh . . . just a minute—here's a man asking about literature." And Phil greeted a be-robed Muslim in Arabic. I had time to muse on the historic animosity between Muslims and Christians. Spaniards equated Muslim Moros[15] of the southern islands with the North African Muslims (Moors) who invaded and ruled Spain for four centuries. However, "Apostle of Literacy" Frank Laubach (who ministered in the Philippines) saw them as humanity needing the Saviour—whatever their violent history of murder and slave trade. OMF's Jonathan Fuller, who with his family lived among Muslims on the island of Maguindanao[16] for several years, points out that Spanish conquest of the Philippines pitted one of the cruelest forms of Christendom against a pastoral people practicing "folk Islam."[17]

---

13. Dr. Parshall has written nine books on Islam. See Bibliography for list.
14. Philippine prostitution involves over 60,000 children and ½ m. women—plus international trafficking.
15. "Moro": Spanish term for Filipino Muslim, variant of "Moor" (from "Mauretania.").
16. Arab spice and silk traders had settled on this southerly island of the Philippines. Pagan rulers along the sea route converted to Islam to strengthen trade ties.
17. See Bibliography: Fuller, Jonathan.

Triumphal Islam Resents Sidelining

But reasons for antagonism go much deeper. While other empires have coped objectively with decline, Muslims, particularly Arabs, nurse deep resentment over the loss of their "Golden Era." By AD 711, Islamic armies had swept victoriously from Morocco to India. For centuries Islam benefited from the arts, sciences, and trades of the cultures Muslims had conquered. Whereas the Greek Alexander had a sense of Manifest Destiny, and Asia's Golden Horde that later sacked Rome had a lust to conquer, both worshiped pagan gods. Neither had a codified religious creed, or canon. Muhammad gave Islam its canon (the *Qur'an*), and the Mullahs its creed (the *Hadith*, or collection of traditions). These in turn empowered Islamic Arab nationalism during a politcally unsettled era, and provided "divine sanction" for killing non-conformists.

Although Western apologists quote pacific passages from pre-Medina sections of the *Qur'an*, post-Medina sections (which abrogate earlier ones) are at the root of militant attacks on Christians and the countries of Christian missionaries.[18] A new front in the provocative literature offensive opened in 1953, with the volume, *ak-Tabshir wa'l-isti'mar fi bilad al-'arabiyya* ("Evangelism and Imperialism in the Arab World"), published in Beirut, Lebanon, and translated into Russian, Persian, and Turkish. Its thesis is that Christian missionaries (with their schools, hospitals, and bookshops) are the most dangerous agents of Western imperialism. After five centuries of dazzling dominance—when wandering nomads became conquerors—the Arab culture of victimization took over and lashed out at perceived enemies.

As I mused over militant attitudes, I also thought of Islamic communities that want only to practice their Islamic way of life peacefully. I'd met them all over the world and found them to be generous and honest family people. In today's world, it is difficult to keep objective. Christians in countries such as the Philippines face the problem of trying to develop compassionate friendships while being realistic. Missionaries especially are loathe to appear critical.[19]

18. Heather J. Sharkey, Assistant Professor of Asian and Middle Eastern Studies, University of Pennsylvania, selects 17 anti-missionary books as a sampling ("only a fraction"), in *International Bulletin of Missionary Research*, July 2004, p. 104-106. New Haven: OMSC. Several of these books blatantly distort facts, take statements out of context, and quote Christian liberals who have converted to Islam.
19. For more on Islam, see Appendix H.

Risk vs. Security—Finding the Balance

As I sat with Phil Parshall, the Muslims who stopped to chat were moderates. But Phil and Julie were aware of the risks they faced. Just around the corner from Phil's bookstall, militants had shot two Filipino Christians who were telling people about Jesus.

Later, Phil and Julie lost a close friend, shot while in a violent part of the country. John Speers was a Brethren missionary who, with his wife Brenda, who had already served a term in the Philippines, but felt called to work with Phil and Julie among southern Muslims living in the Manila area. For intensive language and culture orientation, the Speers first spent a few weeks with an SIM family on the southern island of Maguindanao.[20] Seeking to understand Islam and relate to its followers, John decided to fast during the same period as Muslim villagers. That meant no food or drink during daylight hours—eating only during the night. Brenda was supportive of him in this.

If Muslims felt they were honoring God by suffering from hunger during daylight, in Ramadan (a lunar month), John could at least refrain from offending them, by abstaining while they fasted. Moreover, he could identify with them in their community life. Fast-keepers felt they were seeking after God, and John and Brenda lived among them to show how to find God through Jesus Christ. Of course, there were mixed reactions, but for the most part, villagers approved.

One day as John was out practising conversational language, four men walked up behind him, one shooting him in the back of the head. "Gaining benefit [in witnessing] from keeping the fast does not come without risks," John had written in *Evangelical Missions Quarterly*.[21] Less than a month after sending the article to *EMQ*, John was dead.

"John and I were like brothers," Phil reminisced. "He was a Jim Elliot in the making!"

"We know who killed Mister John," friendly Filipinos told Brenda Speers and other missionaries. "Just say the word, and we'll kill them!" The missionaries didn't accept their offer.

---

20. The team on Maguindanao included ICF (which entered the Philippines in 1984 before merging with SIM), OMF, SEND (formerly Far Eastern Gospel Crusade), advised by SIL (Wycliffe Bible Translators).

21. J. Speers, "Ramadan: Should missionaries keep Muslim fast?" *EMQ*, Oct. 91, p.356. Wheaton: EMIS.

"I bear no grudge against the man who killed my husband," Brenda told amazed onlookers when she visited the spot marked with her husband's blood. "We came here because we love you!" Although grieving over the loss she and their children had suffered, Brenda felt that God was going to speak in an unusual way through such a sacrifice. She was right—several Filipino Christians (who normally keep their distance from Muslims), volunteered to take Jon's place in showing God's love to Muslims.

"Some might say we should pull out of high-risk areas," Phil told me. "That's not how many national Christians feel. I remember how disappointed our Bengali friends were when most missionaries left under pressure. Bengali Christians *had* to live there!

"Yet we must never pressure anyone to go or stay—each person, each family, has to find God's will in particular circumstances. Missions constantly need wisdom finding the balance between reasonable risk and sensible security. The Apostle Paul told 'supporters' that the Holy Spirit was compelling him to spread the gospel in Jerusalem, even though the same Spirit told him he'd face uncertainty, imprisonment, and hardship."[22]

When the Parshalls went on furlough, my brother and his wife took the Parshall's place, Dave as team leader. He confirmed Phil's reports of unbelievable stress the team underwent: kidnapping threats and extortion demands, missionaries and Filipino associates killed, along with team problems of illness and exhaustion resulting in petty quarrelling. Muslims had vowed to get rid of every Christian working among them; missionaries felt satanic oppression. Every team member had to leave for one reason or another, with the exception of two couples. When Operation Mobilisation's ship, Doulos, called at the local port of Zamboanga, militants lobbed hand grenades into one of their meetings, injuring 30 and killing two.[23] (Patrick and Jill Johnstone of *Operation World* well remember the year, 1991, because their son was then serving on board the Doulos.)

I was to learn more about the religious ideologies that peaceful Filipinos faced.

---

22. Acts 20.22-24.

23. Deborah Meroff, *Footsteps in the Sea*; Elaine Rhoton, *The Doulos Story* (see Bibliography).

Manifest Destiny Meets Jihadists

"They will treat you this way because of my name, for they do not know the One who sent me." "The time will come when those who kill you will think they do God a favour" (John 15.21; 16.2).

THE SOUTHERN ISLAND of Mindanao is the center of an Islamic secessionist movement that has troubled the nation for decades. The Philippine's 7,000+ islands (only 700 inhabited), plus countless hidden coves and jungle-lined rivers, make it impossible for security forces to control what goes on. Untamed wilderness provides haven for Communist rebels, Islamic militants, political terrorists, and drug dealers alike. Reportedly, a cell of Al-Quaeda is based there.

Bodily Sacrifices

The Christian world was shocked when Abu Sayyaf militants (a Maoist splinter group which at one time demanded expulsion of all missionaries from the southern islands) kidnapped Martin and Gracia Burnham of New Tribes Mission as they celebrated their 18th wedding anniversary at an island resort in May 2001. Martin had grown up in the Philippines, where his parents had been missionaries since 1969. The rebels also took others hostage.

For a horrendous year the kidnappers and hostages slept in the jungle, forced to keep on the move. Yet all that time, the Burnhams showed only love toward their captors. On a trek, Martin would offer to help carry part of a young terrorist's load. At night, as a guard shackled him to a tree to prevent escape, Martin would thank him and wish him "Good night!" The couple sang hymns and choruses as they hiked, encouraging fellow captives.

In 2002, government Rangers finally located the terrorists and on June 7 moved in while the hostages slept. Martin died in the crossfire. Soldiers rescued Gracia and the other hostages[1]—gaunt, frail, but alive.

"Martin's peace and politeness always amazed me," Gracia said as she recovered, thankful to rejoin her three worried children. "The day before Martin's death, we sat beside each other during a breather in trekking. We thought of all the things we could give thanks for: our boots, life, every Filipino Christian we could name, our families and friends and churches who were praying for us. Once more we prayed for our captors, with whom we'd been sharing the gospel every chance we had. We prayed that somehow God's Word would enter their hearts, and they'd turn to Christ."

Gracia (whose name means Grace) remembers Martin's quoting Psalm 100, vs. 2: "Serve the Lord with gladness: come before His presence with singing."

"We might not leave this jungle alive, Dear," Martin once confided, turning to Grace and giving her a gentle kiss, "But at least we can leave this world serving the Lord with gladness. We can serve him right here—with *gladness!*" And that's what Martin and Gracia had done.

Such tragic scenes may imply that all the islands are aflame. However, not every Muslim is a militant. One of Dave and Bev Fuller's sons, Jonathan, with his wife, Marilyn, and their three children lived for several years in a coastal Muslim village. It took time to overcome the fears and suspicions that centuries of conflict had built. Hope of some material benefit from these 'Americanos' balanced the community's initial concerns. As Jon and Marilyn shared village life and learned the language,

1. Several hostages as well as Gracia provided these details of the Burnhams' ordeal and witness.

their Muslim neighbors' fears faded. The Fullers became part of the community. In time the village head and elders worked with Jon and Marilyn and their team to develop a community preschool and water project.

It was only when orthodox Muslim teachers came to "purify" the villagers' Folk Islam[2] that problems arose.

"Get rid of those Christians!" the Qur'anic teachers demanded. "They pollute your village. It's like having pigs running around!"

The village leaders quietly yet firmly defended their guests. "How do you expect us to send them away?" they argued. "They have been the means of *ridski*[3] from Allah for our community."

For the Fullers, the village was a hands-on experience in reaching out to Muslims, providing the core of Jonathan's thesis on Islam and Christianity in the Philippines: *Cross Currents.*[4] When Jon and Marilyn left the village for "home assignment," Filipino Christians volunteered to continue their village ministry— in their culture a courageous and sacrificial thing for them to undertake.

Invasions, Wars, Revolutions

That title certainly is apt for the tides that meet in the Philippine archipelago. Worldwide, other "hot zones" have been a focal point of Christendom,[5] Islam, and sovereign power, but this island chain presents a unique juxtaposition.

A chain of more than 7,000 verdant islands stretch 1800 km. (1120 mi.) between Taiwan and Borneo, lying across the vortex formed by the South China Sea (on the West), the Pacific Ocean (on the East), and the Celebes Sea (on the South). Several islands bear distinctly Malayo-Indian

---

2. The Islamic Sufi faith that travelled via Indonesia was distinct from Arabic Islam, absorbing mystic elements as it passed through ancient Persia and the Indian sub-continent's Hindu and Buddhist filters.

3. *Ridski*: blessing.

4. Jonathan Fuller, *Cross Currents* (see Bibliography).

5. See definition under Appendix F: Religions of the World/Christendom (as distinct from *Christianity*).

names, such as Mindanao and the Visayas, their people reflecting a mixture of Malayan, Polynesian, and Chinese features. In fact, China ruled the islands for a brief time and so did Japan during its occupation (WW II). In spite of many tribal wars (or because of oppressive invaders?), Filipinos are generally gentle, a people of light-brown complexion and short stature.

The position of these islands inevitably invited influences from trading powers. Millennia ago, apparently there was a land bridge with the mainland—which historians think dark-skinned pygmies crossed, finding sanctuary in the jungle hills now known as Negros Island. More than 2,000 years ago, the Ifugeros (likely from Taiwan) arrived and terraced the hills of Luzon,[6] lacing them with irrigation canals.

But obviously many influences hop-scotched eastward along the Indonesian islands and the Sulu Archipelago (the Philippine's southern chain) and sought to spread northwards. Early traders brought Hindu and Buddhist elements, followed by Muslim traders, who controlled the Spice Islands' sea trade with Europe. Islamic rule over the southern island of Maguindanao began in 1475, a useful base for Muslim slavers to raid neighboring islands—a little more trouble than buying spices, but slaves fetched a fine price in the Middle East and Europe.[7]

In 1521, Portuguese explorer Magellan landed but was killed. In 1565 the Spaniard Miguel Lopez de Legaspi claimed the islands for Spain, naming them in honor of the king, Philip II, who had commissioned him. It was only some seventy years since Spain had defeated the Muslim Moors of North Africa, who had ruled them for 700 years.

While eager to get in on the East's lucrative trade, Philip must have possessed some moral sensibility. He warned his explorer not to offend or enslave the people (except Muslims, who were already enslaving non-Muslims). Instead, the king commissioned the conquistadors to establish

---

6. The northern and largest of the islands. The terraces still produce bumper rice harvests.

7. Before I get too worked up about such wicked Arab traders, I remind myself that Romans earned a tidy shekel selling some of my enslaved ancestors from the Islands of Anglia (England *et al.*).

trade, sovereignty, and the faith. They told islanders that their only purpose was to bring knowledge of the Holy Catholic Faith—but this wouldn't be possible unless they acknowledged the Spanish king's sovereignty!

Iberian Catholic missionaries (closely tied in with Spain's government) did much to unite the impoverished islands, bringing literature, technology, and medicine. But reaction to the earlier Muslim occupation of Spain now played out in the Philippines. I tried to take an objective view of history:

> At the time, Muslims (whether sea pirates, land bandits, or governments) straddled the East-West trade routes. Europe, emerging from medieval somnolence, looked upon Muslims as a blockade to direct access to the East's riches. Christendom (political power hand-in-hand with religion) saw Islam as The Great Enemy—a view reciprocated by Islam's portrayal of Christendom as The Great Satan.
>
> To Spain, its occupation of the Philippines achieved three ends: (1) overcoming another Muslim ("Moorish") power; (2) extending the reach of sovereign and church to combat the evils of paganism; and (3) opening this section of the trade route to direct access. (Spain considered the islands as a stepping-stone to establishing direct trade with China.)

Inquisition and Revolution

This was the background of the "Christianity" that had arrived in the Philippines. Its confrontational invasion formed the Moros' view of Christianity, and its morbid legalism set the pattern for Filipino Christianity. As evangelical missionaries later arrived, these were the attitudes that faced them.

But the liberty that followed the American Revolution on the other side of the Pacific sparked Filipino interest. Priestly legalism, harsh enforcement, and failure to train indigenous clergy ignited a popular revolution in 1896. Although its leaders tortured and massacred a number of priests, they were rejecting the cruel church, not Christianity. In fact, the rebels declared the Filipino Republic "the first Christian republic in the Orient."

That was the beginning of the end of Spanish authority, for in 1898 Spain lost its war with America.[8] But when USA freed the archipelago from Spain, revolutionaries were stunned that the American Republic seemed to side with the Iberian State Church—re-instating the priests. Revolution turned into reformation as America governed the Protectorate for the first three decades of the 20th c. By 1934, the U.S. committed itself to sponsor The Commonwealth of the Philippines, in 1946 recognizing its Independence. (Muslim leaders in Maguindanao would have preferred remote US rule, rather than coming under rule of the "Christian North.")

The cauldron still boils, though. Moros continue their protest against rule by the "infidel," while over in Spain, North African terrorists claim occasional revenge.[9] But Spain and America seem to have patched up their quarrels even though the Spanish-American War had robbed Spain of its divinely ordained sovereignty over the Philippines and Cuba!

The first **Protestant** venture in the Philippines was by (*surprise!*) two former Catholics, who had become Protestants in Spain. They turned up in 1889 with Bible portions translated (for the first time) in a Filipino dialect. Both fell ill, and the Spanish (still in charge in 1889) put an end to their efforts. As America took over the islands, army chaplains sponsored the YMCA—the first continuing Protestant ministry. Many other Protestants felt they must not leave the Philippines prey to western commerce and vices infesting the Pacific islands. Besides, Christ had commissioned his followers to go into all the world. Didn't that include the Philippines?

By 1901 several denominational societies had established an Evangelical Union to coordinate mission deployment and avoid duplication.[10] Missionaries had compassion for people obsessed with

8. The Spanish-American War was actually over possession of Cuba, but was won in the Philippines!
9. Authorities blamed the 2005 Madrid train bombings on North African terrorists.
10. A general practice on the part of most missions worldwide. Until the 1950s, "comity agreements" did avoid duplication and rivalry, but the drift of people to cities following WWII meant that members of different denominations formed churches affiliated with their particular denomination, regardless of where they moved. Also, as some missions lost an evangelical emphasis (even though they continued to aid social development through schools and hospitals), evangelicals felt free to evangelize anywhere, although usually consulting with groups already there.

religion but without spiritual peace—either in fear of evil spirits or struggling under syncretistic Christian ritual.

"Manifest Destiny" Manifested

It's also true that Christian mission societies were products of their day, and often reflected the assumption (shared by education, politics, and trade) that Western powers had a duty to export their civilization to less developed parts of the world. Today, in our superior (!) wisdom, it's easy to criticize that attitude now, because we look at the world as we now see it, not as explorers and pioneers found it. In their era, the following described much of the Philippines :

- women treated as mules or worse—mules were more valued;
- high maternal death-rate during childbirth;
- high infant mortality and low life expectancy;
- periodic famine, poverty, and endemic disease;
- social segregation (tantamount to caste) and slavery;
- tribal warfare and plundering tyrants;
- creativity suppressed through fear of offending some god or spirit;
- taboos harmful to human life (e.g., eating proteins, and planting banned).

Missionaries were painfully aware of these conditions, but "tolerant society" back home could not imagine such injustice. In the same way, William Carey's reports of appalling conditions had seemed incredible to Europeans. People in the UK couldn't accept Amy Carmichael's early graphic reports; after her first book, she had to tone down her descriptions.[11] German friends of Ziegenbalg (see Ch. 8 re. South India pioneer) refused to print his research about Hindu gods.

But while noting injustice and destructive customs, benevolence was just as well intended then as it is today, as agencies now combat AIDS, infanticide, female abuse, and hunger. However, human pride can pervert altruism into a sense of superiority. If Europeans remembered that the appalling conditions in Asia had once been common in Europe, humility could have tempered conceit.[12] And in fact it did—as shown by the comment of the 16th c. preacher, John Bradford, when he and a friend passed a drunk slumped in a gutter: "There, but for the grace of God, goes John Bradford!"[13]

Noble Savage vs. Superior Civilization?

In his book, *Missionary Methods—St. Paul's or Ours?*[14] Anglican Roland Allen noted the sidetracking of missions from their New Testament course. In the Philippines during the 60s, American theologian, historian, and missionary Gerald H. Anderson sensed an almost subliminal sense of Manifest Destiny among some missions. He felt this "had its roots in the concepts of Anglo-Saxon racial superiority, of America as the center of civilization in the westward course of empires, the primacy of American political institutions, the purity of American Protestant Christianity, and the desirability for English to be the language of mankind."[15]

Secularism and Christianity were in a bind—and nowhere more than in the Pacific. On the one hand, Margaret Mead's "Noble Savage" fit the social evolutionary concept of an innocent world that would get better if interfering missionaries didn't impose their religious mores! On the other hand, Roman and Iberian Catholicism implemented the Pope's "Manifest Destiny." That concept had already driven Islam's expansion (see Appendix H), but it seeped into some Protestant altruism as well.

In returning to New Testament principles, evangelicals had to buck long-established expectations. Manifest Destiny involved denominational control from overseas and financial largesse. As a result, when the C. & M. A. began work in the Philippines (1901), it ran into resentment when it wouldn't pay national pastors from overseas.[16]

---

11. Carmichael's first book was accurately titled, *Things as They Are* (see Bibliography)—no cover-up!
12. Before Europe captured slaves for its colonies, Imperial Rome rated Britons their most stupid slaves!
13. Fuller, *People of the Mandate, op. cit.*, p. 170. Some have condemned Bradford's statement as arrogant, as if Bradford implied divine privilege. Instead, the pastor was *identifying* with the rest of fallen mankind. He knew God's saving grace could redeem anyone—him included. It only required one's acceptance.
14. Roland Allen—see Bibliography.
15. G.H. Anderson, ed., *Studies in Philippine Church History* (see Bibliog.). See also England, John C. *et al., Asian Christian Theologies* (Bibliog.).
16. Fuller, *Mission-Church Dynamics, op. cit.*, p. 36.

More recently arrived interdenominational missions have followed the same self-support policy, and have seen churches develop their giving while avoiding the stigma of being "paid foreign agents." After WW II, a number of Americans who had helped free the Philippines from Japanese occupiers returned as missionaries in order to help the people they had learned to love and respect.

Methodist Gerald Anderson, with his wife Joanne, carried valuable lessons with them as they returned to USA. In 1976, Gerald became Director of the Overseas Ministries Study Center, where missionaries and mission professors could amicably and profitably study and exchange sometimes-conflicting views, aided by biblical exposition. "Jerry" (as he called himself) also sought to revive Methodism's earlier evangelical missionary emphasis by helping to establish the Mission Society for United Methodists, serving on its board for twenty years.

From these islands, with their complex history and population mosaic, have come Christian ministries that also benefit the rest of our world. In the Philippines, Jim Montgomery developed the concept of DAWN (Discipling A Whole Nation). Launched in 1974, it used a multi-media approach to evangelize and teach, with the vision of starting 50,000 churches by the turn of the century. (Although using a typically American "numbers" approach, DAWN did achieve 40,000 by 2000.) In 1978 its goal was to raise up 2,000 missionaries by 2000—a goal it exceeded. Churches in other countries have used the basic concept to motivate members to concentrate on discipleship. A number of training schools prepare Filipino missionaries, who now serve in 77 other islands or countries, with nearly 3,000 serving in 122 agencies.

In the Philippines, Christians make good use of media communications, with their own Christian TV channel, audiovisual films, radio broadcasts, and printing presses. People have viewed and heard the Jesus Film in 25 languages, and another 41 are in progress. So far, 75% of the population has seen the film. Health Communications Resources, sponsored by several Filipino and expatriate organizations, trains lay leaders in promoting village health. The Translators Association of the Philippines, indigenous offshoot of Wycliffe (SIL), lists 60 language New Testaments or Bibles in print, with another 44 language translations in progress.

Gold in the Garbage

"Before you leave, you have to see Smokey Mountain!" said a Filipino friend, Ronaldo. We drove to Manila's infamous landfill dump (since closed). A mile away, I saw smoke of smoldering garbage spiraling upwards as we drove to the base of the largest dump I've ever seen—a "mountain," rhetorically speaking. Poverty-stricken Filipinos discovered "gold" in the garbage. Families foraged for anything they could sell for re-cycling. They lived in shacks of salvaged wood, metal, plastic, and cardboard.

"Can you make a living here?" I asked one scavenging father. He assured us he could feed his five children, and he didn't pay rent! Filipinos are entrepreneurs, even if so many are poor. Still, the polluted air was bad for their health. Many died young of respiratory complications. A Filipino priest, Fr. Benigno Beltran, moved in with the squatters, drawing the government's attention to their plight. The government has since closed Smokey Mountain, and scavengers have moved to other dumps.[17]

Ronaldo told me his church assists one of several pastors who minister to these squatters. Aid agencies help families move off the dumps, into other occupations. On Sunday, we attended Diliman Bible Church, an OMF-related church in nearby Quezon City, capital of the Philippines. Its congregation provides help for both spiritual and physical ministries—all in Jesus' name. The pastor, Dr. Isabelo Magalit—a powerful preacher—later became President of Asian Theological Seminary.

The caliber of young indigenous leadership God is raising impressed me when the executive of the Alliance of Bible Christian Communities of the Philippines (ABCCOP)[18] invited me to meet with them. Typical of a young indigenous church with no traditional ties, they were curious about SIM's indigenous churches in other lands—how were they structured, administered, financed, taught? What was their missionary

---

17. At the time, city landfill sites were often the only space displaced refugees could find to live. The government has since tried to provide better campsites for refugees.

18. ABCCOP lists 450 congregations, 20,000 members, 50,000 adherents—an association initially founded by converts from the work of OMF and SEND (formerly Far East Gospel Crusade—which grew out of the spiritual concern of a group of American soldiers who helped free islanders during WWII). TEAM (formerly Scandinavian Evangelical Alliance Mission) and Regions Beyond Missionary Union (which merged with West Indies Mission to form World Team) have joined with ABCCOP churches.

outreach? These were young, Bible-grounded leaders plugged into meeting poverty's needs, but also finding their way between extremes of syncretism and ritual churchianity. They faced pressures from materialism, politics, and Islamic militancy.

"Before you go, please lead us in prayer," they asked after our discussion. I hardly knew how to pray, apart from using Paul's benediction as he was leaving the young Ephesian church: "I commit you to God and to the word of his grace, which can build you up and give you an inheritance among all those who are sanctified."[19]

Later, as my flight lifted up and over this cluster of lush islands, the scene was disarmingly peaceful. But down below, one of those green specks hid a great tragedy. The side of a mountain ridge had slid down and literally buried—in 30 meters (about 100 feet) of mud and rock—a whole village of some thousand people. The disaster reflected the Philippines' greatest problem: its population may double by 2034.

Iberian Catholicism not only encourages large families but bans any form of birth control. Loggers and developers push further into hill-tribe territory; hungry farmers seek new land for crops, burning off brush cover. All this threatens the existence of ethnic minorities and leaves hillsides unstable on islands inundated with rainfall.[20]

****

Filipinos, some of the happiest people in the world, are loving and lovable, generous in spirit and rich in culture. But the burgeoning population's potential is shackled by a background combination of Iberian Catholic ritual and traditional spiritism,[21] *impoverished by corruption, mismanagement, and crime. However, throughout the islands, Jesus has followers—from hill tribesmen to urban high-techies—who provide witness and leadership, the bright hope of a promising people.*

---

19. Acts 20.32
20. In some parts, the jungle wilderness is fast disappearing due to extensive logging—some illegal but some due to corruption. A century ago, more than half of the land area was forest. Now only 70,000 sq. km. remains under forest. Result: loss of wildlife habitat, devastating flash floods, and mudslides.
21. Iberian Catholic ritualism: sin today; receive a priest's absolution tomorrow (for a fee). Spiritism: sin freely, protected by paying a shaman and wearing talismans, including a crucifix around the neck.

Section – III

EAST ASIA

The famed "Star Ferry" ploughs across the strait between Hong Kong island and the Kowloon mainland.

Sun Like Thunder – **20: Oriental Drama**

The Middle Kingdom's Heart

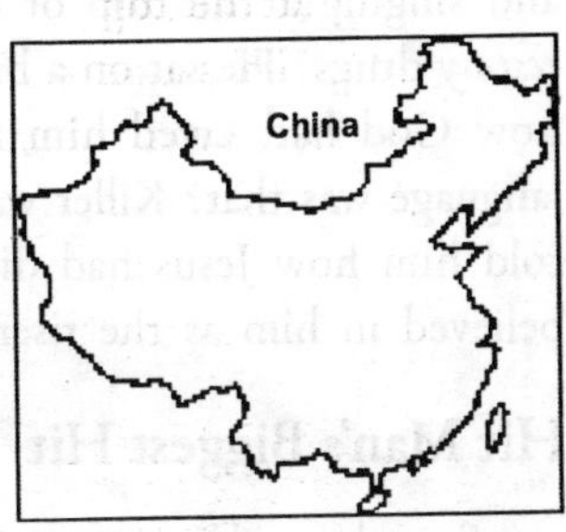

China: Pop. 1,356,939,193

"A highway will be there; it will be called the Way of Holiness . . . The redeemed of the Lord will walk there. . . . Gladness and joy will overtake them, and sorrow and sighing will flee away" (Isaiah 35.5-10).

"EXCUSE ME, GUYS, while I take this phone call from Hong Kong," Kevin Frost called to the other members of his band during a recording session in London. M—[1], a missionary friend, was on the line.

"Can you come to show a Triad gang how to produce an album?" M— was asking. Kevin had read her reports of remarkable things God was doing in Hong Kong. Like Kevin's mother, M— had quite a ministry among prisoners and gang members. But to help a criminal gang make a CD recording? Was this a joke?

No joking, Kevin realized when he heard the details. The hit man of a notorious Triad[2] Gang in Hong Kong, "Killer," had become fed up with his life on the run. He decided to opt out of gang life. Before skipping town, he filled his knapsack with his gang's money. They owed

1. Actual name withheld by request.
2. Triad: British term for criminal gangs who used the triangle symbol of the "Three Harmonies Society" (Heaven, Earth, Man)—originally a resistance movement to overthrow the Manchu Qing Dynasty (18th c.). When the Qing fell, the Triad split up and turned into criminal "triads."

it to him, didn't they, after all the assassinations he'd carried out for them? He booked in at a fancy hotel on another island—under an assumed name, of course.

Enjoying his new life of luxury and anonymity, Killer went out for a stroll one evening, when he heard lively music coming from a large tent. Looking inside, he was amazed to see a crowd of young people clapping and singing at the top of their voices. About what? Were they all on *ecstasy* drugs? He sat on a back row of folding chairs as an evangelist told how God had saved him from criminal life. "Saved"? What kind of language was that? Killer waited around to talk with the evangelist, who told him how Jesus had died like a criminal, in order to save all who believed in him as the risen Saviour.

Hit Man's Biggest Hit

Somehow that went straight to the young thug's heart. After the evangelist prayed with him, he went back to his room a changed man—he was now only Chu Li, but a redeemed Chu Li. He spent the next couple of days reading a Bible he found in the hotel room.[3] He couldn't understand the transformation in his life. In place of anger, he now had inner peace, as if he'd been searching for this all his life. And he wasn't on *ecstasy*!

"What of the money I've stolen?" he wondered. According to what he read in the Bible about confession and walking in the light, he'd have to take that money (or what was left of it) back to the gang and confess his theft. The Triad code vowed death for anyone deserting the gang. Could he tell them? He had to, even if it meant the end of the road. Now he at least knew where he'd be after death.

When he walked into the gang's hideout back in Hong Kong, they waved their sawed-off shotguns and pistols in salute for their hit man. Where had he been? Chu the Killer stood in the middle of the floor and quietly told them he'd found Christ as his Saviour; so he'd come back to confess he'd stolen their money. He was sorry—and he'd leave everything he had, to repay the money he'd stolen.

3. I've found Bibles in hotel rooms all around the world, placed by the Gideons, bless 'em! —WHF

"But guys—I don't belong here any more," he announced. "I'm leaving the gang!" Dropping to his knees on the floor, he prayed for the gang members. Eyes closed, Chu waited for the inevitable bullet through his head. Instead, only silence! Cautiously, he opened his eyes and peered around the room. The gang members appeared stunned. Several bowed their heads.

"Tell us—how does this work?" they asked incredulously. They'd never had a Triad member, let alone their toughest hit man, confess anything. And he was *quitting the gang*? Killer must have run into some powerful stuff!

So tell them, Chu did. If Jesus could find him, holed up in a luxury hotel on another island, God could find anyone. If Jesus could give their hit man assurance of sins forgiven, of eternal life, anyone could find that peace. If Jesus could bring him back to confess he'd stolen their money, anything was possible. The gang heard him out. One by one they too dropped to their knees and ended up trusting in Christ. They asked Chu to start a Bible study for them all.

The Triads had often protected druggies' rock bands. They'd dreamed of starting their own band. A couple of them could strum guitars and one ex-drug dealer was good on drums. Now maybe they could start a Jesus Rock Band! They got involved with a local church music group. Some of them had met "M" during her prison visits, so they asked if she knew anyone who could show them how to produce a quality album. They wanted to get their Good News to gangs they used to shoot it out with. "M" was a prayer partner of Kevin's missionary parents[4] and knew that Kevin had produced several albums for major record groups, written music for London and Broadway hits, and received awards.

Kevin had been to many places with his music industry, but this assignment topped them all. He met the former gang in Honk Kong and helped them record and produce their new music. Within six months, the "Jesus Rock Band" was drawing crowds—not because of their

---

4. Derek and Kathy Frost had been our neighbors in Africa. Derek won global media awards for SIM documentaries, his videos and DVDs competing with international commercial promotions.

latest assassination hit, but because of the converted gang's latest gospel music hit.

World's Most Fascinating City

I could visualize the whole scenario, for I'd been to Hong Kong several times. While missionary pioneers traversed the Old Spice Roads (land and sea routes) the hard way, I took the easy way—a Cathay[5] Pacific airliner that slid in between high-rise buildings (a scary experience in itself, but skillfully handled!).

Hong Kong was still a colony of Britain on my first visit. I stayed with our SIM Honorary Secretary and her husband—Lena and Stephen Lau. When Lena learned I was turning 60, she went out and purchased fresh prawns and vegetables, invited friends and threw a memorable party. With typical Chinese hospitality, Lena cooked up steaming dishes of sweet-and-sour pork ribs, shrimp, *bok choi*, and bean paste-filled dumplings. For the Western guest, a candle-decked birthday cake completed the menu, served with endless cups of Oolong tea.[6] "In Chinese culture, the 60th birthday is very special!" my hosts explained. (Something to do with attaining the age of wisdom?)

Chinese are fastidious shoppers. Anything and everything was available in the high-rise malls—levels of shops stacked on top of each other (no space to build except up). Housewives normally shop every day for fresh vegetable, fruit, fish, and fowl—market vendors keeping the creatures alive until someone purchases them.

In my travels, I discovered how protective regional cooks are of their cuisine, with major differences between North and South. A popular chef in Guizhou province criticized more northerly Sichuan chefs for contaminating spicy stir-fry *gong bao jiding*—even adding peanuts. Unforgivable! However, diets are changing. While China has been the

---

5. Though later applied to China, "Cathay" was a European form of a term derived from the Qidan of Mongolia, who ruled North China from 916-1125. As to the airport, Honk Kong now boasts a modern terminal on Lantau Island, a city expressway link crossing the water on massive floating pontoons.
6. *Oolong*: Xiamen for "black dragon"—tea made from only partially fermented leaves.

world's biggest consumer of dog meat, animal rights groups have made this delicacy less popular, and more people are enjoying dogs as pets, not as their "pet" food.

But the Laus were cosmopolitan—Stephen (from Tianjin in the north) was a mechanical engineer, while Lena (from Guilin/Kuilin in the south-west) was Lecturer in Linguistics at Hong Kong University. Both were active in Christian ministry, Stephen with the Christian and Missionary Alliance; Lena with SIM. They arranged for me to speak in churches, seminaries, missionary training schools, and to InterVarsity groups. I found a vibrant Christian community, ranging from radio programs to student ministries, from university students to graying elders.

Stephen and Lena's high-rise was one of many that looked over the previous haunts of Killer and his Triad gang in the busy harbor. From the Laus' tiny balcony, I viewed passenger ferries and private craft crisscrossing the harbor. Tugs guided a freighter to its berth. Square-sailed junks[7] lined the docks and shores. People lived year-round on many of the junks. South China Sea moisture spiraled upwards like fluffy whipped cream above Hong Kong's high-rise office buildings.

Crowded the city is, but the crowds add to this bustling city's exhilarating atmosphere. Several million mainland Chinese as well as refugees from south-east Asia swell the population. Everything was on the move: vehicles on narrow roads; people on narrow sidewalks. In daylight, passenger planes landed and took off from an airstrip built on reclaimed land, while buses and ferries plied their routes 18 hours a day. Some high-rise buildings were miniature factories, with tinkers and cobblers, tailors and joss-stick[8] makers busily turning out products from single rooms (their combined living and working quarters). Hong Kong has to be the most fascinating city I've ever stayed in![9]

I enquired how this anomalous enclave came into existence. Before Hong Kong reverted to China in 1997, every evening the island's radio and TV stations signed off with the British national anthem, to the surprise of non-Commonwealth visitors.

---

7. Portuguese *jonco,* from Javanese: *jon*—small Chinese sailing vessel.
8. Buddhist prayer incense sticks. Joss: <Pidjin English for Portuguese *deus* (god).
9. Hong Kong's Stock Exchange now outranks New York's in initial public offerings (IPOs).

As 1997 approached, foreigners found it hard to comprehend that many Chinese wanted to stay independent of the mainland. Hong Kong's entrepreneurs were afraid they'd lose their international commerce. Newspapers daily headlined million dollar investments the colony's tycoons were putting their money into overseas.[10] However, to the government of China, it was essential for the nation's sovereignty to reunite Hong Kong with the rest of China. They viewed the 1842 Nanjing Treaty (which, among other things, had ceded the island in perpetuity to Britain) as "unequal" and unfair.

"China's Supreme Leader Deng did agree that Hong Kong could maintain its way of life for 50 years," Stephen and Lena Lau later explained, referring to Deng's reassurance that "horseracing and dancing" (his aphorism for the colony's lifestyle) would continue. Of course, there were a number of pragmatic reasons.[11]

And while the ex-colony shared in the global economic downturn around the turn of the century, it has maintained its entrepreneurial spirit.[12] Typical is its telecoms industry. Telephone companies from around the world stop off in Hong Kong to see its remarkable breakthrough in use of broadband technology, world leader in deploying television over broadband phone lines. Hong Kong still hums along smoothly, with the highest GDP per person in a list of 26 countries, outside of North America and Europe. Currently it is the hub (and chief investor) of China's Pearl River Delta (PRD)—one of China's three most important economic zones. In fact, PRD (population 65m) exports are greater than those of south Korea and India.[13]

Shameful Trade in Opium

As to the West's moral degeneracy, the 19th c. "Opium Wars" shaped the Orient's view. To me, Britain's backing of the Opium trade, in collusion

10. At the time, sending real estate skyrocketing in Vancouver, Toronto, and California!
11. In a list of 159 countries, Transparency International rated Hong Kong 15th least corrupt, vs. the rest of China in 82nd position (*Economist*, Oct. 22, 2005).
12. Hong Kong ranked highest in Canada's Fraser Institute's '06 Economic Freedom of the World Index.
13. It is highly likely readers of this travelogue possess wristwatches, electronics, apparel, footwear, or toys made in the zone.

with France, Russia, the USA, and Chinese merchants, is one of history's most shameful episodes. The iniquitous trade was inexcusable, but it was part of a much larger picture.

For one thing, Britain's gunboats hadn't sailed up the Yellow River to Guanzou in order to sell opium, but to establish a mutual diplomatic and trade zone—one of many "Treaty Ports" eventually opened. The West saw this as restoring China's earlier trade, when China dominated the sea routes.[14] Offshore Chinese wanted to restore that trade, merchants reasoned. The East India Company saw China as a handy market for India's bumper opium crops. Opium was readily available from Chinese smugglers—why not get in on the trade "legitimately," through an official pact? After all, opium was only one of many products Chinese and foreigners traded, and at the time there wasn't public opprobrium—British gentlemen acceptably "snorted" snuff.[15]

The West did not understand China's psyche and implications—what made it hostile to outside knowledge at the time.[16] As a result the West placed China at a crippling disadvantage internally and externally. And no rationale excuses the flood of opium along with other trade items. If anyone points out that Lin Zexu's confinement of foreign traders sparked the British-French trade war against China, the ethical Mandarin Imperial Commissioner was only trying to stop opium trade by confiscating their opium stocks. Not only was it a social evil, but it also drained the supply of silver—thus threatening the Emperor's tax system. (Foreign traders as well as China's government accepted only silver, not the market's copper coins).

---

14. See Chapter 18.
15. Inhaling ground-up tobacco powder.
16. The Chinese ethic was actually very tolerant of everything except change. (Chapter 18 explains the process that led to hostility towards the outside world.) The treaties precipitated crises in China (which portrayed foreign trade as "tribute" by vassal states, in order to preserve the Emperor's sovereignty). Confucian principles divided court advisors: avoid conflict by compromise, or battle insurgent trade. (Cf. "Confucius" in Ch. 18; also Fairbanks's *China*, p. 200—Bibliog.) Western demands for diplomatic equality/powers followed Russia's precedent-setting accord on China's Western border.

Pressured from the West by Russia, from the North by Japan, and from the East by European trade, the Emperor finally signed treaties establishing "free ports"—and opium flooded into China along with other imports. It was a sad day for China, and a disgraceful day for the morality of foreign trading powers. It's true, I mused, "The whole world lies in wickedness"!

Unfortunately, trade, gunboats, and opium converged in China's collective consciousness to form a stereotype of the West. Innocent Protestant missionaries were tainted with that perception as they arrived on the traders' fast-sailing "clippers" (often the only viable way). The connection is understandable. In the Philippines, Iberian Catholic missionaries had arrived as an integral part of military force. Monks became officials of government. It was a convenient arrangement, for the State not only protected the Church but also controlled it—ensuring mutual support between Church and State.

So when Protestant missionaries began arriving in the Far East, China assumed the missionaries had the same cozy imperial relationship. Truth is, missionaries often opposed the policies of their own governments. Missionaries viewed benign neglect ("Don't disturb the natives—we want to trade with them!") to be as harmful as active aggression. Sometimes they landed in prison for speaking against destructive actions and customs (such as opium trade and foot-binding; in other lands, slavery and wife-burning), which their own governments conveniently overlooked for the sake of trade.

Missionaries Arrive in *Gunboats*?

As to the misinformed slur, "Missionaries arrived on gunboats," Nestorian missionaries had arrived that way a thousand years earlier—but the "gunboats" belonged to Muslim-Arab officials establishing diplomatic relations with China! Arabs controlled the Indian Ocean trade routes of the day, and they appreciated Nestorian missionaries as cultural advisors and language translators (from the missionaries' prior contacts). Arab *dhows* provided safety from pirates—often Arabs themselves.[17]

---

17. Of all world sea-lanes, *The Economist* lists the South China Sea as still most piracy-prone (April 26/06).

Because Western imperialism in China is relatively recent (and therefore uppermost in our judgment), we tend to lose the perspective of history—as if China's preceding centuries did not suffer from outside interference and humiliation. As I'd be finding out (see next chapter), China had been assailed by wave after wave of invaders from Inner Asia—some of whom set up Dynasties in China. In demanding extraterritorial rights[18] in the Treaty Ports, Britain, France, Holland, Portugal, Russia, and USA followed the precedent of Turks and Arabs in Central Asia and Africa. And, in spite of inequalities, China did benefit from such things as (for instance) Britain's suppression of "duty-free" smuggling, and collection of import duties under foreign diplomatic supervision. Such surrogate action was in keeping with Confucian minimalist central administration.

I tried to be objective in judging a previous era. The shameful factor was not in opening mutual trade or requesting exterritorial rights (several Asian nations already had agreements on these). The evil was in Britain's complicity in the iniquitous opium drug trade. Although I had nothing to do with that, as a Christian Westerner I feel the shame, even centuries later.

Yet I also perceived shards of light entering that murky era. For instance, one of China's foremost anti-opium philanthropists, Chen Su Lan (1885-1972) was the son of parents whose lives had earlier been shaped by Methodists missionaries. Chen's widowed mother, a nurse trained by Methodists, had fled inland when a gunboat sailed into the port city of Fuzhou. There Chen studied at a college headed by a Methodist missionary. At considerable personal risk, he fought the government's opium trade and founded the Anti-opium Clinic in Fuzhou. After fleeing from invading Japanese, he formed a trust that later gave land to Scripture Union and a Methodist children's home and church. Chen founded the Chinese Young Men's Christian Association. The address he once gave on the role of Christianity in emancipating women was most memorable.

Learning of such lights shining in darkness helped me balance the "in-your-face" stereotype of "missionaries and opium sailing together into China on gunboats!"

---

18. *E.g.,* Application of a nation's own laws in charging or protecting its citizens living within the enclave. In the case of Europeans, this sheltered them from indiscriminate action by a host nation, which at the time may not have recognized due legal process or human rights.

From Eden to Ur to China?

The Mandarin name for China, Zhong Guo, means "Middle Kingdom." To Asia's Central Plain dwellers, it was the *world's* geographic middle. On the perimeter: western Turkic invaders; northern marauding Mongol and Manchu horsemen; southern forest dwellers across the Himalayas; island raiders on the eastern edge. To Confucian elders, all were "barbarians." Only the orderly Middle Kingdom dwelt in peace with the spirits. Only *their* shamans knew how to control the *yang* and the *yin,* which affected the fortunes of man. The Middle Kingdom provided the balance between competing cosmic forces.[19]

But where had China's earliest ancestors come from? Chinese and Jews both have the world's longest preserved history, with ancient Chinese characters predating Abraham or Moses, around the era when the first pyramids were constructed.

"I have now come to the conclusion that the ancient Chinese were one of the many original nations dispersed at the Tower of Babel," states Chan Kei Thong of Shanghai, in *Faith of Our Fathers.* (See Bibliography.) He points out that the first emperors of China were monotheists, and practiced animal sacrifice as substitutionary atonement for sin, similar to Old Testament rites. The ancient Chinese character for "sacrifice" combines symbols for "bull, lamb, unblemished, spear." Symbols for "lamb" and "me" form "righteousness."

And so, it is possible that China's ancestors migrating eastward carried with them belief in one, eternal God. Later, in a world full of malevolent spirits and many gods, Jews traveling the Old Spice Road reinforced the concept that God, not forces of nature, created the universe. Contrary to superstitious beliefs that had developed, many Jewish merchants and travelers believed that the living God had placed man and woman upon the earth. It was the loving Lord God who sought to restore humanity from the pit of sin—a radical concept for Hindus and Buddhists!

---

19. Buddhism arrived in the 1st c., influencing Chinese thought. Buddhism teaches that to achieve Enlightenment (escaping from the cycle of birth after birth), one should react neither negatively nor proactively, but seek "the Middle Way" of Sublimation.

I later found evidence of that witness back in Toronto, where I reside. The Royal Ontario Museum preserves several artifacts from a Jewish synagogue once located in the former national capital of Kaifeng.[20] The leader of a local synagogue, Rabbi Debra Lansberg, told me about taking a group to China, to check out the actual site. The rabbi showed me photographs of the large stone monument now preserved in Kaifeng's museum. Its inscription describes the arrival of the Jews (likely Persian-Jewish merchants tracing their lineage back to the Babylonian Dispersion). Also recorded is the Emperor's welcome: "You have come to our China. Respect and preserve the customs of your ancestors, and hand them down here . . ."[21]

Moreover, the rabbi found a community who still call themselves Jewish. A typical Chinese hamlet welcomed the Canadian Jews—but many of the 200 or so villagers were definitely not typical Chinese. True, their eyes were oriental, but their faces were unusually long. Almost Abrahamic, I thought after seeing their photos.

"How did their ancestors settle in central China?" I asked Rabbi Lansberg. She'd asked them that, and through an interpreter, the villagers told how their merchant forefathers had traveled the Old Spice Road, married Chinese women, and settled around the capital.

Since the Kaifeng discovery, remnants of Jewish life and worship have come to light all over China. Muslim chroniclers, calling them "Radanites,"[22] claimed that Jews traded all the way from Spain to China's coast. Many settled in waystops along the route, some becoming weavers and dyers of fabrics—especially China's famed silk. At one time, China's coins were bilingual: Chinese characters on one side, Semitic on the other.

What happened to those Jews? A number of them became mandarins, under great pressure to add Confucian concepts to their culture. Intermarriage, floods, wars, and isolation during China's withdrawn

---

20. Sung Empire capital, Kaifeng at the time was likely the world's largest city (1m residents c. A.D. 1,000). Just south of the Yellow River between Beijing and Shanghai, Kaifeng straddles the Old Spice Road, connecting several caravan routes.

21. From "The Jews of Kaifeng," Beth Hatefusoth Museum, P.O.B. 39359, Tel Aviv, Israel 61392.

22. From a Persian phrase meaning, "Knowing the way." The oldest records of China's Jews are a letter written around 718 A.D. in Persian but with Hebrew letters on paper made in China, and a Hebrew penitential prayer from the 8th or 9th c., composed of Hebrew scriptures. (M. Pollak, Bibliog.)

centuries (when their contact with Jerusalem was forbidden) weakened their heritage—even though they hung on to their ancestral identity.

Before the era of the Cross of Christ, how well Jewish travelers communicated the Abrahamic prophecy, we cannot know. We do know that Jewish manuscripts, on paper found only in China, date back to 406 C.E.[23] Marco Polo related meeting Jews in China in 1286. When Jesuit Matteo Ricci (see below) met Jewish community representatives in 1605, *he* assumed they were Muslim, and *they* thought he was Jewish—because of each other's monotheism.

According to the Bible's Genesis record, the Spirit of God "hovered over the waters" of the created globe, so I assume he has also hovered over humanity itself ever since Eden. Old Testament prophets declared that the Lord looks for those who will withstand evil—or "stand in the gap" as humanity rushes headlong over the precipice of iniquity. As mankind degenerated so that "every inclination of the thoughts of his heart was only evil all the time," God had found righteousness in Noah's life. Later, the Spirit somehow lit the flame of faith within Abraham's heart, calling him out of the pagan environment of Babylon and promising to bless all nations through him.

In this saga of God and man, I recognize a biblical principle: *It is God who raises up one and sets down another.* Organization-conscious Westerner though I am, and having taught management seminars, I also have to accept that we cannot manipulate God with our methodology. He is not tied to eras, systems, and human strategies—but like the wind, his Spirit moves as he wills. That's how Jesus explained the Spirit's working to the erudite teacher, Nicodemus.[24]

So as to the spiritual effect Jewish travelers had along the Old Spice Road, we at least know that the Holy Spirit could use the news of the one and only God to cause mankind to "seek the Lord till he be found."[25] Certainly traces of monotheism existed in China long before the first Roman Catholic or Protestant missionaries arrived."[26]

23. Internet: faculty.rmwc.edu/fwebb/buck/bgoleary/jwssl;.httm (2007).
24. John 3.8.
25. Isaiah 55.6.
26. Samuel Hugh Moffett's comprehensive two volumes, *A History of Christianity in Asia* (see Bibliog.). Since historians have thoroughly researched this topic, our travelogue will only summarize events.

Marker of Burial or Victory?

Because we've thought of early Asia as "unreached," it's difficult for us today to realize the extent of Jewish and Christian contacts with the Far East in the early centuries A.D. Before the gospel reached most of Europe, Asian Jews and Christians numbered in their thousands. As early as A.D. 455 (still well before Islam), a Persian embassy, very likely including Jews and Christians, had made diplomatic contacts with the Wei Dynasty inside the Great Wall.

However, Medieval Europeans were aware of the Nestorian Monument as the most dramatic evidence of Christian presence in China.[27] Discovered in 1623 by workmen digging near China's ancient capital, the Goliath-sized block of black limestone features a cross above a lotus blossom. Its inscription tells of a Nestorian missionary's arrival in the capital in 635 (as early as Aidan's mission over in Europe, from Iona to England).

The engraved account describes the T'ang emperor's examination of the missionary's *sutras* (scriptures), which, he declared, "cover all that is most important in life. . . . So let it have free course throughout the empire." Accordingly, the emperor ordered that China's first Christian church be built in the capital. Open-minded, he similarly approved construction of Buddhist, Manichean, Taoist, and Zoroastrian places of worship. During the T'ang Dynasty, China was probably the most civilized country on earth.

Remarkable though the monument is, when Jesuits arrived in the 16th c. they saw no sign of any Christian or church. The monument could have been the tombstone of Christianity rather than an "Ebenezer" of continuing faith and hope.[28] But much more evidence came to light towards the end of the 19th c., when documents comparable in historicity to the Dead Sea Scrolls turned up in a Buddhist cave. Amazed scholars have identified at least nine *Christian* manuscripts, some dating back to the 7th c. The church was more active in China than had been thought.

27. "Nestorian" includes Nestorians doctrinally, or simply Middle East Christians (Syrian, Persian).

28. To remind Israel of God's continuing protection from enemies, the prophet Samuel raised a monument called "Ebenezer," meaning "Hitherto the Lord has helped us." 1 Samuel 7.12.

How much was syncretism and how much was spiritual regeneration, only the Holy Spirit knows. But by the end of the 7th c., there were said to be Nestorian monasteries in every prefecture, with the missionary Alopen elevated to the equivalence of "archbishop" of the Chinese realm.

The monument and documents also indicate the high level that Christians reached in China and neighboring states. The Nestorian priest Issu from Persia became a high-ranking general in the Chinese army. His care for the poor and the sick earned Chinese respect for Christianity. So skilled was he in the Chinese language that even Buddhist monks sought his help in translating the *sutras* they brought from Tibet.

Early mission outreach sometimes resulted from administrative arrangements—with emperors appointing Syrian and Persian Christians as well as Muslims to government posts because of their learning in different fields. The Chinese emperor's Turkic Uighur allies (who now form a province in China's North-West), initially favored Christianity but turned to its syncretistic counterpart, Manichaeism—easier to embrace.[29] That led to Islam's later ascendancy among the Uighur.

What happened to the legacy of Oriental Christianity? Moffett[30] cites too great dependence upon the rulers of the era for patronage. But another familiar reason seems to have been *lack of missionary evangelism and biblical teaching*. Even though many disciples had a personal faith in Christ as Saviour, the general populace viewed this "new religion" as fulfillment of social ideals. Jesus was the "perfect gentleman" of Confucian society: an obedient son, a benefactor doing good to people in need, a wise teacher, a preacher against injustice—and yet willing to sacrifice his life for the good of others.

In the end, Jesus the Savior became simply "the Example."[31] His life completed the *yang* and the *yin* of life's cycle. So the gospel lost its edge. At the same time, the Confucian concept of Jesus as the "Perfect Gentleman" was no match for Islam's aggressive inroads. Many Christians

29. Coming from Persia, Mani combined teachings of Zoroastra, Buddha, Christ, and Greek Gnosticism.

30. *Op. cit.*, Vol. I, p. 303, etc.

31. This syncretistic view has its counterpart elsewhere in liberal theology (such as Liberation Theology).

compromised their faith rather than witnessing boldly. Over in Baghdad, word among both Christians and Muslims was "the church of the Far East has died out."

Rise and Eclipse: Ecclesial and Solar

By the 1500s, however, the changing balance of world power gave opportunity for missionaries from Portugal and Italy to arrive on China's coast. Francis Xavier (whose trail I last crossed in India) had gone on to Japan and from those islands, in 1552 headed for China—but he died *en route*. Five years later, Portuguese priests established a mission in their enclave of Macao (south of Britain's Hong Kong). It would be 30 years later that RC missionaries established work on Chinese territory proper, led by an Italian priest, Alessandro Valignano. I was impressed by Valignano's evaluation of missionary work in India and the Far East—and his consequent policies when he arrived in China:

1. Don't depend on colonial trade connections—more detrimental than helpful.
2. Reach out to the unevangelized, rather than only "the faithful," as Macao had.
3. Do not follow the harsh legalism of Iberian Catholicism.[32]
4. Adopt local culture of Chinese names and clothing; learn the language.
5. Train and appoint Chinese leaders as equals with European priests

Ahead of his day, indeed! Valignano brought in another Italian, Matteo Ricci, to implement his policies. Ricci caused a sensation by giving a watch to a general—apparently an unknown instrument till then. Ricci also won Chinese confidence by his respect for their customs, his use of their language, and adoption of Confucian costume (rather than the Buddhist robes despised by educated Chinese).[33]

---

32. Spain and Portugal (the Iberian Peninsula) instituted the cruel Inquisition against suspected heresy, following the Moorish (North African Arab-Berber) Islamic occupation of the Peninsula (711-1492). See Fuller, *Tie Down the Sun* (*op. cit.*) for effects of similar Iberian Catholicism in Latin America.

33. Colman Chan of SIM states that many officials respected missionaries as "Western Confucian Scholars." Ricci sought to identify Christianity's God with the Confucian *Shangti* ("the Lord on High"). His contextualization led to "the Chinese Rites Controversy" between Jesuits (who accepted it) and Dominicans and Franciscans, who condemned it as syncretism—a debate that continues to this day.

Chinese converts rose to the highest levels of government. Xu Guangshi, a Confucian from the upper classes, met Ricci in 1600. He soon saw that the morality of the Bible surpassed that of even Confucius, and that Christianity was superior to Buddha's teaching. He asked for baptism as a Christian. Ricci encouraged him to study academics further. Xu joined the Imperial Academy and rose to become second only to the emperor. When Muslim mathematicians miscalculated a solar eclipse in the auspicious Imperial Calendar, Xu prevailed on the Bureau of Mathematics to allow a German and a Dutchman, with Chinese colleagues, to review and reform the entire process. This provoked jealousy and persecution of church leaders, but when the German, Adam Schall, forecast to the minute another eclipse in 1644, the church was vindicated.

That eclipse coincided with the beginning of the Manchu Dynasty, and so impressed were the Manchurians, they promoted Schall to the highest level of Mandarin. It was a golden era for the Church, including a towering cathedral built in Beijing itself, although factions of church orders introduced harmful wrangling that led to decline and persecution. Heated controversy arose over contextualization vs. syncretism, the conflict of Confucian rites vs. Christian rites, and the name translators should use for God. Dissension in China reverberated back in Rome, involving the Pope himself. This resulted in censure and (along with other problems elsewhere) in 1773 to the dissolution of the Jesuit Order itself *worldwide!* Most harmful was the effect on the Chinese population of church quarrels—disillusioning many. Ascendant Catholicism experienced its own eclipse.[34]

Other missionaries arrived, some unexpectedly. For instance, Russian Orthodox members found themselves in 17th c. "Peking" after being captured while exploring a disputed area of China-Russia's border. Among them was an Orthodox priest, whom the Chinese allowed to conduct Christian services in an abandoned Buddhist temple. The Russian Christians gained

---

34 China severed its Vatican ties in 1957, imprisoning many local priests but eventually allowing a state-sponsored Catholic Church, with government-appointed bishops. Anticipating the 2008 Olympics, the Pope in '07 cited the situation's "complexity," authorizing those "seeking his blessing" (*Economist* July 7/07).

respect and, with Chinese converts, grew into a community of some 80,000. While contributing to oriental theology and science, however, they neglected any spiritual outreach and eventually died out.

Lesson? *"A sound theoretical basis, together with education and goodwill, are not enough for a substantial and sustained growth of missionary work."*[35] As with the earlier Nestorians, this also applied to other Christian enclaves occupied with piety but failing to evangelize. "Animosity between ethnic groups was no doubt one of the reasons," comments Colman Chan. Christians became isolated and sterile.

History's Divine Strategist

Over the last three centuries, the Divine Strategist has put together several chain links:

1. The first Protestant missionary was Presbyterian Robert Morrison (1782-1834), who went to China under the London Missionary Society in 1807. Today we'd call him a "tent-maker," because he signed on as translator for the East India Company. (Calm down—EIC sold lots more than opium!) That gave him legal status to be in China, which by then had discouraged foreign contacts. Morrison was a prolific worker, translating the Bible into Classical Chinese along with several hymns and a prayer book. He produced a three-volume Chinese-English dictionary, a Chinese grammar, and several tracts.[36]

2. Morrison's legacy wasn't limited to literature. He inspired a German missions student, Karl Gutzlaff (1803-1851), whom he met in London. Gutzlaff sailed for Indonesia under the Dutch Mission Society, intending to evangelize Chinese living in Java and Siam (Thailand). He made several visits along the coast before entering China (in 1833) as a freelance missionary buoyed with visions of a "blitz conversion" of China. (Sounds like some upstart missions I've known—but don't let me be judgmental! I had to recall how God graciously tempered my own youthful zeal with experience—hard lumps and all!)

---

35. Anastasios Yannoulatos, quoted in Stamoolis, *Eastern orthodox mission theology today* (see Bibliog.).

36. Working with colleague William Milne. Classical is different from spoken Mandarin and Cantonese.

Karl's medical work was a forerunner of medical missions in China. He also translated Bible portions into vernacular Chinese. How much he was influenced by the Italian Valignano's earlier indigenous policies, I do not know. But donning Chinese attire and wearing the male pigtail,[37] he recruited Chinese men to distribute tracts and Scripture portions. He didn't supervise his "agents," unfortunately, and although Gutzlaff naively sent supporters glowing reports, most of the agents duped him with false accounts, to receive more payment—and more scriptures on "rice paper" (which fetched a fine market price for rolling tobacco into cigarettes!).

3. However, Gutzlaff's vision in turn stirred Baptist missionary Issachar Roberts, an American. In 1844 he became the first Protestant missionary to evangelize *outside* the foreign trade zone of Canton (Guangzhou)—something that Roman Catholics had done under an earlier dynasty, but a very courageous venture in this new era. While Gutzlaff had been naive about human nature, he rightly foresaw that Chinese Christians were the ones who, ultimately, would evangelize the nation. The indigenous Chinese Union and Chinese Associations grew out of Gutzlaff's vision, as did the Chinese Evangelization Society (CES).

4. Meanwhile, God was preparing the next link in the sequence. When I was a child, James Hudson Taylor (1832-1905) was our family's example of missionary commitment. As a boy in Yorkshire, England, the first JHT heard fascinating stories about China, told by friends of his Methodist lay-preacher father. After his conversion at age 17, the teen started preparing himself for pioneering in China. With Yorkshire determination[38] that would typify his life, the young man began learning Mandarin, purposely ate very simply, and lived in slum housing, sleeping on the bare floor to "toughen" himself up.

5. In 1853, Taylor set off for China, arriving in Shanghai in 1854, where he worked with the non-denominational China Evangelistic Society (CES) headquartered in London. However, he withdrew in 1857, continuing as an independent until 1865. After illness invalided him

37. During their Qing ("Pure") Dynasty (17th to early 19th c), Manchurian invaders from Asia's far northeast made their tonsure mandatory for males: a shaved-back forehead and braided queue. Some Roman Catholic missionaries adopted this custom, as did Gutzlaff and Hudson Taylor.

38. "I won't be druv" (driven by anyone else) was the motto on Yorkshire County's coat of arms.

back to the UK, Taylor discovered the other side of preparation for ministry—spiritual development.

"Hudson Taylor's Spiritual Secret"

Ever since teenage, Hudson (as he was known) had been transfixed by Jesus' cry from the Cross: "*It is finished!*" That being the case, reasoned Hudson, there was nothing else for him to do but accept Jesus as Saviour. Later however, after a term in China, missionary Taylor realized that the Holy Spirit had a continuing work to do within his life. As he struggled with his own weaknesses and the opposition of both friend and foe, a fellow missionary showed him a Scripture motto that changed his whole view of discipleship: "Abide in Christ."[39]

"I have striven in vain to abide in him!" Taylor regretted. "I'll strive no more. Has he not promised to abide in me—never to leave me, never to fail me?" This became known as "Hudson Taylor's Spiritual Secret." Even more than his tenacious pioneering, it has inspired generations of men and women to rest in the same spiritual truth.

While Taylor followed several of Gutzlaff's indigenous practices (referring to him as "Grandfather of the CIM" because of Gutzlaff's principles), the "spiritual secret" he'd learned during his illness stood him in good stead throughout the years. In 1865, revived in spirit and body, Taylor founded the China Inland Mission. Support-wise, at first he followed the CES system—each missionary living off support given individually. Later he followed the system used by Baptist pioneer William Carey in India (see Serampore Covenant in Ch. 10), putting all funds into a support pool. CIM's policy at the time was never to make needs known, "looking to God alone" (hence the term, "faith mission").

When Taylor, his wife, and 20 recruits arrived in China in 1866, his goal was mission outreach in all 18 provinces. By Taylor's death in 1905, CIM had reached that goal, with 825 missionaries, 500 Chinese workers, and 25,000 converts.[40] Among missionary reinforcements arriving in 1885

---

39. From the words of Jesus in John 15.4.

40. In 1865, J. Hudson Taylor outlined his vision in *China's Spiritual Need and Claims*. He is credited with pioneering recruitment of single women for missions. His second wife, Jennie, first foreign woman known to travel into China's interior, assisted in famine relief. (Taylor had to spend considerable time in administration, speaking in Europe and North America on behalf of CIM.)

were the renowned "Cambridge Seven"—university cricketers who became leaders in missions. One of them was the indomitable C. T. Studd—a rugged individualist who practised extreme austerity and blunt speech, often making life difficult for his colleagues. He finally went on to Africa, founding World Evangelization Crusade.

Taylor's closing years endured the sadness of a massacre at the end of the century, in which many CIM and recently arrived Christian and Missionary Alliance missionaries gave their lives during the Boxer Rebellion. A secret society, the Boxers[41] embodied mounting resentment of humiliating foreign invasions, the Opium War, one-sided treaties, and the scramble of other nations to establish spheres of influence.

"Dogs of the Imperialists"

Since missionaries were the most common foreigners that rural peasants saw, they and their converts became the chief target of the Boxers, who determined to rid China of all foreign influence. They considered missionaries "the running dogs of the imperialists."

Drought and unstable government added to mindless blame. Slaughter of foreigners built up in the closing years of the century, commanded by the hostile empress dowager. Among the first victims were women missionaries of the Anglican Church Missionary Society and its related Zenana Bible and Medical Mission.[42] Many Christian Chinese women died because foot binding hobbled their escape from murderous mobs.

"Chinese society of that period was incredibly cruel and ruled by fear," wrote Eileen Vincent.[43] "Priscilla [Studd] wrote, 'Sometimes [girl] babies were thrown on to the mountainside or into pagodas . . . with a hole so that wolves can get the body.'" In particular, Christian converts suffered savage public beatings.

---

41. Boxer: approximate translation of their Chinese name, "Righteous Harmonious Fist."
42. A mission formed in India, founded and operated by women to help women.
43. Eileen Vincent, *C.T. Studd and Priscilla*. Bromley/Gerrards Cross: WEC/STL (OM), 1988.

In 1900, anarchy broke loose, led by the turbaned Boxers.[44] Mobs hounded hundreds of foreign missionaries and thousands of Chinese Christians to their deaths throughout China and even in Mongolia. It was a desperate era. The diary of Eva Jane Price, martyred along with her husband and seven-year-old daughter, eloquently expresses their distress and also their faith: ". . . knees and legs shake in spite of all effort to be brave and quiet, trusting in God . . . 'Fear not, it is all right.' . . . If we die, we die in peace." That was Eva's last entry, June 30, 1900.

In spite of the bloody holocaust, Christianity did not disappear, as it had on several previous occasions under persecution. Church historian Samuel Moffett attributes the church's resilience to the sound faith of Christians, based on Bible teaching. Numbers of Christians actually increased during those years.

Little did the world know that the Boxer carnage was only a foretaste of the Communist pogrom to come. Within half a century, Christians suffered along with the rest of the population in the horrendous Maoist revolution. Though many Chinese Christians begged missionaries to stay, by mid century the CIM, among other agencies, reluctantly realized its presence had become counter-productive—even dangerous—to national Christians.[45]

The saga of the gospel continues in China, across Asia, and around the world. "Only the Holy Spirit could have linked up these people and events so significantly," I thought. Missiologist Ruth Tucker of Trinity Seminary, Deerfield, IL., states, that J. Hudson Taylor "directly or indirectly influenced founding of over forty new mission boards."[46]

---

44. Rosalind Goforth, in *Goforth of China* (Bibliography), documents this and describes the terrifying escape that she and her husband (Presbyterian missionaries) experienced in 1900.

45. CIM stayed through much persecution and loss of life. In 1951, rather than give Chinese colleagues problems by association with foreigners, CIM also withdrew. Last missionaries out, Arthur Matthews and Rupert Clark, were under house arrest and couldn't leave till 1953. After the mission's "reluctant exodus" in 1951, CIM adopted the name, "Overseas Missionary Fellowship," headquartering in Singapore. In 1993 the mission became simply OMF International.

46. Tucker, R., From Jerusalem to Irian Jaya. See David Michel, In God's Way, p. 23. Toronto: OMF.

James Hudson Taylor still inspires men and women to commitment. Concerning the "Back to Jerusalem Movement," while avoiding triumphalism, house church leaders Yun and Xu Yongze comment, "It is as though Hudson Taylor handed a flaming torch to the Chinese church and asked us to continue the race to the finish line."

We may be tempted to look upon the last few centuries as a new breakthrough in an Asia of impenetrable spiritual darkness. But to me the thrill was discovering the divine strategy God has followed *in Asia over the past millennia.*

The ubiquitous portrait of Chairman Mao looks on from the wall of the Forbidden City as the author views Tiananmen Square.

Seeing Better than Hearing

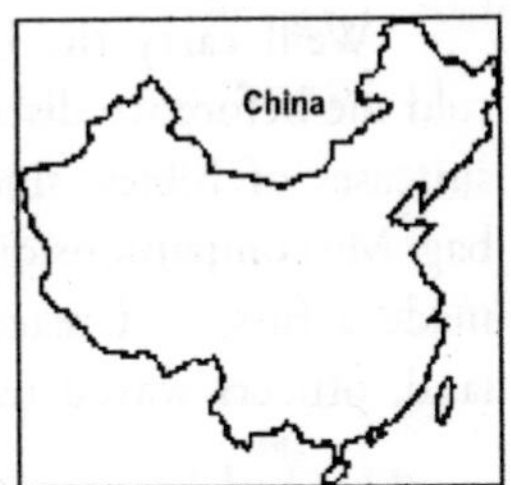

"Come and see what God has done" (Ps. 66:5).

CHINA'S HISTORY WAS FASCINATING, but how were Christians faring there now, I wondered. That was before the mainland had opened to visitors. "You should really go and see for yourself," the Laus urged. And so they arranged for me to accompany a couple of evangelists up the coast.

A ruddy sun was "coming up like thunder" through the haze of the South China Sea when I met the evangelists at the dockside. They turned out to be two women. The older, Hui, was an experienced "Bible woman," who had frequently visited inland. The younger, Lily, had never been across to the mainland but was preparing to be a missionary. I wondered about the etiquette of my traveling with two single women, but apparently it was acceptable—maybe because of my "age of wisdom"! I took heart that SIM's Chinese council had arranged the trip. Lily's father came to the dock to give us his patriarchal blessing as we set sail up the coast to Xiamen—China's tea-port city back in the 1800s.

The two evangelists had stuffed their bags with Bibles and Scripture portions. None of us agreed with any idea of smuggling—even though these were Bibles.[1] We would honestly declare the baggage contents if

1. At the time, importing literature was restricted. For several years the government has authorized printing of Bibles in China. However, with China's vast population, copies were not always available, and we knew of no gift more appreciated by Christians.

customs officials asked, but we did wonder what to expect when we landed. So once on the blue-green sea, the three of us met on the upper deck, in the lee of a ventilator shaft. This being Lily's first trip out of Hong Kong, we prayed that God would calm any nervousness and would guide our footsteps.

"We'll carry the baggage with the literature," the Chinese women told me before we disembarked. "It is better." I'd been carrying one of the suitcases of Bibles, since my own personal effects were all in one small bag. My companions didn't want a foreigner to be implicated if any official made a fuss, and reactions were unpredictable. However, when we did land, officers waved us through Customs without question.

Hui had been to this port before, so she led the way along muddy lanes to find lodging for the three of us at a low-cost hostel. On the path fussy chickens picked at their multigrain cereal, while on a bamboo fence a rooster crowed defiantly. Disgruntled goats rested in the shade of bamboo shacks—in which they would sleep at night, alongside their owners. A laborer balanced two buckets of vegetables on a pole across his shoulders. A mother carried home fresh greens for the evening meal in a backpack, while leading her child with one hand and dragging a protesting goat with the other. Two rosy-cheeked teens, a girl and a boy, chatted on their way home from school, books in backpacks. Young folk strode confidently, while older peasants shuffled along—reflecting (for women) a way of walking in former years of foot binding?[2]

This was not the sophisticated urban life I'd seen in documentaries on the New China. These were ordinary villagers going about their daily routine. Many looked weary, but they were also friendly, making me feel comfortable. Men and women mixed freely; I didn't sense any self-consciousness between the sexes—no flirtatious glances or provocative dress, as in so much of the West. Unlike women in some parts of Asia, Chinese women seemed free and natural.

The hostel manager took one look at me and told the women they could stay, but I'd have to go to the foreigners' hotel, where I would register my passport. The hotel turned out to be several times the cost

---

2. Brian Power, *The Ford of Heaven: A Childhood in Tianjin, China* (see Bibliography).

of the "local" hostel, but the cot-like bed was at least clean. I invited Hui and Lily to have supper with me in the cafeteria. Others were enjoying their noodles.[3] After a bowl of rice, fish, and greens washed down with green tea, we headed off to meet Hui's friends. By word of mouth, she'd informed them we were coming.

The Secret "Upper Room"

Up a back stairway, we climbed to the upper level of a shuttered house, where a group of friendly men and women welcomed us. The evangelists hadn't told me, but I soon discovered that this was in fact a house church. There were a dozen of us in a tiny room.

"They're studying the book of Acts," Hui whispered to me, interpreting an occasional sentence or two. The Bible study leader, she explained, was Dr. Wu,[4] an engineering professor at the local university. A tall, handsome young man was a university student. A young boy—maybe 12, I thought—was a grandson of the professor. During the informal service he was memorizing Bible verses. There were also a couple of middle-aged women and an elderly man.

"Who is *he*?" I asked Hui.

"That is Elder Choi," she replied. "You can talk with him in English—he worked for a British trading company before Communism took over. He became a Christian from reading the Bible when he was young. Dr. Wu is his son, the student his son's son, and the boy is son of his son's son."

"You mean the old man is the great-grandfather of the young boy?" I asked. Hui nodded, not too sure what a great-grandfather was. I silently gave thanks for the gospel seed that had taken root in four generations and was still bearing spiritual fruit.

After a time of meditation, Dr. Wu's wife passed around Chinese pastries and demitasse cups of green tea. Hui told me that the other

---

3. In traditional etiquette, slurping is a compliment to the cook. (Wished I'd known that as a boy, when my parents chastised me for doing the same.)
4. For security all names have been changed.

woman, Han, had just come back from banishment in the countryside. I noticed she spoke a little English, so I went over and sat beside her.

"How long have you been away?" I asked, with Hui interpreting when we needed help.

"For 30 years," Han replied quietly. I thought her eyes were haunting, even though her face expressed graciousness. "The cadres sent me away to the western provinces to work on a collective farm."

"Why did they send you away?"

"I was a secondary school teacher. The cadres said teachers were counter-revolutionaries, so we must go and do useful work."

"That must have been very hard for you!" I said, blinking at the thought. "You were used to teaching students in a classroom, not planting rice."

"It was very hard. My hands were not used to holding a hoe," Han murmured without a trace of bitterness. She only lowered her eyes, as if trying not to remember the pain.

"Yet you still follow Jesus," I pressed gently, searching for some clue to this woman's faith in the midst of trial. "Did you fellowship with other believers—or how did you survive?" I looked in the face of this disciple—so gentle and serene. I tried to imagine what an educated teacher must have endured during 30 years of hard labor, exiled from family and taunted by children who should have been in class—but who no longer had a school to attend. Thirty years!

"I just looked up to God as I transplanted rice and weeded it," Han replied softly. "I had fellowship with my Lord."

For thirty years! Spiritually, I suddenly felt like a miserable beggar in the presence of a saint. Han was only one of millions of educated Chinese who had lived through Mao's terror—dragged from home, office, or classroom by young "revolutionaries," humiliated by public beatings, interrogated for imagined wrongs, jailed, banished, and robbed of family. To say nothing of those who committed suicide or who died of injuries and starvation!

The Great Leap Forward of 1958-1960 was supposed to raise the standard of living for "the oppressed masses" by changing social structure. Instead, an estimated 20-30m Chinese died from malnutrition and famine.

Maybe, the Party Chairman reasoned, it was the culture, not only the system, that needed drastic change. But in the ensuing Cultural Revolution (1966-1976), 400,000 died of malnutrition, and another million were affected physically or mentally crippled. Many officials, including some who had helped Mao Zedong to power, committed suicide.

Only Mao's death in 1976 brought an end to China's Twenty Lost Years, as some have called the Great Leap and the Cultural Revolution's span. "Be vicious!" Mao told the mindless mobs as they bludgeoned thousands to death. Meanwhile the Chairman forced artists to paint huge murals, showing vibrant, smiling young Communists marching towards a bright future. Countries overseas were treated to media pictures of these.

Since then, the Chinese Communist Party (CCP) has re-thought its future and ushered in the era of Economic Reform.[5] I would see more of that in my travels. Just now my mind reeled with questions: How? Why? Who?[6] But the gentle woman offering me another rice cake brought my thoughts back to this "Upper Room." I swallowed, wiping my arm across my eyes.

"Would they sing a hymn before we leave?" I asked Hui, sensing the sacredness of the moment. After checking that windows and shutters were closed, the professor's wife went into the bedroom and retrieved a half-dozen worn hymnbooks from under a mattress. They had no covers, their corners were curled. As these humble disciples sang a Chinese hymn ever so softly, my heart filled with praise and intercession to the Lord. A cathedral choir could not have made any greater impact. It was a benediction. I'd just experienced what Jesus had promised his disciples: "Where two or three are gathered in my name, there am I in the midst of them."[7] I was seeing the gospel in 3D—the living Word—as I'd never seen it back in my own comfortable Christianity.

---

5. Within discrete limits, Christians now have more liberty. However, research, analysis, and discussion of the Mao years are still not allowed in China.
6. For analysis based on my research, see Appendix F: Religions/Secularism.
7. Matthew 18.20.

Finding Liberty in House Churches

As I returned to Hong Kong, I realized that the "Upper-Room" gathering was typical of many "house churches" at the time. (Repression of "house churches still continues, however, and local governments restrict circulation of the Bible.) Alternatively, the government does recognize China Christian Council churches, dubbed the Three-Self churches.[8] For many years they were not known for biblical truth—although they had commendable features of self-support, self-leadership, and self-propagation. Under the Religious Affairs Bureau, the Council's stated purpose was to rid Chinese churches of all "imperialist" influence. The liberal theology of Y. T. Wu, a Union Theological Seminary (USA) graduate, set out to mesh Communism's materialism with Universalism.

The Party, to control churches even as it controlled all other institutions, not only paid church salaries but also regulated where churches could be built and what pastors could teach. The Bureau banned doctrines on such provocative issues as the Second Coming of Christ, and also religious teaching of anyone under 18. However, an estimated 20m adherents attend some 13,000 Three-Self churches, led by around 3,000 clergy. While some pastors preached Christianity without the redemptive Cross, more and more of them now preach an evangelical message while respecting state requirements.

The Bureau also recognizes the quasi-government Amity Foundation, which operates like any other volunteer organization, recruiting teachers from overseas and even providing legal counsel. Annually, Amity's printing presses print some 2m Bibles, readily available to the public in some areas—but not as readily as Buddhist *sutras* and the *Qur'an*. Also, a Christian may have to provide name and address I.D. House church members often report difficulty obtaining a copy. In a remote area, one evangelist hand-copied the village Bible, so he could carry the copy with him as he went to other villages to preach.[9]

---

8. From their origin as the state-approved Three-Self Patriotic Movement.
9. Reported by Roberta Hestenes, President Emeritus, World Vision, USA, in a discussion Dec. 7, 2002.

Rather than be restricted by the state in any way, millions of Christians across China have worshipped in unregistered groups, led by evangelicals the people support financially. At another location in Asia, in an inside room of a gospel agency, I'd already seen a wall map of China with tiny colored stickpins spread all over. Each color represented the number of people known to be worshiping in a group: white, up to ten; yellow, up to 25; green, up to fifty; blue, up to 100; red up to 500; purple, up to 1,000 or more. The agency had received letters from those locations, or Chinese Christians had visited them and reported back. Although in some places pins were more heavily clustered than in others, it seemed there wasn't an area of this vast country beyond reach of a "house church."

"So how many worshipers do all those pins add up to?" I asked Hwa Yuan (pseudo name), the agency's local manager.

"We can fairly accurately estimate 50 million," he replied. "There may be more, but we want to be on the conservative side."[10]

"May I take a photo of the map?" I, the eternal photographer, asked.

"*No way!*" Yuan cautioned. "We don't let anyone photograph that. But we will give you one of the thousands of letters we receive." And he handed me a precious letter written in Chinese characters, but with all names and locations blotted out. I couldn't understand the characters, but I imagined what that letter meant to a disciple on the Old Spice Road.

I knew that one of those purple pins represented Pastor Samuel Lamb's flock, who meet in several rooms in a four-story building, via closed circuit TV. Interestingly, the local police station occupies the ground-floor level.

"They know everything I do," Pastor Lamb told our friends, David and Phyllis Howard[11] when they visited him. "Of course, they regularly call me in for interrogation! I have nothing to hide. Persecution doesn't

10. Since my first visit, the reported number has steadily grown. "Today there are more Christians in China than in any other country on earth," states SIM's Howard Brant after a visit. The government's figure for Christians is 25 million (members of the Three-Self Movement). Actual number may be 100m.

11. Dave was then International Director of World Evangelical Alliance. Ken Anderson tells the full story of Pastor Lamb in *Bold as a Lamb* (Grand Rapids: Zondervan, 1991).

harm true church growth—our worshipers have grown from 30 to 3,000 in number." The pastor had already spent 20 years in prison. Talk about courageous witness—like the early disciples after Pentecost!

Today church groups in China range from a handful of believers to one mega-church of 20,000 adherents—who meet in various houses but are connected in fellowship by closed circuit TV. As China relaxes constraints on non-registered churches, members openly sing and pray aloud. "If officials want to check up, they know where we are, anyway!" explain leaders, conscious they are being unobtrusively monitored.

Chinese Missionaries Travel *BACK* along Spice Road

Many house church leaders are reaching outward in their vision for spreading the gospel—even outside China's borders. For instance, there are now Chinese churches in Siberia—many without pastors. Outreach isn't a sudden impulse, I discovered. Years of following Jesus under repression—as the early disciples did—have honed many of China's believers in their personal commitment to their Heavenly Lord. They take his Commission seriously. To them, it's not a case of "converts of missions becoming mission evangelists." Through many different ways, these Chinese Christians have found the Light of the World, and without any foreigner telling them, they know their Saviour has commissioned them to be "light" in a world of spiritual darkness. They witness very directly, without apology.

These kinds of disciples have a vision: to equip and send out 100,000 Chinese missionaries along the Old Spice Road and its environs—all the way back to Jerusalem.[12] Like the Apostle Paul, they know this may mean trials, imprisonment, even death. Already, several of the first volunteers have been arrested on their missionary journeys, but they were prepared for that. It gave them opportunity, again like the early apostle Paul, to preach to fellow prisoners.

"While we thank God for their commitment, there are problems," comments Colman Chan. "Many have a charismatic zeal to suffer and die

---

12. Hattaway, Paul, *Back to Jerusalem*, 2003. Carlisle: Gabriel Publishing. "Three Chinese House Church Leaders Share Their Vision to Complete the Great Commission."

for their faith, almost as proof of their Christianity. Suffering may come, but as a *motive* for service, it is misguided. As we witness and teach, we must be ready to suffer and die, but it is others who impose it on us—it should not be our *choice*."

Far be it far from me to seem critical of these zealous believers, who have suffered so much! But Chan's comment, coming from an oriental, is insightful. Meritorious suffering and death feature in many religions. Muslim *jihadis* regard death (including suicide) for their faith as the fastest and surest path to Paradise, with its sexy virgins and luscious fruits. Although Christian history cites many believers who chose death rather than renounce their faith in Christ, Christendom (politicized Christianity) can consider suffering, death, and martyrdom as merit points, to be "redeemed" at least with salvation and at most with sainthood. (Shades of Buddhism!)

That misrepresents the prophecy of Jesus to his disciples: "They will put some of you to death" (Luke 21,16). That will happen because, Jesus went on to say, of people's hatred of *him*—not for merit. Believers trust in the *finished* merit of Jesus' death and resurrection. To receive his "Well done!" they need only be obedient and faithful until death, I realized.

Sweet and Sour

Whether about social ills or religious persecution, public reports still must be discreet. The following recent press release reveals sensitivities (names changed, date deleted):

> In —, a judge found house-church pastor Chong and three relatives guilty of "illegal business practices," . . . after new Regulations on Religious Affairs strengthened a ban on illegal religious publications and increased the penalty for printing or distributing them without government approval. Judge Won Cho sentenced Chong to three years, his wife to two years, and her brother to 18 months. Chong's sister was found guilty of concealing illegally acquired goods but escaped prison because she had provided information to police. Chong's mother, now caring for her 5-year-old grandson, told Reuters that the prosecution had not found a single witness to testify that Chong had earned money from the sale of the books. Chong, who

led several house-churches, said the books were printed for free distribution within house church networks. The four were held for 10 months before the case finally went to trial.

Defence lawyers acknowledged that the literature was printed without permission but argued that the defendants could not be charged with "economic crimes" since the Bibles were never intended for sale. A key lawyer on the defence team received notice to suspend his law practice for a year, making an appeal extremely difficult. (He said police have made attempts on his life and harassed his family, and he now faces imminent arrest after releasing two reports on the torture of Falun Gong members and the rights of minorities.) Moreover, a clerk from the court visited Pastor Chong to warn him that his sentence would be increased if he "annoyed" judges with an appeal. Defendants appealed anyway, which the court rejected on December 20 (leaving their verdicts and sentences unchanged).[13]

However, like China's famous sweet-and-sour soup, there are two "flavors" in this bowl. China wants positive publicity overseas; so on the one hand, such press releases could lead to more liberty for minorities. On the other hand, overseas publicity can cause official reaction in China. While the Central Government is increasingly open to what they see as multi-culturalism, the government is also concerned about any movement that might unsettle society. Politicians and generals realize what happened in the former USSR could happen in China—but with ten times the chaos because of the population.

Some government officials don't always distinguish between cults such as the Taiping Movement,[14] the current Falung Gong, and evangelical church groups. They are all seen as outside the established order. There is a state-approved church, isn't there? So officials profess not to understand why evangelicals want to meet separately. Is something insidious involved? Certainly such tensions call for prayer on the part of Christians everywhere for wisdom coupled with harmlessness "as doves."

---

13. Compass Direct, Jan. 2006.

14. Hong Xiuquan proclaimed the Heavenly Kingdom of Great Peace. Untaught, he selected Old Testament passages (picked up from a Protestant Chinese tract), to war against Manchu rule. The "Kingdom" ended in the Taiping Rebellion (1851-1864), with great loss of life and property—discrediting Christianity.

Actually, there are remarkable opportunities for discrete witness *within* the nation's systems. Government welcomes Christians among the thousands of foreign teachers they admit annually—especially at university level. China sought for half a million Teachers of English as a Second Language (TESL) by 2008—the Olympics year. Evangelicals have a reputation for honesty, faithfulness, moral rectitude, and professional excellence.

"For forty years we've been telling students to serve their communities sacrificially," a university president told Jonathan Fuller of OMF. "But nothing they've done matches the sacrificial work of your volunteer teachers and their friends from overseas." A woman official told others on her city council, "Let there be no corruption with the money this agency is sending to help us. I've been overseas and have seen the kind of people who support their work. They aren't rich; they give sacrificially!"

So disciples of Jesus, both Chinese and expatriate, go quietly about their daily work and life, showing themselves to be worthy citizens on earth, even while knowing their "citizenship is in heaven." At the same time, they keep active as "the salt of the earth."

"A century ago, . . . China was THE great mission field of the world," missiologist Patrick Johnstone wrote concerning *Back to Jerusalem.* "Who could ever have believed that after a further 50 years, Communism, and terrible persecution, . . . China might become one of the foremost missionary-sending countries in the 21st century?"[15]

China certainly has the overwhelming manpower and is developing resources, but Johnstone, Jim Taylor, and others concur that this amazing outreach may founder on the same shoals that have wrecked many a missionary movement through the years—materialism. Christian young people, many the product of house evangelism and teaching, are pouring into the cities. Lacking follow-up discipling, they fall prey to the glitter of the new material world and lose their missionary vision.

"The spiritual mortality rate is alarming!" Jim Taylor had told me when I talked with him in Singapore. "It's the same thing that sidetracks Christians in the West.

15. From endorsement on cover of *Back to Jerusalem, op. cit.*

"We have another concern, though," Taylor added. "While heroically volunteering to evangelize the hard places along the Old Spice Road, many of these new Christians make no effort to evangelize unreached groups right around them. Christians overseas need to be discrete in publicizing the Chinese missionary movement, while also more prayerful for the follow-up of new Christians and for their witness in their own 'Jerusalems.'"

The Evangelical Fellowship of Asia notes the same problem throughout Asia—not only in China: the lack of witness to neighbors, particularly in Muslim areas.[16] This of course, is a worldwide problem among Christians.

*****

Old World—New Potential

The Chinese adage was true: *"Hearing something a hundred times is not as good as seeing it once."* After my coastal visit I was eager to see something of the heartland.[17] Flying into Beijing, I stood in Tiananmen Square—site of the annual Day of Mourning for the Dead, observed by Confucians and Buddhists.[18] The Square was a traditional gathering site. Uprisings had begun here in the past, so government was keeping a close eye on it. Reminding me of that, Chairman Mao (although long dead) gazed down from a large portrait on the wall of the Forbidden City at the far side of the Square.[19] But today the only activity was a soldier, rifle over one shoulder, parading across the vast square.

---

16. W. Harold Fuller, *People of the Mandate*, p. 48 (see Bibliography).
17. As mentioned earlier, the author also has a personal interest in China. Nearly a century ago, his father applied to the CIM, but was turned down because of a heart murmur. Instead, he went to Canada and often befriended Chinese work crews, sharing the gospel. Later, the author's brother and one of his sons with their families joined CIM, renamed OMF. –WHF
18. *Tiananmen*: "Gate of Heavenly Peace."
19. So called because of its sacredness in the era of emperors, who resided there. Confucius taught that the Emperor ("Son of Heaven" and chief shaman) had absolute control on earth, directly in line with cosmic forces. Thus, the emperor's palace had been a place of worship for shamans, not commoners.

"Tiananmen," I recollected, had become world-famous in 1989. During a visit by Russia's President Gorbachev, students held a hunger strike to emphasize their call for greater participation in government. A month after the visit, camping protesters and the world press were still camped there. On June 4, while the world watched TV screens in horror, soldiers, fearing open rebellion, opened fire on the students, killing 200 (government figure) and injuring thousands.

Now I was there myself. As I walked across the deserted square, I thought of the university student I'd met in the "house church" before "Tiananmen." Where was he now? I hoped he'd not been among the slain protesters. Since then, China had gone through remarkable transitions, providing a world of possibilities for young people like that student. It was difficult to put together a balanced picture. Seeking to understand China, I hired a cabbie to drive me to one of its most recognizable landmarks: The Great Wall. The view from there would put things into "perspective" in more ways than one.

James Hudson Taylor III chats with SIMers Yu-Guang and Lily Hsieh, joined by his wife, Leone, and the author.

Schoolgirls visiting the Great Wall greet the author before reciprocating by taking his photo.

View Atop the Great Wall

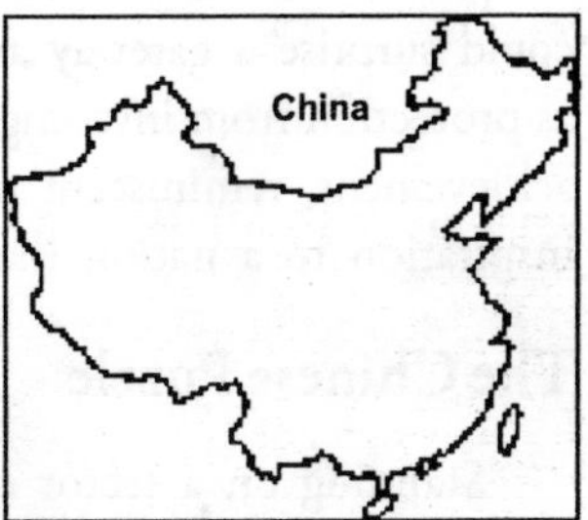

"Who has stirred up one from the east, calling him in righteousness to his service? He hands nations over to him and subdues kings before him. . . . Who has done this. . .? I, the Lord—with the first of them and with the last—I am he" (Isaiah 41. 2-4).

OBVIOUSLY, I WASN'T THE ONLY VISITOR interested in viewing the Great Wall of China. Most were Asian tourists, with an occasional Westerner, strolling along the stone walkway on top of the Wall. A young Chinese aimed a camera at his pretty companion. Probably newly weds, I thought, noting the blushing orchid in the girl's raven-black hair. For romantics, "The Wall" was North America's equivalent of Niagara Falls, so I made gestures about my using their camera to take their photo standing together. They readily accepted and then pointed at the camera dangling around my neck. "Photo . . . you?" they asked haltingly. So I have a record of standing on China's most recognizable ancient site.

Recognizable indeed[1]—for nearly 2,000 miles, snaking across plains and along hilly ridges, from the sea to the desert. In 214 BC, the First Emperor, Qin Shi Huang, may have joined existing state walls to form a kind of partial barrier; but it was some 1,600 years later that the Ming Dynasty completed restoration of the present massive Great Wall. The Emperor's officials ordered village headmen to organize peasants to

1. Discernible even from high-altitude flights, but not, as earlier supposed, from the moon.

construct local sections. Toiling like worker ants, they carted earth, brick, and stone in baskets slung on shoulder poles. Using removable frames, workmen tamped thin layers of clay "fill" hard as concrete to build up a wide core, faced with brick and stone.[2]

Between strategically placed lookout towers, foot soldiers—even chariots—could travel along the cobbled top, protected between low ramparts. Barbarians couldn't scale the Great Wall, but on horseback they could surprise a gateway and breach the defenses. Eventually ineffective as protection from invading hordes, the Wall nevertheless was a Herculean achievement, reminiscent of Egypt's pyramid construction. It is also an inspiration to a nation that is re-building itself by working together.

The Chinese Puzzle

Standing on a sector of the wall that crested a ridge, I looked out across the countryside, trying to visualize this mammoth named China.[3] Everywhere were reminders of the nation's ancient heritage; yet China remained a puzzle to me. How had the Middle Kingdom held so many ethnic groups together and developed such commendable order? How had it produced inventions so far ahead of my own ancestors? (China had a form of steam engine before James Watt was born.)

In spite of such advance, why had China allowed the rest of the world to overtake it in the 16th c.? How could a respectful society allow children to terrorize their elders during Chairman Mao's violent era? While Cambodia's hideous pogrom was any nation's most decimating percentage-wise,[4] it couldn't compare with the extent of China's massacre.

Yet, I knew this vast country was now competing with the rest of the world! How to solve this Chinese Puzzle?

---

2. In this way, "organized labor" built palaces, cities, trade routes, irrigation channels, and shipping canals across China's Central Plane. The tamped-earth method was stronger than *adobe* (from Egyptian *dbt*: "mud brick") that Moses' people made of earth and straw in Egypt. "Landcrete" method today pressurizes laterite soil, but adds minimal cement powder (H. F. Dowdell, *It Just Happened to Happen,* p. 106 (—see Biblio.).
3. From Emperor Qin (pronounced "Chin"), who unified language and peoples 221-210 B.C.
4. Cambodia's pogrom did more than "decimate" (meaning 10%). It wiped out 25% of the population.

South of my vantage point, today's Beijing (yesterday's Peking) was now bustling with building cranes and jackhammers, as well as traffic jams. Excavating for modern projects such as the 2008 Olympics "unearthed" pre-historic sites that yield clues about the early inhabitants of East-Central Asia. In fact, recent "digs" show that China extensively farmed wheat and rice as far back as 2000 or even 2400 BC. Agriculturalists had thought ancient China depended on millet, but the new sites indicate early trade with Western Asia—the supposed source of wheat.[5]

Not far from the city, the Peking Man Cave has long provided fossils and artifacts of the early dwellers on these plains and hills—not grunting ape-men but intelligent members of settled communities that planted crops and made utensils. They even developed the complicated craft of silk-making, from worm cocoon to garment—a Chinese secret and monopoly (thus naming "the Old Spice Road") until smuggled to the West in the 6th c. Even if these "pre-historic" people chose to dwell in caves (or at least bury their dead in them, along with food and utensils to use in the next life), they decorated cave walls with art and artifacts. Intricately sculptured clay and (later) bronze figures depict armies and horses to accompany an emperor into the next world. The Zhoukoudian excavations, southwest of Beijing, have revealed breathtaking art, craftsmanship, and technology.

Attesting to China's ancient culture, is the world's "oldest surviving game of pure mental skill":[6] "Go" is its name in English, *Weiqi* in Chinese. Players move black or white stones across a grid—deceptively simple, yet (unlike chess) no computer program has yet been able to outwit a player. Played at least 2,500 years ago, it has sharpened the minds of peasants, warlords, and emperors alike, equated with cultured society along with the arts. Under various names, the game spread to Japan, Korea, and Tibet.

"Heavenly Dynasties"

I turned and looked westward, where the Wall wound like a serpent from ridge to ridge. Fluffy clouds reached to the horizon. But what were

5. University of Toronto report, Winter 2005-2006. Soybeans, cultivated by China for five millennia, arrived in North America by chance, as ballast in Chinese ships. The US caught on to their nutritional value and is now the world's largest producer of the ancient bean.

6. *Economist*, Dec. 18, 2004.

those rising *cumuli* in the distance? Towering formations, rank upon rank, seemed to take on shape. Were they emperors clothed in billowing brocade robes? Yes—*they must be China's dynasties!* (Isn't the imagination amazing?) Most distant in time was the Zou Dynasty, then the Qin and the Han—including "the Yellow Emperor," mystical ancestor of the Han reputed to have lived some five millenia ago. Closer still were the Wei, Sui, Tang, Sung, Yuan, Ming, and Qing.

I'd heard of their emperors—some benign and beneficent, some crafty and cruel. With unquestioned authority, they could massacre thousands of subjects who seemed a threat. Or they could use their power to change the face of the land with vast public projects. Several arose from outside the central Han core—western Tartar, northern Mongol,[7] and northeastern Manchu, some uninvited, others beginning as alliances to repulse rebellions. Some stayed, intermarried, and became encultured Chinese. Others overthrew their hosts and took over—ungrateful lot!

But while horseback warriors excelled at invading, they fell flat on their faces (or off their horses) when trying to govern other cultures. (Tartars and Mongols were *so-o-o* different, complained their Chinese subjects!) The desperate despots turned to skilled elements from Asia and even Europe—co-opting Jews, Arabs, Persians, Greeks, Romans, and Russians. Near the turn of the 14th c., they roped in Venetian travel-author Marco Polo.[8] USA didn't yet exist, or China might have got in on some exchange program(!).

"Who are the Chinese?" you ask. *Which* Chinese do you want to know about? The slight Cantonese of the South? or the big-framed Manchu of the Northeast, or the sturdy Turkic Uighur of the West? Or other of the 55 Chinese ethnic groups the government lists?[9]

China has not been a backward wasteland. As well as inventions ahead of the West (including paper, gunpowder, eyeglasses, and silk)

---

7. Mongols were the first to make Beijing capital of the Empire.
8. Polo didn't write China's tourism brochures (!), but when you visit Beijing, cross Marco Polo Bridge to reach Peking Man's Cave. See Ch. 19 for more on the developed Chinese societies that astounded Polo.
9. Although Han now comprise over 90% of the population; 55 national minorities make up the rest.

before the end of the first millennium A.D., the nation enjoyed standardized weights and measures, state schools, and an examination system. Movable wood blocks (for pictographs) printed books. Writing was common among the *literati* (who outnumbered the privileged official class). Europe claims for itself several Chinese inventions, according to historian Patricia Fara.[10]

However, East and West did interchange ideas more than we might think. Archeologists have uncovered evidence that bronze, painted pottery, metal agricultural instruments, irrigation canals, mechanical clocks (Chinese used water clocks), two-wheeled chariots, and eye glasses (all items soon employed by China) first appeared in Europe and the Middle East before the Far East used them. So East and West enriched each other.

China Beat Columbus, Magellan, and Cook?

Nevertheless, "West is West, and East is East, and never the twain shall meet," wrote Kipling.[11] For millennia, China insulated itself from the rest of the world. Mountain ranges (the Caucasus, Urals, Hindu Kush, Pamirs, and Himalayas among others) and deserts discouraged mass intermixing, until war or trade forced it. Outside of China, most navigable rivers run north to south, not west to east—the ancient direction of trade. (China's longest river, the Yangtze, flows southeast as if to empty into Southeast Asia's great Delta, until changing its course to the northeast.) Between China's west-east rivers, the Qin Dynasty built north-south transport canals. It further unified the empire with 4,000 miles (some 6,000 kms.) of imperial highway—more than the Roman Empire's.

Chinese sailing craft had no pressing need to venture beyond the coastal fishing waters. Anyway, pirates commanded the sea trade route to the continent's south. The major exception to being landlocked came in the 15th century. Ming Emperor Zhu Di commissioned Grand Eunuch Zheng He (a Muslim from Central Asia) to undertake diplomatic voyages along the Arab and Chinese sea trade routes. Between 1405 and 1435

---

10. Patricia Fara, *Science: A Four Thousand Year History*. Oxford U. Press, 2009.
11. Rudyard Kipling, English-Canadian travel author, 1865-1936. He continued: "but there is neither East nor West . . . when two strong men stand face to face, though they come from the ends of the earth!"

Admiral Zheng conducted seven voyages, boasting the largest flotilla of the biggest ships the world had seen—some with masts 90 feet tall. Their sternpost rudders could out-maneuver the rest of the world's steering oars. Zheng's first flotilla contained over twice as many ships as the (later) Spanish Armada of the 16th c.

Indeed, China dominated the Indian Ocean and Western Pacific, penetrating southward to Java and westward to Ethiopia and today's Kenya—how far south along the coast we do not know. We can speculate that on his next voyage (to be his eighth), Admiral Zheng could have rounded the Cape of Good Hope almost a century before Portugal's Bartholomew Dias succeeded from the opposite direction in 1488.

Chinese seafarers could have discovered Europe before Europe discovered China by sea! Some cartographers now make that claim, based on an ancient Chinese map of the world, dated 1418, that matches a Chinese book describing Zheng's exploits, also dated 1418.[12] Cartographers wonder whether the Chinese Admiral circled the globe (the map does present the world as round, not flat), but they agree that Chinese seafarers visited Australia and New Zealand centuries *before* Captain Cook. Experts note that Chinese maps showing sections of the continents date back to the Kublai Khan, whose forays covered large areas.

Whether the Admiral circumnavigated the world or only a hemisphere, why was there no follow up of China's discoveries after 1433? After all, Europe converted its own later explorations into trade and empire! Although Ming Dynasty seafarers brought a giraffe home from Africa (that should have "heightened" interest in further expeditions!), invasive Mongols distracted the Ming Emperor and consumed his treasury. Some Confucian purists insisted on isolation from foreign contacts. Besides, were officials a wee bit jealous of Zheng's exploits? He was a leader among the eunuchs, who were becoming powerful. Maybe the shamans saw signs in the sky.

Anyway, China's ship of state, at the height of its superiority on the high seas, "battened down the hatches," as we sailors used to do in stormy

12. *The Marvellous Visions of the Star Raft*. Map report from *The Economist*, Jan. 14, 2006.

weather. Like an ancient tortoise (to change the metaphor), China once more withdrew into its isolationist shell, closing down shipyards, banning seafaring, and even destroying Zheng's voyage records (ah—there *was* jealousy!). It would be half a century before Christopher Columbus set out to find the sea route to China (instead discovering the "Americas"[13] in 1492). His three ships *totaled* only one-tenth displacement size of Zheng's largest ship!

China continued in a world of its own, even closing coastal trading centers to discourage piracy.[14] It proved to be an engulfing pot rather than a melding pot for any other culture—such as those of inner Asia's invaders. I wondered what it was about China that could turn invaders into "Chinese," instead of vice versa. Still, why did neighboring ethnic groups as well as distant ones find China to be such a completely different world? What "glue" held together the world's largest population under a series of dynasties that arose and collapsed one after the other? Were there common values that permeated society, from the Emperor down to the family? If so, how could such an ordered society collapse into Communist-era anarchy? And besides, how did China bounce back so rapidly to become a leading world power? (Full cycle: now Chinese warships escort Chinese freighters through the Arabian Sea, to ward off *today's* pirates!)

Fitting the Pieces Together

Questions, questions! My thoughts were in confusion. Confusion? Ah—maybe I'd find the solution in "*Confucian*"! From the Great Wall, I hurried back to Beijing to research one of history's great scholars and philosophers, Confucius.[15]

---

13. "America": thought named for 15c. Florentine, Amerigo Vespucci, who kept journals of Columbus' voyages. Cartographer Mercator (16c.) awarded him the honor. But "America" could have derived from Richard Ameryk, Welsh sponsor of John Cabot (15c. Venetian explorer, Giovanni Caboto). In 15c., new lands were named after a benefactor's *surname*, not the first. If the honor had gone to Columbus' navigator, the continents would have been named "Vespuccia" (Sylvain Fribourg, *Economist* Letters, Sept. 22, 2007).

14. Yet Chinese trade did not collapse. Recent research documents inflows of silver (for currency) from S. America between 1500-1800, and outflows of Chinese silk, porcelain, and tea (*Economist*, Aug. 25/01).

15. Chinese name: K'ung-Fu-tzu, 551-479 B.C.

Hurried, that is, until my vintage taxi died on the highway. Most drivers bought only enough fuel for the current trip—hadn't my driver estimated the right amount? He looked under the hood and solemnly diagnosed that his generator had burned out, so the battery wasn't charging. That left the sparkplugs spark-less. No problem. Producing a made-in-China cell phone, he called back to his Beijing base. "Coming!" he confidently assured me. While we waited ... and waited for the replacement to arrive, I was able to watch the new and the old China passing along the road:

> A peasant pedalled a three-wheeled "truck" loaded with scrap. A fleet of 20 Mercedes Benz cars, the lead one flying a pennant, escorted some VIP from the airport. On the highway shoulder, a short man shouldered new mattresses stacked as high as he was tall. New buses and transport trucks thundered by. Pulling a cart of melon, a melancholy donkey ploddingly ignored traffic, yet no driver blew a horn. The public's mindset impressed me; Communism had at least replaced traditional expectation of privilege with a sense of equality. Affluence and poverty seemed to accept each other as one's lot in life. While I'd seen how garish sex ruled city nightlife, out in the countryside men and women were very decorous, working and travelling alongside each other without flirtatious self-consciousness. (Unless I didn't understand Chinese sexual innuendoes!)

The mechanic showed up, spat on the road, and disappeared (except for his legs) under the "bonnet" (hood) of the car. For exercise, I strolled along the highway shoulder. On a sideroad, a farmer had spread his harvest of red peppers over half the roadway to dry. At the intersection, a woman was selling *bok choy* and cabbage heads—surplus (above quota) that the state then allowed her to sell privately. It was a big step for that generation, which had never known "the open market."

Interesting—revolution was slowly melding into reform. I recollected that years before, Mao Zedong and Chiang Kai-shek had been colleagues in protesting against corruption. A warlord kidnapped Chiang and forced him to form a united front against the Japanese with Mao. According to biographer Jay Taylor, when Mao then had opportunity to destroy the Communist uprising, Chiang (a man of his word) felt he could not betray his commitment.[16] Chiang Mao chose the path of revolution through the Chinese Communist Party, while Chiang Kai-shek chose the way of reform. *Wu* (force) won over *wen* (civil reform). Chiang and his Nationalist Party ended up on the island of Taiwan—which he saw as "providential," allowing him and his son to bring about true reform.

Mainland and island have rattled sabers at each other, yet they've also enjoyed a lot of positive interaction. Taiwan became one of the globe's most export-financed economies, with one quarter of its exports going to China. The island nation has been the world's biggest contract chipmaker. I was interested to see the number of electronic items that bore a Taiwan mark inside. Taiwanese visit China for work, education, or family reasons. An estimated 1m Taiwanese executives have moved to China to operate factories.

In the mid 1900s, the Christian population of this predominantly Buddhist island was estimated at one-tenth of 1%, but official figures now report 3% nationwide, while in the capital, Taipei, the figure may be as high as 10%. In the face of disillusionment over materialism, many Taiwanese are finding Jesus Christ as personal Saviour—some through the vibrant Christians they meet while in *China*. A recent Franklin Graham "Festival" in Taipei reported large attendances and thousands of conversions.[17]]

By the time my taxi started along the road again, I was wondering what had happened to the hopeful age of Confucian philosophy and Buddhist Enlightenment. What could the past teach me about today's society? Even though it is still closely controlled, society at least functions. Back in Beijing, I made sure to tip my cabby, because taxi drivers, though underpaid, have to purchase their own fuel. They not only have to belong to registered companies, but also pay their employers fat commissions.

(That visit of mine was before the current economic "revolution" taking place in China. By the early 2000s, a visitor would be stunned by the development of both urban and rural areas: a network of highways criss-crossing the countryside, a bullet train speeding between

16. J. Taylor, *The Generalissimo: Chiang Kai-Shek and the Struggle for Modern China.* Harvard Press, '09.

17. *Decision*, January 2009.

Beijing and Shanghai, and futuristic buildings displaying China's prowess to impress the 2008 Olympics visitors. But before all that, I was learning about the historical backdrop that made recent development all the more significant. So back to Confucius and Mao.)

China experienced a twisting pilgrimage from Confucius to Mao. Born in 551 B.C. in East China, Confucius came from a noble family. At the time, factions on China's Central Plain and in its foothills were restive, preceding two centuries of warring states. Distraught feudal leaders sought philosophers' counsel. At the time, there was no established religion. The imperial court and mandarins guided the factions through moral ethics—principles and thinking inspired by "The Heavens."

David Landes, in his *Wealth and Poverty of Nations* (see Bibliography), p. 38, explains the result: "It was precisely the wholeness and maturity of the inherited canon and ethic, the sense of completeness and superiority, that made China so hostile to outside knowledge and ways, even where useful." That explained China's withdrawal into itself during the Medieval Period, when it was pressured by rising external powers. But how had that "canon and ethic" become a national viewpoint?

That was where Confucius left his indelible imprint, I learned. In the midst of social and civil unrest, among a fractured people spooked by superstition, he taught the concept of the ideal person, one with a strong ethical sense of propriety, moderation, and the value of social order in the family, workplace, and government. His teaching had a calming effect, dealing with time rather than eternity—for how could we understand the future, he reasoned, if we didn't understand the present? The concept of *tien* taught that mortals could never know "the sky and heavens."

Interviewing Confucius

As a journalist, I imagined interviewing Confucius for the *Shantung Herald* (*SH*). I "found" the venerable teacher sitting on a low wall in the shade of a black locust tree, whittling his bamboo pen as a devotee played haunting melodies on a *guqin* zither.[18] No brocade detracted from the

18. The *guqin's* long neck has no frets; the player plucks its single silk string while sliding a piece of ivory up and down to make the distinctive slurring tones of traditional oriental music.

simplicity of the great teacher's linen gown. Although his shoulders were slightly stooped, his words were unhurried, with the ring of authority. When he looked at me from under drooping eyelids, as if disillusioned with life's glitter, his gaze would have penetrated any ulterior motive on my part, I felt.

Our imaginary interview might have gone like this:[19]

SH: Ni hao (How are you?), K'ung Fu Tzu, Most Honorable Teacher! Thank you for granting this unworthy servant the sublime opportunity of an interview.

C: Please, please! Get up off the cold earth and sit here beside me. Know you not that we all are born equal?

SH: Indeed ... but wasn't your father a nobleman?

C: At one time, yes. However, through others' intrigue, he lost his position and wealth. I was born into poverty.

SH: How did that affect you? I believe your comments could help our many readers, who struggle to find wealth and position.

C: My parents were good people, but I suppose our family's fall from power to poverty did shape my thinking. I realized that privilege is temporal, leaving us at the mercy of jealous enemies who plot against us. But, as our sages say, 'What you cannot avoid, welcome.'

SH: Please go on—but first, do you mind if I write notes? Your golden words are too precious to drop into careless memory.

Stroking wispy grey hairs on his chin, Confucius gestured permission and continued.

C: As I was going to say, we must earn respect by our morality and integrity. When all else fails, those are the strengths of any ruler.

SH: Your teachings are changing brutish and immoral society.

---

19. The *Shantung Herald, like the interview,* is imaginary, but I've sought to convey the views of Confucius authentically though simplified, based on John Hinnells' *Dictionary of Religions*, and other sources. The *Analects* ("Selected Sayings") contain Confucius' actual teachings, collated by his followers after his death. See Appendix F – Religion – Confucianism.

C: Let us say that I seek to bring mankind back to the ancient moral and social traditions of our nation's Golden Ages.

SH: Of course, I should have said you are a transmitter of ancient wisdom. As you traverse the Middle Kingdom, do you advise powerful officials to rule ethically now?

C: If we are all born equal, and if the way to earn respect is through our morality, that applies to all of us—fathers, teachers, officials, even our rulers. To live in peace, we must all respect the ethical authority above us: children their parents, students their teachers, staff their employers, citizens their rulers. We should show humility and kindness to each other.

SH: But our spiritual mediums, the shamans. Don't they bring us good luck?

C: The shamans are only intermediaries—the ones who interact between the unseen powers of the universe and us mortals. They understand the auspices—the signs under which we should plant crops or go on journeys. But they aren't magicians who can bring us luck. They aren't priests who placate the unseen forces.

SH: How then can the Emperor become The Son of Heaven? Are not the shamans the ones who so empower him?

C: Ah, child, you do not yet understand. The cosmos is ordered, and so must life on earth be ordered. The heavens have hierarchies, and so has our world. Through contact with unseen forces, shamans only *discover* who heads up the hierarchy here on earth. Who is the mortal counterpart of the sun. That's what they discover and announce. Ultimate authority resides in the Emperor. Only he has the Mandate of Heaven, the power to rule us. Of course, he retains that power by his ethical example. So if he loses our respect, he must step aside.

SH: My humble apology, O Wise One . . . but did you mention the "heavens"? I've interviewed prophets of Jehovah who've come all the way from Jerusalem. I'm sure they'll be glad that you know about Heaven. They say that's where the Creator dwells.

C: Again, senseless mortal, you do not understand! You see, there is no such *place* as Heaven where we shall dwell. Forget the ancient belief in the "supreme Deity," Shang Ti—he was too remote for anyone to approach anyway. There's no such *being* as a Creator God or a Destroyer Satan. Those are the mistaken concepts of Jews and Taoists. What we are dealing with are forces of the *heavenlies* that govern us earthlings. In the cosmos, the male *yang* force combines with the female *yin* force to produce all that we see around us.

SH: Then how can we control our own lives, Good Instructor?

C: That's what I spend my time teaching. You see, on earth there are two prevailing forces: the *wu* and the *wen*. In our relations, it is much better to follow the way of *wen*, using teaching and diplomacy rather than *wu*, or force. Of course, there are times when force may be necessary: when the stars indicate it and the Emperor orders it.

SH: Thank you for enlightening me. But one more question, Honourable Teacher. In view of your venerable age, I am surprised at your vitality. What is your secret?

C: Ah—you city dwellers! You know nothing. C*hi* is the vital energy force of existence. You must learn how to control it through *tai chi* exercise. Acupuncture can help restore it.

SH: Thank you, Gentle Sir. Indeed I am an ignorant child. But now I must hurry back to meet the next issue's deadline. Oh, may I quote you as the founder of a new religion? It would make a great *headline! The* Herald *would outsell even the* Straights Times.

C: I have never heard of those; they sound as if they are from another planet! Anyway, O senseless scribe, if you understood anything, you would know that my teaching is not a religion. As I told you earlier, it is only the ethical way to follow traditions our fathers brought with them to our land.[20] Your profit motive is wrong. Commerce is not the way of civility, of *wen*. I do not respect the merchant class, trading on the backs

20. Confucian teaching shows traces of Egyptian-Babylonian cosmology, Persian Zoroastrianism, Gnostic Dualism, and Siberian shamanism. Taoism, mentioned in the interview, expressed the opposing views of a contemporary of Confucius, traditionally Lao-tzu, who retained mystical elements from Mesopotamia, including sorcery. While following Confucian ethics, many Chinese also practise Taoism. "Magic" alchemy (purporting to transform base metals into gold) may have led to China's later development of metallurgy.

of people. Look at the hypocrisy of Jewish traders, who lend money to our market sellers—with interest that the sellers can scarce repay. Yet they tell us that Moses condemned usury![21]

"But let us not digress," and the venerable Teacher raised his hand slightly, to signal the end to our session. "Besides, I see others waiting to discuss with me. . . ."

Even this imaginary interview didn't solve the Chinese Puzzle for me. Although I wished that Confucius had known the Creator God and his salvation, I was impressed with the Teacher's high ethical principles. I did wonder—could Confucius' commendable ethics and teaching about the cosmos possibly provide a common thread woven throughout China's dynasties, Mao's Communism, and China's rebirth as a world player? It all seemed contradictory—given the great teacher's ethics vs. China's turbulent history. *Yet maybe . . .*

Confucius Say: "Respect Ancestors, Enjoy Life"

Once again, journalistic imagination enabled me to leap forward one thousand years from the time of Confucius, to interview Chinese citizens. Had the Sage made any difference? I imagined coming upon a little boy flying his kite over his family's rice field. As I approached, he placed his fingertips together, still holding the kite string, and touched his hands to his forehead in respect. About to ask his name, I heard his father calling:

"Fou Tse, the geese are in among the rice. Chase them out—but gently!"

"Yes, Honorable Father," Fou Tse responded, and then apologetically to me: "Please excuse my neglect, Sir." The boy immediately hauled in his kite and raced over to protect the newly transplanted rice seedlings. Then I saw his father walking towards me.

"Excuse this scribe for interrupting your serenity, Honorable Sir," I said to Fou's father as I bowed. "But I am reporting for the *Shantung*

21. Did both Confucius and (later) Muhammad pick up their opposition to interest-bearing lending ("usury") from Jewish caravan travellers, who recited "Moses and the Prophets" around evening campfires?

Herald. I'm writing a feature on the values of our society. I was impressed with the respect that your little boy shows."

"Ah yes—respect, although sometimes he is careless," I imagined Father Fou (FF) replying. "But he is learning to obey without questioning. We all must do that."

SH: I live in the city, where rascals sometimes do not obey authority. Of course, for that folly, they pay with their lives. May I ask, do you have that problem in your village?"

FF: "Seldom. Very seldom. It would not be the way of Confucius. The geese must obey my son, he must obey me, I must obey the Nobles, and they must obey the Emperor—whatever he decides. That's how we balance the heavenly forces in their levels of control: the stars and moon and sun. They're all under the power of the cosmic forces. Our shamans divine signs in the sky to tell us when is the right time to plant or harvest—or marry or travel. We wouldn't dare do anything without having the right signs."

SH: "I notice how you paid respect to the stupa[22] *over there, as you approached me. I presume your ancestors'—maybe your parents'—remains are there?"*

[When I interviewed Confucius, I hadn't noticed these Buddhist tower-mound memorials, but I knew that Buddha had been a contemporary of Confucius,[23] and that the Mahayana form of Buddhism had since come across the Himalayas to China.]

FF: Of course. We must respect our ancestors by placing food, drink, and gifts before their *stupa*. Confucius explained how our departed ancestors travel endlessly through the heavens; so wouldn't they need

---

22. *Stupa*: Sanskrit for cairn, or burial monument.

23. Confucius and Buddha (whose philosophies were remarkably similar: avoid extremes, seek "The Middle Way") arose around the same era as that of Greek philosopher/scientist Aristotle, whose views shaped the Mediterranean world. All three were from "the ruling class" (*i.e.* noble, aristocratic). At first, Confucian scholars rejected Buddha as "western, non-Chinese." In 691, empress Wu Hou imposed Buddhism as the state religion, opposing Christianity. Indian Buddhism entering China was the Mahayana, which included assistance by Enlightened Ones (*Bodhisattvas*) remaining on earth to help others. Nirvana became a state to attain ("beyond description!" so Buddha never mentioned it, monks explain).

provisions? Our people constantly worry about our ancestors, but not as much since the Buddha brought us Enlightenment.

SH: Enlightenment?

FF: Yes, of course. Where have you been? Don't you know how the Noble Buddha explained we could end our ceaseless wandering in the next life by getting off the wheel of life? That would mean becoming Enlightened—feeling no desire or pain, no existence. Even if we don't manage in this life to build up enough good *karma* to achieve that, Buddha has given us hope of eternal peace—Nirvana.

SH: Eternal peace—such as Jesus promised? Those Syrian Christians who've come along the Spice Road have told about a Saviour who gives eternal peace.

FF: Oh, no! What Jesus taught was superstition. The Buddha revealed that there are good Buddhists who could enter eternal bliss, but who have chosen to remain upon earth in order to help others. Maybe Christians would call them saviours. Or maybe they are like the messiah the Jewish traders talk about. We have to care for these good people because they help us men.

SH: They help men? How about women?

FF: If women respect and obey us men, we can share our good *karma* with them. Or by good deeds, women can upgrade themselves and be reborn as males. Of course, there are different levels of males. . . . Anyway, I see that Fou Tse has quarried the geese, so I must prepare one to give our shaman. I want him to give Fou an auspicious sign to start school.

Two Intertwining Strands

The imaginary interview over, I found myself back in today's world.[24] At last, the Chinese Puzzle was making sense. I could see two strands woven throughout China's cord of history: a positive and a negative—a philosophical *yang* and *yin,* if you like. Ironically, the two threads were so interwoven, that positive strands contained negative fibers.

24. Again to avoid travelog becoming treatise, I've imagined dialogue. Confucian/Buddhist beliefs cited are based on John Hinnells' *Dictionary of Religions, op. cit.* and confirmed by Chinese MS readers. —WHF

Confucius promoted important values in family life and society: loyalty, honesty, generosity, and equality in birth. His concept of authority also brought order to a restive population, demanding undivided obedience to authority, regardless of changing politics. Hierarchy of authority implied accountability right up to the heavens.

One down side, however, was the concept of earthly counterparts to heavenly powers. This meant the Emperor—earth's highest authority, enjoyed a "Heavenly Mandate." One of his titles was "Son of Heaven."[25] The Emperor amounted to chief shaman of what functioned almost like a theocracy—the only earthly being with absolute power, backed up by heavenly powers. Because of this, an emperor could promote or demote (not based on privilege but on cosmic auspices), and could order with impunity the slaughter of an entire group or class.

Power of Life and Death

That actually took place in 1380. The Emperor ordered the slaughter of some 40,000 people directly or remotely connected with the family of his prime minister (whom he suspected of undermining his rule). No public outcry. The Emperor was the only one with exclusive access to the cosmos, which must have informed him that the *literati* were plotting rebellion! Besides, Confucian teaching had no concept of judgment after death. Justice must be meted out in this life.

Therefore, an Emperor could behead or beat or castrate[26] an official in public ("Let *that* be an example!")—even if he had done no wrong but was indicted by some event beyond his control (*e.g.*, a typhoon felling a favorite willow). The bubonic plague that swept China in the 14th c. undoubtedly led to the nationwide unrest of that era.[27]

---

25. As already indicated, the Confucian terminology stemmed from Egyptian/Babylonian-style cosmology—controlling the unseen forces of the universe. Neither Confucius nor his contemporary Buddha accepted the Jewish concept of a Creator God or a divine Messiah/Saviour. "Heaven" simply meant "the heavenlies." There was no supernatural being (God)—only forces and influential ancestral spirits.

26. If the humiliated official didn't already have a male heir to placate the heavens on his behalf, castration would leave him to wander hopelessly after death forever, people believed. It was a fate worse than death.

27. Speculation is that Mongol invaders carried the plague to Europe, causing its deadly 14th c. Black Death.

Signs of the heavens, in effect, countermanded the basic equality of all beings. On the positive side, the concept of heaven-earth hierarchy gave parents authority over children, but on the negative, it also gave men absolute authority over women. Shamans divined auspices that granted office or position to a person or group. Confucian views of the innate goodness of mankind led to lack of realism in facing local or national problems—noted by analysts of the era's economic conditions. Confucius relied on pacifist learning instead of military defence against invasion. At the same time, signs in the cosmos legitimised the Emperor's absolute control of everything, including people, income, trade, law, and arts. Later, these factors made Mongol conquest of a weak emperor relatively easy.

In spite of certain benefits to a cosmopolitan society, the over-all result stifled entrepreneurship. While the West sees individual enterprise as liberating (enabling anyone to achieve, with resultant benefits to society as a whole), ancient China saw it as uncontrolled selfishness, not beneficial to society. And indeed it is often so! At the same time, the commendable Confucian concept of every person's responsibility for himself fed into Buddhism's teaching of accruing good *karma,* in order to improve one's status in re-incarnation. Chinese macho society adapted Buddha's elevation of womanhood by changing the precept, "Husband *supports* wife," to "Husband *controls* wife."

In both Confucian and Buddhist teachings, there were traces of the concept of "Limited Good." Anthropologist William Kornfield of SIM once explained it to me:[28]

"The concept has arisen in different parts of the world. In this view, there is only so much good in the world; so if a person receives more than one's share, others are restricted in what they can receive. Anyone who rises above the rest may be attacked for being successful."

The concept of Limited Good held back others from even trying to improve. The Confucian emphasis upon learning was for the sake of knowledge itself, not necessarily for personal advancement.

The downside of Confucian teaching was suspicion; a successful person would threaten others. This resulted in attempts to "cut down tall poppies"—sometimes through paying a shaman to come up with *negative*

28. W. Harold Fuller, *Tie Down the Sun* (see Bibliography).

auspices for a competitor. Personal grievances, ambitions, or bribes could affect interpretations, influencing people and their decisions.

What Turned China Up-Side-Down?

Underneath the elite-imposed Confucian order of society, there persisted a different philosophy: Taoism.[29] Tradition traces it to a contemporary of Confucius, Lao Tsu. The record of his sayings reflects ageless wisdom. Examples: "He who knows others is learned; he who knows himself is wise." "To rejoice in conquest is to rejoice in murder." "Govern a great nation as you would cook a small fish."[30]

Although its origin is questionable, "Tao" is the nameless, unchanging, non-assertive essence and source of heaven and earth. Its concepts are manifold, but it appears to be a mix of magic, mystic rites, and philosophy borrowed from Zoroastrian (Persian) and Babylonian animism. Although, like Confucianism, favouring simplicity and peaceful compromise, it became the *antithesis* of Confucian learning, relying instead on magic and appeasement of spirits. In the face of rigid Confucian order, many peasants quietly practised Taoism, and some elites subscribed to it while professing politically correct Confucian principles. For many, it became a safety net, or perhaps double insurance for success.

Taoism survived because "Tao" (or Ultimate Essence) was not thought to initiate anything. So Taoists resigned themselves to the inevitable, including Confucian rules. This acceptance led to a *laissez-faire*[31] attitude, though it kept Taoists out of trouble. That is, until the invading Mongolian Emperor Kublai Khan rejected its magic and ordered its teachings burned (1281). Eventually the empire that had developed beyond the Roman Empire's prowess, and could have ruled the world by the 12th c., withdrew like a turtle into its shell—while the West developed technology and trade that eventually dominated China itself (at least for a time!).

That may have explained why the Chinese Dragon turned into a Turtle, its head tucked in. But I had a bigger question: How did the Turtle metamorphose into a Serpent?

---

29. Taoism (Daoism): "Teachings of the Way," a word linguistically similar to Greek "Logos" (John 1.1).

30. In other words, don't over-do it!

31. *Laissez-faire*: <French, implying, "Let people do as they please."

The Confucian Confusion

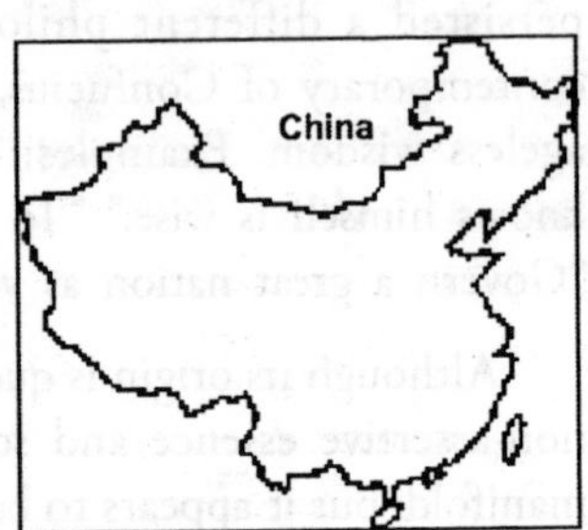

"The fear of the Lord is the beginning of wisdom; all who follow his precepts have good understanding" (Ps. 111.10).

CONFUCIUS HELPED ANSWER my question: *How could Chairman Mao Zedong take absolute control of this amazing nation* (brilliant, ethical, compassionate in many respects) *and commit the most heinous atrocities without compunction?* How could the masses, ingrained with the concept of respecting authority, turn against the authority of parents, teachers, and state? How could children drag their elders out of bed and gleefully slaughter them? How could order turn into anarchy overnight?

Paradoxically, Confucius held the answer. Of course! Hierarchical authority (the essence of Confucius' code of living), while legitimising Mao's authority, also became the enemy to destroy! It seemed contradictory, an anomaly for an ordered society. In fact, it was devilishly Hegelian, the philosophy adopted by Marx-Leninism.[1] While achieving power of life and death as the new Emperor, Mao had to destroy the Confucian social structure that gave him legitimacy but also bound the nation in tradition. Taoism, which, in the interest of "universal order," resolutely resisted change, also had to go. Imprisoning Confucian and Taoist scholars, Mao overthrew traditional respect within family and society.

1. Hegelian: The process of thesis-antithesis-synthesis ("black is white; injustice is justice") that has been used to legitimize atrocities of Stalin, Hitler, and other tyrants. See Chapter 14 re. Pol Pot.

It all became frighteningly clear. Chairman Mao became the new Emperor, the highest power in the Confucian-shaman hierarchy of authoritarian collectivism. The adoring masses were showing obedience to their divine leader. They understood when Mao told them that bourgeoisie (the middle class, landowners, merchants) had held down the proletariat (unskilled peasants). Hadn't Confucius said that all people are born equal? The elite had taught (but conveniently ignored) his principle of "unselfishness"—meaning that no individual should improve his condition above that of the lowest peasant, unless raising that person's level also. Cut down the "tall poppies"— to the "masses," that meant anyone with education. Simplistically, it sounded like Communist ideology.

But the twisted doctrine also had a split personality. While espousing rule by the Communist proletariat, "Chairman" Mao (*i.e.* The Emperor), was the only one who could allow or deny rights. With Confucian idealism, he opposed merchant, landowner, and military classes. But to bolster his own position, Mao also attacked Confucian tradition, morals, and scholars.

Instead of using the military to take control, Mao whipped up the *peasants* to cleanse the nation of such "leaches," using sheer force of numbers. Mindless mobs were only "executing" justice on behalf of the newly mandated Son of Heaven! *Let the heads roll!* Confucius had taught that judgment is here and now—there's no Judgement Seat *after* death. "Be vicious!" Mao exhorted. So his followers, in one fortnight, bludgeoned to death some two thousand in Beijing alone.

Mao—Paranoid Genius

My mind reeled as I learned more about Mao Zedong. As a teenager, he apparently skipped classes because he couldn't follow his teachers' thinking. Events in the islands across the Sea of Japan excited him.[2] Mao devoured translations of books by Western liberals such as Thomas Huxley, Adam Smith, and J. S. Mill. In 1917, a departmental dean in China's premier university, fresh from studies in Paris, attacked Confucius in the

2. Even before WW I, Japan had become an example of oriental power that could compete with Europe in trade—a ruthless model to emulate. But China also resented Japan's expansionism, as the island nation vied with Europe in claiming areas of trade influence in China.

name of science and "democracy," infusing students with the heady spirit of the French Revolution. A student protest in Tiananmen Square in 1919 denounced Confucian family bonds and culture for leading to "the misery of the multitudes."[3] Mao was one of those students, bitter that the government banned the socialist journal he edited.

At first, young Mao favored reform, but in 1921 International Communism's local agent, a Marxist/Leninist Dutchman, helped Mao and other revolutionaries to form the Chinese Communist Party (CCP), founded on revolutionary class struggle. Lenin, they learned, saw "Western Imperialism" as the prop of Western capitalism. If the CCP helped to destroy it, capitalism would fall worldwide. Heady stuff that!

Mao endured great physical suffering while developing a militia and the CCP. Power intoxicated him, and by the time the CPP declared itself the state governing power, he had become virtual Emperor of China. (The proletarian title of "Chairman" was an ironic nod to Confucian levelling of society.) At first a sympathetic world looked upon him as the one to break through China's endemic corruption and stifling traditions. Wasn't Mao destroying the grip of the powerful landlords, and encouraging the rural masses to develop themselves and their country? Liberation, on its way to democracy! Familiar song?

Soon it became apparent that Mao was out to revolutionize society through violence—a ruthless genius in his own evil way.[4] The charismatic leader was ready to take over China.

The nation, in turn, was ripe for Mao's picking. History was on his side: in 581, Emperor Sui had declared an official redistribution of equal fields and collective responsibility—but under *his* central bureaucracy.

So while Chairman Mao told peasants he was putting their welfare into their own hands, in reality they owned nothing and could do nothing unless the Party decreed. Cadres, themselves peasant activists, regulated life. True to human nature, they demanded "perks" and status, benefiting from the productivity of rural slavery. Inexperienced in leadership, they

---

3. The words of Lu Xun, reformist writer (1881-1936). Fairbank, p. 268 (see Bibliography).

4. Jung Change, Jon Halliday in *Mao: The Unknown Story*, portray Mao as unparalleled evil (see Biblio.).

discredited the revolution with ruinous mismanagement, actually lowering the already dismal level of rural living—yet disguising the true production figures. Unskilled peasants rejected all experience and expertise from the past as "bourgeois." In the '50s, there were a million cottage smelting-furnaces, but they produced unusable pig iron!

Mao's purges also followed the violence of other emperors. Circa 230 B.C., Emperor Qin murdered 460 scholars and burned the archives of conquered areas, preserving only his own records. As mentioned, in 1380, Emperor Hong Wu had massacred at least 40,000—possibly 100,000.[5] For Mao, given the population growth, what was so out of place to purge a million "oppressors," out of some billion suffering people?

Struggle: Reform or Revolution?

Mao's communism grew in the power vacuum that followed the collapse of the Qing (Manchu) Dynasty (1644-1912). That vacuum had made way for the 20th c. struggles between reform and revolution. Respected nationalist leader, Sun Yatsen, formed the Nationalist Party (NP) to reconcile the two views. A Methodist reformist, General Jiang Jieshi (Chiang Kaishek)[6] became its leader, but was opposed by the CCP's revolutionary Mao Zedong. The NP ended up on the Island of Taiwan (before then largely Japanese populated), while the CCP dominated the mainland.[7]

The CCP Chairman's power was intoxicating. A psychoanalyst would need to explain what led to his paranoia, but like many tyrants before and since, he suspected even his closest colleagues and inner circle. Transitions taking place in Soviet Communism, including Krushchev's "revisionist" denouncement of Comrade Stalin, increased Mao's paranoia.[8] With much cunning, Mao encouraged "intellectuals" (anyone with at least secondary school education) to criticize their officials—a ploy to weaken the powerful.

5. Fairbank, *ibid*. p. 189 (see Bibliography).
6. The story of General Chiang Kaishek and his wife, Soong Meiling, is well documented by others.
7. On the 70th anniversary of Mao's "Long March" to power, the Chinese government presented TV sets to 80,000 survivors of the March, to solve their "television-viewing difficulties." (*Maclean's* Nov. 6/06.)
8. Roderick MacFarquhar and Michael Schoenhals, *Mao's Last Revolution*. Harvard U. Press, 2007.

But when intellectuals also criticized CCP policies, Mao quickly turned against such "anti-revolutionaries," unleashing a ruinous purge of educated people, even though the state sorely needed them. Mobs destroyed much of China's 3,000 years of artifacts. The paranoid Chairman developed phobias: during a famine launching a crusade to kill all birds (maybe *they* were causing the famine by eating grain!), and another time, all insects. His behaviour became unpredictable and irrational. Sycophant officials surrounding him didn't realize his devilish plans—until he swept them away also.

The Confucian system of respect for authority was not balanced by legal human-rights safeguards (which Confucius opposed). The doctrine of absolute rule legitimised by the cosmos left no room for question or debate. Control of society led to control of thought (Mao's "Red Book"). Equality that denied opportunity, shared poverty instead of wealth. The concept of Limited Good provided a ready basis for extremes of communist egalitarianism.

In the absence of a transcendent Creator God who would sort out the righteous and unrighteous in eternity, accountability stopped at the Emperor's palace. In fact, in the 60s, Mao crowed, "The latest remnants of the Christian faith in this land have been destroyed!" The megalomaniac settled accounts by stamping "PAID" in blood. After all, for Confucius, didn't death end everything?

So there was the answer to my question, "How could this all happen?" ***China's Communism was a natural synthesis of Confucian philosophy, peasant rebellion against elitist and foreign oppression, and Communist dialectic. Mao was the catalyst for revolution.***

Simple? Yes, hideously simple.[9] I remember being appalled, as a young man, by Mao's reign of terror. Yet, if I'd known history, I shouldn't have been surprised. As I thought it through in hindsight, I began to see China's current emergence in a new light.

---

9. "Simple" as Hitler's "Final Solution." My summary uses a yard-wide brush, but there exists a plethora of books on China's history—though research and review were long taboo within China (see Bibliog.)

Understanding this background helped me in viewing China's positive development today.

While we recoil from Mao's brutality, ironically his purges made creation of a new China inevitable. Communism forcibly ended the chokehold of wealthy merchants and landlords on illiterate peasants. It broke the ubiquitous drug trade. Egalitarian ideology gave women new self-confidence, after centuries of male oppression. Because it had such absolute power, the government was able to unify the nation's languages, replacing complicated pictographs with *pinyin*-related characters.[10] At first, literacy and education increased exponentially; superstitions went underground.

But during China's "Twenty Lost Years," schools and universities closed, culminating in the Cultural Revolution. Young zealots destroyed everything they considered old: cultures, customs, ideas, habits—even records. The entire country couldn't have existed much longer as Mao applied Marx-Lenin's self- destructing ideology. As China was sliding into chaos, Chairman Mao's death in 1976 (coinciding with a major earthquake—a devastating omen) came not a day too soon!

New China: *Peaceful* Revolution

With Mao Zedong gone, Premier Zhou Enlai called for "The Four Modernizations," opening the way for *reform* rather than continuing revolutionary mayhem. Then in 1978, Deng Xiaoping (who had himself been "purged" twice) took the helm, quietly introducing a pragmatic slogan: "Seek truth from facts"—a neat secular (scientific) motif that still gave a nod to Buddhist and Confucian concepts of "truth," or knowledge. With 85% of the population literate in basic reading (only the official

10. *Pinyin*, anglicized as "pidjin": <*pin* "to arrange" + *yin* "sound." Chinese pictographs consist of 214 symbols, forming up to 50,000 ideographs. Simplified symbols are usually written vertically in books, newspapers, and formal invitations, from one column to the next on the left. Used with English (in bilingual communication) they have to be written horizontally, reading left to right. Complications arise when there are multiple horizontal lines of characters, as in a paragraph. In theory, the pictographs could read both ways, but context usually indicates which way the writer intends. Don Richardson (*op cit.*, p. 117) cites the Christian significance of Chinese pictographs—many incorporating biblical concepts.

dialect of Mandarin has a written form), the nation was ready to burst forth. Teachers of English were in demand. The state invested millions in state universities, speeding up the education process through multiple overseas scholarships. Returning graduates staffed thousands of new state universities.

While Chinese have risen to the top of academia, ingrained Confucian and Taoist emphasis on rote learning at first slowed creativity. Entrepreneurs who have broken out of that traditional mould (often through overseas exposure) now spearhead China's increasing creativity. The nation's self-confidence showed in its break with global Internet protocols of "domains" (*e.g.* ".org" or ".com"), by independently authorizing new suffixes in Chinese characters. The British Council, in partnership with a Chinese partner, claims that 2m students log on to its website of vocabulary and business English—making it the world's biggest online university.

On an earlier visit to China, I'd seen only government-controlled TV programs in my hotel room; the daily news was canned propaganda. But now, while the government is naturally wary of unrest, I watched a singing competition sponsored by a yogurt manufacturer! In August 2005, some 400m (nearly one third of China's population) viewed the finale. Voting was limited to users of text-messaging mobile phones, so only (!) about 8m cast their ballots to select "the Super Voice Girl." Discussion filled the newspapers. On the radio, I could even listen to one of Dr. James Dobson's Family Counseling broadcasts, and in a bookshop I could buy "Focus on the Family" books. This Chinese Puzzle is full of surprises!

Inevitably, along with unaccustomed education and industry have come relaxing of parental and moral control. Confucius wouldn't recognize today's urban teenagers, but any Westerner would. Whereas prostitution has always been part of Chinese society, nowadays it is flagrantly open in cities, along with raunchy nightlife, drugs, and alcohol. Tobacco usage has also been a tradition, and by the beginning of this millennium, the number of smokers was already estimated at 300 million, more than the total in the entire developed world. The Chinese government makes $10 billion a year in tobacco tax.

Yet, in the Chinese view, libertine Western societies are in no position to lecture on morality. I remembered the shocking case of a Chinese visa student who abducted and murdered 9-year-old Cecilia Zhang in our Toronto neighborhood. Back in his Chinese village, officials testified that he was a good young man who fell to temptations in Canada—"a minefield of sin, where students face violence, immorality, and crime."[11]

Oddly, a poll revealed that 23% of Chinese think extramarital affairs in which no one gets hurt are acceptable (compared to 11% of Britons and 9% of Americans). But Chinese are far more likely to think that monogamy is the natural state for human beings: 70% of them agree, compared with 57% of Americans and 42% of Britons.[12]

Perhaps the vacuum created by years under Communism plus current moral laxity accounts for another surprise: reviving interest in religion. Pan Yue, director of the State Environmental Protection Administration, has even argued in a published article that the Communist Party's traditional view of religion was wrong.[13] The state now allows the once-banned Confucian teaching (with its quasi-religious ethics). Pan suggested that Buddhism and Taoism had helped "social stability" throughout the nation's earlier history. Some officials see the influence of religion in Hong Kong (where Protestant agencies provide the lead in health and other civic services) worthy of emulation. Breaking with restrictive culture (including the subordination of women) is leading many educated young people to look into evangelical Christianity.[14]

Changing official attitudes took me back to my clandestine meeting with Chinese disciples in an "upper room" before restrictions were lifted. And even if all might not yet be open, I gave thanks for the faithfulness and endurance of followers of Jesus.

The "Gung-Ho" Society

"When China awakes, it will astonish the world," Napoleon Bonaparte forecast some 200 years ago. Although "when China re-

---

11. Radio 680 news report, Toronto, July 27, 2004.

12. Sympatico MSN, October 25, 2004.

13. Party members have had to be atheists, but even that requirement could change.

14. *Economist,* Feb. 3, 2007.

awakens" might be more accurate, it was true that I was being properly astonished.

During my visit to Beijing, nowhere did I see a beggar. At the time, preparations for the 2008 Olympics were in overdrive, most financed from state coffers. Bulldozers removed the shanties that used to ring the capital, and tall cranes dominated the city core's skyline, swinging building materials onto project sites day and night.[15] The city's traffic grows more chaotic as 1,000 *additional* cars funnel onto the streets *every day*. The new China was "gung-ho" to show the world its progress.[16]

Today's China is living up to that phrase, hoping the Olympics erased centuries of humiliation, during which the nation felt ignored and disrespected. Ancient Chinese capabilities keep surfacing. For instance, when today's American scientists tried to solve a mathematical problem beyond the processing capability of any supercomputer, they resorted to the Chinese "remainder theorem" described by an A.D. 3rd c. mathematician, Sun Tzu (not the military strategist of that name).[17]

Between 1600 and the early 1800s, China's culture was more advanced than the West's, with larger cities and a higher literacy rate, as well as mastery of the high seas.[18] While some neighbors may be concerned at China's growing power, the nation's leaders feel that they are simply restoring its previous glory. "Peaceful rise," its President Hu calls it. "A renaissance," Singapore's Lee Yuan Yew terms it. In fact, China's economic growth is proving a boon to South-East Asia, as industries there provide parts for Chinese assembly plants. Chinese architects, engineers, and investors are now in demand in Southern Asia, Africa, and the Middle East. Impressive road and rail links will eventually link the nation with ports on the Arabian Sea and the Bay of Bengal.

---

15. "Two-thirds of the planet's construction cranes can be found in China, where 40% of the world's cement is currently being poured." (*Books & Culture*, Jan.-Feb. 2007, p. 15.)
16. "Gung ho" comes from Chinese *gong-he*—acronym for the "Chinese Industrial Cooperative Society," and implies "working together." During WW II, U.S. marines picked it up to mean enthusiasm or zeal.
17. *Economist*, March 24, 2007, re. the work of Jerry Adams of the University of Maryland.
18. *Economist*, March 31, 2007, special report on China, p. 4.

China now boasts the world's largest facility for servicing private planes—for visitors who plan to fly themselves in. Spectators watched Olympic contests in the new stadium (shaped like a bird's nest), or enjoyed the arts in the world's largest opera house—both designed by renowned European architects. At night visitors were awed by spectacular fireworks—a speciality in China, which invented gunpowder. Appropriately, firecrackers are the traditional way to scare off evil spirits at festivals. In Beijing shoppers could "shop till they dropped" in the world's largest shopping Mall.

The nation that once withdrew from the rest of the world has now broken through even the barrier of space: in 2005, China's space agency launched two cosmonauts into space, and announced plans to land on the moon soon.

All this flurry of progress is taking place in a society that many Westerners find difficult to understand—one where cities manufacture computers for the West and yet villagers still use the ancient abacus (low-cost and efficient) to tote up bills in their market stalls. China is a dictatorship, yet aspects of its economy function like a democracy. "It has a kind of state-controlled free enterprise system," explained financier Mark Maxwell after a visit to China. "Our free enterprise and democracy in the West are based on a middle-class majority population. China doesn't have this base. It's trying to bridge the gap between a minority of urban entrepreneurs and a majority of rural peasants still living as their grandparents did." Three-quarters of China's 1.3 billion people live in rural areas.

While major cities boast industrial plants with the latest equipment, 370 workers *a day* die through industrial accidents. Meanwhile, for many villagers, life remains "nasty, brutish, and short," as one report stated. Until economic growth trickles down among the rural population and brings about more general development academically and socially, the government daren't remove controls. The peasants are the ones who would suffer. The alternative would be millions of angry peasants rising up to destroy holders of wealth that seems beyond their grasp. China's leaders don't want to go back to Mao's era!

Economic Reform: Controlled Capitalism

Although the current pace is fast, it didn't develop overnight. Since Mao's day, economic reforms have been slow to take effect. That is understandable, in turning around such a "ship of state." How to bring one fifth of the world's population out of socialist state planning into free trade, without a breakdown in law and order? I had to understand the country's present status against the backdrop of what it was before Communism: opium trade, rampant prostitution, general laziness, religious superstition, fatalism, along with exploitation by feudalism and the worst aspects of mercantilism.[19]

I put myself in the place of government leaders. They'd been through the horrors of revolution, but they didn't want to experience the anarchy the USSR had suffered with Stalinism's collapse. Studying the disastrous dissolution of the Soviets, they concluded that its political change had outpaced economic growth.

Did I have a simplistic concept of Communism vs. democracy? State control of everything, including thought and religion, was obviously abusive and counter-productive. But while wanting to take their place in the global economy, China's leaders had chosen "controlled capitalism" (one could term it) rather than risk the anarchy of a massive population unfamiliar with the personal responsibility that true liberty requires (if it is not going to destroy itself).

There were other problems: endemic corruption and protectionist regulations. So while China's officials wanted change to set the wheels in motion, Chinese entrepreneurs were afraid of erratic officialdom, and foreign investors hesitated. One unheralded person who helped to bring about change was a Southern Baptist businessman, Dwight Nordstrom, heir to a family fortune made by a pharmacy chain. In a business discussion in the 1990s, Chinese finance officials asked Nordstrom how he felt he could be of help.

---

19. As I'd found in South America, Communism demonized "Capitalism," which the people never experienced apart from a few discreet entrepreneurs. The real monster was exploitive *mercantilism.* Fuller, *Tie Down the Sun, op cit.* (p. 309, etc.) See also Juan Isaias, *The Other Side of the Coin* (Bibliography).

"I happen to be from a wealthy family and am willing to help you find foreign investment," he told the authorities; "but you'll have to agree on two things: No red tape and no bribery."[20]

Authorities accepted his offer and challenge, and some observers credit him with furthering China's positive attitude to foreign investment—which is generating economic growth. Whether that is so or not, Nordstrom has encouraged some dozen companies to build plants in China, together employing around 8,000 people.[21] That's not many in a country of over one billion. But it reflects changing official attitudes.

The New Entrepreneurs

Europeans once thought of China as a producer of "knock-off" copies of goods produced by the West. That still may happen, but Chinese entrepreneurs have broken the mold. A prime example is Jack Ma, founder of the globe's largest business-to-business Internet system, Alibaba. Still in his early forties, he is already a challenge to even Google and Yahoo! In fact, Western companies seek to follow his pattern of success.[22]

China currently boasts the world's second largest economy, which is forecast to be larger than USA's by 2027, and twice as large by 2050. Even now it is the biggest I.T. exporter *to* USA—although America is the country that designed I.T. "protocol" and invented the electronic computer and transistor! China produces and consumes one-quarter of world steel, one-half of global cement, and one-third of its fuel. It has the world's largest foreign currency reserves, ahead of Japan.[23] China is now concerned about instability arising from its over-heated economy. But economists worry about what *doesn't* appear in China's public budget: upwards of $90 billion in hidden military spending annually.[24]

---

20. Report by R. Gupta, SIM Conference on Asia, 2005. *The Economist* (August 4, 2007, p. 55) suggests that the Confucian view of society inadvertently contributes to bribery: family and friends first, then "face," finally the law. Common disguise for soliciting a bribe: "The man with the key is not here."
21. Reported as example of lay ministry, 40th anniv. of School of Intercultural Studies, Fuller Seminary, '05.
22. *Economist*, September 26, '06.
23. Foreign investment, however, also raises Chinese concern about foreign control. For more discussion on Asia and the world economy, see Appendix I.
24. U.S. Pentagon estimate, 2006.

Although India's low wages and English speakers attract outsourcing, China has the edge in flexible labor and financial laws. It has the second highest energy consumption (although taking three times more energy to produce a product than does USA, still the world's largest manufacturer).[25] To secure adequate energy supplies for its burgeoning industry, China has energy contracts with such ready partners as Brazil, Iran, Russia, Sudan, Venezuela, and Zimbabwe. Of course China also has contracts with Europe and North America, but more for goods and services than raw materials. "Down-Under" neighbor Australia supplies coal and plutonium—the latter for nuclear power generation, to help relieve China's chronic electricity shortages.

"If you want one year of prosperity, grow grain. If you want 100 years, grow people," a Chinese proverb states. That lies behind massive development of universities, which number more than in any other nation. China, along with India and other emerging nations, has in effect doubled the global workforce. That in turn is radically changing not only industry but also the social environment in Western countries. There is a positive side—inflation and interest rates would be much higher were it not for the cheaper goods arriving from overseas labor markets. The downside, of course, is the pain of social upheaval in the West as employment moves to Asia.

There couldn't be a more graphic illustration of today's industrial global revolution than the story of IBM's personal computer (PCs). Although there were forms of PC earlier, in 1981 IBM introduced its popular PC that became the industry's standard. But in 2004, IBM decided to shelve its PC hardware manufacturing to concentrate on services and other innovations. The purchaser? A Chinese company, Lenovo, paid IBM $1.25 billion for the business. With lower labor costs, Lenovo is now churning out some four million PCs annually. And Lenovo's founder, working with other entrepreneurs who survived the Cultural Revolution, has helped change government attitudes and business actions. Dalian,

25. China is now the world's biggest air polluter, commissioning two new coal-fired power plants per week. World demand for low-cost goods means more pollution from manufacturing. However, government has introduced environmental targets—such as up to 65% reduced energy consumption for new buildings.

North-East port city, houses Japan's outsourcing call-center in China, along with Dell, G.E., Microsoft, and SAP. Dalian boasts 22 universities, with 200,000 students enrolled.

A homegrown example of entrepreneur is China's Nine Dragons paper company. Bypassing American and British companies to become the world's largest paper producer, it was begun by a woman (yes—in a man's world!). Starting out some 15 years ago in Hong Kong, Mrs. Cheung recycled waste paper for packaging materials before moving up into papermaking. With plants in China's South, East, and West, Mrs. Cheung has become the world's wealthiest woman entrepreneur.

Hopes raised and dashed

Although global monetary policy increasingly is shaped not in London, Paris, or Washington but in Beijing, industrial growth also involves problems.[26] As Asia's rural areas develop, more youth need employment. The Asian Development Bank estimates that by 2015, China's labor pool will grow 7% annually. Europe and North America have lots of work for low-cost labor, but many new industries in China are now utilizing the same automated industrial machinery the West used to lower its own costs! To employ its increasing labor force, China is developing internal markets. One indicator of their growth is the 100 million Chinese who log on to the Internet daily. Even seniors find personal "blogging" sites help them keep in touch with society.

However, haste to overcome rural poverty can have its tragedies. In the 1990s, officials in central China's Henan Province encouraged peasants to sell their blood, to be returned to them after the plasma had been removed. It sounded like an easy source of income but resulted in a disastrous health scandal. In the process blood became contaminated with HIV/AIDS, infecting thousands of clinic patients as they received contaminated blood or plasma. Instead of anticipated wealth, entire communities have been devastated.[27]

26. *The Lenovo Affair: The Growth of China's Computer Giant and its takeover of IBM-PC*, by Ling Zhijun. London: John Wiley, 2006.

27. *Economist*, Jan. 20,2007.

China's dilemma is that it must keep up the pace of economic growth in order to maintain social stability among restless peasants—some 700 *million* struggle with poverty. Economic development means unprecedented migration to cities. Until recently, the ratio of rural to urban population was 80 to 20, and rising expectations increased migration to the cities, raising the ratio to 50/50.

China now has the world's most populous city: Chongqing, in Sichuan Province, with 30 million residents—and growing![28] Nationwide, every year 17 million babies are born. This rapid grow puts great strain on food supply, transportation, education, and social services (health, welfare, care of elderly). It also adds to rising crime, straining police and judicial systems. And back in the villages? Parents, moving to cities to find work, leave children with grandparents, creating a deprived society at home.

However, the economic downturn at the first of this century created another problem—factories laid off millions of workers, who returned to their villages penniless but with expectation of better living standards. That threatened to unleash urban unrest.

"Go West!"

Xinjiang, largest and most westerly province, has 5,500 km. of frontier bordering eight mostly Muslim countries. The province has been China's show-window for domestic (internal) development. Beyond the cities, gas and oil pipelines cross grassy plains on which peasants tend herds and sleep in traditional *yurts*.[29] But cities boast new factories, shops—and Pizza Huts—while shiny bicycles and cars fill the streets.

Dotting city skylines, pagodas of Buddhist temples poke up between Islamic muezzin towers and Russian Orthodox spires. Although there was no Uighur evangelical church in 2007, Christian evangelists and aid workers find many ways to help the people. One short-term team keeps

---

28. In contrast, this *one* Chinese city has nearly as many people as all of Canada (world's second largest country)! Chongqing has the distinction of being "Woman Town." District gates declare: "A woman never makes a mistake," and even tourists will have to keep rules set by its female council—or else wash dishes!

29. *Yurt*: Turkic, "home."

busy as exchange teachers, even supplying ethnic minority students with books, desks, chairs, and backpacks. Local officials invited the team to assist in medical clinics.

These have more than economic significance. Home to Turkic Uighurs, Kazakhs, and other descendents of Central Asia (yes—related to those hardy ancestors who sacked Rome and terrorized Eastern Europe in the 5th c.), the area on a couple of occasions has declared itself East Turkestan.

During the Soviet era, Moscow feared Chinese expansion into the same areas that the USSR was absorbing, and fed border republics with fears of Chinese takeover. China already faces an enormous task unifying 456 ethnic groups countrywide, and is very wary of separatists groups. Uighur Muslims are mostly Sufis, whose mystic worship of Allah sits ill with the Communist Party's atheism. Arms and drugs cross the plains from Pakistan and Afghanistan. Unemployed youth high on drugs and looking for a cause is the last thing China wants on its restive borders. Pilgrimage to Mecca is still illegal (but the government does sponsor "official" trips, which are well supervised).

Hence the government's "Go West" policy: industry, schools, hospitals—and ethnic migration to create an "ethnic balance." China's majority Han people head West from the crowded eastern coastlands. Xinjiang, the New Western Frontier, welcomes NGOs that can help with development. Boom times, they believe, spawn a satisfied population and lead to a more open and tolerant society.[30]

Changing Traditions, Changing Values

China has a different worry at the other end of the age graph. While restrictions on family reduced the nation's burgeoning demographics, in 2009, there were 32 million more males than females.[31] Sex-selection contributes to this: at 18-weeks' gestation, many mothers use ultrasound to discover the gender of the fetus. Desiring a male heir, mothers may abort female fetuses. The preponderance of males may add to rising crime rates,

30. SIM and OMF are among the NGOs the government has asked to help.
31. Figures from *OneNewsNow* 4/18/09.

prostitution, marketing of females, and increase in homosexual practices. However, for some time rural areas have been flexible on the policy, and there are official hints that the government may scrap it by 2010.

But the most worrying result the aging population faces is the below-replacement birth rate.[32] (That's a new problem for China, where one million babies are born each year!) The trend means that by 2050, one-third of population will be over 60—the ratio of working people to retirees falling from its 2004 level of six to just under two. That will make any social security system (provided by family or state) more difficult to maintain.

On top of the changing rural/urban ratio, secularization affects the whole nation. The Cultural Revolution destroyed many traditional values. Not only does the new generation have a gap in history and traditions, family mores do not hold back criminal tendencies as they once used to. Families themselves are often riven by "virtual marriages" on the Internet—straying spouses may carry on emotional romances with several Internet suitors whom they will never meet.

"It's emotional adultery," states "Jamie" Hudson Taylor (JHT IV), who helps government schools recruit men and women in the professions.[33] "Sad—but it shows the need for Christian witness and Biblical teaching these days in China. In fact, the societal demands of China's economic growth, including migration to the cities, present the greatest challenge the Church of Jesus Christ has ever faced in China."

"Jamie" (so known by OMF to distinguish him from his father, "Jim," whom I had met in Singapore) told us about asking one official if he'd want teachers from overseas. JHT's heart sank when the official pointedly asked if they'd all be Christians, but he truthfully answered, "Yes."

"That's good!" continued the official, while Jamie started breathing again. "We wouldn't want any other teachers from overseas. Christians have shown they are not only capable but also responsible. They set the students a good example for living."

32. A fertility rate of 2.1 enables a population to replace itself. By 2004, China's rate was 1.69.

33. Taylor and colleagues specially welcome overseas Chinese. Indigenes dub them "sea turtles."

Patrick Fung, the medical doctor who became OMF's General Director in 2006,[34] underlines the need for Christians, whether Chinese or missionaries from other lands, to be involved in "incarnational ministries," as OMF's founder put it. That means integrating one's faith with one's profession.

"It needs courage as well as wisdom," explains Patrick, who knows that in China everyone's activity is monitored. "But as we show forth Christ in 'the market place,' others will ask why we are different from the world. OMFers incarnate the gospel by working *alongside* Chinese Christians, not *under or over* them, setting an example in evangelizing and discipling. For all our work in Asia, we're praying for 900 new members like that, this year!"

Dr. Fung points out the interchange that is going on between church groups. "Urban migrants are constantly moving from the interior to coastal centers, where they often live in bewilderment," he reports. "It is encouraging to see how inland pastors also move to the coast in order to minister to them."

Command Economy

China has made its decision. After centuries of invasion by "barbarians" and humiliation at the hands of "foreign merchants" (anathema to all Confucian principles), the nation that produced *literati* ahead of Europe, is taking its rightful place in the family of nations. That means a leading role, whether in politics, industry, or even mercantilism! *The orient has awakened!*[35]

However, I could sense a tension in today's command economy: (1) In one way, it's not contrary to Confucian dictum: *the Emperor has decided*. China shall lead the global economy. Obey! (2) In another sense, mercantilism and industrial competitiveness don't really fit Buddhism or Confucian thought. Shaman? Maybe. New concepts mingle with ancient traditions, to get the best of both worlds! Architects carefully design lobbies to benefit from the most auspicious angle to catch the flow of

34. Dr. Fung was studying overseas when the Lord challenged him to minister with OMF. Currently, 80,000 students from the People's Republic study in New Zealand alone, with another 80,000 in U.K.

35. The general term "Orient" traces through Sanskrit back to Greek: "to arouse" or "rise." Aryans brought their Sanskrit to South Asia, having added Greek words picked up during migration.

good influences and allow evil forces to exit right on out the back door. Today's entrepreneurs use the brightest ideas and technologies from both East and West. But behind the scenes, the Communist Party carefully controlls the nation, blocking "counter-revolutionary" Internet ideas, and shaping young minds by guiding public opinion.

Anyway, China's leaders would sort out the *yang* and the *yin*. It was time for me to leave for Mongolia. Short of money by now, I stopped at a wayside stall for breakfast before heading to the airport. I wolfed a bowl of noodles, washing it down with ginseng tea.[36] No meal service on the flight into Mongolia, I'd heard, so those noodles would have to do, even if the "shrimp-*flavored*" loops would make any real shrimp shrivel up.[37]

At the airport terminal, signs warned: "No Smoking or Lighting." Another sign assured passengers: "Safely Baggage Inspected." My departure card, which I was to surrender to Frontier Defence Inspection, gave nine occupations to choose from. They included Professional, Farmer, Worker, Jobless, and Other. I checked off "Other."

No one asked me *which* "other."

---

36. The chopsticks I used were two out of 45 billion pair used and tossed annually. Recently I learned that in 2006, China imposed a 5% tax on disposable chopsticks. Have to save trees! Now I know why China is interested in my own country's softwood lumber industry!
37. "Shrimp" in fact means "to shrivel" in Old Norse/Low German.

****

On Mongolia's plains, horsemen corral their steeds outside their domed yurts.

Golden Horde Shines Again[1]

[The Lord]"whistles for those at the ends of the earth. Here they come, swiftly and speedily!... their horses' hoofs seem like flint" (Isaiah 5:26,28).

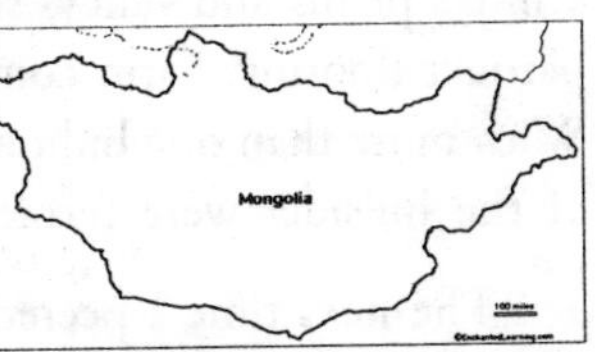

Mongolia: Pop. 3,083,289

MY ONLY WAY INTO "OUTER" MONGOLIA[2] was by MIAT, a Mongolian flight available on Tuesday, Thursday, and Saturday. With both schedule and money tight—I was thankful to be booked on Thursday's flight. My problem had been that Thursday was the only day the Mongolian consulate in Beijing was open to obtain a visa. At the time, I could not get one outside of China.

I *had* to board that Thursday flight, so I arrived at the sparse office before it opened, ahead of a small line of traders and travelers from China and other nations. In any nation, I don't like to stick out like a pushy foreigner, but while Communist Chinese don't like officiousness, they do respect officialdom. So when the Consul appeared, without apology I waved my letter from Mongolia's Ministry of Information, inviting me to conduct a seminar for Mongolian reporters. I glanced at my watch . . . I still had to fight Beijing's traffic to the airport, and board the flight scheduled to depart in a few hours.

I breathed more easily when the stoic consul stamped my application in several places, front and back. Picking up a larger rubber stamp, with a final impressive flourish, she entered a visa in my passport.[3] I sensed that

---

1. As noted earlier, *horde* comes from Mongol-Turkic, *ordu* ("camp"—or a khan's/chief's residence).
2. "Outer" because a province of northern China is also called Mongolia ("Inner Mongolia").

each impact of the official rubber stamps announced that newly independent Mongolia has authority over who crosses its borders. However, the nation on the northern plateau could use all the help it could get, so the Consul let me in. After "racing" (at tortoise speed in slow traffic) to the airport, I found that my flight had been delayed.

When our venerable Russian Ilushin aircraft (a converted military plane) did take off, I looked down on a farming mosaic. Every inch of China's plains and valleys seemed to be cultivated—like green and brown parquet flooring. Farm communities dotted the landscape between fields. With more than one billion people to feed, every plot was precious. Some of the hillsides were terraced to the top.

The next time I peered out the vibrating aircraft's window, I saw no green—only haze or dust, with patches of sandy desert. Beginning in China's Inner Mongolia and stretching across into Mongolia, the wasteland beneath us was the third largest desert on earth (1,295,000 sq. km; ½ m. sq. miles). Covering nearly half of Mongolia, the Gobi increases by more than 200 km. per year. That's the Gobi I'd read about in the travelog by my boyhood heroines, Francesca French and Mildred Cable.

Cable! My mind went back to the tobacco salesman I'd met on the flight out of Nepal— Michael Cable. What a potential market he'd find in China, I reflected, with some 30% of world tobacco consumption![4] I remembered how he'd sheepishly admitted that Mildred was his great-aunt. In fact, she was an English pharmacist and midwife who had also studied surgery. But she didn't fly over the hot sands in the comfort of an airplane, as I was doing. Members of CIM with a burden for Mongolia, Sisters Mildred and Francesca along with Eva French (all in their fifties), traveled that rugged stretch of the Old Spice Road by mule-drawn cart laden with Chinese and Mongolian Scripture portions.[5]

---

3. Travelling the globe, I realized that rubber stamps provide bored officials an exaggerated sense of power ("to go or not to go"), repeatedly slapping their official endorsement on travelers' documents.

4. But Michael would face the Republic's near monopoly of the 350m. smokers' market.

5. Their books: (1) *Through Jade Gate and Central Asia;* (2) *Something Happened;* (3) *The Gobi Desert.*

Adopting Chinese dress, they *lived* in oases among "Ínner" Mongolia's nomads, braving 48-hour dust storms, with temperatures dropping from 45 C (113 F) in summer to –40 C/F in winter. They stared-down war chiefs, endured capture, and once saved the life of a wounded brigand leader. At the time "Outer" Mongolia itself was closed to missions, but during the first half of the 20thc., the women sent gospels in with Mongol travelers. It was not until 1990 that the outside world was able to look in and see fruit of those seeds.

And how did those intrepid pioneers sum up their ordeals? "The meaning and reality of Christ have become intense," they wrote. "He is Saviour, Guardian, Friend—Way and End. We have lacked nothing." As a boy, I didn't need cartoon heroes. Missionaries like those captured my imagination. Talk about high adventure! I wondered if I could ever call myself a missionary!

Now missionaries *from* China and Korea courageously serve in the Gobi. In their isolated felt "tents," they pray for entry to the hearts of the surrounding nomads—and slowly they've been making friends. Andrew Ng, Deputy, International Director for East Asia and Pacific Area, told me about visiting them. "We chewed rock-hard yak meat and drank fermented-milk tea,"[6] Belinda Ng commented—but their fellowship couldn't have been sweeter! The desert sand reminded the Ngs of Niger's sub-Sahara a hemisphere away, where they've served in SIM's hospital.

I also heard of a Korean table tennis champion who intentionally lived in a Gobi village, where she shared her Christian faith while coaching villagers in the game. (During Russian occupation, table tennis competitions were big!) She even played against a Mongolian champ, who later professed faith in Christ. The gospel message bounces in many different ways!

Skeletons of a Past Era

As our flight landed at the capital, Ulan Bator, I wondered what gospel witness was there; it was the early '90s. But first I had to decipher

6. Unrefrigerated, milk slightly ferments—and stirred in with stale butter fat, gives tea a rancid flavor.

immigration forms. That presented a challenge, because they all were still in Russian.[7] From filling out similar forms in different languages around the world, I guessed what to write on each line and which box to check. When other passengers, puzzled, asked me what the form meant, I handed them my filled-in form to get the idea. In those fast-changing days, I reckoned that no one in Mongolia would ever look at them anyway.

And maybe I was right. Before the '90s, Mongolia had been the eastern showpiece of Communist Russia (enabling the Red Army to keep an eye on China's northern frontier). From Beijing to Moscow is a train trip of 8 days[8] on the Trans-Siberian Express, and air transport was not always reliable. So Marxist *apparatchiks* had run the eastern flank of the USSR from bleak blocks of Stalin-era offices along unimaginative grids of desolate avenues in the capital, Ulan Bator.

One helpful heritage from the Communist era was central heating for blocks of those high-rise offices and apartments. In the high-rise hostel where I stayed, I warmed my supper (a package of noodles) on the steam-heated radiator. The steam came through tunnels from a mammoth plant set between ten boxy apartment buildings. However, if your building was not hooked up to the system, that posed a problem—as one church group later discovered. They planned to build a youth center beyond reach of tunnel heat and piped water. Environmental laws prohibited burning coal. God answered prayer unexpectedly, when the town mayor offered to sell a building hooked up to the system.[9]

In Ulan Bator, the tunnels provide street children refuge. Thousands of unwanted, abused, or rebellious urchins beg, scavenge city dumpsites, and sell themselves for sex. At night, many boys and girls crawl down manholes to spend nights in warmth and safety. They pass around bits of food and dregs of vodka bottles they've scrounged or stolen. Children sing themselves to sleep with a sad refrain: "Our hearts are full of sadness—where are the parents to care for us?"

---

7. My visit was just after Russia's departure. Mongolia's government services are now greatly improved.
8. The USSR, from Baltic to Bering Sea, covered 11 time zones, nearly halfway around the world.
9. SIM Short-term Team Report, Mongolia, 2007.

Police round up stray children and incarcerate them in gulags. An InterServe missionary asked a 13-year-old inmate if he could play chess. As he nodded assent, his eyes filled with tears—no adult had ever asked him to play. He walked over to a corner and cried.

A cousin of mine had been executive secretary of Britain's Save the Children Fund, so I was glad to find that agency active, along with several adults who seek to rehabilitate children at risk. One was an Irish advocate, Christiana Noble, through her Christiana Noble Foundation.

Exploring the city, I found that the Russians had provided a museum. I was fascinated to view a 20 cm.-long (8") dinosaur egg as well as a dinosaur skeleton found in the Gobi. With all its controls, the Communist era did produce positive results: equal opportunities for both men and women, breaking of stifling religious superstitions, opening up society to change, providing basic food, medication, and housing—even if the people had no freedom to choose where they'd like to work.

But with the collapse of the Berlin Wall and the USSR, Moscow lost interest in propping up a puppet state with few natural resources. Mongolia became pretty much an orphan state. China hadn't thought too kindly of Mongolia anyway, since it seceded from China in the Russian-backed revolution of 1921. At the time of my visit, offices had only occasional staff, and shop shelves were mostly bare. A bookshop on the main boulevard was sparsely stocked with second-hand books. When I asked for Mongolia's Little Red Book (The Constitution of the Mongolian People's Republic), the clerk rummaged under the counter to find a copy of the once mandatory Communist reading for the masses. No one wanted it now. Though it was marked $1.00, the clerk asked for only ten cents.

"The Great October Socialist Revolution, which marked the beginning of mankind's transition from Capitalism to Communism, was a turning point in the history of the Mongolian People's age-long emancipation struggle . . ." the preface read. It cited "the fraternal socialist aid of the Soviet Union." Actually, the state had never known real capitalism. In traditional *communalism*, herders freely ranged the steppes to graze their herds, never owning a plot or pasture. That actually made Marxist take-over easy (although it soon proved repressive to free-ranging grazers), but recent change from state collectivisation to free enterprise was proving traumatic.

The new constitution of 1992 renounced Marxism but recognized only three official religions: Lama Buddhism, Shamanism, and Islam. It restricted certain freedoms. National and international reaction led to a review that at least conceded the right of church registration and of an agency to disseminate religious teaching "in line with those of [registered] religious institutions."

In the economy, aid agencies largely filled the gap left by departing Russians. But in the '90s, summer drought conspired with heavy winter snowfall and ice crusts[10] to kill off most of the cattle—the main livelihood of the nomadic people. Traditional cooperatives would have helped soften the blow, but now herders had no such recourse.

Moreover, after 400 years of Chinese domination, Communism had given Mongolians aspirations to grandeur that ended in disillusionment. Unfortunately, young people considered pastoralism backwards. The Asian Development Bank favors private ownership of land, but lack of an adequate road network concentrated herders around cities, over-grazing limited pasture. Chinese mining companies press for mining rights—a threat to the fragile environment of Mongolia's plains. Resultant inflation adds to problems.

Such are the economic woes of a beautiful people with a proud history. As I walked along the main street, the failed dream seemed reflected in a partly constructed glass-faced convention center and hotel (initially financed by the Aga Khan), now waiting for a buyer with $14 million to complete.[11]

"The Flail of God"

I remembered reading about the era of an earlier Khan, Genghis Khan ("Lord of the Earth"), who unified central Asia's nomadic tribes in 1203. Unspeakably cruel and yet a genius at organization,[12] the Great Khan fully believed he was divinely appointed to conquer the world—

10. Termed *zud*, ice crusts prevent animals from digging out fodder from under the snow.
11. The building has since become one of many spanking new towers in downtown Ulan Bator.
12. Mongols traditionally used a democratic process, electing khans (chiefs) through deputies in councils known as *kuriltai/khurals*, which then elected parliament. Since Communism ended, this process continues.

didn't the shamans tell him so? Subduing Central Asia, he turned in fury on the Muslim world after Shah Mohammad of Khwarizm robbed and murdered a caravan of Muslim merchants traveling under Genghis' protection in 1218. He proclaimed himself to Muslim captives as "the flail of God"—punishment for their sins. Muslims called the eastern barbarians, "the accursed of God."

Back then, Mongol horsemen swept across the plains. An appointed khan ruled Persia and advanced towards Egypt, on the way nearly annihilating Islamic fanatics known as the Assassins. Razing Baghdad in 1258, they reportedly caused 2m deaths, including that of the Caliph, Islam's last global leader.[13] Another khan pushed northwards on the Volga, his gold-braided tent earning his warriors the nickname, "Golden Horde."[14]

Mongol rallying cries crumbled resistance and created history's largest contiguous land empire, stretching from the Arctic Ocean southward to Indonesia's Straight of Malacca and from the Pacific westward to Eastern Europe. Mongols, as well as the Turkic tribes they rallied to their cause, had grown up in bare subsistence, living on wild meat, curds, and *kumiss* (a fermented mare's milk brew). These hunter-warriors had learned to survive by warfare in the steppes' harsh climate, waiting out icy storms in their felt-covered *yurts* made from the hair of their animals, stitched together with animal sinews, and stretched over poles laced together at the top.

Not only exporting terror, they inadvertently introduced caviar to Western Asia and Europe—salted eggs of sturgeon fished from their frigid lakes. Caviar would keep in saddlebags for months, spicing up food the wild warriors scrounged along the war trail. Ironically, some of the pickled roe, finding its way to royal tables further west, became an expensive delicacy. Mongolians were first to domesticate sheep, goats, horses, and camels ranging over their grassy plains, without a fence for 3,000 km. (1,900 miles)! Those endless grasslands astounded

13. So reported by the 14th c. historian, Maqrizi in *The Mongol Conquests*—see Bibliography.

14. Label given to Mongols who overran Eastern Europe in 13th c., ruling Russia until 1486.

19th c. explorers with their massive herds of gazelle and wild ass—which have now dwindled to an estimated 1.5m. (Extinction threatens the two-humped Bactrian camel, native only to Mongolia and northern China.)

In the Great Khan's heyday, the fierce demeanor and unintelligible speech of his horsemen struck terror into other nations. European artists depicted Mongols as hideous savages feasting on the limbs of victims. However, Mongolian conquests curbed marauding tribes along the Spice Road, thus promoting Eurasian trade. Unfortunately, Mongolian armies also carried with them from China "The Black Death." The plague wiped out entire communities in Europe, which had no resistance to its ravages.

Early Mongol conquests also produced a new ethnic group—the Tartars,[15] as Mongols settled down among conquered Slavs, Turks, and Russians. They developed a new breed of horse, crossing their stocky Mongolian steeds with leaner, longer-legged Arab horses, resulting in endurance coupled with speed. Mongols are credited with inventing the deadly compound bow and leather stirrup—enabling warriors to aim their bows behind them while galloping at full tilt. The era also gave the world a new scourge: Timur Lang,[16] who rose to power in 1369, terrorizing Central and Western Asia.

Egyptian Mamluks[17] eventually stopped the Mongols' westward drive, pushing them east of the Euphrates. This spared Europe from being overrun. Genghis' empire had reached its zenith, and thenceforth consolidated itself in the East. Genghis' grandson, the Kublai Khan (1215-1294), established the Mongol Yuan dynasty of China. Kublai unified the feuding tribes that had divided China for 350 years. He valued Chinese culture, and employed a Tibetan lama to provide his own Mongolian people with their first alphabet, but it didn't catch on. More moderate than previous khans, he handed out free grain to disadvantaged peasants and appointed Chinese administrators.

---

15. *Tartar/Tatar*: from Persian—a Turkic inhabitant of Tatar Republic in Russia and Siberia. By association, "Tartar" has come to mean a formidable person of violent temper.
16. Timur Lenk: Turkic—"Timur the Lame," angry conqueror Europeans referred to as Tamerlane.

Yet under the surface, the Empire was beginning to crumble. Luxurious living in China softened Mongolian soldiers. By the early 15th c., the Empire's energy was spent. Conquest, not government, was the Mongols' genius. True, as Mongols returned to their *yurts* on the northern plains, they left behind massive projects such as waterways, roads, and a nation-wide courier service connected by 10,000 post houses. But the khans created class distinctions by favoring Mongols, Persians, and Turks over ethnic Chinese as officials and merchants. They also neglected agriculture to the point of impoverishing the peasantry. Worst, they left a legacy of tyranny that stifled future progress. The once affluent East struggled to subsist while the backward West broke out of its shell.

Amazing Twists of History

But that turn-around resulted partly from a strange twist of history—or was it a divine design that the shamans had never foreseen? Genghis Khan had stated, "We Mongols believe that there is but one God, by whom we live and by whom we die." During Kublai's reign, the Khan welcomed representatives of nations and religions to his court. In 1266, two Venetian merchants, Niccolo and Mateo Polo, missed their way on the Old Spice Road and turned up in front of the Great Khan.

However, they somehow impressed the short and stocky Kublai. He asked the Polo brothers to return home and bring back one hundred Europeans learned in religion and the arts, and if these could prove the superiority of Christianity, he and his people would be baptized. There would be more Christians in his realm than in all the rest of the world! By the way, could the Polo brothers also bring him back a little holy oil from Jerusalem?[18] Kublai was always hedging his religious bets—that's why he kept a stable of 5,000 astrologers and shamans, and also invited Lamas from Tibet to convert Mongolia.

The Polos did return to Kublai's court in 1275. But a couple of monks they'd managed to recruit from the Vatican lost heart along the Old Spice Road, fleeing back to Europe. Instead of one hundred learned men, all the

---

17. Mamluks: an Egyptian Muslim military ruling class.
18. Jewish merchants as well as Muslims had long spread news of the holy city, "Jerusalem."

Venetians could produce was a bottle of holy water and a few papal letters—a major gospel opportunity tragically missed.[19] (In the 19th c., Europeans did attempt to take the gospel to Mongolia. British Congregationalists heroically penetrated the area and in 1818 compiled the first Tibetan-Mongolian dictionary. It was hard slogging—23 years of effort resulted in only four converts. Between 18171841, the London Missionary Society had two missionaries working among Buryat Mongolians.)

Meanwhile, here's another amazing twist! Niccolo's 20-year-old son, Marco, accompanied his father on this journey. Kublai employed him on the spot, making him his special envoy. For the next 17 years, Marco journeyed throughout Mongolia, China, and other accretions of the empire. Venice had been one of Europe's most cultured cities, but the world Marco now explored was beyond any European's imagination. Marco's eyes popped at the affluence, the industry, the technology, and the arts of this exotic world.[20] In one year, he counted 20,000 ships sailing up China's Yangtze River with cargo from Java, Sri Lanka, and India. Arab seafarers took tea, spices, textiles, and artefacts back along the Old Spice Sea Route.

When Marco eventually returned to Europe, authorities slapped him in jail for recounting what they considered to be misleading fantasies. Marco used prison time to good purpose, dictating his travelogue to a scribe. Publication of *A Description of the World* shook Europe with reports of stones that burned (coal), other stones that exploded in the air (gunpowder fireworks), rock-hard shiny clay plates (porcelain), fire-resistant fiber (asbestos), commonly used paper money made from bark (Europe valued only metal coinage), and other outlandish claims. At Marco's deathbed in 1324, the priest administering the Last Rites pled with him to retract his "invented fables" or face eternal consequences.[21]

---

19. Much earlier Christian monks had attempted to reach the Mongolian Plateau but were repulsed.
20. Using mirrors, Chinese focussed the sun's rays to light fires—a simple technology currently being developed in the West to generate heat to drive electric generators!
21. I understood the incredulity of Marco's report, for I once heard Ethiopian evangelist Markina report to his remote village about visiting USA. Villagers laughed in disbelief at stories of travel under the earth like a mole (a subway/underground) and men playing ball in a field where night turned to day. On a farm, a cow filled 1½ milk buckets *daily* (local cows squeezed out 1½ cups). Markina could have visited Mars!

But Europe was already bitten with Eastern Trade Fever. Although today we tend to condemn the West's forcible opening of China to trade in the 1800s, Chinese merchants and the rest of the world welcomed revival of the voluminous two-way "free trade" that China had enjoyed with the Middle East and Europe 500 years earlier.

The down side of Marco Polo's story is that in place of Jesus' disciples, Buddhist monks arrived. Initially, Buddhism made inroads among the noble class, but eventually throughout the land. In the 17th c. monks founded Urga around the Temple of the Living Buddha. By the 20th c., about 50% of the male population were monks living in monasteries.[22]

Another surprising twist took place in 1920, when *a Russian*, no less, became the last Khan of Mongolia! That was during the Russian civil war. Freiherr von Ungern-Sternberg, a *German*-born dissident tsarist army officer, invaded Mongolia and installed himself as Khan—hoping to use the country as his base to take back Russia from the Bolsheviks. But his 130-day rule ended when the Red Army captured and shot him.[23]

Communism took over Mongolia's capital in 1924, using genocide to eliminate educated and religious elements. Through 70 years of repression, they ruthlessly dragged monks from their retreats, destroying all but four monasteries out of thousands. They even changed Buddhism's Urga[24] ("Big Yurt") to Ulan Bator (Red Hero). But once the USSR collapsed, Mongolia threw out its Communist rulers, and Buddhism revived. While the nation's underlay is shaman, now nearly one quarter calls itself Buddhist.

No doubt we would have planned things differently—but the Bible reminds us of God's "fullness of time." Call it Divine Design, if you like.

My Unlikely Assignment

My own visit to Mongolia started back in Canada when I received an unlikely letter from Mongolia's Press Attaché, inviting me to conduct a seminar for journalists in Ulan Bator!

---

22. BBC World News July 30, '03.

23. James Palmer, *The Bloody White Baron: The Extraordinary Story of the Russian Nobleman Who Became the Last Khan of Mongolia*. London: Faber and Faber, 2009.

24. *Urga*: "Big Yurt" or tent.

I later learned that Frank Tichy, brother of an SIM missionary in Africa, became acquainted with government officials through his development work in Mongolia. He knew the problems of switching from a centrally planned Soviet-style economy to a market economy, so he understood when the Attaché, Chimadorge,[25] fretted that journalists didn't know how to research and write news stories objectively. They'd learned to depend on controlled propaganda releases. Chimadorge, once a government minister, lost his post when Communism collapsed. Since then he'd found Christ as Savior. Tichy told the Attaché about on-the-job training I'd given for several missions.

That's how I found myself in Mongolia. The airport I'd just left in China wouldn't allow anyone to take a photo—but upon landing at the airport in Mongolia, Korean visitors were happily snapping each other's photo in front of the main terminal. The few soldiers I did see were waiting for a bus. No secret police questioned me on the street as I walked along dictating my impressions on a pocket recorder.[26] No informant listened in as I later met with a group of eager young journalists at the Ministry of Information.

Communism had at least left the nation with a high adult literacy rate—97%. The problem just then was to provide current reading material. One young man was enjoying the challenge of publishing his own newspaper. He started with $50 and was sole owner and staff. To pay the print bill, he gave the printer free advertising space. Other adverts and a charge per copy covered remaining costs and made a small profit.

But to young journalists, schooled under Marxism, life was confusing. No central government gave them press handouts. How could they find a story on their own? Would they be punished for original thinking?

The new breed of journalists had another problem—how to use their press freedom responsibly. In the absence of censorship, they concluded their job was to tear apart anyone in authority or a position of responsibly. The press was definitely turning "yellow"—just like newspapers of America's Wild West Frontier era.

25. Many Mongolians had no surname; some added a meaningless initial to distinguish between individuals.

26. On another continent, I have been detained for doing just that.—WHF

My seminar was fairly basic: news sources, objective reporting, handling controversy by reporting both sides, and structure of a news story (journalism's five Ws: What, When, Where, Who, Why). Rudimentary, but the budding reporters thanked me for coming.

In closing the seminar, I said I'd like to pray for their nation and their work. My interpreter giggled as she tried to translate that—her background of Communism, overlaid on Buddhism, did not have room for a personal deity. However, the group listened politely to what was likely the first public prayer in the Ministry of Information.

I dropped over at the offices of JCS—the registered name of Joint Christian Services. I wasn't sure if I'd found the right place: a massive brass wall figure of Lenin's head, adorned with hammer and sickle, confronted me in the spacious lobby. But it was O.K.—the new government had made available to JCS the abandoned Russian Cultural Center, with its Red era symbols firmly embedded in the entrance wall. JCS, a non-profit enterprise established in 1992 by eight Christian agencies, was committed to "make Christ known by word and life,"[27] while providing services. World Vision's David Andrianoff, of Russian parentage, was just the right man to start JCS under the Trade and Industry Ministry.

JCS has set up business co-ops, health care, and education programs. It staves off starvation for entire stranded communities during famines, provides day-care for children, rescues many a mother in childbirth, provides marriage counselling, teaches business skills, and runs a rehab program for alcoholics.[28] All in the name of Jesus. Its constitution includes room for Christian instruction, under Mongolia's freedom-of-religion clause. Its Gobi-Altai project (assisting nomadic herders) has won the government's "best NGO project" award.

Missionaries from many nations and agencies fill strategic posts in the nation—many facing the world's greatest climatic extremes, so

27. Founding partners: InterServe, Mennonite Board of Missions, MTI (Korea), Ministry to the Unreached, OMF, Orebro Mission, SIM, and YWAM. Tear Fund, World Concern, World Vision and others soon joined.

28. An estimated 20% of the population is alcoholic (five out of six families affected), according to JCS.

different from their temperate native climes. Typical was SIM's Director for Mongolia, Ariel Ceballos who, with his wife Connie, taught at Union Bible Training Centre, the only government-recognized Bible school. The Ceballos were from the Philippines. Other team members taught English as a second language. Mongolians Siga and Oyuna, who came to Christ through invitation to a Bible study, were key team members.

"The Church Scene is a Mess!"

During my visit, I was able to see first-hand the tensions faced by an infant church. It has since matured greatly, but at the time, it reminded me of Paul's description of the Church in Corinth. Warren Willis, then local director of Campus Crusade's "Jesus Film" Project,[29] heard that I was vice-chair of World Evangelical Alliance and asked if I would meet with several concerned Korean pastors.

"Most of the church scene is a mess. The Lord guide!" was his encouraging parting as I set off to learn more about the church in Mongolia.

The government had just expelled a couple of Korean pastors—but not because they were pastors. Whereas they'd entered on business visas, they actually spent all their time preaching. The government rightly saw this as visa mis-use. But other pastors had come through the proper channels and faced no problem from the government. Their problem was an internal one—factions within the churches. Among them were nit-pickers—including one who split a church by decrying the way the pastor cut the Communion bread.

Some dozen church groups competed to claim the same converts as their members. An American missionary added to the complex scene by setting up his own evangelical association that claimed to be nation-wide but excluded certain valid churches.

Oh yes, there still was another little problem: the merits of one Bible translation versus another. One used shamanist terms.[30] I'd seen that

29. As a registered educational charity, "Jesus Film" showings have had great response nationwide.

30. Currently there are three New Testament translations, two controversially using different terms for God. The average Mongol does not understand a Bible translation in classical Mongolian. There's a Cyrillic script New Testament, and German linguists are working on a version in traditional vertical script.

approach in Bangladesh and other lands, and it was always a point of contention. Another group attracted many pastors with foreign funds. Others refused the largesse.

Help! Suddenly I wished for the Wisdom of Solomon—but all I could do was to share with the pastors the experience of churches in other lands—how they faced division, rivalry, and misunderstanding through much prayer and loving consultation together. I advised against trying to fight any group. The Devil didn't mind who did what—he only wanted to cause public disunity and quarrelling. These pastors had plenty to keep them busy and productive as they followed the leading of the Holy Spirit. We recognized the truth of James' words: "Where you have envy and selfish ambition, there you find disorder and every evil practice." We prayed instead for "the wisdom that comes from heaven."[31]

But along with tensions of a developing new church life (that older churches still have!), I saw encouragements—the vibrancy of first-generation Christians. Before 1990, when Mongolia turfed out its Communist rulers, there were perhaps four known disciples of Christ. In the next ten years their number doubled and tripled and grew a hundred-fold. Perhaps some 20,000 Mongolians worship in some 60 churches and another 100 informal congregations.[32] Though churches are chiefly in the three major cities, Christian groups now exist in all 18 provinces, outnumbering Buddhist groups and sparking a backlash.

On 1st October 1992, a consortium of 9 mission agencies was formed to do development and holistic work in Mongolia. Together with others of like-minded bodies, these encouraged the unity of the local churches and formation of the Mongolian Evangelical Alliance, which today has over 450 churches under their umbrella. The original consortium grew to 16 agencies.

After centuries of exclusion, in only a decade the gospel has exploded from pioneering infancy to church adulthood—although needing much teaching and training of leadership. So rapid was the change that friends of ours whose calling as rudimentary pioneers took them to Mongolia in

31. James 3.13 – 18.
32. Southern Baptists were the first denomination to receive official registration of a church.

1990, by 2000 were looking for another country in which to "pioneer." Not that there wasn't plenty to do in helping the church grow to maturity. That reminded me of the Apostle Paul's most exacting ministry back in Asia Minor, in the first century: the care of the churches!

"Please Forgive My Sins!"

At JCS I was able to interview one of the early believers who spoke English. Dageema's statuesque build bespoke some Russian ancestry, but her jet-black hair and eyes like dark olives set in high cheekbones were definitely oriental.[33]

Dageema's parents had been multi-layered in their beliefs. Shaman[34] spirit-worshipers like most Mongols, they kept their spirit shrines while nominally accepting Tibetan-style Buddhism. When faced with any problem (surely the result of some bad *karma*), they'd pay a Buddhist monk to pray for them—hoping to reduce their *karma* debit account that might bring them back as animals or snakes or even flies in their next incarnation. After a brutal Communist campaign in 1937 against such religious superstition, they paid lip service to Marxism. State TV warned against foreigners who confused the people with religion.

Trained as a teacher, Dageema lost her job because of TB infection. While recuperating, she studied English on her own and got a job as a tour guide. One day she overheard a Korean in a tour group talk about a personal God who loves us so much that he gave his only Son for our salvation. This so amazed her that she later spoke to the unseen God very simply: "Please forgive me for my sins and guide me."

Dageema didn't understand that something special had happened, but when she told a group of visiting Korean teachers, they were so enthusiastic and happy for her that she realized her decision must be important. She went with them to their Eternal Light Church. When she heard their singing and worship, she started to cry.

---

33. Typical gradated mix of Slav West and Sino East across N. Asia's 11 time zones, from Baltic to Bering.

34. *Shaman*: Siberian priest/priestess who uses magic for healing and divining hidden information.

At the church, a man working with JCS invited her to work for the cooperative agency. Through her translation work, she grew in understanding of the Christian faith and witnessed to her unemployed husband. He blamed her for not earning a higher wage with the government, but after she prayed that he'd find a job—and he did—he stopped criticizing her and listened to the gospel. Because of so much corruption around him, he found it hard to believe that her Christian faith can overcome dishonesty and other evil.

"I know that's the work of the Holy Spirit," explained Dageema, brushing a straying strand of raven hair away from her eyes.

At first the sudden spread of the gospel in a land only recently open to Christians seemed surprising—until I learned more of Mongolia's history. Records suggest that Nestorian[35] Christians from Persia had a hand in providing the script for the unwritten Mongolian language of Genghis Khan, via the Uighurs on Mongolia's western border. Through the same influences, Uighurs also provided the basis for his laws—which became as sacrosanct as the Ten Commandments. The expansionist emperor took a Christian wife—one of three Christian sisters who left a lasting mark upon the Far East. The son of one of those wives became a Mongol Great Khan, or Emperor.[36]

The more I learned of the past, the more I realized the Divine Design of the Holy Spirit, choosing channels, times, and seasons, which Jesus told his disciples were "in the hands of the Father." Meanwhile, the disciples were to witness for their Saviour, to the ends of the earth—that included all along the Old Spice Road. So what I saw happening in Mongolia should not have surprised me, really. When disciples fulfilled their responsibility, anything could happen! The surprising element—the disheartening, dismal fact of history—was the earlier failure of followers of Jesus to be his witnesses.[37]

---

35. As mentioned earlier, "Nestorian" was a generic (not always doctrinal) term simply meaning "Eastern."
36. Chapter 18 on China has already discussed early Christian influences through these channels.
37. See Acts 1.7 for basis of this paragraph.

Long-lost Cousins Return with Gospel!

Most interesting was the amazing way the gospel had come full cycle—beyond the wildest imagination. Many of the Mongolian and Chinese faces I saw could have been so-called Amero-Indians of North and South America.[38] Many have since become followers of Jesus, and recently they've become burdened for the spiritual needs of their cousins in Asia.

"In Mongolia, the people immediately identified with us tribals," Richard Twiss writes in his book, *One Church Many Tribes*.[39] "They spoke of legends about Mongol hunters who travelled to the north and east and never returned; they believed we were descendents of those hunters . . . . They trusted us . . . we were able to share the gospel story freely." Surprises for us, but not for the Holy Spirit!

Before leaving Mongolia for Korea, I wanted to explore a little. A tall, square-jawed Mongolian, Ming, agreed to show me something of his country. He, an intelligent university student, had just become a Christian. "Why?" I asked.

"Buddhism didn't make sense, Islam was crazy, and Communism had proved itself ineffective," Ming explained. "So the alternative was Jesus Christ." I felt like saying that Jesus was more than an alternative—he was the Saviour, but only for sinners! However, now was not the time to nitpick! Ming had learned enough about the rest of the world for him to become an angry young man. He was disillusioned by all systems. He trusted nobody. I could tell that his heart ached for his country.

"We can't go around begging for handouts all the time!" Ming complained. "We've got the resources—land, gold, some of the best coal, 90% literacy—but we are penniless. Although people now have high

38. Called "Indians" by European explorers who thought they'd arrived in Asia when they stumbled on the New World. Now known by ethnic names, these aborigines also call themselves, "First Nations." They crossed from Asia on a prehistoric bridge of land or ice at the Bering Straight, or along the Aleutian Islands and down North America's west coast before filtering eastward.

39. R. Twiss, *One Church Many Tribes*, p. 203 (see Bibliography). Rick and Laura Leatherwood, who worked with Dave and Bev Fuller in the Philippines, confirmed that Navajo Christians who visited Mongolia could communicate in their native language.

expectations, they'll have to change their mindset before they'll do anything useful."

I paid mileage on a JCS Jeep for Ming to drive me around to see a cross-section of Mongolian life. (Ulan Bator holds 25% of the nation's population.) Old men sat on a bench, thoughtfully puffing on clay pipes. Rosy-cheeked schoolgirls tossed their pigtails as they sat giggling in a sunlit doorway. A battered Russian-built garbage truck clattered by, honking to let householders know they should bring out their garbage and dump it in the truck. The driver poked it in further with a hoe—the compactor mechanism wasn't working.

We stopped outside a butcher shop long enough for me to look inside. The paint on the outside was peeling. Inside was the smell of meat—but the display cases were empty. Hungry customers had snapped up the meat long before noon. Life was hard, a humorless scramble to even exist. I'm glad to hear that life for many has since improved.

Home, Home on the Range!

Ming drove me out to the wide flat plains of the Mongolian Steppe. There wasn't a fence in sight, right to the horizon. Most of this landlocked country is 1500 meters (4,900 ft) above sea level, with mountain ranges in the West. The sun arched high in the blue sky, which stretched to the horizon, where it kissed a low line of hills. Naked rock outcroppings girded themselves with nature's furs—dark evergreens. The road bridged a river that drains across Mongolia's nearby border into Siberia's Baikal Basin.

Since I hail from the Great Lakes area of North America, Lake Baikal fascinated me. I heard it holds 20% of the world's known fresh water—as much as all five of the Great Lakes together, yet it has a surface area only slightly larger than the five's *smallest*, Lake Ontario! Reason? Baikal is the deepest lake on Planet Earth.[40] For centuries, geologists have puzzled over Baikal's formation, but now consider its sheer stone sides to be "a rift basin," formed by a cataclysm of the earth's tectonic plates that folded

40. 1,940m. (6,365 ft.) at one point, with an average depth of 758m. vs. Lake Superior's 147m. (world's largest *surface* area). Although fed by 336 rivers, Baikal has only one surface outlet.

the earth's crust in a deep fault. Environmentalists worry about an oil pipeline Russia and China are planning. Its initial route skirted the highly seismic south end of the lake.

In the Tunguska region of Siberia, there's further evidence of a cosmologic cataclysm. In 1908, historians tell us, Tunguska experienced a huge explosion, heard for hundreds of miles, now near the convergence of three major rivers. Shamans would have a different explanation, but cosmologists say that one of the cosmic rocks that hurtle through space struck the area. They consider it a "smaller" asteroid (50-100 meters across), of the kind that may ram into earth every thousand years. Such clutter the universe, along with larger asteroids. May their ilk land on a deserted plain, not a city!

Bringing me down to earth was a pastoral scene of children herding sheep and cattle,[41] as we followed the verge of a sloping valley. Further off, horsemen raced along the valley floor just like their ancestors, uttering war cries in practise for their upcoming annual cultural festival. Amid a ring of round tents, muscular braves, stripped to the waist, competed in a wrestling match. Outside hut clusters, strips of blue cloth fluttered from piles of rocks—shaman-blessed good luck charms.

"May we visit one of those *yurts*?" I asked. Ming pulled off the road, bounced across the fresh green sward of Spring, and stopped outside a traditional hut—woven white felt stretched over a top wooden lattice resting on a central pole. Its igloo design resisted winter's high winds better than a flat-sided tent. Whenever the family needed to move to better pasture—say in winter or drought—they collapsed the lattice, wrapped the felt "tent" around it, and transported it on horseback. Roofing rods were painted the red and blue of the nation's flag, and the doorframe was orange.

Inside, the *yurt* was spotlessly tidy, with a bed and small table set on a wooden platform. In the middle, an iron stove heated the *yurt*. We greeted a pig-tailed mother as her wide-eyed toddler peered from behind her skirt. The woman's busy hands were knitting sheep's wool she'd spun on her wheel. These rural dwellers of the Steppe seem content to live as

41. Livestock outnumbers population by at least 12 to one.

their ancestors have, unlike their frustrated city cousins. All Mongols seem to have ruddy cheeks from their plateau's high altitude and fresh climate.

Back on the road—the only one across the plains at the time[42]—Ming and I continued our conversation. We discussed disillusioned youths' alcoholism and drug addiction. We talked about ingrained atheism, resurgent shamanism, and Buddhist backlash. "What's going to hold back the church?" I asked.

"I'm a believer," Ming replied, his dark eyes flashing; "but I have problems with the churches. They are fighting among themselves. Other religions or ideologies won't succeed in blocking the gospel. If anything does, it will be quarrelling between Christians. I'm fed up and don't want anything to do with it!" Ming was typical of many Mongol youth. In the social, political, and economic confusion of the new Mongolia, Christ's disciples will lead them to faith only through personal integrity reflecting God's Word.

"Look—the Trans-Siberian Express!" Ming exclaimed, pointing to a puff of smoke on the horizon. We watched the passenger/freight train crawl into sight, snake along the valley, and disappear over a ridge. I felt for the intelligent, good-looking but angry young man beside me: would the train of progress stop for him and his country? More important than his faith in humanity, would his faith in Christ fail not?

Off to the Hermit Kingdom

Next day my flight took off for Beijing, en route to Korea. I prayed it wouldn't meet the fate of the Mongolian airliner that had recently crashed into a mountain peak. Investigators eventually found the crash site on a snow-covered slope. All the passengers had died. The plane's black box, which would have recorded any corrective warning from the tower and the aircraft's final moments, had no tape in it. This proud country of the Great Khans, that had once received tribute from China, Egypt, India, Persia, and Russia, at the time *couldn't afford tapes!* My heart bled for this courageous nation.

---

42. Planning a national road grid has been one of the Joint Christian Services' projects.

Dr. Young Jun Son, Director of Korea's Missionary Training Institute, welcomes the author to teach church-mission relations and management/leadership development

Hermit Gets Engaged

"You are the light of the world. . . .let your light shine before men, that they may see your good deeds and praise your Father in heaven" (Matthew 5.14,16).

Korea: Pop. 49,975,564
North Korea: Pop. 26,451,118

When I answered the gentle knock on our hotel room door in Seoul, an attractive young woman beamed as she asked something—what, I didn't know. I couldn't understand Korean and she couldn't understand English. Lorna, who was able to accompany me on this visit to Korea, joined in the exchange of "signs and wonders" (that is, hand signs and wondering what they meant). Fortunately, hand language is much the same anywhere. We concluded it was Lorna the woman wanted, and Lorna was to accompany her—where or for how long, we had no idea. To add to Lorna's adventure, we happened to be in a city of 10m we'd never visited before!

Courageous woman, Lorna. In Africa, she was one of the few women who dared drive through the chaotic traffic of Lagos, Nigeria's overgrown port city. In South America, she accompanied an unknown hotel attendant into a den of thieves to retrieve my stolen wallet. (I didn't know about this adventure till I returned from researching ancient ruins!)

But now we recollected seeing this attractive young woman, Kim,[1] when we arrived at the airport. She was the wife of one of the pastors

1. "Kim" seemed the name of every third person—Korea's equivalent of "Jones" or "Smith." South Koreans radiate an exotic attractiveness—a handsome oriental mix reflecting centuries of intermarriage with Chinese, Japanese, and even Russian occupiers.

who had invited us to come to tell their Prayer Fellowship For Muslims (PFFM) about the work of missions. Kim thoughtfully took Lorna to experience local culture, while I stayed in our hotel room to prepare my discussion notes.

Kim introduced Lorna to a cultural tea ceremony—sipping ginseng from colourful ceramic bowls, with rice cakes to eat. For the food, no fingers—only chopsticks.[2] To Christians, it was only a relaxing tradition, with no connection to Buddhism, which had introduced the ceremony to the Orient to induce a peaceful frame of mind through meditative ritual. And indeed, after the whirl of travel, Lorna found it very relaxing.

Amazing Transformation

The Korean War had awakened the nation to the rest of the world. "I've never seen such an amazing transformation in a nation!" a Reuter's correspondent had told us on our flight into Seoul. "In the Sixties, Koreans were a down-trodden people. For centuries invaders had overrun them, so they isolated themselves. It's no longer 'the Hermit Kingdom.' You'll find an aggressive, ambitious nation, *ready to engage the world*."[3]

Just *how* aggressive, Lorna (yes, she returned to our room all in one piece!) and I later discovered when we went exploring our downtown street. Trying to be a gentleman, I held a shop door open for a woman—and was just about run over by the stream of shoppers who kept pressing through. I soon realized that in the new urban Korea, you had to look after yourself—polite or not. Yet oriental courtesy was still alive. As we left the shop, sales clerks politely bowed farewell to us.

When Lorna and I visited an outlet mall, it was almost like predestination or at least foreknowledge, to see styles (and the predetermined "in" color) that shoppers back home wouldn't even know about for six months! European and American designers "outsource" their fashions to Korea and other Asian countries with low labor costs.

---

2. Traditional Korean chopsticks are different from both Chinese and Japanese, being shorter, smaller.

3. The UN's current Secretary General, Ban Ki-Moon (member of a small indigenous church), epitomizes Korea's amazing transformation into a respected industrial power and international power broker.

Another world, the Communist North, loomed just miles north of Seoul. Before the Korean War, the heavily industrialized northern part was the peninsula's powerhouse (and useful Far East ally for Stalin), whereas southern peasants barely subsisted and seemed to have no future. Although Korea has a history of invading armies, Communism's onslaught from the north indelibly scarred the nation—splitting it into two.[4] Across the demilitarized zone brokered during the Korean War, guards on both sides keep vigilant watch. Ironically, the North's junta brutally suppresses religion but substitutes virtual worship of its dictator, "Our Dear Leader."

In the mid-1900s, no one could have imagined the complete turnaround of economies north and south of the cease-fire line. Now the psychopathic North is a country "with a past but no future"—yet too dangerous to ignore.[5] On the other hand, one indicator of South Korea's *domestic* progress is that it has Asia-Pacific hemisphere's highest rate of household Internet connections—70%, compared with an over-all figure of 10%. Korean car manufacture has made its own name and ranks seventh in the world, with plans for new factories in America, Europe, and China. Samsung Electronics has overtaken Japan's Sony in stock-market capitalization.

Along the southeast coast, the world's three largest shipbuilders testify to Korea's remarkable rise from the poor cousin of pre-war Korea (before its division into North and South) to its current economic leadership. South Korea accounted for almost 40% of new ship orders in 2006, and neighboring China and Japan covet its highly qualified engineers.[6]

---

4. South Korea, backed by the US, had been about to win the war (which would have kept the Korean peninsula unified). Apparently Stalin was prepared to abandon the conflict, but China's Mao sent in 300,000 troops to support Kim Il Sung. (John Lewis, *The Cold War: A New History*. See Bibliography.)

   Through the centuries, Korea has been a pawn of China, Japan, Mongolia, and Russia.

5. Kongdan Oh and Ralph Hassig, *North Korea: Through the Looking Glass.* Quoted in *The Economist*, Dec. 18, 2004, they state "perhaps 2m died of famine and related disease in the 1990s (out of 22m population), and up to 200,000 political prisoners and their families are confined in harsh labor camps."

6. *Economist,* Nov. 10, 2007.

Most of the financial capital is tied up in a few giant family conglomerates (called *chaebol*). That's an increasing political problem, given the Korean public's rising expectations of democracy and business ethics. But after authorities began prosecuting against corruption, the founding families seem to have noticed. Current family patriarchs have tipped billions of *won* ($millions) into public coffers. With their companies, they've even apologized "for causing public concern." None of this has slowed down Korea!

In education, Seoul's Yonsei University reflects the nation's confidence. "Since 1885, Yonsei stands as one of the most distinguished educational institutions of high learning in Asia," states one of its advertisements in an international magazine

In the West, we hear political outbursts against the USA, and Korea has pockets of demonstrators on call—that's the headline stuff of TV newscasts. However, we didn't find antagonism among the general population. Instead, English-speaking pastors told us how grateful they were to America for freeing their nation. "We can never forget the 30,000 American soldiers who gave their lives for our country!" they told us.

When our hosts took us on a tour of a factory, I noticed workers laughing as they glanced our way. "What are they saying?" I asked.

"They say you look like President Jimmy Carter," our guide explained. "One of them just asked if their visitor brought any peanuts!" (I doubt the President would have been flattered!) More than the workers' humour impressed me however: they were aware of world news, with the ex-President's global jaunts on behalf of poverty-affected areas. And they hadn't missed the trivia detail of Carter's humble peanut-farmer origins in Plains, Georgia.

"Where's the Toughest Challenge?"

Unable to do research in the starving North, I was encouraged to hear of the emergency food and medicines that Christians in Korea, China, and Japan are able to ferry into North Korea. Surprisingly,

Christian professors staff an inter-Korean university (based in the North's capital)—offering the nation's only graduate program. Although all radios are supposed to be fix-tuned to state broadcasts, people secretly receive Christian programs beamed from outside the country. The Korean Evangelical Alliance estimates that in North Korea 100,000 believers exist "underground," in spite of the regime's brutal repression of religion.

Bells rang in my head as I reflected on the North's similarity to Chairman Mao's era in China. The state twisted Confucian principles to underlie its ideology: group think, regimented ethics, enforced leveling of society, no God—only the Emperor, with absolute power. Yet from infancy, citizens also learn that the Emperor is Elder Brother, the epitome of "the perfect gentleman," the example of morality. "The Korean people absolutely worship, trust, and follow the General as god," the Workers' Party newspaper stated, referring to the nation's leader. The only other "deity" recognized is *Dankun*, considered to be the earliest ancestor of Koreans.

Was God prepared for this? In his economy, tremendous spiritual awakening had occurred throughout the Peninsula prior to the Communist invasion. It prepared Christians for the rigors of war and dire persecution thousands would suffer. Believers experienced what the Apostle Peter meant when he wrote to "those who have suffered grief in all kinds of trials."[7] The spiritual awakening was a return to the solid foundation missionary pioneers had laid.

Although Nestorians and Roman Catholic emissaries had visited Korea earlier, it was not until 1884 that Protestant Christianity arrived on the (then undivided) peninsula.[8] In preparation, John Ross Scott had worked with Koreans in China to provide a Bible translation. Presbyterian and Methodist pioneers established churches on foundations that have endured till this day:

---

7. 1 Peter 1:6. Verse 7 continues: "These have come so that your faith—of greater worth than gold, which perishes even though refined by fire—may be proved genuine and may result in praise, glory, and honor when Jesus Christ is revealed."
8. In 1593, a Jesuit had arrived as chaplain of a failed Japanese invasion. Eastern (Russian) Orthodox missionaries sought entry the end of the 19th c., receiving visas in 1900.

1. Christ Jesus as the only Saviour and Lord, received through repentance and faith.
2. The Holy Scriptures as the sole authority and doctrine of the churches.
3. Prayer as the primary duty of believers.
4. *Giving as a Christian responsibility.*[9]

Meeting today's followers of Jesus, Lorna and I realized the solid work the pioneers established. Our host, the PFFM, was one of several small volunteer organizations of men and women who, having received the gospel, were now zealous to obey their Lord's commission: "Go into all the world." To them, the tougher the challenge, the better!

With North Korea bristling just miles away from these Christians, I would have thought their priority would be evangelism among Communists. But PFFM already knew about outreach to the North. These young believers were strategists. Reading about the rigors of discipleship in Muslim lands, they realized that Islam presented a much greater global challenge to missions than Communism ever would. In fact, Islam has *converted* many Koreans working in Saudi Arabia. Returning to Korea, these become missionaries in reverse. In Seoul alone, there are now several dozen mosques.[10]

So PFFM looked up agencies working among Muslims and invited SIM to meet with them. Although not supported by any denomination, these businessmen and women put Lorna and me up in a hotel and paid for our meals—all out of a desire to learn more about reaching Muslims with the gospel.

Blossoming Believers, Harassed Disciples

Such commitment refreshed us who came from jaded Christian nations. I remembered hearing that when Billy Graham preached in Seoul, the city's largest stadium overflowed into the neighbouring park, with the largest public gathering in history. Christians rose early in the morning to pray, and they witnessed on the streets. A decade later, at

9. *Prayer News,* Fellowship of Faith for Muslims, April-July, 2001.
10. *Operation World* estimates Korean Muslims as 20,000.

Lausanne's Continuing Committee on World Evangelization (CCOWE)[11] held in Korea in 2000, some ten thousand men and women stood in commitment to Christ's Commission, wherever and whatever that might mean.

Every Sunday, at least 15 megachurches are *each* attended by 12,000 or more people— some many times that number.[12] On a subsequent visit to Korea, I attended the famed Yoido Full Gospel Church in a suburb of Seoul. I arrived just as an earlier sitting poured out of the main auditorium. As other thousands poured in, I would have been too late to find a seat in the next session if I hadn't been a foreigner. As I tried to follow the surge of worshipers jamming the doors, an usher saw this Caucasian and thoughtfully pointed towards a stairway to a balcony bearing the sign: *English Translation.*

Sure enough, I found a seat among other foreigners, donned a set of headphones, and sat back to enjoy the service. The pastor, David Yonggi Cho, had been born into a Buddhist home and had studied Eastern Religions. But after finding Christ as Saviour, he attended an Assemblies of God Bible College. Dramatic recovery from TB set him on a charismatic course and further theological studies. But the service I attended could have been in any Baptist church back home! It was only one of five sittings held that day, with a total of some 150,000 in the auditorium or adjacent halls through closed-circuit TV.[13]

However, I had a nagging sadness as I walked out of that service. The sun shone, but an ominous shadow loomed out of the North. How could I enjoy such freedom of worship, with its uplifting songs and joyous message from an open Bible, while just a few miles away, disciples hungered for even a verse of Scripture and a handful of rice?

---

11. A ministry sponsored by the Billy Graham Association.

12. Mark A. Noll, quoted in *Books and Culture*, December 2001, p. 22. Ten of the largest church congregations in the world are located in Seoul. Johnstone (*op cit.*) states re. Korea: "The first Protestant church was planted in 1884. By 1984 there were over 30,000 churches, and over 60,000 by the year 2000." Christians now constitute some 35% of Korea's population.

13. Total Sunday attendance has since grown to 250,000; with an estimated congregation of ¾ m. Yoido is actually a cluster of congregations, which hold joint services at the mother church on Sundays.

I felt guilty for fellowshipping with multitudes of believers, when across the border isolated disciples of Jesus prayed in secret. They'd be arrested if even three or four met together, or shot if caught with a Bible. "Prosperity gospel" didn't fit North Korea. "Lord—how long?" I breathed. Flourish? Could the church even *survive* under those awful conditions?

I knew the answer when I read the five principles North Korean disciples recite when a few of them do get together in secret:

1. Persecution and suffering are our joy and honour;
2. We want to accept ridicule, scorn, and disadvantages with joy in Jesus' name;
3. As Christians, we want to wipe others' tears away and comfort the suffering;
4. We want to be ready to risk our lives because of love for our neighbours, so they also become Christians;
5. *We want to live our lives according to the standards set in God's Word.*

I wouldn't wish their circumstances on anyone, but all at once I knew that First Century Christians were still living along the Old Spice Road—all the way across on Asia's eastern coast. I also had to admit that these dear believers know their Lord in a way that I don't. Yes, I can rejoice in the church flourishing in lands of liberty, but I give thanks for distressed disciples who are faithful even unto death. They belonged in the suffering Church in Smyrna ("I know your afflictions and poverty"), rather than the blossoming early church ("praising God and enjoying the favor of all the people").[14] But both of those churches were part of the history of the Body of Christ upon earth.

New Lessons for Old Missions

Korea has been "an inspirational model for mission in Asia," according to Susan B. Harper.[15]Asia's vibrant Christianity certainly proved very

14. Rev. 2.8 and Acts 2.4247 respectively.
15. Susan B. Harper, *In the Shadow of the Mahatma—Bishop Azariah and the Travails of Christianity in British India*, p. 89. Grand Rapids: Eerdmans, 2000.

uplifting for me, a Westerner. I'd preached on the Macedonian Call[16] and written a book on the relations of Church and Mission.[17] But Korea was an entirely different chapter. Contrary to critics' scenarios of western religious imperialism barging in on hapless people, early *Korean evangelists* were the ones who laid the groundwork for later *foreign missionaries.* That is a story with many surprising strands.

Suh Sang-Yun (*So Saw*) was one of those evangelists. Born in 1849 near the border with China, he crossed over to Manchuria to sell red ginseng roots for medicinal potions. When he himself fell seriously ill, a Scottish missionary in China took him to a hospital for surgery. Through this incident he became a Christian and helped the Scottish missionaries *in China* translate the Bible into Korean. He secretly carried Bibles on his trading trips back to Korea, where he and his brother distributed them. Result? By the time American missionaries arrived in 1884, there were a number of Christian believers—some seventy in Suh's hometown of Sorae.[18]

Later, in the late 20th c., it was *Korea* that called on Western missions—not to send them more workers, but to show them how to *send their own* missionaries to other lands. In that respect, it was similar to other parts of Asia where messengers of the gospel had planted the Good Seed centuries earlier; the church had grown, and now disciples wanted to obey their Lord by reaching out to others.

Recent mission arrivals in Asia, such as my own agency, acknowledged the dedicated ministries of earlier men and women from many nations. Certainly 50 years ago, SIM's International Council of that era had no intention of ministry in Asia. It was already fully occupied elsewhere. As in its introduction to Southern Asia, SIM responded to Far East invitations almost reluctantly—certainly very cautiously. Although calls came from Asians, SIM sought the advice of nationals and of sister missions already involved in South-East Asia and the Far East. The signals were all green!

---

16. Apostle Paul's response to the Macedonian's call, "Come over and help us!" (Acts 16.9).
17. W. Harold Fuller, *Mission Church Dynamics* (see Bibliography).
18. A. Scott Moreau, ed., *Evangelical Dictionary of World Missions*, p. 917 (re Korea, by Bong Rin Ro). Grand Rapids: Baker Books. ISBN 0-85364-995-2.

Korea had many lessons to teach an international mission. First of all, the nation had its own problems. Zeal was not lacking. Funds to send young volunteers to other lands were not lacking. The main problem lay in Korea's unusual insularity. In spite of frequent invasions from other nations, Korea was a very homogenous state. Ethnic loyalty was a prime virtue. Invaders hadn't stayed, even though their soldiers obviously left behind a trail of pregnancies. The result was an oriental race of mixed features, but society was homogenous, not cosmopolitan. At the time, few Korean mission volunteers had training in cross-cultural missions—or in survival in another country and culture.

A familiar pattern developed in the '80s: a Korean church would send an enthusiastic volunteer to another land, all expenses paid. The starry-eyed missionary would obey Jesus' command to "go into all the world." This age of opportunity would soon end; they must hasten to declare the gospel message! But over on the distant shore they faced reality. Uninstructed and lonely, the self-sacrificing novice faced isolation, misunderstanding, and often hostility. Without language and culture orientation, and without customary fellowship with fellow Koreans—the well-meaning volunteer often became disheartened, returning home spiritually and emotionally broken. The volunteer's church, in turn, lost heart in its mission outreach.

Zeal Needs Knowledge

It reminded me of the Apostle Paul's phrase in a much different context: "Zeal not based on knowledge." Korean pastors soon realized the need for both knowledge and zeal. They saw the wisdom of serving with experienced international agencies that could instruct and guide them, caring for their needs in a strange land. With typical Korean action, eager men and women began to turn up at the office doors of sending missions in Europe and North America. Ready for a challenge although not really prepared to cope with it, they'd often ask for "the most difficult mission field in the world."

SIM's Ian Hay, General Director at the time, began receiving calls from Korea. These came through missionary leaders who had ministered at Korean conferences.

"A year apart, mission professors Walt Baker of Unevangelized Fields Mission and John Gration of Africa Inland Mission both told me of Koreans enquiring about ministry to Muslims," Hay recalled.[19] "Quite separately, both advised the Koreans to ask SIM!"

On his way to take part in the "Lausanne" Pattaya conference in Thailand, Hay traveled via Korea and stayed with friends serving with The Evangelical Alliance Mission (TEAM). who introduced him to the Koreans who had been enquiring. One couple, Sam and Sarah Kang, in 1981 became SIM's first Korean members, serving in Nigeria before providing administrative help in Korea. Even though SIM had worked cross-culturally for nearly a century by then, Korea proved to be a new cultural learning experience! Dr. Hay goes on to explain:

> "Rather than establish our own SIM organization in Korea, we decided to work through Korean church groups while gaining experience initially. I met with denominational leaders to sign an historic document of partnership between the Hap Dong Presbyterians and SIM. That was a cultural experience. Everything was done very formally at a huge table with flowers in the center; the denominational leaders sat on one side while my wife, June, and I sat on the other as we very formally signed documents.
>
> "We learned cultural distinctions by trial and error. We had to have separate agreements with each of the denominations that send missionaries to us. It seemed logical to link Koreans with the nearest SIM office, which then was Singapore. Only later did I learn the cultural gross error. Because of history, Koreans were not pleased. We reasoned all Asians are Asians. By no means. So we linked Korea to Australia, but that wasn't the best either. Koreans needed direct contact with International—no other "home" office in between.
>
> "As General Director, until then, when I sent any official document around the Mission, I would send it in both English and French, because of our francophone areas of ministry. When we linked up with Korea, I assumed Koreans would appreciate our translating

19. Ian Hay, SIM's General Director Emeritus, letter to Harold Fuller, July 29, 2005. It was Dr. Hay who commissioned Lorna and Harold to visit Korea.

documents into Korean. To my amazement, Koreans were not pleased. Translation implied their English was poor. I'd insulted them!"

SIM Australia and Singapore offices did, however, play an important part in developing links with a "coordinating committee" in Korea. On October 2, 2000, SIM Korea became a full-fledged "sending office." By 2006, 85 Koreans were serving with the mission in 17 countries, with others waiting to go. Its Council reflects a cross-section of men and women, clergy and laity. Each Council member brings a wealth of experience and insight. For instance, there's Rev. Myung Hyuk Kim, Ph.D. Born in North Korea, Kim escaped imprisonment and possibly death when guards accosted him and other teens crossing the border. His companions stopped when challenged, but Kim kept running. He's never heard of the fate of his companions, but he prays for the day when he can preach the gospel in the North. Meanwhile, he is active not only on SIM's Council, but with Korea's Evangelical Alliance, the Evangelical Alliance of Asia, and other agencies.

Prayer Mountains and Tongue Twisters

"You're fortunate that your first Korean members were Sam and Sarah Kang," one of those leaders told Ian Hay after the signing ceremony. The man was Young Jun Son. He himself had served as a cross-cultural missionary under InterVarsity Christian Fellowship in USA, and had ministered in Africa, Asia, Europe, and South America before returning to Korea to marry an American Presbyterian missionary, Mary Lou.

Together they served in student and pastoral work, but their hearts ached as they saw zealous volunteers fly overseas, "crash-land" spiritually and emotionally, and return to Korea in defeat, discouraging the supporting churches that had sent them out. So when Korea's Hap Dong Presbyterians asked the Sons to help solve the problem, they agreed to do their part. They established the Missionary Training Institute (MTI) in Seoul.

That's how SIM, OMF, and other missions received invitations to send experienced missionaries for a few weeks at a time, to lead mission workshops at MTI. Ian Hay asked me to participate, and I found myself once again landing in Korea. But how was I going to locate our contact at the airport? I needn't have worried.

"WELCOME DR. FULLER!" I couldn't miss the large sign at the arrivals lounge. Holding it aloft was Young Jun Son himself, who had come to meet me at the airport. In fact, he and Mary Lou took me into their own home—the house previously occupied by Presbyterian missionary-theologian Harvey Cox. The Sons and their four children provided a delightful international atmosphere, but I had to become acculturated to the wider Korean scene. The morning after my arrival, when I came down to breakfast, I learned that Young Jun was just returning from his morning prayer meeting at the local church. In fact, he had risen at 4.30 a.m. That happened every morning. I felt apologetic for missing prayer time, although I was still struggling with jet lag.

"Don't think you should get up early with me," Young Jun reassured me as he sat down to a bowl of muesli after returning from early prayers. "Mary Lou doesn't. With us Koreans, it's cultural to rise early to pray."

So I relaxed, especially when I noticed the head of the house retreating to his bedroom after breakfast, for a nap before we both set off for the MTI course. No one would denounce praying early in the day—but I learned that it followed a Confucian-Buddhist pattern. Koreans would rise before dawn to meditate—preferably on a hilltop, closer to ancestral spirits hovering in the sky. Christians brought new meaning to the practice of prayer with retreats to "Prayer Mountains"[20] But I heard the MTI principal urging course members *not* to spend nights in prayer—they had to stay awake in classes the next day!

"Why did you say SIM was fortunate to have the Kangs as our first Korean members?" I asked Young Jun. We could discuss sensitive issues freely, both of us having served internationally.

"Christians here don't lack commitment, but they think they can jet off to other parts of the world and find acceptance just as they would at home among their own people," he explained.[21] "They don't realize the

20. Korea's "365-24 Prayer Movement" recruits intercessors for prayer chains right through the year. Currently there are 3,500 in 128 prayer teams. In 2006 organizers invited Patrick Johnson, founder-editor of *Operation World,* to speak at their annual retreat. To encourage intelligent intercession, they are translating all or part of *Operation World* into Russian, Mongolian, and Kazakh.

21. A recent example of this was a group of —Korean Christians who went to Afghanistan for humanitarian work in a remote village. The Taliban kidnapped them all, killed two men, and eventually released the rest upon receiving ransom money.

rest of the world may think differently. At the same time, they tend towards individualism and pride. Churches keep splitting. Denominations keep splintering. We're glad the gospel has spread so rapidly, but pastoral training hasn't kept pace. So there are thousands of churches run by elders without theological training. For some, a church is their kingdom.

"But Sam and Sara Kang have a humble outlook," he added. "They work with others. They're good listeners as well as witnesses. So your first experience with Koreans has been positive." We readily agreed.

MTI's vision was to immerse Korean mission candidates in a cross-cultural experience. That's why Dr. Son and his colleagues invited missions from other lands to participate in a one-year orientation course. They assigned me the daily Bible studies for a month, plus a course in time-management. On another visit, when I lived in the MTI dormitory with course members, I taught administration and writing.

Eating dried fish for breakfast and spicy-hot *kimchi*[22] with rice at most meals was a cultural experience! During my research in the Orient, I'd already caught on to chopsticks for survival. But in Korea I learned cultural sensitivities: community over individuality, respect for anyone older, continued use of formal titles—even among close friends.

A major benefit from the visits of missionaries was the use of conversational English as an international language. In fact, MTI asked missions to send teams of young people—some just out of secondary school, to live among the course members. SIM's Australia and New Zealand offices send volunteers during their summer break "Down Under." Europe and North America send teams during their summer—cultural immersion for all.

Even though Korea has 100% literacy, and these members were all university graduates, it was extremely painful for their Korean tongues to form English words. An intelligent M.A. graduate would struggle to pronounce my name, usually with a strangled expression. By the same

---

22. Chilli-hot cabbage pickle, without which no Korean meal is complete. Recent research by the University of Minnesota credits an element in cabbage with reducing some forms of cancer, particularly breast cancer.

token, few foreigners ever learn to speak Korean fluently—a unique verbal exercise.[23] Surprisingly, the language is related to Hungarian and Finnish. Apparently a linguistic group, moving northwards from Mesopotamia millennia ago, split at the Caucasus Mountain range. Some migrated westward and some traveled eastward, seeking pasture for their flocks.

Overcoming the language barrier, "English Camps" have been one effective way of ministry. Dave and Rosalie Hodges of Canada tell about leading an international team of students to staff a camp (as it closed, a number of youth had committed their lives to missionary service):

> We saw a remarkable change in our students from shyness and nervousness on the first day of camp to 64 enthusiastic, confident people by the end of camp. . . . But we learned more from them than we taught them. We found it is impossible to out-give Koreans!

Suiting Up

For my first session with MTI, I had just flown in from Down Under. I had been glad of my winter suit in New Zealand and Australia, but it was summer in the northern hemisphere, and monsoon winds turn the appendix-shaped peninsula into a sticky oven. From our earlier visit, I knew that Koreans expect proper attire in church. No worshipper would wear jeans to a service, and a pastor had to be properly suited up. But in a classroom, I reasoned to myself, I'd be able to teach in shirtsleeves. Otherwise I'd suffocate from heat in the absence of air conditioning. Fortunately, I mentioned my plan to my interpreter, explaining that (in a gesture of formality) I'd still wear a tie.

"Oh, sir," he replied, a trifle shocked that I'd even suggest it; "our teachers *always* wear a suit coat!" Lecturers must not give any hint of informality. Sweat dripping off the end of my nose, I had to teach in the sunshine blazing through the classroom windows—which seemed to amplify the heat. (Talk about "the hothouse effect"!) I knew I had to exchange my winter suit for lightweight clothing. That evening, I asked Young Jun if he could recommend one of Seoul's fast-service tailors. Next morning during a class break, Young Jun called me to his office.

---

23. Cultural placement of the tongue is one factor: note its position when saying "Korea" vs. "Kolea."

"This is Kim Chong, the tailor," Young Jun introduced the man holding a tape measure. Right there, the tailor measured me, showed me swatches of summer-weight material to choose from, and said he'd be back the next day. Sure enough, 24 hours later in the principal's office, "Instant-Tailor" Chong tried the basted suit on me for a fitting. The following morning I donned my lightweight suit, complete with my name hand-stitched on the inside pocket (including, in honorific Korea, "Rev." preceding my name). And the cost of the only custom-tailored suit I've ever possessed was less than an ill-fitting polyester product "off the rack" back home!

The course members were handsome people, their oriental eyes set above high cheekbones. They were also beautiful in spirit—the cream of the crop for mission service. Once a month they provided their own cultural treat for visitors—an evening of traditional dances and singing, in full cultural costume. Koreans, I decided, were the Welsh of Asia, their strong voices blending in harmony. And prayer sessions were an uplifting experience. In a prayer meeting or Sunday service, a time of prayer was the signal for everyone to pray at once! Impassioned voices filled the assembly hall with guttural sounds and explosive outbursts. Their pleas to God mounted louder and louder like the roar of a waterfall; until the leader struck a bell—and the gathering fell silent.

The careful mentoring of MTI and other training courses has turned the dream of the ten thousand CCOWE volunteers into a reality. By the year 2000, nearly 10,000 Koreans were serving as missionaries. They continue to go, many as missionaries to their own Korean people who have found employment in other lands.

In contrast to the warmth of my first visits to Korea, my last visit was in winter, when prevailing winds change direction and bring sub-zero temperatures from central Asia. No problem—I once more called on the tailor who had made me that summer suit. Same made-to-measure procedure, but this time the material was fine wool—light for traveling yet warm. Then as a farewell gift, MTI gave me a wad of *won* currency notes to pay for the new suit! Talk about generosity!

This time, after my sessions at MTI, Young Jun Son took me on a preaching tour around the nation. Churches ranged from village groups to mega-churches in industrial centers.[24] At each church, we sat down to eat with believers—always with *kimchi*, of course! This "breaking of bread" (not a ceremonial bit of wafer and a communion cup but a full meal) was an important aspect of Korean fellowship.

"Foot Washing" in a Snow Storm

Our most memorable visit was to an island off the tip of the peninsula. A blanket of snow had fallen during the night, and a bitter wind blasted us. Telephone lines were down, so we hadn't been able to communicate our arrival time to Pastor Kim Chew.

Not to worry, Young Jun assured me. When we turned up unannounced, Pastor Kim switched on the loudspeaker that normally played hymns and chimes for the villagers. Now she[25] broadcast the news of our arrival. By the time a round-bellied stove warmed the little frame chapel, Kim's parishioners had braved the blizzard to worship with us.

As elsewhere, these country worshipers paused to pray whenever opening the Scriptures—just as Israel did when reading (or hearing) Psalm 67:1.[26] I knew that, before I stood in any church pulpit, I had to remove my shoes. But in this rural church everyone also kicked off shoes during prayer. So of course I did. As I knelt on the freezing floorboards, a woman took the woolen shawl from her shoulders and wrapped it around my legs and feet. The act of kindness, her equivalent of washing my feet, brought tears to my eyes.

And Kim? She went on to prepare herself for ministry with SIM in South America. Assigned to Chile, she wondered how she could meet Chile's new visa requirement of some profession other than "missionary."

---

24. Korea's export policy makes it a world trade competitor. No wonder it has the world's largest shipyard.
25. Yes, Pastor Kim was a qualified "Bible Woman" and impressive preacher.
26. "May God be gracious to us and bless us and make his face shine upon us," is a request for the Lord's blessing upon the reciting of his Word, as indicated by *Selah* ("Meditate upon this") following it.

No problem, SIM's Pacific Andes Area Director wrote back. Hadn't she supported herself at seminary by keeping honeybees? The country of her appointment was eager for someone to show their rural people how to convert wild honey harvesting into viable bee-keeping and honey-processing. Pastor Kim Chew received a visa and soon found a bountiful spiritual ministry in South America.

Visiting Korea blessed me. As I turned toward Japan, I remembered it had colonized Korea from 1910 to 1945. Several of the countries I'd just traveled through had feared and loathed Japan because of its brutal invasions. It didn't seem so long ago that I was on a warship headed for the Japanese theatre of war. How much had changed since World War II? Was I ready to be surprised?

At the center of industries and commerce, Tokyo hums with activity.

Land of Rising Sun Sees New Light

"From the rising of the sun to the place where it sets, the name of the Lord is to be praised" (Psalm 113.3).

Japan: Pop. 127,315,474

DUMBSTRUCK, I DOFFED MY HAT, bowing my head before the skeleton of the Hiroshima Industrial Promotions Hall. "Skeleton" was the word, for its naked iron framework rising into a gaunt dome was the area's sole structure left standing after the world's first atomic bomb attack had detonated directly above it. The Hall had been "Ground Zero," the eye in the firestorm that blew out in every direction from this point.

The Industrial Hall now formed the centerpiece Hiroshima's Peace Memorial. Except for stunning photographs of the surrounding city (like a field of straw flattened by a tornado), I couldn't have imagined the devastation. Now gleaming towers mark the rebuilt city.

What the photos didn't show were the faces of astonished men, women, and children—standing even a mile away—whose eyeballs melted and dribbled down their scorched cheeks as people instinctively looked towards the bomb's searing light, seconds before the deadly blast itself blew them away. Some 140,000 died immediately; other thousands languished in agony from the radiation.

As I tried to imagine the carnage, a class of uniformed schoolchildren visited the nearby memorial shrine of a 12-year-old girl who had courageously lingered on for months, inspiring the nation not to give up in its recovery. No giggles or chatter came from the children, each making a respectful bow in front of their heroine's statue after silently adding a folded-paper crane to a shoulder-high pile of *origami* birds.[1]

Japan's Rape of Asia

I wondered how things could come to such a gory conclusion! Then I realized how the nation had hunkered down in its mountainous redoubts, isolated from the realities of the developing world. With their proud Samurai traditions, they smarted from centuries of humiliating attacks and the disintegration of their mainland fiefs—which they'd considered their divine right. The nation's 1868 Meiji Restoration revived the nation's confident imperial ethos, and its victories in the Sino-Russian war and WWI turned the island nation into a regional power. When contrary Western liberal influences (imbibed from Europe's Enlightenment) threatened Japan's war machine, its aristocratic/warrior tradition surfaced under the umbrella of WWII. The nation re-discovered its "Manifest Destiny," and Japan's rape of Asia was on.

Long before the US declared war on the nation, Japan's harsh militarism had earned the universal hatred of invaded neighbors. At one time, Japan had 1m troops in China, where *at least 15m Chinese died*. In southeast Asia, *5m died*.[2] Even after Hitler's war machine collapsed and the West targeted the Eastern Front, Japan continued its atrocities, preferring suicide to surrender. Led by their "Divine Emperor," the warlords dreamed of world domination.

Japan's WWII militarism was perfectly rational to Japan's generals. The Shoguns felt self-assured their divine Emperor would restore and expand their nation's honor and empire.[3] Well-funded shamans, with no little self-interest, assured Japan's warlords the gods were with them. While hapless neighboring nations cringed at unprovoked aggression, the militia's bloodcurdling cries of "*Tora! Tora! Tora!*"[4] announced the restoring of the nation's glory.

1. *Origami:* "folded paper." A proverb states, "The crane lives for a thousand years." Therefore it is a symbol of long life, a suitable wish for a patient, or in Buddhism, for a departed one in the next life.

Traditional bombing raids made no difference. The gods would reward any who died in defending Japan's divine calling. American forces, the main players in the Pacific theater, knew that only a cataclysmic event would end the carnage. Average Westerners found it hard to understand, for while the media had kept them acutely informed about the Nazi holocaust (ghastly, though mild in comparison), Asia hadn't hit the headlines in the same way. Europe was war-weary, slow to understand and quick to misjudge (perhaps even to this day) the need for America's knock-out punch—dreadful as it had to be in order to stop further atrocities.

But at first even Hiroshima's atomic firestorm didn't convince Japan's war machine to quit. Nippon[5] was invincible, shamans assured the Emperor; its gods would yet be victorious. Hiroshima, a minor industrial centre, could be sacrificed. However, when the next atomic bomb flattened the major port of Nagasaki, warlords knew they faced a holocaust they hadn't dreamed of. August 15, 1945, they and the Emperor surrendered.

In that moment, Japan committed national *hara-kiri*.[6] Its glorious Army, pride of the Samurai nation, lost face, and its deified god-emperor became a mortal—a constitutional monarch. The disillusioned nation descended into psychosis! It was now a malnourished, occupied nation, defeated by the powers it had arrogantly set out to conquer.

On August 6, 1945, I'd been standing under an anti-aircraft ("Ack-Ack") gun platform of our Canadian warship in the Pacific when, over

2. That civilian carnage contrasts sharply with America's loss of 100,000 troops during the Japanese war.

3. Made me think of our world's current tensions, as radicals in the Middle East dream of restoring their divinely appointed Caliphate.

4. *Tora*: "Tiger!"

5. Nippon: known as Japan in English.

6. *Hara-kiri*: ritual disembowelment, sometimes decreed by a court of law for a convicted *samurai*, and the preferred alternative to losing face through surrender. Why had the *Emperor* not committed suicide? Since the Emperor was a god, he had the privilege of transmuting into human form, disowning his deity and even his status as emperor. Why wasn't Hirohito tried as a war criminal? The threat of Far East Communism made Hirohito more valuable alive than dead—warning of aggression's folly and (through Japan's reformation) an example of the peaceful path to national success.

Japan, a single US bomber dropped the first A-bomb out of a clear sky. Our flotilla was under a radio blackout, in case lurking submarines might detect a signal, but semaphore code signalled the news from one ship to another. Later, as we awaited our fleet Commander's orders, the second bomb fell. Shortly after, our ship's radio crackled into life with a stunning message: *Emperor Hirohito Surrenders to General McArthur.*

With a cheer, we tossed our sailor caps into the air—our fleet could head back into a Canadian port instead of toward Japan! Demobilizing on Canada's West Coast, we returned to civilian life—in my case, preparation for mission service. Many of my fellow students at Prairie Bible Institute turned out to be veterans of service in the Pacific. All over North America and Europe, enrolment in Bible schools and seminaries suddenly ballooned with men and women who had witnessed Asia's suffering—and wanted to take part in its physical and spiritual healing.

Staff of missions that had been working in China began to return to that land and its neighbors. David Michell's poignant story, *A Boy's War,*[7] tells how Japanese soldiers incarcerated him and children attending a missionary school. Michell later returned to Japan as a missionary before becoming OMF director in Canada. His most inspiring memory from those years of deprivation was the godly example of fellow prisoner and Olympic Gold Medallist Eric Liddell.[8]

America, the nation whose atomic bomb finally brought Japan's war machine to an abrupt halt, wisely moved in to help the nation replace militarism with economic power. That was wise strategy, for a shattered Japan could have sought recovery in Stalin/ Maoist-style politics. Instead, reconstructed Japan became a stabilizing factor in the Far East—one of the world's most generous benefactors, donating and lending funds to impoverished nations. Economists state that Asia's subsequent economic rise stemmed from Japan's economic recovery. (See Appendix I.)

---

7. See Bibliography.
8. Oscar-winning "Chariots of Fire" portrays the 1924 feat of Liddell one year before sailing for China with the London Missionary Society. (See David J. Michell, *The Spirit of Eric Liddell.* Toronto: OMF.)

"Tora, Tora, Tora!"

But back in 1941, the spine-chilling war cries of Japanese bomber pilots drew back the curtains on Japan's earlier tragi-drama. Until then, the Western Hemisphere had been the theater of World War II. But Dec. 7, 1941, when Japanese Wing Commander Mitsuo Fuchida cried "*Tora, tora, tora!*" Japan's planes and ships knew they had achieved complete tactical surprise over the US forces on Oahu Island. US Navy radios at Pearl Harbor, Hawaii, crackled into life—and the Pacific war front opened up.

What I didn't know for many years was that Fuchida later became a Christian evangelist!

Captured, the Japanese pilot had ended up in a US prisoner-of-war camp. He and other prisoners couldn't understand why an 18-year-old girl visited the camp regularly, seeking to do anything she could to help them, within the rules of the prison.

"Why are you so kind to us?" a puzzled prisoner at last blurted out.

"Because Japanese soldiers killed my parents in the Philippines," Margaret Covell answered softly. Fuchida and his fellow prisoners were stunned. To them, the concept of *katakiuchi*[9] revenge made Margaret's forgiveness and kindness incomprehensible. Was she being disloyal to her parents? Or did she know a secret about life and death they didn't know? At times she tried to tell them about a God who loved them.

When freed, Fuchida went in search of Margaret's secret. He learned that her parents had escaped from Japan and taken refuge in Baguio, where Japanese soldiers found them. The soldiers mistook their small domestic radio for a communication device and sentenced them to death. As the Covells knelt, blindfolded, awaiting the swish of the sword to behead them, they prayed for their captors. When Fuchida heard that, he wondered where he could find such peace? One day he accepted a New Testament from an evangelist. For the first time he read the story of Jesus' death on the Cross. He was amazed to read, in essence, the same words that Margaret's parents had prayed for their captors: "Father, forgive them, for they know not what they do."

---

9. *Katakiuchi*: "Attack enemy"—a revenge concept, even if it takes many rebirths to do so completely.

Weeping, the tough suicide bomber realized Jesus had prayed not only for those who crucified him, but also for the whole world. He kept reading and put his trust in the Saviour. Fuchida went on to study the Bible and became a Christian leader.

Call to Missions: "Come Over and Help Us!"

While America sought to fill the power vacuum that Japan's surrender had left in the delicate balance of Far Eastern nations, General Douglas MacArthur, who had accepted the surrender, realized the nation's emotional and spiritual psychosis. He called for "10,000 missionaries and 10 million Bibles" to help bring healing. "Japan cannot have a democracy without Christianity,"[10] he believed, thinking of Christianity's democratic values vs. Japan's shaman-influenced warrior culture.

Many Christian war veterans, including this author, entered missionary training. Some returned to the Orient with the gospel instead of bombs.[11] Mainline denominations formerly active in Japan responded—but for several, interest in missions had waned, except for social causes.

What of interdenominational missions? As noted in earlier chapters, China Inland Mission, hounded out of China, had regrouped—in 1951 becoming Overseas Missionary Fellowship (OMF), with a strong vision for reaching Asia. But to head into Japan so soon—wouldn't that hinder work in surrounding nations brutally mauled by Japan's soldiers? Feelings ran high. And how would the Japanese feel? During WWII former missionaries to Japan had accompanied the West's troops as non-combatant chaplains.

However, SIM's General Director of the time, Guy Playfair, also heard MacArthur's call. Years before, as an athlete from Canada's

10. At first the Emperor offered to make Japan a Christian nation. General MacArthur replied that people could come to Christ only voluntarily—not by decree (Billy Graham, *Just As I Am*, p. 194). United Bible Societies responded to the call for Bibles. MacArthur declared, **"As I look back . . . [to] when modern civilization trembled in the balance, I thank a merciful God that he has given us the faith, the courage, and the power from which to mold victory." (R. Jason News Service, Fonthill, ON, July 4, 2009.)**

11. Several formed new missions with this specific purpose: including Far Eastern Gospel Crusade (later called SEND), and Christian Nationals Evangelism Commission (later called Partners).

hard-bitten Prairies, he'd prepared for the Olympics but instead had responded to the challenge of Africa's need. A man of vision and hands-on action, he was now ready for the urgent challenge of Japan. SIM had no "baggage" of serving in countries Japan had invaded. Playfair visited Japan in 1947 to see for himself, returning convinced this was God's moment for Japan. A donor even sent in $5,000 (a princely sum in those post-war years!) to enable SIM to open work in Japan. Surely God wanted SIM to help with the task!

Playfair's councils in Africa agreed with him, but home councils put on the brakes. Tensions grew, causing at least one council member to resign. Africa offices (which would be most affected by such an expansion) called for a step of faith; whereas sending offices feared that their visionary General Director was ramming the decision through.[12] They pointed out that projects in Africa were unstaffed; some months the mission couldn't pay allowances—and yet unsupported candidates waited to go to Africa.

So Playfair's plea to enter Japan went unmet. Greatly disappointed, he sent the $5,000 to his fellow mission leader, Oswald J. Sanders, then General Director of CIM-*cum*-OMF.

"Did you know how God used Guy Playfair's letter and that donation to help direct OMF?" Dr. Sanders asked me years later. I hadn't heard.

"Our International Council members were meeting in New Zealand," Oswald explained. "We were really in a quandary about Japan. We didn't doubt the urgent need, but we doubted the wisdom of hurrying into the nation that had been Asia's greatest nightmare. What effect would our ministering in Japan have on our reception by other nations we were just beginning to reach? What were our priorities?"

I understood on a smaller scale, for in Africa sections of the church had been upset with our giving time to other tribes who had been traditional enemies—or who were looked upon as inferior! The grace of

12. Hector A. Kirk, Field Secretary, SIM, West Africa, *Japan and the S.I.M.* Jos: Niger Press, 1950. Kirk bluntly described the tension and (to disprove the allegations against Playfair) called for a member vote.

God had a lot of work to do *within* churches as well as among unreached peoples.

"So we threw ourselves upon the Lord for his direction. Kneeling by our chairs, like the early apostles, we cried out, 'Neither know we what to do!' Anyway, how would God show us the answer to such a complex question?"

How indeed? As OMF Council members rose from their knees, a secretary handed the General Director an airmail envelope. Opening it, he found an international money order for $5,000. Halfway around the globe, SIM's General Director had scrawled a note: "Please use this to survey the needs in Japan. God bless. Guy."

"Unmistakable guidance!" OMF concluded. For Oswald Sanders, it was a classic case of God's answering even before his people called[13]—the letter had been on its way a week but just arrived while Council members were wrestling in prayer over the complicated question: "Enter Japan or not"? For Guy Playfair, it was a case of "Man's disappointment is God's appointment." SIM's councils had no idea that one day SIM missionaries would work as colleagues alongside OMF missionaries *in Japan*!

Today Japanese missionaries serve with SIM not only in Asia but also in distant lands, such as Tanzania in East Africa. One of the first from Japan was Michika Aoba, whose father was a Shinto priest, her mother a spiritist. "As a child, I could see there must be only one God—if there were any at all," Michika said. A talented Tokyo tour guide fluent in several languages, she joined the staff of Swissair and saw the world. She also trusted in Christ as Saviour and while studying in Zurich, heard missionaries report about the needs of the world.

Michika ended up serving with SIM in Nigeria as a teacher. Swarms of flies in the village bothered this hygiene-conscious Japanese. "But my students didn't seem to notice my racial background. In fact, being more used to Europeans, I found the ways of my *North American* colleagues the biggest adjustment!" Michika laughed.

13. Isaiah 65.24: "Before they call, I will answer; while they are still speaking, I will hear."

Criminal Invites Pioneer *Missionary*?

That's *recent* history, but when did the gospel *first* enter Japan, and who was the first missionary? Japanese historian Saeki writes that the first Middle Eastern Christian missionaries reached Japan in 199 AD, and Nestorians came in 515, a thousand years before Xavier.[14] Dr. Saeki also mentions that a Mongolian helmet inscribed with a cross, and a Mongol envoy who might have been Christian, could hint at Christian contacts in the 13th c., but Saeki and other scholars do not give credence to any continuing Christian presence at the time.[15]

In the 16th c., Dutch, English, French, German, Portuguese, Russian, and Spanish [alphabetical but not chronological order] merchants raced to establish trade with the remotest potential market at the time: Nippon. But that century's first missionary arrived on a Chinese junk, responding to the persistent appeal of a Japanese criminal! I thought of the way that God used a harlot in the history of Israel as I heard about the criminal Yajiro, on the run from justice. He traveled to Malaya to beg Francis Xavier to bring the gospel to his people.

Missions historian Samuel Moffett relates that Yajiro (or Anjiro), sought refuge in a Buddhist monastery after causing a man's death (likely accidentally in a brawl). Finding no peace of heart, Yajiro fled the country on a Portuguese ship, whose captain told the distraught youth that a Portuguese missionary in Malacca could help him spiritually. After a roundabout journey, Yajiro finally found Xavier, who responded in 1549 by sailing to Japan with two other priests, three Japanese, and a Chinese Christian.[16]

At the time, civil war had fractured society. Rampant corruption, immorality, and warring Buddhist monks had disillusioned people.[17] With Xavier's arrival, feudal leaders eagerly hoped to gain material benefit from the Christian monk's nation. Historians called the ensuing years, "Japan's Christian Century." Xavier wrote glowingly of Japanese as the best people he had ever met among "unbelieving nations," while at the same time

14. Kenny Joseph, *Jiro and Jesus in Japan.* Unpublished (REAPJapan1@aol.com).
15. P. Y. Saeki, *The Nestorian Documents and Relics in China.* Tokyo: Maruzen, 1951.
16. Samuel Hugh Moffett, *Christianity in Asia,* Vol. II. Maryknoll: Orbis Books, 2005, pp. 69, 70.

condemning their immorality and idolatry. Other historians confirm that Japanese society showed more decorum than the brawling seamen on Europe's ships. In fact, Japanese found white traders' wares inferior to their own![18]

Although the people often misinterpreted Xavier's message as another Buddhist sect, he and his colleagues established a reputation for Christian compassion: an orphanage (as an alternative to infanticide), a home for the homeless, and Japan's first surgical hospital. Several Christian generals served in the army. But, Jesuits struggled against syncretistic tendencies of converts trying to keep one foot in two separate worlds: Christian and Shinto/Buddhist.

Nearly a century of amazing Christian growth suddenly ended with a horrendous backlash. In 1614, the government, feeling threatened by what they saw as a foreign faith and the military power behind it, proscribed Christianity. Although the Jesuits, joined by the Franciscan Order, had disassociated themselves from the profitable Portuguese silk trade, the government of the day turned on them, accusing them of undermining their religion and planning to invade Japan. Thousands of Christians were imprisoned and killed (including 26 publicly crucified)—culminating in the massacre of nearly 40,000 Christians in 1638.[19]

Japan had had a higher percentage of Christians in the 16thc. than at the end of the 20c. Moffett notes. What happened? Suspecting an undermining authority in the church, the Emperor evicted the missionaries. The land that had seen such amazing acceptance of Christianity turned into one of its greatest hellholes for disciples. Persecution included devilish torture and death for those who refused the

17. Xavier esteemed Japan's culture, but condemned depravity of its monks, whose celibacy led to homosexuality, in his view. (Concise *Dictionary of the Christian World Mission,* p. 669. Bibliog.)

18. G. Milton, *Samurai William: The Adventurer Who Unlocked Japan*. London: Hodder- Stoughton, '02.

19. The castle of Hara on the Shimabara Peninsula fell to invaders. Masuda Shiro Tokisada defended the fortress with 37,000 Christians, who fought valiantly to the end—even the women and children. All survivors were beheaded, except Yamada, a "Judas" who opened the castle gate to the enemy.

edict to recant. To all appearances the church died out. Moffett, son of Presbyterian missionaries in the Orient, and a missionary himself, cites a reason other than persecution:[20] although 16th c. missionaries introduced the printing press[21] and published writings on science, grammar, and poetry as well as Christian subjects, there is *no record of a printed Bible translation.*

At the time, the Vatican insisted on Latin for the Bible (as Islam has insisted on Arabic as the only language for disseminating its scriptures). In the 14th c., England's state church had banned John Wycliffe's English-translated portions, and in the 16th c. had executed William Tyndale, burning his translation.[22] Japan closed down to the rest of the world and would have to wait until the 19th c. for its first printed Bible.

Hidden Christians Emerge

Nearly three centuries later, when Commodore Perry's smoke-belching naval ships loomed over the horizon in 1853, Japan was fractured into some 300 small provinces, each the fiefdom of a prince supported by a warlord. For 2½ centuries Tokugawa shoguns had ruled the islands under extreme feudalism amounting to a strict caste system. The quarreling princes quickly signed a Treaty of Commerce with America, each hoping to get in on imagined riches of trade.[23] Slowly, Christian disciples began to emerge from obscurity. In 1859, almost 300 years after Xavier's arrival, the Paris Foreign Missionary Society (an RC mission) met a group of

20. Moffett, *op cit.*, Vol. I, p. 361, recognizes persecution and oppression as factors in the decline of Middle Eastern churches. But he also cites the loss of missionary vision. Those were also factors in the rapid decline of Japan's 17th c. church under Shinto and Buddhist rulers. However, Moffett singles out Japan's lack of a printed Bible translation as a major factor (*ibid*, Vol. II, p. 83).
21. Block printing was used on the Chinese mainland in the 10th c.; movable type was first used manually during 11th c. Ch'ing Li period. However, Germany's Johannes Gutenberg was first to use it in a mechanical printing press (15th c.), making mass printing possible. Portuguese brought it back to Japan.
22. As stated, Linguist-Anthropologist Lamin Sanneh credits Protestant missionary translations for the more rapid (although later) spread of Protestant Christianity than of Roman Catholicism. (See Sanneh, Bibliog.)
23. A different picture than that of the "imperialism" depicted by America's critique. Neither was the US alone in seeking trade. European countries also sought benefits.

believers who led them to a community of thousands of "hidden Christians" who had secretly kept their faith.

Two samurai clans restored the monarchy in 1868, shattering the caste system. They proclaimed a teenager as *Meiji* (ruler), pressuring him to ban Christianity as an "evil sect," restricting Buddhism, and reviving Shinto as the national faith. However, the youthful ruler preferred reformers, and by 1873 Japan opened once more to Christian activity as part of the price of trade benefits.

Presbyterians, Methodists, Congregationalists, and Anglicans were the forerunners of a number of Christian agencies who came through this door that finally opened. Although they did not manage the unified profile they'd hoped for, they did accept the Statement of Faith of the World Evangelical Alliance.

And what happened to that missing element, the Bible in a Japanese tongue? The Holy Spirit was at work, prompting several attempts. Bible portions had sold well. But it was 1879 before the New Testament appeared in Japanese, and 1883 for the Old Testament. Catholics lagged behind their Protestant counterparts, not completing their Old Testament translation until 1959.

Unlooked for help came from the chaplain to the Russian consulate in Japan, Nicolas Kassatkin. The Russian Orthodox priest was a courageous witness for the gospel. He even took on a samurai named Sawabe, who challenged him to a verbal dual (intent on killing the Russian if Sawabe did not win the debate). The priest's soft answers shook the samurai to the extent that Sawabe continued discussions with Nicolas and eventually became a devout believer in Christ and defender of the Christian faith, resulting in the secret conversion of several high-ranking Japanese.[24]

But Nicolas felt that the only available Japanese Bible, produced by Protestant missionaries, was too colloquial and foreign in terminology.

24. At the time, it was illegal even to study Christianity, let alone become a Christian. Sawabi was a Japanese "Apostle Paul."

His superior, Bishop Innocent, missionary to Alaska and the Aleutian Islands, encouraged Nicolas to study Japanese. The erstwhile chaplain produced a version of the New Testament that relied more on Chinese and archaic terms—more fitting, Nicolas felt, for the Holy Scriptures.

Following earlier evangelistic attempts in Japan, was this now God's "fullness of time" for the islands? It seemed the Holy Spirit had Japan in the spotlight, bringing together, in effect, the work of an international consortium of translators from Asia, Europe, and North America. Personally unknown to each other, they made the Word of God available in the language of the people.

Samurai's Son Becomes an *Apostle*?

While critics trot out the tired accusation that missionaries entered Japan at the point of Imperialist guns,[25] it was the feudal lord (*daimyo*) of Higo, Kyushu, who in effect brought in a lay Christian, retired America army captain, Leroy L. Janes.[26] The captain's assignment was to teach citizens modern military tactics as a corollary of Western trade. Janes opened his school for Samurai[27] boys in the military town of Kumamoto.

Captain Janes, a member of the Reformed Church of America, wasn't a member of any mission board at the time, and he didn't go around preaching, but his godly character intrigued his students. Although he knew military tactics, he wasn't the typical warrior they expected him to be. They were full of questions, but Janes waited three years, when the boys could understand his English better (for he never mastered Japanese), before he began to answer questions about his faith. His wife, a daughter of India's pioneer medical missionary doctor, John Scudder, spent nights in prayer for the salvation of the boys who studied

25. As explained earlier, the only logical means of arrival was on British naval ships (even as Muslim teachers had arrived on Arab gunboats).

26. That was in the early 1870s. Janes was not the only retired officer Japan recruited to teach. Col. W. S. Clark was another. These two are credited with Christianity's spread more than any missionary of the era.

27. Japan's warrior aristocracy.

under her husband.[28] Authorities didn't object to Janes' lessons from the Bible, because they thought those would convince the young Samurais of Christianity's folly.

I remember as a young boy gazing at an autographed photo of a distinguished-looking Japanese on a wall of our home—why it was there I didn't question. People from different parts of the globe passed through our home. To my parents, the whole world was a mission field. Later I learned that the Japanese had stayed in our home when I was a toddler. He was Evangelist Tsurin Kanamori, and my father had arranged his itinerary on North America's West Coast.

Now in Japan, I discovered that this Kanamori had been Captain Janes' brightest student. Out of curiosity, the young Samurai and several classmates visited Janes on Sundays (which Janes always observed as a day of rest) to hear him explain the Scriptures. Janes encouraged them to memorize Scripture, and several boys quietly became believers in Christ. Kanamori was among them, at 18 the eldest.

One day while explaining about the Apostle Paul's missionary travels, Captain Janes looked directly at Kanamori and asked, "Is it not a glorious thing to imitate such a man as Paul?" From then on, Kanamori became known as Paul Kanamori, for early Japanese Christians normally adopted a name from the Bible.

Pledge: Follow Jesus till Death

When the students' parents and friends heard, the adults fiercely opposed the boys' spiritual decisions. Friends ostracized them. One mother drew a dagger she kept in her bosom and threatened to kill herself unless her son recanted. Kanamori's father disowned him. But the fiercer the persecution, the more determined the boys became. Meeting on a local mountaintop January 30, 1876, 40 of them pledged to follow Jesus until death—whatever others did to them.[29] Their favorite hymn was one

28. Information about Captain Janes and Evangelist Kanamori is from P. Kanamori, *Paul Kanamori's Life Story* (see Bibliography). Re. John Scudder, see Chapter 9 on Sri Lanka.

29. Thus the boys gave Christian meaning to the traditional Samurai oath of fealty to the gods.

they'd heard Captain Janes and his wife sing around their home: "Jesus, I my cross have taken, all to leave and follow Thee." They became known as the Kumamoto Band.

"We'd never met a missionary or evangelist; we didn't know what a church or a pastor was," Kanamori later recalled. "We only knew that Jesus died and rose again for us, calling us to be his disciples. We didn't understand, but the Holy Spirit was at work."

In fact, today we'd call it a revival, for when the boys returned from vacation for the new school year, they were so full of the gospel they immediately started leading new students to the Lord. For the first week, the principal had to suspend regular studies because the boys all wanted to study the Bible.

The young Christians went home on weekends and witnessed to families and friends—even to Confucian scholars (for they had all been Confucian). Kanamori's elderly Confucian teacher had been his loving mentor, but when the patriarch saw he could not refute his former student's preaching, in rage he forbade him ever to return. However, after the scholar died, his own grandson became a vibrant Christian preacher. Regeneration was spawning a spiritual revolution.

Kanamori remembered how his Samurai grandfather had presided over an annual feast in which villagers trampled on a buried Roman Catholic icon. The Samurai imprisoned anyone who refused. Government notices warned: "Belief in the evil religion of Jesus is strictly forbidden." In the 19th c., by the time of the revival at Capt. Jane's school, government had become more tolerant; persecution came mainly from the boys' families.

Kanamori and his fellow disciples realized that the RC icons were part of a formal religion, but something different had transformed their own lives. From the Scriptures, they knew it was the regenerative work of Christ. In time, they met two other groups of evangelical students that had sprung up in Japan: the Yokohama and Sapporo Bands. Together, these later formed the Congregational Church in Japan.

"Higher Criticism" Destroyed His Faith

That was the first phase of Paul Kanamori's pilgrimage. He regretted the second phase, but it was a commentary on the effect of nominal Christianity not only in Japan but also throughout Asia—imported from the West! Jo Niishima, the founder of Doshisha, Japan's first Christian university, was also from the Kumamoto Band but had absorbed Unitarian doctrine while studying in America. He invited Kanamori to teach Theology at the university. To prepare, Paul read volumes of European books, most of which were by modernist authors. "Higher Criticism" slowly eroded the faith he had once held so strongly. It destroyed the credibility of Scripture and in turn the deity of Christ Jesus. Therefore, Jesus was simply a model to admire and follow—not the Saviour.

As I read Kanamori's later account of the systematic destruction of his faith through European rationalism, my mind went back to the discussion I'd had with the Yogi disciple in India. The source was the same: Europeans espoused Aryan concepts and elevated man above God, rationalism above revelation. Accordingly, Buddha, Muhammad, and Jesus were on the same plane—models of perfect manhood for all to strive after! As Kanamori absorbed this heresy, theological liberals in the West praised the erstwhile Japanese evangelist for his new "enlightened views."

"I was a backsliding prodigal son of my Heavenly Father for many years," Kanamori wrote in his memoirs.[30] Not that he performed evil. In fact, he threw himself into active social reforms in government service. It was some twenty years later that the death of his beloved wife, a faithful follower of Jesus, awakened him to the emptiness of life without the living Saviour. Paul Kanamori returned to his spiritual moorings.

That is when people began to call Kanamori, "The Dwight L. Moody of Japan." He was known for his single message—a presentation of the gospel that took three hours to deliver. He preached all over Japan (and later in North America) to vast crowds. In a weeklong series, rather than change his message for the second and succeeding night, he asked the crowds to stay home after they'd heard him, so a different crowd could hear the same message. He kept meticulous statistics of attendance and decisions for Christ.

---

30. Kanamori, *op cit.*, p. 34. (Kanamori was born 1857, died 1945.)

As he grew older, he published a book, *The Christian Belief,* which became a best seller. Throughout his ministry, Paul Kanamori remained humble, closing his autobiography with the Scripture, "Not by might, nor by power, but by my Spirit, saith the Lord."

Japan's 1889 Constitution had made Shinto[31] the state religion and a patriotic duty. The Roman Catholic Church allowed its members to take part in rites at Shinto shrines—portraying them as culture and patriotism. Major Protestant churches followed suit, in line with the theological liberalism promoted by Kanamori for two decades. Like their counterparts later in Hitler's Germany, most Christians felt obliged to show loyalty to the ruler and his war machine above the lordship of Christ. If they voiced any goal, it was simply for a benign "peace" rather than a vibrant Christianity that would stand up for justice and mercy. There were disciples, however, who suffered the consequences of standing for righteousness. Pastors who refused to worship the Emperor died in prison.

Meanwhile, the Holy Spirit was working out a strategy above any war machine's. While many post-war missionary ventures pioneered in a new generation, their evangelism actually meant a return to the almost forgotten era of only half a century earlier, when Evangelist Paul Kanamori had preached to vast crowds in every province of the land.

"Flee to the Mountain!"

In a sense, my colleague, Dr. Tadashi (Joshua) Tsutada was a third-generation product of that earlier awakening, for his grandfather had received the gospel, and his father had been a pastor. Joshua, who became principal of Japan's Emmanuel Bible Training College, and I became friends as members of the International Council of World Evangelical Alliance. Joshua told me how Japan's WWII attacks on Hawaii and Hiroshima came full circle in his own life.

Joshua married a daughter of the Japanese submarine commander, Captain Yokota, who had fired the first torpedo into the US aircraft

31. *Shinto*: "Way of the Gods," ancient worship of nature and the deified Emperor. Shamans and shrines supposedly eased tension between male forces of the sky ("heavenlies") and female forces of the earth.

carrier Saratoga as it sailed off Hawaii, July 11, 1942.[32] But their marriage involved an amazing series of events. Captain Yokota's wife, Mutsuko, had come to the Lord as an eight-year old through an Alliance missionary's Bible study. Mutsuko wanted to be a missionary herself, but later settled down as Captain Yokota's wife. While her husband was serving in the navy, Mutsuko provided a home for their three girls in Hiroshima.

When the Captain died overseas, life became so difficult for Mutsuko that the widow considered suicide, but the Holy Spirit reminded her of her earlier commitment. The Lord seemed to tell her to raise her children so *they* would become missionaries, as she had originally wanted to be. She found work with her sister, a medical doctor who managed a hospital in the center of Hiroshima.

One day a voice told her, "Flee to the mountain!" Her sister told her not to fear anything—Hiroshima was a smaller city on the West Coast and wouldn't be under any threat of attack. But the voice persisted, so one afternoon Mutsuko, with her daughters, loaded her suitcases on a truck travelling to the other side of the range beyond the city.

The next morning at 8.20, the atomic bomb detonated—some 300 meters (100 yards) from the hospital where Mutsuko had worked.

Mutsuko and her children were by then safe beyond the hills, but her medical sister's life also was spared, because when the blast leveled the hospital, she was working in the basement. That protected her from the worst radiation, and a heavy beam protected her from falling debris. On the spot the medical doctor dedicated herself to the Lord. She treated many radiation victims, but 27 years later died of radiation herself.

"That's amazing, but how do *you* fit into all that?" I quizzed Joshua.

"Ah! Mutsuko re-married and her three daughters did become missionaries—one to Kenya, one to Jamaica, and I married the third. We served in India at Yeotmal Seminary before Emmanuel Bible Training College called me to be their principal."

Later, Joshua was the logical choice for the Japan Evangelical Association to head up their first delegation to a conference of the

32. USS Saratoga suffered several attacks but sailed throughout WW II.

Evangelical Association of Asia (EAA), held in Singapore in 1987. It wasn't easy for Japanese believers, who had to pass Singapore's shrine commemorating the slaughter of ten thousand Singaporeans machine-gunned by Japanese soldiers. And it wasn't easy for other delegates to sit next to delegates from their erstwhile invader. But the greatest test came during the opening ceremony, marked by a parade of national flags to demonstrate the international unity of the assembly.

Joshua begged off marching beneath his nation's flag, because to many evangelicals, the flag's rising sun had been a Shinto symbol of the "divine" emperor. Instead, Pastor Tsutada read greetings from the churches in Japan. Dropping the letter to his side, with his voice quivering, he apologized for his country's aggression against the nations represented at the conference.

"My Hatred Melted"

"We are deeply sorry for what happened during the Second World War!" he confessed, head bowed. "The church in Japan was very small and young at the time. There was very little we could do to stop the war."

The room was hushed. Delegates dropped their gaze to the floor. Joshua took a deep breath and went on to explain that a number of pastors had languished in jail during the war—some had even died—because they refused to bow to the edict declaring the war to be divinely inspired.

"My father was one of those imprisoned pastors," Joshua added softly. "But I'm not excusing my country." His voice broke, tears streaming down his face. Before he could sit, Singapore's respected Christian patriarch, Dr. Benjamin Chew, grasped his arm.

"I was a young doctor at the time and saw the atrocities," Dr. Chew recounted. "I wished I could just let the injured Japanese soldiers in the hospital die, but I had to be true to my medical oath. Then one day I saw a Bible on the bed of a dying enemy soldier.[33] I asked if he were a Christian, and he nodded. In that moment my hatred melted, and the

33. Actually, a number of Japan's military (including suicide bombers) were Christians, who struggled with a sense of fulfilling national duty vs. their commitment to Christ. Emiko Ohnuki-Tierney recounts in *Kamikaze Diaries* (University Chicago Press, 2007) how one pilot wrote: "When I fly, I'll sing hymns."

young soldier and I had daily fellowship until he slipped away to his Saviour. Our bonds in Christ crossed all racial barriers."

The room of delegates, from countries that had suffered hundreds of thousands of casualties at the hands of Japanese invaders, melted in sobs of contrition. The once-formal delegates ended up embracing each other! And Asian Christians showed their forgiveness of Japan and acceptance of Joshua by electing him Chairman of the Evangelical Fellowship of Asia's Executive Council. Since then, the Japan Evangelical Association, though small, makes its voice heard. It helped persuade the government to compensate Korean women who had been forced into prostitution (as "comfort women") by Japanese troops.[34]

Japan had opened a new chapter in its story book.

---

34. It was seven years later, on June 6, 1995, that the Japanese government for the first time expressed "deep remorse" for attacking its neighbors. On August 14, 1995, the 50th anniversary of Japan's surrender, the Prime Minister issued an apology to the whole world for the "tremendous damage and suffering to the people of many countries." (Fuller, *People of the Mandate, op. cit.*, pp. 45-47.)

****

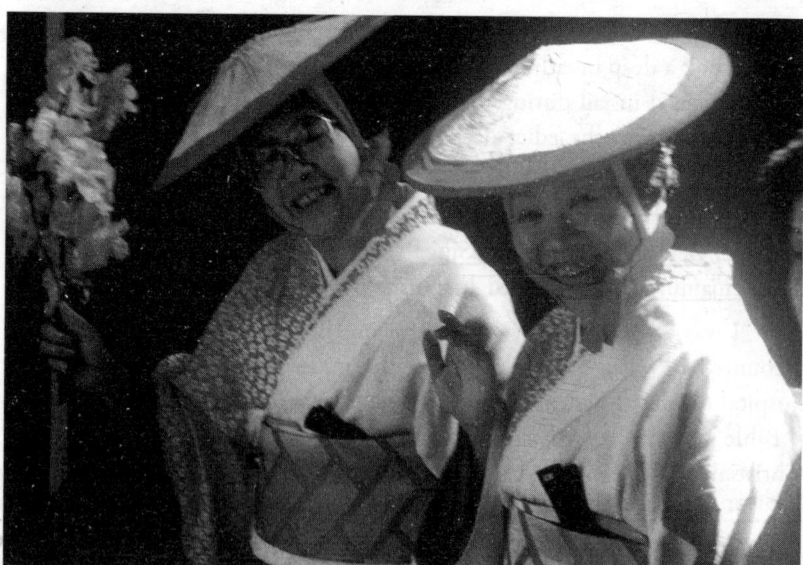

Fresh from a Geisha festival, two women greet the visiting cameraman.

Ancient Japan's New Chapter

"Our struggle is not against flesh and blood, but against . . . the spiritual forces of evil in the heavenly realms" (Eph. 6.12).

I WAS NOW SEEING the new Japan. The most significant newscast I watched on TV showed a Japanese envoy chairing peace talks between Sri Lankan officials and "Tamil Tiger" rebels. The warrior state had become peacemaker!

Although Japan is rightly proud of its history,[1] and controversy raged over state visits to the nation's leading war shrine, a sure sign of democracy has been newspaper articles examining Japan's wartime record. During the nation's recovery, a number of Christian agencies set up offices and Bible schools in Japan. Friends of ours, Ken and Betty Roundhill opened a training center in their home. Betty had gone from our church to Japan under the Central Japan Pioneer Mission. There she met and married New Zealander Kenneth Roundhill of World Evangelization Crusade (WEC). Seeing the need for Japanese leadership in the churches and missions, Ken and Betty devoted all their efforts to a discipleship ministry.

On our way from Korea (see previous chapter), Lorna and I dropped in on the Roundhills, at the time living in Japan's former capital of Kyoto.

1. The world's oldest monarchy, "The Chrysanthemum Throne"—unbroken male lineage of 2,600 years. Tradition states it descended from the Sun Goddess, Amaterasu (symbolized on Japan's flag).

Historic forts and monasteries filled this emperor's capital. Statues of Buddha benignly surveyed milling crowds. In monasteries, effigies of *bodhisattvas* (explained in Ch. 14 re. Thailand) flanked his placid image.

I was intrigued by Kyoto's *Hoodo* rock shrine, for it reminded me of sacred rocky columns on North American plains. "Plains Indians," migrants from Asia, had brought them; to this day, many believe that nature spirits and ancestors indwell the unusual shapes. They even call them "*hoodoos*."[2]

Kyoto's most famous resident, at least for *literati*, had been Murasaki Shikibu—prototype of all novelists, although she lived a thousand years ago. Member of the ruling clan around the end of the first millennium A.D., she immortalized culture covering three generations in the engaging *The Tale of Genji*. While Europe was still a cultural backwater, a 1008 Japanese diary mentioned the book—making it the world's first known novel. Japan's macho males didn't oppose the female author, because at the time they considered fiction writing frivolous—not for men! (Or were they secretly enamored by the story's flagrant sexiness?)

Rather than using Chinese, favored by the intelligentsia, Murasaki wrote in the Japanese *kana* syllabary of the common people. Scribes hand copied the pages as she wrote, the method used until the printing press came to Japan in the 17th c. Now one thousand years after its first appearance, multiple copies continue to roll off presses—a global record, apart from the Bible. Today's novelists measure their work by the standards of Murasaki Shikibu, with spin-off tales of the hero. Recent years have seen films, a TV series, a CD-ROM edition, and translations in other languages, and spin-offs of *Genji* Tea, sweets, lectures, and even a *Genji* symphony. A popular *Manga*-style cartoon edition has sold 17m copies—and still selling.

Learning How to Take a Traditional Bath

Although many Japanese live in a modernized world far removed from the scenario of the *Genji* series, we found that our friends, Ken and

2 Webster's Dictionary surmises the word derives from "voodoo," since some Afro-Americans also worship such rock columns. Webster apparently didn't know the Japanese source.

Betty Roundhill, had actually built their house in a style more traditional than some Japanese homes we later visited. Taking off our shoes so as not to damage the thick padded straw mats, for dinner we sat on the edge of a sunken recess in the floor, with our legs beneath a low table. A screen decorated with the famed "Willow Pattern" separated us from the rest of the room, giving a cozy feeling.

After we enjoyed a light supper of raw salmon rolled in seaweed and nesting in boiled rice, Ken and Betty invited us to have "first soak" in the evening's bathwater.[3] That indicated we were their "guests of honor."

"Before sitting in the square tub, first soap yourself," our hosts explained to us puzzled novices. "Then rinse off from the bucket on the floor before sitting in the tub to relax. The rinse water will run down that drain hole in the floor." It turned out to be a relaxing experience. Then we slid the paper wall of our bedroom closed and fell asleep on straw-filled pallets on the floor.

The Roundhills told us amusing stories of the clash of cultures. One visiting preacher, in the best Western tradition, began with a humorous story. As it became complicated, his Japanese interpreter asked the preacher to tell the whole story without waiting for translation—and the interpreter would then explain it to the audience. After the story, the Japanese spoke only a minute before the audience burst into laughter.

After the service, the visitor was impressed that the audience had caught the point so quickly. "Oh," explained the translator, "I simply said you had told a story they wouldn't understand, but if they laughed you would be happy and go on with your sermon!" True Japanese gracious culture—say or do what is pleasing to the visitor.

Understanding surface indicators of deep currents in Japanese culture, Ken and Betty ministered not only to Japanese but also to missionaries in other lands through their training book, *The Life and Work of the Missionary*.[4]

---

3. Japanese are very conscious of personal hygiene and privacy. Japan introduced to the world the touch-less toilet. In place of toilet tissue, water jets spray from inside the toilet to clean one's *derriere*. No hands! In some public lavatories, a generator provides "white noise" to block out embarrassing sounds. Another invention "launders money": automatic teller machines (ATMs) clean money with antimicrobials.

4. Roundhill, K. (see Bibliography).

They were able to explain, for instance, how to place furniture in a room. In traditional houses of yore, it made sense to cluster everything in the middle of the room, away from the paper partitions.[5] At the same time, it gave everyone a sense of community, closeness, and "belonging." Lorna and I could imagine how isolated and uncomfortable Japanese visitors in Western homes might feel—for no accountable reason. Aren't we being friendly enough greeting them by their first names (No!) and passing snacks to them as we try to chat (No!) across the empty space in the middle of the room (No again!)? To us, our room looks "uncluttered." To a Japanese newcomer, it could look uninviting—even repelling.

Such subliminal signals explain a lot about Japanese society—including the two-level formal and informal levels of the psyche. Japanese who have lived overseas or have mixed with internationals for some time politely tolerate our rudeness, while we tend to think oriental society somewhat inscrutable—and wonder why people fail to respond to western outgoing friendliness ("brashness," a Japanese might call it) and directness. (Actually, Japanese culture is personally warm and informal within one's community, but in official contacts, it operates on a formal basis that appears "starchy" to foreigners.[6])

The Roundhills told Lorna and me about an unexpected cultural twist—this time among missionaries. As Japanese men and women, trained by the Roundhills, applied to join WEC, veteran members became concerned that the Japanese would find out the level of their mission salaries, or "allowances." This wasn't as racist as it sounds. WEC operated on its own financial concept of "faith"—meaning that no missionary (even if asked) ever told even a supporting church how much monthly support he/she would need for living expenses, had no promised level, and didn't even let colleagues know of any shortage. It was a rigorous life of complete faith, which the Lord honored with amazing supply.[7]

---

5. The Western phrase, "The walls have ears," took on real meaning for us in Japan!
6. In *Beyond Culture*, Edward T. Hall explains the bases for these cultural signals. I recommend his books on culture to anyone working cross-culturally, in any part of the world (see Bibliography).
7. I believe God can call some to live like that (I grew up in such a home). I deplore pressure fund-raising for God's work. However, in the "static" of today's society, missions need to state needs honestly—so involving supporters in responsible giving.

Why, then did those expatriate missionaries object to nationals becoming members? The expatriates feared that nationals would observe how little their missionaries actually had in material things (including food supplies). That could become a subtle form of solicitation, violating their faith principle, they felt!

Lorna and I had stayed in the home of one of a Japanese couple, who had been missionaries. We wondered how Japanese Christians felt about going to evangelize in a country which (at that time) was 16% Christian, when their own country was perhaps 1.5% Christian.

"We and our church wouldn't have missed that experience for anything," the couple replied. "Christ commissioned his disciples to be missionaries; that includes Japanese. We can learn from other lands, and we can witness for Christ in other cultures."

Bridging the Oriental-Occidental Divide

With enquiries from Japanese increasing, SIM invited experienced church leaders and laypeople to form a sending council in Japan. The Mission's East Asia Director at the time, Andrew Ng, invited me to accompany him and Singapore Board member Loh Hoe Peng to the inauguration.

We met in Tokyo with the Japan Evangelical Association and other respected leaders.

Our generous hosts served tempting *hors d'oeuvres,* including *sushi* rolled in rice and wrapped in seaweed, followed by a sumptuous Japanese banquet: *Miso* soup, *tempura* vegetables, *sukiyaki* beef—the works! (In all my travels, I was glad no one served me *Fugusahi,* a seafood delicacy but toxic unless expertly prepared. I learned that the fish contains enough *tetrodotoxin* to kill 30 diners!) Waitresses in *kimonos*[8] and red-vested waiters served us in a splendid hall decorated with paper lanterns. Traditional pen-and-brush drawings of dragons, sacred black-necked cranes, and Mount Fuji graced the walls. Pastors and elders then formally commissioned their missions council to the task, followed by a time of prayer.

---

8. *Kimono*: lit. "wearing thing," imported directly into English as "kimono," a loose outer garment.

Later, Andrew, Hoe Peng, and I walked to our lodgings for the night. Cyclists streamed past us through the narrow streets. Mirrors at "blind corners" warned vehicles of oncoming traffic. Pedestrians bowed in thanks to motorists for stopping. Bunches of plastic flowers decorated lampposts. Garish neon signs, enlarged Japanese characters, and paper lanterns lit up the night. Signs included Sony and Toyota—of course!

"Look—Chinese food!" my two companions suddenly cried, spotting a smaller sign almost hidden by the others. Regardless of the late hour and our earlier banquet, we simply had to stop for a bamboo basketful of mouthwatering prawns steamed in rice flour, chased down with chrysanthemum tea. And the chopsticks were squared and flat-nosed—not round and pointed.[9] I could see how, even in the Orient, there's nothing like *native* fare. After all, that's true of any of us. This gastric sidelight helped me see how I, like most westerners, tend to think of "East Asians" as monolithic, when they aren't.

Elephant and Giraffe in *Japan*?

Andrew and Hoe Peng returned to Singapore, but I was able to stay to explore Japan a little. It was fascinating to see how cultural differences come right down to regions within a single country, indeed to communities—even to professions within communities.[10] In fact, some historians change the debate of whether early Japanese were a race, to "*When* did Japanese become a separate race?" That question may upset the national and religious pride of this island kingdom, but Japanese archeologists and anthropologists are unearthing evidence that the islands were once linked to the mainland, stretching in one continuous arc from Manchuria and Korea southward to the Philippines—and possibly Indonesia. They are discovering not only continental artifacts and human fossils but also mammals (hairy bison, elephant, giraffe, and deer)—the latter dredged out of the inland sea now separating Japan from China.

9. The difference between traditional Chinese and Japanese chopsticks.

10. Missiologist George Peters (quoted in Ch. 15) made this point in *Evangelism Explosion* (Bibliography). Although agreeing that Christians are "all one in Christ Jesus," he observed that people tend to respond to evangelism in groups of the same profession or background (where they feel comfortable). As they mature in Christ, they more readily accept people of other backgrounds and mix with them.

Early human settlements reveal Japan's patchwork quilt of racial backgrounds—from ancient aborigines[11] to descendants of Polynesian islanders who fished further and further northwards. Many were already of racially mixed lineage. Sinking seabeds and rising volcanic lava isolated these from their forebears. Captives from wars with China, Korea, Mongolia, and Russia have added to the mosaic of sizes, skin tones, and faces—ranging from delicate doll-like features (tiny nose, rose-bud mouth, slits for eyes, and white skin) to ferocious samurai faces (square chins, shaggy eyebrows, wide nose, heavy upper lip, handsome dark skin).

Farmers, who followed streams into valleys where they could grow crops, became further isolated by mountain ridges. This led to a plethora of sub-cultures throughout the islands.

In much the same way as Europe's wandering tribes on the other side of the world created the admixture of the British Isles, a miscellany of Asian wanderers melded into the Japanese "people."

Even though historians are still exploring Japan's past, the islands are indeed an ancient land. Early Chinese chroniclers wrote of the domain of Yamatai in the islands, ruled over by a queen—who became deified as Japan's Sun Goddess. Later, China's northern Mandarin referred to Japan as "Land of the Wa" ("little people")—although in southern China (Canton), people were also short in stature. Officially, China called the islands silhouetted in the rising sun *Jih-pen* ("sun-rise"). Venetian Marco Polo, traveling through China, translated that as "Jipangu" (the last vowel, as usual, not pronounced). That stuck with the rest of the world as Japan (*Nippon* or *Nihon* to Japanese).

From the Asian mainland came iron, gunpowder, rice, and horses (some of their bridle ornaments tracing back to Scythia in Western Asia/ Eastern Europe—birthplace of the Aryans?). Japan's multi-cultures reminded me that we all have come from somewhere else, and that we all benefit from the sharing of cultures throughout the centuries!

---

11. Inhabiting Hokkaido Island in the north, Ainu (also called Ezo) had big frames, white-skin, and heavy beards—a wandering Caucasoid tribe that survived crossing the continent from west to east? Very hostile, to the Japanese they were brutish barbarians, although Emperor Kammu (781-806) admired their warriors. "One Ainu warrior is worth 1,000 Japanese soldiers," he said. See J. E. Kidder in Bibliography.

The islands' disparate population coupled with their isolation produced two driving characteristics: on the one hand, a warring culture of survival, and on the other hand, pretensions of imperial power. Combined, these driving forces spurred the island kingdom to foreign excursions, which in turn led to its humiliation.

Revolution Becomes Reform

This background helped me understand the Japan around me—including the proliferation of cults and sects, and government suppression of them. I also learned more about militarism in the national psyche. The long swords and the sharp daggers that warriors used to wear had religious significance. As in several Indian[12] and Persian religions, metal itself supposedly was imbued with supernatural power. Sword-makers fasted and offered sacrifices to the gods when forging weapons, and both emperors and shoguns presented ceremonial swords to shrines. Sword-wielding samurai repeated the magic mantra their form of Buddhism prescribed.

Death itself was ritualized, and suicide became an honorable way out—especially for a leader facing defeat.[13] Japan has one of the highest suicide rates. Instructed by the legally produced *Complete Manual of Suicide*, group suicides (aided by the internet) tripled in one recent year.[14] Agreeing on a day, the group "meet" and snuff out their lives through exhaust or charcoal-stove fumes. Favourite spot: facing sacred Mount Fuji. The government attempts to police web sites.

A recent Gallup poll reflects today's attitudes: roughly 1/3 of the nation believe there is no afterlife (death is the end of all things). More than half agree that one cannot have a personal relationship with God and communicate with him. Fully 2/3 of adults think that no one hears their prayers, but praying makes them feel better anyway.

---

12. Even in Western countries, Sikhs insist on their religious right to carry a small dagger (indwelt by the god of iron) under their turbans. No doubt airport security has a slight problem with that custom.

13. *Hara-kiri* or *seppuku*: lit. "Belly cutting" or disembowelment, was the preferred method. See earlier note explaining why Japan's defeated Emperor Hirohito did not need to commit suicide.

14. ABC News, Nov. 28, 2000; BBC News Aug. 23, 05. In 2003, suicides topped 34,000.

Japan, like most nations, is still changing. On Sunday, the three of us visitors divided forces and attended three different churches. Many churches have only half a dozen members, although the ones we visited were larger.[15] Church growth is a slow process in a Shinto nation, where people work from sunrise to sunset. But in the church in which I preached, I noted that young people with electric guitars and drums had taken over the "worship" section of the church. Very untraditional—but typical of today's "mod" urbanites with their latest gadgets.

In fact, the younger set admire anything "American." Popular *Manga* comic books depict Japanese characters as blond-haired, with Caucasian features. At a kiosk frequented by "blond" spiked-haired Japanese teens, I asked the name of sushi and rice take-out food. "Kalifornia" the salesgirl replied. Of course—fast-food! Clever marketing has turned the seaweed-wrapped rolls into a national craze for *Setsubun*, the coming of spring, to bring good fortune and repel demons. TV adverts repeat the legend of a famous samurai who won a battle after swallowing a sushi roll. Of course, one has to face the prescribed direction while swallowing it. Seven-Eleven, Japan's largest convenience chain, can scarcely keep up with demand at *Setsubun* time. Movies and books from the West's pop culture feed Japan's urban teens with titles such as *Harih Pottah*—Japanese translations of J. K. Rowling's best-sellers.

Today's culture happily mixes hamburgers and "flies" (fries[16]) with sushi and the tea ceremony. However, education doesn't neglect traditional skills. One girls' school rates applicants on their dexterity with chopsticks. The test: picking up seeds and marbles.

Everyone in Tokyo, a megalopolis of 34 m., seemed on the go, milling in and out of traffic and gleaming office towers flanked by traditional kiosks.[17] We dropped in at TEAM's Word of Life, which has its own printing presses, bookshops, and film/TV production studios. (Shamanism,

---

15. Christians of all descriptions number about 2 m., out of a population of some 127 m. Birthrates are declining even as the population ages.

16. While Westerners have difficulty over some Oriental sounds, Japanese often interchange "l" and "r."

17. Tokyo's Gross Domestic Product (GDP) ranks first in a list of cities worldwide, projected for 2020. It also is one of the most expensive cities in which to live.

I discovered, refers to "the word" as a source of mystical power, providing a bridge for evangelicals to introduce the Living Word, Christ.) We found WEC's Christian Literature Crusade (CLC) bookshops busy.

Post-war Tokyo had become a center of Christian activity, with radio, TV, film, and literature ministries—to be expected in a nation more literate (almost 100%) than either Britain or USA. Some 90% of Japanese can tune in to Pacific Broadcasting Association's "Light of the World" programs, started by Akira Hatori—a Japanese student at Fuller Seminary, Pasadena, when Toronto's People's Church helped him raise the needed start-up funds in the 1950s. A Christian university helps train for pastoral and missionary service. "Tent-maker" missionaries have a ready opportunity with the Ministry of Education, which annually employs 2,000 English teachers to assist in secondary schools. As to social concern, Tetsunao Yamamori reports that two-thirds of Japan's churches contribute to his Food for the Hungry fund.

Seesaw: Emperors vs. Shoguns[18]

Japan's history over the past century is remarkable by any measure—an isolated feudal and fractured people, humiliated in world conflict and with few natural resources, became the region's first democracy, rising to be a world power. Therein lies the romance of an exotic history. When the WW II Emperor died in 1989, his only living son became emperor—and made world headlines by marrying a commoner! Today's royalty traces back more than two millennia—longer than any other known royal line—but through male heirs. A female descendant marrying a commoner must opt out of the royal family.

Yet the royal line hasn't always ruled. Nippon's history has been as fractured as its rocky islands—centuries of feudal rivalry, foreign attacks, and never-ending struggle between metropolitan nobles and provincial warlords. "Patricians" and their emperors considered the warriors unlearned "barbarians" who destroyed Buddha's peaceful way of life. Warrior *samurai* despised royalty and nobles for their wasteful opulence and corrupt living on the backs of peasants.

---

18. ***Shogun***: Governor from the *Samurai* (lit. "Those who serve"—that is, by the sword) class.

So control of the nation constantly seesawed between emperor/ noble vs. governor/warrior. Eventually, destructive struggles forced both patricians and provincials to respect each other—emperors for preserving the nation's arts and culture, and shoguns for their pragmatic administration, judicial fairness, and centralized unification—even if imposed by force.[19] The Emperor was fully occupied with endless ceremony and ancient ritual to placate the gods, so he needed the Shogun's governing ability.[20] The Shogun, after giving rein to merchants and artisans, saw his need for learned courtiers and culture in order to maintain trade and diplomatic relations.

The accommodating Japanese overcame religious tensions in the same way. Nobles embraced Chinese Buddhism for its knowledge and promise of "enlightenment," making it the state religion in the 8th c. after a Korean monk, Gyogi, identified Shinto deities with Buddhist counterparts. It was total syncretism, making ascetic Buddhism (which traditionally denies this world's pleasures) compatible with Shinto's focus on securing success and happiness upon earth! Warriors depended upon myriad *kami*[21] for personal power and victory in battle. But everyone—patrician and provincial—was comfortable with a national syncretism of Tibetan Buddhist enlightenment, Japanese Shinto spirit-worship (animism), and Chinese Confucian rules for living. People held funerals at solemn Buddhist shrines but performed weddings at merry-making Shinto shrines—often built side by side for convenience.

I saw this syncretism on the fantasy Island of Miyajima, in a quiet tidal bay off Hiroshima. Eerily, at high tide the Itsukushima Shrine (built 593 A.D.) seemed to float on the water. No metal nails held together this picturesque temple dedicated to three Shinto sea goddesses. Fern and

19. The shoguns assured human rights for even landless peasants and women, and through the samurai reduced coastal and highway robbers and marauding gangs that once terrorized the countryside.

20. In fact, ceremonial rites so occupied emperors that at times one would resign in order to take up more practical administrative duties. The ruler would replace himself with a puppet—often a child. And, as explained earlier, the emperor, being divine, had the power to change into a mortal or back into a god.

21. There are some 8 million spirits of nature residing in trees, rivers, rocks, mountains, wind, thunder, and lightning. People sacrifice to these and pay shamans to interpret their will.

bamboo framed the shrine, with sacred Mount Misen San as backdrop. Inside the five-storied pagoda (a sacred bell hanging from each upturned gable), reclined a painted Buddha figure, and seven other Buddhist shrines around the island added to its enchantment. Troupes of monkeys loped among trees over the heads of some 2,000 deer—all possessed with spirits, monks assured us.

Obviously monks, nuns, and officials are still human, and in the 8th c., reformist Emperor Kammu found it necessary to purge their ranks of immorality and corruption. Separating Buddhist monks and the Shinto state, he introduced fair taxation and a police force.

Appeasing the Spirits

After the devastating earthquake of 1257, a Buddhist reformist proclaimed that it was judgement for the corruption and arrogance of other monks and their followers. His new Lotus Sutra sect was the only true way. All others were "hellish" and "lies." Another reformer, Nichiren, warned that unless people followed the Lotus Way, other calamities would follow, including an invasion—which Mongols later attempted. The Lotus Sutra became the main scripture and nation-wide sect. An import from India, it took its place with the Hindu gods Brahma and Indra. Archeologists have unearthed figures similar to Hindu deities, with multiple limbs and heads. Their ferocious expressions would scare any dragon off into space![22]

Of course, religious divisions threatened the power of warrior monks, who feared the loss of income and disciples. They unleashed private armies and pressured the government. Sometimes the Emperor simply moved his capital away from their power base.

But two attempted Mongol invasions in the 13th c. left the nation bankrupt, with agriculture untended.[23] Government collapsed. At the same time, a new wind was blowing, with freedom that shoguns had

---

22. Also associated with India are "Ashoku bells," after India's first Buddhist ruler, Ashok. Locals so dub ancient cast bells (likely presumed magical) found embedded on plateaus overlooking fertile fields.

23. Mongols had superior numbers, but devastating typhoons smashed the invader's navies both times.

introduced. Earlier simplification of the adopted Chinese *kanji* pictographs into a phonetic alphabet form[24] made reading easier and learning available to all. People realized that one didn't have to withdraw into monastery cloisters in order to pursue "enlightenment." *Samurai* liked this interpretation, because it broke the control of monks, who had amassed estates and built private armies. It also confirmed *samurai* belief in the ability of individuals to better themselves through hard work—whereas the patrician depended on privilege, inheritance, and corruption.

A succession of Buddhist sects arose: Heian Buddhism, such as Shingon school by Kuhkai and Tendai school by Shinran, and then Kamakura Buddhism such as Pure-land school, which promised Paradise, but believed that Hell was one possible destination of re-incarnation. Another sect was Zen Buddhism, which rejected ritualism and asceticism, instead promoting hard work and meditation. Its teachers would often kick and beat disciples—in order to free them from self-deception, they helpfully explained(!).

Another sect taught devotees to repeat the name of Buddha 70,000 times daily to ward off evil spirits. Need help? Inscribe Buddha's name and prayers on strips of paper and tie them to bushes. Since wind is a spirit, each flap in the breeze "recites" the prayer for them. (Ahead of their day for harnessing wind power?)

If I wished, I could drop a prayer into a prayer wheel and pay a monk a few *yen* to turn it. That was a daily occupation for some monks, who paced alongside rows of large cylinders containing prayers or mantras, always turning them clockwise. Over-busy Japanese workers can make good use of this pay-as-you-go (to work) system.

I remembered that, back in the West, perhaps the best known Eastern cult is the Unification Church founded by Sun Myung Moon, known as "Moonies." But I found that Buddhist splinter groups proliferate. Sohka Gakkai is one of hundreds of new Shinto sects. The government

24. Buddhist monk Khukai had earlier developed this *kana* system, paving the way for Japan to become the world's most literate society. The most widely read newspaper, *The Yomiuri Shimbun* (over ten million copies), began in the late 1800s.

25. "AUM" >from Hinduism; some Buddhists use it as a mantra in contemplating "Ultimate Reality."

estimates there are some *220,000 cults and sects*. The twisted views of AUM[25] Shinrikyo (founded only in 1984 by a Tibetan-style guru) in 1995 led its devotees to flood Tokyo subways with deadly sarin gas, killing twelve commuters and injuring six thousand.

To me, the most attractive sect has to be *Shingon* ("Easy Way") introduced by Monk Khukai. He determined that attaining Buddha status requires no ritual. Man by his very existence is a budding Buddha. "*That was easy!*"

In fact, in a kind of Gnosticism, when a Japanese dies, family members believe that person becomes a Buddha (*hotoke*)— no matter how wicked his/her life. So to show respect (and thus avoid being punished by the departed), family kneel before the ancestral altar (*butsudan*), perhaps several times a day, offering food and outlining the day's activities (for protection). This is such a part of culture that even if a person also attends a church service, he may see nothing incongruous in performing the shrine ritual.

"If a Nail Sticks Up . . ."

Although back in 1587 Shogun Toyotomi Hideyoshi decreed the expulsion of all Christian missionaries—and there have been other clampdowns on Christianity—today the nation has freedom of religion. However, so central are Shinto and Buddha to Nippon culture, that turning *from* them to embrace any other faith is simply out of the question. Want to be a Christian? "Sure, Christians are nice. I'll just add belief in Jesus to my traditional beliefs!" *That was easy!*

"If a nail sticks up, it will be hammered down," Japanese culture decrees. That's why Japan puzzles Westerners, who almost worship individualism. It explains why Japanese seem inscrutable. It also explains why they naturally are so pleasant and cooperative—and yet they find genuine conversion to Jesus Christ as Lord and Saviour so cataclysmic. A national survey outlines eight rules governing Japanese—nationally, *always*, the secular researcher claims:[26]

---

26. Hiroshi Yoshida, *The 100 Residents of the Village 'Japan.'* Reported in WEC's *Go*, Summer 2004.

1. Never say a blunt "yes" or "no."
2. Be aware that people are watching.
3. Do what the manual says.
4. Take only the good bits of religion—and do it on the quiet.
5. Go to shops where there are lines. The rest probably aren't worth going into.
6. Distinguish between real intention and outward appearance.
7. Strive for uniformity, normality, and balance.
8. When you meet someone you don't know, smile!

So Japanese culture establishes a unified universe—the spirit heavenlies are one with the physical world, in which fauna and flora are one with humans—and therefore everyone on earth should have the same beliefs.[27] Society is consensual, founded on *wa*, harmony.

All this left me with a big question. *If conformity typifies the soul of Japan, how was it possible for Emperor Akihito to marry a commoner—against millennia of royal tradition?* In my news magazine, the obituary of a Quaker widow clued me in.[28] What did she have to do with Prince Akihito?

The Prince and the Quiet Quaker

After Japan's surrender, General McArthur encouraged Emperor Hirohito to search for an American tutor for his 12-year-old son, Akihito. Remarkably, the royal "headhunters" bypassed capable teachers with bilingual skills and landed upon a quiet widow whose Scottish forebears had emigrated to Philadelphia: Elizabeth Gray Vining. A Quaker, she was as surprised as anyone. She didn't know Japanese, but she had written fascinating children's books. No doubt that caused the search team to employ her.

Anyway, the young prince and the middle-aged tutor soon bonded: Elizabeth taught him English, and Akihito taught her Japanese. But as Vining implied in the title of her autobiography, *Windows for the Crown Prince*, more was involved than learning ABCs. The quiet Quaker

27. Judith Snodgrass, *Presenting Japanese Buddhism to the West*. Chapel Hill: University of North Carolina Press, 2003. Snodgrass shows how this Eastern thought system influenced Western liberal inclusiveness.
28. *Economist*, December 11, 1999, p. 81.

introduced the impressionable boy to independent thinking—he could explore and judge everything for himself, not (as tradition required) turning to courtiers about the simplest detail. Yes, as an individual in God's eyes, he could even risk making a mistake! It was O.K. to be a nail sticking up for what he knew was right.

This was revolutionary, given Japan's monoculture in which traditional schools deduct marks for errors but do not reward achievement. However, the lad's royal father approved. So when the Prince married the girl he fell in love with while playing tennis, the only foreigner invited to the wedding was Elizabeth Vining! But did the Shinto-backed government accept Vining's intrusion into the royal household? Definitely—demonstrated by honoring her with The Order of the Sacred Crown. Japanese royalty does not interfere in government, but Emperor Akihito's openness to the outside world undoubtedly has set an example for these once-isolated islands.

"The Miracle of Japan's Recovery" reflects several Christian values unrecognized by most observers. They have "opened windows" not only for the Prince but also for the nation, as I'd find out in my further travels in Japan.

Tokyo's famed "Bullet Train" pulls into Tokyo station.

Sun Like Thunder – **28: "The Ends of the Earth"**

East and West *Do* Meet!

"In the east give glory to the Lord; exalt the name of the Lord, the God of Israel, in the islands of the sea. From the ends of the earth we hear singing: 'Glory to the Righteous One'" (Is. 24.15,16).

I STILL HAD MANY QUESTIONS begging for answers before I left Japan. How did these islands, on the outer edge of massive Asia, develop a culture all their own? How did such an ancient land, devastated by war, take its seat among today's global leaders in so many ways? For trivia, did Japan's culture make it the world's largest producer of robots? But more important to me, what was the state of the Church in the land of *Shinto*?

A little sightseeing came first for this meeting-weary traveler. I found that a quick way to view the countryside was from the world-famous Bullet Train. At speeds of up to 180 mph, we slipped smoothly between cities. I was amazed at the clocklike precision of the streamlined train. At each station, we stopped precisely where carriage doors opened exactly aligned with markings for passengers to enter each carriage door.

On the train, I was still learning about Japanese culture. The train's toilets were marked "Western Style" and "Japanese Style." Curious to know the difference, I peeked in the latter and found it was the squat type—no seat. I found the foreigners' "convenience" more convenient. But culture is culture. Later, while I waited to use "Western Style," an elegantly kimonoed and coiffed lady came into the passageway, awaiting her turn. When "the little room" was vacant, out of courtesy I gestured for her to go ahead of me. However, she politely declined and pointed to the "Japanese-Style" door. The lady obviously preferred tradition over Western "comfort."

On this train trip, I looked forward to seeing fabled Mount Fujiyama, an extinct volcano among Japan's 60 active cones.[1] In my parents' home, a painting of Fuji had excited my boyhood imagination. But now the sky was overcast. I could see no further than the string of trackside villages whizzing by. Putting away my telephoto camera, I contented myself with addressing postcards of Japan's sacred mountain, to send family and friends.

Suddenly a cry echoed throughout our passenger coach. Were gangsters attacking us? Everyone rushed to the other side of our carriage to look out the windows. Startled, I too looked out. The clouds had parted to reveal a breath-taking sight: *Mount Fuji!*

In the distance, the snow-clad cone appeared to float above a base of clouds and mist, like a surreal monarch on his throne. I now understood how Japanese believe that resplendent Fuji-san was a sacred deity. Annually, thousands of pilgrims visit numerous shrines and temples on it slopes. For me, apart from viewing the mountain, the greater thrill was to know the One who had set in motion the titanic forces that resulted in such grandeur!

Rice Race Goes "Techy"

But a cloud curtain again veiled Fuji as our train continued snaking between hamlets and wide patches of vivid-green "paddy" (rice fields). The countryside was a constant kaleidoscope of tradition and modernity. At times, tall chimneys of a modern factory formed a backdrop to bent forms of peasants under cone-shaped sunhats cultivating the rice. The islands' climate and topography are ideal for rice production. At one time rice fed not only the nation but also hungry neighbors. Because only a quarter of the land is flat enough for field cultivation, hillsides are terrace-planted.

1. Until the 18th c., Fuji (3,766 m. / 12,367 ft.) also was active, earning its local name, "Fire Mountain."

This island nation that once sought to dominate the world through militarism, in fact achieved global supremacy through the economy. Although with less than three percent of global population, the nation enjoys ten percent of global GDP.[2] It ranks among the top in microelectronic, photographic, video, auto, steel, and shipbuilding industries, to say nothing of the latest export—*sudoku* puzzles, that have become a global craze![3] Their number grids edge out crossword puzzles in some newspapers and pulp magazines.

I was surprised to discover that Japan was the original source for what became "The Green Revolution" that I'd heard of in India. One of General MacArthur's staff in Japan, a wheat expert, collected wheat samples, including one species, Norin 10, that grows only two ft. tall (instead of the usual four). A scientist in Oregon crossed Norin 10 with other wheat grains to produce other short-stemmed varieties. Meanwhile, Norman Borlaug, a scientist experimenting in Mexico, crossed Norin 10 and other grain to grow heads that produce three times the normal yield. By 1963, Mexico's wheat crop was six times greater—and that's when India's M. S. Swaminathan invited Borlaug to try the same in India. The rest of the story came to be called, "The Green Revolution"! (See Chapter 11.)

Agriculture shaped early Japan's group mentality, as farmers had to share water sources in difficult geographic areas.

"That required patience, diligence, and cooperation" explained Pastor Joseph Ogawa.[4]

Others point out the combined effect of Shinto, Confucius, and Buddhism on the national self-image, all emphasizing conformity—no *tall poppies*. Some traditional views are ingrained: rejection of prominent

---

2. Wealth is very regional, however. Islands in the far North and South face unemployment, poverty.
3. *Su-doku*: literally, "single number." A player fills in missing numbers, one to nine randomly but in vertical and horizontal rows, totaling 81 squares. Numbers must occur only once in any given line; but in each of nine sub-squares dividing the entire box, figures one to nine must also appear—each only once. (*Aficionados* debate whether this game of logic originated with an 18th c. Swiss mathematician's game.)
4. Dr. Ogawa, served with OMF in Indonesia, was Dean of Singapore's ACTI, member Asia's Evangelical Alliance council, chair Japan Evangelical Alliance—now chair SIM's Japan Council. He and his wife have children serving in overseas missions.

individuals, a feeling of guilt if one is not working, failure considered a shame rather than a learning step towards success. *"Only one who avoid* [*sic*] *wasting time can get profit,"* an office sign reminded me.

Before WW II, this combination of uniformity and labor caused many Westerners to regard Japan as a nation of expert copiers—marketing copies of Western inventions and plastic toys for children. But now *kaizen* (continuous improvement) drives Japanese industry to develop agriculture and industry beyond the accepted norm. Whether the basic concepts are their own or foreign doesn't matter.

Example. When scientists in the West gave up researching for commercially viable light-emitting diodes (LEDs), Japanese scientists plodded on. After a series of trials by a number of scientists, Shuji Nakamura, working in the laboratory of a small chemical company, in 1993 produced the world's first bright blue LED. At the time, he had no doctorate, had never published a research paper, and worked for an unknown company based in the least populated of Japan's four main islands. He went on to create LEDs of other colors, which you now see in your flat-screen TV and in many traffic lights.

Nakamura's company rewarded him with a $200 bonus,[5] but today the global market for LEDs exceeds some $10 billion. Nakamura's discoveries even enable you to replace your light bulbs with illuminated wall panels.[6]

"Nice Doggie!"

Japan, the world's second largest manufacturing country (USA is first), leads the world in production of industrial and domestic robots.[7] These including robotic pets and personal nurses. In fact, Japanese cannot understand why the rest of the world doesn't catch on to these latest two. There's an interesting reason that combines today's innovativeness and yester-year traditions.

5. Nakamura has since moved to the University of California, and recently won a $7m patent settlement.
6. *The Economist*, Sept. 23, 2006. Japan, a major environment polluter in the '60s, now leads in hybrid car and solar panel production.
7. Although the Czechs provided the word *robota*: "forced labor."

Japan produces and uses more robots than any other nation, and stocks almost half the world's supply. Religion and culture explain why. Shinto belief makes no distinction between the animate and inanimate. Just as spirits dwell in rocks and trees, they also must live in robots. Not that a spirit makes a robot move—literate Japanese understand technology—but a machine becomes just as "living" as an animal or human being (in somewhat the same way as a child thinks of its dolly or teddy as living). If it looks like a dog, barks like a dog, wags its tail like a dog—it must be a dog! Technicians can program a robot terrier to respond to its owner's specific commands. Best of all, you don't have to feed it or stoop and scoop! Just charge its batteries at night, and in the morning it can wake you up with the whine, bark, or music of your choice. The ideal companion for seniors! And a lot less expensive to "employ" than a qualified person, these days.

I wondered how a robot nurse works. This is where culture enters. Japanese are increasingly aggressive in today's global market, but traditionally, they don't like to appear too forward—or to have a nurse they have to talk with. Why not? The Japanese psyche can be very empathetic, if not somewhat neurotic. Your average Japanese is wondering what you're thinking when he or she says anything. This can leave a person trying to second-guess the other person's response. (My homespun chatting must have come across as very crass and unfeeling!)

Enter a robot nurse, to whom you don't have to talk—or if you do, you don't have to worry how to phrase your request. The robot is programmed and won't talk back. It scans the patient's face, to detect any change from a happy expression to a sad one. It monitors pulse, blood pressure, and temperature, automatically dialling the duty medic if the I.V. drip is running low or a medical crisis looms. It can even extend strong "arms" to help a human nurse turn the patient over. Unquestionably, the preferred bedside form of care! (And cheaper for the hospital than employing more staff. No pension!)

There are robots for personal entertainment. Warrior-minded males can purchase (for a measly $1,105) a warrior robot that contains

17 motors and comes with a 100-page manual. Using remote controls, men can play war games on a "virtual" battleground. The perfect gift for a more domestic older adult would be a cuddly poodle, doll, or even a remote-controlled fish that any aquarium would be proud of. Sociologists (and of course toy-salesclerks) claim robot-toy baseball players help bring together fathers and sons—notoriously alienated.

But the robot industry, with its advances in technology, has branched out. Now robots can fly, fetch, carry, converse, do most factory jobs, and perform surgery (under supervision, of course!). Japan displays its inventive thinking not only in technology but even in the food domain: sorting fruit, making salads, and butchering. And to assist the robots, Japanese horticulturalists solved the problem of handling unwieldy oval-shaped watermelons that waste packing (and refrigerator) space. Developing *square* watermelons solved the problem!

But technology serves not only adults. Schoolchildren need their own TV channel? No problem: a dedicated satellite in geo-synchronous orbit (always over Japan) beams WOWOW programs to their sets! However, the low birth rate (with its decreasing infant population) accounts for an interesting cultural twist: **cat cafes**. In Tokyo, one of these popular cafes, The Calico, features 20 cats of 17 different breeds. While enjoying tea or coffee and a snack, a customer may pet one of these feline attractions, who contentedly purr while rubbing up to lonely visitors.

Work Ethic

As to the stereotype of Japanese as diligent "copy artists," Joshua Ogawa helped me understand the background, as well as Japan's current spirit of initiative:

"In the past, Japan's culture and education maintained 'the harmonious society' but also hindered creative thinking. The group or organizational body was traditionally more important than creativity. However, we're now seeing a combination of group thinking and individual initiative."

Although business schools may now question Japanese management systems, Austrian-American management guru Peter Drucker (1909-2005) promoted such long before the West began to emulate them in the '80s.

In fact, our word for a powerful, wealthy business leader came from Japanese *Taikun*.[8] In turn, if the Tokyo stock market plunged, Japanese bankers would call it a *shokku*.

By the turn of this century, Japan experienced the world's greatest percent increase in goods and services. Japan along with China tops the world in official reserves. The world's richest Asian at the turn of this millennium was no longer an oil prince, but a Japanese businessman, Masayoshi Son. And as car owners are finding, General Motors' lead has been replaced by Toyota—acclaimed as the world's most advanced manufacturer, with large car plants in USA.

In Japan's frenzied corporate world, businessmen and women have no time for religious worship (a problem churches as well as shrines face), but worshipers of Buddha and Shinto easily fulfill their obligations to shrine and monastery with gifts and paid surrogates. Firms are financing research (aided by Sony scientists) in "life force" (animism's *ki*) at Tokyo University. A survey asked businessmen trapped in the corporate world what they, in the next life, would most like to return to earth as. "A bird," was their favorite response.

"Japanese have developed a thoroughly post-modern view, with 75% of adults and 86% of teens feeling that right and wrong are determined by the circumstances of the situation," Dr. Ogawa points out. "A Gallup poll revealed that 75% of adults and 85% of teens agreed they sometimes tell lies if they have to do so; 85% of teens and 64% of adults often wonder why they exist.

"Young people have lost the purpose of life. They cannot follow the over-committed lifestyle of the older generation. They feel remoteness and social distance, showing their shallowness in spiritual matters and compromise with ungodly moral choices. All this leads not only to secular nihilism, but also to religious nihilism in the form of cultic revitalization."

Ogawa questions the percentage of Christians listed in some polls. "Not wanting to offend, many Japanese may reply affirmatively to a

---

8. *Taikun,* now archaic in Japanese, entered English vocabulary a century before Drucker's interest. Drucker also passed on American management techniques to Japan. His collection of Japanese art testified to his appreciation of the nation's culture.

question about Christian beliefs, yet they may be including such beliefs along with their Shinto worship, or they may have left an earlier profession of faith in Christ, thus inflating percentages. For Japan, the more difficult problem is how to *maintain* the Christian faith throughout life."[9]

Tradition plus modernity add up to complex challenges for the gospel. Helping Christians maintain their spirituality throughout life is one that churches face. Yet the gospel has penetrated culture. For instance, Christian Japanese have their own rationalization for hard work:

> *[Jesus] worked as a carpenter until he was thirty years of age, and during his three-year ministry he worked hard. Even on his holidays he helped people and healed the sick. ... Some people came to Jesus and asked, "Don't you rest even on a rest day?" "No, God always works; if God rested, the world would fall; therefore, while God works I work also." According to Christ, therefore, daily living was religion.*[10]

As to my earlier question about Japanese Christians, relatively so few in number, serving in other lands, Ogawa lists positive benefits [11]

1. There are aspects that can be realized only by workers from those countries that have been mission fields themselves.
2. West and East, North and South can complement each other in the work for the Kingdom. Asians can fill in that which Westerners have left undone.
3. After years of service overseas, a number of Japanese have become leaders in home ministries, bringing new insights and visions which could never have been obtained by serving only in Japan.
4. As Asians serve with Westerners in other lands, the gospel can be presented in a more balanced way—not just the gospel from the West.

But SIM's Japan Council chairman is by no means a Japanese nationalist. He sees a definite advantage having missionaries *from other*

9. Though Japan's population is about 125m, polls list religious adherents as some 220m—Japanese can claim to be both Buddha and Shinto followers, simultaneously. Joshua K. Ogawa, *Unlimited Purpose*. Singapore: OMF, 1985. Also, "The Task of Evangelization in 21st c. Asia," Asian Lausanne Conference on Evangelism papers, May 2006.
10. Toyohiko Kagawa, *New Life through God*. New York: Fleming H. Revell Co. 1931

lands come to Japan to help evangelize his own country, and to strengthen Christians. That, he says, really globalizes the gospel.

Driving Globalization

In thinking of secular globalization, I have to smile (paternalistically, no doubt!) at protesters who blame wicked Western capitalism for overpowering the rest of the world—the impoverished world. Actually, Japan, China, India, and other Asian countries are the ones driving globalization—and the West had better not retreat into protectionism or it will find itself like China in the 14th c. To help truly poverty-stricken nations, we need to do more than throw money at corrupt governments. We'd better encourage reform and help develop self-sustaining skills.

Japan has been the globe's most generous donor—and a wise one. I was interested to learn that Japan's public broadcaster, NHK, donated TV and radio equipment to Iraq—including a series of programs on Japanese engineering that should inspire reconstruction in that war-devastated country. At the other end of Japanese products is, well, "dirt." Construction jobs dig up 30 million tonnes of it annually. Builders use a "lot" as landfill in new coastal sites, such as Osaka Bay's airport built on an artificial island. But Tokyo's ***Shimbun*** newspaper published an appeal by tiny Tuvalu (averaging only two meters above sea level) in the South Pacific for some of the stuff. That kingdom wants to raise (so to speak) its chances of surviving global warming.

Japan's high literacy rate and large budget for Research and Development gave it an early edge over China's vast population advantage. Increasingly, Japan is competing in world markets with specialized technology. It has even become a major partner with America's Boeing in producing the 787 Dreamliner, built with ultra-light composite materials.

For a while, inflation (fueled by some of the globe's costliest housing) threatened Japan's advantage.[12] Then with boom times came shortages.

11. See Joshua Ogawa, *op cit.*

12. For several years, Tokyo was the world's most expensive city to live in. To beat rising costs, some Japanese industrialists outsource their manufacturing to less expensive South-East Asian lands. Yet Japan has the lowest income-tax rate among industrialized nations.

Car manufacturers ran short of steel, halting production at three of the largest manufacturers. Japan faces a new threat, the same as Europe's problem: the birth rate (one of the world's lowest) is not replacing an aging population. In 2005, 54% of women in their late 20s were single.[13] By 2030, for every retiree, Japan will have only two workers; by 2050, for *two retirees* only three workers. Percent of people over 65 is already the world's highest—due to reach 30% by 2025. Japan's current 127m. population is predicted to fall by one third in the next few decades. At current fertility rates, the last Japanese would die by A.D. 2800!

At the same time, major firms guarantee employment for life, reducing opportunities for youth. While pensioners account for a major slice of the national budget and are living longer,[14] the younger generation do not have the technological skills their seniors have. Add to that Japan's resistance to low-wage foreign replacements. (Robots are cheaper than Filipina nurses, and don't need visas). Japan has a mandatory health insurance system and ranks first in World Health Organization's chart, with the world's lowest infant mortality rate. But as the nation experiences some of Europe's stagnating problems, the government is considering reforms to its financial systems, strengthening Japan as a financial center—since the nation no longer can depend on employment in manufacturing (many Japanese companies produce their goods in lower-cost neighboring countries). An aging population requires higher rates in order to live off savings—that requires attracting foreign investment.

Economists also suggest that Japan, Germany, and Italy (all with aging populations) could increase their labor pools by encouraging women to work outside their homes. But no one knows the social cost. Commendably, family values still play a major role in Japan's society. Only 1% of births are to unwed mothers,[15] compared with 30% in USA.

---

13. *National Post*, quoted in *Servant*, Issue 72, 2005. Three Hills: Prairie. While the downside in Japan's society is a low marriage rate, the upside is that only 1% of births occur outside of marriage (compared with 62% in Iceland!). This reflects two main factors—stigma of illegitimacy, and ease of abortions.

14. Japan has the world's highest life expectancy. More than 25,000 Japanese are over 100.

15. However, as noted, abortions are easily obtained. And while the ratio of worker has shrunk to four to one retiree, by 2030 pollsters forecast the ratio will be only two to one.

Already, however, traditional attitudes are losing their hold on urban teens. Half the arrests for felonies in a recent five-year period involved teenage youth. As a result, Japan's Diet (Parliament) has reduced adult court trials to the age of 14. Wealthy "lost kids" act out the violence of video games—which echo Japan's militaristic heritage. Best-known producer of violent films was Kinji Fukasaku (died 2006), who directed scenes in "Tora! Tora! Tora!" (the film about Pearl Harbor). His last film featured students taken to an island, each supplied with a weapon, and told to kill each other. Kinji described it as *emotional release*—"because Japanese don't feel hope anymore."

Increasing alcohol consumption (declining elsewhere on the globe), reflects this hopelessness.[16] Consumer groups join ranks with the government in combating the problem. Two mobile systems sell telephones with built-in breathalyzers, which inform operators where the user is. "Driving agents" do a brisk business taking intoxicated customers home; another driver follows with the owner's car.

Whatever reasons overseas observers see for Japan's increasing national anxiety, several Japanese authorities[17] cite the following:

1. Self doubt that the 1980s' affluence was based on real fundamental strengths;
2. Collapse of euphoria over the new success as economic worries grew;
3. Major bankruptcies;
4. The Aum Shinrikyo cult's poison gas attacks;
5. Self confidence shaken by the Kobe earthquake.

(Events 4 and 5 occurred just before the turn of the century, interpreted as ill omens of the spirits.)

Although Japan scores highest in student performance globally, educators blame increased classroom indiscipline on over-busy fathers

---

16. Japan's health ministry reports almost 2% of population are alcoholics. *Economist,* Feb. 17/07.

17. Among these, historian Naoki Inose; popular author Haruki Murakami; and Heizo Takenaka, government economist—quoted in *The Economist*, March 29, 2003, p. 37, re Japan's self doubts.

and doting mothers, who leave discipline to school authorities. Others say that excessive TV watching is breaking down Japan's group values. All agree that not only earthquakes are unsettling Japan.

Perhaps the biggest blow to the self-confidence of Japan's business community, with its high value placed on integrity, was architect Hidetsugu Aneha's falsification of earthquake resistance data in his designs. (He blamed cost-cutting.) His admission not only sent the nation's building reputation reeling but also condemned hundreds of buildings to be destroyed and rebuilt.

The nation is also concerned over its nuclear power plants, which generate a third of Japan's electric power. All are in an area of "significant seismic activity." Most have survived earthquakes undamaged. However, there have been disasters and "cover ups," shutting down several plants and stalling authorization of new ones needed to meet population and industry needs while reducing fossil fuel emissions.

Disillusionment and anger disturb Japan's outwardly placid society, asserts an academic Japan-watcher.[18] National anxiety showed up when several Japanese who had gone to help street children in Iraq were released by their captors. Back home, their psychiatrist noted that the kidnapping wasn't their most stressful moment. The worst came upon their return, when they faced a nation angry that the Japanese hostages had caused so much trouble and embarrassment! With true Buddhist sentiment, the freed captives apologized to their own country.[19]

Two Remaining Questions

Remaining on my to-do-in-Japan list were two personal questions I'd had since boyhood. Growing up, I'd been impressed with men and women who went to Japan under the Japan Evangelistic Band (JEB), which merged with the Central Japan Pioneer Mission (CJPM). Calling a mission a "Band" made sense after I'd heard of "bands" formed by early student converts in Japan. My father had been chairman of CJPM's

---

18. J. Nathan, *Japan Unbound: A Volatile Nation's Quest for Pride and Purpose.* NY: Houghton Mifflin '04.
19. ABC World News, April 24, 2004.

Canada Council. I was a little curious to know what happened to the missionaries who had passed through our home, and the small groups of believers we'd prayed for.

While interviewing Shin Funaki, President of Tokyo Biblical Seminary, I learned that his father had been CJPM Chair in Japan at the same time that my father chaired its Canadian Council. Over *demitasse* cups of ginseng tea, we compared notes about our fathers and their counterpart positions. We also discussed the spiritual health of Japan's churches. As Chair of Japan's Evangelical Association (JEA) at the time, Shin Funaki was a member of the Board that had published the JEA's Declaration on the Fiftieth Anniversary of WWII. In it, the JEA not only repented of "the sins" of the churches during WWII, but also apologized to neighboring nations, asking their forgiveness.

In contrast to imperial militarism, the JEA's Declaration on the Fiftieth Anniversary of WW II stated: "In the power of the Holy Spirit, we go forth to fill Japan and the world with the gospel." That was the gospel of the Prince of Peace. JEA's Declaration was further confirmation of the spirit that Joshua Tsutada had shown back in Singapore.

Sitting in the office of Dr. Funaki, I quizzed him about sending Japanese missionaries to other lands. Was it really practical, or was it simply "the thing to do," I wondered.

"Definitely we need to send out missionaries," he replied. "Of course, Jesus commanded us to do so. We must not neglect our own needs, but our churches could become self-centered without a vision for other lands.

"There's a lot of Western materialism affecting our country, which makes us wonder why we don't see more missionaries bringing spiritual influences. Sometimes we think *your* countries must be mission fields."

Some Western missionaries had tried "Evangelism-in-Depth" methods in Japan, but they'd failed. Why? I asked. Shin explained that while mass evangelism might produce visible results (most Japanese want to be cooperative), such "converts" usually don't last.

"You have to remember that Japanese culture has no knowledge of the Holy Creator. If there's no conviction of sinning against him, there's no repentance—only shame for a perceived error. Therefore, a person feels no need of a *Saviour*. We have to work one-on-one, teaching the reality of a holy God who loves them so much that he sent the Savior!"

I began to understand the slow pace of church growth in Japan. Official census figures for the number of Christians often are higher than church membership indicates, but that reflects hesitation to affiliate with a church because of social stigma and peer pressure. Actually, many Japanese tune in to Christian radio and TV and read Christian literature.

*****

Town's Terrors Overcome

"DO YOU THINK I could meet anyone who remembers JEB and CJPM pioneers?" I asked. "When I was a boy, several passed through our home in Canada."

Dr. Funaki introduced me to a pastor who as a boy had worked for several of those early missionaries. On our way to a range of hills, the pastor and I drove past rice "paddies" and screened-off golf driving ranges sandwiched between housing clusters.[20] Then we started climbing towards a mining hamlet in the hills above Karuizawa, north-west of Tokyo. To the left of the winding mountain road, bare Japanese maple branches formed a lattice backdrop for twisted *Matsu* pines poking between snow-covered rocks. Finches and teals flitted between their branches. To our right, a sheer cliff plunged down to an icy stream foaming over rapids. The raw beauty seemed straight from an ink-and-brush silk panel. The only element missing was a sacred crane.

Yet disaster lurked among these picturesque cliffs. Pennants and strips of paper inscribed with prayers fluttered at the edge of the road where vehicles had plunged into the ravine. Mineshaft cave-ins, earthquakes, forest fires, and howling blizzards were bad enough in themselves. But villagers believed something more sinister caused these disasters: ancestral spirits roaming the skies. Their children or

---

20. Golf is popular, but, ironically, players fear making a hole-in-one. It is such a sign of good luck that the golfer must lavishly entertain his friends. Accordingly, golfers buy insurance *against* such expenditure—four million golfers annually tote up more than $2 million on golfing policies!

grandchildren must have dishonored them in some way, and this is how ancestors took revenge! Small shrines in front of dwellings were not just out of respect for the departed, not just "ancestor worship." Villagers *had* to make offerings to placate ancestors' anger over their progeny's errors.[21]

How could anyone tell these folk—so placid on the surface—about Jesus? I tried to imagine our conversation:

"*Konnichiwa*! [Hello!] I've come to tell you about God's love," I'd begin, as a general, non-confrontational opener.

"Which god are you talking about, Fuller-Sensei? There are so many."

"I mean God the Father. He sent his Son, Jesus, to show us God's love."

"Oh yes—we've heard that Jesus was a good teacher, although of course he never reached the level of Buddha. Our famous Japanese teachers taught us Tendai, *the Middle Way of Shinto and Buddha. And* Shingon *includes the great gods, Brahma and Indra."*

"Jesus did more than setting an example of goodness—he *gave* himself for our sins."

"We haven't sinned—we've only made mistakes, and shamans show us how to correct them. But tell us about Jesus. You say he died. Please, did he commit hara-kiri *suicide?"*

"The Bible says we all have sinned, but Jesus died in order to pay for our sins."

"Bible? Our scriptures are the Lotus Sutra *and other sutras. They tell us how we can achieve Enlightenment so we'll stop coming back to this world of trouble. If we respect our ancestors and the spirits with offerings, they will forgive our mistakes."*

---

21. The Taika Reform (7th c.) blamed people's poverty on the custom of burying family treasure along with parents, to ensure ancestors' happiness. To avoid this loss of wealth, reformers encouraged cremation. Families kept ashes (*shari*) in miniature pagodas (*shari-to*), still squandering considerable wealth—some designed with exquisite gilded filigree. Grave robbers found ancient burial mounds to be "goldmines."

"The Bible agrees that we should honor our father and mother, but they can't save us. Jesus can because he *lives!*"

"Stop, stop! Don't you know that our ancestors are listening? Don't you know what they can do to us? Even Confucius said we must appease ancestors for the mistakes of their children. That's the only way we can have peaceful life."

The gospel seemed so impossible to explain to Shinto followers! My evangelical clichés would wash off an ancestor worshipper like water off a crane's back. I felt useless as I went to stay overnight with a Japanese couple who spoke no English—and I spoke no more than a local greeting.

But my spirits rose when I noticed their well-worn Japanese Bible. We shared a common language—our Christian faith. After my rinse-and-soak tub (you guessed it—I was honored to go first), I slipped into an embroidered purple silk *kimono and* tied its red sash. After recording my notes for the day, I fell asleep under a padded quilt. In the morning, to keep my legs warm at breakfast, my hostess considerately draped a heavy cloth over my legs and my feet while I ate.

Mrs. Kumori was *too* considerate—she'd thought her guest would expect an "American" breakfast. The good lady must have gone into the city to buy eggs, coffee, jam, and sliced bread for toast. Of course she laid out her best knife and fork instead of chopsticks. Bowing in grateful appreciation, I tried to explain that I'd enjoy their *regular* food for lunch. My hostess understood my gestures, and at noon a whole fish eyeballed me from a plate of noodles and tofu. Soy sauce and green seaweed pickle garnished this delicacy, which I enjoyed with authentic pointed chopsticks.[22] Jasmine tea replaced the coffee. It was real *washoku*.[23]

Just as I was leaving for a meeting in the nearby wooden chapel before returning to Tokyo, I stumbled on a cultural nicety. As any Westerner might do, I commented on a hand-inscribed wall plaque mounted on antiqued wood, hanging by the front door. My hosts explained that its *kanji* characters quoted 2 Corinthians 6.2: "*Now is the acceptable time;*

---

22. Chinese chopsticks have flat sides and are chisel-ended, not pointed.
23. *Washoku*: Japanese food. Western food is *youshoku*.

now is the day of salvation." Next thing I knew, they handed me the plaque, insisting I accept it. Only later did I learn that if a visitor admires something in one's home, the owners will present it as a gift. Japanese hospitality!

Meanwhile, some thirty villagers traipsed through falling snow to meet this stranger from beyond the rising sun. Although nearby Karuizawa city has grown into a busy center,[24] a foreign visitor was a rare sight in the mining hamlet snuggled high in the hills above it. The plaintive sound of a single-stringed *ichigenkin* zither filled the wooden chapel with Japanese worship tunes. A sputtering pot-bellied stove bravely combated the chill air. As they gathered, young and old softly sang, "*Shu wa subara shii!*" ("God is so good!"). An interpreter introduced me with the usual honorifics.

"Anyone Remember Burnett-san?"

"Does anyone remember Miss Burnett and Miss Parr?" I asked after giving appropriate greetings. Immediately several hands of elderly folk went up. Faces, wrinkled from decades of hard labor, broke into wreaths of smiles. Needless to say, today's "foreign visitor" was accepted—I was a friend of their beloved pioneer missionaries!

But for me, the moment was special for another reason. I was beholding the fruit of gospel seed planted decades ago by two women, in an era of male dominance.[25] In this rough mining hamlet the seed had grown and born fruit even through oppressive regimes and brutal wars. Memories exploded in my brain: my father's friend, evangelist Paul Kanamori; the women missionaries who'd visited our home; our bedtime prayers for this very village! (Why was I choking up? Must be the altitude!)

Far from Japan's military conquests and the devastating A-bomb, these humble disciples were faithfully following Jesus at the eastern end

24. Decades earlier in Karuizawa, Methodist Kanzo Uchimura had spurned formal "churchianity" with his "Non-Church Movement." He disbanded any group of followers who set themselves up as a church body.

25. Early missions discouraged women from entering "macho" Japan. Buddhism banned women from some activities, including climbing mountains, but *pre*-Buddhist kingdoms had female as well as male rulers.

of the Old Spice Road. Christ had conquered the terror of angry ancestors and demons. Spiritual regeneration had worked a quiet revolution in these mining families. They loved the Creator instead of fearing Shinto spirits or Buddhist forces of nature. Eternity held an assured hope rather than the hopelessness of endless re-incarnation.

As this little flock sang softly to the sliding notes of the zither, I marveled how the gospel in a mining town and family prayers on another continent had anything to do with each other. Ah—the answer was grace, God's grace, that allows us somehow to be involved in *his* divine design.

But right now, I still had one burning question—a question I was too embarrassed to ask. Lillian Burnett was a very massive woman. (Think sumo wrestler, but female.) It wasn't her fault; she had a glandular problem. She didn't let it hold her back from being a missionary, although she seldom returned home. When she came to our home on one of her rare furloughs, I thought she must intimidate the slightly-built villagers in Japan. Indeed, with such a handicap, should she have ever gone as a missionary? I didn't need to ask. After the service, as we sipped roasted-barley water, old-timers crowded around to tell how much they loved both Lillian Burnett and Dorothy Parr.

"Burnett-*san* must have found it difficult living among us," they volunteered without my asking. "But we knew she loved us. She was our spiritual mother!" That was it! The love of Christ, shown through clay vessels, overcomes differences of race, language, and even personal impediment. Leaving the wooden chapel through the snow, I found myself literally following in the footprints of Jesus' disciples on the Old Spice Road. I felt privileged to see the results of the ministry that my father had prayed and worked for in Canada—but which he'd never seen first-hand.

Still, as other Japanese later became part of the mission that I was working with, warning bells rang in my head:

> "Integrating Japanese missionaries will require us to understand their context," I reported to SIM's International Council. "Their background, a mixture of several oriental religions, is mystical and philosophical rather than doctrinally theological. Family relations

include the father's absentee role and women's unobtrusive role. Work ethic, community, and team concepts will differ radically from Western values of self-fulfillment and individualism. These different attitudes can spell problems in a clash of cultures, or they can be a challenge to understanding and tolerance. I believe we can learn from each other's values, and this can be a meaningful application of our professed desire to communicate cross-culturally."

It's true—East is East, and West is West, but Kipling's remedy of "two strong men" being able to bring the two together wasn't the way of Jesus Christ. His Gospel enables us to meet and learn from each other. We become "all one in Christ Jesus!"

****

AS I HEADED FOR THE AIRPORT at the end of my trek across Asia, that summary applied to all the continent's cultures, I knew. But now dawn was staging a show fit for an Emperor. Gray mist lingering upon the restless ocean turned purple and pink. Magenta and crimson splashed across the sky. I almost heard trumpets announce the guest performer's debut on stage as the sun's orange orb burst over the eastern horizon: "Ta-da! A new day has dawned!"

> *"The people living in darkness have seen a great light; on those living in the land of the shadow of death, a light has dawned." "Jesus said, 'I am the light of the world. Whoever follows me will never walk in darkness, but will have the light of life.'"*[26]

"Lord, may many more in Japan—and in Asia—find the Light!" I breathed, dazzled by the rising sun's gold shekels spilling across the ocean, right to the water lapping my feet.

Challenges lay ahead in this Land of the Rising Sun. Framing the incoming tide, a vermilion-colored Otorri gate (two horizontal camphor wood beams on twin vertical poles) protected the shore from invading evil spirits. Its pagoda roof would send them shooting back into space,

26. Isaiah 9.2 and John 8.12.

27. Whaling is part of the nation's identity, the meat providing protein. Although global whale conservation limits or bans commercial whaling, Japan harvests whales for "research," officials state.

while offerings to the spirits of nature welcomed benign forces. Along the coast, ancient stone monuments appeased the spirits of dead whales.[27] After all, hadn't a "divine wind"[28] once saved the country from Mongol invaders?

Japanese rightly worry about impending calamity for their chain of ridges thrust up from the sea by subterranean plates. Nearly 2,000 km. (over 1,000 miles) long, the land is active with volcanoes, earthquakes, and sometimes devastating tidal waves. In 2004, a quake even derailed a bullet train! There's another threat: Japan's cities bulge with 75% of the population, and because several cities are built on land reclaimed from the sea, Japan has been a key participant in the Pacific *tsunami* warning system.[29]

****

I stood on Japan's Pacific shore and watched *the dawn come up like thunder* indeed—as if a floodlight on the emblematic sun emblazoned on the nation's flag flying from a nearby flagpole. Bursting up from an endless horizon, the red orb reminded me that Jesus had commanded his disciples to be his witnesses to "the uttermost parts of the earth."[30] In earlier centuries, disciples standing where I stood would have concluded they'd arrived at "the uttermost." Japan's archipelago formed a closing bracket to their known world. What seemed like a world away, the opening bracket for my tramp across Asia had been far to the West at Pakistan's Khyber Pass in the Hindu Kush, where the sun *almost seemed to go down with the roll of thunder.*

28. A devastating but timely typhoon, which Japanese defenders gratefully dubbed *kamikaze* ("divine wind"), turned back the Mongol invasion of 1274.
29. As noted in an earlier chapter, *tsunami* is Japanese for "harbor wave."
30. Acts 1:8 AV.

EPILOGUE

SUN LIKE THUNDER – **29: EPILOGUE**

Satan's Vs. God's Designs

"You will know the truth, and the truth will set you free" (John 8.32). "I am the way and the truth and the life. No one comes to the Father except through me" (John 14.6).

ONLY MONTHS HAD PASSED since I stood at the Khyber Gateway—some three thousand miles (4,000 km.) due west as the crow flies. But the travel span seemed more like centuries—so much had happened on my circuitous route, covering further thousands of miles. I could scarcely believe what I'd seen. From the jet vapor trails high above the Khyber Pass and India's international telecom centers, to Japan's robot nurses, our world had indeed changed. On my hotel TV, I saw news clips of London and New York, showing noisy protesters against globalization, and realized how hopelessly out-of-touch they were with the reality of Asia.

Although sounds, smells, voices, and scenes filled my head, more powerful emotions filled my heart. I needed time to think through everything. Beyond the exotic, what had I really seen? What did it mean? In the end, could any divine design come out of this vast kaleidoscope of culture?

There *was* a common thread: Back in Eden (which many locate in the Middle East somewhere), Satan had dangled before mankind the prospect, "You shall become as gods." I had seen that tempting but misleading promise pop up in religions right across Asia. But I had also seen the Holy Spirit working in the lives of God's servants, who were being "conformed to the likeness of his Son"—the Lord Jesus Christ.[1]

Nagging Questions

Why hadn't the gospel at times done better in winning Asia and the rest of the world to Christ? Shinto followers might think the Apostle Paul agreed with them when he wrote about "principalities and powers in heavenly places." Although he exclaimed, "I can do all things through Christ who strengthens me!" the Apostle was hardly triumphalistic when he also wrote, "There are many adversaries." He suffered shipwreck, hunger, and beatings—and perhaps most hurtful, desertion by colleagues such as Demas.

As in other parts of the world, across Asia I'd met valiant disciples of Jesus, and also those who had messed up. Yet for Paul the bottom line was this: "The important thing is that in every way, whether from false motives or true, Christ is preached" (Phil. 1.18).

After all, at the outset of Jesus' earthly ministry, Satan had tried to thwart the purpose of the Son of God through the wilderness testing. Again, in Calvary's dark hour Satan thought he was victor. Unseen powers apart, human nature was certainly in the mix I'd seen across Asia. How was I to make sense of the hodgepodge of religious pretensions—mankind's attempts to manufacture a human path of salvation rather than accept the Way, the Truth, and the Life? Instead of accepting or simply rejecting Jesus, why did people *hate* him and his disciples? They hadn't hated Confucius or Buddha. No one put *them* to death. But of course—Jesus himself forecast that; it is the nature of evil to hate good.

Moreover, while recognizing well-intentioned reformers in a number of faiths, what was I to do with the pompous posturing I'd seen among supposedly saintly monks, gurus, venerable teachers, and

1. Romans 8.29

even pastors, whose private lives belied any spirituality? I sensed the abject hopelessness of religions that teach unknown re-cycling, or others that promise eventual paradise—if Gabriel can balance one's good deeds against one's bad deeds? I'd seen pride in religious rites unaccompanied by repentance of the sinner—for whom the Heavenly Father waits patiently with the gift of salvation. I prayed that in my own contacts, others would see humility—not arrogance. No. Better still, may they see Jesus.

I still ached over the injustice of women's abysmal suffering at the hands of men, of adults exploiting children, of men destined to servitude and abuse because of the accident of birth. Fatalism that acquiesces with avoidable calamity left me feeling helpless.

AND YET, there stayed with me memories of the delightful people who inhabit Asia—the shy smiles of appreciation for the simplest help or recognition, the gracious patience in desperate conditions. Each person in each country had an inborn desire for affection, for security, for fulfillment. As a disciple of Jesus, standing at the end of the Old Spice Road, I knew who could fulfill those desires. In the words of the Saviour, I could tell the woman at the well how she could find the water of life. In Jesus' name, I could give that rich young man ruler the "one thing" he lacked.

I ended my travels frustrated that I couldn't get through to those men and women and children. I was only passing through. I could only observe the human longings and see forces that provided noxious water and a stone in place of bread, that drove children away, that supplied the rich enquirer with yet another material rite he didn't need. "Lord," I breathed, "please send your messengers of the gospel to these dear people."

Traversing the Old Spice Road (and its side trails) conjured up nightmares of rapacious dictators, warring princes, arrogant entrepreneurs, groveling masses, and sore-covered pilgrims. It was enough to drive any visitor to despair. But a Japanese proverb reminded me, *"You can never see the sun rise by looking in the West."* For hope for Asia, I needed to look in the right direction—at what God is doing right across this vast continent.

It was this very world that the Son of God purposely entered and gave his life to redeem. I lifted my heart in thanksgiving for Jesus, our Saviour, and for the faithful disciples who had trekked across this same continent millennia before I was born. I thought of the thriving pockets of believers way back then, and of those I'd just been worshiping with. At every turn of the Spice Road I'd seen Jesus' footsteps in pilgrimage of his disciples!

They were obedient to the Commission of their Lord: *"All authority in heaven and on earth has been given me. Therefore go and make disciples of all nations . . .. And surely I will be with you always, to the very end of the age."*

There *is* a Divine Design; God *is* sovereign. Isaiah had said it all:

> *". . . from the rising of the sun to the place of its setting, men may know that there is none besides me. I am the Lord, and there is no other."*

APPENDICES A - J

Appendix A (Cf. Chapter 7)

Seeds of Greatness Blossom: Ramabai's Mukti Story

THE GREATEST WOMAN produced by Modern India," Prof. A.B. Shah of the State Board for literature and Culture in Maharashtra, India, called her. **Indian social reformer D. K. Karve wrote, "Pandita Ramabai was one of the greatest daughters of India."**

The remarkable story of Pandita Ramabai demonstrates the great potential of Indian women—and what any nation forfeits by suppressing them. I was intrigued to read her story, republished by my Indian friend, Vishal Mangalwadi.[1] Ramabai's family pilgrimage reminded me of the Roman centurion, to whom God sent the Apostle Peter. It also reminded me of the Apostle Paul, who, distressed by the idol worship, pointed out that creation was a *witness* to God's kindness. Idolaters should therefore turn from idols to the living God.[2]

A High Caste Woman's "Enlightenment"

Born in a forest ashram[3] in 1858, Ramabai Sastri was related to the ruling family (*Peswa* —Prime Minister) of Pune in Western India. But before the age of 17 she was the lone family survivor of one of India's periodic famines. Her Brahmin (high caste) parents had bequeathed this slight, gray-eyed girl precious gifts: unquenchable courage, an enquiring mind, and disillusion about Hindu gurus—most of whom they regarded

1. MacNicol, Nicol, *What Liberates a Woman?* (Introduction by Mangalwadi). New Delhi: Nivedit, 1996.
2. Re. Peter, see Acts 10. Re. Paul, see Acts 14, 17, and Romans 1.
3. A religious retreat center. The Forest was the third highest level of Brahmin existence on earth.

as repulsive fakes. But there was more.

Ramabai's father, Anant Sastri, was a Brahmin scholar whom admirers had showered with gifts of gold and even an elephant from Nepal. He forfeited his wealth and prominence to seek God in a forest *ashram* (group study retreat) high in India's *Western Ghat* hills. Although he never found the Unknown God, as he was starving to death he made his youngest daughter, Ramabai, promise to continue the search. (In the face of much opposition, he had encouraged her to study Sanskrit—the "sacred" language traditionally banned to women—thus enabling her to learn it.)

Earlier in Pune (Poona), Anant had picked up the revolutionary idea that Brahmin women should be allowed to learn Sanskrit—language of the gods forbidden to women. Anant broke the rules and taught his wife and daughters the sacred, complex language so they could read the Hindu scriptures. After Anant's death, Ramabai's mother continued to teach her the sacred classics. Although only a teen orphan, Ramabai could debate even with Brahmin *pandits* (learned ones). So impressed were they with her cultured bearing and knowledge of the classics that they honored her with the title of *Pandita*. Her listeners' gifts supported her as she travelled..

At the same time, she found it impossible to believe in the very things the classics had taught her about the gods. The writings revealed that ancient women were not denied learning. Her mistrust of Hinduism turned to rage as she observed widow burning, abuse of females (banned from reading or writing), and the wretched fate of lower castes. Since they could never improve themselves, she felt that the system accounted for her people's backwardness: "No spirit of daring, no ardor, no enterprise, no self-reliance, no anything!" Women, she felt, were "helpless victims of indolence." She longed to open "the eyes and ears of those who long have dwelt in the prison house of ignorance."

Meanwhile, Christian Indian scholars helped her to understand their faith. Finally she felt she'd found "a superior religion." Travelling to England and USA, she hungered to know the living God. She came across a copy of the Gospel of Luke, and Christian friends (Indian and expatriate) helped her understand it—so different from Hindu writings. Ramabai finally trusted in Christ as her Saviour and Lord. She then gave herself to helping widows and other women at risk. Speaking engagements overseas gave her many new friends who later supported her ministries. The home she founded grew into the Ramabai Mukti Mission, where girls were trained in crafts. Many enquired about Ramabai's faith, and she gladly opened the Word of God to them.

Although during her lifetime many Hindus blamed Ramabai for the destruction of women,[4] she was always a true Indian patriot. She was the first woman ever to address the National Social Congress (in 1899). In 1989, India's government finally issued a postage stamp in honor of the Pandita. Professor A.B. Shah of Maharashtra State explains why:

> *Pandita Ramabai Saraswati*[5] *(1858-1922) was the greatest woman produced by Modern India and one of the greatest Indians in all history .... a pioneer in the fields of women's education and social reform .... She was the first to introduce the kindergarten system of education and also the first to give a vocational bias to school education in India. Most important of all, she was first to rebel against the inhuman slavery to which widows were subjected in Hindu society, [laying] the foundations of a movement for women's liberation.*[6]

The gospel brought to bloom seeds of greatness sown by her parents. This accomplished woman passed that gospel on to the women who found asylum with her. "If it was possible for [God] to save such a great sinner as I am, he is able to save others," the Pandita told them. "*The only thing that must be done by me is to tell people of him, and of his great love for sinners, and his great power to save them.*"[7]

---

4. To their thinking, Ramabai damned women to bad *karma* by freeing them from male domination.
5. Hindus called her Saraswati (goddess of language, literature, learning). She rejected the idolatrous title. Her full married name was Ramabai Dongre Medhavi.
6. MacNicol, *op. cit.*
7. Basil Miller, *Pandita Ramabai, India's Christian Pilgrim*. Grand Rapids, Zondervan, 1949. For a recent dissertation on the Pandita's life, see Keith J. White, *Pandita Ramabai (1858-1922): A Re-evaluation of Her Life and Work*. Cardiff: University of Wales, April 2003 (unpublished).

Appendix B

Commonalities of Religions — A Summary

Religion: a system of beliefs and observances that relate a human to the supernatural,

distinct from spiritual regeneration ("the New Birth" provided by Jesus Christ)—although some religions teach a doctrinal regeneration based on rites and self effort.

Commonalities:

1. For everything real, there may be a counterfeit.
2. Every religion's beliefs and culture are protected by
   a. Vested interests
   b. Cherished belief
3. Every religion believes it is the superior or only true way to God.
4. Religions are used for political purposes; some are imposed by force or law, by political elite in order to secure support of the unlearned proletariat.
6. Both learned and unlearned, rational and irrational, devout and secular, are among followers of religions—for different reasons and with different commitment.
7. No religion is monolithic. Basic religion has sub-cultures and beliefs. These are created by dynasties, reforms, heresy, syncretism, personal "revelations," and superstitions.

8. A religion includes loyalty to a leader, clan, system, nation, tradition, chauvinism, culture, way of life, or worldview.
9. All religions (whatever their origin) have been hi-jacked by vested interests that have modified, distorted, codified, and embellished the original. Vested interests impose and protect religions from change—for financial, social, or political reasons.
10. All religions proselytize, whether overtly or covertly. Some do so through evangelism and voluntary response; others forcibly through coercion. Some by marriage requirements, social and legal restrictions, taxation, or exclusion from certain privileges. *E.g.* Offspring of a Jew married to a non-Jew must be raised as a Jew. A non-Hindu can become a Hindu only through supposed re-incarnation (which will depend on accruing good *karma* in the previous life).
11. Religions that seem tolerant and universalist, nevertheless can be intolerant or "superior" to others looked upon as "separated brethren."
12. All religions seek to provide a complete system to:
    a. Explain the world and universe.
    b. Explain suffering and cope with it.
    c. Manipulate (control) forces deemed to affect human life.
    d. Provide the source and objective (beginning and end) of individual life, rationale for existence, and answers to the questions: "Where did we come from? Where do we go?"
    e. Provide reward and punishment.
    f. Seek to explain or at least identify the unknown and unknowable.
    g. Provide comfort in bereavement.
13. All religion is affected by human reason or imagination/superstition, even though truth may be incorporated. .
14. All religions teach, imply, or are undergirded by acceptance of the transcendent— whether an external force, power, deity, spirit, or internal power of the mind over matter (sublimation).

******

Christendom and Christianity:

"Christendom," as here defined, is a system of belief and worship that is associated with Christian faith but encompasses externals of institutions and systems that seek to supplement or even substitute for Christ's work of grace, which one receives in response to faith alone.

The Christian faith (as it derives from Christ and not from human reasoning) also includes a number of positive elements incorporated in some other religions: *e.g.* worship of the supreme God, service to fellow beings, personal rectitude, belief in life after death (albeit with assurance).

Evangelical Christianity provides:

1. Vicarious once-for-all sacrifice for sin.
2. Redemption of the sinner.
3. Peace with God now and assurance of eternal life.
4. Behavior-changing regeneration that makes possible being "conformable" to God's will.

Christianity as here defined is often termed "evangelical" (from "evangel"—the Gospel of Jesus Christ). Although it may be expressed in some religious systems, it does not depend upon a system of religion but rather upon the regeneration of the Holy Spirit.. But increasingly, it also includes a number of experiential concepts not always based on biblical Scripture.

******

Religion and Wisdom: God has given humans reasoning powers, resulting in meditation, poetry, and philosophy about life. In each religious culture, we find words of beauty and wisdom. Solomon wrote, "The words of wise men are like goads" (SS 12.11). Asia's cultures are rich in philosophy, some more so than materialistic "Western" cultures.

However, when it comes to understanding eternity, man's reasoning becomes imagination, for he has no revelation of the unknown apart from what the eternal Creator reveals. The same is true of moral things, in guiding our lives upon earth. If the only guide to behaviour is human reason, we can end up in superstition or vain striving to attain goodness. Without God's laws and grace, we have no way of dealing with sin; in fact, we may have a distorted concept of sin and morality.[1]

To be fair to non-Christian religions, we must recognize the lofty ideals, the artistic expressions, and the ethical value in many of them. They express the intelligence and moral insights the Creator embedded in the human mind (in contrast to the animal kingdom).[2] But we also must not equate these natural aspects with saving grace. In fact Christendom itself provides us with many noble thoughts and a system of seeking morality, righteousness, and eternal bliss. But it, as well as non-Christian religions, cannot provide us the *way* of salvation from sin apart from the redemptive work of Jesus Christ, God incarnate. Religions, including Christendom, provide what all human philosophy does—a system of coping with earth's problems and fears. Religions without Christ the Redeemer cannot provide cleansing from sin, daily empowering for righteous living, and assurance of eternal life.

Religion and Human Condition: A safari across Asia can cause the traveler to suspect that whatever God has planned for Good, Satan does his utmost to corrupt—though Satan promised Adam and Eve they'd not only gain knowledge of Good and Evil but also become as gods!

Today's burgeoning populations, deteriorating environments, and virulent pandemics are worry enough. But would humanity have wiped itself out before now if it had not been scattered around the globe? Even before Babel, while mankind had one language, universal evil was so great that God sent the Flood and commissioned a fresh start. Satan turned even that into defiance at Babel.

Yet each linguistic group retained the knowledge of God[3]—if people would only seek him! However, Satan misleads even that incipient

1. Example: One ethnic group in Papua New Guinea bases social status on deception of others. (See Bibliography: Richardson, Don, *Peace Child*)
2. Humanists equate these natural characteristics with innate goodness ("God within us all"), contrary to the Bible's statement that "the heart is deceitful above all things, and desperately wicked" (Jeremiah 17.9). The point is that sin has warped man's nature so that his loftiest thoughts are prostituted to serve his pride.
3. Eccles. 3.11, so well illustrated in Don Richardson's *Eternity in Their Hearts.* (See Bibliog.)

awareness through man-made rites, idols, and superstitions that promise Paradise. After millennia of man's trashing every opportunity to find Truth, God personally entered our world, dwelling with us as the Eternal Son, in order to help us know "The Way, the Truth, and the Life."

Only *know*? The knowledge (*gnosis*) of ancient sages redeemed no sinner. The sacrifices, mystic mantras, sacred rites, and pilgrimages of Asia have never regenerated a sinful heart. Neither can Christendom's philosophy. We can give thanks that God stepped in and provided salvation for us—salvation we can accept through repentance and by faith in Jesus Christ.[4]

Amazingly, we can return to one "language," for Jesus brought regenerated humanity a universal "language of love" transcending all division. I experienced that in my travels in Asia, enjoying fellowship with Christians whose language I could not understand.

In contrast to that spiritual oneness, the languages of the world have finally come full circle back to one secular binary language—an amazing but simple sequence of zeroes and ones! Is an Apocalypse of global revolution and destruction now ready to break upon us?

— WHF

---

4. Appendix F explores Religions and the distinctives of Christianity.

Appendix C

Buddha's Elephant: God's self-revelation in Christ

Buddha used to tell a parable about a rich king who wanted to entertain his courtiers. He commanded that an elephant be brought in, and several blind beggars, one at a time. The first blind beggar touched one of the elephant's legs. As he felt around it, he declared: "This is a pillar." The next beggar touched the tail of the elephant and commented: "This must be a rope." Another beggar put his hands on the elephant's ear by accident and said: "This is a palm leaf, waving in the wind." The next one grasped the trunk of the elephant and exclaimed in fear, "Perhaps it is a snake!" Onlookers rolled around in hysterical laughter: "These blind beggars are so stupid, that they can't tell it is an elephant!"

Siddhartha Gautama, who later was called Buddha ("The Enlightened One"), told this story to illustrate "the mystery of human religion" and the futility of trying to understand the whole truth—which no one can grasp.

A lot of people today support this Buddhist understanding of religion—"the Theology of the Elephant." People seem to appreciate the humility of anyone who says, "A person cannot know anything precise about truth." This is still public opinion, ever since the European Enlightenment, ever since the great poet and philosopher Gotthold Ephraim Lessing wrote to his publisher in a letter stating: "If God held the truth in his right hand, and perpetual searching for the truth in his left hand, then I would fall humbly into his left hand, saying: "Father, give (me), because all truth is just for you alone."

But something happened in the Temple in Jerusalem that has radically changed the question about the possibility of knowing God. A young couple went to the Temple, the woman holding a baby in her arms. Suddenly, an old man walked up to them, took the child in his arms without asking, looked at it and prayed: *"Lord, now my eyes have seen your salvation. Now I may die in peace; my eyes have seen your salvation."*

This is the crucial difference between the Theology of the Elephant and the Theology of the Child in the Manger. Buddha recognized something essential with regard to the religions. The possibilities of the natural man are those of religion, the Theology of the Elephant. We cannot, from our tiny frog-like perspective, grasp the reality of God. But the Absolutely Other, which came into the world as Jesus, is this: that God took on human form, that God became a baby, like us, so that we can see him as one of our own. Because we cannot come to God—not even with our knowledge and understanding—God came to us.

Now it is clear: we can see a human being, touch him, ask him questions, get to know him, talk with him, have a part of his being—and this not just in a fragmentary way, but entirely. The record of Jesus is about a man with whom we can be on a first name basis, one to whom we have immediate and direct access. This is the wonderful message of the Gospel, which begins with the nativity, when God took upon himself this human form and gave us this gift that mankind could touch and see. So that the one who considers Jesus of Nazareth may know: "Here I am encountering the Living God, who is, at the same time, limitless."

From the human perspective of the history of religions, Buddha was initially correct with his Theology of the Elephant: the natural man with his own means alone, can grasp the divine only in a fragmentary fashion, if at all.

–Anonymous

(See Chap. 10, 12 and Appendix F, regarding "The Buddha" and Buddhism. — WHF)

Appendix D (See also Appendix F: Asia's Religions)

Witness through the Ages

WESTERNERS don't usually think of Central Asia as an ancient sphere of missionary activity. However, even in the first century of the Christian Era, the Apostle Thomas spread the gospel to India (see Ch. 6). Before the end of the first millennium there was extensive missionary outreach to the land of Slavs and Tartars.[1] About the time Mohammad was extending Islam's influence in the Middle East, Eastern Orthodox missionaries were braving ruthless warlords to take the Gospel to the Slavic people and right into Russia, resulting in the birth of the Russian Orthodox Church.[2] In the 17thc. just outside Moscow, the Church built a replica of Jerusalem's Old City, visited by Slavic pilgrims on their way to "the Holy Land."

True, there were major doctrinal disputes. Nevertheless, disciples of Jesus Christ pressed on in the footsteps of earlier Jewish travelers who had carried the news of the one and only true God across Asia's steppes and mountain ranges—right into Mongolia, China, and Korea. They even crossed along the Aleutian stepping-stones into North America. The astounding thing is that in later centuries, even the Orthodox Church ignored this gospel heritage.[3]

---

1. Persian names applied to the vast region of Central Asia between the Yellow Sea and Dnieper (E. Europe), peopled by Turkic tribes considered wild and ruthless.
2. Eastern Orthodox, Nestorian, and Syrian church distinctions have often been blurred, their labels interchanged. But along the Old Spice Road, I saw the legacy of Jesus's disciples in each discipline.
3. Colleague James J. Stamoolis, documents this in *Eastern orthodox mission theology today* (Bibliog.).

Witness—and Satan's Distortions

Pre-Christian era writings at times appear to refer to Christ. Christian missionaries of Universalist leanings sometimes used these references to consider some non-Christian religions as "other ways" to God.[4]

Similarly, reference to God as Creator appeared among South America's ancient Inca traditions. Roman Catholics attempted to use these to introduce Christianity to South American peoples. Animistic Pacha Mama became the Virgin Mary. However, instead of turning traditional worshippers to Christianity, the result was syncretism—religion that absorbed ancient pagan concepts within the new Christian forms imposed by their conquerors. In such cases, even when Christendom was active in new areas, Satan often distorted the gospel, making it only one more religious system.

In Medieval centuries in Asia, mission sometimes resulted from political arrangements—with emperors appointing Syrian and Persian Christians as well as Muslims to government posts because of their learning in various fields. As mentioned in Chapter 17:

> Russian Orthodox members arrived in 17th c. "Peking" after being captured while exploring a disputed area of China-Russia's border. Among them was an Orthodox priest, whom the Chinese allowed to conduct Christian services in an abandoned Buddhist temple! The Russians gained respect and grew into a community of some 80,000. However, while contributing to oriental theology and science, they sadly neglected any spiritual outreach.

Lack of evangelistic outreach not only left Christians passive and open to encroachment by the non-Christian world around them. Lack of witness also reflected loss of spiritual life within the church. If it had been alive with the Spirit of Christ, it would have been concerned for others' spiritual needs, even as the earliest Christians were. For example, before his conversion, Jewish rabbi Saul of Tarsus was hostile to Jesus and his disciples. After conversion from religious orthodoxy, he became "the Apostle Paul," displaying a Christian sense of responsibility to witness for his Lord wherever he traveled.

---

4. Max Muller, CMS: *Christ in Ancient Vedas*, p. 203 re. "precious stones among the rubbish."

Lesson? "A sound theoretical basis, together with education and goodwill, are not enough for a substantial and sustained growth of missionary work."[5] This also applied to Roman Catholic and Protestant enclaves that occupied themselves with piety but failed to reach out with the gospel. They became isolated and sterile.

Missionary Imperialism?[6]

"Imperialism" has been a much-used derogatory term for a couple of centuries. Americans "resonated" (as they say so creatively) with the term, because their British[7] founders had rebelled against Imperial Britain and gained Independence. They then extended their own empire over much of North America and across the Pacific as far as the Philippines. Marx and Lenin employed the term as handy currency among the "downtrodden masses," but Communism then sought to extend its own imperial suzerainty around the globe.

Until World War II, the British took pride in an "enlightened" Empire that spread more widely than African, Asian, European, and Latin American imperialists had earlier established. After 1945, post-war diplomacy made Imperialism anathema. War-weary Britons seemed almost ashamed of their once much-lauded imperial history.

What has that to do with a book on Missions? Regrettably, missionaries have found themselves tarred with the same brush as imperialists. Even today, intractable governments accuse Non—Governmental Organizations (NGOs, as missions along with other charities are known) of being "spies" (read "imperialists"). Yet missionaries do not represent their own governments but Jesus' "kingdom not of this

5. Orthodox missiologist Anastasios Yannoulatos, quoted in James Stamoolis, *Eastern orthodox mission theology today* (Bibliography).

6. Global ambition by any ideology or religion naturally raises the point of Christianity's teaching that Jesus Christ is ruler of the universe, and that his rule will one day be recognized by all nations. Other religions make similar claims. How do we know which to believe? What's their difference? I seek to address those valid questions in Appendix F. Also, see note at end of Appendix H: Islam—comparison of Islamic conversion by force and Christian conversion resulting from spiritual conviction.

7. The author's father, British missionary to N. America, admired Americans ("the most generous people in the world"), while ribbing them that their greatest American, George Washington, was an Englishman!

world." They even sometimes seem apologetic about their nationality/culture, to avoid the "imperialist" slur!

Unrecognized are missionaries who have purposely given up their own national identification to live with "the down-trodden masses," who have stood up for liberty where there has been none, and who have pressed their own governments to grant dignity and freedom to oppressed peoples.

Understandably, missionaries do not rise to their own defense, because they serve a Leader who was misunderstood, facing hatred and infamy meekly "as a lamb." It may be better that messengers of the gospel should remain misunderstood rather than becoming arrogant—if that indeed is the trade-off. But there is a place for a study of missiology that documents the non-imperialistic role of missionaries. The stereotype seems supported by Constantine's political cry, "By this sign [the Cross] I conquer." Also there were the politically motivated Medieval Crusades, and the politico-religious stance of the Roman Church (note Appendix F and H re. distinction between *Christendom* and *Christianity*).

In the West, where humanistic ideology threatens to wipe out all public religion and has destroyed much traditional morality, people tend to be amused at Christian witness. (Note the laughable stereotypes in many a movie.) But attitudes are different in parts of Southeast Asia, where Communist governments and traditional religions react to the gospel like a raging water buffalo to a red flag. A news release states:

> "Christians remain the most persecuted religious group in the world today. According to the World Evangelical Alliance, persecution and discrimination are the daily reality for more than 230 million Christians in more than 60 countries around the world. They are denied their basic human rights and suffer discrimination and violence simply because of their religious beliefs.
>
> "While we remain largely free to practice and profess our faith here in Canada, the lives of a growing number of Christians around the world are in danger. One woman imprisoned for her faith in Jesus was recently asked about her sentence. She responded, "I was sentenced

> to two years in prison...The verdict was 'Believes in God.' I remain guilty." The daily suffering of these Christians goes largely unnoticed. No national newspaper headlines, no prime-time television interviews inform us of the injustices perpetrated upon those that name Jesus as their Lord. . . . Theirs is the promise that though persecutors can imprison, torture, or even kill, nothing they will face can remove them from their Father's love.[8]

Even in the West, neo-liberalism now espouses oriental faiths along with a pseudo-spiritual "Christianity" that includes "Jesus" (as a model for humanity) but rejects Christ and his salvation.

This irrational hatred of the gospel reveals Satan's determination to prevent the redemption of humanity from his grasp. He incites fierce opposition to the Saviour and his disciples—whether from ideology or religion. After all, the Devil wanted to be "like the Most High. He promised Adam and Eve they would become "like God, knowing good and evil"[9] ("Enlightenment"?) if they rebelled against God's sole restriction.

Today, Satan's seduction continues on the Old Spice Road, but Jesus' disciples continue to witness for their Lord.

— WHF

---

8. International Day of Prayer for the Persecuted Church (IDOP), World Evangelical Alliance, 2005.
9. Genesis 3.4.

APPENDIX E

SIM Resource Materials on Asia

SIM Country Profiles and Infopacks provide detailed summaries of statistics for each country of ministry. SIM's magazine, *Serving in Mission Together* (in Asia, *SIMNow*), features news of mission personnel, countries and ministries. Presentation of SIM ministries is also available on CDs and DVDs, and on the Internet: sim.org, and *www.simeast.com.*

Address enquiries to your local SIM national office or to SIM International, 1838 Gold Hill Road, Fort Mill, SC 29708, USA. **Office Addreesses** (apart from Africa and S. America):

Australia: P.O. Box 42, Penshurst, NSW 2222, Australia. *sim.australia@sim.org.au*

Bangladesh: Box 8123, Mirpur Dhaka 1216, Bangladesh

Canada: 10 Huntingdale Blvd, Toronto, ON M2J 4S5 *gregg.bryce@sim.org*

China and S.E. Asia: P.O. Box 104, Chianag Mai 50000, Thailand

East Asia: SIM East Asia Ltd., 116 Lavender Street, 804-09 Pek Chuan Bldg., 338730 Singapore. *info@simeast.com*

France: SIM France, Alain & Christiane Soudrain, Quartier Les Mains, 84860 Caderousse, France. *sim.france@sim.org*

Italy: Randy Seamon, Via Calatabiano 18, 00122 Roma, Italy. *postmast@sim.ch*

Korea: Hak-Jin Chun, 8602 Econo-Charmant B/D, Sungman City 463-805, South Korea *director@simkorea.org*

Mongolia: JCS International, P.O. Box 189, Ulaanbaatar 210351, Mongolia

New Zealand: P.O. Box 38-588, Howick, Manukan 2145, New Zealand *info@sim.org.nz*

Pakistan: Clive Barker, Businessmen's Colony, Rahim Yar Kahn, 6422, Pakistan

Philippines: MCPO Box 2016, 0706 Makati MM, Philippines

Switzerland: SIM International, CP 4051, CH-2500 Biel/Bienne 4, Switzerland *postmast@sim.org*

Thailand: C-SEA, P.O. Box 014, Chiang Mai 50000, Thailand

U.K.: SIM-UK, Wetheringsett Manor, Wetherinsett, Stowmarket, Suffolk. IP14 5QX *info@sim.co.uk*

Country Statistics

Unless otherwise stated, statistics in *Sun Like Thunder* are chiefly from *Operation World, 21st Century Edition,* by Patrick Johnstone and Jason Mandryk, with Robin Johnstone.

For further statistics and details, see *Operation World* (Bibliography).

Appendix F

Asia's Religions

[See also Appendices D: Witness through the Ages; G – Christianity; and H - Islam.]

TRAVELING along the Old Spice Road, visitors realize the major role religion has played (and continues to play) in the formation of Asia's cultures and peoples. Religions originating in Asia have now spread around the globe. Questions inevitably arise:

How did such multiplicity develop? What effect do religions have upon Asia today? Can we join the dots? In view of Christianity's claims *vis-à-vis* the exclusive claims of other religions, how can we know which to follow?

Can we support the following thesis? *All religions are responses to common human needs, but Christ Jesus (God incarnate, not a religious system) is the only Way, the only Truth, and the only Life to meet those spiritual needs fully.*

[Lest reference to any religion seem negative, I assure readers that I respect people of all faiths, as well as those of no religious belief. Among our neighbors in North America's most cosmopolitan city, we have friends who are Buddhist, Hindu, Jewish, Muslim, Orthodox, as well as agnostic and evangelical. WHF]

The "Evolution" of Asia's Religions[1]

PERSISTENCE OF RELIGIOUS BELIEF mystifies secularists, who thought the 18thc Enlightenment should have consigned religion to dusty archives as a curious relic. Evolutionists, always insisting

1. *Religion*: Originally the word (Latin: *re-ligare*) meant "to bind"—an obligation, duty, whether secular or sectarian. Thus it is used in the New Testament. Today, it refers to a so-called "faith system": "An institutionalized system of religious attitudes, beliefs, and practices" (Miriam-Webster).

that there's a secular, naturalistic explanation for everything, have recently explained that even "spirituality" is an evolutionary development! Therefore human DNA must have developed "a God gene" as a "coping mechanism" that is essential to the very "survival of the fittest"—our advanced level of animal existence. Rationalists agree that only humans are able to contemplate the transcendental and self-transcendental (call "spirituality").

"Is God in Our Genes?" a cover feature in a national magazine asked. "A provocative study asks whether religion is a product of evolution."[2] The feature cited *The God Gene: How Faith is Hardwired into Our Genes*, by molecular biologist Dean Hamer, who claims to have isolated one of the genes responsible. To him, "We're a bunch of chemical reactions running around in a bag."

To be fair, the magazine, *Time*, also quotes *The Book of Ecclesiastes* (3. 11): "He has also set eternity in the hearts of men, yet they cannot fathom what God has done from beginning to end." In the following essay, we look briefly at the *development* ("evolution" in that sense) of religion throughout the history of Asia and our world.

****

IN THE BEGINNING, there was no religion. Or to be more precise, in the beginning was God, and the creation he pronounced "good" did not need the structure of a religious system. Adam and Eve instinctively loved God with all their hearts and minds and souls. Worship of the Creator God was part of their nature, not yet corrupted by sin. God did not have to require that they do anything other than enjoy his presence and each other's company.[3] However, the Creator did make one stipulation. It was not a ritual they had to perform. It was only the simplest test of the couple's complete love for their creator: *avoid* eating the fruit of one single tree set amid the cornucopia they could enjoy in the Garden.

2. *Time*, Canadian edition, October 25, 2004.
3. Millennia later, Jesus stated that these requirements were the essence of the Law of Moses, which sought to guide sinful humanity back to a right relationship with the Creator (Matthew 22.37; Romans 13.8-10).

Why make such a stipulation, small as it was? God had given mankind a most precious ability—to *choose.* In caring for their global garden, Adam and Eve would need to make decisions based on choice, so here was the definitive opportunity to choose.

Choice proved that God was not a divine tyrant who had created a robot that would mechanically love him.[4] Without an alternative to loving God fully, spiritual choice would be meaningless. Man should love the Lord out of free will. So God provided one tree in the midst of the Garden, a tree that would remind mankind and the surrounding creation (angels and all) that Adam and Eve really did love the Lord their God, their Creator, with all their heart, soul, and mind. Leaving that tree alone was no problem; they didn't need that tree. It didn't restrict their diet or their freedom. It proved their *freedom* to make moral decisions involving the use of reason and logic. That identified humanity.

It was only after the Great Deceiver[5] had beguiled mankind into rebelling against God, that humanity developed religion.[6] Adam and his immediate progeny apparently knew enough about God's will to recognize sin and understood forgiveness of sin.[7] As mankind proliferated, however, man's own fears, desires, imagination, and reason developed systems of cultic religion far removed from loving God with all the heart, soul, and mind. Sinful nature wasn't satisfied simply with *not* loving God (as if that alternative could stand alone). Soon mankind was destroying itself in mutilation, human sacrifice, murder, and profligacy—often as religious ritual.

In the midst of a confusing mix of man-made doctrines and rituals, God chose a powerless nomad to father a nation to preserve knowledge

---

4. Without mankind's having ability and opportunity to choose, critics would blame God for making man a mechanical toy programmed to obey him.
5. Jesus described Satan as "the father of lies from the beginning" (John 8.44). The Apostle Paul calls him The Great Deceiver.
6. Religion: likely from Latin, *religare*, "to restrain"-by inference, to regulate. I use the term to mean a system regulating life on earth and trying to control the unknown—particularly one's fate after death. WHF.
7. Note the story of Cain and Abel (Genesis 4).

of the sovereign God. Although other races and cultures at times had glimpses of an eternal God, Jehovah used Jewish lineage as his human channel for incarnating his eternal Son, Jesus Christ, for the salvation of mankind.

In spite of human failings, the nomadic father of that nation, Abraham, had personal faith in God's promises. He earned the title, "Father of Faith." Through Abraham's descendent Moses, God provided not only the Ten Commandments but also a complex system to regulate life and faith for the Jewish nation. More than one religion traces its origin to Abraham.

Religion has had a series of major reformers. Many religions have some element of divine truth, but also incorporate man-made superstitions and rituals with the hope of obtaining eternal merit. Zoroaster sought to direct idolatrous thought towards a paramount god, while retaining animistic beliefs (such as the sacredness of fire). Greek Athenians, among their sacrifices to idols and spirits, preserved an altar to "The Unknown God." Gnostics replaced mindless pantheism with objective knowledge. Siddhartha, founder of Buddhism, sought to reform Hindu idolatry, but replaced it with taboos leading to a nihilist "Enlightenment." Judaism rejected idolatry for monotheism, as did Islam, but both substituted ritual for faith. "Christendom" (as distinguished from evangelical Christian faith) rightly refused emperor worship but replaced the Emperor with the Pope, who was *de facto* ruler over the Holy Roman Empire.

Religion makes man feel "OK" by following a set of disciplines. There remains no need for divine redemption. After all, it was the orthodox religious leadership of the day that crucified Jesus, who came to redeem mankind.

****

(The following major religions are listed in the chronological order in which they first appeared in Asia's history.)

PAGANISM: For our summary, we'll use this term to mean anything other than worship of the one true God. That includes nature worship (sun, moon, stars) animistic spirit worship, shamanism, and idolatry. Later, we'll consider major religions and ideologies that have developed specific creeds—including monotheistic religions that worship one Supreme Being but do not accept God's provision of salvation through Jesus Christ by grace, received through faith.

How did paganism develop, considering the earlier history of faith? Adam and Eve had personal knowledge of their Creator. Enoch "walked with God." But by the time of Noah, evil was so pervasive that "every imagination of the thoughts of man's heart was evil continually." God found it necessary to start afresh with Noah's family. Result of mankind's sinfulness was the Flood, giving the possibility of a new start for the human race. But mankind continued to reject God's salvation, forming various man-made systems.

Sumerians were an early example of human religion—placating spirits and gaining favor with their man-made idols. As the Apostle Paul later explained, they abandoned worship of the Creator for the created thing—the sun, moon, and stars. They degenerated into self-destructive superstition, included sacrificing infants to "the gods."

ZOROASTRIANISM: Zoroastrianism, apart from Judaism, is history's oldest monotheism. Its 6thc. BC founder, Zoroaster, was reputed to be from Eastern Persia (Iran). He rejected the gods of Indo-Iranians, taught that the righteous would go to Heaven and the wicked to Hell. He believed in individual judgment after death, on the basis of one's good or evil deeds, and in a universal judgment after a resurrection. He sought to reform idolatrous Sumerian religion, teaching that the supreme god, Ahura Mazda ("the wise god"), required good deeds for help in his cosmic struggle against evil.

Legend says his birth was prophesied, and that the supreme God protected him when evil tried to destroy him as a child. Although Islam eventually all but wiped it out, for over a thousand years Zoroastrianism was the world's most powerful religion, the official religion of three empires. Traces remain among minorities (called *Parsees*) in Afghanistan, Pakistan, and India.[8]

---

8. Readers will recognize several similarities to Christianity, but the same elements exist in several religions—undoubtedly due to global spiritual needs and Satanic devices to anticipate and simulate truth.

HINDUISM:[9] "We can only surmise how and when the Hindu religion and caste system started," J.E. Dodla, Indian scientist, points out. "Hindus claim that their religion is 100,000 years old, but the high literary value of their *Vedas*, as well as descriptions of culture and civilization existing at the time, suggest a more recent beginning (although still in the B.C. era).

Dodla, who has studied Hinduism in depth, also explains the caste system: "Early Western historians didn't understand Hinduism's development. The Hindu religion introduced the caste system, dividing society into five classes according to a hierarchical descending order—four recognized classes and one unrecognized class, as follows:

1. *Brahmana* (Brahmin, the priestly and educated class).
2. *Vysya* (Business class).
3. Kshatriya (Warrior class)
4. Sudra (Farming and artisan class).
5. Panchama ("Panchama" means 5th category). There is no name for this class; they are called *Panchamies* or *untouchables. They are* the labor class, involved in menial jobs (in the sight of Hindu society). It consists of two sub-castes:
   (a) *Mala. Cremating, burying, farming, and out-door servant labor, etc.*
   (b) *Madiga. Scavenging* (they have to physically carry out the "night-soil"), *shoe making, mending, etc.* They are looked down upon as *"beef eaters."* These are Hindus.

"Since the Panchama communities were called *"untouchables,"* Mahatma Gandhi (a Vysya) "up-graded" their identity by naming them *Harijans* to get their support of his struggle for India's Independence. After Independence, the Indian Constitution named the two communities *Scheduled Castes.* Recently they are called Dalits.

---

9. **The philosophers who shaped Hinduism into a religion:** (1) In *Bhagavad Gita* (AD 650-680), Sankara Acharya introduced Advaitha Vedanta Philosophy. *Advaitha*: 'no two'—*i.e.* a god's spirit (Bhagawan's Atman) and human spirit are one. (2) In A.D. 1100 – 1150, Ramanuja Acharya introduced Dvaith Philosophy. *Dvaitha*: 'two'—*i.e.* god and human are *different* spirits. —Pradeep Kumar Chidiyawala, 'Introduction' to *Bhagawad Gita*. Gita Gyan Mandal: Hyderabad 1991. (Cited by J.E. Dodla.)

"The communities that did not come under the Hindu purview of caste system were named in the Indian Constitution as *Scheduled Tribes:* Forest and Hill Tribals, Nomads, Aborigines etc. They are not Hindus, but worship spirits and their own gods."

"There is no 'converting' to Hinduism. If one identifies himself as a Hindu by worshiping Hindu gods, then he *is* a Hindu, but he also has to identify himself with one of the Hindu castes."

An Eclectic Religion: This eclectic form of religion developed from Sumerian idolatry. Joshua R. Thambiraj[10] posits that Aryans brought the religion of the Baals, with its pantheism and myths, to the Indian sub-continent in oral form, coalescing into the *Vedas* and *Upanishads* sometime between 500 BC and 500 AD—written only some 1,400 years ago. (Aryan Sanskrit suggests a link between *Deus* and *Deva.*) Though more recently presented in the West as only healthy breathing exercises, Yoga "offers" ancient postures of Baal worship.[11] Yoga's goal is to suppress all bodily impulses till "the inner self" achieves union with the Ultimate Reality. That amounts to Nihilism.

Although wrapped in polytheism, Aryan belief did not have any basis of spiritual regeneration. Instead, its existential super-man philosophy, along with different class levels of birth, imposed the tyrannical lowest caste system on the sub-continent's Dravidians and aborigines. In turn, influencing the Aryan overlay was the ancient Hindu belief in *karma*—the effects inherited from good and bad deeds governing destiny (i.e., the next level of *Janma*, or rebirth). "Reincarnation" is a term reserved chiefly for gods. Such depended on observing *Dharma* (deeds duties). As various streams of humanity pressed eastward, those who migrated south of the Caucasus and Himalayas pressed, wave upon wave, into the narrowing funnel of the Indian sub-continent. Today one billion people speak some 180 languages plus dialects. [As India's middle (economic) class grows,

---

10. Joshua Raj, *A Biblical Approach to Indian Traditions and Beliefs*. Singapore: Genesis Books, 2008.

11. Y*oga* >Sanskrit: *union* (with gods, spirits)—"Ultimate Reality." Body movements are "offered" to such. *A sitting posture in Yoga is named the "L*otus Position"—from the water lily that reportedly grew out of **Brahma's** navel **and** formed the seat of **Laksmi** , the goddess of wealth.

caste distinctions become blurred, but in reality they also continue; for instance, in cities, Dalit (formerly termed "Untouchable") ghettos provide Dalits their social network.]

So Hinduism is essentially an umbrella for many sects and forms of religion. Although it recognizes a trimurthies of the three paramount gods—Brahma (Creator), Vishnu (Sustainer of Creation), Shiva/Siva/Parameswar (Destroyer)[12] —it embraces millions of gods and goddesses. It also includes ten reincarnations of gods, or Avatars who destroy evil and save devotees. Vishnu carries the three-pointed "trident" (or trisul)—which also appears in the hand of the Greek and Roman sea-god (King Neptune).

As mentioned below (under "Christendom"), "Liberal" Protestant theologians recognized this polytheism, but pointed out that some forms believe in an ultimate "Absolute" god. They pictured this as the core of Hindu belief, requiring only "enlightenment" to reveal God the Father.[13] Therefore they saw Hinduism as an oriental "way" to the Eternal God, not realizing Hinduism's ultimate objective—*moksha*, paradise/sublimation. In Christian terms, this smacks of Satan's lure in Eden: "Eat of the forbidden fruit, and you shall become as gods."

Now Hinduism embraces values from Communism to Universalism (but not Christianity)—any philosophy or religion that might increase one's good *karma* and earn better status in the next re-birth. Although Hinduism emphasizes the *dharmic* concept of religious duty, it believes that mankind lives in an age of *maya* (illusion) composed of cosmic vibrations. Educated Hindus view Quantum Theory as supportive of *maya.*

Although India's "secular" state is based on tolerance of diverse religions (required by the nation's constitution), some observers feel that Hindu nationalism—which wants to impose Hindu religious beliefs on the country—reflects Aryan/European fascism rather than human values.

---

12. Vishnu's son, Manmadh, is alleged to have great sexual powers, leading devotees to venerate the genitals of the idol, which represents lustful sex (J. E. Dodla).

There's one aspect of Hinduism rarely mentioned: flagrant sex. Male devotees copulate with temple prostitutes as an act of worship of female and male deities. Murals and statues depict Vishnu and other gods naked except for chastity belts that emphasize the genitals. Male sperm contained the gods' gift—the germ of life, didn't it? So orgasm must be an act of religious worship, making the sex act (*kamam*) an integral part of Hindu worship. And so it has been throughout history, before the Flood and featuring in the excesses of cultures such as Nineveh, Sodom and Gomorrah, and Babylon. It shows up in Christendom as well (noted in Appendix G).

BUDDHISM:[14] The reformer, the Gautama Buddha was born into affluent nobility in highly superstitious Nepal (that location is sometimes disputed). Seeking to overcome the subcontinent's complex idolatry, he warned followers against starting a new religion. Buddhism is a form of Gnostic Aryanism, teaching existential self-improvement to upgrade one's status—until released from the wheel of re-incarnation, attaining eternal sublimation (transcendence). It fulfills Satan's attractive seduction of Adam and Eve: "You will become as gods."

How's this for a definition of Buddhism? "There is a part of all of us—a divine spark—which antedates the demi-urgical creation; ... through a gift of knowledge—basically coded words—a mass of believers can ascend the various levels of heaven, and eventually reunite the sparks . ..."[15] *It actually describes, in part, ancient Gnosticism—long before the Gautama Buddha lived!*

So what? Living in Nepal and India, would Buddha have known about the Gnostics of the Mediterranean North Shore? Easily! Gnostics, Jews, Zoroastrians, and Nestorians were among travelers on the Old Spice Road and its environs branching into India's sub-continent. Research by Calcutta University's Dept. of History posits that Buddha's near ancestors may have travelled the Old Spice Road widely, having access to the world's learning and superstitions.

---

13. Liberal theologians cite the Apostle Paul's reference to the Athenians' and Corinthians' idol worship (Acts 17, 1 Corinthians 8). However, Paul accompanied those references with condemnation of idolatry and with a clear presentation of Jesus Christ, the only Way of Salvation.
14. For "Peoples of the Buddhist World," see www.gmi.org/buddhist.
15. Jeremy Lott, *Books and Culture*, November/December 2002, p. 36, defining early Gnosticism.

Beyond tracing the views of Buddha, many of Buddhism's adherents as well as liberal Christians strain to link Buddha (b. 563 BC) and Jesus Christ with each other in teaching—though such scholars admit that Buddha and Jesus had widely differing views on the nature of man, God, and salvation. On an island in Vietnam's Mekong Delta, near a Buddhist monastery, stand gigantic statues of Buddha and Jesus, arms around each other. Anecdotes have arisen about Buddha, attributing miraculous conception and birth, and calling him "God of Gods."

Marcus Borg, a liberal Christian scholar, was convinced that Jesus and Buddha were earth's two "greatest holy beings," who taught their followers "the Way" of "enlightenment." In *Jesus and Buddha*[16] he collates some 200 purported "parallel sayings." However, many are contorted to seem "parallel." And since Jesus (as well as Gautama Buddha) was well informed about both current and ancient philosophies, in announcing "the Kingdom of God" he naturally couched his language in terms people understood,

> In some lands, a Buddhist background can affect the views of Christian converts. Steve Taylor, Evangelical Fellowship of Thailand, lists several skewed concepts: (1)God is detached, one of several powers, great but maybe not Lord; (2) he can be manipulated, requiring repayment for his favors and payment for one's mistakes. Taylor says theological schools should address these unbiblical views.[17]

But back to Buddhism itself. The Gautama broke from Hinduism's idolatry yet retained such core beliefs as *karma* and rebirth. For some time, Buddhists don't consider "self" a reality but a human delusion,[18] so their ultimate goal is "emptiness" (*maaya)*—"a final blessed state marked by the absence of desire or suffering." Life is *empty of meaning*, requiring *freedom from views.* Such "enlightenment" can be attained through meditation (*sankhya yoga*)—an import from Hinduism, which at first opposed Buddhism, even chopping off heads and arms of Buddhist statues.)

16. Marcus Borg, ed. Berkeley: Ulysses Press, 1997.
17. *Evangelical Missions Quarterly*, Vol. 37., No. 1, Jan. 2001. Wheaton: IL. p. 72.
18. An ancient concept on which Mary Baker Eddy based her 1879 Christian Science sect.

Buddhist "liberation" ultimately leads to annihilation, "suppressing all activity of body, mind, and will, that the self may attain liberation from them."[19] Some Buddhist sects employ the Hindu mystical sound of "aum" ("om") to promote this meditative state of mind. (Note explanation under "Hinduism.") Though "nihilism," even that label is unacceptable, being a position or view!

The counterpart of evolution's attempt to explain spiritual experience as chemical activity,[20] Buddhism perfectly matches the basic traits of *self-transcendence*. Hamer (cited above) lists those as (1) *self-forgetfulness* (ability to become entirely lost in an experience); (2) *transpersonal identification* (feeling connected to a larger universe); and (3) *mysticism* (openness to things not literally provable). We can identify these in so-called "spiritual" experiences (including drug-induced ones), but they do not describe the salvation and worship of Jesus Christ experienced by evangelicals. As the Apostle Paul noted, "[God] has also set eternity in the hearts of men, yet they cannot fathom what God has done from beginning to end" (Eccl. 3.11).

JUDAISM: By the time of Abraham, whose family lived between the Euphrates and the Tigris Rivers, society had degenerated into almost total paganism. Abraham grew up in a society that sought to placate evil spirits and earn salvation by good deeds. God's covenant with Abraham, from which Judaism developed, was God's corrective of the idolatry of Abraham's culture. Abraham was not to follow that departure from the truth. (While testing Abraham's obedience, the *aborted* offering up of Isaac not only rebuked the human sacrifices of the culture Abraham had left, but also pointed to the vicarious sacrifice of the Eternal Son, Jesus Christ.)

The devout lives of those who embraced the Abrahamic covenant and later followed the Law of Moses attested to their faith in the living God. God instituted the Ten Commandments through Moses as an antidote to the pagan worship from which his people had just escaped.

---

19. Miriam-Webster's dictionary (11th edition).
20. Reference to DNA in opening paragraph of this Appendix.

The law was not intended to be a way of salivation, but rather to lead mankind to repentance and to "the faith of Abraham" (Galatians 3.9). The "Patriarchs," psalmists, and prophets were only a few whose names have come to us in the annals of Jewish history. But the followers of the God of Abraham, Jacob, and Isaac (Jewish and Gentile) are countless.

Regrettably, the penchant of man to try to earn his own salvation through self-effort infected the Jewish faith, culminating in ritualistic Judaism. Notable in certain Orthodox Jewish circles is belief in the sacredness of phylacteries worn on the head and fringes on the garments, as well as the merits of kissing the *Me'zuzah* markings on the house doorpost.[21]

As Jesus later told the Pharisees and scribes, "You invalidate the Word of God by your tradition that you have handed down" (Mark 7.13). The Apostle Paul (Rabbi Saul), himself fully learned in the Jewish Law, reminded his Jewish parish that the Law, which held its followers "prisoners," was not given to "impart life," but to "press" us to Christ as the fulfillment of the Law, "that we might be justified by *faith*" (Galatians 3.21-25).

GNOSTICISM: So-called "Wisdom" (Knowledge[22]) sects have existed for millennia, turning up in different forms. Gnostics taught that esoteric knowledge—revealed only to cult leaders or their initiates—was essential to enter the after-life. One group believed that the Jewish Jehovah God was evil, and that he created an evil world.

The Apostle Paul warned the early Christians of the Greco-Roman world against following "a different gospel—which is no gospel at all" (Galatians 1.6,7) but was based on "wisdom"—referring to the esoteric wisdom of Gnosticism. The Nag Hammadi "Gnostic gospels," remnants of which have been discovered recently in North Africa, were a collection of purported sayings (rather than the contextual narrative style of Matthew, Mark, Luke, John). Traces of their teaching can be found in Islam and other religions.

---

21. S.B. Rohold, *Jewish Life and Longing*. London: Pickering and Inglis, c. 1924.

22. *Gnosis*: Greek, "knowledge."

CHRISTIANITY: See Appendix G. This also refers to Christendom (mentioned below under "An Ecumenical Chimera") as institutional religion related to (but distinct from) Christian faith.

ISLAM: See Appendix H. Although arising in Asia, Islam is treated separately in this overview as a major religion that requires separate analysis.

SIKHISM:[23] Indian Guru Nanak founded this monotheism about A.D. 1500. It contains traces from Judaism, Buddhism, Christendom, and Islam, rejecting idolatry and caste. However, it retains strong superstitions, from its Hindu background. Males wear a turban containing a wooden comb, and a small metal dagger in their belts—these days a miniature one, as a symbol of resistance, although earlier it was for protection from fierce persecution. Generally peace loving, Sikhs work in high-security areas (*e.g.* airports in Western lands), and have been among Britain's most loyal battalions.

SECULARISM/HUMANISM: Darwinism and Buddhism share the same philosophy—that there is no God (that is, no supreme being); mankind achieves his own "salvation" (*i.e.* betterment) through his own self-effort. However, while Buddhism believes in a cycle of births after death, secular Darwinism believes that death ends all for each individual. The only meaning in life is to achieve one's goals in the pursuit of happiness.

Secularists, particularly in Europe in the 18th to 20th centuries, sought to "reform" the errors of Christendom. Many intellectuals saw only the excesses of a Christendom that amounted to superstition and oppression—not the release from spiritual and intellectual bondage that the Holy Spirit could bring. During the same era, dubbed "The Age of Reason," there were outstanding scientists who did in fact trust in Christ as Saviour and Lord, and who used their release from the Medieval Church's superstitions to pursue scientific research. But for other intellectuals who became agnostics and atheists, man's progress could be secured only by "rational" science that did not accept God as Creator, let alone Redeemer.

23. *Sikh*: Hindi, Urdu "disciple."

This reaction to Christendom replaced God (who was seen as a mythical being) with man himself. "God was dead," philosophers such as Diderot and Nietzsche decided. Hermann Hesse (1877-1962), son of a German Lutheran pastor, became enamoured with Eastern thought and Karl Jung's psychoanalysis. His novel, *Siddhartha,* later made into a sensuous film in India, widely influenced German and Indian intellectuals and students with its romanticized, idealistic portrayal of Buddhism. It included instruction in achieving "enlightenment." Awarded the Nobel Prize for Literature in 1946, Hesse became something of a cult figure.[24]

Recently, *The End of Faith: Religion, Terror, and the Future of Reason*[25] by philosopher Sam Harris dismisses Christianity (and all religion) but endorses Buddhist "spirituality." Global best seller, *A New Earth—Awakening to Your Life's Purpose,* by German "spiritual teacher" Eckhart Tolle, follows the same confused path. Full cycle: Asia-Europe-Asia. As history attests, this sequence led away from spiritual reformation and redemption to secular revolution.

Some systems of religion ultimately end in solipsism and nihilism ("self" is the only reality in this world—the only "god"—but since self is meaningless, it ends in nothingness). That being the case, to correct problems on this earth, even if they are only apparent, violence is quite legitimate. An example of this appeared in a 19th c. Russian party named "The Nihilists," renowned for assassination and terrorism.

An Ecumenical Chimera

Religions have been fracturing Asia, a prime example being the political Partition of Pakistan (majority Islamic) and India (majority Hindu). Yet all religions share some common values—if not the existence of God, at least certain moral standards. Ecumenists, many of them good souls rightly concerned about sectarian divisiveness, share a vision of creating peaceful harmony among all religions. Couldn't Christians find bridges of understanding—even common truths among all religions? For instance,

---

24. Hesse could just as well have re-printed the popular 2nd c. Gnostic heresy of Valentinus, who combined elements of mythology, Eastern mysticism, Hellenism, Platonic dualism, and Christianity. Only a few devotees would attain to *Pleroma*—ultimate fullness of divine life. It was essentially Buddhism!

Judaism worshipped Jehovah as the one and only God. Muslims recognized the sovereignty of the one God, the historical person of Jesus, and the importance of the Bible as a holy book. Early Aryan/Hindu scriptures spoke of the sacrifice of the perfect Man as the way of salvation, and Buddhism taught moral values akin to Christianity—indeed Jesus fit their concept of the ideal man. What more could one ask for?

Christendom

Liberal theologians—often kind-hearted, compassionate souls—had already disavowed the uniqueness of Christ as too bigoted and exclusive to be worthy of the love of God for a pluralistic world. The Bible was great literature, even as were the *Qur'an* and *Upanishads,* but please don't claim biblical Scripture to be the *inerrant* Word of God! That's an archaic view, they implied. Liberalism grasped at the hope of a world religion. If every faith contained commendable values, every religion could indicate a way to God.

To theologically liberal-leaning Christians, this was what Jesus meant in his prayer, "that they all might be one." Several errant Anglican (Episcopalian) priests accept both Christianity and Islam as "Abrahamic faiths." South Asia, with its eclectic Hinduism, seemed to promise true Ecumenism. Liberal theologians published harmonies on dialogue and reconciliation. Professors wrote books on comparative religions.[26] A Hindu scholar, Raja Ram Mohan Roy, an early convert to Unitarianism, translated the gospels into Hindi, omitting doctrines and miracles that non-Christians wouldn't understand or accept. He crafted a "universal theology" acceptable to nominal Christianity ("Christendom") and Hinduism.[27]

That strengthened universalism ("all mankind will be saved, in this life or the next"), which bounced back to India with liberal missionaries in following decades. Some churches expunged mention of sin, the Virgin

---

25. Free Press, 2005. In *The End of Religion*, Bruxy Cavey rebuts Harris' distortion of Christian faith, explaining futility of "religion" vs. effectiveness of Christ's life in a believer. (See Bibliography.)
26. See Bibliography.
27. Alvin Austin, in *Evangelical Studies Bulletin.* Wheaton: ISAE, Spring 1997.

Birth, Christ's cleansing blood, and the Resurrection from their hymns and Sunday school materials. Hinduism's plethora of beliefs and gods had references to morals, judgment, and eternal reward that liberal theologians could relate to a "sanitized" universalism.

Unfortunately many did not understand true Christian unity, based on the uniqueness of Christ's deity.[28] Although they may have recognized that history contained God's "redemptive analogies," they mistook religious systems for ways of salvation. In fact, they kept the husks of Christian tradition, but lost its kernel of spiritual life. The Apostle Paul describes such as "having a form of godliness but denying its power." Liberal theology is a comforting, tolerant view, but a tragic chimera. The test of any spiritual system is not whether it meets man's earthly aspirations

The Unique Mediator

All religions have sought "mediators" to help them in this life and the next. Pagan "witch doctors," Buddhist Bodhisattvas, Hindu Babas, Jewish Patriarchs, and Roman Catholic saints were supposedly able to do that. But biblical Scripture tells us "there is one God, and one mediator between God and man – the man Christ Jesus."[29] He is the unique Mediator, because, although he is God, he gave himself for the sake of his fallen creation. He not only redeemed believers but also gave them his Holy Spirit to be more than religious—to live *regenerated* lives upon this troubled earth. While other religions have indeed influenced Christendom, it is interesting to realize that the emergence of the Christian faith influenced Asia's religions to "restructure and redefine their beliefs, often borrowing Christian techniques and worship styles."[30]

****

Asia not only has given rise to the world's major forms of religion but also to many of their variations. — *W. Harold Fuller*

---

28. Ian Hay helpfully studies this question in *Unity and Purity*. Toronto: SIM International, 1983
29. I Timothy 2:5
30. *Books & Culture*, Sept.-Oct. 2006.

Appendix G

Christianity vs. Christendom

[Although Appendix F: Religions refers to Christianity, we give more analysis and commentary in this separate file, because the topic has so many ramifications today.]

CHRISTIANITY is not the same as *Christendom* (see Appendix F - Religions)—at least, not in my book! *Christianity* rests upon salvation by *faith alone* in Jesus Christ as Saviour. *Christendom* practices many different rituals—some of precious significance helpful to worship–but in themselves none providing the spiritual regeneration every sinner needs. In discussion with a learned Pharisee, Jesus Christ aptly portrayed spiritual regeneration as being "born again." This, Jesus explained, was not achieved by religious dogma or ritual, nor by physical birth or human effort, but by the Holy Spirit's spiritual regeneration (John 3:1-18).

People who receive Christ's redemption by faith may also practice certain rites for purposes of identifying with their Saviour (water baptism) or remembering his death (Communion service), but not in order to earn salvation or divine grace. In this sense, therefore, our discussion does not include Christianity as a "religion" (in keeping with the definition of "religion" as a system).

By that same definition of "religion," although *Christendom* includes worship of Jesus Christ, it often has become a system dependent upon ritual as a means of receiving divine grace, including salvation. But it also connotes political power—something Christ's disciples never experienced. That happened after Emperor Constantine believed the sign of the Cross enabled him to win in battle. The Edict of Milan (313) gave Christianity legal status, but it soon led to acceptance of the state church as the religious voice of "the Holy Roman Empire." The Church of Rome retained ("baptized?") the religious trappings of Rome's pagan era, including its "holy days," vestments, icons, temples, and its political capital. These all were remnants of religions and philosophies the empire had absorbed—from animism and idolatry to Gnosticism. The latter grew out of Greco sects that AD added so-called "Christianity" to their pantheon in the first century.[1]

It was a paradigm shift for a previously banned "sect," suddenly catapulted to power and prestige. "Power corrupts," and for those who succumbed to its temptations, "The Church" changed from a marginalized body commissioned by Jesus to look outwards. Instead it became a politically-empowered organization that looked inwards, intent on preserving the *status quo* and enhancing its own aggrandizement. During a visit to Rome, I viewed the remarkable contrast between Christendom and Christianity. In St. Peter's Cathedral, massive pillars and gold ornamentation framed the high altar, before which devout pilgrims bowed and made the sign of Christ's cross. At appointed times, a priest recited a "Christianized" mantra, burning incense before the altar and wafting it over kneeling supplicants.

If I found "Christendom" above Rome's cobble-stone surface impressive, what I found in the Catacombs underground filled me with awe. Threading my way along tunnels burrowed in the stone and clay, I pictured early Christians taking refuge there. Flickering clay oil lamps lit the dank burial niches where they met to worship "the Light of the world." Their faith could mean their death in the Arena, yet for them it meant eternal life. What a heritage we have, I mused!

Early followers of Jesus weren't used to pomp and ceremony; the Apostle Paul referred to them and himself as "the off-scouring of the earth." They didn't even call themselves "Christians"; their critics used that term to label them (Acts 11.26), probably in derision.

In contrast to politicized Christendom, evangelicals have never had a Pope. They appeal directly to Christ, who the Bible states is Head of the Church. Usually, individual "congregationalist" churches administer

---

1. See N. T. Wright, *Judas and the Gospel of Jesus.* (We can give thanks that in some quarters, Roman Catholicism has itself experienced reform, and now includes an evangelical element. –WHF)

discipline through their own congregations, ministers, and theologians. Denominations appeal to the council or presiding officer of their respective association.

Liberty vs. Legislation

It is difficult for adherents of legislated religion (such as non-evangelical Christendom, Judaism, or Islam) to understand a Christian's "liberty in the Spirit." Accustomed to ritual observances to win religious acceptance, legalists equate Christianity's spiritual life with promiscuity—and all too often the loose living of some professing Christians verifies that supposition. Muslims, for instance, may categorize Christians as profligate sinners because of the unrestricted environment in which they live. Non-Christians do not understand how a "born-again" Christian can live a moral life surrounded by an immoral society. Jesus explained that God intentionally leaves a Christian to continue living "a light shining in darkness" of such an environment—a witness to the redeeming power of their Lord.

The Apostle Paul stated: "The letter [legalism] kills, but the spirit gives life." He also warned: "Do not use your freedom [from the ritualistic regulations of the Jewish Law] to indulge the sinful nature. . . . Live by the Spirit and you will not gratify the desires of the sinful nature" (Galatians 5.13,14). Lest a person use "liberty" as an excuse for continuing in sin, Paul further instructed converts to examine themselves to make sure they were living the faith they professed (2 Cor. 13.5). The Christian faith is not vested in a building, an icon, a mantra, or a legislated moral code. It is an *incarnation*—the Spirit of Christ living within a person, transforming human frailty "into the likeness of Christ." Christianity is not a religion making God like ourselves—that is, formulating a god according to *our* concept of what a divine being should be. Rather, it is God making us *in his image.*

In other words, God's Holy Spirit at work within a person is more powerful than legislated external prohibitions. Although religious restrictions are commendable, in the end they do not assure conformity. Adherents find ways of bypassing the restrictions. God seeks to transform a person spiritually rather than simply making him conform to religious ritual (Romans 12. 1,2). That is the meaning behind being "born from above."

Christianity and Christendom Are Different?[2]

Critics of Christianity often confuse it with Christendom. They do not realize the distinction and equate all Christianity with the bigotry and political expressions of Christendom, including its excesses (*e.g.* the Medieval Crusades—which sought to gain followers and territory by force).

Frank Laubach (1884-1970), often labeled "the Apostle of Literacy," was one who understood the stark difference between Christendom and Christianity. As a missionary among the Islamic Moro people in the Philippines (see cha. 16) early in his ministry, he soon realized the need to disassociate the gospel message from the "Christendom" that Spanish forces had imposed—a religion of cruel suppression in the name of "The Church." Laubach wrote: *"If we can untangle Christ from the terrible handicap of Christendom, which has kept so many millions from him, we will be doing the Moros a priceless service."*[3]

Critics write books that cite violence and wars fomented by religions.[4] Secular critics forecast the end of religion as science explains life. Genius (and paraplegic) Stephen Hawking, outstanding scientist of the 20th c., sees no use for religion as he explains the origin and sustenance of life. He places the Christian faith in the same category as all religious superstition.

While on the one hand secularists decry "religion," many people are espousing "spirituality"—the current "in word." But it has a dangerous sequence, so well outlined by N. T. Wright: "First, a 'quest for the divine,' which turns out to be the quest for self-discovery, leading to a religiously

---

2. For one treatment of this divergence, see Alan Kreider in *Speaking About What We Have Seen and Heard*, chapter 2, "The Early Church and the Christendom Shift." Jonathan Bonk *et al*, eds. (Bibliog.)
3. Frank C. Laubach, *Thirty Years with the Silent Billions.* Manila: Laubach Literacy, 1960., p.38.
4. Very true. Of course, secular philosophy (such as Communism, Nazism, and Saddam Hussein's secular regime in Iraq) has also caused violence and war. Unfortunately, violence is a human vice, showing up in sectarian enmity. Bruxy Cavey in *The End of Religion* (see Bibliography) cites a news report of recent Hindu-Muslim violence that equals any Crusade atrocity.

propagated existentialism in which "discovering who I am," as the primal obligation, leads to the secondary obligation of "being true to who I am"—even if that means being false to all sorts of other things."[5]

What critics of Christianity do not understand is the transforming work of the Holy Spirit, already mentioned. They can point to many examples of failure by Christian leaders and quasi-superstitious rituals of churches, but they also equate Christianity with the outward trappings of what masquerades as Christianity. They have never experienced the transforming power of the Holy Spirit, which can turn a sinner into a disciple of Christ.

But, you may protest, we know Christians who are as bad as anyone—greedy, corrupt, proud, deceitful, immoral! Moreover, they seem to spend more time quarrelling among themselves than bearing witness to the Holy Spirit's unity.

All this is sadly true. A disgraceful example has been Christendom's continuing turf wars over "the Holy City" of Jerusalem. Greek Orthodox, Roman Catholic, Armenian, Coptic, Syrian, and Ethiopian Orthodox monks have long fought over "rights" to sacred sites—while Muslim neighbors watch with some bemusement. (Actually, Turkish Ottoman rule protected the sacred sites from disrepair more than some of Christendom's fiefs have done.)[6]

Islam and even some Christians continue to cite the so-called "Christian Crusades" as another example of arrogance on the part of the Church. "Crusaders" were not following the teaching of Jesus, who told his disciple Peter to "put up the sword."[7]

On the personal level, regrettably there are faithful church members who claim to be evangelicals, —yet they do not evidence holy living. Whether their belief is real enough to have received the promise of

---

5. N. T. Wright, *Judas and the Gospel of Jesus,* p. 129. Grand Rapids: Baker Books, 2006.
6. *Books & Culture* March/April 2009 review of Raymond Cohen, *How Christians Came Together to Rescue Their Holiest Shrine.* Oxford University Press, 2008.
7. Cited by pacifists who refuse to serve in armed forces. However, the Lord's instruction had nothing to do with fulfilling one's duty to serve his country, which is only rendering to Caesar that which is Caesar's.

redemption or not, only God knows. Is it head knowledge, a mental acquiescence? One thing is clear, the Holy Spirit does not control their lives. Jesus told his disciples how to discern true believers: "By their fruit you shall know them." Scripture tells us that "the fruit of the Spirit is love, joy, peace ... " (Galatians 5.22). Christians not living in right relationship with God do not evidence that fruit.

Medieval Christians reacted to a depraved world by isolating themselves in monasteries and convents. But stone walls could not keep out sinful nature. Evangelicals know they should live in this world as living witnesses to God's power over sin. Instead of cloistering themselves, God calls them to dwell in a sinful world without being part of its sins. In earth's show-case, they are citizens of Heaven. And therein lies a danger—that a disciple of Jesus can become so "heavenly minded that he is of no earthly good" (as someone has put it). But embracing salvation personally (as has to happen in the transaction of regeneration) must not end up as a kind of monasticism—withdrawing from one's society. Jesus told his disciples, as he still tells us, that the spiritually regenerate disciple must be "salt and light" in the present world.

How Can This Happen?

Yet, as we realize our human frailties, our plight can be as real as that of the Roman jailor who pleaded, "How then can I be saved?" *How then can we become Spirit-filled? It seems impossible!* It *is* impossible for human nature to achieve—only the Holy Spirit can bring us to the end of our self-striving and make us Christ-like. For many, it may take a cathartic experience to make us abandon our self-righteousness and accept the victorious spiritual life only the Holy Spirit gives.

After all, Christianity is *Christ in us, the hope of glory.* That's what critics of Christianity do not understand. They look for a formula, a do-it-yourself religion. Instead, we can receive salvation and spiritual life only through a personal meeting with God, through Christ's Holy Spirit. Salvation is an internal transformation, not an external conformity to any formula. Each man and woman and child has to meet with the Spirit of God in repentance and faith.

And how shall we know when we have done that? Again, there is no formula. It is not *religion*; it is a life—*Christ's life living in us.* If we stray, the Word of God will convict us of sin and unrighteousness, bringing us back into living relationship with God. Then the inner witness of the Holy Spirit gives us peace.

Jesus used a significant term in talking with Nicodemus, the religious lawyer who met with him in secret: "You must be born again!" This religious man, who had sought to keep the Law of Moses and live a life pleasing to God, asked with some incredulity, "Master, how can that be?" Typical of human reasoning, he thought in terms of *doing* something, such as being physically re-born—obviously impossible. Jesus explained that in contrast to physical birth, spiritual re-birth (that which connects us with the Spirit of God) does not come from human effort but from "above"—from the Spirit of God.

That is what sets true Christianity apart from religion: not a system, formula, human effort, but the Holy Spirit regenerating us, bringing us back into personal relationship with God. Those who have not experienced this will never understand it, for only the Holy Spirit can make it happen.

"Other Gospels"

While many today have rediscovered the meaning of the Cross of Christ, wily Satan has twisted its symbolism to mean (in the eyes of "oriental religions") western culture—even though Christianity came out of Asia. Since Judaism, Hinduism, Buddhism, and Islam all infuse their societies with their own religious morals, their followers assume that Christianity does the same (as indeed "Christendom" has done). Therefore, to many non-Christians, Christianity represents individualism (neglect of family), immoral promiscuity, and drunkenness. Non-Christians do not discern the difference between Christianity and Christendom, so genuine Christian witness comes up against roadblocks.

Christendom: As a man-made religious system, Christendom refers to biblical Scripture, but not as its sole authority. Even Scripture is subjected to some church edict. Christendom includes sects that follow human philosophy—whatever fits the needs or superstitions of any group. Most distortions subtly change living faith to a religious system, but there are also radical distortions that seem hard to believe! For instance, a quasi-Christian Nestorian sect, the Yezidis of Iraq (numbering some 2,000) has recently turned up in a refugee camp. They worship Lucifer, whom, they believe God has forgiven. He now runs earthly affairs as "the Peacock God."[8] In turn, this distortion has roots in an ancient branch of Gnosticism.

Unlike evangelical Christianity, some forms of Christendom validate "sainthood" (bestowed by the Vatican on those who have performed a miracle). Devotees pray to saints for health or success in this life, and for souls of the dead. In essence, a saint takes the place of Mahayana Buddhism's *Bodhisattvas*—good souls who delay their entry to *Nirvana* in order to help humans on earth. Orthodox Catholicism is also similar to other religions as systems of good works: good deeds must outweigh bad deeds, or else be expurgated in the fires of Hell. (In such a view, prayers, deeds, and gifts to the church by other people can hasten their release from purgatory.)

While there are fine evangelical Roman Catholics who trust in Jesus Christ as the one and only mediator between God and man, the RC church as a whole represents Christendom—a politicized hierarchical system. As such, its diplomacy embraces other religions in a syncretistic way.

One example is RC's official view of Islam: *Lumen Gentium*, a major Vatican II document states: ". . . the plan of salvation also includes those who acknowledge the Creator. In the first place amongst these there are the Mohamedans [*sic*], who, professing to hold the faith of Abraham, along with us adore the one and merciful God, who on the last day will judge mankind."

Unlikely as it might seem, Christendom includes those who accept the Hindu concept of sex (described in Appendix F). A prominent Canadian author, clergyman of a major denomination, stated in a TV series: "In sexual intercourse there is a losing of oneself, a taking up of oneself into the other and into a third something—into God himself ... a way of knowing God."[9]

8. Books and Culture, May/June 2002, p. 34
9. *Harpur vs. Hancock*, Hantsport: Lancelot Press, 1994, p. 157.

Ecumenism: Divisions within the churches and their constant wrangling disturb good-hearted Christians, who long for unity. They cite Christ's prayer for believers, that "they might be one." Undeniably, among Christians there are "fighting fundamentalists" who enjoy a good theological scrap. They exhibit an almost pharisaic penchant for "jots and titles," forgetting the role of the Holy Spirit who brings harmony regardless of differences (such as attitudes to women).

However, while evangelicals decry division based on sectarianism, they adhere to the essentials of biblical truth (e.g., salvation only through faith in Jesus Christ). Recently evangelical Anglicans published *Anglican Essentials*[10] in order to spell out doctrines they saw as the essence of their Christian faith. Similarly, following "Higher Criticism" at the turn of the 20th c. (which trashed biblical teaching), evangelicals in the major denominations met to state the basics (or "fundamentals") of the Christian message. Two diverse reactions followed: (1) certain simplistic groups used these as a basis for a zealous literalism[11]; (2) liberal critics coined the disparaging term, "fundamentalism." However, World Evangelical Alliance more recently reiterated basic Christian beliefs.[12]

Some ecumenists believer that Christianity is only one way to God, and that all other religions lead to heaven. They ask, "Would a loving God limit salvation to acceptance of the Christian gospel? How about those who have never heard of Jesus Christ? Important question. However, one thing we do know is that, as Peter told his erstwhile jailers, "Salvation is found in no one else, for there is no other name . . . by which we must be saved."

Yet, some may wonder how the Old Testament (written before the incarnation of Jesus) gives many examples of people finding faith in the eternal God's salvation. Noah and Abraham were outstanding instances. They didn't expect their sacrifices to "earn" them salvation. Rather, their "burnt offerings" expressed their repentance and their faith in Jehovah

---

10. G. Egerton, *Anglican Essentials—Reclaiming Faith Within the Anglican Church of Canada* (Biblio.).

11. Even though these agreed with the basics of faith, the Apostle Paul's phrase, "zeal without knowledge" seems applicable (Rom. 20.2).

12. W. Harold Fuller, *People of the Mandate*, 181 (App. C). Carlisle: Cumbria/Baker: Grand Rapids, 1996.

God's forgiveness. Those "believers" did not trust in the names of the many pagan gods of their cultures.

Old Testament sacrifices also presaged the sinless Son of God's death for our sins "in the fullness of time." Yet because God is timeless, Christ's sacrifice was a reality before the "foundation of the world." In every era, the Spirit of God has been at work, bringing men and women to the knowledge of eternal life. It is the Holy Spirit, Jesus explained, who convicts "the world of guilt in regard to sin and righteousness and judgment."[13]

Neo-liberalism: This current hybrid of liberal theology now parades in the garb of "progressive evangelicalism." It professes to follow Jesus, but not Christ—too "Christian"(!). Abandoning Marxist idealism, according to Peter Jones of Christian Witness to a Pagan Planet, neo-liberalism is now "spiritually progressive, combining evolutionary theory, geo-politics, medieval mysticism (The Cloud of Unknowing) and ancient Gnosticism (The Gospel of Thomas)" (*www.cwipp.org*).

In their pursuit of love for everyone (which we should all espouse—but from a foundation of truth), ecumenists can be very inclusive in their theology. After all, Jews, Christians, and Muslims all trace their roots back to Abraham! Recently in India, one denomination opened its synod with ecumenical prayers in the names of the Hindu god Shiva, Gautama Buddha, Islam's Allah, and Jesus Christ. No doubt the synod felt a cozy sense of brotherhood and pious tolerance.

"Falling Away"

The Apostle Paul warned against "falling away" from the truth of the gospel. In past decades, a popular form of Christianity has swelled certain churches. Yet major apostasy may be in the making, as increasing government restrictions in the West could cause social persecution and cause many shallow followers to desert their churches.

But why do the children from godly families desert their parents' faith, some becoming antagonistic? There could be a number of causes. However, one can result from harsh attitudes of the earlier generation.

13. Scripture basis for this and previous paragraph: Rom. 1.16-32; 3.9-26; Gal. 4.4; 1 Peter 1.20; Heb. 11.

In some cases, the children of ardent evangelicals may react to the single-mindedness of parents. For instance, a new Christian may react so strongly against his former godless living, that he presses his personal faith upon his children in a radical way. The parent (let us call him Generation A) feels he is acting in the spiritual interests of his own children, but they (Generation B), raised in the new spiritual environment, may not appreciate their parent's ardency. Generation B has not known the godless life from which their parents have been so radically converted. They naturally feel that "the world" around them is attractive, not the den of evil depicted by parents. Therefore, parents' ardent faith may come across as intolerant of others. Wanting to be tolerant, Generation B may still retain a personal faith in Christ's salvation, but not with the conviction of their parents. For the grandchildren (Generation C), regeneration may become simply "spirituality"—a vague catchall that could include everything from liberal theology to Buddhism.

Tolerance is a virtue, but if it is not based on solid conviction of Christian teaching, it can soon become compromise and even *acceptance* of non-Christian views. Therefore Generation B may be permissive in spiritual matters when raising their own children (Generation C): "We'll let our children decide what they want to believe." In contrast to coercion, that of course is to be commended. However, it may become Utopian—believing that truth will always triumph. Without clear biblical teaching on spiritual issues, Generation C can be misled by "the heart, which is deceitful above all things."

And so, as Generation B seeks to correct the seeming intolerance of their parents' zeal, it may neglect to lead Generation C to find salvation itself. While shedding the outer shell of intolerance, Generation B may not pass on the kernel of the Gospel.

Why Persecution?

Throughout history, various minority groups have been persecuted for different reasons—religious, ethnic, cultural, commercial, political, land ownership, etc. Jews are one group that has suffered everything from mild ostracism to violent pogroms. Civilization opposes extremists in any religion, decrying violent acts of customs that deny human rights and are counterproductive or even harmful to devotees. Hindu customs of widow burning and female infanticide come to mind as examples. However, while western society opposes such customs, it is tolerant towards those who choose the Hindu belief system in its benign aspects.

But while the social projects of Christians (such as famine relief or anti-AIDS programs) win plaudits, Christianity as an evangelical faith often evokes resistance and even hatred. That hatred is remarkably universal—on the part of secularism and religions. This should not come as a surprise, for Jesus himself stated that "the world" hated him "without a cause." (Indeed, his life on earth was sinless, marked by doing good and speaking such truth that even his enemies said, "Never man spoke like this man.") He also told his disciples, "All men will hate you because of me."[14] In referring to them while praying to God the Father, Jesus said:

> "I have given them your word and the world has hated them, for they are not of the world any more than I am of the world. . . . As you have sent me into the world, you have sent them into the world. . . . I pray also for those who will believe in me through their message." (John 17. 14-20.)

Why should Christians suffer persecution? Satan, who masterminded the seduction of God's creation, sees to it that followers of the living God face animosity and persecution.

> *"They will treat you this way because of my name, for they do not know the One who sent me," Jesus told those who followed him. "The time will come when those who kill you will think they do God a favour." (John 15.21; 16.2.)*

Christendom often accuses evangelical Christians of evangelizing—*of all things(!)*. One reason is that the gospel, while being "Good News" (meaning of the word), involves conviction of sin and repentance. That riles people who prefer a "feel-good" religion. Most people prefer to be left undisturbed in their traditional religion, and resent anyone who presents an alternative. Islam in particular regards Christians as infidels worthy of death. But **Ramon Llull** (1235-1315), missionary to Muslims and martyr

14. Luke 26.17.

for Christ, stated, "Death has no terrors for a sincere servant of Christ who is laboring to bring souls to a knowledge of the truth."

Jesus commissioned his disciples to "go into all the world and preach the gospel." That command actually builds on God's call to Abraham, "the Father of Faith." Abraham's descendants trace his posterity to the Incarnation of Jesus Christ and to all his spiritual children (Galatians 3.6-9).[15]

*****

THE EVANGELICAL FAITH sums up the relationship that reconnects lost humanity to the Eternal God—changing us from being "dead to sin" to being "alive to God in Christ Jesus."[16] *As the Apostle Paul, a learned rabbi formerly depending on religious rites for acceptance with God, put it: "I no longer live, but Christ lives in me. The life I now live in the body, I live by faith in the Son of God, who loved me and gave himself for me."*[17] —WHF

15. Islam re Sonship of Jesus Christ, see Kenneth Cragg, *The Qur'an and the West*, p. 146 (Bibliography).
16. Romans 6.11.
17. Galatians 2.20.

Appendix H

Islam — "Submission to the Will of Allah"

ORTHODOX ISLAM believes that everyone is born a Muslim, but that many become "infidel" through others' influence. Accordingly, in the Final Judgment, everyone will again become Muslim or be eternally damned. To persuade unbelievers (by use of any means) to turn to Islam does them a favor, fulfilling Allah's will. How did this develop?

MUHAMMAD IBN ABDULLAH (570-632), founder of Islam, was born into one of the many aristocratic merchant families of the city of Mecca, Arabia.[1] At the time, Arabs were riven by many clans and tribes. Their main occupation was nomadic—sheep and camel herding. However, as experts in desert living, many were skillful camel drivers, employed by the wealthy camel-train owners of the Middle East and its surrounding nations. These transported spices, perfumes, diamonds, and silk along that section of the Old Spice Road (sometimes called the Silk Road).

Muhammad's father died before his birth, and his mother died when he was only six, leaving him without the benefit of being raised by his own parents. After a few years as a shepherd, the young Muhammad attached himself to several of the traders' caravans, first as an assistant and then a capable camel-train driver employed by Bibi Khadijah,

1. Contrary to tradition that Mohammed was an illiterate nomad—a view used to support Islam's basic claim that Angel Gabriel must have transmitted the *Qur'an* directly "because Mohammed was illiterate."

wealthy widow of Ubaidullah, an Arab who had converted to Ethiopian Orthodox Christianity while taking refuge in Ethiopia.[2] Even though the widow was almost twice Muhammad's age, eventually the two fell in love and married. This placed Muhammad at the center of the widow's expanding trade empire—traversing the busy camel routes between the Yemen, through Mecca, Gaza, Jerusalem, and northwards to Damascus.

Mecca was the Arab's center of animist religion, learning, politics, and commerce—a busy crossroads on the Old Spice Road. Through its bazaars passed merchants and goods from Africa, Europe, the Middle East, and the Far East—as well as followers of other religions. Although portrayed as a "pure religion," Islam reflects ancient Zoroastrian veneration of the elements and spirits, Hinduism's new moon (a part of Vishnu's headress) and Mecca's pagan *Ka'aba*. There are traces of Jewish monotheism and ritual, Greek and Roman philosophies, along with heretical teachings of Christian sects (including Nestorians, Copts, and Armenians).[3]

Islam also reflects early Gnostic dualism (leading to asceticism). It shows up in Muslim public prayers and rituals (such as Ramadan "fasting"—refraining from food during daytime, while feasting at night). The *Qur'an* is similar in style to the Nag Hammadi "Gnostic gospels" (remnants of which have only recently been discovered in North Africa)—a collection of sayings, rather than the narrative style of Matthew, Mark, Luke, and John. Muhammad lived before there was an Arabic translation of New Testament writings.

During the day, caravan travelers shared information and ideologies; after sundown, incantations and creeds mingled with the crackle of campfires. Arabs worshipped a multitude of gods—in fact, one for every

---

2. Abdiyah Akbar Abdul-Haqq, *Sharing Your Faith with a Muslim,* p. 14 (Bibliography).

3. Also reflected in earlier writings of other religions. Muhammad's maid was a Coptic Christian, who would know the Arab version of the Nativity of Jesus, which Muhammad incorporated in *The Qur'an*. (W. St. Clair-Tisdall, *The Sources of Islam,* Preface. *See* Bibliog.) Throughout the Arab world, in Rome's North African colonies and other lands, there were respected Christian communities. (Mecca Christians had their own cemetery.) Some were cultic, Gnostic, or legalistic; some accepted Jesus as a prophet but not as divine. Paul warned against teaching "a different gospel, which is really no gospel" (Gal. 1.7 NIV).

day of the year (Arabs counted 360 days in their year). But Muhammad had also had contact with *Hunafa* Arabs, a pre-Islamic group who traced their ancestry back to Abraham's Ishmael, and rebelled against Mecca's idolatry.

Gabriel Dictates the Qur'an

Muhammad often resorted to a cave north of Mecca,[4] where he pondered the disunity, corruption, and idolatry of his people. His brilliant mind tried to sort out a world of diverse religions. This "static" contrasted with the stillness of the desert, its relentless sun drenching each evening sky with the colors of an artist's masterpiece. At night, the vast canopy of the starry vault made him wonder about the Unseen—an omnipotent God? Later tradition has it that Muhammad thought he heard a voice telling him: "*There is only one God, and Muhammad is his only prophet.*"[5] It is said he identified the voice as that of the angel Gabriel, who continued appearing in visions, commanding him, "Recite."

With his animistic background, Muhammad feared he was possessed by desert *jinni* (spirits), but his wife assured him that he was indeed being called of God as a prophet. Therefore he believed that Gabriel gave him divine instructions, quoting from a golden tablet inscribed by the finger of God.[6] It is said that Muhammad's keen memory absorbed the instructions, and he repeated them to relatives and neighbors. His followers later compiled these recitations in the *Qur'an* (Arabic: "recitation"), which became Islam's most holy book.

---

4. Giving Muhammad contact with ascetics of other religions (Muir, Pref. in W. St. Clair-Tisdall, *ibid.*).
5. Although now Islam's essence, this is not included in Muhammad's original message (J. Miller, SIM).
6. Therefore the Qur'an is considered sacred only in its original Arabic characters. Tradition surrounding the *Qur'an* has shades of Moses receiving the Ten Commandments written by the "finger of God" and of the Apostle Paul receiving revelations. According to Orthodox Christian tradition (which Muhammad would have heard), God revealed the *Pentateuch* to Moses all at one time. As to Paul, his teachings were inspired, not dictated (as the *Qur'an* claims to be).
7. Some sources describe Warqa as an Arab convert to Judaism before becoming a (Coptic) Christian.

One of his wife's cousins, Warqa ibn Qusayy, was a Christian[7] who frequently related Bible stories and texts. Muhammad remembered many passages and knew about the Old Testament prophets and about Jesus. Warqa, impressed with the young man's opposition to idolatry, encouraged Muhammad to believe he was called to be a prophet.

Although Muslim traditions differ widely, the core of the *Qur'an's* teaching is very simple: complete submission (Arabic: "*islam*") to the one Supreme Being in everything. Thus there can be no division of religion from the secular, as is the case in much Western thinking.[8] According to Islam, its form of religion must control every aspect of life—including eating, entertainment, sex, and social, judicial, and political activity. One's daily life is ordered by decree—Islamic law, or *Shari'a*—not by inner moral discernment resulting from spiritual regeneration.[9]

While submission has come to mean fatalism among many Muslims, others oppose this interpretation, considering submission to God as discipleship rather than fatalism. Muslims exhibit genuine human emotion of sorrow in the face of suffering and death. On the other hand, as in other cultures, public grieving can become a social symbol—the more vehement, the greater the tribute to the memory of the deceased.

Accompanying complete submission to Allah, Islam considers five religious duties to be incumbent upon every Muslim (often referred to as The Five Pillars of Islam):

1. Profession of faith.
2. Prayer.
3. Fasting.
4. Almsgiving.
5. Pilgrimage.

---

8. In fact, most Westerners today insist upon the separation of religion and society ("church and state") as the only way to protect society from "religious bigotry." This is one reason Western Christendom and Islam have difficulty understanding each other or sharing in one democratic society.
9. *Shari'a* defines ordering of life, giving Arabs an external judicial system, even as Levitical Laws provided Israel with its judicial system. (Appendix G: *Christianity*, explains inner spiritual change.)

Jihad—Violent or Moderate Struggle?

Some Muslim theologians add *jihad.* That could mean either moral struggle or violent warfare. Moderates use earlier Qur'an passages to support the more benign "struggle" concept—which includes the personal spiritual struggle of the soul. Terrorists and their supporters refer to later passages that endorse violence: *Sura 8:12: "Allah shall cast terror into the hearts of the infidels. Strike off their heads, strike off the very tips of their fingers."* Sura 8.60 exhorts the faithful to *"strike terror into the enemies of Allah"*; Sura 9:5 commands: *"Slay the idolaters wherever you find them"*; Sura 9:123: *"Make war on the infidels who dwell around you. Deal firmly with them."* Muhammad commanded, *"Whoever changed his Islamic religion, then kill him"* (Bukhari, vol. 9, bk. 84, no. 57).

Tolerant societies may see only Islam's pietistic posturing—for instance, alms-giving, unpretentious white robes, and five daily prayer sessions, with worshippers bowing foreheads to the ground. But for many, the humble posturing may be only a meritorious exercise to earn the reward of Paradise; none of it changes the proud human heart. Tolerant societies may not realize the intolerance and pharisaic self-righteous ethos of Islam—even though Islam is not alone in that kind of religiosity.

Many Western commentators note that Muslims in several countries seem to be turning from violence to a moderate interpretation of *jihad*—moral "struggle." In order to encourage this, some countries have even allowed *Sharia*-governed communities, unaware of violence that may be preached in mosques. Robert Spencer, scholarly observer of Islam, sees the new Muslim tactic as response to strong Western reactions against violence. Instead, Islamists seek to infiltrate democracies and eventually gain dominance politically.[10]

At the same time, there are genuine non-violent moderates and reformers who need encouragement. These include prize-winning Sayed al-Quimani (Egyptian) and Abdullahi an-Na'im (Sudanese). *Jihadists* have threatened both with death for their liberal views.

---

10. Robert Spencer, *Stealth Jihad: How Radical Islam is Subverting America without Guns or Bombs.* New York: Regnery Publishing, 2009.

Western apologists should indeed defend moderate Muslims—and the author has several such Muslim friends. But apologists need to remember three basic tenets that shape Orthodox Islam:

1) Later passages in the *Qur'an* "abrogate" earlier ones.[11]
2) It is acceptable to lie to infidels (*i.e.* non-Muslims).
3) In the final analysis, everyone will become a Muslim, or face eternal damnation.

Of course, there is no such thing as monolithic Islam, and certain of the above views may not describe the Islam that Westerners know. However, in the absence of a global leader, the *Qur'an* and *Hadith* provide uniform orthodox teaching and control. Outside Arabia, local cultures add their own color to Islamic *practices*. As a sacred duty, Shi'as (predominant in Iran) add recognition of their *Great Imam* (or "Religious Teacher," missing since the 12[th]c. but momently expected to re-appear).

In 2008, the Iranian parliament approved the "Islamic Penal Code," whereby any woman who left Islam would be punished with life in prison and any man with execution. Nearly two hundred parliamentarians supported the bill, seven opposed it. The world's reaction, including that of the United Nations, to this contravention of international laws has been screamingly silent.

Iran is in fact merely attempting to institutionalize what is already reality in Egypt, Pakistan, Sudan, Saudi Arabia, and the Gulf states. Even in areas of the Islamic world where Christianity has traditionally been tolerated (such as Palestine and Iraq), conversion from Islam is still seen as socially and morally criminal—incurring the death penalty.

Under *Sharia* (Islamic law), a woman can ask for a divorce, but only the man can grant the request, and he can refuse, according to a book, *Sharia, Cruel and Usual Punishment*, by Egyptian-born American author Nonie Darwish. In addition to apostasy (leaving Islam), adultery, theft, or drinking alcohol are punishable by beheading, stoning, amputation of limbs or flogging.

11. Scholars have different views about abrogation, but Islamic scholar Ernest Hahn (Fellowship of Faith to Muslims) confirmed to the author that this is the governing rule of hermeneutics in Islamic theology. Some critics may argue that in Christianity, the New Testament abrogates the Old. However, the NT explains how Jesus "came not to destroy" the Mosaic Law, but to *fulfill* it. The OT foretold his coming to do that.

Very basic to orthodox Islamic culture is denial of "creativity." In fact, the Arabic word for *creativity* is the same as the word for *heresy*: "bida." This is in keeping with the concept that Allah has decreed everything to do with life, and mankind must not innovate or alter what is prescribed in the sacred writings. (It is true that evangelical Christianity accepts the Old and New Testaments as divinely inspired *in their original manuscripts*, not to be altered by "contextualization." But Christianity encourages creativity as a God-given talent to be used.)

Reform Movements in Islam

This is not the place to repeat the subsequent history of the development of Islam, except to mention that Muhammad and his followers came to believe that he was successor to Jesus and was the last of the prophets. The *Qur'an* was the completion of God's revelation and was superior to the Bible, they claimed. Wealthy merchants resented Muhammad's preaching against their mercenary greed and the idols that drew pilgrims to the city. Bedouins feared the wrath of the idols and spirits that Muhammad condemned. Expelled from Mecca, Muhammad fled to (what became) Medina.[12] As his following grew, his army eventually was victorious over Mecca. Through trade, teaching, and conquest, Islam subsequently spread along the arteries of the Old Spice Road. To benefit from Islam's influence, entire countries (including Persia, which became Iran) quickly sued for peace, "converting" ancient cultures to Islam *en bloc*.

Muhammad saw himself only as "the warner" of coming judgment, in the tradition of Amos and Jeremiah. He never professed to be the way of salvation and did not claim miracles other than the *Qur'an* being a miracle in itself. (Later commentators did attribute miracles to him.[13]) This merchant-turned prophet, whose nickname meant "The Trusted One," sincerely sought to overcome the degeneracy of his people. In a

12. Muhammad's expulsion parallels the Jewish Exodus from Egypt—"coming out" and "beginning anew," with suffering culminating in escape: for **Judaism** (through Moses); for **Islam** (through Muhammad).

13. Tradition also holds that "Muhammad is the quintessence of love for God and therefore the most sacred being on earth" (Kenneth Cragg in telephone link with OMSC Leadership Forum, Dec. 2006), making any slur on his name an unforgivable sin, greater than disparaging "the Unknown God."

time of great ethnic upheaval, he proved to be a remarkable leader, uniting warring tribes and replacing the divisions of nations and races with a sense of unity within a grand "brotherhood"—the *umma* of Islam. In place of the uncertainties of placating evil spirits and vengeful gods, Muhammad provided a tangible system to attain to an Islamic Paradise through works that brought a new discipline to tribal life.[14]

However, Muhammad foresaw the splintering of Islam into many sects—72, according to Abul Kasem, an ex-Muslim author (nirribilli@gmail.com). Kasem also quotes *Qur'anic* references to what he terms Islam's "cannibalism"—destructive infighting between the sects. (Sounds like fulfillment of the prophecy regarding Ishmael: "His hand will be against everyone and everyone's hand against him, and he will live in hostility toward all his brothers.")[15]

Although Islam began in Arabia, a persistent aspect of Orthodox Islam has been its required "Arabization." There are many different cultures reflected among Muslims, but Irshad Manji (a Muslim) in *The Trouble with Islam* (St. Martin's Griffin, 2005) refers to Islam's insistence on reading the *Qur'an* in Arabic (in order to be genuine), obligatory (if physically possible) pilgrimage to Mecca and facing toward Mecca in prayer, and its attitude to Jews and women. (See Appendix I re. Islam's attitude to women.)

Arab development is inextricably linked with Islam, because of the religion's strictures. For instance, *The Economist* (July 25, 2009) reports that for two recent decades, Saudi Arabia, the United Arab Emirates, Kuwait, Syria, Jordan, and Egypt together registered 367 patents in the U.S., while over the same period, Korea registered 16,328 and Israel 7,652. And the number of books annually translated in Arabic in all the Arab world is but one-fifth of the books translated into Greek by Greece.

Such comparisons might seem irrelevant except for the Arab world population explosion. Improved health, medical, and social conditions have resulted in a higher survival birth rate that is slated to increase the population by 40%. The median age in the most populous states is the

---

14. For ritual's importance, see Kenneth Cragg, *The Qur'an and the West*, pp. 108-09, 116 (Bibliography).

15. Genesis 16.12

mid-20s. With the world's highest rates of unemployment, this presages social unrest as incumbent conservative families try to reign in the ambitions of younger populations. But those ambitions have been awakened by Arab communication media, such as *al Jazeera*. Where there *is* nominal democracy, "parliament" often is a facade, and elections usually serve to ensconce absolute Islamic rule. Add to this mix competing Muslim sects, and the Arab world's future will be interesting—to say the least!

Islam's Allah and Christianity's God—Same?

Isn't Islam's Allah the same as the God of the Bible? It is true that Arabic derives "Allah" from the Aramaic *Elah* or Hebrew *Eloah/Elohim.* But whatever differences there may be in the way monotheistic Jews, Christians, and Muslims worship, Islam's Allah is not the same as the God of the Bible. One major difference is that, unlike Jehovah God of the Bible, Islam's Allah can renege on a promise: to say that he cannot, would limit Allah—who can do anything he wants! "Capricious" would describe Islam's Allah. (Muslims who argue that "Jehovah God" also changes his mind, overlook the fact that Jehovah responds to true repentance with forgiveness. Also, Jesus did not change the Law but *fulfilled* it, making a new Covenant possible.)

Beyond that basic difference, Muslims deny that Jesus Christ was God Incarnate. Christ a Prophet? Yes, but nothing more than a prophet. Muslims believe Muhammad and was the greatest and final prophet. Did God provide for our salvation through the death and resurrection of his "only begotten son"? No, Muslims insist—to them, even the thought is blasphemous.

The concept of prayer is another major difference. Whereas a Christian may offer up a spontaneous prayer—whether in worship, petition, or thanksgiving—at any time of day and in any posture, a Muslim must adhere to a regulated recitation at specified times of day, and always facing toward Mecca. Originally, Muhammad recited the prescribed prayer three times a day, always facing toward Jerusalem, but later changed his ritual position to face in the direction of Mecca. After his death, his successors expanded the number of times to five: before dawn, *before* the sun reaches its zenith (never at its zenith), between noon and sunset, after sundown, and after darkness has fallen.

How ever one tries to describe Islam, some Islamists may object to one thing or another. The fact is that, as in Christendom, there are many different forms of the religion, depending on local culture and teaching. For instance, Sunnis reject Ahmadiyyas, looked upon as an aberrant sect—even though they are the most aggressive Muslims in spreading their faith in the West.

Islam became a corrective to certain excesses of the Middle East in his era. The new religion reduced profligate prostitution, alcoholism, and usury—all rampant in society. While we commend such ideals, we also recognize that "religion" (whatever its label —Islam, Christendom, Hinduism, or other) has never transformed sinful human nature. Only Christ's Holy Spirit can. (See Appendices F and G re. Christendom vs. Christianity.)

This still leaves unanswered the question: "How did Islam expand so rapidly in its first century, overcoming ancient empires such as Persia?" There'd been successive waves of rulers. One despot seemed as bad as another! Anyway, why should we care? Several factors being repeated *today* in Europe made Muslim take-over easy. Social malaise had set in. Orthodox Christianity was weak—much of it lacking evangelical faith. Why resist the intruders' doctrines, as long as people could practice their own "faiths"? Thus weary empires and cultures crumpled like rows of dominoes. In Iran (Persia), Christians and Jews who did not convert to Islam could live in peace, (pursuing their religions and trade) by paying tribute tax. The Muslim state tolerated them as *dhimmi.*[16] After all, didn't a Divine Mandate destine Islam to rule the world? It was an example of Manifest Destiny (defined in chapter 16).

The West needs to realize that Islam, given this kind of expansive background, today considers Europe and the Americas simply *jahiliyya* (pre-Islamic)—ripe for Islam's dominance. [For further analysis of Islam, see W. Harold Fuller, *"Evolution" of Religion.* Available from SIM's web: https://simnet.sim.org/international%20archives]

16. *Dhimmi*: >*dhamma*, a derogatory verb, meaning "to blame, find fault."

Appendix I – Women

The Age-Old Battle of the Sexes[1]

[NOTE: In Western cultures, several explicit references to sexuality in this appendix may seem crude or out of place. However, since they are simply part of life in the cultures under consideration, we include them here without any intention to be crude. Regarding the status of women under different religions, see also Appendix F: Religions.]

BATTLE OF THE SEXES? If it *is* a battle, it's been a one-sided one most of the time. Adam began the blame game when he told the Creator that his disobedience was Eve's fault. Ever since, male pride may seek to bolster its ego by denigrating females.[2] Whatever the religion, it seems males thank their deities they were not created female!

But was the Fall of Man from the innocence of the Garden of Eden a one-sided affair? Although the Genesis tale reports that "the Serpent" approached Eve, the couple must have been together. (Since God gave to Adam the care of Eve, where was he when the Serpent tempted his wife—standing beside her?) Scripture does not suggest that the female alone was in the transgression. Instead, the Bible blames "Adam" (as the person representing the human race) for the entry of sin into the world through disobedience to God (Romans 5.12). And whatever the sequence of temptation and sinfulness, the fact of "the New Creation in Christ Jesus" is that Christ's death and resurrection removes all guilt, and the Holy Spirit makes everyone, both men and women, equal in standing before God. To insist on the superiority of men over women is to perpetuate

---

1. See also Bilezikian, Gilbert, *Beyond Sex Roles.* Grand Rapids, MI: Baker Academic, 2006 Ed.
2. The term "help-mate" is a distortion of the statement that God made Eve as a "help" *meet* (*i.e. suitable*) for Adam. And the word "help" is the same as is used to describe God as "our *help* in ages past."

the curse of the Fall of Man – the curse that Christ Jesus removed in his redemptive act.

Such teaching goes against male pride. From the physical standpoint, men almost seem to forget that no male would be alive were it not for the woman in whom he, as a foetus, took form, through whom the infant was born, and whose body provided nourishment and constant care to sustain the fragile new life. It is the mother who provides the infant's initial environment.

Instead of honoring women, male-dictated religions even deem a woman ceremonially "unclean" during the ten days surrounding her menstrual cycle[3] (again, without which no man could be born). So from conception to death, females are made to feel inferior—ironically, because of the very assets they possess: oestrogen's chemistry, organs of reproduction and nourishment, perspicacity, empathy, affection. Instead, males ignore, marginalize, mutilate, and even kill them. Symbolic of this in many cultures and their religions, a female foetus may be aborted and a widowed female may be abandoned to die. In between these "terminals," the female's existence is full of labor, pain, and sorrow. Many women endure this simply as "a woman's lot," a view taught by some religions. Men need to understand and make life more bearable for women.

Islam considers that male sperm (semen) is a divine, sacred emission. Because semen in itself is seen as the essence of life, males are automatically superior to females.[4] Such attitudes ignore the strategic female genetic production of "the egg," without which male semen remains lifeless.

Although certain societies and religions practice male discrimination against females, such has been true of human relations throughout history. However, while the Old Testament prescribed death for an adulterous woman, it applied the same death penalty to male adulterers. So when a woman was brought to Jesus without the guilty man, Jesus did not condemn her but told her not to continue sinning (John 8.3). Jesus' acceptance of women on par with men defied male custom.

---

3. Under Mosaic Law, this was for protection of the woman and as a hygienic precaution against disease.
4. Kenneth Cragg, *The Qur'an and the West*, p. 33 (see Bibliography).

Among some evangelicals, the counterpart of totalitarian religion's ban of women from their holiest sites, is banning women from supposed "leadership" roles in the church, such as deacon, elder, minister (which originally meant "servant"), and preacher. Although this is changing, for some, teaching children down in the church basement is about the limit of female "leadership."

Although Evangelical Christians have done much to elevate womanhood, yet some still mis-apply the Bible's teaching on male-female relationships. One author has written a book popular in certain marriage discussion groups, *Men Need Respect, Women Need Love*. This polarizes the two, feeding egotism in males (as respected leaders and therefore superior) and confirming subjectivity of females (as "objects" to love, and consequently often inferior). The above book's author does not intend that, but masculine testosterone infers it. The truth is that women need respect from men, and men need love from women more than ego-building "respect." True respect has to be earned—not demanded or legislated. Otherwise it becomes only obeisance from subjects. Love that is not based on respect turns into pity or abuse.

Do males feel "threatened" by admitting that women possess outstanding abilities? Historian Patricia Fara cites inventions by women, which have been credited to men.[5] —including, for some, leadership? Do men protect their sense of superiority, so they won't feel inferior? (If so, what does that imply about their seeming self-assurance?) It is fairly easy for the male's aggressive psyche to dominate the female's natural caring psyche—the very element that equips women for child rearing. Reduced to chemistry, it is a case of testosterone vs. oestrogen!

Of course, whether male or female, we all need affirmation. The paradox is that above all, we all need to die to the self-life that drives every human being. (The paradox is that human nature strives to promote itself, whereas the self-life must die to itself so that Christ's life—his Holy Spirit—can fill us, using our God-given abilities as he wills.) It seems that males, with their masculine pride, find that extra difficult. That's why the Apostle Paul so explicitly outlined the essence of the

5. Patricia Fara, *Science: A Four Thousand Year History*. Oxford U. Press, 2009 (also cited in Ch. 18).

Christian life as a death-and-life process: dying to self through accepting Christ's death, not just once for all as Redeemer, but constantly through his Holy Spirit in the believer. "Dead to sin, alive unto God."[6]

Gender Prejudices

Poets and artists have extolled the external beauty of women. Solomon did also, but went beyond the external to describe the beautiful character of womanhood. Cultures have had their own concepts of beauty. For instance, in some African cultures, obesity added value to a woman—that made her more voluptuous and, it was thought, fecund. In several tribes, "ornamentation" included extended earlobes and lower lips, stretched by wooden disks. In ancient China, bound feet ("the three-inch golden lotus") were the epitome of female culture, a sign of being well bred in contrast to the "crude-looking" wide feet of peasant laborers.

"Of course, there was no need for them to go out to shop or work; if they did go out, they would be carried in a litter—today's version of a chauffer- driven car!" comments former Hong Kong University Lecturer in Linguistics, Lena Lau.

Moral/sexual purity, whether in a single man or single woman, is precious, of course, and we would not want to trivialize the importance of virginity. However, in some cultures, no matter if a husband has lost his virginity (by committing fornication) many times before he married, that is never questioned. Rather, to many a prospective groom, theirs is the all-important question: "Is my fiancé a virgin?" To assure suitors in some cultures, parents pay a medical practitioner to physically examine their daughter's genitals—a humiliating experience for any woman. Or would-be husbands may send prospective brides for medical certification.[7] Such "proof" becomes a symbol of male ownership—little to do with true love.

Recently a Muslim in France received annulment of his marriage because the bride falsely claimed to be a virgin—but a court ordered a review of the case as gender discrimination.[8] Some forms of Islam use the

---

6. See Romans 6 – 8 for Paul's explanation of this paradox and solution.
7. Without going into medical explanations, it is sufficient to state that the bodies of some females lack traditional "proof." This has led to false accusations, humiliation, and (in some cultures) even to death of innocent women. In Medieval times, some European brides would take a capsule of blood to their marriage bed and break it at the appropriate time—to "prove" their virginity!

cell phone to make divorce simpler. A husband can now send the required triple pronouncement ("I divorce you!") in a text-message, from anywhere in the world—and the divorce is complete!

Most religions—including those that do not exploit women—impose restrictions. Orthodox Judaism bans men from listening to recordings of women singing traditional Hebrew chants.

Orthodox Islam's legislated cover-up and isolation of its women, while posing as protection of females, becomes a symbol of male control, disguised as "submission" to Allah.[9] It actually makes the man "owner" of the woman, a property—screening her from societal interaction with the general populace (apart from protected circles of women). Although a *burqa* protects a woman from exploiting her body in public—which immorality we'd condemn—in effect it totally banishes a woman and the feminine gifts God has given her, intended to complement masculinity.

However, segregating women really reflects a *male* problem. Christian men know how they must constantly "walk in the spirit and not the lust of the flesh," as the Apostle Paul instructed. Pure thoughts arise only from the Holy Spirit's living in the believer. In a legislated religion that does not know inner spiritual regeneration, the solution is to cover up the object of lust. Yet, though sex may not be publicly displayed, sinful men are still lustful.

Some moderate Muslims reject the mandatory veiling of women, which the *Qur'an* does not require. During the debate over whether France should allow wearing of the Muslim headscarf in government schools and offices, in 2008 Cities Minister, Fadela Amara, boldly commented about the *burqa*: "It is not a religious sign but the visible sign of a totalitarian political project preaching sexual inequality."[10] An Afghani ruler apparently introduced the *chadri*, veiling head and face to keep the public from seeing his wives' faces.

---

8. *Economist*, July 19, 2008.

9. A Montreal mosque, though stating on its website that wearing the hair-covering *hijab* was voluntary, went on to specify: 'by removing your *hijab*, you have destroyed your faith. Islam means submission to Allah in all our actions. Those who refuse submission cannot be called Muslims.' Tarek Fatah, *Chasing a Mirage: The Tragic Illusion of an Islamic State.* Quoted by Robert A. Jason, Christian News, May 27, '08.

Punishment for moral infractions further reveals discrimination against women For instance, an Islamic court in Saudi Arabia recently sentenced a 19-year-old woman to *200* lashes (plus six months in prison), even after a group of seven men had gang-raped her because they found her in the company of an unrelated male in the dark. (The rapists were sentenced to prison for two to nine years, but without lashes.) The government (defending itself as "virtuous" and the sentence as "based on God's book") revoked the license of the lawyer who represented the woman in an appeal of the barbaric sentence.[11]

Saudi macho society is showing slight changes: King Abdullah has promoted reformers and even appointed the nation's first female minister—responsible for women's education. But women are still not allowed to drive a car!

"Women in Pakistan live in fear," Amnesty International reported 2009. "They face death by shooting, burning, or killing with axes if they are deemed to have brought shame on the family. They are even murdered by their kin if they are raped, for which they, as they are thereby deemed to have brought shame."[12]

Hindu society, may not have social restrictions such as Islam has, yet Hindu men exhibit obsessive control through the number of "honor killings" of women by male relatives suspicious of a woman's infidelity. On the other hand, freedoms of secular and so-called "Christianized" society come with the price of promiscuity in entertainment and real life. Throughout the world it is the controlling male who goes free!

While, as a result of various factors, there are women who initiate promiscuity, females become the real victims of male promiscuity. Modern society itself constantly stimulates a man's sexual drive, which some men indulge wherever possible—unless restrained by ordinance (as in Islam) or inner moral rectitude (ultimately, the redemptive work of the Holy Spirit).

---

10. *Economist*, July 19, 2008. It is true that the *Qur'an*, while requiring modest dress for both men and women, does not mandate the *burqa*. It originated in ancient Arabia, where both men and women might wear it during sandstorms.

11. *Toronto Star*, Nov. 25, 2007.

12. Lorrie Goldstein in *Toronto Sun*, March 7, 2009.

In the final analysis, male denigration of females reveals weakness, not strength. Some, to bolster their "macho" image, denigrate females. Also, an unrestrained male, sexually stirred by the sight of a female, may subconsciously feel vulnerable, wanting to satisfy his sex drive. Blaming the woman for stimulating his desire, he may solve the problem either by licentiousness or by requiring the woman to cover herself—sometimes to the extent of becoming invisible (other than as a black tent) in society. Between those extremes is insistence that women wear some sign of subjection—such as a headscarf or veil—supposedly to show subjection to God. But *who* is their *de* facto master, or "god"—males who keep them in bondage?

Superior Ability?

The Creator did not intend male and female to be in competition, but for each to contribute to the whole of society. Male and female abilities complement each other. Removal of either from any aspect of society creates a vacuum, a missing element, and is harmful to humanity.

Take the Taliban, for instance. Found chiefly in Afghanistan, these males had lost their mothers during Afghan's struggles. Most members of an entire generation grew up without knowing the love of a mother—or even a father, as many were orphaned or grew up under the care of a male fighter. Instructed by Islamic male ideology, youth grew up as women-hating religious zealots. (Passages of the *Qur'an* teach male-female equality, though with different gender roles.)

Men base their superiority on physical strength and skill. Muscular strength, no one will deny they have—although neither will anyone argue that the boxing world champion is intrinsically superior to a whiz kid in a wheel chair. But skill? Apart from the inestimable contribution that mothers make in home care, there are other pluses. A lead article in a news magazine[13] posits that in the world economy, females may be a better investment. Girls earn better school grades than do boys, and (on average) more women than men go on to university. More British women than men, by far, train to be medical doctors, and, on average, women financial investors receive higher returns than do men. Of surprise to

13. *Economist* April 15, 2006, page 16.

men, statistics show that globally, women contribute more to the world's economy than men, because of their care of family and the home, as well as in industry and professions.

Countries that discriminate against women, the article's author points out, would do well by investing more in the education of women, who in turn will raise healthier and better-educated children. Besides, educated women prove more likely than men to spend money on learning and health than on armaments. And in countries suffering workforce attrition from aging populations (*e.g.* Germany, Italy, Japan), women—who universally live longer than men— especially before and after raising a family could greatly relieve the employment problem without affecting birthrates. (Sweden and USA have a higher birthrate than Italy and Japan, although they also have a greater percentage of women who handle more than housework.) As to social implications, many people use the Internet at home instead of going out to work, reducing absenteeism among parents of school-age children. Today homemakers use many timesaving devices in housework.

******

IN THE BEGINNING, the Creator intended neither male domination nor feminism. It was sin that introduced the male-female tensions that plague the world. In Christ, the Apostle Paul assures us, "there is neither male nor female" (Galatians 3.28). That does not teach "unisex," but neither does it allow for superiority and inferiority. God has given both males and females their respective roles in his plan for the human race. Both have their individual strengths to contribute to the whole. It is high time that evangelicals speak out publicly against the abuse of women and discrimination against them. This is a global crime against God's creation, accounting for more female deaths than the AIDS pandemic.

For instance, Western society may pretend that abortion is a woman's right, exercising her freedom—but in this ultrasound era, it leads to the increasing disappearance of "the girl child." In Asia, where male progeny is preferred, selective abortion of female fetuses has increased, and immigrants have taken the problem with them to the West.

Are Christians concerned? Our lack of response reflects our oft-unrecognized lack of esteem for womanhood. Whereas the Cross removed the curse imposed in Eden, we can perpetuate it in our male-female relations. So the Battle of the Sexes (or the struggle between them) continues!

—WHF

APPENDIX J

Asia and World Economics

NOTE: Most of this Appendix on Asia's Economies was written before the global economic downturn in the first decade of this century. East and the West blamed each other for the world-wide recession, but at Press time it was too early to forecast its effects or duration. The following explains the phenomenal rise of Asia's economies before the recession.

GLOBALIZATION SOMETHING NEW? Actually, trade along the Old Spice Road was an early form of it. In the first century BC, for instance, Eastern noodle-making interchanged with Middle East wine-making—so did certain technology, such as making watches (West) and paper (East). Such intermingling of cultures continues to be at the heart of globalization: China is now the biggest producer of wheat (originally from the Middle East); India produces the most peanuts (originally from South America). And as for tea, coffee, cocoa, and tobacco—well, you know the rest of their "global" story.[1]

We cannot understand the global economy, or even the economy of one's own nation, without understanding what is happening in Asia's economies. Western economists now keep active desks in Asia. "Emerging economies" (EC) include developing countries in all continents, although Asia, because of its size and resources, represents the highest percentages.

---

1. While tea, coffee, and cocoa contribute to society in positive ways, tobacco continues to leave its tragic trail. Asia accounts for half the globe's annual 5m. deaths caused by tobacco—originally from South America. Not satisfied with that, one Western tobacco company now produces clove-flavored cigarettes for Indonesia (fifth-largest tobacco market), which traditionally uses cloves as a flavor additive.

In 2005, population of EC countries represented over 85% of world population, had nearly 70% of global foreign-exchange reserves, but consumed only some 50% of global energy and accounted for some 40% of exports. Those and other percentages are rapidly increasing. Asia now has the bulk of the globe's foreign exchange reserves.[2]

Reversing the Balance?

This means big changes in the balance of global trade and prosperity.[3] However, for nations such as China, it really is only returning that country to the economic leadership it enjoyed during the Medieval era.[4] At the end of the first millennium, A.D., Asian economies (EC) monopolized 85% of global Gross Domestic Product (GDP). In the early decades of the 20th c., its proportion had shrunk to 40%, while today's "developed economies" had increased to nearly 60%. By 2025, some economists estimate, that balance will again be reversed, 60% to 40%.[5]

China has been key player in this turn around, also providing lessons in principles of global trade. Eighteenth-century China was still the world's largest economy—seven times as large as Britain in GDP. Observers will have their own political views on the effects of Western imperialism, but in essence, the Chinese Emperor Qianlong made a decision that effectively cut China out of global trade and the expansion of his nation's economy. For some 200 years China remained isolated and increasingly poverty-stricken. In contrast, today's China is a leader in global trade. Observers hope its leaders will make sure its economic growth is not confined to an elite but is spread over the entire populace. Unfortunately, the nation's headline prosperity has been enjoyed chiefly by a tiny educated minority; although wealth spilled over to millions of uneducated "peasants," they have been the first to suffer from decreased consumer spending by the West.

---

2. *Economist*, Sept. 2, 2006.
3. Example: Hong Kong's Stock Exchange recently outranked New York's initial public offerings (IPOs).
4. See Chapter 18.
5. Figures are from "A Survey of the World Economy," *Economist*, September 16, 2006.

What is the biggest factor in bringing about this shift in global economy? Observers think it is mainly due to the use of the Internet, making trade and industry easier across political and geographic boundaries. This is especially true in service industries; an operator in Delhi or Shanghai may handle a telephone inquiry in London or New York. But it is true of technology: for instance, the American-designed Apple iPhone is assembled in China from components made in Japan (the screen) and South Korea (the flash memory). Of course, global down-turns consequently have a domino effect on them all.

Employees and unions in the West rightly worry about the effects of "off shoring" and globalization. We share the concern of our hardworking friends in the Southern U.S., for instance, who have worked in local factories all their lives. Most were untrained for other employment, and they have children in college. Fortunately many companies provide scholarships for laid-off employees, to train for other careers. But for many, the blow is severe. Pundits prophesied the doom of the West as the Far East rose, but the global downturn of 2009 made the future uncertain. Policy-wise, governments need to keep in mind the lessons that China learned from two centuries of isolation. Saving local jobs for a short period could eventually prove disastrous economically. Economic growth builds upon competition, not protectionism.

What Is Really Happening?

There is going to be pain—but not without gain. Constantly changing balance of trade and of labor costs affects traditional economies. The new tigers in Asia changed the nature of the game. Their massive labor force[6] reduced prices for consumers in the West (otherwise inflation in this century's first decade would have been out of sight), but in most cases, those companies do so by using the technology and industrial equipment the West designed—although they are beginning to develop their own technology. The West invented and produced these in order to be more competitive—which is what Asia is doing, even if it means taking away industrial jobs from the West. However, while the American and British

6. When China, India, and Central Asia embraced open marketing, global labor suddenly doubled.

industrial revolutions doubled incomes over half a century, China did so in a single decade. Asia (largely China) now has a larger middle class (necessary for economic growth—see below) than "the West""—reverting back to the East's preponderance (in that category) over the West in the 1600s.

But besides lowering consumer costs in the West, Asia's new industries also employed people—some producing raw materials, some in industry, some in marketing—creating new markets for goods and services from Asia as well as the West. Asians watching TV and the Internet long for these "other world" items and services. So globalization increased global wealth, at the same time that aging populations in rich countries would have slowed it down. The new East-West competition also spurred innovation in richer countries. Pain comes in the re-structuring that accompanies this new wealth and its production, both in the West and in the rest of the world—and in global consumer-spending fluctuations.

Currently, USA has the largest economy of any country (GDP, in purchasing-power parity), but by 2049, China is forecast to tie with USA in GDP. Excluding gold, Japan and China already vie for the world's largest financial reserves, although USA still leads in science and technology.

So economists believe that expansion of global trade, increasing the power of "emerging economies," will benefit the entire world. Although it will mean reconfiguring "developed economies" (DE) it should mean that people and governments in EC countries will have more money to spend on whatever DE countries have to offer in such things as products, services, education, health, and technologies. The genius of both economies will show up in their ability to develop what each other needs but, for various reasons, cannot yet supply in sufficient quantity.

As well, sustaining global growth will depend on availability of resources—new as well as traditional: such as energy-saving technologies and environmental preservation. Demand for oil, water, and timber presents new problems throughout Asia, as well as in other parts of the globe. China, the world's biggest coal producer and a major oil importer, is about to become the world's greatest air polluter. Its leaders are showing concern for environmental problems, but they always face risk of social unrest if they do not meet the aspirations of the nation's emerging masses.

Growth Factors: Aristotle (1[st]c BC) identified the growth of a middle class as best for a nation's economy. Asia's expanding middle class (a working population set between the extremes of dire poverty and vast wealth) fulfills the Greek philosopher/scientist's view. Several factors combined to produce Asia's economic growth:

1. *Population.* Obviously, massive populations present a great consumer market (China alone has over half-a-billion cell phone users). But large populations can hold back growth unless accompanied by other factors. The government is well aware that in economic down-turns, unskilled and unemployed millions can present a colossal political problem.
2. *Education.* Rural populations still lag behind in having adequate schools and staff, although governments are increasing investment in educating their people. Because of so much competition between nations, educating an undeveloped nation needs a jump-start. But a middle class, open change and often agitating for it, seeks education for self-improvement.
3. *Overseas higher education and training.* Asian nations have taken advantage of scholarships and programs in Europe and North America, at the highest levels of science and other disciplines. In this way, Asia (and other continents) are doing what made Europe and North America strong in the past—using wealth in other areas (in this case, educational "wealth") to enhance its own.
4. *Entrepreneurship.* Combining the benefits of education and marketing requires the greatest use of entrepreneurship—fuelled by the middle class concept of "meritocracy," rather than entitlement. India and China are not lacking in these: witness leading businesses and industries in both countries. In fact, there are people like Vinod Khosla, graduate of the Indian Institute of Technology. Indian-born, he made most of his billions in Silicon Valley, USA. Khosla helped to found Sun Microsystems (a major competitor with Microsoft), and

became a partner in Kleiner Perkins—famous for investments in AOL, Amazon, Compaq, and Google. Khosla is now crusading to reduce the world's dependency on oil by developing efficient substitutes.

5. *Increasing openness to competition.* There are many other Asians making a success of business and industry in the West, but for them to succeed in their own countries involves one more factor: removal of protectionism and archaic financial restrictions and structures in their Asia homelands. Although India and China have about the same populations at present, China presents the more attractive ambience for entrepreneurs (found chiefly among the middle class) because of removal of many restrictive measures (although currently with government supervision—"controlled democracy?"). However, in a government-controlled society, competition risks backlash by vested interests.

6. *Financing.* Entrepreneurs need finance in order to construct buildings, do research, manufacture, and market products. Either domestic (internal—from financiers or banks or government) investment, or external (foreign). Because of China's population and its less restrictive regulations, entrepreneurs are attracting that kind of investment. Once these new businesses or services start up, they will continue turning the wheel of re-investment, growth, marketing, and profit. All that means a developing market but, most importantly, employment (in order to staff the new businesses and services).

7. *Honesty.* There is a moral factor—more than moral issues of protecting the environment so that our children have air to breath, water to drink, and land on which to grow food. We're thinking more than the moral factor of liberty—to choose where to live and how to be employed.

   At the top of the moral-factor list is probity: honesty. That rules out corruption, including bribery, use of shoddy materials, misrepresentation of products and services (call them "scams"). Without these, opportunity, entrepreneurs, financing, and competition will throw any sector off the cycle. Trust will collapse. The people and their nation will lose.

8. *The Internet.* As noted, Internet communication has revolutionized globalization—linking markets with manufacturers and increasing "just-in-time" production. But ironically, at times the Internet has misled financial services, as powerful computers crunch data fed into them for "quantitative analysis," at times creating virtual "bubbles" and fuelling recession.[7]

Any Nation Can Do It

With care, any nation can pull out of poverty by getting on this cycle—given growth in consumer spending, and provided a totalitarian government or repressive culture/religion does not choke off progress. After Nigeria gained independence, President Nnamdi Azikiwe told the nation, "Now it is your responsibility to work, to build, to develop our nation. Grow something, make something, trade something—and if your land can't grow anything, you can at least make bricks out of the mud, sell them, and buy food and clothes!" That was before oil was discovered in commercial quantity. Azikiwe's formula was self-help, instead of relying on a colonial power or blaming someone else for starving the nation.

All over Asia there are instances of countries that have followed one of two ways: (1) Blame someone else for your problems, and try to blow them up, or (2) Work to develop one's own nation with whatever assets it may have (whether rice or oil or manufacturing or services.) As Dr. Azikiwe might add: "If you have only rocks, develop tourism to come and enjoy the view!"

So North Korea, once the more prosperous part of the Korean Peninsula, languishes under tyranny (that threatens the rest of the world), while South Korea, the poorer half, competes with the rest of the world in producing wealth that the whole nation enjoys. (Sure—the West enabled it to do that. But who helped North Korea become a Stalinist nation, pouring in 300,00 troops to defeat any liberators?)

There are many other examples of the choices that nations make economically as well as politically. Algeria, once a terrorist state known for making bombs (including one that blew up an aircraft over Europe),

---

7. *The Economist* Special Report on Finance, Jan. 24, 2009, p. 10.

has now made peace instead, developing the nation and relating to the family of nations. Next door, poverty-stricken Morocco may not have oil, but the brightest Moroccans are making money (and employ camel drivers among other nomads) from burgeoning tourism. South Africa has become a leader among African nations, whereas Zimbabwe (once called "the breadbasket of Africa") was starving to death while its megalomaniac president quaffed wine in his isolated "palace." There *is* a choice nations can make (except nations where government stifles freedom.)

As to inflation in prospering nations, bankrupt Zimbabwe's hyper inflation demonstrated that inflation may be caused by other factors, such as artificial price increases not related to improved products or output.

Leading the Pack

JAPAN: Back in the 17th and 18th centuries, Japan introduced "forward contracts" and "futures trading"—which more recently the West considered its own financial service innovations. After World War II, America helped Japan recover economically through US government and private investment, as well as providing innovative technology (*e.g.* transistors, the core of TV and radio production). This enabled Japan to lead Asia's economic and academic scene. However, resultant largesse has contributed to increased cost of living, reduced birthrate (therefore population), and aging workforce. Nationalist Japan, instead of importing workers, seeks to maintain its ethnic *status quo* by investing both capital and expertise in neighboring countries. So Southeast Asia produces many components of Japan's vehicles sought by cost-conscious Westerners, while Japanese engineers and entrepreneurs give oversight.

However, in Japan family-run conglomerates and entrenched traditions of "seniority" reduce incentives. In a system rewarding tenure rather than performance, mediocre senior management may go unchallenged, while performance among younger workers may be unrewarded. Reforms are on the way, but the country is overly reliant on exports. Believing that global demand would continue, companies built up surplus resources, using an over-valued yen. When global demand slumped, Japan found its capital tied up in expansion coupled with job losses and unemployment.

CHINA decided to sit in the front row of post WW II world assemblies. To help accomplish this, it now has the most universities of any nation, and the highest rate of investment. Results show up in gleaming high-rise city towers as well as (increasingly) in small village industries. The government is very aware of what can happen if the poor masses rise up against the wealthy fringe. So China is building some 24,000 km (15,000 miles) of expressways and 20 nuclear power stations, bringing the total to 30 by 2020, to spread wealth and improve living conditions.

But in China's push for rapid progress lies a danger—of which the Prime Minister[8] as well as financiers are aware: excess production based on politically-motivated loans. Much of the finance has come from state coffers (economists aren't sure what percentage, since the large banks are state owned). This is not bad, except that the state has encouraged (or pushed) banks to make large loans without adequate research, so that interest rates are not based on viability (consumption and risk). Eager business prospectors build and manufacture before the market has developed, with the result, for instance, that China now *overproduces* steel tonnage equal to the entire output of developed nations (a third of its output is *excess*). That (coupled with plunging profits) simply means: steel companies won't be able to sell their current inventory, let alone next year's output. Therefore the industries (steel is only one of the borrowers) will default in repaying loans, and banks will be in trouble—which will affect the nation's economy and future investment.

That's only one worry in China! Other concerns include unemployed university graduates (more than 6m a year), and rising unrest among urban populations lured by consumerism—laid off by global recession. At the other end of the social spectrum, shortage of skilled artisans, managers, and technicians cannot meet the demands of burgeoning industry. These two polarized factors press the watchful state to keep the wheels of production turning even as labor costs increase. One benefit is to move (until now) eastern sea-board industries inland, taking advantage of lower rural labor costs—but also increasing transport-marketing costs. Result of the equation? *China no longer has the lowest labor costs in Asia.*

---

8. In a speech to Parliament March 2006.

Socialist China has another interesting complication: how to maintain "a harmonious society" as disparity grows between the newly rich and the peasant population. As the 2008 Olympics approached, Party watchdogs complained about affluent spenders becoming "intoxicated with comfort" and "sinking into depravity." In Beijing, the Party targeted billboards displaying luxury goods, as well as a whole range of lavish living—from diners leaving food on their plates to millionaire suburban homes.[9]

INDIA: Among India's peoples (soon the world's largest population) are brilliant minds and capable entrepreneurs. American companies, in particular, have made use of this "brain bank" in such things as data outsourcing centers. But although it has fewer such developmental needs compared to several other Asian lands, it has other problems. India's massive bureaucracy, onerous labor laws, and factionalised parliament often end up passing only platitudes. (China's flexible authoritarianism enables it to enforce the good advice of its economists.) India's government knows the hard decisions it needs to make in order to free up the nation's economy, and enforcement of its high standards is weak. Vested interests block sensitive bills from being passed in the cumbersome court systems. Throughout the nation, endemic bribery, destructive culture, caste quotas, paralysing religions, and family businesses stultify the best of the nation's intentions. Socialist provisions help garner voters, but special interest policies such as free electricity for farmers are counterproductive. "Ferocious" corruption in corporate (family) governance often leads to run-away financial manipulation, according to Indian accountant Saurabh Mukherjea.[10]

However, barriers to growth are crumbling. India has developed certain sectors remarkably—such as its Internet services. Tata & Sons owns Britain's Tetley Tea, and Tata Steel is making similar international acquisitions. Individual entrepreneurs are creating successful enterprises. Although the burgeoning middle class blurs caste importance, in reality the need for social networking preserves caste identity as peasants congregate in their own sections of towns. If the nation can control

9. *Economist,* June 2, 2007.

10. *Economist,* Jan. 17, 2009.

soaring wages and inflation, and loosen up its systems, it does have potential to be truly "India Shining." Meanwhile, tourism uses the slogan, "Incredible India."

SOUTH-EAST ASIA: The nations sandwiched between China and India increasingly benefit from the global economy. Their lower-cost labor produces many parts for their big neighbors' assembly plants. India's current over-supply of engineers enables Southeast Asian workshops to produce goods for China's burgeoning consumer market, financed by Chinese banks. And Big Brother's largesse (China now has the world's largest financial surplus) reduces the neighbors' concern over China's power. However, with prosperity comes inflation—affecting competition. And recessions in the West immediately affect "Asia's millions," as factories lay off workers.

ISLAMIC NATIONS: Nations that follow *Shari'a* law (such as Bangladesh, Indonesia, and Pakistan) are a major exception to the economic factors Asia faces. In those that rigidly apply Islamic economic principles (banning speculation and interest charges), economic growth is restricted—although oil-producing nations are currently awash with cash. However, moderate Muslims find ways of circumventing religious restrictions. (For instance, Islamic payment of 5% down to secure a futures option with three months to pay the balance, isn't much different from a non-Muslim's speculative fixing of the futures option.)

TODAY, Asia makes a fascinating and instructive study in economies—and the picture continues to change. Consider one possible circular problem affecting China:

1. Unemployment causes political unrest, until manufacturing for export raises living standards of entire communities.
2. These *nouveau riche* can then afford—and demand—better living conditions and wages—causing inflation.
3. Inflation increases the cost of manufacture, and therefore exports—causing global companies to move to lower-cost neighboring countries.
4. In China, where supervision is a major problem because of the population's size, some producers try to reduce costs by using inferior ingredients.

5. Global markets may complain and reduce purchase of China's exports.
6. Government catches up with the miscreants and closes them—causing unrest.

There's another problem looming: pollution of the atmosphere. China is now number one emitter of greenhouse gasses.[11] Acid rain affects one-third of China's farmland. Both China and India contribute to the melting of the Himalaya's glaciers, which supply their largest rivers with life-giving water. This threatens over a billion people dependent on those rivers for irrigation as well as fish food. Down on the coast of Bangladesh, rising sea levels could drive some 35 million refugees inland by the middle of this century. Result of all this? *Starvation, plagues, massive population unrest, political instability.*[12]

What has Asia's economy to do with the central topic of this book, *Following Jesus on Asia's Old Spice Road*? It means that more than ever in history, Asia is in flux—presenting conditions in which the gospel can meet the spiritual needs of peoples undergoing traumatic change. In economic terms, Christians in Asia (though welcoming experienced disciples from elsewhere) will be able to finance their gospel outreach "on Asia's Old Spice Road" and worldwide. In Asia, the sun really does seem to *come up like thunder*.

*****

Economist Mark L. Maxwell Comments on Economics:

"Global Interconnectedness, or re-coupling of the globe. Without question, this is related to international trade policy that has followed the Internet's information flow.

"What do falling house prices in the West have to do with China's urban unemployment? *There are multiple connections:* Consumption in

11. China's rebuttal to critics is that some 30% of the pollution results from manufacturing goods for the West. To western nations, that only confirms the number of industrial jobs transferred to China!
12. Though a concern, glacial melting and other global warming may be a cyclical phenomena that is being politically manipulated. So suggests columnist Lorne Gunter, in National Post, Canada, Jan. 20, 2010.

America is being satisfied by production in China. Marginal consumption in America is being financed by debt (core consumption is begin financed by income). This was largely a case of borrowing by people who should not have been borrowing, from lenders who should not have been lending. A major investor in US debt is the Chinese government and related companies. When Americans ran out of borrowing capacity, consumption had to drop. The biggest ticket item on the consumer list is a house; so when America's buying dropped, house prices dropped, and mortgages soared higher than the value of the mortgaged house.

"*The conclusion*: At this point the world is awash in surplus capacity. Greed seems to be at the heart of most of the world's heart-aches: consumption in the western world, corruption at the top of most governments, excess capacity around the world, and sub-quality products (such as some North American cars). *The cure is restraint*—living within one's means and making products that serve others well. (A version of "Do unto others as you would have them do unto you"?)

"Actually, China has done a good job of responding to the consumption demands of the world. Its political system has not hampered its ability to generate quite acceptable products at good value, and in the process has allowed many people to be employed, some of whom have become very wealthy. Communism is a form of government which can work for commerce (as in China) or can destroy commerce (as in Cuba, USSR). On the other hand, some democracies do not help commerce (Nigeria being one example).

"Neither system is God-ordained. Both can honor God or provoke him greatly. Israel is an interesting example of a country that has been a theocracy, a socialist monarchy, and is now a democracy. The sad thing is that there are many examples of human rights abuses in history, regardless of form of government.

"In India, caste (right of birth ensuring a person's position) will naturally result in under-employment of millions, with organizations run by people who may not be the best at the job: probably one of the world's largest wastes of a natural resource! Arguably, India's buried treasure is in its lower classes and non-castes. Liberate those resources and India, already a mighty force, could truly be a formidable force in global economics.

Bibliography

A

Abdul-Haqq, Abdiyah Akbar. *Sharing Your Faith with a Muslim.* Minneapolis: Bethany Fellowship, 1980.

Adeney, Miriam. *Daughters of Islam.* Downers Grove: IVP, 2002.

Ahmed, Nazmuddin. *Islamic Heritage of Bangladesh.* Bangladesh: Government of People's Republic of Bangladesh, 1980.

Aikman, David. *Jesus in Beijing: How Christianity Is Transforming China and Changing Global Balance of Power.* Washington: Regnery, 2003.

Allan, J. D. *The Evangelicals: An Illustrated History.* Grand Rapids: Baker Book House, 1989.

Allen, Roland. *Missionary Methods: St. Paul's or Ours.* London: World Dominion 1912.

Anderson, Courtney. *To the Golden Shore: A Life of Adoniram Judson.* Rochester: American Baptist Historical Society, 1956.

Anderson, Gerald H. and Stransky, Thomas F., editors. *Mission Trends No. 3. Third World Theologies.* NY: Paulist Press, and Grand Rapids: Wm B. Eerdmans Publishing Co., 1978.

Athyal, Sakhi. *Indian Women in Mission.* Bihar: Mission Educational Books, 1995.

Azariah, V.S. *Christian Giving.* London: World Christian Books, republished 1955.

B

Bell, Dorothy. *Nannie's Story . . . In Weakness, Strength.* 1979. Privately published by Mrs. George Bell, 82 Murray Crescent, Cobourg, Ontario, CA. K9A 2V9.

Bentley-Taylor, David. *Java Saga, Christian progress in Muslim Java.* London: OMF, 1975.

Bentley-Taylor, David. *The Weathercock's Reward.* Singapore: CIM/OMF, 1967.

Bergquist, James A. and Manickam, P. Kambar. *The Crisis of Dependency in Third World Ministries: A Critique of Inherited Missionary Forms in India.* Madras: Christian Literature Society, 1974.

Bilezikian, Gilbert. *Beyond Sex Roles.* Grand Rapids: MI: Baker Academic, 2006 Ed.

Bista, Dor Bahadur. *Fatalism and Development: Nepal's Struggle for Modernization.* Calcutta: Orient Longman Ltd., 1991.

Bonk, Jonathan J., *et al.* eds, *Speaking About What We Have Seen and Heard—Evangelism in Gobal Perspective.* New Haven: OMSC, 2007. ISBN 0-9762205-4-7.

Borg, Marcus, ed., *Jesus and Buddha.* Berkeley, CA: Ulysses Press,1997.

Bourdeaux, Michael. *Gorbachev Glasnost & the Gospel.* London: Hodder and Stoughton Ltd., 1990.

Bradnock, Robert (editors). *South Asian Handbook.* Travelers World Guides, 1993.

Buntain, Huldah. *Treasures in Heaven.* Springdale: Calcutta Mission of Mercy, Whitaker House, 1989.

C

Cable, Mildred; French, Francesca. *Ambassadors for Christ.* Chicago: Moody Press, n.d.

Cable, Mildred, and French, Francesca. *The Making of a Pioneer.* London: Hodder and Stoughton, 1949.

Cairns, Earle E. *Christianity Through the Centuries.* Grand Rapids: Zondervan Publishing House, 1954.

Cameron, Julia (ed). *God's grace to nine generations.* Singapore: OMF, 1999.

Carey, Sammy Pierce. *William Carey.* London: The Carey Press, 1923.

Carpenter, Joel A. and Shenk, Wilbert R., editors. *Earthen Vessels.* Grand Rapids: Eerdmans, 1990.

Cash, W. Wilson. *The Expansion of Islam.* London: Church Missionary Society, 1928.

Chamberlin, Margaret. *Reaching Asians Internationally, A history of International Missions.* Wayne: International Missions, Inc., 1984.

Chan, Kei Thong, *Chien Kai Shek—Faith of Our Fathers.* Shanghai: Orient Publishing Center, 2006.

Chang, Jung, and Halliday, Jon. *Mao: The Unknown Story.* New York: Knopf, 2005.

Chapman, Colin. *Islam and the West: Conflict, Co-existence or Conversion?* Carlisle: Paternoster, 1998.

Chan, Kei Thong, *Faith of our Fathers*. Shanghai: ???, 2006.

Chao, Jonathan (editors). *The China Mission Handbook*. Hong Kong: Chinese Church Research, 1989.

Cherry, W. H. *Outstretched Hands.* Cheshire: Ceylon ad India General Mission, Wright's Ltd., UK. 1960.

Clark, Dennis E. *The Life and Teaching of Jesus the Messiah.* Elgin: Dove Publications, 1977.

Cormack, Don. *Killing Fields, Living Fields*. London: Monarch Books, 1997.

Covell, Ralph. *Pentecost of the Hills in Taiwan.* Pasadena: Hope Publishing House, 1998.

Cox, F. A., *History of the Baptist Missionary Society, 1792 to 1842.* London: T. Ward & Co., 1842.

Cragg, Kenneth, *Muhammad and the Christian*. Maryknoll: Orbis Books, 1984.

Cragg, Kenneth, *The Qur'an and the West.* Washington: Georgetown U. Press, 2006.

D

Dalrymple, William. *From the Holy Mountain: A Journey Among the Christians of the Middle East*. New York: Henry Holt, 1998.

Davis, Catherine L. *The Spirits of Mindoro.* East Sussex: OMF, Monarch Books, 1975.

Davis, Walter Bruce. *William Carey, father of modern missions.* Chicago: Moody, 1963.

Dawson, Mary. *Bearing Precious Seed.* London: Ceylon and India General Mission, n.d.

DeHart, Joel. *The Upper Hand, God's Sovereignty in Afghan Captivity.* Islamabad: 1994.

Dennett, Bill, *Sharing God's Love with Muslims: Effective Guidelines for Christians.* Adelaide: SPCKA, updated 2006. ISBN 1 876106-11-5.

Deshmukh, I. O. *The Quest of Truth*. Pune: Shalem Printers, 1988.

Deshmukh, I. O. *The Gospel & Islam.* Bombay: Gospel Literature Service, 1982.

Djoeandy, Omar. *Redefining Success*. Nairobi: Nairobi Chapel, 2002.

E

Eastman, Roger. *The Ways of Religion*. New York: Oxford, 1999.

Ellingsen, Mark, *The Evangelical Movement.* Minneapolis: Augsburg, 1988.

Ellwood, Agnes. *Living Harvest*. Toronto: Ceylon & India General Mission, 1956.

England John C. et al., *Asian Christian Theologies: A Research Guide to Authors, Movements, and Sources*, Vol. 1-3. Delhi: ISPCK; Maryknoll, N.Y.: Orbis Books, 2002-2004.

Eubank, L. Allan. *Dance-Drama Before the Throne: A Thai Experience*. Chiang Mai: TCF Press, 2004.

Ewing, John W. *Goodly Fellowship: A Centenary Tribute to the Life and Work of the World's Evangelical Alliance 1846-1946.* London: Marshall, Morgan, Scott, Ltd., 1946.

F

Fernando, Ajith. *The Christian's Attitude Toward World Religions.* Wheaton: Tyndale, 1987.

Fernando, Ajith. *The Supremacy of Christ*. Wheaton: Crossway Books, 1995.

Fitzsimons, Lionel. *Panorama Pakistan*. Middlesex: International Christian Fellowship, 1980.

Francis, T. Dayanandan (editor). *The Christian Witness of Sadhu Sundar Singh, A Collection of His Writings.* Madras: The Christian Literature Society, 1989.

Freeman, Derek. *The Fateful Hoaxing of Margaret Mead: A historical analysis of her Samoan research.* Boulder: Westview Press, 1999. First published as *Margaret Mead the Heretic: The making and unmasking of an anthropological myth.* Victoria: Penguin Books, 1996.

Fuller, Jonathan. *Cross Currents*. Manila: OMF Literature, 2006.

Fuller, Olive, *Better to Give*. Chicago; Moody Press—"A Dohnavur Book" 1965.

Fuller, W. Harold (editor), *Global Crossroads.* Manila: OMF, 1998.

Fuller, W. Harold. *People of the Mandate.* Carlisle: WEF, Paternoster, 1996.

G

Gilchrist, John. *Muhammad - the Prophet of Islam.* Mondeor: MERCSA, 1994.

Glover, A. E. *A Thousand Miles of Miracle in China.* Chicago: Moody Press, 1959.

Gnanakan, Ken. *Managing Yourself.* Bangalore: ACTS Trust, 1993.

Goforth, Rosalind. *Goforth of China.* Toronto: McClelland & Stewart, 1937.

Golden, Arthur. *Memoirs of a Geisha.* Toronto: Vintage Canada, 1998.

Goldsmith, Martin. *Islam & Christian Witness.* Downers Grove: InterVarsity Press, 1982.

Greeson, Kevin. *Camel Training Manual.* Bangalore: SUDHINDRA, 2004.

Griffiths, Michael. *Changing Asia.* Herts: Lion Publishing, 1977.

Guang, Pan. *The Jews in China.* Guang Dong: China International Press, 2001.

H

Hale, J.R. *Renaissance Exploration.* New York: W.W. Norton, 1968.

Hale, Thomas. *A Light Shines in Central Asia.* Pasadena: William Carey Library, 2000.

Hale, Thomas. *Living Stones of the Himalayas.* Grand Rapids: Zondervan, 1993.

Handojo, Hanna. *Assignment: Cuenca.* Manila: OMF, 1994.

Hankins, Gerald W. *A Heart for Nepal*: The Dr. Helen Huston Story. Winnipeg: Windflower Communications, 1992.

Harper, Susan Billington. *In the Shadow of the Mahatma: Bishop V.S. Azariah and the travails of Christianity in British India.* Grand Rapids: Eerdmans, 2000.

Hefley, James and Marti. *By Their Blood, Christian Martyrs of the 20th Century.* Milford: Mott, 1979.

Hatefutsoth, Beth. *The Jews of Kaifeng.* Tel Aviv: Nahum Goldmann Museum, 1948.

Hattaway, Paul. *Back to Jerusalem.* Carlisle: Piquant, 2003.

Hawker, David. *Kanchi Doctor, Ruth Watson of Nepal.* London: Scripture Union, 1984.

Hemming, G. A. *Advancing Together: a Tale of Two Missions.* London: Internat. Christian Fellowship, n.d.

Hesse, Hermann. *Siddhartha.* India: Macmillan, 1973.

Heydt, Henry J. *A Comparison of World Religions.* Ft. Washington: Christian Literature Crusade, 1976.

Hoefer, Herbert E. *Churchless Christianity.* India: Asia Programme-Advancement, Training, Studies, 1991.

Hsueh, Yu Kwong,, *You Guided My Life* (transl. Lily Ho Hsueh). Singapore: SIM East Asia, 2008.

I

Isaias, Juan. *The Other Side of the Coin*. Grand Rapids: Wm. B. Eerdmans, 1966.

J

Jenkins, Philip, *The next Christendom: the coming of global Christianity*. New York: Oxford, 2002

Johnson, David L. *A Reasoned Look at Asian Religions.* Minneapolis: Bethany House Publishers, 1985.

Johnstone, Jill. *You Can Change the World.* Ft. Washington: WEC International, 1992.

Johnstone, Patrick, Jason Mandrik, with Robyn Johnstone, *Operation World* 21st Century Edition. Milton Keynes/Tyrone: Authentic Media (STL), 2007. ISBN 978-1-85078-357-2.

K

Kanamori, Paul. *Paul Kanamori's Life Story*. London: Pickering & Inglis, 1925.

Kane, J. Herbert . *A Global View of Christian Missions from Pentecost to the Present.* Grand Rapids: Baker Book House, 1979.

Kemp, Hugh P. *Steppe by Step.* London: OMF/Interserve, Monarch Books, 2000.

Kehrberg, Norma. *The Cross in the Land of the Khukuri.* Kathmandu: Ekta Books, 2000.

Kidder, Jonathan Edward. *Ancient Japan*. Oxford: Elsevier-Phaidon, 1977.

Kidder, Jonathan Edward. *Japan Before Buddhism*. London: Thames and Hudson, 1959.

King, Winston L. *Buddhism and Christianity—Some Bridges of Understanding.* Phil.: Westminster, 1962.

Koshy, T.E. *Brother Bakht Singh of India*. Secunderabad: OM Books, 2003.

Kroeger, Richard Clark and Kroeger, Catherine Clark. *I Suffer not a Woman*. Grand Rapids: Baker, 1992.

Kuhn, Isobel. *Ascent to the Tribes.* Chicago: Moody Press, 1956/Singapore: OMF 2000.

Kuhn, Isobel. *Nests Above The Abyss*. Singapore: OMF, 1947.

L

Lambert, Tony. *Resurrection of the Chinese Church.* London: Hodder, Stoughton, 1991.

Landes, David S. *The Wealth and Poverty of Nations.* New York: W. W. Norton & Company, 1998.

Lane, Denis. *One World, Two Minds.* Singapore: OMF, 2004.

Larsen, Ron. *Mercy in Mural.* London: Poona and Indian Village Mission, 1967.

Larson, Warren Fredrick. *Islamic Ideology and Fundamentalism in Pakistan.* Lanhaam: Univ.Press, 1998.

Lattourette, K.S. *A History of Christianity, Volume I.* New York: Harper & Row, 1975.

Lattourette, K.S. *A History of Christianity, Volume II.* New York: Harper & Row, 1975.

Legge, James. *The Notions of the Chinese Concerning God and Spirits.* Hong Kong: Register Office, 1852.

Liao, David C. E., editor. *World Christianity, Eastern Asia.* Monrovia: Missions Commun.Center, 1979.

Lindell, Jonathan. *Nepal and the Gospel of God.* Kathmandu: United Mission to Nepal, 1979.

Lingenfelter, Sherwood. *Transforming Culture.* Grand Rapids: Baker Books, 1998.

Locke, Trevor & Rona. *Tribals for Christ.* Bangalore: Indian Evangelical Mission, 1992.

Love, Fran and Eckheart, Jeleta, (editors). *Longing to Call Them Sisters*—Ministry to Muslim Women. Pasadena: William Carey Library, 2000.

Love, Rick. *Muslims, Magic, and the Kingdom of God.* Pasadena: William Carey, 2000.

Lowe, Chuck. *Territorial Spirits and World Evangelisation.* Fearn: Christian Focus (for OMF), 1998.

Luzbetak, Louis J. *The Church and Cultures.* Pasadena: William Carey Library, 1970.

Lyall, Leslie T. *Come Wind, Come Weather.* Chicago: Moody Press, 1960.

M

Maberly, Allan. *God Spoke Tibetan*. Rockwall: Evanel Bible Translators, 2001.

Mangalwadi, Vishal. *India: the grand experiment*. Surrey: Pippa Rann Books, 1997.

Mangalwadi, Vishal. *Missionary Conspiracy, Letters to a Postmodern Hindu*. Carlisle: OM, 1996.

Mangalwadi, Vishal. *Truth and Social Reform*. London: Nivedit Good Books, 1996.

Mangalwadi, Vishal. *When the New Age Gets Old. Looking for a greater spirituality*. Downers Grove: I InterVarsity Press, 1992.

Mangalwadi, Vishal. *The World of Gurus*. New Delhi: Vikas Publishing House, 1977.

Mangalwadi, Ruth and Vishal. *William Carey, a tribute by an Indian Woman*. Mussoorie: Nivedit,1993.

Mangalwadi, Vishal and MacNicol, Nicol. *What Liberates a Woman? The story of Pandita Ramabai – A Builder of Modern India*. Calcutta: Association Press, 1986.

Marozzi, Justin. *Sword of Islam, Conqueror of the World*. New York: Harper Collins, 2004.

Marshall, Paul. *Their Blood Cries Out*. Dallas: Word Publishing, 1997.

Matthews, R. A. *Born for Battle, Studies in Spiritual Warfare*. Singapore: OMF, 1978.

Mawdudi, Abul Ala. *The Punishment of the Apostate According to Islamic Law*. (English translation by Husain, Syed Silas; and Hahn, Ernest.) Mississauga: VOM, 1994.

McPhee, A. G., *The Road to Delhi*, Bishop Pickett Remembered 1890 -1981. Bangalor: SAIACA, 2005.

Medearis, Carl, *Muslims, Christians, and Jesus*. Bloomington: Bethany House, 2008.

Michell, David J. *The Spirit of Eric Liddell*. Toronto: OMF Books, 1996.

Miller, Sheila and Murray, Ian. *The Gods Must Be Angry*. Singapore: OMF, 1990.

Moffett, Samuel Hugh. *A History of Christianity in Asia*, Vol. I. San Francisco: HarperCollins, 1992.

Moffett, Samuel Hugh. *A History of Christianity in Asia*, Vol. II. Maryknoll: Orbis Books, 2005.

Moreau, A. Scott Moreau, ed., *Evangelical Dictionary of World Missions*. Grand Rapids: Baker Books, 2000. ISBN 0-85364-995-2.

Morton, Sue. *Angels in the Rafters.* Chiang Mai: Murree Christian School, 2002.

Moyer, Elgin S. *Who was who in Church History.* New Canaan: Keats Publishing, 1974.

N

Neill, Stephen; Anderson, Gerald; Goodwin, John; *Concise Dictionary of the Christian World Mission.* London: USCCL, 1970.

Neudorf, Eugene. *A Light to All Japan*, the story of Susan Dyck. Camp Hill: Christian Publications, 1998.

Nevins, Joseph. *A Not-So-Distant Horror: Mass Violence in East Timor.* Cornell: Cornell U. Press, 2005.

Nicholls, Bruce J (editor). *The Unique Christ in our Pluralist World.* Carlisle: WEF, Paternoster, 1994.

Nicholls, Kathleen. *Asian Arts and Christian Hope.* New Delhi: Select Books, 1983.

O

Oh, Kongdan; Hassig, Ralph C. *North Korea - Through the Looking Glass.* New York: Brookings, 2000.

Olsen, Viggo and Lockerbie, Jeanette. *Daktar, Diplomat in Bangladesh.* Chicago: Moody Press, 1973.

P

Padinjarekara, Joseph. *Christ in Ancient Vedas.* Kerala: India Mukti Mission, 1984.

Page, Sydney, H. T. *Powers of Evil.* Grand Rapids: Baker Books, 1995.

Paget, Kathleen. *Out of The Hand of The Terrible.* Toronto: CIGM, 1949.

Palin, Michael. *Himalaya.* London: Weidenfeld & Nicholson, 2005.

Parrinder, Geoffrey (editor). *World Religions from Ancient History to the Present.* N.Y.: F. on F, 1971.

Parshall, Phil. *Bridges to Islam.* Grand Rapids: Baker Book House, 1983.

Parshall, Phil. *The Cross and the Crescent.* Wheaton: Tyndale. 1989.

Parshall, Phil. *The Fortress and the Fire.* Bombay: Gospel Literature Service, 1975.

Patterson, George N. *The China Paradox, Christ versus Marx.* Milton Keynes: Word Publishing, 1990.

Perry, Cindy. *A Biographical History of the Church in Nepal.* Wheaton: Church History Project, 1992.

Peters, George W. *Indonesia Revival—focus on Timor.* Grand Rapids: Zondervan Publishing House, 1973.

Pollak, Michael. *Mandarins, Jews, and Missionaries: The Jewish Experience in the Chinese Empire.*

Philadelphia: Jewish Publication Society of America, 1980.

Pollock, J.C. *Hudson Taylor and Maria.* Grand Rapids: Zondervan, 1962.

Power, Brian. *The Ford of Heaven: A Childhood in Tianjin, China.* NewYork: Signal, 2006.

Prabhakar, B. A. (editor). *Into the Seventies with Christ, All India Congress on Evangelism.* EFI, 1965.

Pudaite, Rochunga. *The Book That Set My People Free.* Wheaton: Bibles for the World Press, 60187.

R

Raddon, Jean. *Life on the Roof.* Strathfield: Christian Women's Conventions Int'l, 1975.

Radhakrishnan, S. *Religion and Culture.* Delhi: Vision Books, 1968.

Raj, Sunder. *The Confusion Called Conversion.* New Delhi: TRACI, 1988.

Ramachandra, Vinoth. *Gods that Fail.* Carlisle: Paternoster, 1996.

Randall, Ian, *Spiritual Revolution—the story of OM.* Bletchley: Authentic Media, 2008.

Reed, Barbara Flory. *Beyond The Great Darkness.* Singapore: OMF, 1987.

Rhoton, Elaine. *The Doulos Story.* UK: OM Publishing, 1997.

Richard, D. John. *Asian Church Leaders.* Evangelical Fellowship of Asia, 1989.

Richardson, Don. *Eternity in Their Hearts.* Ventura: Regal Books, 1981.

Ro, Bong Rin (editor). *Christian Alternatives to Ancestor Practices.* Taiwan: Asia Theo. Association, 1985.

Ro, Bong Rin; Nelson, Martin L. (eds). *Korean Church Growth Explosion.* Wheaton: Asia Th. Assoc. 83.

Robert, Dana L. *American Women in Mission*. Macon: Mercer University Press, 1996.

Roy, Olivier. *Globalized Islam, the Search for a New Ummah*. New York: Columbia U. Press, 2004.

S

Sanders, J. Oswald. *Prayer Power Unlimited.* Chicago: Moody, 1977.

Sanneh, Lamin. *Translating the Message*. Maryknoll: Orbis Books, 1989.

Sasson, Jean P. *Princess* (treatment of Women in Saudi Arabia). London: Bantam Books, 1993.

Seunarine, J.F. *Reconversion to Hinduism Through Suddhi*. Madras: Christian Literature Society, 1977.

Shorrosh, Anis A. *Islam Revealed.* Nashville: Thomas Nelson, 1988.

Smedes, Lewis (editor). *Ministry and the Miraculous: a Case Study at Fuller Theological Seminary*. Pasadena: Fuller Theological Seminary, 1987.

Smith, Alex G. *Siamese Gold, The Church in Thailand.* Bangkok: OMF Publishers, 1982.

Sng, Bobby E. K. *In His Good Time, The story of the church in Singapore 1819-1992.*

Singapore: Graduates Christian Fellowship, 1993.

St. Clair-Tisdall, W. *The Sources of Islam*. Edinburgh: T. & T. Clark, Dec. 1900 Edition.

Staines, Gladys. *Burnt Alive*. Mumbai: Gospel Literature Service, 2000.

Stamoolis, James J. *Eastern orthodox mission theology today*. Eugene: Wipf and Stock, 2005.

Stiller, Brian C. *Critical Options for Evangelicals*. Markham: Faith Today, 1991.

Stone, Anthony Philip. *Hindi Astrology: Myths, Symbols and Realities.* New Delhi: Select Books, 1981.

Stone, Anthony Philip. *Light on Astrology*. Bombay: Gospel Literature Service, 1979.

Story, Jay, *Memoirs of a Pilgrim.* Indore: Sat Prachar Press, 2008.

Sunderaraj, Francis. *To God be the Glory, 40 years, Evangelical Fellowship of India.* EFI, 1991.

T

Tagore, Rabindranath (John Thorpe, trns.), *Let My Head Bow Down.* Charlotte: SIM Archives, c. 1960.

Taylor, Dr. and Mrs. Howard. *By Faith: Henry W. Frost & China Inland Mission.* Singapore: OMF, 1888.

Thampu, Valson. *AIDS: Heresy and Prophecy.* New Delhi: TRACI, 1993.

Thyaharaj, Venkateswara. *A New Motive for Living.* Bromley: Pilot Books, 1997.

Tiplady, Richard (editor). *One World or Many?* Impact of globalisation on mission. Pasadena: WCL, 2003.

Titus, Murray. *Islam in India and Pakistan.* New Delhi: Munshiram Manoharlal Publishers, 2005.

Toliver, Ralph. *Gold Fears No Fire.* Singapore: OMF, 1986.

Trevor, Hugh. *Multi-Channel Japan.* Sevenoaks: OMF, 1970.

Tucker, Ruth A. *From Jerusalem to Irian Jaya.* Grand Rapids: Zondervan, 1983.

Twiss, Richard. *One Church, Many Tribes.* Ventura: Regal Books, 2000.

Tzu, Sun. *The Art of War.* New York: Bantam Doubleday Dell, 1983.

V

Veith, G. E., Jr. *Fascism: Modern and Postmodern.* Mussoorie: Nivedit Good Books, 2000.

Vencer, Jun. *Poor is No Excuse.* Exeter: World Evangelical Fellowship, Paternoster Press, 1989.

Vincent, Eileen , *C.T. Studd and Priscilla.* Bromley/Bulstrode: WEC/STL (OM), 1988.

W

Wang, Mary. *The Chinese Church that will not Die.* Wheaton: Tyndale House Publishers, 1972.

Weerasingha, Tissa. *The Cross & the Bo Tree.* Taiwan: Asia Theological Assoc., 1989.

Wellman, Sam. *Amy Carmichael.* Uhrichsville: Barbour, 1998.

White, Keith J. *Pandita Ramabai (1858-1922): A Re-evaluation of Her Life and Work.* Cardiff: University of Wales, April 2003 (unpublished).

Williams, Esther. *Sacrifice or Investment?* Bangalore: Outreach Publications. IEM, 1985.

Williams, Theodore (editor) *Together in Mission.* Bangalore: World Evangelical Fellowship, 1983.

Wiseman, Ray. *Disciples of Joy. Anand Chaudhari's spiritual journey.* Brampton: Partners Int'l, 1998.

Wiseman, Ray. *I Cannot Dream Less. Chris Marantika.* Brampton: Partners Int'l Canada, 2003.

Wolpert, Stanley. *Gandhi's Passion: The Life and Legacy of Mahatma Gandhi.* London: Oxford Un., 2001.

Wraith, Ronald; Simpkins, Edgar. *Corruption in Developing Countries.* Lond.: George Allen Unwin, 1963.

Wright, Don, editor. *Operation Japan.* Tokyo: Operation Japan Publishing Com., 1997.

Wright, N. T., *Judas and the Gospel of Jesus.* Grand Rapids: Baker Books, 2006

X

Xin, Xu. *The Jews of Kaifeng, China.* Jersey City: KTAV Publishing House, 2003.

Y

Yamamori, Tetsunao. *Church Growth in Japan.* Pasadena: William Carey Library, 1939.

Yohannan, K.P., *Revolution in World Missions.* Carrollton: Gospel for Asia. ISBN 978-1-59589-001-6.

Yun, Brother, Hattaway, Paul. *The Heavenly Man.* London: Monarch Books, 2002.

Z

Zacharias, Ravi. *Jesus Among Other Gods.* Nashville: Word Publishing, 2000.

Zaehner, R. C. *Hinduism.* London and New York: Oxford University Press, 1966.

Index

1. Persons

2. Places

3. Subjects